'91

Object-Oriented Programming
Systems, Languages, and Applications

OOPSLA '91

Conference Proceedings

Edited by Andreas Paepcke

acm
PRESS

Sponsored by the Association for Computing Machinery's
Special Interest Group on Programming Languages (ACM/SIGPLAN)

The Association for Computing Machinery
11 West 42nd Street
New York, New York 10036

ACM SIGPLAN NOTICES (ISSN 0362-1340) is published monthly by the Association for Computing Machinery, Inc., 11 W. 42nd St., New York, NY 10036. The basic annual subscription price is $20.00 for ACM Members. Second class postage paid at New York, NY 10001 and at additional mailing offices. Postmaster: Send change of address to SIGPLAN NOTICES, ACM, 11 W. 42nd St., New York, NY 10036.

ORDERING INFORMATION

Orders from nonmembers of ACM placed within the U.S. should be directed to:

Addison-Wesley Publishing Company
Order Department
Jacob Way
Reading, MA 01867
Tel: 1-800-447-2226

Addison-Wesley will pay postage and handling on orders accompanied by check. Credit card orders may be placed by mail or by calling the Addison-Wesley Order Department at the number above. Follow-up inquiries should be directed to the Customer Service Department at the same number.

Please include the Addison-Wesley ISBN number with your order:
A-W ISBN 0-0201-55417-8

Orders from nonmembers of ACM placed from outside the U.S. should be addressed as noted below.

Latin America and Asia:
Addison-Wesley Publishing Company, Inc.
Reading, MA 01867, U.S.A.
Tel: 617-944-3700;
Cable: ADIWES READING;
Telex: 94-9416

Canada: Addison-Wesley Publishing (Canada) Ltd.
36 Prince Andrew Place
Don Mills, Ontario M3C2T8, Canada
Tel: 416-447-5101

Australia and New Zealand:
Addison-Wesley Publishing Company
6 Byfield Street
North Ryde, N.S.W. 2113
Australia
Tel: 888-2733;
Cable: ADIWES SYDNEY;
Telex: AA71919

United Kingdom, Republic of Ireland, Africa (excluding North Africa) and South Africa:
Addison-Wesley Publishers Ltd.
Finchampstead Road
Wokingham
Berkshire RG11 2NZ, England
Cable: ADIWES Wokingham;
Telex: 846136

Continental Europe, the Near East, Middle East, and North Africa:
Addison-Wesley Publishing Company
De Lairesstraat, 90
1071 PJ Amsterdam
The Netherlands
Tel: 020 76 40-44
Cable: ADIWES AMSTERDAM
Telex: 844-14046

ACM Members: a limited number (copies are available at the ACM memb discount. Send order with payment to

ACM Order Department
P.O. Box 64145
Baltimore, MD 21264

ACM will pay postage and handling (orders accompanied by check.

Credit card orders only:
1-800-342-6626

Customer service, or credit card orde from Alaska, Maryland, and outside th U.S.: 301-528-4261

Credit card orders may also be placed mail.

Please include your ACM memb number and the ACM Order number wi your order.

ACM Order Number: 548911
ACM ISBN 0-89791-446-5

Welcome to OOPSLA'91

On behalf of the OOPSLA'91 conference committee, I am pleased to welcome you to the sixth annual conference on Object-Oriented Programming: Systems, Languages and Applications.

Five years ago, OOPSLA was organized to provide a forum for those interested in exploring, and exploiting, the object-oriented paradigm. The conference was designed to bring together the best research and the best practice in order to accelerate the practical use of object technology. OOPSLA'91 carries on this tradition.

The success of OOPSLA is directly due to the hard work of the volunteers serving on the conference and program committees. I have been particularly fortunate to have experienced hands who knew what it would take to make this a technically rewarding event. To all of you, my sincerest thanks.

I would also like to acknowledge the solid support of ACM and SIGPLAN. OOPSLA'91 has benefited from the talented people at ACM and the committee is grateful for their contributions. We thank SIGPLAN for its sponsorship and for distributing both the Proceedings and the Proceedings Addendum.

The committee members also wish to thank their employers and sponsors for supporting their volunteer work. Putting together a conference of this size and quality demands both personal and professional sacrifice and we appreciate their cooperation.

Finally, we thank all of you – the presenters, session chairs, exhibitors and active participants. We hope you will find this conference to be stimulating and fun.

John Richards, Conference Chair, OOPSLA'91

Conference Committee

Conference Chair
    John Richards, *IBM T.J. Watson Research Center*
Program Chair
    Alan Snyder, *Hewlett-Packard Laboratories*
Audio/Visual
    Robert M. Livingston, *Steinbach & Company*
Demonstrations
    Sam Adams, *Knowledge Systems Corporation*
Education Chair
    John Pugh, *Carleton University*
Exhibits
    Timlynn Babitsky & Jim Salmons, *JFS Consulting*
Local Arrangements
    Naomi Nielson, *Servio Corporation*
Panels
    Ralph Johnson, *University of Illinois at Urbana-Champaign*
Press Relations
    Jeff McKenna, *McKenna Consulting Group*
    Ed Niehaus, *Niehaus Public Relations*
Proceedings
    Andreas Paepcke, *Hewlett-Packard Laboratories*
Proceedings Addendum
    Jerry Archibald, *IBM Research*
    K.C. Burgess Yakemovic, *NCR Corporation*
Publications/Publicity
    Dexter Sealy, *On Technology*
Operations Chair
    Daniel E. Steinbach, *Steinbach & Company*
Registration/Conference Information
    Carole Mann, *Gentleware Corporation*
Student Volunteers
    Suzanne Skublics, *Object Technology International*
Treasurer
    David N. Smith, *IBM T.J. Watson Research Center*
Tutorials
    Jon Hopkins, *Synetics Software Corporation*
Workshops
    Kent Beck, *MasPar Computer Corporation and First Class Software*

The OOPSLA'91 Technical Program

Object technology continues to be a subject of great interest and activity. This year, over 200 papers were submitted to OOPSLA from all corners of the globe, compared to 194 submissions to last year's joint conference with ECOOP. Considering that ECOOP '91 received 129 submissions, the increase in reported activity worldwide this year is dramatic!

To ensure a fair and informed selection process, each submitted paper was reviewed by at least three members of the program committee or a trusted associate. For this year's program, the committee selected 23 outstanding papers, 17 with a research focus and 6 reporting on experience using object technology. The research papers cover a broad spectrum, including languages, implementation, environments, types, software engineering, concurrency, and persistence.

As object technology plays an increasing role in commercial software development, it is important to report on and evaluate its effectiveness in practice. Such evaluations are a valuable contribution to knowledge and help direct the next stage of research. This year's program includes a new forum for oral presentations by practitioners reporting on their real world experience using object technology. I hope that many of these reports will lead to technical papers at future OOPSLA conferences.

To assist prospective authors of technical papers for future conferences, the program committee decided to reprint the guide to authors that I prepared for this conference; it appears as an appendix in these proceedings.

I would like to thank the members of the program committee for their efforts in putting together the technical program. I would also like to thank the other reviewers, who are listed on the following page. I also gratefully acknowledge Andrea O'Brennan, Dennis Dougherty, and Maria Barraza for administrative support and Kevin Wentzel for computer tool development; it was only with their help that this task could have been accomplished.

Alan Snyder, Program Chair, OOPSLA'91

1991 Program Committee

Chair: Alan Snyder, *Hewlett-Packard Laboratories*

Grady Booch, *Rational, Inc*
Luca Cardelli, *DEC SRC*
Pierre Cointe, *Rank Xerox*
William Cook, *Apple Computer, Inc.*
Gail Kaiser, *Columbia University*
Henry Levy, *University of Washington*
Henry Lieberman, *MIT*
Mark Linton, *Silicon Graphics, Inc.*
Ole Lehrmann Madsen, *Aarhus University*
Ron Morrison, *University of St. Andrews*
Eliot Moss, *University of Massachusetts*

Mayer Schwartz, *Tektronix, Inc.*
Guy Steele, *Thinking Machines Corporation*
Jacob Stein, *Servio Corporation*
David Thomas, *Object Technology International*
Mario Tokoro, *Keio University/Sony CSL*
Chris Tomlinson, *MCC*
Dionysios Tsichritzis, *University of Geneva*
Jeannette Wing, *Carnegie-Mellon University*
Rebecca Wirfs-Brock, *Tektronix, Inc.*
Akinori Yonezawa, *University of Tokyo*

Other Reviewers

Lars Bak
Bill Bregar
Eric Brown
Phil Cannata
Jeffrey Chase
Amer Diwan
Christophe Dony
Ed Felten
David Garlan
Philippe Gautron
Richard Hudson
Michael Huhns
Norman Hutchinson
Jørgen Lindskov Knudsen
Greg Lavender

Jacques Malenfant
Claus Nørgaard
Jens Palsberg
Christian Queinnec
Rajendra Raj
John Reynolds
Elmer Sandvad
Michael Schwartzbach
Bob Shaw
Evan Smith
Lynn Andrea Stein
Michael Travers
Randy Trigg
Darrell Woelk

Papers and Panels

Tuesday, October 8, 1991

Welcome and Keynote Address
Session 1: 8:00am-9:30am

Implementation
Session 2: 10:00am-11:30am

Environments
Session 3: 1:00pm-2:00pm

Experience Papers I

Session 4: 2:30pm-4:00pm

Types

Session 5A: 4:30pm-6:00pm

Panel

Session 5B: 4:30pm-6:00pm

Wednesday, October 9, 1991

Panel
Session 6A: 8:00am-9:30am

Panel
Session 6B: 8:00am-9:30am

Software Engineering
Session 7: 10:00am-11:30am

Concurrency and Persistence
Session 9: 2:30pm-4:00pm

Thursday, October 10, 1991

Panel
Session 11: 8:00am-9:30am

Language
Session 12A: 10:00am-11:30am

Experience Papers II
Session 13: 1:00pm-2:30pm

Panel
Session 14A: 3:00pm-4:30pm

Panel
Session 14B: 3:00pm-4:30pm

Making Pure Object-Oriented Languages Practical[*]

Craig Chambers

David Ungar

Stanford University[**]

Abstract

In the past, object-oriented language designers and programmers have been forced to choose between pure message passing and performance. Last year, our SELF system achieved close to half the speed of optimized C but suffered from impractically long compile times. Two new optimization techniques, *deferred compilation of uncommon cases* and *non-backtracking splitting using path objects*, have improved compilation speed by more than an order of magnitude. SELF now compiles about as fast as an optimizing C compiler and runs at over half the speed of optimized C. This new level of performance may make pure object-oriented languages practical.

1 Introduction

In the past, object-oriented language designers and programmers have been forced to choose between purity and performance. In a pure object-oriented language, all computation, even low-level operations like variable accessing, arithmetic, and array indexing, is performed by sending messages to objects. Although a message send may cost only one indirection more than a procedure call, a message send may cost much more than an *inlined* procedure call. Unlike a statically-bound procedure call, a message send refers to no single target method, and so the compiler cannot simply expand its destination in-line. Pure object-oriented languages thus exhibit high call frequencies which interfere with good performance.

For example, the fastest commercial implementation of a pure dynamically-typed object-oriented language, ParcPlace Smalltalk-80[*] [GR83], runs a set of small C-style benchmarks at only 10% the speed of optimized C; this implementation contains techniques developed by Deutsch and Schiffman [DS84] that are widely considered to be the state of the art in software techniques for building fast implementations of pure object-oriented languages.

Even statically-typed (but pure) object-oriented languages like Trellis/Owl [SCW85, SCB+86], Eiffel [Mey86, Mey88], and Emerald [BHJL86, Hut87] must overcome the overhead of dynamically-dispatched message passing.[**] Static typing allows the compiler to check that an object will understand every message sent to it and perhaps to use a somewhat faster dispatching mechanism to implement messages. However, because an instance of a subclass can always be substituted for an instance of a superclass, and because subclasses can provide alternate overriding method implementations, static type-checking cannot determine in general the single target method invoked by a message. Since static typing alone does not enable static binding and inlining of messages, it cannot significantly reduce the overhead of message passing.

Hybrid object-oriented languages such as C++ [Str86, ES90] and CLOS [BDG+88] short-circuit the overhead (and consequently the benefits) of passing messages by including statically-bound procedure calls and primitive, non-object-oriented data types for simple things like numbers, arrays, and cons cells. These data types are accessed via built-in operators or procedure calls that are automatically inlined by the compiler to achieve good performance. However, it is only within pure object-oriented languages that the benefits of

* This work has been generously supported by an IBM graduate student fellowship, an NSF Presidential Young Investigator award, and grants from Sun, IBM, Apple, Cray, Tandem, NCR, TI, and DEC.

** Authors' present addresses: Craig Chambers, Department of Computer Science and Engineering, Sieg Hall, FR-35, University of Washington, Seattle, WA 98195; David Ungar, Sun Laboratories, MS 29-116, 2550 Garcia Ave., Mountain View, CA 94043.

* Smalltalk-80 is a trademark of ParcPlace Systems, Inc.

** Even these "pure" languages restrict common built-in types like `integer` and `bool` to be non-object-oriented to get better performance.

object-oriented programming universally accrue for all code in a program. This fundamental trade-off between purity and performance has prevented the many programmers who need high performance from fully enjoying the benefits of object-oriented programming.

Over the last few years we have been working on bridging the gap between the performance of traditional languages and the performance of pure object-oriented languages. We are developing new implementation techniques and compiler optimizations for our implementation of SELF [US87], a pure dynamically-typed object-oriented language even harder to compile efficiently than Smalltalk-80. The following chart summarizes our progress to date, compared against optimized C (faster execution speed is higher on the graph, and faster compilation speed is farther to the right on the graph):

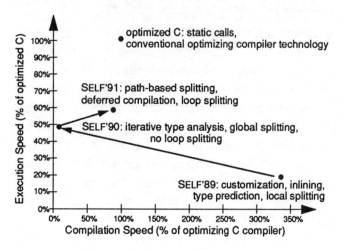

In 1989, we presented early results [CU89, CUL89] showing how our SELF system ran the same set of small C-style benchmarks at 20% the speed of optimized C, twice as fast as the ParcPlace Smalltalk-80 system. In 1990 we described more recent work [CU90] in which our SELF system ran the same benchmarks at 40% the speed of optimized C, another factor of two improvement over the early SELF system and a factor of four faster than ParcPlace Smalltalk-80. Unfortunately, the new techniques were slow: compiling a single benchmark took from tens to hundreds of seconds, and one technique, loop splitting, took an exponential amount of time and space and so could only be applied to the smaller benchmarks. Since our compiler runs dynamically at run-time to conserve compiled code space and

minimize start-up time after a programming change, the sluggishness of the compiler sapped the overall performance of our system. Users could not tolerate minute-long pauses for compilation during interactive use.

This paper reports on work we have done this last year to re-engineer our techniques. New type analysis algorithms replace the expensive backtracking approach of the previous SELF compiler with path data structures to extract the same type information at a much lower cost. Additionally, the new system defers compilation of uncommon cases until they actually occur at run-time. As a result the compilation time of our optimizing SELF compiler has improved from a few minutes per benchmark to a few seconds, and we have been able to compile all our SELF code with full optimization. With this improvement, compile times for SELF now compete with those for optimized C. Gains in compilation speed are usually purchased at the expense of run-time performance, but the run-time performance of our new system has actually *improved*, to over 50% the speed of optimized C. Now that our optimization techniques have entered the realm of practicality, we hope that language designers and users can safely adopt a pure object-oriented model with message passing as the most basic mechanism for computation and rely on implementation techniques like ours to provide a level of performance, both run-time and compile-time, competitive with hybrid object-oriented languages and even traditional languages.

Section 2 presents an overview of the structure of the SELF compiler. Section 3 illustrates many of our new techniques using an excerpt from the bubblesort benchmark. Section 4 completes the discussion of our new techniques by extending the example to include a loop. Section 5 relates current run-time performance, compile-time performance, and compiled-code space costs for the current SELF compiler, the previous SELF compiler, the ParcPlace Smalltalk-80 system, the ORBIT optimizing compiler for T (a dialect of Scheme), and optimized C. Section 6 describes the status of our SELF implementation with hints of current and future work. Section 7 completes the paper with a brief discussion of related work.

2 Overall Structure of the SELF Compiler

Before explaining our new advances in type analysis and compilation, it is necessary to review the matrix in which they are embedded. Readers who are familiar with our past work may wish to skip this section.

2.1 Dynamic Compilation

The SELF system employs *dynamic compilation* to obtain better run-time performance than an interpreter while reducing compile-time and code-space costs over a conventional static compiler; dynamic compilation in SELF is similar to dynamic translation in the Deutsch-Schiffman Smalltalk-80 system [DS84]. When a programmer types in a program, a *parser* (corresponding to the Deutsch-Schiffman compiler) translates it into a simple byte-coded intermediate representation. Later, when the program is invoked, a *compiler* (corresponding to the Deutsch-Schiffman translator) compiles and optimizes the program, caching the resulting object code for future use.

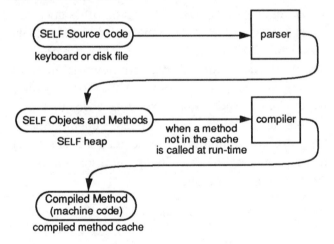

2.2 Customization

Dynamic compilation offers new opportunities for efficient implementation not available in a traditional static compilation world. Although many classes* may inherit the same method, the SELF compiler compiles a separate, *customized* copy for each of them. In each copy, there is but a single class for self, and this knowledge

---
* Since SELF has no classes, our implementation introduces *maps* transparently to the user to provide similar information and space efficiency as classes [CUL89]. Thus in our system customization is based on the internal map of the receiver rather than its class. We will continue to use the class terminology in the rest of the paper for pedagogical reasons.

allows the compiler to replace all dynamically-bound messages sent to self (such messages are a large fraction of the messages sent in SELF programs) with statically-bound procedure calls. Once a message has been statically-bound, more conventional techniques like inline substitution (*inlining*) can be used to reduce the overhead of the message even more. If the target method of the message is short (as is frequently the case in pure object-oriented languages), static binding and inlining can speed the message by an order of magnitude or more, especially if the inlined method can be optimized further in the context of the call.

2.3 Types in the SELF Compiler

Customization provides type information that enables compile-time message lookup for all sends to self. To perform similar optimizations for messages sent to other receivers, the SELF compiler performs *type analysis* to infer the exact class of message receivers. Like traditional data flow analysis, SELF's type analysis propagates the type binding information through the control flow graph. Unlike traditional data flow analysis, SELF's type analysis is interleaved with other techniques like message inlining and message splitting (described in section 3.3). These other techniques transform the control flow graph while the type analysis is labeling it. The need to label and transform the graph simultaneously empowers and complicates our techniques.

A type in the compiler specifies a non-empty set of values. A variable of a particular type at a particular point in the program is guaranteed to contain only values in the type's set of values at run-time at that point. The following table shows the different kinds of types used in the SELF compiler, chosen to support the optimizations.

name	set description	static info	source
constant	singleton set	compile-time constant	literals, constant slots, true and false type tests
integer subrange	set of sequential integer values	integer ranges	arithmetic and comparison primitives
class	set of all values with same class	format and inheritance	self, results of some primitives, integer type tests
unknown	set of all values	none	data slots, message results, up-level assignments
union	set union of types	one of several types	results of some primitives
difference	set difference of types	exclude certain types	failed type tests

3 Type Analysis

To compute the static type information necessary for optimization, the compiler builds a mapping from variable names to types at each point in the program (i.e. between every node in the control flow graph). We will illustrate this process with a code fragment taken from the inner loop of the `bubblesort` benchmark that exchanges two elements in a vector (or any other collection that responds to `at:` and `at:Put:`):

```
| aTemp |
. . .
aTemp: (aCol at: i).
aCol at: i Put: (aCol at: j).
aCol at: j Put: aTemp.
```

Each node in the control flow graph may alter the type bindings as type information propagates across the node. For example, a declaration of a local variable such as `aTemp` adds a new binding to the type mapping. Since local variables in SELF are always initialized to compile-time constants, each binding will initially be to some constant type. In our example, there is one local, `aTemp`, initialized to `nil`.

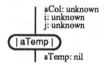

3.1 Type Prediction

Next the compiler must generate code for the first `at:` message. Since the receiver is `aCol`, and since the type of `aCol` is unknown, the compiler cannot statically determine the target method. However, the compiler predicts that there is a good enough chance that the receiver of `at:` is a vector to make it worthwhile to optimize this case. So the compiler inserts a type test for `aCol` before compiling the `at:` message.

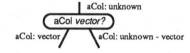

Now that two cases have been separated, the compiler is free to lookup and inline `at:` for the vector case along the left branch; it must still generate a full message send for the non-vector case. The inlined `at:` primitive includes a type check and a bounds check for the subscript argument, which result in two more branches.

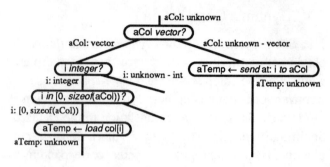

3.2 Deferred Compilation

In the code generated for vectors, there are two branches that lead to primitive failure: one for a non-integer subscript argument and another for an out-of-bounds subscript argument. Just as the compiler is imbued with the knowledge that the receiver of `at:` is likely to be a vector, it is also informed that primitive failures are unlikely. In fact, they are so rare that it is not even worthwhile to spend time compiling code for them.[*] Accordingly, the SELF compiler defers compiling code for these uncommon cases, generating instead a stub that invokes the compiler. This optimization is new with the current SELF compiler.

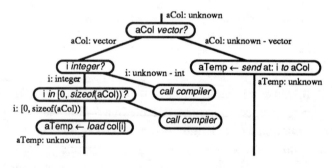

Deferred compilation of uncommon cases dramatically reduces the time required for type analysis and conserves much compiled code space. In addition, deferred compilation of uncommon cases speeds and simplifies

---

[*] We would like to gratefully acknowledge John Maloney for pointing this out to us.

register allocation. In most traditional allocators (especially the faster ones), a variable is allocated to a single location for its entire lifetime. If the variable must survive across a call, then the allocator may require that the variable be allocated to a stack location for its entire lifetime rather than a register. In SELF code, many more calls remain in uncommon-case branches than in common-case branches, and so a variable cannot be allocated to a register only because of some calls in uncommon branches that the variable must survive. The performance of the common-case branch under such a register allocation strategy thus is adversely affected by the mere presence of uncommon branches, even if they are never executed. The previous SELF compiler attempted to solve this problem by allocating uses independently and allowing a variable to migrate to different locations during different portions of its lifetime, but this implementation was very slow. Deferred compilation of uncommon branches allows the new SELF compiler to use a simpler, faster register allocator.

In the rare case that the stub for an uncommon branch is executed, the compiler generates code for the uncommon branch in a separate compiled code object called an *uncommon branch extension*. This other routine reuses the stack frame created for the original common-case version and returns to the same place where the original common-case version would have returned to. When compiling such an uncommon branch extension, the compiler becomes very conservative. Since its predictions have been wrong for this method once already, it assumes it does not know much about the probabilities of the cases within the extension. All uncommon branches are fully generated in an uncommon branch extension (uncommon branch stubs are not used). This prevents recursive uncommon branch stub invocations which could lead to lengthy compile times. Also the compiler is biased in favor of saving compile time rather than generating better code when compiling an uncommon branch extension.

3.3 Message Splitting

The compiler has finally compiled the first at: message, splitting with respect to aCol's type. It must now decide whether to merge the two control flow paths back together or to keep them apart. The two paths have different type information, and knowing this information may allow the compiler to optimize later messages (this is particularly true in this example in which there are three more messages sent to aCol). But keeping the two paths split apart takes up more compile time and compiled code space; this extra effort is wasted if the compiler won't end up making use of the information (such as if there were no more messages sent to aCol). Good heuristics for resolving this problem are central to achieving good run-time performance and good compile-time performance.

3.3.1 Eager Splitting: Never Merge

One extreme strategy would always keep branches apart and split everywhere possible (except at loop head merge nodes); we call this strategy *eager splitting*. Eager splitting has the advantages that it promises the best possible code quality and very simple forward-only type analysis. Unfortunately, the size of the control flow graph grows exponentially, and so pure forms of eager splitting are not practical. We have investigated several approaches to limiting the "eagerness" of this strategy, but with only limited success.

3.3.2 Reluctant Splitting and Paths: Merge Now, but Save the Information

An alternative strategy merges branches as soon as possible, but saves enough information to remove the merge later and split if need be. This *reluctant splitting* strategy allows the compiler to avoid unnecessary splitting.

The previous SELF compiler saved enough information using *merge types* (union types that implied that a merge node created the union) to decide whether or not to split the control flow graph, but could not split the merged type binding information into two more specific sets of type bindings. Hence, it had to reanalyze each of the split paths every time it split a merge to recalculate the split type information. Although such reanalysis occasionally revealed an opportunity for further optimization of a split path that was not possible in the original merged path, the backtracking nature of reanalysis made it very slow.

Our new type analysis algorithms implemented in the current SELF compiler do *not* reanalyze the parts of the control flow graph modified by splitting. As a result, the time to do type analysis becomes roughly linear with respect to the size of the resulting control flow graph. To split the type information as well as the control flow graph and avoid reanalysis, the new compiler uses a more detailed representation of type information based on *path objects*. Each path object represents a unique path through the control flow graph, and type information is conditional for particular path objects. At a branch node each path object splits into two separate paths, one per branch successor; at a merge node paths are not recombined (that would defeat the purpose of paths!) but instead are simply collected together to form a set of paths in the merge's successor node. A path object in reluctant splitting is analogous to a control flow branch in eager splitting, and consequently reluctant splitting using path objects has the potential for the same quality of type analysis as eager splitting, but at a fraction of the cost.

Once merge type information is replaced with per-path type information, splitting can be couched in terms of separating the subset of the possible execution paths that have a particular type binding (or combination of type bindings, or any other kind of information accumulated during type analysis, such as available expressions for common subexpression elimination) from those paths that do not. The new type information along the two split branches is easily calculated by simply filtering the type information by the appropriate set of path objects. Splitting is now much faster than the previous SELF compiler; copying the control flow graph nodes is relatively inexpensive, and paths relieve the compiler of the time to reanalyze the split control flow graph.

Of course, the path data structures have an associated cost in compiler complexity and compilation speed. At every branch node, the number of path objects doubles (one path along each outgoing branch for every single incoming path object), potentially leading to an exponential blow-up of paths that could swamp the compiler's type analysis. To combat this possibility, our compiler combines paths that have identical associated type information, since they will never be split apart. Fortunately, we have not observed exponential blow-up with this *global reluctant splitting* strategy for the SELF programs we have written so far.

To further reduce both overall compilation time and the risk of exponential blow-up, the SELF compiler normally uses a more conservative *local reluctant splitting* strategy. This approach forcibly combines all paths together into a single path after any control flow graph node that generates machine instructions, such as a message send node or a branch node but not an assignment node or a merge node. This has the effect of replacing each set of path-specific types with a single union type for the resulting combined path, thereby sacrificing some precision of type information to keep compilation fast. In the cases where this early path combining makes a difference, local reluctant splitting saves up to 30% of the compile time at a cost of up to 30% extra run time over global reluctant splitting [Cha91]. Perhaps surprisingly, global reluctant splitting sometimes enables optimizations which significantly shrink the size of the control flow graph and consequently occasionally compiles *faster* (and runs faster) than with local reluctant splitting.

Here is our example up through the first merge, this time with the path information.

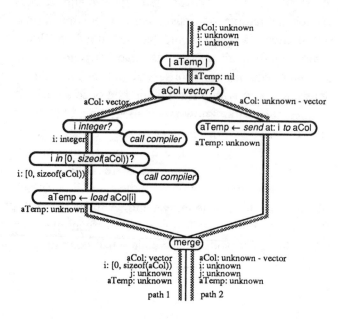

Now it is time to start using the paths. The compiler must generate code to send `at: j` to `aCol` and put the result in an anonymous temporary, called `t1` here. The type of `aCol` after the merge is either a vector (along path 1) or a non-vector (along path 2). Since the compiler keeps these two types separate using paths, it can do something more intelligent than inserting another type test to see if `aCol` is a vector. The compiler can use the path information to delay the premature merge until after the `at: j` message by *splitting* the merge and the `at: j` message into two copies, one along path 1 and one along path 2. In the path 1 case, `aCol` is known to be a vector, and the compiler can inline the `at: j` just as it did in the preceding `at: i` message. Along path 2, the compiler knows only that `aCol` is definitely not a vector, and so must fall back onto generating a full message send.

Now the compiler is faced with `aCol at: i Put: t1`. Again it splits path 1 from path 2, but this time the path objects uncover a hidden opportunity: the elimination of the type and bounds check of `i` along path 1. This extra type information about `i` is available because the compiler uses paths to recover the types of variables other than the one being split on. Paths support similar optimizations for the last message, `aCol at: j Put: aTemp`, as the next figure shows.

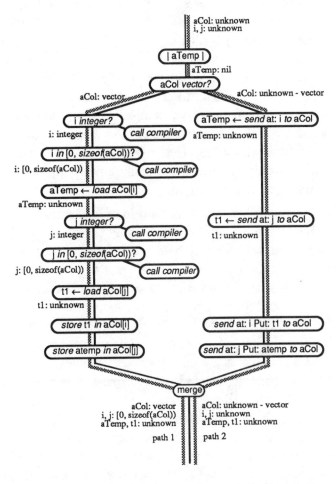

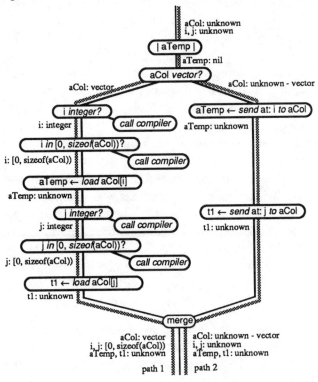

Every redundant type and bounds check has been eliminated, no effort has been wasted compiling uncommon cases, and none has been expended to reanalyze types after splits. Deferred compilation of uncommon branches and reluctant splitting based on paths enable these results.

4 Optimizing Loops

The previous example is taken from the inner loop of the `bubblesort` benchmark. Our techniques work especially well to optimize programs containing loops, frequently compiling *multiple versions* of a loop, each version optimized for different combinations of types.

Our type analysis technique for compiling loops is called *iterative type analysis*. The compiler first compiles the body of the loop assuming some type bindings at the loop head computed from the types at the loop entrance (the branch entering the loop from the top). It then checks to see whether the types computed at the loop tail are compatible with the loop head; if so it connects the loop tail to the loop head and is done with the loop. If the types are not compatible, the compiler attempts to split the loop tail to create a loop tail that is compatible with a loop head. If splitting won't help, then the analysis iterates, compiling a new loop body assuming more general types.

Compatibility of loop tails with loop heads must be defined carefully to preserve opportunities for optimization. Even though a loop head may have more general types than the types at a loop tail, and thus would be acceptable as a connecting loop head, the compiler avoids connecting a loop tail to any loop head that has less class type information. For example, if a loop head has some variable bound to the unknown type, while a loop tail has the same variable bound to the integer class type, the compiler will treat the loop head as incompatible; this ensures that the knowledge that the variable is an integer at the completion of the loop can be exploited in subsequent iterations. To avoid expending too much time and space on separate versions of loops, the compiler allows a loop tail to have a constant or subrange type while the loop head only has a class type (of the same class, of course); this sacrifices only a small amount of type information but saves a lot of compile time and compiled-code space.

Both the current SELF compiler and the previous SELF compiler follow this same plan when compiling loops. However, they differ in the details of how they answer the following questions:

- *What should the initial type bindings be at the head of the loop?* The previous SELF compiler simply assumed the same types as the loop entrance. The current SELF compiler uses *early generalization* of constant and subrange types to the enclosing class types for any variables assigned within the loop. This usually saves an iteration over the simpler strategy used in the previous SELF compiler, although it occasionally sacrifices some type information.

- *What should the compiler do when it cannot connect a loop tail to any loop head?* The previous SELF compiler would replace the inadequate version of the loop body with a new fresh copy, with all split loop heads merged back together. It then allowed normal splitting to split the loop head back apart. This approach had the advantage that loop bodies should be quite compact, and since the previous SELF compiler didn't defer compilation of uncommon branches it ensured that all uncommon branches got merged together quickly to save compile time and compiled-code space. Unfortunately, the compiler ended up reproducing a lot of analysis to split the loop bodies apart over and over each iteration, and the backtracking type analysis was excruciatingly slow and space-consuming when reanalyzing split loop bodies. This compile-time performance problem hindered our ability to debug the compiler and its voracious appetite for compiler temporary space prevented us from compiling multiple versions of loops on any but the smallest benchmarks.

The current SELF compiler avoids these pitfalls by adopting a simple, fast strategy. When a loop tail isn't compatible with any loop head, the compiler simply "unrolls" the loop for that one loop tail; the other versions of the loop remain unaffected. This strategy matches our forward-only type analysis scheme both in implementation simplicity and compilation speed. Its drawback is that in some situations this unrolling strategy uses more compiled code space, since there is no sharing of code among separate loop bodies. With deferred compilation of uncommon branches, this has not been a problem in practice.

We will illustrate these points by embedding our example within a simple endless loop; for the sake of simplicity we will ignore the loop counter testing and incrementing code that would be part of the real inner loop of the `bubblesort` benchmark.

After compiling the loop for the first time, the control flow graph has one loop head, which could accept any types, and one loop tail with two paths.

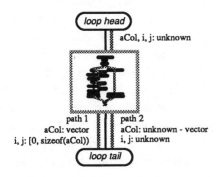

Although the compiler could choose to merely connect the tail up to the head, that would lose class type information on path 1, so the compiler splits path 1 off from path 2, and connects the loop tail for path 2 back to the head.

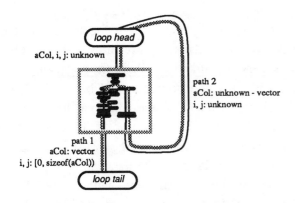

After connecting up the non-vector path, the compiler must generate code for the remaining path. Along this path the compiler already knows that aCol is a vector and that i and j are integer subranges.* This more specific type information enables a shorter, faster version of

---

* In a more realistic example, i or j would be assigned within the loop and the compiler would generalize their types to the integer class type, so that the version of the loop to be compiled would handle more potential loop tails. In this pedagogical example, neither i nor j is assigned and so their types are left unchanged.

the loop to be generated with no type tests or bounds checks.

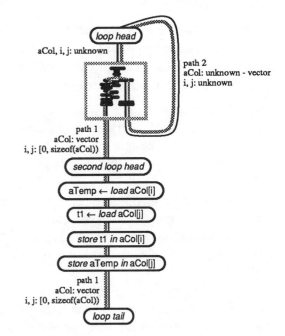

At this point, the types at the last loop tail are an exact match for the second loop head, and so the loop tail can be connected to the second loop head to finish our example.

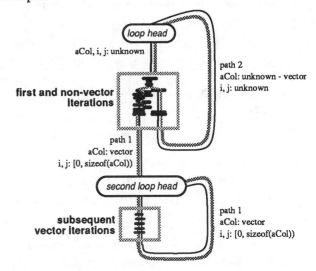

At this point the compiler has ensured that most of the executions of the loop will be as good as can be. It has in effect compiled a separate version of the whole loop for the common case that aCol is a vector, hoisting the type test out of the subsequent iterations into the first iteration. All this has been accomplished without costly backtracking in the type analysis.

5 Performance Results

5.1 Methodology

In order to evaluate the performance impact of deferred compilation of uncommon cases and non-backtracking type analysis with loop unrolling and path objects, we compared the performance of three versions of SELF:

- SELF'90 is last year's SELF system [CU90], lacking both deferred compilation and non-backtracking type analysis. Partly because of lengthy compilation times, this system could not generate multiple copies of loops.

- SELF'91 (not deferred) is the current system, with non-backtracking type analysis, but with deferred compilation disabled. This system can be compared to SELF'90 to isolate the effect of non-backtracking type analysis.

- SELF'91 (normal) is the current system including both deferred compilation and non-backtracking type analysis. This system can be compared to SELF'91 (not deferred) to isolate the effect of deferred compilation. Both SELF'91 configurations used local reluctant splitting.

To measure execution and compilation times for a SELF benchmark, we first flushed the compiled code cache and then ran the benchmark 11 times. Consequently, the first run of the benchmark includes both compilation and execution, while the remaining 10 runs include only execution. Therefore, we calculate the execution time by taking the arithmetic mean of the times for the last 10 runs and calculate compilation time by subtracting the mean execution time from the time for the first run.

In order to evaluate the practicality of pure object-oriented languages, we standardized the processor, a lightly-loaded Sun-4/260 SPARC-based workstation, and measured several other systems:

- The standard Sun C compiler with optimization enabled (using the −O2 option) established a goal for run-time performance. The graphs present performance relative to optimized C. (Appendix A contains the raw data.) Compilation time for optimized C includes the time to read and write files but not the time to link the resulting .o files together.

- In order to compare our approach to implementing a pure object-oriented language with competing approaches, we measured the ParcPlace Smalltalk-80 system (version 2.4) incorporating the Deutsch-Schiffman techniques [DS84].[*] As far as we know, this is the fastest implementation of any other system in which nearly every operation is performed by sending a dynamically-dispatched message. Variable accesses and some low-level control structures do not use messages in Smalltalk-80, unlike SELF.

- In order to compare our techniques against other systems supporting generic arithmetic, we also measured the ORBIT compiler (version 3.1) [KKR+86, Kra88] for T [RA82, Sla87], a dialect of Scheme [RC86]. ORBIT is well respected as a good optimizing compiler for a Scheme-like language. These data are labeled T/ORBIT (normal). Since nearly all benchmarks for Lisp-like systems measure programs that use integer-specific arithmetic, we also measure a version of the benchmarks using unsafe integer-specific arithmetic (e.g. fx+ and fx< in T) and explicit indications to the compiler to inline certain functions (define-integrable in T). These data are labeled T/ORBIT (integer only). Compilation time includes the time to read and write files but not the time to load the generated file into the running T system.

In some ways, comparing these systems is like comparing apples to oranges. Our measured SELF system includes support for message passing at the most basic levels, user-defined control structures at the most basic levels, generic arithmetic, robust error-checking primitives, and support for source-level debugging. All these features are available in the SELF versions we measured. Neither the C version nor the T versions of the benchmarks use message passing or user-defined control structures, neither C nor the integer-specific version of T support generic arithmetic, neither C nor T compiled using ORBIT perform error checking for all primitives, and neither the optimizing C compiler nor T compiled using ORBIT support source-level debugging. We have directed much of our effort toward developing optimization techniques that coexist with the advantages of the SELF language and environment; programmers no longer need to choose between semantics and performance.

---

[*] Compile time and compiled code space measurements for Smalltalk-80 are unavailable.

We measured the eight Stanford integer benchmarks [Hen88] and the Richards operating system simulation benchmark [Deu88]. The C version of the `richards` benchmark is actually written in C++ version 1.2, translated into C using the standard `cfront` filter, and then optimized using the Sun C compiler. Only a few of the object-oriented features of C++ are used; for example there is only a single virtual function call (C++ terminology for a message send) in the entire benchmark. In the charts below we report the average results for seven small Stanford integer benchmarks and `puzzle` and `richards` separately; this separates the benchmarks into rough "equivalence classes" based on benchmark size. Raw data for each benchmark may be found in Appendix A.

5.2   Results

The graphs to the right show the execution speed, compilation speed, and code density for our benchmarks, normalized to optimized C. Bigger bars are better.

5.2.1   Non-Backtracking Type Analysis and Deferred Compilation of Uncommon Cases

Comparing SELF'90 to SELF'91 (not deferred) reveals that eliminating backtracking speeds up compilation by a factor of two to four. Run-time performance and compiled-code space efficiency are roughly comparable for the two systems. Since other aspects of the SELF compiler and run-time system also changed between these two systems, it is difficult to make precise comparisons, but we can conclude that this technique succeeds at reducing compile times without significant penalties for the other metrics.

Comparing the two versions of SELF'91 with and without deferred compilation of uncommon cases reveals that this technique is an unqualified success, boosting compilation speed by up to a factor of 10, while simultaneously improving both execution performance and code space efficiency. In conjunction with non-backtracking type analysis, deferred compilation improves compilation speed by more than an order of magnitude over the previous SELF system.

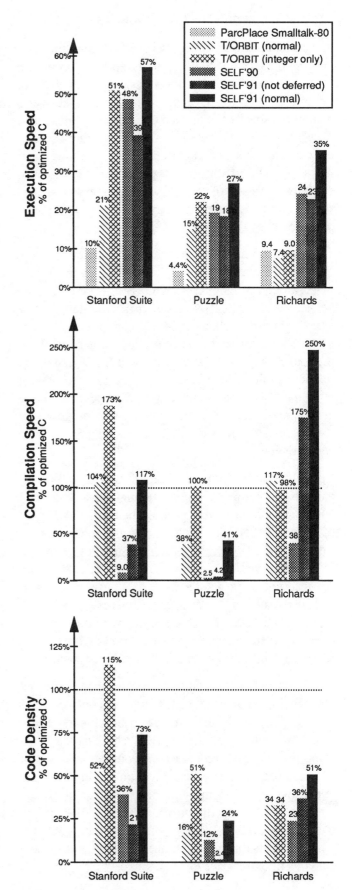

11

5.2.2 Comparing SELF to Other Systems

The current SELF compiler runs the small Stanford integer benchmarks at well over half the speed of optimized C and more than five times faster than ParcPlace Smalltalk-80. The `puzzle` benchmark runs at over a quarter the speed of optimized C, again five times faster than Smalltalk-80. The `richards` benchmark runs at over a third the speed of optimized C, four times faster than Smalltalk-80; this level of performance is achieved partially because of recent work primarily by Urs Hölzle on extending the SELF system to speed polymorphic messages [HCU91].

These measurements suggest that our techniques would improve the speed of generic arithmetic even in non-object-oriented languages. Our SELF system runs between 50% and 250% faster than "normal" T programs compiled using the ORBIT compiler, and faster by 10% to 20% than even hand-tuned integer-specific T programs. Our results show that such hand-tuning and restricting of programs is no longer necessary to achieve good performance, and we would hope that future benchmarkers no longer resort to such violations of their languages in search of favorable performance comparisons.

Compilation speed for the current SELF system is comparable to optimized C and the normal version of T and ORBIT, is about half the speed of the restricted version of T and ORBIT, and is over twice the speed of C++ (recall that `richards` is written in C++). Part of SELF's compilation speed efficiency is because it does not read and write intermediate files but instead compiles native machine code directly into the same address space as the compiler. This avoidance of intermediate files and their accompanying overhead is one of the advantages of a dynamic compilation-based system.

SELF uses only a third more code space than optimized C for the small Stanford benchmarks and only twice as much code space for the `richards` benchmark. These results are better than the T/ORBIT combination when compiling normal T programs. We consider this amount of space usage to be reasonable, considering the relatively low cost of memory in today's workstations and the greater functionality provided by the SELF system over C and even T. We hope that these measurements allay any fears that our techniques require unreasonable amounts of extra space to be effective.

6 Implementation Status

The techniques described in this paper primarily were implemented in the SELF system in the summer and fall of 1990. We have been freely distributing this system, known as SELF Release 1.1, since January 1991. Over 150 sites around the world have a copy of our SELF implementation, and several medium-sized projects in SELF have been pursued by people outside our group.

Two compilers are distributed with this system: the latest SELF compiler described in this paper and the original SELF compiler described in [CU89] and [CUL89], which is less optimizing than the latest SELF compiler but compiles faster. When using the previous SELF compiler described in [CU90], a user would have to take a coffee break during a compilation, and many programs would fail to compile. With paths, the elimination of backtracking in the compiler's type analysis, and deferral of the compilation of uncommon cases, compile times for the latest compiler are merely distracting. To minimize this distraction, we are investigating adaptive recompilation strategies that reserve optimization for heavily-used methods [HCU91]; a crude form of this which first compiles methods using the original SELF compiler and later recompiles often-used methods using the latest SELF compiler is the standard configuration of our current system.

7 Previous Work

Other systems perform type inference over programs without explicit type declarations. ML [MTH90] is a statically-typed function-oriented language in which the compiler is able to infer the types of all procedures and expressions and do static type checking with virtually no type declarations. Researchers have attempted to extend type inference to object-oriented languages, with some success [Wan87, Wan88, Wan89, OB89, Rou90]. These approaches use type systems that describe an object's interface or protocol, not the object's representation or implementation. This abstract view of an object's type is best for flexible polymorphic type-checking, but provides little information for an optimizing compiler to speed programs. Our type analysis is more akin to traditional data flow analysis than type inference, in that it computes precise, time-varying, representation-level types for objects suitable for optimizations.

A different approach is taken by the Typed Smalltalk project [Joh86, JGZ88]. Users must annotate programs with type declarations for instance variables, class variables, global variables, and primitives, and then either run an inferencer to compute the types of methods and local variables [Gra89, GJ90] (which, like type inference in ML, provides the compiler with little information to support optimizations) or hand-declare selected methods and local variables with more specific representation-level type information. This representation-level type information is used by the TS optimizing compiler to perform run-time type casing and message inlining.

Published performance results for TS indicate that small Typed Smalltalk programs with explicit user-supplied type declarations run between five and ten times faster than Smalltalk programs executed by the Tektronix Smalltalk interpreter on a Tektronix 4405 68020-based workstation. Rough calculations based on the speed of the Deutsch-Schiffman Smalltalk implementation on a similar machine indicate that the TS optimizing compiler runs Typed Smalltalk programs about twice as fast as the Deutsch-Schiffman system runs comparable untyped Smalltalk-80 programs. This published result is still somewhere between two and three times slower than that achieved by our current SELF compiler, even though users do not add any declarations to SELF programs.

Recent unpublished performance results for very small benchmarks (smaller than any of the benchmarks we report in this paper) indicate that the current speed of Typed Smalltalk is close to the speed of our current SELF system, but unfortunately the current Typed Smalltalk system does not support generic arithmetic (integer arithmetic primitives do not check for overflow) [McC90]. Much of our work has been directed towards supporting both good performance and the complete language semantics; we found generic arithmetic particularly difficult to support efficiently in our SELF system and developed deferred compilation of uncommon branches and path-based splitting partially in response to this challenge.

8 Conclusions

The current version of the SELF compiler is both *effective* and *usable*. It executes small benchmarks at well over half the speed of optimized C, five times faster than the fastest existing implementation of any other pure object-oriented language with similar features, and with a compilation speed that is currently comparable to the optimizing C compiler. This new-found level of performance, both run-time and compile-time, hopefully will convince other language designers and language users that pure object-oriented languages are now practical.

The key technical contributions over our previous work on the SELF compiler are careful design and implementation of splitting strategies that rely only on path-based non-backtracking type analysis and deferred compilation of uncommon branches. Non-backtracking type analysis leads to up to an order-of-magnitude improvement in compilation speed by avoiding time-consuming reanalysis of split branches. Path objects are critical to realizing this non-backtracking goal without degrading the quality of the type analysis. Iterative type analysis is sped up further by eagerly generalizing the types of assignable local variables before loop analysis and by simply unrolling new copies of loops for loop tails that don't match any loop heads rather than starting the whole loop analysis over from scratch. Deferred compilation of uncommon branches exploits the skewed execution frequency distribution by only compiling those parts of the control flow graph that are likely to be executed. This technique increases compilation speed by nearly an order of magnitude and even improves execution speed by simplifying the type analysis and easing the register allocation problem. Deferred compilation fits in quite well with the on-demand dynamic compilation strategy used in our SELF implementation.

While the current SELF implementation is now usable and reliable, it still remains slower than desirable. We are pursuing techniques to reduce compiler pause times further, hopefully to the point at which SELF users forget that the compiler even exists.

Acknowledgments

We would like to express our heartfelt gratitude to the other members of the SELF group for their contributions and support: Urs Hölzle, Bay-Wei Chang, Ole Agesen, and Randall B. Smith.

References

[BHJL86] Andrew Black, Norman Hutchinson, Eric Jul, and Henry Levy. Object Structure in the Emerald System. In *OOPSLA'86 Conference Proceedings*, pp. 78-86, Portland, OR, September, 1986. Published as *SIGPLAN Notices 21(11)*, November, 1986.

[BDG+88] D. G. Bobrow, L. G. DeMichiel, R. P. Gabriel, S. E. Keene, G. Kiczales, D. A. Moon. Common Lisp Object System Specification X3J13. In *SIGPLAN Notices 23(Special Issue)*, September, 1988.

[CU89] Craig Chambers and David Ungar. Customization: Optimizing Compiler Technology for SELF, a Dynamically-Typed Object-Oriented Programming Language. In *Proceedings of the SIGPLAN'89 Conference on Programming Language Design and Implementation*, pp. 146-160, Portland, OR, June, 1989. Published as *SIGPLAN Notices 24(7)*, July, 1989.

[CUL89] Craig Chambers, David Ungar, and Elgin Lee. An Efficient Implementation of SELF, a Dynamically-Typed Object-Oriented Language Based on Prototypes. In *OOPSLA'89 Conference Proceedings*, pp. 49-70, New Orleans, LA, October, 1989. Published as *SIGPLAN Notices 24(10)*, October, 1989.

[CU90] Craig Chambers and David Ungar. Iterative Type Analysis and Extended Message Splitting: Optimizing Dynamically-Typed Object-Oriented Programs. In *Proceedings of the SIGPLAN'90 Conference on Programming Language Design and Implementation*, pp. 150-164, White Plains, NY, June, 1990. Published as *SIGPLAN Notices 25(6)*, June, 1990.

[Cha91] Craig Chambers. *The Design and Implementation of the SELF Compiler, an Optimizing Compiler for Object-Oriented Programming Languages*. Ph.D. thesis, Stanford University, in preparation.

[DS84] L. Peter Deutsch and Allan M. Schiffman. Efficient Implementation of the Smalltalk-80 System. In *Proceedings of the 11th Annual ACM Symposium on the Principles of Programming Languages*, pp. 297-302, Salt Lake City, UT, 1984.

[Deu88] L. Peter Deutsch. Richards benchmark source code. Personal communication, October, 1988.

[ES90] Margaret A. Ellis and Bjarne Stroustrup. *The Annotated C++ Reference Manual*. Addison-Wesley, Reading, MA, 1990.

[GR83] Adele Goldberg and David Robson. *Smalltalk-80: The Language and Its Implementation*. Addison-Wesley, Reading, MA, 1983.

[Gra89] Justin Owen Graver. *Type-Checking and Type-Inference for Object-Oriented Programming Languages*. Ph.D. thesis, University of Illinois at Urbana-Champaign, 1989.

[GJ90] Justin O. Graver and Ralph E. Johnson. A Type System for Smalltalk. In *Conference Record of the 17th Annual ACM Symposium on Principles of Programming Languages*, pp. 136-150, San Francisco, CA, January, 1990.

[Hen88] John Hennessy. Stanford benchmark suite source code. Personal communication, June, 1988.

[HCU91] Urs Hölzle, Craig Chambers, and David Ungar. Optimizing Dynamically-Typed Object-Oriented Programs using Polymorphic Inline Caches. In *ECOOP'91 Conference Proceedings*, Geneva, Switzerland, July, 1991.

[Hut87] Norman C. Hutchinson. *Emerald: An Object-Based Language for Distributed Programming*. Ph.D. thesis, University of Washington, 1987.

[Joh86] Ralph E. Johnson. Type-Checking Smalltalk. In *OOPSLA'86 Conference Proceedings*, pp. 315-321, Portland, OR, September, 1986. Published as *SIGPLAN Notices 21(11)*, November, 1986.

[JGZ88] Ralph E. Johnson, Justin O. Graver, and Lawrence W. Zurawski. TS: An Optimizing Compiler for Smalltalk. In *OOPSLA'88 Conference Proceedings*, pp. 18-26, San Diego, CA, October, 1988. Published as *SIGPLAN Notices 23(11)*, November, 1988.

[KKR+86] David Kranz, Richard Kelsey, Jonathan Rees, Paul Hudak, James Philbin, and Norman Adams. ORBIT: An Optimizing Compiler for Scheme. In *Proceedings of the SIGPLAN'86 Symposium on Compiler Construction*, pp. 219-233, Palo Alto, CA, June, 1986. Published as *SIGPLAN Notices 21(7)*, July, 1986.

[Kra88] David Andrew Kranz. *ORBIT: An Optimizing Compiler for Scheme*. Ph.D. thesis, Yale University, 1988.

[McC90] Carl McConnell. TS performance data. Personal communication, October, 1990.

[Mey86] Bertrand Meyer. Genericity versus Inheritance. In *OOPSLA'86 Conference Proceedings*, pp. 391-405, Portland, OR, September, 1986. Published as *SIGPLAN Notices 21(11)*, November, 1986.

[Mey88] Bertrand Meyer. *Object-Oriented Software Construction*. Prentice-Hall, New York, 1988.

[MTH90] Robin Milner, Mads Tofte, and Robert Harper. *The Definition of Standard ML*. MIT Press, Cambridge, MA, 1990.

[OB89] Atsushi Ohori and Peter Buneman. Static Type Inference for Parametric Classes. In *OOPSLA'89 Conference Proceedings*, pp. 445-456, New Orleans, LA, October, 1989. Published as *SIGPLAN Notices 24(10)*, October, 1989.

[RA82] Jonathan A. Rees and Norman I. Adams IV. T: a Dialect of Lisp or, LAMBDA: the Ultimate Software Tool. In *Proceedings of the 1982 ACM Symposium on Lisp and Functional Programming*, pp. 114-122, August, 1982.

[RC86]   Jonathan Rees and William Clinger, editors. *Revised³ Report on the Algorithmic Language Scheme*. In *SIGPLAN Notices 21(12)*, December, 1986.

[Rou90] Francois Rouaix. Safe Run-Time Overloading. In *Conference Record of the 17th Annual ACM Symposium on Principles of Programming Languages*, pp. 355-366, San Francisco, CA, January, 1990.

[SCW85] Craig Schaffert, Topher Cooper, and Carrie Wilpolt. Trellis Object-Based Environment, Language Reference Manual. Technical report DEC-TR-372, November, 1985.

[SCB+86] Craig Schaffert, Topher Cooper, Bruce Bullis, Mike Kilian, and Carrie Wilpolt. An Introduction to Trellis/Owl. In *OOPSLA'86 Conference Proceedings*, pp. 9-16, Portland, OR, September, 1986. Published as *SIGPLAN Notices 21(11)*, November, 1986.

[Sla87] Stephen Slade. *The T Programming Language*. Prentice-Hall, Englewood Cliffs, NJ, 1987.

[Str86] Bjarne Stroustrup. *The C++ Programming Language*. Addison-Wesley, Reading, MA, 1986.

[US87]   David Ungar and Randall B. Smith. SELF: The Power of Simplicity. In *OOPSLA'87 Conference Proceedings*, pp. 227-241, Orlando, FL, October, 1987. Published as *SIGPLAN Notices 22(12)*, December, 1987.

[Wan87] Mitchell Wand. Complete Type Inference for Simple Objects. In *Proceedings of the Second Annual IEEE Symposium on Logic in Computer Science*, pp. 37-44, Ithaca, NY, June, 1987.

[Wan88] Mitchell Wand. Corrigendum: Complete Type Inference for Simple Objects. In *Proceedings of the Third Annual IEEE Symposium on Logic in Computer Science*, p. 132, Edinburgh, Scotland, July, 1988.

[Wan89] Mitchell Wand. Type Inference for Record Concatenation and Multiple Inheritance. In *Proceedings of the Fourth Annual IEEE Symposium on Logic in Computer Science*, pp. 92-97, 1989.

Appendix A   Per-Benchmark Raw Data

The SELF'90 run time and compile time data are as reported in [CU90]. That system was not completely debugged and could not compile more than one copy of a loop. The system later was fixed and could compile more than one version of a loop, but was even slower to compile than the published system and still could not compile the larger benchmarks without running out of compiler temporary memory space. Compile times and code size data are not available for Smalltalk-80. The C version of richards is actually written in C++, preprocessed into C, then compiled with an optimizing C compiler; this partially accounts for its relatively slow compilation speed.

Run Times (ms)	Smalltalk	T (normal)	T (int only)	SELF'90	SELF'91 (no defer)	SELF'91 (normal)	C (optimized)
bubble	2700	1000	340	320	680	230	200
matrix multiply	4600	2500	900	700	640	600	280
perm	1400	1200	280	200	360	230	110
queens	860	640	240	260	250	180	92
quicksort	1300	1500	650	330	440	270	130
towers	1000	730	310	440	300	350	190
treesort	1100	1300	960	960	1000	930	870
puzzle	16000	4500	3100	3600	3900	2500.	690
richards	7700	9800	8100	3500	3200	2800.	730

Compile Times (s)	T (normal)	T (int only)	SELF'90	SELF'91 (no defer)	SELF'91 (normal)	C (optimized)
bubble	2.7	1.3	22	16	1.8	2.9
matrix multiply	3.0	1.5	30	9.8	3.8	2.9
perm	2.1	1.0	20	5.3	2.2	2.8
queens	3.4	1.6	25	8.2	4.6	3.1
quicksort	3.4	1.7	120	10	2.5	3.0
towers	3.4	3.5	7.6	1.9	1.3	3.7
treesort	3.5	2.4	7.0	6.5	2.1	3.9
puzzle	24	9.1	360	220	23	9.1
richards	12	14	36	7.7	5.4	13

Code Size (Kb)	T (normal)	T (int only)	SELF'90	SELF'91 (no defer)	SELF'91 (normal)	C (optimized)
bubble	4.7	1.9	5.9	21	2.2	2.7
matrix multiply	5.4	2.1	8.3	12	4.0	2.5
perm	3.6	1.3	7.1	7.9	2.9	2.4
queens	5.2	1.7	8.0	12	5.0	2.5
quicksort	5.8	2.7	10	20	3.6	2.8
towers	6.5	3.5	7.4	5.3	3.3	3.1
treesort	5.8	3.6	7.2	12	3.6	3.3
puzzle	32	9.9	41	210	21	5.0
richards	18	18	26	17	12	6.1

Parallel Generational Garbage Collection*

Ravi Sharma [†]

Mary Lou Soffa

Dept. of Computer Science
University of Pittsburgh
322 Alumni Hall
Pittsburgh, PA 15260

Abstract

With the advent of parallel systems, opportunities for efficiency exist that have yet to be exploited, especially in the area of garbage collection. In this paper, a parallel generational garbage collection algorithm is presented that extends previous work by exploiting opportunities for parallelism in the garbage collection process itself. A prototype implementation of the parallel generational collector was developed and its execution simulated to determine its efficiency. For a certain class of programs, the parallel generational collector performed up to 67% less copying than a parallel copy collector and reduced elapsed times up to an additional 12%; corresponding reductions in overhead for the ongoing program were also observed.

1. Introduction

Recent developments in parallel architectures and software indicate a growing interest for implementations of object-oriented languages on parallel systems.[3, 12, 17, 19, 24] Parallel architectures such as the Sequent Symmetry,[15] Encore Multimax,[8] and DEC Firefly,[21] utilize multiple processors operating in parallel on a shared global memory. The introduction of parallelism has presented opportunities for efficiency that have yet to be exploited, especially in the areas of storage management and gar-

bage collection. High overhead, reported to be as much as 20% of the execution time, may be involved in the allocation and reclamation of the many objects created and destroyed by object-oriented programs.[1, 6, 22] The work presented in this paper reduces the high overhead in automatic garbage collection by utilizing a generational scheme to exploit opportunities for parallelism in the garbage collection process. Current parallel collection algorithms only exploit the possibility of allowing the ongoing program's computation to progress simultaneously with the garbage collection. However, the availability of many multiple processors also suggests the application of parallelism within the garbage collector itself.

The generational scheme for garbage collection lends itself naturally to the problem of automatic storage reclamation on parallel systems. A generational collector segregates dynamically allocated objects according to their ages into generations within the heap in order to concentrate its efforts in collecting the younger generations, which is where the major proportion of garbage is gen-

* This work was partially supported by the National Science Foundation under Grant CCR-8801104 to the University of Pittsburgh.

† Please direct all correspondence to this author's present address: AT&T Bell Laboratories, Room 2K-115, 480 Red Hill Road, Middletown, NJ 07748. Phone number: (908) 615-4273, FAX number: (908) 615-2882, email: sharma@mozart.att.com

erated.[14,16,22] Parallelization of such a generational scheme can occur on two fronts. First, garbage collection should be allowed to take place in parallel with the ongoing program. Second and more important, parallel tasks within the collector could simultaneously collect garbage in several generations. The method presented in this paper parallelizes a generational scheme for garbage collection for use on a shared-memory multiprocessor architecture. A medium-grained synchronization technique, based on paging in virtual memory systems,[1] is combined with the object partitioning nature of generational systems to achieve improved efficiency. The algorithm is designed to operate on shared-memory multiprocessor architectures, but is also applicable in a timeshared uniprocessor environment that has paging of virtual memory. The parallel generational collection algorithm and a parallel copy collection algorithm were implemented and their performances simulated using a number of mutators. Experimental results are given comparing the performance of these two collectors.

Early work in parallel garbage collection algorithms began with the study of "on-the-fly" garbage collection schemes, which involve two processors operating on a common memory in such a way that one processor (the *mutator*) performs the "useful" work and the other (the *collector*) reclaims unused storage. Algorithms developed for on-the-fly garbage collection were used more as examples in proof techniques for parallel programs than in practical and efficient garbage collection systems.[2,7,9,11] These algorithms parallelized the traditional mark-and-sweep collector, and thus inherited its deficiencies, primarily the need to access a large number of objects, including both the live and dead objects.

Copy collection algorithms avoided the costly phase of accessing dead objects within mark-and-sweep collectors.[5] This cost was eliminated by moving the live objects to a new area of memory, so that the previous area of memory would be free for subsequent copy collections. A generalization of the copy collection algorithm on a shared-memory multiprocessor was developed for an

implementation of Multilisp.[10] Each thread of a Multilisp program interleaves its execution with calls to the collector. However, in order to maintain synchronized access to objects in the system, each object is equipped with its own lock, and special hardware support is necessary to realize the required efficiency. The Pegasus collector[18] is a concurrent collector that also implements this algorithm, but in a time-sharing fashion on a uniprocessor system. As with the Multilisp implementation, the Pegasus collector maintains per-object locks to ensure the atomicity of object updates. Another drawback is the collector's reliance on the time-shared nature of execution in order to ensure the absence of obsolete pointers into the collected space. These restrictions decrease its applicability on a multiprocessor.

Recent work in parallel collection investigated the use of the medium-grain locks on the pages in virtual memory systems instead of finer-grained per-object locks for synchronization.[1] Operating on stock commercial uniprocessors and shared-memory multiprocessors, this technique allows computation to progress simultaneously with a copy collector except when accesses are made to objects on a page not yet scanned by the collector. Figure 1 gives a view of the memory layout of this algorithm during a collection.

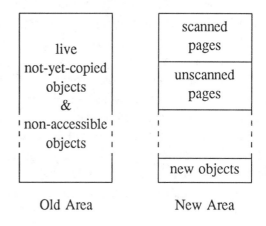

Figure 1. Memory layout for the parallel copy collector.

At the start of a collection, the root objects are copied into the new area and the virtual memory protection for the pages in the new area containing the root objects are set to "no-access". The mutator threads are then resumed, along with a collector process and a page fault trap handler. Whenever the mutator attempts to read an object that has not yet been scanned by the collector for references to the old area, a page fault trap occurs, the handler immediately scans the objects on the requested page for references to objects that need to be moved to the new space, and control is subsequently returned to the mutator. Meanwhile the collector process also scans the pages in the new space for references to objects that require relocation. As a page is scanned by the collector, its virtual memory protection is set back to "access". A locking mechanism consisting of a single lock provides the exclusive access to shared information that is read and updated by both the collector process and the trap handler. Large objects are managed by a *crossing map* technique that indicates when an object crosses the boundary between pages. This crossing map is consulted when a page trap is handled to find the page preceding the faulty page that begins with a fresh object.

Generational garbage collectors are copy collectors that attempt to eliminate the drawback of frequently copying stable objects. Based on the observation that many young objects die quickly while older objects continue to live,[14, 16, 22] the simple copy collection algorithm was altered to partition objects into generations based on the age of an object. Each generation is allocated its own area of memory. Younger generations are copy collected without disturbing older ones, permitting younger objects to be collected more often and reducing the time and effort spent on copying older, more stable objects. All new objects are allocated from the youngest generation, and objects are advanced (*tenured*) from younger to older generations based upon their survival through a number of collections.

The invocation of a collection (a *flip*) for a generation k generally results from the amount of available free space within the generation falling below some preset threshold[14, 16, 22] or due to some scheduling criteria.[23] To allow a generation k to be collected without traversing older generations, a table of backward references (references from objects in older generations to those in younger generations) in k must be maintained for consistency when collecting objects in k. A *remembered set* is used to indicate those older objects that make such backward references, as these references point to possibly live objects within the generations being collected. The burden of maintaining these tables of intergenerational references falls on some store instructions[14] and on the collector itself.[22]

When collecting a generation k, forward references (references from objects in younger generations to those in older generations) as well as backward references must be reconciled. One solution to handle references from younger generations is to extend the remembered set for generation k to contain objects that have references into generation k regardless of their relative age. This solution results in an explosion in the size of the remembered sets as, in general, there exist more pointers from younger generations to older ones than vice versa. The other solution, as implemented by Lieberman & Hewitt,[14] is to collect all younger generations as well as generation k so that object references will remain correct. In other words, when collecting a generation k, it becomes necessary to collect all generations $i \leq k$ in order to avoid prohibitive growth of remembered sets due to inclusion of references from younger generations. The extra time required to perform the collection of generations up to and including k is offset by the fact that generation k is less frequently collected relative to those younger than k.

2. Parallel Generational Garbage Collection

Our parallel generational algorithm employs multiple collectors working in parallel to make efficient use of the underlying architecture. The incremental nature of the algorithm is a direct result of using the virtual memory synchronization technique. Computation is allowed to progress during the garbage collection phase. Advancement of an object through the generations is based on its survival through a number of collection phases.

The algorithm subdivides the work of the collector during each collection phase through the use of intermediate generations. In order to maintain pointer consistency while collecting a single generation k, pointers from objects in generations younger as well as older than k must be reconciled. The method presented here works similarly to that of Lieberman & Hewitt[14] by collecting all the generations up to and including k, but collects these generations in parallel.

Allowing the collection of each generation $i \leq k$ to take place in parallel implies the use of locks to maintain synchronization between the parallel tasks, and thus the possibility of deadlock is introduced. Deadlock occurs when a circular wait condition exists among a set of tasks such that each task of the set requests a lock that is in control of another task in the set. Deadlock is avoided in our algorithm by using different classes of locks that control access to separate variables of each generation.

The utilization of intermediate generations also involves design choices concerning the remembered set. One possibility associates a remembered set with each generation i containing objects in generations greater than i that refer to objects in i. As noted earlier, this method is inefficient. Our algorithm uses a *collective remembered set* to reduce the proliferation of remembered sets and the requisite amount of work to manage them. This technique requires that only one set be maintained for all of the generations in the system. The collective remembered set consists of the pages that contain objects that have backward pointers into generations younger than their own. When a collection is performed on generations 1 through k, pages in the remembered set are scanned only if they belong to a generation greater than k. This method of scanning remembered set pages avoids the consistency problems among individual remembered sets for each generation. The collective remembered set is similar to the *page-marking* scheme used by Moon.[16]

2.1. Memory Layout

Memory is divided into several generations, one of which is called old space (*OS*). The old space contains those objects tenured from each of the generations by virtue of their survival through a number of collections (or scavenges). These objects have very long lifetimes and are virtually permanent in the system.

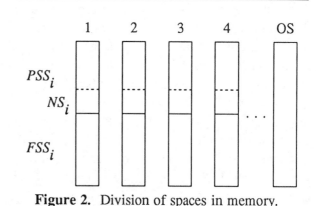

Figure 2. Division of spaces in memory.

Table 1. Glossary of Components for Generation i.

RS	the collective remembered set
RS'	the not-yet-scanned remembered set
PSS_i	the past-survivor space for generation i
PSS_i'	the not-yet-scanned past-survivor space
NS_i	the new space for i
FSS_i	the future-survivor space for i
OS	the old space

Each generation i is divided into two spaces, the past-survivor space (PSS_i) and the future-survivor space (FSS_i). PSS_i contains an area called the new space (NS_i) from which new objects or objects advanced from a younger generation are allocated. The past-survivor space also contains objects that have survived previous scavenges of the generation. The future-survivor space is typically empty during the execution of the mutator and is used when collecting live objects in the generation. A collection of generation i begins with the exchange of PSS_i and FSS_i and continues with the copying of reachable objects from the "new" FSS_i to the empty PSS_i.

Figure 2 gives a pictorial view of this memory layout. While the different spaces of each generation have been portrayed with equivalent sizes, this situation is not the case in general. The spaces of the youngest generation can be expected to be the largest size, as newly created objects are allocated within this generation. The spaces of the other generations may be smaller, since objects are located there only due to tenuring activity.

2.2. The Algorithm

The algorithm is presented in pseudo-code in the following figures, using sets to describe the collections of objects within various spaces. The set of pages containing objects that have backward references is called the collective remembered set (RS). In general, a collection of generation i begins with the exchange of PSS_i and FSS_i. Reachable objects are copied from the currently "full" FSS_i to the now empty PSS_i. Also, new objects are allocated from the new PSS_i. After all the reachable objects in FSS_i are copied, those that remain are garbage and are reclaimed by considering the entire FSS_i to be empty, ready for subsequent collections in the generation. The following invariants are maintained by the algorithm:

GC1. The mutator sees only PSS and OS pointers in its registers.

GC2. Objects in scanned pages contain PSS and OS pointers only.

These invariants allow objects in the not-yet-scanned pages to contain FSS pointers in addition to PSS and OS pointers. As objects are copied from FSS to PSS, the pages in PSS containing these objects are marked as *unscanned*. When the unscanned pages are scanned, FSS pointers on the page are updated to PSS pointers by copying the referenced object to PSS, thus maintaining invariant GC2. Invariant GC1 is maintained by the function that initiates a collection phase as well as by a page trap handler that traps requests to pages that may still have FSS pointers within them.

A garbage collection phase is invoked by a call to the function Flip(k) (see Figure 3). Flip initiates a collection on the first k generations by exchanging the roles of the past-survivor and future-survivor spaces of these generation and

copies the root objects to the new past-survivor space. As with other copy collection algorithms, the root objects are those objects that are directly accessible to the mutator. Objects that qualify as root objects include those currently in the machine registers, those saved on the run-time stack, etc. Only those root objects that are in the generations being collected are copied. Invariant GC1 is maintained as the mutator now has only PSS or OS pointers in its registers. By copying the root objects, the pages on which they reside are marked as unscanned, thus maintaining invariant GC2.

```
Flip( k ) {
    suspend all mutator threads ;
    if a previous collection is still running then
        wait for its completion ;
    for i := 1 to k loop
        swap( PSSᵢ, FSSᵢ ) ;
    for all root objects o loop
        if generation of o <= k then
            forwardObject( o );
            update pointer to o's new location ;
        endif
    RS' := { P ∈ RS | generation of P > k } ;
    RS := ∅ ;
    for all pages P ∈ RS' loop
        mark page P as unscanned ;
    spawn parallelGC( k );
    resume mutator threads ;
}
```

Figure 3. The Flip operation.

More specifically, Flip performs the following actions: (1) temporarily suspends all mutator activity, (2) waits for the completion of the previous garbage collection phase (if necessary), (3) exchanges the roles of the past and future spaces in the first k generations, (4) copies the root objects residing in the first k generations, (5) determines and marks as unscanned those pages in remembered set that are in generations older than k, since those pages contain objects that need to be scanned, (6) spawns the garbage collection process parallelGC(k), and (7) resumes the suspended mutator activity.

As the algorithm progresses, the remembered set is updated in so far as pages that no longer contain any backward references are removed from the set. Backward references within objects are removed due to updates to object references by the mutator or due to the eventual advancement out of younger generations of the objects that are the result of backward references.

The parallel collection algorithm, `parallelGC(k)`, is initiated by `Flip` and works by spawning a collector process for the remembered set and one for each generation participating in the collection (i.e., generations $1, 2, ..., k$) (see Figure 4). Initially, none of the pages in the remembered set have been scanned (and thus they are shown as belonging to RS') and the root objects copied by the flip operation are in one of PSS_i' for $i \leq k$. Once the remembered set and the past-survivor spaces for all generations $i \leq k$ have been scanned and all live objects in those generations have been copied, then the roles of the past-survivor spaces and the scanned future-survivor spaces of the participating generations have been completely interchanged (or flipped), and the collection phase is over. All remaining objects in FSS_i are garbage and each FSS_i is considered free. The remembered set undergoes some changes due to this algorithm; pages that no longer have references to younger generations are removed from RS, and new pages may be added to RS as a result of tenuring.

```
parallelGC( k ) {
  loop
    spawn rsCollect() ;
    spawn gc(i) for all 1 ≤ i ≤ k ;
    wait for rsCollect and all k gc processes to
      finish ;
    exit loop if RS' = ∅ and for all i PSS_i' = ∅ ;
  end loop
  for i := 1 to k loop
    FSS_i' := ∅ ;
}
```

Figure 4. Top-level of the parallel garbage collector.

Two routines comprise the next level of our collection algorithm. One routine (`rsCollect` depicted in Figure 5) repeatedly scans the contents of each page in the (not-yet-scanned) remembered set, searching for references to objects that need to

```
rsCollect( ) {
  for all pages P ∈ RS' loop
    let i be the generation associated with P ;
    lock l_i do  scanPage( P );
    RS' := RS' - { P } ;
}
```

Figure 5. The collection of the remembered set.

```
gc( i ) {
  for all pages P ∈ PSS_i' loop
    lock l_i do
      scanPage( P );
      PSS_i := PSS_i ∪ P ;
      PSS_i' := PSS_i' - P ;
    enddo ;
}
```

Figure 6. The collector for generation i.

```
gcTrap() {
  loop
    trap( mutator, P );
    let i be the generation associated with P ;
    lock l_i do  scanPage( P );
    resume( mutator );
}
```

Figure 7. Trap routine to detect references to unscanned objects.

be relocated. The other routine (`gc`) is the scanning routine that essentially copies live objects as it traces out the directed graph of these live objects within the generation from those objects already placed in the past-survivor space of the generation but have not yet been scanned (see Figure 6). One instance of this routine is created for each generation participating in the collection.

Locks l_i, n_i, and f_i are used to synchronize access to the past-survivor space PSS_i, to the new space NS_i, and to PSS_i' for forwarding actions, respectively. As noted earlier, using a single class of locks to access each of these spaces leads to deadlock. The consideration of using only two classes of locks per generation likewise leads to deadlock. For example, using a lock l_i for PSS_i and a lock n_i for NS_i and PSS_i' leads to deadlock between the process for a generation that needs to advance an object to the next generation and the process for collecting the older generation that has a reference to the younger one. The other cases similarly lead to deadlock. In addition to the possibility of deadlock, using only one or two classes of locks can inhibit the amount of parallelism that can be exploited by a generational collector.

The collector sets the virtual memory protection of the pages of the unscanned areas to "no-access". These areas include pages that contain objects in the not-yet-scanned remembered set and the pages to which the `Flip` operation copied the root objects. Whenever objects are placed in PSS_i', their pages are marked as not-yet-scanned, as are the pages added to RS'. If the mutator tries to access an object that has not yet been scanned, it will generate a page-access trap. This trap is fielded by the collector and is handled by `gcTrap` (Figure 7). The offending page is immediately scanned for references to objects that need to be relocated, after which control is returned to the mutator. It is this scanning that maintains invariant GC1 by allowing the mutator to see only PSS and OS pointers.

The routine `gc` operates on a page-by-page basis, calling upon `scanPage` to scan the objects on a page (Figure 8). `scanPage` in turn calls upon `scavengeContentsOf` for each object on the page. In `scavengeContentsOf`, an individual object is scanned for references to other objects that require relocation (see Figure 9). Only the referents in the future-survivor space of a generation participating in the current collection phase need to be relocated. These objects are relocated (while at the same time forwarding pointers are left in their place) and pointers in the original object are updated. If a referent has already been forwarded, then only its pointer is updated to indicate its new location. This routine is also in a position to determine whether or not the page containing the original object belongs in the remembered set, since it can determine if any referent is in a younger generation. This determination is performed after the object's referents have been relocated.

`forwardObject` determines the space to which an object is copied when it is collected. If the object has survived enough scavenges, it is tenured to the next older generation. When an

```
scanPage( P ) {
  return if P is marked as scanned ;
  while there are objects o ∈ P to scan loop
    scavengeContentsOf( o );
  mark P as scanned ;
}
```

Figure 8. The per-page scanning function.

object is copied (or collected) to a different space, a forwarding pointer is left in its old location so that other references to this object can be properly updated. In the cases where an object is relocated to a generation that is not participating in the current collection (i.e., generations > k and OS), the contents of that object also need to be scanned to maintain consistency. Such cases are handled by placing the object in RS' and marking the page in which the object resides as unscanned. The object will subsequently be scanned by either `rsCollect` or `gcTrap`.

The mutator's involvement with the garbage collector occurs in two ways. The first is the allocation of storage for an object (Figure 10). All objects are allocated in generation 1, and objects enter the other generations by virtue of advancement. However, if the allocator notices that the free space for generation k is approaching zero then it invokes the garage collector by calling the `Flip` operation.

The decision of which generations to involve in the collection can be more complicated than shown in Figure 10, and should be tailored to provide effective and efficient storage management for the particular situation or application at hand. The problem is to pick a k such that generation k is the oldest generation that is nearing saturation and requires collection. The tradeoff here is between an early collection of a generation and bypassing the collection of a generation that will soon require it. The balance struck between these two conditions has an impact on the efficiency of the collector since collecting a generation too early would waste garbage collection effort and not collecting a generation near saturation would precipitate a second collection quickly.

```
scavengeContentsOf( o ) {
  for all objects o´ pointed to by o loop
    j := generation of o´ ;
    if j ≤ k and o´ ∈ FSS_j then
      forwardObject( o´ );
      update o to indicate new o´ location ;
    if o now refers to a younger generation then
      RS := RS ∪ { o } ;
  endloop
}


forwardObject( o´ ) {
  return if o´ was already forwarded ;
  j := generation of o´ ;
  if age of o´ < tenuringThreshold then
    lock f_j do
      PSS_j´ := PSS_j´ ∪ { o´ } ;
      mark page P containing o´ as unscanned ;
      leave forwarding pointer in old o´ ;
  elsif j = MaxGenerations then
    lock n_OS do
      OS := OS ∪ { o´ } ;
      mark page P containing o´ as unscanned ;
      leave forwarding pointer in old o´ ;
    enddo
    RS´ := RS´ ∪ { o´ } ;
  elsif j = k then
    lock n_{j+1} do
      NS_{k+1} := NS_{k+1} ∪ { o´ } ;
      mark page P containing o´ as unscanned ;
      leave forwarding pointer in old o´ ;
    enddo
    RS´ := RS´ ∪ { o´ } ;
  else
    lock f_{j+1} do
      PSS_{j+1}´ := PSS_{j+1}´ ∪ { o´ } ;
      mark page P containing o´ as unscanned ;
      leave forwarding pointer in old o´ ;
  endif
  FSS_j := FSS_j - { o´ } ;
}
```

Figure 9. Functions for object scan and forward.

The mutator's other involvement with the collector is in the management of the remembered set. Certain store instructions in the mutator are responsible for discovering backward references as they are created, and the pages into which these backward references are placed are included in the remembered set. This monitoring of references can and does occur quite independently of an ongoing collection phase.

```
allocate( ) {
  if free space for some generation k
       < spaceThreshold then
    Flip( k );
  if there is an ongoing collection then
    lock n_1 do
      allocate storage for object in NS_1 ;
      return pointer to this storage ;
  else
    allocate storage for object in NS_1 ;
    return pointer to this storage ;
}
```

Figure 10. Object allocation in the mutator.

2.3. Deadlock Avoidance, Termination, and Correctness

Allowing the collection of each generation $\leq$ k to take place in parallel introduces the possibility of deadlock. The possibility of deadlock exists since locking mechanisms are used to synchronize access to the various spaces of each generation. There are three types of locks used: lock l_i is used to control access to PSS_i, lock f_i is used to control access to $PSS_i´$, and lock n_i is used to control access to NS_i. Deadlock can occur between two tasks if one task controls a lock requested by the other task and the first is waiting for a lock in control of the latter. Thus a circular waiting condition exists and deadlock occurs. This condition extends to multiple tasks, each waiting for a lock in control of the next. We now show that the various tasks of the algorithm request locks in such a way that no circular wait condition exists and deadlock is avoided.

Claim: *The locking mechanisms of the parallel generational garbage collector avoid deadlock.*
Proof: Consider the sequence in which locks are requested by the tasks of the system during a collection phase. rsCollect acquires a lock l_i for some i, then after a series of calls to scanPage, scavengeContentsOf and forwardObject requests either lock f_j for some $j \leq k$ or lock n_{k+1}. gc (*i*) acquires locks in the same manner. The mutator, during the course of its execution, may either activate gcTrap, which also acquires locks in the same manner or invoke allocate, which

23

only requires a lock n_i. As no task requires more than one lock of any type at a given time, deadlock can only manifest itself among the different locks in the system. The graph in Figure 11 represents the dependencies among the types of locks in this algorithm. Since there are no cycles in the graph and no task holds a lock forever, no circular wait or deadlocked condition can occur. □

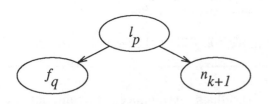

Figure 11. Dependences between locks (for any p and $1 \leq q \leq k$).

In order to prove the correctness and termination, it is necessary to note that all of the set union and set exclusion operations in the parallel garbage collector described above are atomic actions (as in Dijkstra et al.[7]). The atomicity of these actions in an implementation on a multiprocessor would not be difficult to ensure as multiprocessors typically provide single instruction memory locks. Race conditions that exist among the tasks of the collector are removed by the test for completion in `parallelGC`.

Given the absence of deadlock, it is now possible to show termination of a parallel collection phase.

Claim: *Once initiated, the parallel generational garbage collector terminates after a collection of k generations.*
Proof: The parallel generational garbage collector is initiated by the `Flip` operation. Directly before spawning `parallelGC(k)`, the situation in memory is as follows:

$RS = \varnothing$
$RS' = \{$ pages in generation $> k$ that may contain objects
      with backward references $\}$
$PSS_i = \varnothing$
PSS_i' may contain some root objects
$NS_i = \varnothing$

`Flip` continues by spawning `parallelGC(k)` and resuming the mutator. `parallelGC` repeatedly spawns `rsCollect` and k `gc` tasks, waits for their completion, and checks the termination condition. This condition is simply that there do not exist any not-yet-scanned objects (i.e., all PSS_i' sets and RS' are empty).

The actions taken by `rsCollect` involve removing and scanning the pages from RS', and possibly updating and placing them in RS. The consequences of these actions may result in the addition of not-yet-scanned objects into some PSS_i' or pages into RS' (and, of lesser interest, objects into NS_{k+1}). Each `gc(i)` scans PSS_i', copying objects to PSS_i, and may also result in the addition of not-yet-scanned objects into some PSS_i' or pages into RS'.

The mutator's involvement is restricted to `gcTrap` which works like `gc`, `allocate` which interacts with NS_1, and some store instructions that interact with RS. The latter two cases do not affect any PSS_i' or RS'. Since (a) only unscanned objects are placed in PSS_i' and RS', (b) there are only a finite number of objects in memory, and (c) deadlock does not occur, `rsCollect`, `gc`, and `gcTrap` eventually scan all the unscanned objects and `parallelGC` terminates. □

We now proceed to prove a claim of correctness. To reiterate, the collector works by placing known "live" objects that are not-yet-scanned into one of PSS_i' or their pages into RS', and then scans these objects for further references to "live" objects. The invariant GC1 which states that the mutator see only PSS and OS pointers is maintained by `Flip` and `gcTrap`, and the invariant GC2 which states that objects in the scanned areas contain PSS and OS pointers is maintained by `rsCollect` and `gc`.

Claim: *The parallel generational collector correctly achieves its objective by copying all the objects that are live at the time of the flip by the end of the collection phase.*
Proof: Note that the root objects are the bases from which all live objects are available to the program. The root objects that exist in generations $\leq$

k are copied into PSS_i'. Consider the graph of live objects traced by beginning with the root objects that reside in generations $> k$. This graph may cross into generations $\leq k$, and given that RS is properly implemented, the crossover points of paths in the graph from generations older than k to those younger would be represented by various objects on the pages in RS'. Note that there may also be pages in RS' due to objects on unaccessible paths, but objects along these paths will not be reclaimed until the older generations are collected (i.e., these objects are presumed live).

The paths of live objects beginning on pages in RS' are traced first by `rsCollect` and then by either or all of `rsCollect`, `gc`, and `gcTrap`. Likewise, the paths emanating from those root objects already copied into PSS_i' are first traced by `gc(i)`, and then by either or all of `rsCollect`, `gc`, and `gcTrap`. The maintenance of the GC invariants by `rsCollect`, `gc`, and `gcTrap` result in the copying and scanning of all live objects emanating from the root objects.

In order to complete the proof of correctness, it remains to show that RS is properly implemented.

Claim: *RS is correct, i.e., all objects that have a reference to a younger generation are on pages that are members of RS.*

Proof: There are only two cases that result in an object o having a reference to a younger generation. The first case is by some store instruction in the mutator. Since the mutator checks for this occurrence and immediately adds the pages that have such references to RS, the page containing o is correctly placed in RS. The second case is as a result of tenuring. By `forwardObject`, an object o may be tenured and placed either in a PSS_i' or in RS'. The former set is handled by `gc` (or by `gcTrap`) and the latter set is handled by `rsCollect`. Since the objects in PSS_i' and RS' are actually scanned by the collector using the function `scavengeContentsOf` that explicitly checks for backward references and adds the pages containing such objects to the RS, the page containing o is correctly placed in RS. $\square$

3. Performance Evaluation of Parallel Collection

A performance evaluation study of the parallel garbage collector was conducted to determine the efficiency of the collection method. A simulator of a shared-memory multiprocessor was utilized in the implementation in order to facilitate instrumentation and experimentation. The simulator was built using the C programming language on a Sun Microsystems 3/50 workstation. The multiprocessor model was developed with routines that simulated shared-memory and the virtual memory mechanisms required in order to appropriately implement the parallel garbage collection algorithm. Features such as the object representation and allocation, access to the root objects and remembered set, the garbage collection trap handling mechanisms as well as the parallel generational garbage collector itself were included to simulate an object-oriented language implementation. The various mutator programs that operate on this shared-memory multiprocessor model are also written in C, calling the allocation and updating routines of the simulator as necessary.

The performance of the parallel generational garbage collector is evaluated via comparison against the performance of a parallel copy collector.[1] This comparison is performed by executing various mutator programs with the two garbage collection systems within the simulator. The comparison of the two parallel collectors demonstrates the differences between the two methods of garbage collection. As such, the work performed by the garbage collector is a primary measure of interest. This measure is calculated as the total number of bytes that was moved or copied during garbage collection. Another comparison made is the overhead imposed on the mutator program by each parallel collection method, and includes measures such as the number of flips, number of page traps related to garbage collection, number of root objects, and the number of backward references. These measures indicate the amount of interference between the mutator and the collector, and this interference is materialized in the form of execution overhead on the part of the mutator.

25

Since the results presented below were generated by a simulator, they allow comparison of the different algorithms in a relative rather than an absolute sense. The simulated execution times were generated by profiling the code executed by the simulator, and as such, are intended for comparison across simulation runs. Percentages of execution times for operations within a single simulation run are not a conclusive indicator of corresponding operations on a parallel machine since the actual operations will exhibit different runtime percentages. For example, the *time for locks* measure in the tables is the total time spent by the simulator in the functions that simulated the acquiring and the releasing of locks. On a typical parallel machine, these operations are realized in hardware and would be expected to take a smaller percentage of the execution time when compared to the function call-return mechanism of the simulator. This smaller percentage would only translate to an even smaller amount of overhead imposed on the mutator than that indicated by the simulation results.

3.1. System Parameters

Particulars about the garbage collection systems are presented in this section. An unlimited number of processors is simulated by allowing all ready-to-execute tasks in the system to immediately proceed. This method exploits the maximum parallelism allowed by the algorithms. A small memory size of 64K bytes is managed by the collector. Pages in virtual memory were set at 128 bytes in size, in accordance with the smaller pages sizes of Moon's system[16] and those of Wilson & Moher.[23] For the generational collector, memory is divided equally among two generations and an old space. This setup for the parallel generational collector requires at maximum five processors (three for the generations, one for RSCollect, and one for the mutator program) for the amount of parallelism exploited by the algorithm. Objects are advanced to the next generation after surviving three collections. The choice of three as the tenuring threshold gives a good medium between Moon's system[16] and Ungar's system,[22] and also follows the findings of Wilson & Moher.[23]

As noted earlier, the decision as to which generations to involve in a collection is not a simple one. For purposes of the simulations conducted here, two thresholds were defined, spaceThreshold and nearSpaceThreshold. The former is used to indicate when a generation absolutely had to be collected, while the latter is used to indicate that the generation could participate in a collection without a loss of effectiveness. After several initial runs of the simulator with the mutator programs described below, assigning the percentages 75% to spaceThreshold and 67% to nearSpaceThreshold provided a good measure by which to determine the generations to collect for an effective and efficient implementation.

Appel, Ellis, & Li's parallel copy collection algorithm[1] is derived from the constraints of using only one generation and no tenuring. However, the single generation is given a memory size that is the equivalent to twice the size of a generation in the other methods. This large single space typifies the situation of copy collection systems. Due to the nature of Appel, Ellis, & Li's algorithm, only two processors are required, one for the mutator and one for the collector.

3.2. Mutator Programs

In order to compare parallel generational collection against parallel copy collection, the characteristics of mutator programs in general were first examined. Previous empirical observations of programs that depend heavily on dynamically allocated storage showed that older objects accessible to the program tend to remain accessible while young objects tend to quickly become garbage.[14, 22] This observation allows the characterization of mutator programs that depend heavily on dynamically allocated storage by using two factors: the amount of long-lived objects and the amount of short-lived objects generated by the program. These two factors divide programs into four groups:

1. small amounts of both long-lived and short-lived objects,

2. a large amount of long-lived objects and a small amount of short-lived objects,

3. a small amount of long-lived objects and a large amount of short-lived objects, and

4. large amounts of both long-lived and short-lived objects.

The first two groups are not very interesting when considering the performance of garbage collectors as garbage collection is not necessary. Programs that belong to the last two groups are the most interesting for garbage collection studies. The large amount of short-lived object storage allocated by programs in these groups generates enough garbage so that garbage collection is necessary. The mutator programs used in the following experiments can be categorized into one of the latter two groups.

Five mutator programs were utilized in experiments to determine the effectiveness of the collection method. The first two mutator programs belonged to group three of the above list. The first program computed Ackermann's function, more specifically Ack(3,5). This program allocated on the heap all of the parameters passed between instances of the heavily recursive Ackermann's function as well as the activation records for each instance of the function. The second program involved the execution of the quicksort algorithm in a functional way; lists were used instead of arrays. The lists in this mutator were partitioned by copying, i.e., two new lists were created, each containing a copy of the corresponding value in the unsorted list. This quicksort routine was executed on a list of 1024 randomly chosen integers.

Collectors that use a generational scheme when reclaiming storage for programs of group three can be expected not to perform as well as copy collection methods. In comparison with copy collectors, generational collectors tend to be involved in more collection phases since by dividing memory into generations, the younger generations are quickly filled with short-lived objects. As only a few objects survive the collection phase, the time necessary for this copying at each phase remains similar for both methods. Thus, copy collectors seem to be a better storage reclamation strategy for programs that exhibit the characteristics of group three.

Recall however that the performance of copy collectors degrades as the number of objects surviving a collection phase increases, since the time for copying increases and less storage is freed, resulting in additional collection phases. Generational collectors have the ability to cope with the increase of long-lived objects and can be expected to perform better for programs belonging to group four. The next set of mutator programs is intended to highlight this performance increase, and includes representatives of applications in artificial intelligence, compilers, and simulation.

The third mutator program implemented a neural network of three levels, each level with 24 nodes. Each of the nodes on the first level was connected to half of the nodes on the second level, and each of the nodes on the second level was connected to half on the third level. The network was run for sixteen input trials, a small number of trials for a network of this moderate size but sufficient to exercise the runtime garbage collector. The fourth mutator program emulates a solution to a data flow problem used by compilers in alias detection, optimization, and parallelization.[4, 13, 20] The mutator program emulated the pattern of dynamically allocated objects and their use to match the pattern generated by a lifetime analysis algorithm operating on a program of seven procedures. The fifth mutator program utilized a discrete event simulation model of a retail center such as a grocery store or a discount store. The focus of this model is the transactions generated at computerized cash registers and a main inventory control system in response to entering each item to be bought by a customer. The store is modeled with ten cash registers with customers arriving approximately every two minutes, spending approximately ten minutes shopping to purchase approximately fifteen items. The model is run for three hours of simulated time.

3.3. Simulation Results

The results of the simulation runs with the mutator programs described above are presented in this section. The following tables use the abbreviations PAR_GC and PAR_CC to refer to the parallel generation collector and the parallel copy collector, respectively. Table 2 presents the results of the simulation runs with mutator programs from group three.

Comparisons between the two parallel collectors reveal the expected result in favor of copy collection. The parallel generational collector PAR_GC performed more work than the parallel copy collector in that 32.7% more copying and 78.2% more collector time for Ackermann's function and more than twice the amount of copying and over three and a half times the total collector time for Quicksort was required by the generational scheme. This greater amount of work imposed additional overhead on part of the mutator than PAR_CC, 3.9% more for Ackermann's function

Table 2. Simulation Results for Programs from Group Three.

	ACKERMANN		QUICKSORT	
	PAR_CC	PAR_GC	PAR_CC	PAR_GC
bytes allocated	339 504	339 504	45 207	45 207
bytes copied	14 608	18 834	17 118	31 577
bytes tenured	-	556	-	7705
bytes reclaimed	333 660	335 616	39 206	40 288
elapsed time	37.64	38.80	4.94	5.97
mutator time	36.08	36.08	4.37	4.37
mutator overhead	4.1%	7.0%	11.5%	26.8%
processor time	37.78	39.11	5.56	9.82
collector time	1.70	3.03	1.19	5.42
# flips	34	63	5	12
time for flips	.64	1.06	.04	.03
avg. # root objs	107.2	106.6	11.6	11.5
avg. # backward refs	-	0.0	-	108.8
GC scanning traps	35	64	100	177
time for traps	.08	.20	.46	1.14
time for locks	.84	1.46	.07	.43

Table 3. Simulation Results for Programs from Group Four.

	NEURALNET		LIFETIME ANALYSIS		RETAIL	
	PAR_CC	PAR_GC	PAR_CC	PAR_GC	PAR_CC	PAR_GC
bytes allocated	444 240	444 240	299 431	299 431	151 972	151 972
bytes copied	102 504	61 614	166 699	43 517	154 392	67 736
bytes tenured	-	10 260	-	11 785	-	23 000
bytes reclaimed	341 736	439 878	294 269	292 825	142 684	133 212
elapsed time	59.81	61.57	42.50	39.86	55.81	49.03
mutator time	55.10	55.10	35.64	35.64	45.57	45.57
mutator overhead	7.9%	10.5%	16.1%	10.1%	18.3%	7.1%
processor time	63.09	71.38	53.67	47.35	57.38	54.62
collector time	7.99	16.28	18.03	11.71	11.81	9.05
# flips	53	89	45	59	29	34
time for flips	.11	.12	.16	.22	.09	.04
avg. # root objs	5.0	5.0	12.5	11.2	7.5	7.4
avg. # backward refs	-	59.0	-	21.1	-	6.7
GC scanning traps	723	936	614	565	1215	795
time for traps	2.87	1.30	4.78	1.84	5.80	2.17
time for locks	1.73	5.05	1.92	2.16	.58	1.25

and 15.3% for Quicksort. For Ackermann's function, total processor time was increased by 3.5% by PAR_GC over PAR_CC while the total elapsed time increased by 3.1%, indicating that little additional parallelism was exploited. Similarly for Quicksort, the total processor time increased by 76.6% for PAR_GC over PAR_CC but the total elapsed time only increased by 20.9%. Notice also that the number of flips for PAR_GC are almost twice the number executed by PAR_CC. This ratio is due to the fact that PAR_CC has twice the amount of memory to fill before a collection is initiated, and this ratio is typical of applications that generate a lot of short-lived objects and few long-lived objects such as Ackermann's function and Quicksort. The 82.9% and 77.0% increases in the number of garbage-collection-related traps for PAR_GC reflects this fact as well.

The results indicate that a scant few objects were tenured by the generational collector during the simulation runs since nearly all of the heap-allocated objects were quickly discarded by the mutator. This lack of tenuring resulted in little object partitioning, contributing to the reduced effectiveness of the generational scheme for this experiment.

The next three sets of simulation runs highlight the benefits of generational collection. Table 3 presents the results for mutator programs from group four. In the neural network program, the parallel generational collector only performed 70.1% of the work performed by the parallel copy collector, and the ratio of flips dropped below 2.0 to 1.7. This reduction in work was achieved in the generational collector by tenuring the objects that represented nodes in the neural network, thus partitioning the longer-lived nodes from the shorter-lived edge weights. The reduction in work by PAR_GC also limited the increase in mutator overhead to 2.6%, the increase in total elapsed time to 2.9%, and the number of traps to 29.5%, while the total processor time increased by 13.1% and the total collector time increased by 103.8% over PAR_CC. The larger amount of work performed by the copy collector also increased the interference with the execution of the mutator, as evidenced by

ratio of the number of GC-related traps to the number of flips. The copy collector experienced a ratio of 12.0 traps per flip, while the parallel generational collector resulted in only 8.0 traps per flip.

The 54.7% less time for traps is attributed to the added parallelism of PAR_GC as in many of the traps, PAR_GC was already in the midst of scanning the page, thus reducing the waiting time by the mutator for page scanning. The increase in locking time is also explained by two reasons, both due to this parallelism. The first is that the added parallel nature of PAR_GC has increased synchronization concerns over PAR_CC. The other is that the mutator program voraciously allocates storage for the changing edge weights, and the contention for locking is magnified by PAR_GC.

The benefits of generational collection come to the fore in the simulation runs involving the lifetime analysis program and the retail center program. Even though the number of flips for PAR_CC is less than that of PAR_GC in the lifetime analysis program, the ratio is now at 1.3 more flips for PAR_GC for typically half the memory allocated before a flip. The work performed by PAR_GC in the amount of bytes copied is only 33.2% that of the copy collector. This reduction also appears in the reduced total processor time of 11.8% and reduced total collector time of 35.1% for PAR_GC over PAR_CC. The effects on the mutator are a reduction in total elapsed time of 6.2% and a reduction in mutator overhead by 5.0% for PAR_GC over PAR_CC. Because of the larger amount of time spent in copying, PAR_CC incurs additional costs in interference with the mutator; 13.6 traps per flip compared to 9.6 traps per flip for the parallel generational collector. While locking time increased slightly (12.5%) for PAR_GC, PAR_CC had 8.7% more traps and cost more than one and a half times than the cost for PAR_GC in order to service them.

Similar results were observed for the retail center program. The parallel generational collector performed 58.8% of the work of the parallel copy collector with a reduction by 11.2% in mutator overhead and 12.1% in total elapsed time. The ratio of flips between the parallel collectors was at 1.2 for this simulation run. The doubled locking time for PAR_GC did not detract from the 62.6% decrease for servicing a 34.6% reduction in garbage-collection-related traps for PAR_GC over PAR_CC. The copy collector's interference with the mutator amounted to 23.8 traps per flip, while the interference between the mutator and the parallel generational collector was limited to 13.8 traps per flip. PAR_GC, by tenuring the longer-lived objects in the retail model to an older generation that is scavenged less frequently, is able to avoid unnecessary work. This fact is supported by the reduction in total processor time by 4.8% and total collector time by 23.4% for PAR_GC over PAR_CC.

The differences in effectiveness between PAR_GC and PAR_CC are portrayed by the plot in Figure 12. This plot maps the average number of bytes that survive each collection against the work performed by each collector in the total number of bytes copied by the respective collector. The data points in the plot were gathered from the five sets of simulation runs discussed above. The trends shown in the plot are fairly typical of the differences between copy collectors and generational collectors, sequential or parallel. In particular, note that as the amount of live data per collection increases, the work performed by a copy collector increases beyond that of the generational collector, as the generational collector is able to reduce the unnecessary frequent scanning of large numbers of live objects.

4. Conclusions

This paper describes a parallel storage reclamation algorithm that parallelizes a generational scheme for garbage collection for use on a shared-memory multiprocessor architecture. A prototype implementation of the parallel garbage collector was developed to determine the efficiency and the effectiveness of the collection method. Experi-

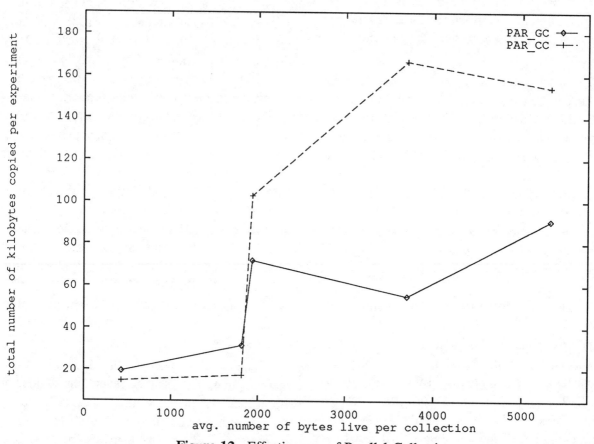

Figure 12. Effectiveness of Parallel Collection.

ments with this implementation have indicated that multi-generational parallel collection has the potential for making more efficient use of an underlying shared-memory computer architecture. The mutator and the collector are also operating in parallel, so the incremental nature of the system is preserved. The simulation results show that when compared against a parallel copy collection algorithm, the parallel generational collector performs better for a certain class of programs, namely those with larger amounts of longer-lived objects. For these programs, the parallel generational collector performed up to 67% less copying than a parallel copy collector and reduced elapsed times up to an additional 12%; corresponding reductions in mutator overhead were also observed.

Further tuning of the parallel algorithm can be achieved by investigating the division of memory spaces among the different generations. Evenly dividing the spaces results in several processors of the computer system working on the collection at once, while proportionately dividing the spaces allows some processors to be free of the collection before the others. In the latter division, the mutator can continue its computation with additional processors simultaneously with the collection that is still taking place on a reduced number of processors. For example, allocating a smaller number of pages to the older generations and a larger number of pages to the younger generations allows the collector to quickly scavenge the older generations and continue with the mutator while the younger generations are still being scavenged. Thus, even though the same amount of combined time is spent on garbage collection, the actual work of the mutator can make progress with more continuous processor time.

This uneven division of memory has another advantage for parallel generational collection. As the size of the younger generations increases and the size of the older ones decreases, the generational collector takes on more of the characteristics of a copy collector. For programs that exhibit characteristics amenable for copy collection, uneven division of memory in this fashion can help a generational collector cope with the greater amount of short-lived garbage.

References

1. Appel, Andrew W., Ellis, John R., and Li, Kai, "Real-time Concurrent Collection on Stock Multiprocessors," *Proceedings of the SIGPLAN 88 Conference on Programming Language Design and Implementation*, pp. 11-20, Atlanta, GA, June 1988.

2. Ben-Ari, Mordechai, "Algorithms for On-the-fly Garbage Collection," *ACM Transactions on Programming Languages and Systems*, vol. 6, no. 3, pp. 333-344, July 1984.

3. Bershad, Brian N., Lazowska, Edward D., Levy, Henry M., and Wagner, David B., "An Open Environment for Building Parallel Programming Systems," *Proceedings of the ACM SIGPLAN Symposium on Parallel Programming: Experience with Applications, Languages and Systems*, pp. 1-9, New Haven, CN, July 1988.

4. Chase, David R., Wegman, Mark, and Zadeck, F. Kenneth, "Analysis of Pointers and Structures," *Proceedings of the 1990 SIGPLAN Conference on Programming Language Design and Implementation*, pp. 296-310, White Plains, NY, June 1990.

5. Cohen, Jacques, "Garbage Collection of Linked Data Structures," *Computing Surveys*, vol. 13, no. 3, pp. 341-367, September 1981.

6. Detlefs, David L., "Concurrent Garbage Collection for C++," Technical Report #CMU-CS-90-119, Dept. of Computer Science, Carnegie Mellon University, May 1990.

7. Dijkstra, Edsger W., Lamport, Leslie, Martin, A. J., Scholten, C. S., and Steffens, E. F. M., "On-the-Fly Garbage Collection: An Exercise in Cooperation," *Communications of the ACM*, vol. 21, no. 11, pp. 966-975, November 1978.

8. Duncan, Ralph, "A Survey of Parallel Computer Architectures," *IEEE Computer*, vol. 2, no. 23, pp. 5-16, February 1990.

9. Gries, David, "An Exercise in Proving Parallel Programs Correct," *Communications of the ACM*, vol. 20, no. 12, pp. 921-930, December 1977.

10. Halstead, Robert H., "Implementation of MultiLisp: Lisp on a Multiprocessor ," *Conference Record of the 1984 ACM Symposium on LISP and Functional Programming*,

pp. 9-17, Austin, TX, August 1984.

11. Kung, H. T. and Song, S. W., "An Efficient Parallel Garbage Collection System and its Correctness Proof," Technical Report, Dept. of Computer Science, Carnegie-Mellon University, September 1977.

12. Lang, Charles Richard, "The Extension of Object-Oriented Languages to a Homogeneous, Concurrent Architecture," Ph.D. Dissertation, Technical Report 5014-TR-82, Computer Science Department, California Institute of Technology, 1982.

13. Larus, James R. and Hilfinger, Paul N., "Detecting Conflicts Between Structure Accesses," *Proceedings of the SIGPLAN 88 Conference on Programming Language Design and Implementation*, pp. 21-34, Atlanta, GA, June 1988.

14. Lieberman, Henry and Hewitt, Carl, "A Real-Time Garbage Collector Based on the Lifetimes of Objects," *Communications of the ACM*, vol. 26, no. 6, pp. 419-429, June 1983.

15. Lovett, T. and Thakkar, S. S., "The Symmetry Multiprocessor System," *Proceedings of the 1988 International Conference on Parallel Processing*, pp. 303-310, August 1988.

16. Moon, David A., "Garbage Collection in a Large Lisp System," *Conference Record of the 1984 ACM Symposium on LISP and Functional Programming*, pp. 235-246, Austin, TX, August 1984.

17. Moss, Eliot, Liskov, Barbara, Yonezawa, Akinori, Thomas, David A., and Hewitt, Carl, "Object-Oriented Concurrency (Panel Discussion)," *Addendum to the Proceedings of the 1987 Conference on Object-Oriented Programming Systems, Languages and Applications*, pp. 119-127, October 1987.

18. North, S. C. and Reppy, J. H., "Concurrent Garbage Collection on Stock Hardware," *Proceedings of the Third Conference on Functional Programming Languages and Computer Architecture*, pp. 113-133, Portland, OR, September 1987.

19. Pallas, Joseph and Ungar, David, "Multiprocessor Smalltalk: A Case Study of a Multiprocessor-Based Programming Environment," *Proceedings of the SIGPLAN 88 Conference on Programming Language Design and Implementation*, pp. 268-277, Atlanta, GA, June 1988.

20. Ruggeri, Cristina and Murtagh, Thomas P., "Lifetime Analysis of Dynamically Allocated Objects," *Proceedings of the 15th Annual ACM Symposium on Principles of Programming Languages*, pp. 285-293, San Diego, CA, January 1988.

21. Thacker, Charles P. and Stewart, Lawrence C., "Firefly: A Multiprocessor Workstation," *Proceedings of the Second International Conference on Architectural Support for Programming Languages and Operating Systems*, pp. 164-172, Palo Alto, CA, October 1987.

22. Ungar, David Michael, "The Design and Evaluation of a High Performance Smalltalk System," Ph.D. Dissertation, Comp. Sci. Division of Dept. of EECS, University of California-Berkeley, March 1986.

23. Wilson, Paul R. and Moher, Thomas G., "Design of the Opportunistic Garbage Collector," *Proceedings of the 1989 Conference on Object-Oriented Programming Systems, Languages and Applications*, pp. 23-35, New Orleans, LA, October 1989.

24. Yonezawa, Akinori and Tokoro, Mario, *Object-Oriented Concurrent Programming*, MIT Press, Cambridge, MA, 1987.

Using Key Object Opportunism
to Collect Old Objects

Barry Hayes

Stanford University
Department of Computer Science
Stanford, CA 94309
bhayes@cs.stanford.edu

Abstract

Object allocation and deallocation data gathered for the Cedar system on Xerox Dorados supports the weak generational hypothesis, *newly-created objects have a much lower survival rate than objects that are older.*

The survivors at all collections thresholds are highly organized; large clusters of objects are allocated at roughly the same time, and live for roughly the same length of time. By cleverly selecting representatives from the clusters and examining the reachability of these key objects more frequently than the cluster itself, the storage system can use the death of these key objects to find good opportunities to collect the clusters they represent.

1   The Generational Hypotheses

Some observations of the relative lifetimes of newly-created objects and older objects leads to the weak generational hypothesis [Han77]. This hypothesis seems to hold across a wide variety of systems: *newly-created objects have a much lower survival rate than objects that are older.* This led researchers to develop storage management systems based on this hypothesis, the time-based generational collectors [LH83, Moo84, Ung84].

The designs of these are actually based on a leap of faith to the strong generational hypothesis: *even if the objects in question are not newly-created, the relatively younger objects have a lower survival rate than the relatively older objects.* These collectors allow many generations and segregate objects into multiple classes by age, not just "new" and "old." As objects age, they are promoted from one generation to the next, and at some point they may be "tenured" in a generation where the time-based collector will never attempt to collect them.

2   Methodology

Over a period of four months, the code in ten Dorados [Pie83] at Xerox PARC was modified to record object allocation and deallocation. The mutator code comprises a wide variety of applications including compilers, mail and network servers, editors for graphics and text, debuggers, file servers, and window managers [SZBH86]. All users incorporated a large number of applications in their daily lives, and storage traces covering more than a few hours include allocations from many different tools.

Nearly all of the mutator code is written in Cedar, a Modula-like language developed at Xerox. Dynamic storage is an integral part of the language, but it is not used as part of the primitive operation set, as are Smalltalk's message send and Lisp's cons. All object allocations are explicitly included in the Cedar code.

Deallocation is done by a deferred reference-counting collector [Rov85]. Pointers to allocated objects can be unambiguously identified except for those pointers on the stacks and in the registers. These regions are treated conservatively, so a bit-pattern on the stack that looks like a pointer to an allocated object will keep the object from being deallocated.

Care was taken to ensure that the monitoring code would not interfere with the performance of the mutator. Some slowdown was inevitable, but users reported little interference with their work. At the end of this paper are summaries of three sessions from three different users. The graphs in the paper are from the session on the machine named Shangrila.

Dorado users invoked monitoring code after the machine was booted and fundamental modules were already running. Objects created before the monitoring began did not have their creations recorded. These objects produce deallocation records but no allocation records. Likewise, objects created while the monitoring code is running but that survive past system shut-down have allocation records, but no deallocation record. Some objects have neither an allocation record nor a deallocation record. These objects were created before the monitoring began and survived until the system was shut down.

There are relatively few objects in these classes, compared to total objects allocated, but some of these classes are large compared to the number of bytes that survive for a long time. For Shangrila there are roughly 15 megabytes of storage where both the allocation and deallocation are seen, and only 1 megabyte of objects seen at allocation and surviving to system shut-down. If a time-based system tenures even 5% of the 15 Mb that should not be tenured, it would amount to 0.75 Mb of the tenured space, nearly as much as the 1 Mb alive at

the end of the test.

Nonetheless, *unless otherwise stated, all graphs and measurements refer only to objects seen at both allocation and deallocation. All other allocations and deallocations have been filtered out of the data.*

The chief unit of measure is the byte. Object sizes will be given in bytes, and objects will be treated as collections of bytes. The unit of time is also a byte. One byte allocated will advance the clock one tick. The storage system defers deallocating objects until a user-specified amount of new storage has been allocated. Usually, the collector runs either every 8 kb or every 16 kb. Deallocation times for objects are no more accurate than the frequency of collections, and the conservative treatment of the stack artificially extends the lifetime of some objects.

3   Analysis of Lifetime Data

Figure 1 shows the cumulative fraction of objects that are deallocated by a given time for the trace of Shangrila. The results of the traces are similar to results published elsewhere [Sha87, UJ88, DeT90]. The weak generational hypothesis holds. The curve rises quickly and has a sharp knee. Only 1% of the bytes survive past 721 kb of allocation, and the bend in the curve is sharp. When 5% of the bytes survived, the system had to wait for 204 kb to be allocated before half the objects were free, but at 1% the half-life is 731 kb. The reclamation rate has decreased sharply between these two points.

Cumulative graphs show the benefits of generational collection on new objects. But the quick rise and long flat tail also hide features about the objects. Since the graph exceeds 95% for most of its extent, the features in the old 5% of the bytes will be swamped.

Figure 2 shows the upper 2.5% of Figure 1. The tail of the curve seems flat in Figure 1 because the large volume of storage released by an early age swamps the details of the tail, but in Figure 2 the details are clearer. Figure 3 shows the same data again, but not cumulatively. Table 1 shows the time since allocation, in kb allocated, needed to

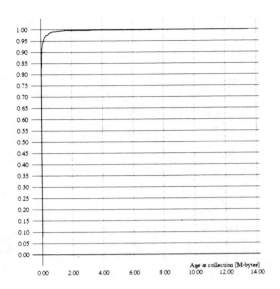

Figure 1: Fraction of Objects Reclaimed by Generational Collections

% surviving (approx.)	Megabytes surviving	Threshold (kb)	Half-life (kb)
100%	16.209	0	8
50%	7.918	8	9
20%	3.977	16	17
10%	1.614	45	111
5%	0.808	155	204
2.5%	0.404	359	265
1%	0.162	721	731
0.5%	0.080	1452	1313
0.025%	0.040	2641	4646

Table 1: Survival Thresholds

reach a given survival rate, and the time that must elapse after that point for half of the remaining objects to be collected. Since object collection times are only accurate to about 8 kb, there is more precision than accuracy in the data.

4 The Strong Generational Hypothesis

Observations of generational collectors has shown a law of diminishing returns. While the youngest subset of objects has a low survival rate, a longer wait is often less useful. Multi-generation collectors

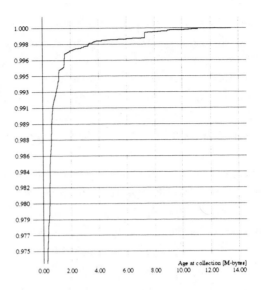

Figure 2: Fraction of Objects Reclaimed by Generational Collections [detail]

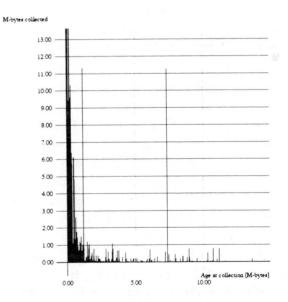

Figure 3: Bytes Collected by Age

show a large drop in reclamation rates from generation to generation, and are often pragmaticly limited to two or three time-based generations.

If object ages had no predictive value in guessing object lifetimes, the survival rate for every age would be the same. In that case, equal-sized generations would allow older objects in later generations exponentially more time to age than objects in younger generations, and the volume of data promoted should *decrease exponentially* with each generation.

For example, assume the death rate is a constant 95% per minute for all objects and does not vary with object age. To ease the calculations, assume that each generation is 1 megabyte and the allocation rate is a constant 1 Mb per minute. Once a minute the youngest generation is collected, and 5% of it, 50 kilobytes, is promoted to the next generation. The second generation will fill after twenty minutes. But the bytes in generation 2 have ages uniformly spread between 1 and 20 minutes. Of the objects that have been in this generation only one minute, 5% will survive. Of the objects that have been in this generation two minutes, only 0.25% will survive, and so on. The expected surviving volume from generation 2 is about 1/19 the volume from generation 1, and with each later generation the rate should be expected to decrease by a factor of 1/19.

If older generations are larger than younger generations, as is the case in many collectors, the older generations will fill even more slowly, the old objects will have even more time to age, and the reclamation rates for later generations should be even larger. The data from this and other studies [Sha87, DeT90] does not show this exponential effect from generation to generation, and so the observed diminishing returns must be due to changes in the death rate as objects age. There are no careful studies of these rate changes, nor analyses of multi-generation collectors that would allow the rates to be deduced, and the strong generational hypothesis better quantified.

The rate changes must be large to account for the missing exponential promotion curve. If the half-life were only linear with age, equal-sized generations would be expected to promote equal volumes independent of the ages of the objects they contained. The Dorado data seems to have a roughly linear relationship between age and half-life, but not clear enough to give full support.

In any case, the spectacular differential in reclamation rates between very new objects and slightly older objects is absent at later times. The strong generation hypothesis is a "folk-model" of generational collection and may not agree with actual system behavior. If a system wants good indicators of lifetimes of older objects, better ones than age are available.

4.1 The Collection Game

Garbage collection can be seen as a two player game, like roulette with an unfair wheel. But even more than with roulette, garbage collection is always a winning game for the house, and a losing game for the collector. A collector loses points for every unreachable object it fails to find, but gets no points for unreachable objects it does find.

Time-based collection is based on the observation that the wheel is unfair. If black comes up more often than red, it would be a good strategy always to bet on black and not red. Since young objects are unreachable more often than old, it is a good strategy to attempt to collect young objects and not old. And this strategy pays off handsomely.

Key object opportunism is based on the observation that the spins of the wheel are not independent events. When the ball finally falls in red, this is a sign that the odds have changed, and red is now likely to appear. When a key object finally becomes unreachable, this is a sign that the odds have changed, and some old objects are likely to be free.

A time-based collector always bets on the young objects. Key object opportunism allows a collector to adjust its bets to account for streaks.

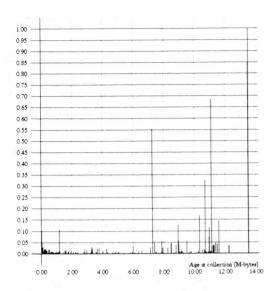

Figure 4: Instantanious Collection Rate

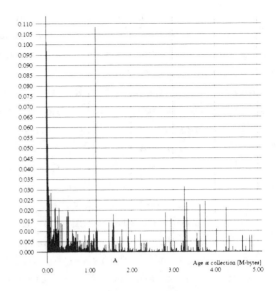

Figure 5: Instantanious Collection Rate [detail]

5 Collection Rate

To emphasize the older objects, Figure 4 shows the lifetime data as instantaneous collection rates for all ages. Bytes are grouped by their age at collection rounded down to a kilobyte. The instantaneous collection rate is the number of bytes that are collected at some age divided by the total number of objects that survive that long or longer. The strong generational hypothesis would require that this function be strictly decreasing. Figure 1, Figure 3 and Figure 4 show exactly the same data; each graph can be derived from the other.

When the volume of bytes remaining is low, individual objects have a large effect on the collection rate. In the extreme, when the oldest object is collected, the collection rate is 100%. In comparing Figure 3 with Figure 4 notice that the spikes near 1 Mb and 7 Mb both represent releases of about 11 kb, but the first is a collection rate of 10% per kb and the later registers as 55%. Likewise, the three rising tall spikes between 10 and 11 Mb each represent less than 1 kb. It is a good idea to examine both the collection rate and the actual volume to see if a spike is significant.

If only small objects were allocated between two 8k collections and they were collected at the same time, each object would have a creation time equal to the number of bytes allocated before it, but all the objects would have the same deallocation time, since they were collected by the same incarnation of the garbage collector. The lifetimes are truncated to kilobytes, so these objects would show up as 8 peer groups, each with a similar deallocation rate.

When there are objects larger than 1 kb, all of the bytes in the object are given the same creation time, and when large objects are released this shows as a tall, thin spike. Short, broad spikes show a large number of smaller objects being deallocated.

Figure 5 is a detail of Figure 4, showing just the collection rates up to 5 Mb allocated. There are two sources of high rates. First, the spike may be the result of freeing an object larger than 1 kb, like the spike near 1.2 Mb. Second, the spike may be the sum of several clusters of objects from different collections, but all with the same age, like the "generational" spikes under 0.5 Mb.

5.1 Significance of High Collection Rates

There may be some trend for spikes in the collection rate to get less frequent as objects age, and this might lend some support to the strong generational hypothesis. The sum of the spikes in a much larger set of traces might smooth the graph and the smoother curve might be more like the monotone decreasing curve predicted by the strong generational hypothesis.

One might reasonably ask if the spikes are merely the result of having a small data set and are not significant. If more data were included there would be other spikes, and perhaps the sum of all of the spikes would yield a constant survival rate. This is unlikely.

Even a small spike needs a huge volume of objects to make the collection rate constant. In the Shangrila data set, only about two thirds of the data that lives past 1535 kb survives to 1578 kb due to a series of spikes marked "A" in Figure 5 [1]. The collection rate is between 1% and 0.5% within that range, but is lower almost everywhere before the spike. There are many similar spikes in the Shangrila data set, and the other data sets look similar.

An object living to time t will have no effect on collection rates for ages greater than t. The object will uniformly lower the collection rates for ages less than t. Therefore, to make the collection rate from zero to t constant, only objects younger than t need be considered.

Assume a spike at time t of collection rate r, and accounting for b bytes of storage deallocated. Since the rate is r and b bytes were freed the total number of bytes surviving t or longer must be $b \times r^{-1}$.

The spike would vanish when all ages from zero to t have collection rates equal to r. At time $t - 1$ there would have to be $b \times r^{-2}$ bytes, and so on. To account for all times from zero to t will take $b \times r^{1-t}$ bytes. These allocations would bring the collection rate level with the spike, but only for times less than t. This could also bury smaller spikes at times less than t, so it is not necessary to sum over all spikes to make the collection rate monotone;

burying a spike that is both large enough and late enough will do.

For the particular spike on Shangrila, collecting at the 1% level from age zero to 1535 kb and still having 81 kb survive would require $81,000 \times .99^{-1534}$ bytes of allocation. This is $380,000$ Mb, about twenty thousand times the size of the data set, and would require about 30 Dorado-years to create, yet this spike is niether very large nor very late.

The spikes are a genuine feature of the data, reflecting clustered releases of bytes. They are not a feature that would go away with longer or more traces. Some of them may get smaller if the data included objects seen at creation *or* deallocation, rather than requiring both, but there is not enough discarded data to reduce the spikes significantly.

6 Allocation Clumps

The "generational spikes" in the collection rate for young objects are a prominent feature. When that is removed, the most prominent feature of the data is that the deaths of objects created at nearly the same time are closely correlated; there are clusters of objects of the same lifetime.

The clusters can be seen as a direct consequence of the way programs are written. There are usually only a few static pointers into a large structure, allowing programs to traverse the structure starting at a few points, like the head and tail of a list or the root of a tree. Other pointers into the structure are created dynamicly as long as the structure is actively used. When the structure is no longer in use, the only remaining pointers point to these root objects; the cluster is reclaimed when these pointers are deleted.

In a cyclic program, this rewriting can happen because a new cycle has been entered. The variables used to hold the root pointers now must be used to hold the pointers to the new cluster associated with the new cycle. If the root pointers are on the stack, they will be destroyed when the procedure using the cluster returns. The clustered release of objects is a consequence of using a roughly

---

[1] In this data set, 80,930 bytes survive to age 1535 kb or older, but 27,090 of these are collected by age 1578 kb. The allocation record for each object includes a complete stack trace at the time of allocation. By going over the allocation records for the 2,237 objects, we can see that almost all of them are the result of a mail message discarded 15 minutes after it was composed and sent.

static number of variables to access a large cluster of dynamic storage.

By seeing how well the age at deallocation of one object correlates with the age of the objects deallocated at nearly the same time, one can get an idea of the magnitude of the clustering. As would be expected, the clustering is tight when all objects, young and old, are examined. Since most objects become unreachable quickly, these objects' ages are highly correlated. Figure 6 plots the difference in age between successively deallocated objects, in kilobytes allocated, against the number of bytes with that difference. More than 80% of the bytes are in objects within 1 kb of the previous object, and the 90% spread is between plus and minus 8 kb. This clustering would be even tighter if rather than successive deallocations, "nearly successive" deallocations were considered. An object of some unusual age might be deallocated between two objects not its peers, but a peer might be very close by.

The surprise is that even if the young objects are ignored, the correlation is strong. Figure 7 again shows the volume of objects with various age differences at collection time, but this time only the 1% of the objects with the longest lifetimes are counted. More than 60% of the bytes come from a spread of ±1 kb, and 75% differ by less than 8 kb. The old 1% of the objects have a half-life of 731 kb, so the system can't count on having them become unreachable soon, but when some become unreachable, others are likely to follow.

7 Opportunism Using Key Objects

There are two kinds of opportunism: the first looks for an opportunity to trigger *hidden* collections, the second looks for an opportunity to trigger *efficient* collections. Key object opportunism is of the second kind. A storage system can exploit the first kind of opportunism by scheduling short collections immediately after processor-bound jobs and looking for non-interactive periods to schedule long col-

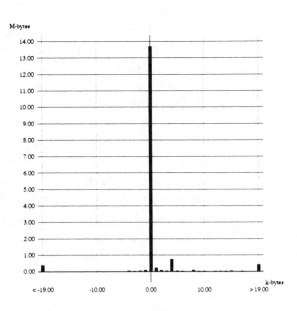

Figure 6: Difference Between Ages

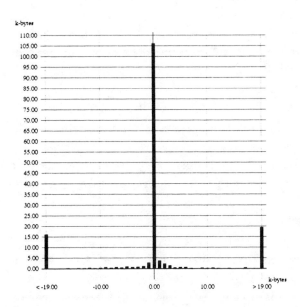

Figure 7: Difference Between Ages: Old 1%

lections [Wil88].

Key object opportunism triggers partial collections based on the clustering behavior of the data. When a cluster's collection time can no longer be predicted from its birth time with accuracy, it is promoted out of the time-based generational scheme altogether. Only later, when the key objects are unreachable, will the system try to collect the cluster.

Since the clusters are not certain to be wholly unrelated, there may be pointers from one cluster to another, and this cross-cluster information must be retained. The literature contains many methods to do the bookkeeping for heaps split across separate areas for both copying and non-copying collectors, and ways to make the clustering more well behaved [Bis77, BGH+77, DWH+90]. The bookkeeping alone does not make a storage management system; it only tells *how* to collect a given cluster. The system also needs information to know *when* to collect a cluster.

A good time to collect a cluster is when the root objects are unreachable. Since the root objects are the usual path in accessing objects in the cluster, when they are free the cluster can likely be collected. This is, of course, not always easy to find out. If a cluster is a tree with back-pointers or a circular list, the root objects can become inaccessible but still be pointed to, but the pointers will all originate from within the cluster; all of the cross-area pointers to the root object are gone.

Key object opportunism puts the root objects in areas distinct from the areas for the cluster, and uses the bookkeeping and collection results on the root areas to predict the results of a collection on the cluster. The collection of the cluster can be delayed until the portents are good.

If the root objects are subject to collection, the system knows when they are free. But even without collecting the roots, the cross-area pointers database can be treated as a 0/1 reference-count for whole areas. When there is a pointer to an area, some object in it has a non-zero reference count. When there is no pointer to an area, all objects have no external references. Updating the

bookkeeping is like doing deferred reference counting.

7.1 An Example

Figure 8 shows how a sample cluster and its key interact with the collection system. This example assumes a copying collector to simplify the bookkeeping, but a collector can do the bookkeeping without doing the copying [DWH+90].

a) A cluster, in this case a tree, is created in the area reserved for new and young storage. The objects in the "new" area tend to die quickly, and tend to be written more than old objects. In a pure form, access to the cluster would be through the key objects only, in this case the root of the tree. The only access to the root is through a global pointer held in an old object or other global variable.

b) After the cluster has passed some age or survived some number of collections, it is copied out of the young area. But rather than being copied to an age-segregated area, each cluster is moved to an area of its own. The time-based generational collector will try less frequently to collect the cluster. In a standard time-based generational collector, this is the "promotion" step.

The key objects for the cluster are copied to a separate area. The collector will continue to try to collect the key objects, but the remainder of the cluster will be promoted and faced with fewer or no collection attempts.

c) It may be that not all the objects will be copied from the young area at the same time, as they may have a range of ages, and objects created later may be hung from various branches of the tree.

Bishop-style copying can be used to try to promote new objects to an appropriate keyed area rather than to a general "old" area, or the objects can be self-identifying, indicating which

41

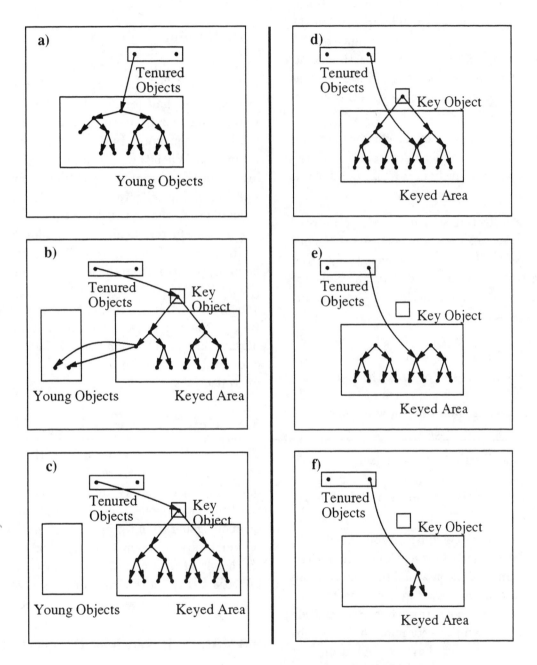

Figure 8: An Example of Key Object Opportunism

cluster they would like to belong to when they are promoted.

d) When the mutator is done with the cluster it writes the variable leading to the key object. In a cyclic program, this will happen when the next cycle stores a pointer to the new root. A program aware of the garbage collection strategy might explicitly zero the pointer, just as cycles are broken for reference-counting collectors.

Pointers to other parts of the cluster may continue to be active, either because a part of the cluster is being actively saved, or a pointer was created which was never zeroed.

e) Since the collection system has not promoted the key objects, they are not out of harm's way. Eventually, an un-referenced key objet will be reclaimed. At that time, the collector can take this as a strong "hint" at an opportunity to collect the associated keyed area.

Note that the collector can not simply deallocate all of the objects in the cluster, since some of them may still be alive through pointers that bypass the key objects of the cluster. The bookkeeping information will show all of these cross-area pointers.

f) A collection over the keyed area is, in this case, fruitful. Most of the objects in the cluster are not saved by outside pointers and can be reclaimed.

The collection system must embody a policy to handle those objects that live longer than their keys. A simple solution would be to copy those objects to a permanent tenured area to wait for the next full collection, but Bishop-style copying will attempt to combine the saved objects with the cluster they are rooted in, and this might also be a successful tactic.

8   Finding Key Objects

Some key objects are root objects, those objects through which accesses to a cluster are usually made. These turn out to have interesting properties reflecting the life-times of their clusters. But other objects may have these same properties, signaling an opportunity for cluster collection.

8.1   Random Selection

A collector could simply promote only half the objects that had lived past the tenuring threshold and use the other half for keys [Wil90]. There will be some correlation between the fraction of garbage in the half not promoted and the fraction in the half promoted. When the collector notices an unusually large number of unpromoted objects of roughly the same age being collected, it could then examine the objects promoted at the same time.

For any cluster, being split randomly wouldn't be likely to produce a good indicator. There would be many pointers from the promoted half to the unpromoted half, and the unpromoted objects would appear reachable. Keeping a large random fraction of the old objects unpromoted would put a burden on the collection system, but a small random fraction seems unlikely to be a good indicator for collections.

8.2   Key Discovery

The collector could gather information in the generational phases that would help to uncover some of the keys without any human intervention. When the time-based collector copies a group of objects from one generation to the next, it could keep track of which objects seem to be the root objects, like the heads of lists and the roots of trees. If a single object stays in this role for several generational copies, perhaps it really is a root object.

8.3   Stack-Based Key Objects

A key object can not be unreachable at the time the cluster is promoted; if it were, it would be collected then. But at some future time it becomes unreachable. This can not happen if there are pointers to it from objects that are neither freed nor altered. A pointer from a static object would tend to indicate that the object pointed to is not a key object, but an object pinned only by volatile pointers would be an excellent candidate.

This suggests a much better heuristic to monitor the stack activity and schedule collections than either monitoring the height of the stack [Wil89, Wil91] or the number of pops from the stack [LH83].

Consider an object that is pointed to only from a stack frame. When the routine associated with that stack frame returns, the object will be collectible unless the routine makes a special effort to save that pointer, perhaps by returning it as a result. A generational collector could promote young objects by first following all pointers from the heap, and only then tracing from the more volatile registers and stack. The first level of objects reachable from the registers and stack would be likely to make excellent keys for objects reachable from only the stack and other objects of similar age.

In the special case of a highly functional or applicatave language, the lifetimes of objects may be more stack-like than would be suggested from the traces of Cedar, a Pascal-like side-effect language. The intuition that heap allocation should be stack-like comes from functional languages.

If stack-based keys were added, a collector would know from the pattern of free objects in the keys how low the stack had dipped between the marking of the keys at the previous collection and their freeing at the current one. It could use this information to schedule a collection of the objects created since the invocation of the routine associated with the lowest dip in the stack.

8.4 Serendipity

Key objects need not even be in the clusters they monitor. An object or small cluster might hold supplementary data about a large cluster. This object is not actually in the cluster, but has a lifetime similar to that of the large cluster. The semantics of the application that creates a cluster can imply that an object is a good candidate.

An examination of the objects promoted by the generational collector and deallocated by a collection over the older generations can show blind spots in the generational collector. If a particular application is allocating a large volume of storage that is promoted and then later becomes free, but there is no obvious root or serendipitous key, the application can be changed to allocate a single object whose sole purpose is to serve as a key. A coincidence can be planned.

8.5 Hint-based Key Objects

Other key objects can be indicated by cycles of human use. There is nothing in the semantics of the editor, compiler, and debugger to suggest that people often use these tools cyclicly, but the cycle arises out of human work patterns. This means that when a program developer begins to debug, there may be key objects in the debugger that trigger a collection of the compiler structures. The two applications are connected not in their formal semantics, but only in their use by people.

It is hard to imagine that a connection through human use could be found easily. This suggests that a collector would benefit by being able to take "hints" about collections, including suggestions from applications about which objects would be good key objects for which clusters. This would increase the communication an application writer could have with the collection system. Including no hints limits the collector to discovering keys on its own.

9 Survival Tables

Tables 2 through 4 condense the information for three of the Dorado traces. First is a short list of characteristics of the trace. I have not done enough analysis to find the major allocation-producing activities in each trace, but the users were asked for traces during "typical days" at work. The short job discription of the users might suggest what that involves.

In each table, the information about survivors to various ages is halving the size of the survivors

43

Machine: Shangrila
User: Lab manager
Time: 11 hours
Volume: 16.209 Mb
Objects: 1.018

| Old storage | | Thresh-old | Half-life | 75% cover |
%	Mb	(kb)	(kb)	(kb)
100	16.209	0	8	±1
50	7.918	8	9	±5
20	3.977	16	17	±8
10	1.614	45	111	±14
5	0.808	155	204	±9
2	0.404	359	265	±5
1	0.162	721	731	±8
0.5	0.080	1452	1313	±72
0.25	0.040	2641	4646	±186

Table 2: Shangrila

Machine: Bennington
User: Programmer
Time: 28 hours
Volume: 12.697 Mb
Objects: 0.844 M

| Old storage | | Thresh-old | Half-life | 75% cover |
%	Mb	(kb)	(kb)	(kb)
100	12.607	0	9	±1
50	5.937	9	10	±1
20	3.093	18	14	±3
10	1.251	39	36	±5
5	0.623	75	316	±8
2	0.314	352	3733	±16
1	0.125	4681	383	±5
0.5	0.062	5063	1714	±15
0.25	0.031	6775	998	±24

Table 3: Bennington

at each step. For each cut-off, the table lists the volume of data involved [sometimes only a few kb], the age cut-off in kb allocated that reclaims all but the given volume, the wait from then in kb allocated until about one half of the remaining objects survive, and the spread in kb allocated that covers 75% of the objects. The spread that covers 50% of the objects is comperable to a half-life, but it is almost always 1 or 2.

10 Conclusions

Sudden short upswings in the collection rate of a storage system are indicative of clusters of bytes becoming unreachable at roughly the same time. When these bursts occur past an age horizon of a generational collector, the bytes contribute to old garbage. The old garbage can be reclaimed by a collection of the old objects, but when there is a large volume of old, live data, collections over it are unattractive.

The unreachable clusters can be deallocated by a collection system by carefully selecting some objects, the key objects, and quickly promoting all

Machine: Saratoga
User: Support staff
Time: 4 days
Volume: 17.441 Mb
Objects: 1.033 M

| Old storage | | Thresh-old | Half-life | 75% cover |
%	Mb	(kb)	(kb)	(kb)
100	17.441	0	8	±1
50	8.583	8	13	±2
20	4.331	20	42	±3
10	1.742	87	129	±2
5	0.870	216	236	±4
2	0.434	452	1108	±10
1	0.174	4002	538	±10
0.5	0.066	4540	311	±12
0.25	0.037	4584	7389	±5

Table 4: Saratoga

others. When the key objects are unreachable, this is a good indicator that the entire cluster is also unreachable.

11 Thanks

The researchers and support staff of Xerox PARC have done much to support this work. Russ Atkinson, Bob Hagmann, Carl Hauser, Peter Kessler, and Mike Spritzer were my chief navigators for the trip through the Cedar system. Hans Boehm, Alan Demers, and Mark Weiser were eager to talk about garbage collection issues. Sharon Johnson managed always to find disk space for the unreasonable volume of data I was generating. Lorna Fear did more support work on my behalf than I could ever repay.

This research would not have been possible without the volunteers who allowed me to slow down their Dorados with my data-gathering code. Thanks go out to Rick Beach on Shangrila, Peter Kessler on Bennington, Subhana Menis on Saratoga, and Steve Wallgren on Fremont and many others. Both Steve Wallgren and Polle Zellweger went far beyond the call of duty and endured unreliable and painfully slow beta-test versions of the code. Willie-Sue Orr helped make the difference by gritting her teeth and making an alteration to the Dorado micro-code, a task few would have dared.

Thanks are also due to Paul Wilson, Hans Boehm, and Norm Adams for commenting on early drafts of this paper and moral support.

This work was funded by Dr. John Koza, the Northern California Chapter of ARCS, Inc., and Xerox.

References

[BGH+77] Alan Bawden, Richard Greenblatt, Jack Holloway, Thomas Knight, David Moon, and Daniel Weinreb. Lisp machine progress report. Memo 444, August 1977.

[Bis77] Peter B. Bishop. Computer systems with a very large address space and garbage collection. Technical Report TR-178, Laboratory for Computer Science, MIT, May 1977.

[DeT90] John DeTreville. Heap usage in the Topaz environment. Technical Report 63, Digital Systems research Center, August 1990.

[DWH+90] Alan Demers, Mark Weiser, Barry Hayes, Hans Boehm, Daniel Bobrow, and Scott Shenker. Combining generational and conservative garbage collection: Framework and implementations. In *ACM Symposium on Principles of Programming Langauges*, pages 261–269, January 1990.

[Han77] David R. Hanson. Storage management for an implementation of SNOBOL4. *Software: practice and experience*, 7(2):179–192, March 1977.

[LH83] Henry Lieberman and Carl Hewitt. A real-time garbage collector based on the lifetimes of objects. *Communications of the ACM*, 26(6):419–429, June 1983.

[Moo84] David A. Moon. Garbage collection in a large lisp system. In *ACM Symposium on Lisp and Functional Languages*, pages 235–246, August 1984.

[Pie83] Ken Pier. A retrospective on the Dorado, a high-performance personal workstation. In *Proceedings of the 10th Annual International Symposium on Computer Architecture*, Stockholm, Sweden, June 1983.

[Rov85] Paul Rovner. On adding garbage collection and runtime types to a strongly-typed, staticly-checked, concurrent language. Technical Report

CSL-84-7, Xerox Corporation, July
1985.

[Sha87]   Robert A. Shaw. Improving garbage
collector performance in virtual memory. Technical Report CSL-TR-87-323,
Computer Science Laboratory, Stanford University, March 1987.

[SZBH86]   Daniel   C.   Swinehart,
Polle T. Zellweger, Richard J. Beach,
and Robert B. Hagmann. A structural
view of the Cedar programming environment. Technical Report CSL-86-1,
Xerox Corporation, 1986.

[UJ88]   David Ungar and Frank Jackson.
Tenuring policies for generational-
based storage reclamation. In *Object-
Oriented programming: systems lan-
guages and applications*, pages 1–17,
September 1988.

[Ung84]   David Ungar.   Generation scaveng-
ing: A non-disruptive high performance storage reclamation algorithm.
In *ACM SIGSOFT/SIGPLAN Practical Programming Conference*, pages
157–167, April 1984.

[Wil88]   Paul   R.   Wilson.   Opportunistic
garbage collection. *SIGPLAN Notices*,
23(12):98–102, December 1988.

[Wil89]   Paul R. Wilson. Design of the opportunistic grabge collector. In *Object-
Oriented programming: systems languages and applications*, pages 23–35,
October 1989.

[Wil90]   Paul R. Wilson. Personal communication in discussion at OOPSLA '90, October 1990.

[Wil91]   Paul   R.   Wilson.   Some issues and
strategies in heap management and
memory heirarchies. *SIGPLAN Notices*, 26(3):45–52, March 1991.

Integrating Information Retrieval and Domain Specific Approaches for Browsing and Retrieval in Object-Oriented Class Libraries

Richard Helm and Yoëlle S. Maarek

I.B.M. Thomas J. Watson Research Center,
P.O. Box 704, Yorktown Heights, NY 10598

Abstract

New techniques for browsing amongst functionally related classes, and retrieving classes from object-oriented class libraries are presented. These techniques make use of two potent, and readily available sources of information: the source code of each class, and its associated documentation. We describe how the integration of information retrieval techniques based on document analysis, and domain specific approaches based on code analysis, permits the construction of class retrieval tools based on natural language queries, and new kinds of browsing tools based on class functionality rather than inheritance. The chief advantages of this approach, compared to previous approaches, are that information about classes is acquired automatically and cheaply – no human intervention is required to acquire information about each class; and it is readily scalable and extensible – classes can be added to the library with very little effort.

1 Introduction

The emergence of large collections of reusable, domain specific, object-oriented software components poses new problems for the software engineer. Of particular interest in this paper, are the problems of how to locate and retrieve appropriate components, and how to meaningfully browse and navigate amongst functionally related components. A promising approach to solve these problems is to equip the software engineer with automated component retrieval and browsing tools.

Central to such tools is the component repository, which contains the actual reusable components, and, more importantly, information about these components which enable tools to retrieve and discriminate between related components. There are a number of important design issues in building a component repository and providing associated tools.

The first is *what information is to be represented about components and how this information is to be organized.* To effectively choose a component requires a deep and detailed understanding of the diverse knowledge about the components functionality [6]; only with detailed knowledge about a component's functionality can a tool discriminate between related components. This knowledge not only includes an understanding of what a component does, but ranges from an understanding of how a component interacts with other parts of the software system, to language-level typing constraints.

The second and probably most crucial design issue is *how to acquire and represent this information.* The question is whether or not this information is to be acquired automatically or manually. The ease of acquisition clearly effects the extensibility and scalability of retrieval tools as component libraries evolve.

Lastly, there is the issue of *how the user is going to query the repository for desired components.* It is important to ensure that the effort required for the user to locate and select components be smaller than the effort in implementing the desired class from scratch [17, 22].

There have been numerous efforts to build automated retrieval tools. These can be broadly classified into two groups according to the approach adopted for acquiring and representing information about components – they are the information retrieval approach and the knowledge-based approach.

In the information retrieval (IR) approach, all information is provided by its natural language documentation. It is automatically extracted from it, via a statistical analysis of the distribution of words therein. With this approach, no semantic knowledge is used and no interpretation of the document is made. The goal is to characterize the document rather than to understand it. There have been relatively few efforts in this direction: [2, 3, 7, 14].

In contrast, the domain specific approach has been very popular in the software community [1, 5, 8, 17, 21, 19]. In this approach, most of the information is provided by a domain expert. Knowledge-based systems are often "smarter" than IR systems: some of them are context sensitive and can generate answers adapted to the user's expertise. As a tradeoff, they require extensive domain analysis and a great deal of pre-encoded and manually provided information to produce adequate semantic descriptions of the components. This impacts detrimentally on the scalability and extensibility of the repository.

The authors previous experience in building repositories, and browsing and retrieval tools based on a pure information retrieval approach [14], and a pure knowledge-based approach [8] led us to conclude that an IR-based approach presents clear advantages in terms of cost, portability and scalability in building a repository, and because they support natural languages queries, in terms of ease of posing queries. We believe IR tools should be systematically used whenever natural language documentation is available. However, to approach the expertise of knowledge-based systems, aspects of their domain specific techniques are required, particularly when knowledge about components can be acquired automatically at low cost. In particular, IR-based tools should take advantage of domain specific information when this information can be acquired at low cost.

Object-oriented class libraries present a unique opportunity to apply an integrated approach to browsing and retrieval. Documentation about each class allows us to apply IR techniques, and the rich structure of class libraries implied by inheritance and part-of hierarchies declared in component source code allows us to automatically and effectively apply additional knowledge about components to enhance the retrieval and browsing processes. In this integrated approach, domain knowledge plays two roles. It is used during the construction of the repository to define the association between an indexable document and a component. It is also used during the retrieval stage to enhance the set of returned candidate components.

This paper describes how the integration of information retrieval techniques based on document analysis, and domain specific approaches based on code analysis, permits the construction of component repositories, class retrieval tools based on natural language queries, and new kinds of browsing tools. The chief advantages of this approach, compared to previous approaches, are that information about classes is acquired automatically and cheaply from readily available sources– no human intervention is required to acquire information about each class; and it is readily scalable and extensible – classes can be added to the repository with very little effort. We describe these techniques in the context of the InterViews C++ X11 graphic toolkit [12] — an object-oriented class library of reusable user interface components.

Reflecting the two separate issues of building a component repository, and browsing and retrieving components from the repository, this paper is broadly organized in two parts. The first, concerned with building a repository, is described in Section 2. The second, concerned with browsing and retrieving issues, is described in Sections 3 and 4. These sections give examples of the retrieval and browsing tools in use, Section 5 evaluates our approach in terms of retrieval efficiency and effectiveness. Section 6 concludes.

2 Constructing the Component Repository

A component repository contains the classes to be reused and their documentation, and more importantly the information about each class which allows them to be retrieved and browsed. In this sense, a component repository contains as only one of its parts, the class library. As mentioned previously, to construct the component repository we make use of two sources of information, the source code of each class, and its associated documentation. The source code is analyzed to build a *program database*, the documents are analyzed to produce a *document index file*. The program database, and the document index file both appear in the component repository. See Figure 1. We now describe, in turn, how these parts of the repository are constructed.

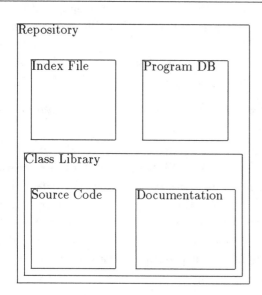

Figure 1: Component Repository

2.1 The Program Database

The program database is generated by parsing the source code and generating information about the classes according to some data model of the programming language. The data model defines the significant relations between entities (classes, methods, variables, etc.) such as "derived-from", "member-of" relationships. The resulting program database can then be used by many tools, such as those presented here, or class browsers, which also access the repository.

Our current implementation stores information about classes as a Prolog database, which can be accessed via logical rules which capture the important relationships between program entities. A more detailed description will be found in [10].

2.2 The Document Index File

To construct the document index file we use techniques from Information Retrieval (IR). Before describing this process in detail, we present a brief overview of the process of building an information storage and retrieval system. A more detailed introduction to IR can be found in [18] and [20]. We then describe how domain specific information from the class library is used to enhance this construction process.

Overview of IR Approach

The IR approach to constructing a repository consists of analyzing a document from a universe of documents, called the *corpus*, in order to extract the *indices* that best characterize the document – see Figure 2. The set of indices extracted from a document forms a *profile* of that document. The production of indices (the indexing stage) is crucial. An indexing scheme has to be chosen in order to select the most representative indices. One technique is to consider an *index* as a word or a set of words that occurs with a significant frequency in the document – a numerical weight that represents the relative importance of the index can then be associated with each index in a profile. From the document profiles, an inverted file index is produced to allow efficient storage and subsequent retrieval of documents.

Document profiles are used to classify and compare documents during retrieval and browsing. For document retrieval, the user specifies a query in free-style natural language which is then indexed using the same indexing technique used for the original documents. The profile extracted from the query directs the repository search. Various ranking measures can then be used to select the best candidate for a particular query [20]. For browsing, profiles can be organized into browse or cluster hierarchies, (See Figure 4) using clustering techniques [20]. This allows the user to see the similarities between documents.

Using Domain Knowledge

In our context, we are interested in building profiles for each class in the repository. As information retrieval techniques only use information from documents to build their characterizing profiles, we must

$$[\text{document}] \rightarrow \boxed{\text{Indexing}} \rightarrow [\text{profile}] \rightarrow \boxed{\text{Storing}} \rightarrow [\text{repository}]$$

Figure 2: Typical repository construction

consider the following issue – *what document is to be associated with each class?* This association, or *mapping* is important in two respects. Firstly, during repository construction, it is used to define the profile associated with each class. Conversely, during retrieval and browsing this mapping is used to go from indices back to the classes. We now describe the issues in defining the mapping between class and document in the context of indexing the InterViews manual pages. A sample manual page for the InterViews class **Frame** is shown in Figure 3.

There are many choices of documentation to associate with a class. Each choice effects the indexing of classes and the candidates retrieved. A key consideration is how to exploit the relationships that exist between documents imposed by the underlying classes described in these documents. Unlike other corpora, such as the UNIX manual pages which have few relationships between documents (other than "See Also"), the documentation for a class library has a rich structure. Foremost, are the relationships between documents imposed by the class inheritance hierarchy. Other relationships such as "part-of" and "type-subtype" define additional structure. In defining the mapping from document to class the question is how to exploit this structure, if at all. Some of the issues that must be considered are:

1. *What is the structure of the documentation for each class?*

   Each manual page for InterViews gives an overview of the class, and then a description of its significant methods. See Figure 3. A "See Also" section may sometimes appear. The issue is, what parts of this documentation are to be indexed?

   After some experimentation, we used just the introductory description of the class, and the description of each method from the manual pages. We found that the general description of the class was not sufficient. Much valuable information may be contained in the method descriptions. We deliberately ignored the "See Also" section as this tended to refer to the classes of instance variables of the documented class.

2. *Does a manual page describe a number of classes?*

   The manual page for **Frame** also describes its subclasses **TitleFrame**, **BorderFrame**, **ShadowFrame**, and **MarginFrame**. This complicates the document class mapping. In fact, we did not associate any document with the subclasses of the class described in a document. The program database allows us to infer a mapping from these subclasses back to their superclass's documentation.

3. *What is the role of the documentation of a classes superclass?*

   In practice, the complete documentation for a class includes the documentation of all its superclasses. The question arises, should this documentation be included in the indexable material associated with a class?

   Despite our initial expectations, we found that documentation of superclasses should not be included as part of the indexable material. We found that superclass documentation, especially of "rich" superclasses, such as that for class **Interactor** (containing 2860 words), tended to overwhelm the documentation of simple sub-classes, such as that for the class **Banner** (containing 152 words). This resulted in a browse or cluster hierarchy which was overly similar to the class hierarchy. This is unsatisfactory because we wish to obtain relationships between classes other than the inheritance relationship.

4. *How much program syntax should be included?*

   Method and instance variable names often indicate their function. Should these names appear as part of the documentation that is to be indexed? We decided to include method names as part of the indexable material. We felt that for InterViews, these names were sufficiently close to English and adequately reflected their function to warrant their inclusion.

5. *What is the significant vocabulary?*

   The documentation of class libraries suffer the problem that it assumes class and method names as part of its vocabulary. Automated techniques for analyzing text in such cases must be made aware of this library-specific vocabulary. For indexing the InterViews manual pages, we treated all class names, and public member function names as part of the vocabulary. This vocabulary was obtained from the program database.

With the above considerations in mind, we create the document to associate with each class by a simple shell script that strips out typesetting commands, embedded code, and sections we do not wish to be indexed. The resulting document, along with the significant vocabulary is then indexed as described in the next section.

2.3 Automatic indexing of class documentation

Having decided on the document to associate with each class, the document can then be indexed.

In order to extract information from the class documentation, we use the indexing scheme introduced by Maarek and Smadja in [15], developed by Maarek, Berry and Kaiser in [14], and embodied in the Guru IR system for software libraries [13]. The atomic indexing unit in this scheme is the *lexical affinity* (LA). An LA between two units of language stands for a correlation of their common appearance [4]. In the Guru scheme, a set of LA-based indices (or *profile*) is built for each document by performing a statistical analysis of the distribution of words not only in the document, but also in the corpus formed by the set of all the documents in the repository.

ρ-value	LA
0.10	construct frame
0.10	frame interactor
0.08	frame margin
0.08	construct interactor
0.08	banner frame
0.07	horizontal vertical
0.06	margin vertical
0.06	horizontal margin
0.06	banner title
0.06	frame surround
0.05	focus input
0.04	fall shadow
0.04	outline shadow

Table 1: Ranked LAs for the **Frame** class

First, LAs are automatically extracted using a co-occurrence compiler, and then those LAs which have a high resolving power in the document with respect to the corpus are selected as indices. The resolving power of an LA (w, w') in a document d is defined as $\rho = P_d \times \text{INFO}(w, w')$ [15], where P_d is the frequency of the LA (w, w') in document d, and INFO is the quantity of information of the two words w, w' in the entire corpus. Taking into account the quantity of information of words, as defined by information theory, permits us to reduce the influence of context words. Table 1 shows LAs ranked by normalized ρ-value for the manual page of class **Frame** shown in Figure 3.

Thus, we can automatically generate from a set of documents, a corresponding set of LA-based normalized profiles. From these profiles, an inverted file index is produced: every index points towards a list of pairs (d, ρ), where d is the document whose profile contains the index and ρ is its corresponding normalized resolving power. The inverted file index, and a dictionary[1] that stores the quantity of information of the words occurring in the set of documents, form the library repository. Both the inverted file index and the corpus dictionary are stored in the repository as a set of files for later

---

[1] This dictionary termed the *corpus dictionary* is necessary for indexing the query at retrieval stage in the same way the documents were indexed.

Frame, TitleFrame, BorderFrame, ShadowFrame, MarginFrame – surrounding interactor

DESCRIPTION

A frame is a monoscene subclass that outlines another interactor. A title frame provides a banner in addition to the outline and highlights the banner when the frame contains the input focus. A border frame draws the outline using a solid pattern when it contains the input focus and using a gray pattern otherwise. A shadow frame draws an outline with a drop shadow. A margin frame surrounds its component with horizontal and vertical glue.

PUBLIC OPERATIONS

Frame(Interactor*, int width = 1)

Construct a frame. If the given interactor is not nil, it is inserted as the frame's component. The frame extends *width* pixels outside of the interactor.

TitleFrame(Banner*, Interactor*, int width = 1)

Construct a title frame with the given banner.

BorderFrame(Interactor*, int width = 1)

Construct a border frame.

ShadowFrame(Interactor*, int h = 1, int v = 1)

Construct a shadow frame. The *h* and *v* ShadowFrame parameters specify the width of the horizontal and vertical shadows, respectively. Positive values for these parameters specify shadows falling to the right and below the interactor, respectively; negative values specify shadows falling to the left and above.

MarginFrame(Interactor* = nil, int margin = 0)
MarginFrame(Interactor*, int margin, int shrink, int stretch)
MarginFrame(Interactor*, int hmargin, int vmargin)
MarginFrame(Interactor*, int hm, int hshr, int hstr, int vm, int vshr, int vstr)

Construct a margin frame. The first constructor puts rigid, fixed-sized glue around the component, while the second surrounds it with fixed-sized glue of the given shrinkability and stretchability. Independent horizontal and vertical margins are set with the third constructor. The last constructor allows full specification of the margin frame's horizontal and vertical margins, shrinkabilities, and stretchabilities.

virtual void HandleInput(Event&)

A frame listens for OnEvent and OffEvent to detect when it has input focus. When an OnEvent is received, Frame::Handle calls Highlight(true); when an OffEvent is received, it calls Highlight(false). For any other event, it calls HandleInput. Frame::HandleInput does nothing.

virtual void Highlight(boolean)

The base class Highlight operation does nothing.

PROTECTED OPERATIONS

Frame(Interactor*, int, int, int, int)

This constructor is used by subclasses to explicitly set the widths of each line in the outline. The integers specify the width of the left, bottom, right, and top lines, respectively.

SEE ALSO

Banner(3I), Event(3I), Glue(3I), Scene(3I)

Figure 3: Manual page for the InterViews class **Frame**

access by the retrieval and browsing tools. These tools are described in the next section.

3 Browsing Amongst Related Classes

The characterizing profiles produced during repository construction provide information about relationships between classes. By defining a measure of similarity between classes based on the profiles, and by using a numerical clustering technique [14] based on this measure, we can then automatically generate a clustering or *browse hierarchy* that displays the degree of similarity between classes. This degree of similarity is purely drawn from the class documentation rather than from the class structure. Therefore, the browse hierarchy we produce is different from (and should be considered as being orthogonal to) the class hierarchies – the browse hierarchy provides a means to browse amongst functionally rather than structurally related components. This capability is not found in current class browsers.

The potential of clustering based on functionality can be seen if we study the browse hierarchy generated from the InterViews class library given in Figure 4. The browse hierarchy may be interpreted using the following rules.

1. *The similarity of a class to another is given by how far to the right of their common parent node they appear.*

   Classes **StringEditor** and **TextEditor** are thus more similar than classes **StringEditor** and **StrBrowser**.

2. *The similarity between classes is greater the further away from the root is the location of their common parent.*

   Thus, classes **StringEditor** and **TextEditor** are more similar than say **Message** and **Subject**, the latter appearing closer to the root of the browse hierarchy.

There are a number of interesting points about the InterViews toolkit that we can discover from the browse hierarchy in Figure 4. Most significantly, many obviously functionally similar classes are clustered together in this browse hierarchy. For example, the editor classes, **StringEditor** and **TextEditor**; those dealing with tables, **StringTable** and **Table**; bitmaps and rasters, **Bitmap** and **Raster**; and the container classes **Deck**, **Viewport**, **Box** and **Tray**. Often, these classes are not closely related in the InterViews class hierarchies shown in Figure 5. Of particular interest are the following clusterings which illustrate the power of this browsing.

1. The classes **Painter, Graphic,** and **GraphicBlock** are closely related — they are all concerned with drawing graphics on the screen. What is significant is that these classes appear in InterViews in three totally different class hierarchies, those rooted at classes **Resource, Persistent,** and **Interactor** respectively. It is not clear how this similarity could be ascertained by a conventional class-oriented browser.

2. The classes **Adjuster, Panner, Scroller,** and **Perspective** are related. The first three of these classes implement functions for the scrolling and panning of windows. They all do this via a **Perspective** object. What is significant is that these classes are unrelated to each other within their class hierarchy, and moreover, the class **Panner** is implemented as a container object, in fact as a subclass of **Scene**, but gets its behavior because it contains (or "buys") a number of instances of **Adjuster**. Once again, it is not clear how this similarity could be found by a conventional class-oriented browser.

Those readers familiar with InterViews will no doubt find other relationships of interest in this browse hierarchy.

In our implementation, internal nodes in the browse hierarchy may be collapsed to see all leaves rooted at it. This displays at one point, all classes which are similar at that level of clustering. Alternatively, the tree may be expanded, so that all leaves appear at the same level, providing more detail about the clustering process. We note that the clustering techniques used to build this browse hierarchy may also be directly applied to other measures of class similarity such as those used by the affinity browser of Pintado [9, 16].

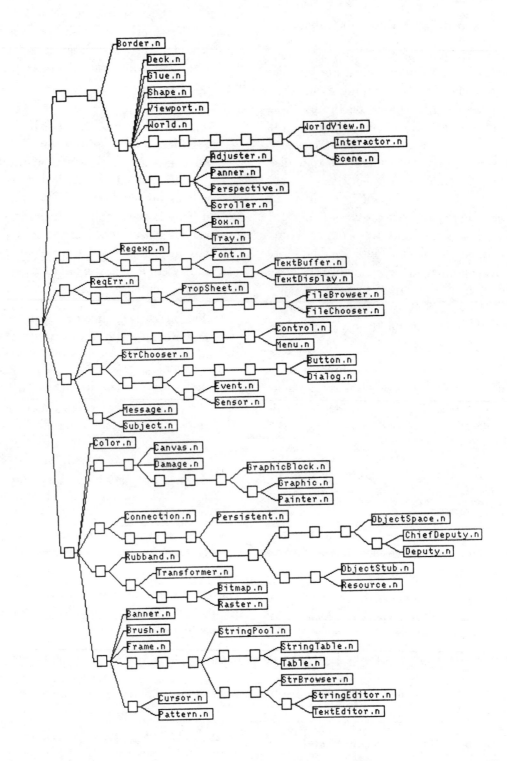

Figure 4: Browse hierarchy for InterViews manual pages

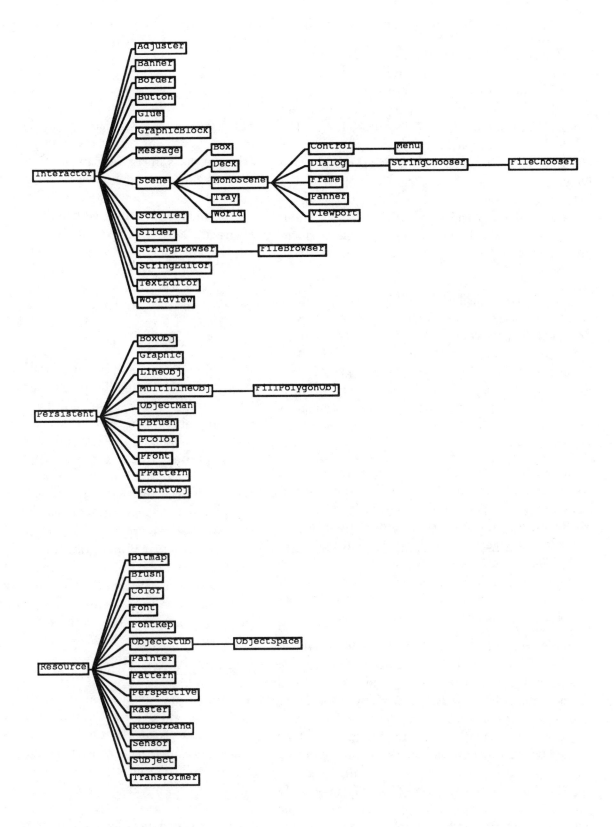

Figure 5: Class hierarchy for classes in InterViews manual pages

4 Component Retrieval and Browsing

To retrieve a component, the user gives a query in natural language and the query is indexed as if it were just another document. A profile of this query is produced which directs a lookup in the document index file in the repository. A list of profiles ranked by their degree of similarity to the query's profile can then be easily identified by using the inverted file index structure. The measure of similarity used is the same as the one used in building the browse hierarchy. This provides an ordered list of candidate classes – via the inverse of the class to document mapping – ranked by degree of similarity to the initial query.

Figures 6 and 7 display two different snapshots of sessions with the retrieval tool. The upper left window is the query window. Whatever is typed there is sent as a query when the appropriate menu item is clicked. Then, a list of candidates ranked by relevance to the query is returned in the top right window. The histogram next to the window gives feedback as to how closely the returned candidates match the query.

Simultaneously, the documentation corresponding to the candidate which best matches the query is displayed in the bottom left window. The user can click on returned candidates to browse their respective manual pages. The user can also cut and paste text from manual pages into the query window to further refine their query as they learn more about the components and the terminology used to describe the components.

The user may also view, in the bottom right-hand window, the candidates functionally related (ranked again by degree of similarity) to the one displayed in the bottom left window. This allows the user to browse amongst related classes. The related classes are not exactly in the same relationship as those classes which appear in the browse hierarchy in Figure 4. The latter is constructed by a pairwise global analysis of the similarity between *all* classes. In contrast, the classes which appear in the "Related Classes" are obtained by a local comparison to the *one* given class. Both browsing via global analysis and local analysis are of value, and give different perspectives of how classes are related.

4.1 Enhancing the Retrieval and Browsing of Candidates

Recall that, for InterViews, not every class in the library could be associated with a document. This is because manual pages often describe a number of classes via an abstract class. This is not a deficiency in InterViews, but rather represents a realistic situation for class library documentation. It is of little value to document every class in a library because many classes will have similar functionality which will be adequately captured in a description of their abstract class. One example is the manual page for the abstract class **Frame**. One consequence of not having a complete document to class mapping is that the retrieval tool's coverage of classes in the repository is incomplete. This means that only those classes with which we could associate a document, can be retrieved.

How then can we improve upon the candidates returned to get a better coverage of the class library? The key here is to use the information about relationships between classes, which are stored in the program database, to further enhance the candidates returned to the user. Essentially, after initially retrieving candidates based on their documentation, the system suggests further candidates using information about relationships between components (see Figure 8) in the class library. We now describe two simple ways to do this using inheritance and part-of relationships. We remark that although, at the time of writing, the program database implements the following capabilities, their integration with the retrieval tool is incomplete.

Exploiting Inheritance

The inheritance relationship is the major structuring mechanism of a class library. Thus, an abstract class is always at the root of the portion of the inheritance hierarchy containing its concrete sub-classes. This property can be used in two ways. Firstly, whenever an abstract class is retrieved, its concrete sub-classes can also be suggested as candidates by traversing the class hierarchy. For example, retrieving the abstract class **Frame** as a candidate allows its concrete subclasses, **TitleFrame, ShadowFrame** etc., to be retrieved. Secondly, to browse amongst concrete classes that do not have

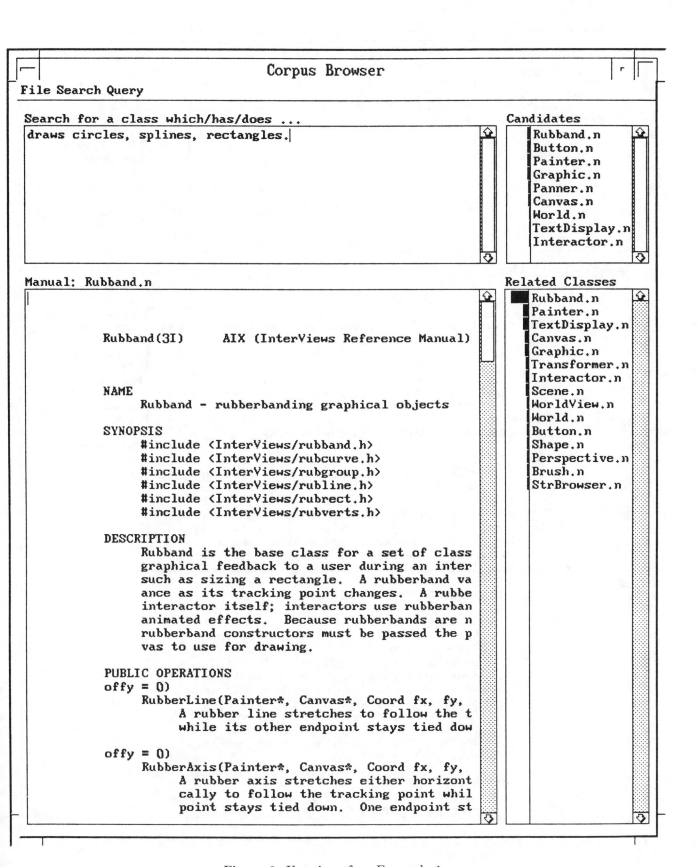

Figure 6: User interface Example 1

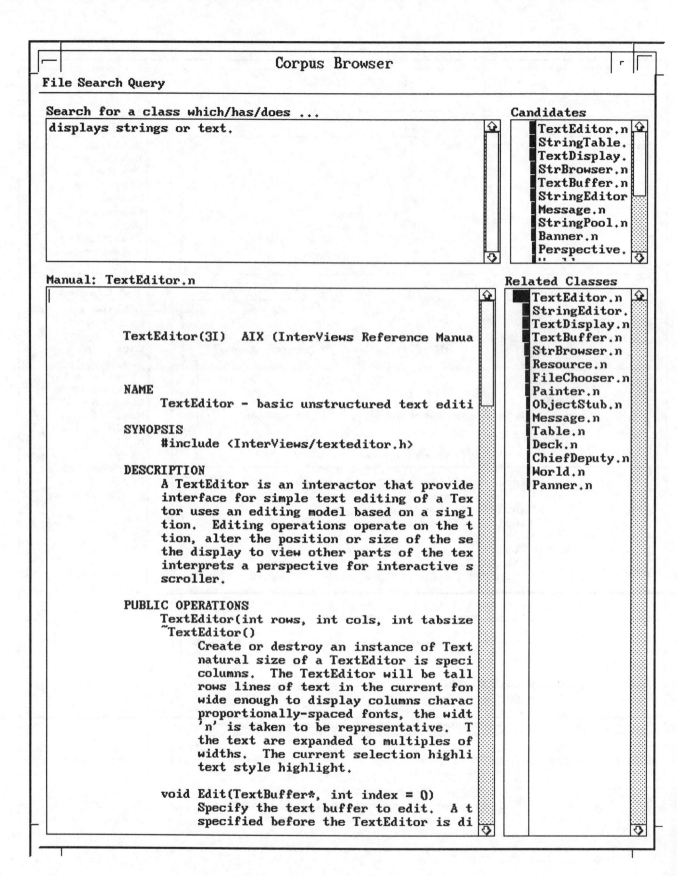

Figure 7: User interface Example 2

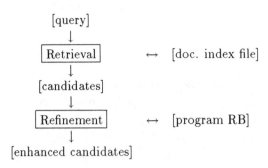

[query]
↓
Retrieval   ↔   [doc. index file]
↓
[candidates]
↓
Refinement   ↔   [program RB]
↓
[enhanced candidates]

Figure 8: Retrieval from Library

manual pages (*e.g.*, **BorderFrame**), we can use the nearest abstract superclass for which there exists documentation (*e.g.*, **Frame**). In this way, information about abstract and concrete classes can be used to make up for the lack of documentation for every class in the class library.

Exploiting Sub-parts

The other major relationship in a class library is that between a class and its instance variables – the "part-of" relationship.

We can make use of this relationship when retrieved candidate classes appear as *functionally significant* parts of other classes: that is, when they are instance variables of a class and this class "buys" or acquires their functionality. For example, in InterViews, the class **Panner** contains numerous instances of the class **Adjuster**. Because each **Adjuster** manipulates the view of a window, the class **Panner** also manipulates the view of a window. Thus, when the class **Adjuster** is retrieved, as it is a functionally significant part of the class **Panner**, **Panner** should be suggested as a candidate.

These part-of relationships can often be inferred from the source code. A potential problem is that parts are often dynamically created and only exist explicitly as local variables within some method. That they are then functionally important for the containing object is difficult to ascertain automatically. One way around this problem is through coding standards which make explicit significant parts of classes[2].

---

[2]In InterViews 2.6 the **Adjusters** do not appear as in-

4.2   Further issues concerning reuse

The candidate classes returned by the retrieval tool are retrieved solely by the profiles of their associated documentation. However, a retrieved class cannot be simply reused based on its functionality inferred from its documentation – other factors, such as the class's type, its location within a class hierarchy, and in which contracts [11] it participates, all determine its suitability for reuse. Given the set of returned candidates, it is important to be able to understand, classify and view them in terms of these factors.

To be able to do this requires new tools and capabilities. These capabilities are somewhat outside the scope of the tools presented here. Notwithstanding this, we propose some simple ways in which the retrieved classes can be organized and classified using simple extensions of existing tools. We concentrate on how inheritance, types and contracts can give more information about the classes.

Inheritance and Types

In languages like C++, class hierarchies define the types of objects. Retrieved classes belonging to different class hierarchies are of different types, and cannot be used interchangeably. For example, the classes **Rubband, Painter** and **Graphic** returned from the query "*draws circles, splines, rectangles*" in Figure 6 occur in different class hierarchies. To display these retrieved classes as a linear list is unsatisfactory. Ideally, the retrieved classes should be displayed in a way which highlights the fact that they appear in different class hierarchies.

Additionally, finer grain relationships can also be displayed via an affinity browser [9, 16]. The information required to display class hierarchies, and class affinities as in [16] is readily ascertained from the program database.

Contracts

Contracts [11] describe how classes are designed to cooperate and work with each other in behavioral compositions. If retrieved classes can participate

---

stance variables of **Panner**, but are created dynamically. Thus it is difficult to infer by static analysis that they are functionally significant to **Panner**. A simple redeclaration of class **Panner** would fix this.

in a contract with each other, this fact should be presented to the user as well.

For example, the query "*incremental scrolling and zooming by manipululating a perspective*" returns as the top five candidates **GraphicBlock**, **Perspective**, **Scroller**, **Adjuster**, and **Panner**. These classes are designed to work together — the classes **Scroller**, **Adjuster**, and **Panner** all scroll or zoom a **GraphicBlock**. They do this via a **Perspective**. In [11] we define contracts *AdjustView* and *AdjustViewWithFeedback* which capture this cooperating behavior between these classes. In presenting these retrieved classes to the user, it is desirable that the fact that they participate in these contracts is made evident, perhaps by displaying a graph which captures their behavioral dependencies.

5 Evaluation

The repository construction tools described in this paper are fully implemented in C on an RS/6000. Currently, the various retrieval and browsing components, are implemented in C, C++, Prolog, and InterViews on an RS/6000, but as yet, are not fully integrated with each other and with other tools such as class browsers. A full integration involves numerous user-interface and visualization issues that we have not yet fully addressed.

In order to evaluate the performance of our system we consider two criteria:(1) efficiency and (2) retrieval effectiveness.

Efficiency

The repository construction requires approximately one minute on an RS/6000 to generate the repository for about 60 InterViews classes. The construction stage could be made faster. However, this is not a crucial problem since (1) it is done off-line and (2) the real bottleneck is the semi-automated identification of the documents to be fed to the IR component, *i.e.* the mapping between documents and classes.

During retrieval, response time has to be fast enough to make the system convenient and attractive to use. In all the repositories we have built (some of them counting about 1000 components) the average response time was below 1 second, and

therefore reasonable as far as user's need is concerned. We are currently evaluating efficiency on larger scale repositories.

Effectiveness

To evaluate the performance of our system we can use the standard IR evaluation method based on recall (proportion of relevant material retrieved) and precision (proportion of retrieved material that is relevant). These are relative, rather than absolute, measures and require comparison with other systems. Unfortunately, there are no other systems in our domain for comparison. However, the IR component of our tool has been previously evaluated and its performance compared to INFOEXPLORER, a hypertext-based library system for AIX on the IBM RISC System/6000 [14]. There it was determined that this IR-component achieves a recall rate as high, and a precision rate 15% better than INFO-EXPLORER, while being less expensive to build and requiring less storage space. This performance will likely be improved upon once we make complete use of the information in the program database.

6 Conclusion

We have presented new techniques for browsing amongst functionally related classes, and retrieving classes from object-oriented class libraries based two sources of information: the source code of each class; and its associated documentation. The chief advantages of this approach, compared to previous approaches, are that most information about classes is acquired automatically and cheaply – no human intervention is required to acquire information about each class; and it is readily scalable and extensible.

Ultimately, the success of the approach presented here will be determined by the availability of class library documentation and source code, and the integration of the retrieval and the browse tools with other tools such as class and affinity browsers, and application builders.

We hope that the kind of tools we have proposed will be attractive enough to motivate programmers to write documentation in a consistent format to permit extraction of appropriate sections, and to write compilers which generate the necessary code analyses required to fully automate the class to document mapping and the refinement of candidate process.

7 Acknowledgments

Mark Kennedy participated in the design and implementation of the inverted file index. Frank Smadja, Dan Berry and Gail Kaiser collaborated in the original design of the LA-based indexing scheme.

References

[1] B.P. Allen and S.D. Lee. A knowledge-based environment for the development of software parts composition systems. In *Proceedings of the 11th ICSE*, pages 104–112, Pittsburgh, PA, May 1989.

[2] S.P. Arnold and S.L. Stepoway. The reuse system: Cataloging and retrieval of reusable software. In W. Tracz, editor, *Software Reuse: Emerging Technology*, pages 138–141. Computer Society Press, 1987.

[3] B.A. Burton, R. Wienk Aragon, S.A. Bailey, K.D. Koelher, and L.A. Mayes. The reusable software library. In W. Tracz, editor, *Software Reuse: Emerging Technology*, pages 129–137. Computer Society Press, 1987.

[4] F. de Saussure. *Cours de Linguistique Générale, Quatrième Edition*. Librairie Payot, Paris, France, 1949.

[5] P. Devanbu, P.G. Selfridge, B.W. Ballard, and R.J. Brachman. A knowledge-based software information system. In *Proceedings of IJCAI'89*, pages 110–115, Detroit, MI, August 1989.

[6] G. Fischer. Cognitive view of reuse and redesign. *IEEE Software*, July 1987.

[7] W.B. Frakes and B.A. Nejmeh. Software reuse through information retrieval. In *Proceedings of the 20th Annual HICSS*, pages 530–535, Kona, HI, January 1987.

[8] D. Gangopadhyay and A.R. Helm. A model-driven approach for the reuse of classes from domain specific object-oriented class repositories. Technical Report RC14510, IBM Research Division, March 1989.

[9] S. Gibbs, D. Tsichritzis, E. Casais, O. Nierstrszand, and X. Pintado. Class management for software communities. *Communications of the ACM*, pages 90–103, September 1990.

[10] R. Helm. An architecture for semantic, distributed, extensible source code and repository browsing. Technical Report In Preparation, IBM Research Division, 1991.

[11] R. Helm, I. Holland, and D. Gangopadhyay. Contracts: Specifying behavioral compositions in object-oriented systems. In *Object-Oriented Programming Systems, Languages and Applications Conference*, Ottawa, Canada, October 1990.

[12] Mark Linton. *InterViews Reference Manual*. CSL, Stanford University, 2.4 edition, 1988.

[13] Y.S. Maarek. An information retrieval approach for building reuse libraries. In *First International Workshop on Software Reusability*, Dortmund, Germany, 1991.

[14] Y.S. Maarek, D.M. Berry, and G.E. Kaiser. An information retrieval approach for automatically constructing software libraries. *Transactions on Software Engineering*, 1991. To appear.

[15] Y.S. Maarek and F.A. Smadja. Full text indexing based on lexical relations. An application: Software libraries. In N.J. Belkin and C.J. van Rijsbergen, editors, *Proceedings of SIGIR'89*, pages 198–206, Cambridge, MA, June 1989. ACM Press.

[16] X. Pintado. Selection and exploration in an object-oriented environment: The affinity browser. In Dennis Tsichritzis, editor, *Object Management*, pages 79–88. Centre Universitaire d'Informatique, Universite de Geneve, 1990.

[17] R. Prieto Diaz and P. Freeman. Classifying software for reusability. *IEEE Software*, 4(1):6–16, January 1987.

[18] G. Salton and M.J. McGill. *Introduction to Modern Information Retrieval*. Computer Series. McGraw-Hill, New York, 1983.

[19] W.F. Tichy, R.L. Adams, and L. Holter. NLH/E: A natural-language help system. In *Proceedings of the 11th ICSE*, pages 364–374, Pittsburgh, PA, May 1989.

[20] C.J. van Rijsbergen. *Information Retrieval*. Butterworths, second edition, 1979.

[21] M. Wood and I. Sommerville. An information retrieval system for software components. *SIGIR Forum*, 22(3,4):11–25, Spring/Summer 1988.

[22] S.N. Woodfield, D.W. Embley, and D.T. Scott. Can programmers reuse software ? *IEEE Software*, July 1987.

Portia: An Instance-Centered Environment for Smalltalk

Eric Gold
Mary Beth Rosson

User Interface Institute
IBM T.J. Watson Research Center
P.O. Box 704
Yorktown Heights, New York 10598

Abstract

Smalltalk environments should accommodate programmers' conceptualizations of objects as independent, communicating agents by providing tools that allow them to work directly with instances. This paper discusses the requirements for such an environment, assesses the standard Smalltalk environment in this respect, and describes an enhanced Smalltalk environment called Portia which provides additional facilities for interacting with instances.

1 Introduction

Object-oriented languages necessitate extraordinarily complex and rich software environments. Like other kinds of languages, there is a need for software tools that help write code, debug a running application and interact with files, but the special nature of object-oriented languages imposes other requirements for the environment as well. In particular, the environment needs to provide facilities for interacting with objects after they have been instantiated.

We contend that a development environment should mirror the programmer's style of thinking by emphasizing the importance of objects. If designing and implementing an object-oriented application

means building a representation of communicating objects, then programmers should be able to create and manipulate that representation (cf. Beck & Cunningham, 1989; Booch, 1986). If programmers work with objects in their mind, then they should work with objects on the screen. We call an environment oriented toward explicit interaction with instances an *instance-centered environment*. An environment is instance-centered insofar as it provides facilities for working directly with objects to debug, understand and create applications. Any activity geared towards working with an instance or group of instances is called an *instance-centered activity*.

Currently, programmers' use of the Smalltalk environment revolves around the Class Hierarchy Browser[1]. The typical style of programming is to write a meaningful amount of code -- enough to support the execution of some part of an application. Only once the code is written, might a programmer use the Debugger or Inspector to test and debug the code. Even with the Smalltalk environment, the act of writing code is not that much different than writing code in any other language; the programmer cranks out line after line, method after method. During this process, the power of all the Smalltalk tools that work with instances is put on hold.

---

[1]Although all points made in this paper apply to both Smalltalk/V and Smalltalk-80, the terminology is in terms of Smalltalk/V. The Class Hierarchy Browser is Smalltalk-80's Standard System View and the term "pane" is synonymous with "view."

OOPSLA'91, pp. 62–74

Sometimes, however, programming code can be composed in the context of a running example in which instances can be used along with the code to work through the programming task (Schneider, 1990; Doucet & Pfeffer, 1989). Every Smalltalk programmer appreciates those times in which modifications to code were done in the Debugger, while in the context of already existing objects. In those cases, snippets of code could be evaluated on the spot and modifications could be tested without writing or modifying any other method. This is the instance-centered approach to code development; this paper investigates whether this style of using specific objects while debugging code can be extended to all code-writing activities.

Object-oriented programmers often come across situations requiring the understanding of some object; this is a precursor to testing, reusing and generalizing objects. Here too, the Class Hierarchy Browser usually serves as Smalltalk programmers' most important tool. Most likely, a programmer understands an object's behavior by studying the programming code that implements that behavior.

In many cases, existing objects can furnish a wealth of information about their behaviors. In general, the Smalltalk environment supplies two ways to understand the workings of an instance. First, the programmer can browse the connections between instances and, second, the programmer can isolate an instance and send it a message noting what it does or what it returns. At issue, here, is how well Smalltalk supports this instance-centered approach and what additional support would improve the current environment.

Smalltalk is a language well-suited for experimenting and prototyping. Again, using the Class Hierarchy Browser, incremental changes can be made to the programming code. In contrast, the instance-centered approach is to experiment with objects that are already part of a working application (cf. Smith, 1987). Smalltalk allows programmers to make changes to running applications by changing the instance variables of existing objects and by sending messages, with the aid of the Workspace, to these objects; in this way, programmers avoid working with the programming code. This paper examines how this support can be strengthened.

This paper introduces an enhanced Smalltalk environment called Portia and discusses how the environment supports instance-centered activities. Portia sits on top of Smalltalk/V PM and runs on an IBM PS/2 under OS/2. This environment has been in development for more than eighteen months and the current robust prototype is used by about a half dozen people at IBM Research. A number of applications have been developed with Portia including a multiple regression statistical package and general statistical tools. Each new version of Portia is built with the previous version.

All of the examples used throughout this paper are based on a Smalltalk implementation of a slot machine. A schematic of the design and a screen shot of the slot machine's interface appear in Figure 1. The design consists of a SlotMachine, three Wheels, several SlotIcons, an Outcome, a Coin, a CoinBox, and a PayoffKeeper. To start the slot machine, a user types an amount of a bet in the pane labeled "bet" and then presses the Spin button. The three list panes show the final position of the three wheels with the chosen SlotIcons highlighted. The pane labeled "payoff" shows the winners' payments. After pressing the Spin button the SlotMachine creates a new Outcome and passes it and a Coin, as arguments, to the first Wheel. This Wheel, which points to a Collection of SlotIcons, spins itself, chooses a SlotIcon at random, and passes the Coin and a modified Outcome to the second Wheel which then repeats the first Wheel's actions and passes off to the third Wheel. After spinning itself, the third Wheel notifies the PayoffKeeper which asks the Outcome to determine, in collaboration with the selected SlotIcons, whether the player has won and posts any resulting payment.

The paper is organized as follows. Section 2 describes what kinds of facilities and tools are necessary for interacting with instances and what kinds of instance-centered activities are and are not supported in Smalltalk's standard environment. Section 3 offers a tour of the Portia environment and section 4 includes some examples of its use. Finally section 5 gives some concluding remarks.

Smalltalk to further enhance programmers' abilities to work directly with instances.

Bringing useful objects together in a text area - The Smalltalk Workspace is an important tool for working with instances. The Workspace is instrumental for the use and understanding of objects and for testing Smalltalk expressions. The Workspace depends on instances but is nonetheless limited in its support of

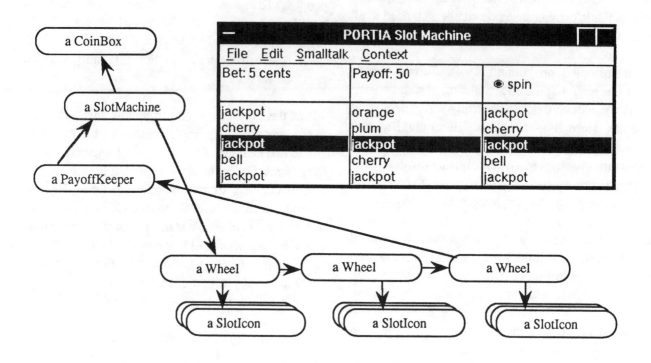

Figure 1. The Slot Machine's Interface and Design

2 Requirements for an Instance-Centered Environment

This section describes how instance-centered activities are facilitated and inhibited by the standard Smalltalk environment and extracts general characteristics required by an instance-centered environment. This paves the way for the next section, on the new Portia environment, which builds on

instance-centered activities.

The major limitation is how instances become part of the Workspace. Certain classes of objects like Numbers and Strings as well as global variables can simply be typed into the text area and then used. Because class objects are global, they can create new instances that also can be used in the Workspace. Some objects, however, are difficult to define in a particular Workspace.

Consider the example of the slot machine. Suppose a programmer wishes to understand the behavior of a CoinBox object. Using information from the Class Hierarchy Browser such as what messages the CoinBox understands and what arguments are sent with those messages, the programmer could use the Workspace to experiment with such an object. For instance, evaluating the expression CoinBox new hasTooManyCoins would confirm that the message elicits the return of a Boolean. Inspecting the CoinBox reveals the number of coins that have been dropped in the box, thus giving insight to the workings of the method hasTooManyCoins.

Now consider how the CoinBox becomes part of the Workspace's text area. Perhaps, as described above, a new CoinBox is created in the Workspace but a simpler solution might be to use the CoinBox that is part of an already working slot machine. After all, the creation and initialization of the CoinBox could be cumbersome and might require, as arguments, other instances that are not easily created or imported into the Workspace.

When inspecting an object, one of the Inspector's text areas is set up so that self refers to the inspected object; this object, and the objects pointed to by its instance variables, can be used in that text area. A CoinBox, then, can be used in a text area if a programmer can find one to inspect. This solution, though, raises a new problem. Commonly, a programmer does not wish to work with one particular object in a Workspace but with a collection of objects that may not be connected to each other; inspecting an object can only bring that single object into the text area. So, a programmer could not use this method to work jointly with a CoinBox and a Coin unless the Coin could be created in the Inspector's text area.

The Debugger portrays a temporal slice of a running program; this tool lists the stack of methods waiting to finish execution, displays the code associated with each method and provides a way to inspect the receiver and arguments for each method. The Debugger can be an ideal tool for bringing together into one text area a group of objects with which the programmer can accomplish instance-centered tasks. Interrupting the SlotMachine's execution in the method spin , for example, can set up a text area with a Wheel, an Outcome and a Collection of Coins.

Nonetheless, there is no guarantee that the instances needed by the programmer can be captured by a Debugger. One problem occurs when all of the objects required are not part of the same application; working with a slot machine's CoinBox and a new kind of object, a PinballMachine, is such an example. Another problem is that the programmer may want to work with a particular collection of objects before an application is far enough developed to meaningfully invoke the Debugger. Moreover, the Debugger requires the programmer to analyze the code to find the correct spot to stop the execution, a potentially difficult and time consuming task.

These difficulties with Workspaces, Inspectors and Debuggers point to a general requirement for an instance-centered environment -- the ability to move any object between any two tools or from a working application to a tool. Just as a word processor allows text to be copied, moved and pasted, an instance-centered environment should permit objects to be grabbed, moved and dropped. With such capabilities, any set of objects could be gathered together in any tool.

Finding instances - A medium-sized application typically involves tens of thousands of objects. Of these, perhaps one or two dozen might be important and interesting enough to work with directly. With the ability to move objects once found, the question of how those objects are found in the first place becomes especially relevant. How does the programmer find a SlotMachine, CoinBox or Wheel?

The Smalltalk environment offers several ways to find instances. Of course, the Debugger, Inspector and Workspace can all access the objects that make up an application. Additionally, all classes respond to the message allInstances by returning a Collection of all existing instances of that class. Even so, these facilities are hampered as described in the following paragraphs.

Many objects are created and destroyed as an application executes; a particular object may not exist at a given time. Consequently, the Inspector, Workspace and use of allInstances will not locate an object that has not yet been created or has been garbage-collected. The Debugger can stop an application at a point for which a given object exists but then the programmer is saddled with the same problems outlined in the previous section.

The Inspector is an excellent tool for finding objects but its use is awkward. Often, a programmer must chase pointers from object to object and in the process creates a long chain of Inspectors. This is time consuming, clutters the screen and requires the programmer to find a path from some starting object to the desired final object.

Another problem is distinguishing between instances of the same class. Because many kinds of objects identify themselves simply by their class name, knowing whether a particular instance is the one sought after can be difficult. Often, the programmer must resort to looking at its instance variables (or perhaps the instance variables of its instance variables) to identify a particular instance, and even this might not be enough information. For this reason, the use of allInstances is of limited use in finding particular instances.

Suppose the programmer wants to change the Collection of SlotIcons pointed to by the slot machine's second Wheel so that it contains a greater number of jackpot icons. This modification would change the characteristics of the slot machine so that the machine would pay off more often. Using allInstances would return a Collection of three Wheels (or more if there are many slot machines) with no straightforward way to tell which one is the second wheel.

An object-oriented environment could spur instance-centered activities by including new ways to find particular instances. In addition to making what is offered by standard Smalltalk less tedious, such an environment could include support for catching objects as they are created, preventing them from being destroyed, and providing ways to distinguish instances of the same class.

Working with programming code - Sometimes programmers need to bring a group of objects into a text area so that they can evaluate snippets of programming code; this is necessary for understanding, testing and debugging that code. This is precisely the role played by the Debugger, but in some cases the Debugger is not an adequate tool for this activity. As discussed already, the Debugger often cannot work when parts of the application are missing or incomplete or when the programmer wishes to test the code within a context that the application is not likely to supply. Commonly, a programmer may wish to test parts of a method even before the method is entirely written or before the code successfully compiles. Even when the method is complete, other parts of the application could remain unwritten. At other times, the programmer may wish to test the code with arguments not used in the application; perhaps some code normally runs with Strings as arguments but the programmer wants to test it with Symbols instead. Additionally, the programmer may wish to take advantage of objects that can be found in some other tool; working with the code in another tool, like the Workspace, may be simpler than invoking the Debugger.

Consider, for example, the code shown in Figure 2. This is a method in PayoffKeeper that takes special action when three jackpots come up on the three Wheels; the code rings a bell for a jackpot and checks to see if the payoff is so large that some money must be withheld for the IRS. Invoking a Debugger on this code might not be possible if, for instance, the user interface for the slot machine was not yet written. Since jackpots occur infrequently, catching this code in the Debugger could require spinning the slot machine over and over again.

An instance-centered environment could support this by allowing the programmer to bring the necessary objects *to the code*. This is possible if the environment supports locating and moving objects as described above and includes ways to attach objects to the tokens in the code. For the code shown in Figure 2, objects must be attached to anOutcome, aCoin, anIRS, and self.

Sometimes, the programmer cannot attach certain kinds of objects to the code because those objects have not yet been implemented. This problem can be solved by implementing objects that behave in a limited way (i.e. act as stubs). This solution,

```
takeActionOnJackpot: anOutcome withBet:
  aCoin notifying: anIRS

anOutcome isJackpot
  ifTrue: [self withhold:
    ((aCoin pays: anOutcome payoff) *
    (1- (anIRS withholdingProportion:
      anOutcome)))).
  4 timesRepeat: [Terminal bell]]
```

Figure 2. Sample Programming Code.

however, requires considerable work; an environment that lessens this work would reinforce instance-centered activities.

3 A Tour of Portia

The Portia environment is designed to provide the support and facilities suggested by the previous section. This environment relies on new tools, modifications to current Smalltalk tools and new object behaviors and manipulations. These enhancements enable programmers to find existing instances, move them from tool to tool or from application to tool, and associate them with programming code. The environment overcomes deficiencies in the current Smalltalk environment,

organizes and displays information about particular objects, and offers new facilities that allow for instance-centered activities.

3.1 Interactions with Objects

To support enhancements to Smalltalk tools and the use of new tools, Portia relies on modifications to how objects are manipulated and to how they behave in the environment. This section explains those modifications.

New object manipulations - To allow for moving objects from one tool to another and from an applications to a tool, Portia supports two object manipulations called *Grab* and *Drop*. Nearly every Portia tool includes an option to grab an object used for that tool or to drop an (already grabbed) object into that tool. So, for example, an object found in the Debugger can be grabbed and then dropped in a Workspace. In addition, the model underlying every pane can be grabbed from that pane by selecting Grab Model from the appropriate menu.

New object behaviors - In addition to the behaviors implemented for a particular application, all Smalltalk objects take responsibility for such language-related behaviors as making copies of themselves and such environment-related behaviors as how they print themselves. Portia includes new behaviors that enhance the way objects interact with the environment; these new behaviors include *name*, *mark* and *hold*.

All objects name themselves when receiving the message objectName:. If an object has a name, the name is used as its printString. The name is a way to identify those objects that are most important in an application and to refer to them when using a Workspace. Marking an object makes it easy to identify later; this is used when working with a new tool called the Locator (see below). An object is marked by sending it the message mark. Both naming and marking objects help distinguish them when working with many instances from the same class. Holding an object makes it available for use at

67

a later time. Sending the message <u>hold</u> places the receiving object in a new Portia tool called the Repository; this tool is described in detail below.

Intervention objects - Programmers may need to work with a set of objects where some of them have not yet been implemented or do not yet work correctly. In these cases, they can use a new kind of object called an *intervention object*. An intervention object implements no behaviors of its own but responds to every message by opening a window, called an *intervention window* (see Figure 3), in which the user can specify how the intervention object should respond to that message. This is especially useful when working with programming code in a text area.

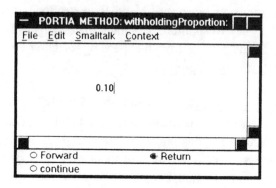

Figure 3. An Intervention Window.

The Intervention Window consists of a text area and three buttons labeled <u>Return</u>, <u>Forward</u> and <u>Continue</u>. The programmer specifies an object by creating, in the text area, an expression for evaluation. If the user chooses <u>Return</u> the intervention object will return the result of evaluating the expression; if the user chooses <u>Forward</u>, the object specified by the expression will handle the message sent to the intervention object. Once the choice is made and the expression set up, execution resumes by pressing the <u>Continue</u> button.

3.2 Portia Tools

The Portia environment adds two new tools to Smalltalk's repertoire called the Locator and the Repository and enhances Smalltalk's Workspace and Class Hierarchy Browser. These tools are described here.

The Portia Workspace - The Portia Workspace retains the functionality of the Smalltalk Workspace but also works with objects imported from other parts of the environment, supplies objects for other tools, attaches objects to Smalltalk expressions, supports multiple text selection, displays information about objects used in the tool, allows for the naming and marking of objects, interacts with other tools, and organizes multiple Workspaces.

Figure 4 shows the new Portia Workspace. The left-hand pane is the text area and corresponds to the Smalltalk Workspace. To conserve screen real estate, multiple invocations of Workspaces are handled by a single tool; the upper right-hand pane organizes and switches between Workspaces. The lower right-hand panes supply information about objects brought into the Workspace and how those objects are bound to the expressions typed in the text area.

Objects are brought into and out of the Workspace by grabbing and dropping them. Selecting the menu item <u>Drop Object</u> places the most recently grabbed object in the Workspace; the dropped object then can be referred to by its name. Objects are automatically grabbed when performing a <u>doIt</u>; the result of the evaluation can then be dropped elsewhere in the environment. The pane labeled "dropped objects" lists the objects dropped in the Workspace.

The Workspace can also be set up so that any expression or snippet of code can be evaluated. This involves specifying what <u>self</u> refers to, assigning objects to argument names and defining temporary variables. Highlighting an expression and choosing <u>Set Self</u> from the menu identifies the result of evaluating that expression as the object referred to by the string self; the set object is identified as indicated in the figure. Once set, the object's instance variables can be referenced as well. Highlighting an argument name before dropping an object into the Workspace binds the dropped object to that name; this information is displayed in the pane labeled "objects attached to text." Additionally, highlighting a list of temporary variables and selecting Set Temps frees the programmer from declaring these variables for each evaluation of an expression. This functionality along with a new ability to select text that is not contiguous supports the evaluation of arbitrary chunks of programming code in the Workspace.

instance-centered facilities of Portia are required for this feature; without specific objects, the environment would not know which of the many kinds of objects that might respond to a particular message should be selected for the Browser's class.

The Class Hierarchy Browser - The Class Hierarchy Browser's text area uses the same kind of Pane as the Workspace's text area and so offers the same functionality. This is useful since the Browser supplies programming code; when bound with specific instances, the code can be used in an instance-centered way.

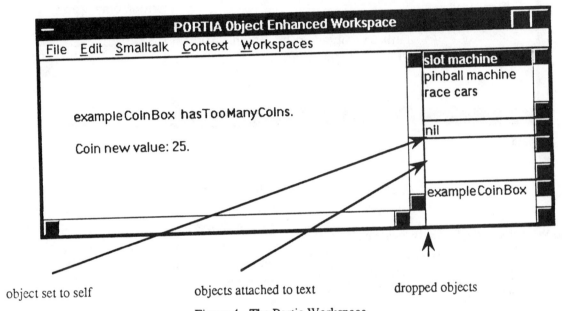

Figure 4. The Portia Workspace.

The Workspace permits programmers to name or mark objects. Highlighting an expression and choosing Name It from the menu prompts the user for a name and then attaches it to the object returned from evaluating the expression. Mark It works in a similar way.

Information in a Workspace can be used for starting up a new Class Hierarchy Browser. By choosing an expression in which the receiver and each argument evaluates to an object, the programmer can open a new Browser with the class set to the class of the receiver and the method set to the message sent to the receiver. Open Browser initiates this action. The

The Browser has been enhanced in a number of ways. Several new features make the binding of instances to programming code easier in the Browser than in the Workspace. The Portia Browser associates separate groups of instances with each method; switching between methods switches between those groups of instances. Setting self while in one method sets self for every method in the same class. Additionally, choosing New Browser from the Workspace not only opens a new Browser with the class and method selected but also sets self to the receiver and attaches the appropriate instances to the argument names.

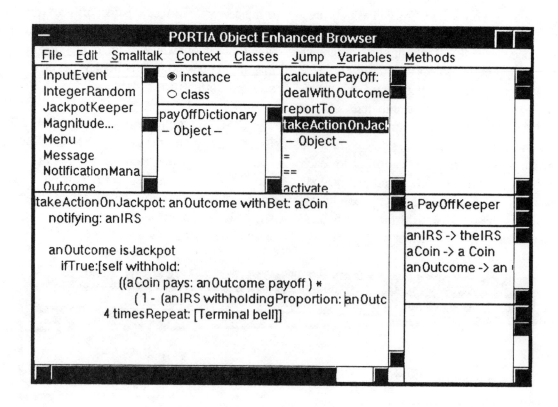

Figure 5. The Portia Class Hierarchy Browser

Like the Workspace, the Portia Browser includes new panes that indicate how <u>self</u> is set, what instances have been dropped and what instances are attached to argument names. Figure 5 shows the Enhanced Class Hierarchy Browser.

The Browser implements a number of features that help programmers navigate through the hierarchy; only one of them will be mentioned here. A feature invoked by choosing the menu item <u>Jump to Expression</u> is similar to the <u>New Browser</u> feature found in the Workspace. Highlighting an expression in the Browser's text area and then selecting this option causes the Browser to select the class specified by the receiver in the expression and call up the method that corresponds to the message sent to that receiver.

<u>The Repository</u> - The Repository's primary purpose is to gather and hold objects (cf. Khoshafian & Valduriez, 1987, Parsaye, et al., 1989). As shown in

Figure 6, the repository consists of a left subpane containing a list of classes and a right subpane containing a list of held objects. Any object listed on the right side can be grabbed and moved to any other tool.

Objects can be brought into the Repository in several ways. First, any grabbed object can be dropped into the tool. Second, every object in the Portia environment responds to the message <u>hold</u> by placing itself in the Repository. Also, the result of any expression evaluated in a Workspace can be held in the Repository by highlighting the expression and choosing <u>Hold It</u> from the Workspace menu. Using the left-hand pane, class objects can choose, at random, an instance of that class for placement in the Repository. Finally, again using the left-hand pane, classes can be instructed to use reflective techniques (Foote & Johnson, 1989, Osterbye, 1988) to place new instances in the Repository as they are created.

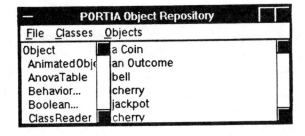

—	PORTIA Object Repository	▯▯
File Classes Objects		

Object | a Coin
AnimatedObj⌐ | an Outcome
AnovaTable | bell
Behavior... | cherry
Boolean... | jackpot
ClassReader | cherry

Figure 6. The Repository

Class objects can monitor the creation of new instances in three ways. First, classes can be asked, by choosing Hold Next from the menu, to put the next instance created by that class into the Repository. Second, classes can hold every object as they are created by that class, by issuing Hold All. Finally classes can be instructed to maintain a pointer to the most recently created object of that class. This is done by selecting Keep Most Recent; choosing Hold Most Recent deposits that object in the Repository.

The Locator - The Locator is a specialized tool for finding particular instances. This tool starts with a user-specified object, called the *starting object*, and considers the objects pointed to by that object, the objects pointed to by each of those objects and so forth. The resulting network of objects is often rather large so the Locator filters this network according to programmers' instructions. The final result is a list of objects, any of which can be grabbed and moved to other tools.

Figure 7 shows the Locator. The middle left-hand pane holds a list of objects that can be used as the starting object; choosing one of these selects that object as the starting object. Objects are included in the list of starting objects by choosing a menu item that drops the most recently grabbed object into the

Locator. The rightmost pane holds a list of located objects and the remaining lists and buttons present ways to filter the generated network of objects.

The generated network of objects can be filtered in three ways. First, the lower left-hand window contains a list of classes; choosing one of these classes filters the network for instances of the selected class. Second, the Locator can filter the network for instances of a class that has been added since the system's delivery. This filter is invoked by pressing the New Classes button. Finally, pressing the Marked button filters the network for objects that have been marked.

4 Using the Portia Environment

This section returns to the examples introduced in section 2 and details how they could be done using the Portia environment.

Understanding the CoinBox - Experimenting with an object in a Workspace is one way to understand how that object behaves. Building a new CoinBox in the Workspace would be difficult because many instance variables need setting. Another approach, encouraged by the Portia environment, would be to start up a slot machine and use its CoinBox. The Locator provides a convenient way to grab that particular object. Figure 7 shows a Locator with a SlotMachine selected as the starting object. The SlotMachine could have been grabbed from the SlotMachine's interface (Figure 1) and dropped in the Locator. By choosing the New Classes button, the tool generates the list of objects shown in the figure. Finding the CoinBox in this list is easy, but if the list were so long that searching it was cumbersome, then the selection of CoinBox from the list of classes would have reduced the list to one entry.

The CoinBox can then be grabbed from the Locator, dropped in a Workspace, and named. Here evaluating expressions like exampleCoinBox hasTooManyCoins gives information about whether a method works, what kind of object a method returns, and how the behavior of an object changes when the state of the object changes.

Initially, the CoinBox is empty so the instance variable coins points to an empty Collection. To further test the CoinBox, the programmer may wish to use a coin box with some coins in it. There are many ways to do this, but the easiest way also demonstrates an important consequence of an instance-centered environment. Because the CoinBox belongs to a running application, using that application's interface can modify the object under

Coin; consequently, highlighting aCoin in the Workspace and choosing Hold It puts that Coin in the Repository where it will be easily available when needed.

Modifying a Wheel - The idea here is to change one of the Wheels, so that it contains all jackpots; this increases the chances of winning a jackpot on a spin of the machine. This modification involves creating a new Collection containing only SlotIcons set with jackpot symbols, finding a Wheel, opening an

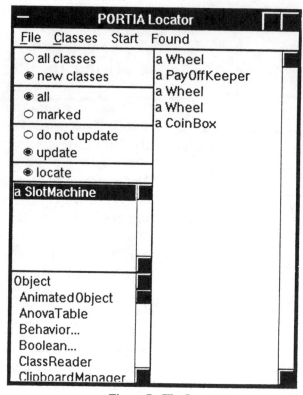

Figure 7. The Locator

consideration. Thus, entering a bet using the slot machine interface modifies the CoinBox sitting in the Workspace. An instance-centered environment allows the programmer to interact with an application's objects using either the software tools or the application's interface.

A Coin could also be added to the CoinBox by creating one in the Workspace and evaluating the expression exampleCoinBox acceptCoin: aCoin. The third example described in this section also uses a

Inspector on that Wheel, moving the new Collection to the Inspector's text area, and setting the Wheel's instance variable icons to the new Collection.

A Wheel can be found using the same techniques used to find the CoinBox; Figure 7 shows that three Wheels were included in the list built from the SlotMachine. Any of those Wheels could be selected and then inspected by choosing the menu item, Inspect It. Using the Locator to mark the Wheel will prove helpful if the programmer later wishes to find the same Wheel and change it back to its original state. The SlotIcons can be found in several ways; one way is to select this class in the left hand pane of the Repository, choose Hold All and start up a new slot machine. With this instruction, SlotIcons are put in the Repository as they are created (see Figure 6).

SlotIcons' printStrings indicate whether they are set with a jackpot symbol or some other symbol so choosing a jackpot from the list of SlotIcons is straightforward. The jackpot SlotIcon can be moved to a Workspace so that an OrderedCollection containing just jackpot SlotIcons can be created. This Collection can then be dropped into the open Inspector thus modifying the Wheel.

Modifying a PayoffKeeper- Recall the example in which the programmer modifies the code in PayoffKeeper for the method takeActionOnJackpot:withBet:notifying: (See Figure 2). Here, the Portia environment can be used to attach instances to the code and modify, test and debug the code in the context of a working application even when the use of a Debugger is not possible. For this example, the programmer needs to find the appropriate instances, bring them together, and attach them to the programming code.

To begin, the programmer opens a Class Hierarchy Browser to the code shown in Figure 2. Then, the programmer grabs the PayoffKeeper from the Locator (see Figure 7) and uses it to set self in the Browser. The programmer finds an Outcome by selecting the class Outcome from the Repository's list of classes, choosing the menu item Hold Next and spinning the slot machine. The Outcome can then be moved from the Repository to the Browser and dropped on the argument anOutcome. Remember that a Coin was already put into the Repository; that object can now be moved into the Browser and dropped on aCoin (see Figure 5).

Next, the programmer attaches an instance to the argument anIRS. If the code implementing IRS has been written a new IRS object can be instantiated in the Workspace, grabbed and dropped on the

Browser's text area. Once done, the objects and code can be experimented with and tested by evaluating snippets of the code in the Browser.

Sometimes, however, a programmer will write code which depends on objects that have not been implemented. In these cases, the use of Portia's intervention object will still permit the programmer to try out the code. Dropping an intervention object on anIRS and then evaluating the expression 1 - (anIRS withholdingProportion: anOutcome) will result in the opening of an intervention window like that shown in Figure 3. The title bar of the intervention window shows that the IRS was sent the message withholdingProportion: . The programmer responds by filling in for the IRS and setting up an expression, in the intervention window which evaluates to an object that the IRS could return when implemented. Here, typing 0.10 in the intervention window results in the evaluation of the expression to 0.9.

5 Conclusion

Portia offers programmers new ways to work with object-oriented programming languages. In Portia, code tends to be generated in the context of a concrete application. New code is often tested as it is written; sometimes a whole method is tested, sometimes the code is tested line by line, and sometimes a fragment of a line is tested. Although working with a specific set of instances suggests that the code would not be as general as for standard Smalltalk, just the opposite is true. The instance-centered nature of the browser motivates programmers to experiment with and understand their code. Because changing the attachments is easy, trying out the code in a variety of situations is straightforward.

Modifying the state of an object can change the behavior of a running application; this encourages programmers to tinker with their software without modifying or adding any code. Instead of changing the code at a point where an instance variable is set, a programmer might set that instance variable, using available tools, to point to an already existing instance. Consequently, the programmer does not need to find the appropriate spot in the code where an instance variable is set or write new code to set it. Moreover, the result of the modification is usually seen immediately and the application is less likely to be restarted.

A doctrine of object-oriented programming is that once an object's behavior is implemented, the programmer only needs to consider *what* an object does, not *how* it does it. Understanding the behavior of an object by browsing the code forces the reader to learn how the behavior is implemented in pursuit of an understanding of what the behavior does. In contrast, direct interaction with an instance provides much information about what it does while sparing the programmer the need to read the code.

In sum, the Portia environment helps Smalltalk programmers work with objects in the environment as they generate code, experiment with an application, and understand the behaviors of objects. Portia adds to the standard Smalltalk environment new ways to manipulate objects, new object behaviors, specialized software tools, and enhancements to existing tools, all of which are geared toward facilitating interaction with instances.

Acknowledgements

Thanks to Jerry Archibald, Julia Hough, John Richards and Dan Walkowski for many helpful comments. Smalltalk/V is a trademark of Digitalk and Smalltalk-80 is a trademark of ParcPlace Systems.

References

Beck, K., & Cunningham, W. (1989). A laboratory for teaching object-oriented thinking. In N. Meyrowitz (Ed.), *OOPSLA'89 Conference Proceedings* , (pp. 1-6). New York: ACM.

Booch, G. (1986). Object-oriented development. *IEEE Transactions on Software Engineering, SE-12*, 2, 211-221.

Doucet, A. & Pfeffer, P. (1989). A debugger for O2, an object-oriented language. *TOOLS '89. Technology of Object-Oriented Languages and Systems Proceedings*, 559-571.

Foote, B., & Johnson, R.E. (1989). Reflective facilities in Smalltalk-80. In N. Meyrowitz (Ed.), *OOPSLA'89 Conference Proceedings* , (pp. 327-335). New York: ACM.

Goldberg, A. (1984). *Smalltalk-80: the interactive programming environment*. Reading MA: Addison-Wesley.

Khoshafian, S., & Valduriez, P. (1987). Persistence, sharing and object-orientation: a database perspective. *Proceedings of the Workshop on Database Programming Languages*.

Osterbye, K., (1988). Active objects: an access oriented framework for object-oriented languages. *Journal of Object-Oriented Programming*, 1, No. 2, 6-11.

Parsaye, K., Chigrell, M., Khoshafian, S., & Wong, H. (1989). *Intelligent databases: object-oriented, deductive, hypermedia technologies*. New York: John Wiley and Sons, Inc.

Schneider, M., (1990) . FAST - a stepper in an object-oriented programming environment. *Visualization in Human Computer Interaction: Seventh Interdisciplinary Workshop on Informatics and Psychology, Selected Contributions*. Springer Verlag, 105-122.

Smith, R., (1987). Experiences with the Alternate Reality Kit: an example of the tension between literalism and magic. *IEEE CG & A*, 7, No. 9, 42-50.

Developing a GUIDE Using Object-Oriented Programming[†]

Joseph A. Konstan and Lawrence A. Rowe

Computer Science Division
University of California
Berkeley, CA 94720
konstan@cs.berkeley.edu and larry@cs.berkeley.edu

ABSTRACT

PICASSO is a graphical user interface development environment built using the Common Lisp Object System (CLOS). This paper describes how CLOS features including multiple inheritance, instance methods, multimethods, and method combinations were used to implement the system. In addition, the benefits and drawbacks of CLOS development are discussed including code quality, maintainability and performance.

1. INTRODUCTION

This paper describes the object-oriented programming techniques used to develop the PICASSO graphical user interface development environment (GUIDE). The PICASSO system is composed of approximately 40,000 lines of Common Lisp [11] using the Common Lisp Object System (CLOS) [7][11]. Several programming techniques from the PICASSO implementation that take advantage of features in CLOS are presented. In addition, the benefits and drawbacks of using CLOS and these techniques for developing a GUIDE are discussed.

PICASSO is composed of an interface toolkit, an application framework, and a set of development tools. The toolkit provides the resources to create graphical user interfaces for the X window system [10] using Common Lisp. In addition to providing CLOS objects for standard X resources (e.g., windows, fonts, colors, graphics contexts, etc.), the system defines CLOS objects for toolkit widgets. Different types of widgets (e.g., text, tables, pictures and drawings) are implemented as classes in CLOS. A large library of predefined widget types is provided including: radio buttons, pop-up and pull-down menus, check boxes, scrolling tables and text, and graphics [9]. In addition, new widgets can be defined by PICASSO users and they can then be used interchangeably with the predefined ones.

The PICASSO application framework [8] provides higher-level programming constructs for building applications. The framework provides abstractions for *forms* (the electronic counterpart of paper forms), *frames* (forms combined with pull-down menus to implement a major mode of an application), *dialog boxes* (modal interactors that are controlled with buttons) and *panels* (nonmodal dialog boxes used to implement alternative views of the data displayed through a frame). CLOS objects are defined for these abstractions. These framework objects are called PICASSO Objects (PO).

The application framework also defines a data model for programming interfaces. PO's are like procedures in a conventional programming language. They may define local variables and constants, they are lexically scoped, and they may be called and passed parameters. Five types of parameter passing are supported to implement different types of sharing including value, reference and value-result. Due to the asynchronous nature of user interfaces, PICASSO also supports value/update parameters (the callee is updated if the caller's variable changes) and value/update-result parameters.

[†]This research was supported by the National Science Foundation (Grants DCR-8507256 and MIP-8715557), 3M Corporation, and Siemens Corporation. Joseph Konstan was also supported by a National Defense Science and Engineering Graduate Fellowship granted through DARPA.

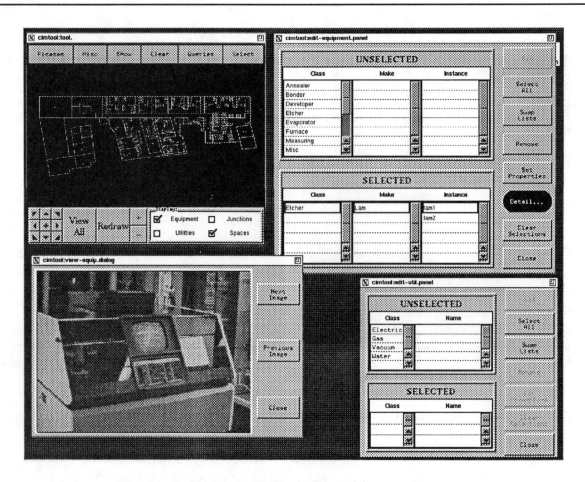

Figure 1: CIMTOOL: A Tool for Managing IC-CIM Facilities

A constraint system is provided that allows the programmer to specify arbitrary constraints between variables and object slots, and the propagation system keeps them up-to-date. For example, constraints are defined between variables in a PO and widgets that display their value to the user. This constraint system is similar to the constraint systems in ThingLab [2] and in Garnet [5]. Lazy evaluation of formula-constrained data is also provided to enhance performance. For example, a button that displays a certain rapidly-changing value when pressed can use lazy evaluation to avoid processing values that are not displayed.

PICASSO has been used to develop applications in semiconductor manufacturing and education. In addition to developing other applications, development continues on the system itself (e.g., a direct manipulation application builder) and on integrating hypermedia capabilities into applications (e.g., animation, audio, and full-motion video). A PICASSO application that displays and controls information about an integrated circuit manufacturing facility is shown in figure 1.

CLOS is an object-oriented programming system built on top of Common Lisp. It provides classes and methods found in most object systems along with a number of features not provided in simpler object systems. For example, CLOS supports: 1) multiple inheritance of both attribute slots and methods, 2) instance methods (i.e., methods specialized for a specific object), 3) multimethods (i.e., methods that discriminate on more than one argument), and 4) method combinations (i.e., factoring code into methods combined at runtime). This paper describes how these features were used to implement the PICASSO system.

The remainder of the paper is organized as follows. The next three sections discuss the use of multiple inheritance, instance methods, and method combinations.

Section 5 discusses the benefits derived from and difficulties encountered using CLOS. And, section 6 presents conclusions.

2. MULTIPLE INHERITANCE

This section describes several ways that multiple inheritance was used to simplify the PICASSO code. In CLOS, classes may inherit slot definitions, including slot attributes such as default values, and methods from any number of superclasses. If more than one parent defines a slot or method with the same name, an inheritance order, called a *class precedence list*, is used to determine the slot or method inherited. For a given class, the class precedence list is determined by the order in which the superclasses are specified in the class definition. This list is followed in a depth-first fashion, but search is cut off by a common superclass. For example, figure 2 shows a set of class definitions employing multiple inheritance and figure 3 shows the class inheritance graph for these definitions. An instance of class F has three slots. Slot-3 has a default value of 31, as is specified in the definition of class F. Slot-2 has a default value of 21, not 20, because D precedes C in class F's class definition. Slot-1 has a default value of 11, not 10, because F inherits from B before inheriting from the common superclass A.

Thus, in this example, the complete class precedence list for F is (F, D, C, B, A). In addition to using this order to search for methods and slot definitions, CLOS uses this list for call-next-method, the mechanism

```
(defclass A ()
    ((slot-1 :initform 10)))
(defclass B (A)
    ((slot-1 :initform 11)))
(defclass C (B)
    ((slot-2 :initform 20)))
(defclass D (A)
    ((slot-2 :initform 21)))
(defclass E (C D)
    ((slot-3 :initform 31)))
(defclass F (D C)
    ((slot-3 :initform 31)))
```

Figure 2: Class Definitions

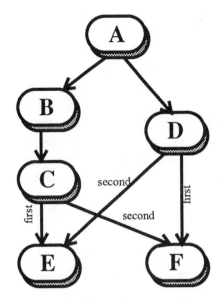

Figure 3: Class Inheritance Graph

for invoking the same generic function in a superclass.

Multiple inheritance is used to improve code sharing among classes and to localize code that might need to be modified. Multiple inheritance was used in PICASSO to implement factored behaviors and abstract classes.

We use the term *factored behaviors* to refer to separating the different roles that objects play into different superclasses. For example, output and input behaviors are separated into the classes **gadget** and **widget**, respectively. A text gadget can display text but cannot receive input. A blank button that can be pressed, but displays nothing is a widget. Interface objects, which we generically refer to as widgets, inherit from both classes. Most text fields can be edited and therefore mix the behaviors of the display-only text gadget class with the editing behaviors of the text widget class. And, most buttons mix display behavior (i.e., displaying a text label or picture in the button) with input behavior (i.e., detecting and responding to mouse button presses). Titles and other decorative trim in a form cannot be changed by the user so they can be implemented by a gadget.

The first implementation of PICASSO did not factor input and output behaviors into different classes. As a result, it was difficult to improve the performance of widgets that did not need all of the input behaviors associated with the class **widget**. Specifically, the perfor-

77

mance of text labels and of menus was unacceptably slow. Factoring the behaviors allowed us to separate out the more costly event-handling and input-oriented behaviors and to use lightweight text and picture gadgets for higher performance.

Later, we introduced synthetic gadgets for very-high performance areas where even a gadget was too inefficient. Synthetic gadgets are not CLOS objects. They are display lists with the correct methods defined on them. They are similar to glyphs in InterViews [3] and are used in PICASSO for elements in tables and menus. This iterative process of continual factoring for the sake of performance has happened several times in the development of PICASSO.

It is virtually impossible to implement cleanly factored behaviors without multiple inheritance. A single inheritance system forces the programmer to specify descendant behavior as a customization of a single parent. PICASSO widgets, however, tend to inherit from at least two superclasses, both of which define many slots and methods. Figure 4 shows the class hierarchy for some typical widgets. A **text-widget**, for example, inherits behaviors from the **text-gadget** class that displays text and from the **widget** class that incorporates all of the behaviors of X windows (e.g., event handling). In single-inheritance systems, one of these behaviors would have to be incorporated into text-widget in a different way.

Factoring behaviors produces classes that can stand alone (e.g., they can be instantiated) and combined together to mix their behaviors. However, sometimes classes are created that will never be instantiated. They define code used in other classes. We call these classes *abstract classes*. Two reasons for using abstract classes are to modularize code and create mixins.

Abstract classes helped modularize the code behind the PICASSO application framework. Figure 5 shows the class hierarchy for the PO classes. The classes **picasso-object**, **top-level-po**, and **callable-po** are never instantiated. Instead, **picasso-object** holds code common to all PO's (e.g., call and return semantics, lexical and variable-holding behaviors, and grouping behaviors inherited from **collection-widget**). **Top-level-po** adds the special behaviors needed by PO's that are displayed directly on the root-window as opposed to being contained inside other PO's (i.e., tools, panels, and dialog boxes). **Callable-po** adds the behaviors of PO's that are called like functions and coroutines (i.e., frames, panels, and dialog boxes). By using abstract classes and multiple inheritance, these behaviors are separated into distinct modules. Otherwise, code would either have to be duplicated (by placing the common behaviors in each **picasso-object** subclass) or moved into the superclass

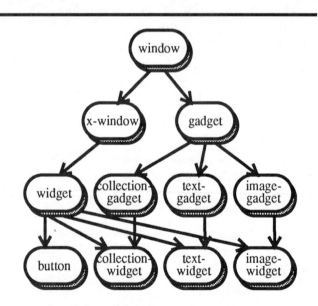

Figure 4: Widget/Gadget Class Hierarchy

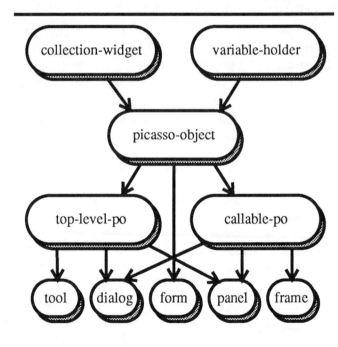

Figure 5: PICASSO Object Class Hierarchy

picasso-object and then selectively enabled when needed. Duplicating code causes maintenance problems and moving code into **picasso-object** hurts both performance and code maintainability by making superclass behaviors dependent on their subclasses.

Mixins are behaviors that can be added into any of a number of other classes. They are "mixed in" by creating a new class that inherits from both the original or base class and the mixin class. Mixins have two major benefits in developing a GUIDE such as PICASSO. First, they allow behaviors to be shared among classes that are otherwise distantly spread across the class hierarchy. Second, they allow easy prototyping in situations where behaviors may or may not belong in certain classes. As an example, the behavior of holding variables (and therefore being a lexical entity) in PICASSO is defined by the mixin class **variable-holder**. It was clear through most of the development of the framework that PO's should be variable holders, but it was not clear whether any other entities should also be variable holders. Specifically, collections which hold other widgets for grouping behaviors and tables could arguably benefit from holding variables. For development purposes, variable holding behaviors could easily be mixed into these classes to explore this option.

Designing mixin classes is trickier than designing ordinary classes because an effective mixin should not disturb the other operations of the class it is being mixed into. A mixin must not conflict with the slots and methods that may be defined in any class except where necessary for the operation of the mixin. In this case, **variable-holder** required a single slot to hold the variable table and a single accessor method for that table. The rest of the class hierarchy was not permitted to use that slot or method name.

Multiple inheritance greatly simplifies the development and maintenance of a large system such as PICASSO. There are some cases, however, where multiple inheritance is too cumbersome to use. The main disadvantage of mixins is the combinatorial explosion in the number of classes that must be defined if all of the behaviors defined in the mixin classes can be combined orthogonally. This large number of classes reduces the maintainability of the code by requiring developers to understand a great number of classes and to code all mixins orthogonally to prevent conflicts in common descendants. A large number of classes is also inefficient

since the creation of a class that may not be needed wastes both processing time and memory. Some object systems support dynamic classes which are instantiated at run-time as needed. Dynamic classes remove the run-time inefficiency of a large class space by allowing classes to be specified as a list of superclasses. The next section presents an alternative solution to this problem that uses instance methods.

3. Instance Methods

Instance methods discriminate on the value of an argument rather than the class of the argument. They define a behavior for a single instance of a class. Slot-value methods define a behavior for all instances of a class that have a specific value in a particular slot. CLOS provides an *eql* method structure that can be used to implement instance and slot-value methods.

Instance methods are used in PICASSO to implement the propagation system that constrains slot values to be equal to the result of specified functions of other slot values.[1] The Lisp form `setf` is used to set slot values with the expression:[2]

$$(\text{setf } (\textit{slot-name object}) \textit{ new-value})$$

This form invokes a method named (`setf` *slot-name*) that takes the new value and the object as arguments and discriminates on the class of the object. `Setf` methods can be written just as any other methods.

A simple implementation of propagation can use the `setf` method for all classes to check whether the change requires a propagation to occur when any slot value is set. This solution is inefficient, even with caching, since setting a slot value must be a fast operation and relatively few slots have propagations that depend on them. By using instance methods, the propagation behavior is added only to the specific slots of objects that need to propagate their changes. These are the slots and objects referred to as arguments in the function used to constrain another slot.

In this case, the preexisting setf method for an object slot is augmented by defining an **eql** *around* method.

---

[1] Propagation also constrains PICASSO variables, but since variables are implemented as CLOS objects the same mechanism can be used.

[2] Technically, `setf` is a macro that expands into functions and methods depending upon the target being set.

Around-methods, discussed in more detail in section 4, wrap themselves around primary methods. They are invoked first, and the primary method is called under their control. After the primary method returns, control returns to the around-method. In other words, the around-method specifies code to execute before and after the primary method. For propagation, the following method is dynamically defined for any object slot that must be propagated:

```
(defmethod (setf slot-name) :around
       (value (self (eql object)))
    (unless (equal (slot-value self 'slot-name) value)
       (call-next-method)
       (propagate
           (gethash unique-key *prop-table*))))
```

The argument list for this method indicates that it applies for any value, but only for the specific object designated. The body of the method checks first to assure that the slot value indeed changed to cut off loops. Then, the primary method is called to update the slot value. Notice that this approach insures that any error checking, side effects, or other processing will be done. Once the primary method returns, the around-method calls the propagate function to pass on the changes to whatever slots have registered interest in this slot value.

Custom setf methods are used for virtual slots and **PICASSO** variables. Virtual slots are implemented as methods to access and update a value without actually storing the value. The setf method does not check for a change since no old value can exist. **PICASSO** variables, for efficiency, always propagate since most variables have propagations. This example illustrates another benefit of instance methods: different variants of the method can be defined to optimize cases that do not deserve their own classes.

Slot-value methods are also used to overcome the problems of combinatorial class explosion introduced by multiple inheritance. The different slot values define a set of *virtual classes* each of which has the same slots and class-discriminating methods but different slot-value methods. The following two examples show how virtual classes reduce the number of classes in the system and make changing classes faster and easier.

Geometry management is the process of sizing and laying out windows within a parent window. This process is implemented in **PICASSO** by a geometry manager that is bound to a collection. A geometry manager includes a data structure that holds layout hints and a collection of routines that pack children within a collection when called. A geometry manager also has routines that respond to asynchronous changes to the children in the collection (e.g., adding or removing a child), requests from children for different sizes, and notifications that the collection itself is being resized. Approximately ten geometry managers are provided in **PICASSO** (see figure 6) and new ones can be added by defining the appropriate functions.

The obvious implementation defines an abstract class for each geometry manager and mixes that class into the base collection classes to yield a different class for **packed-collection-gadget, rubber-sheet-collection-gadget**, etc. This approach leads to 30 or 40 new classes and even more classes if subclasses of collections (e.g., **form, table**, etc.) may be defined with each of these geometry managers. It also makes it more difficult for a user-defined geometry manager to be fully incorporated into the system because the user must add many new classes.

CLOS provides two solutions to this problem. One solution is to create these classes dynamically as they are needed. Classes can be dynamically created rather easily with a metaclass protocol feature that allows a class to be inserted into another class' superclass list. While this solution is a perfectly reasonable implementation, a different solution was used in **PICASSO** because the metaclass solution results in less obvious code and greater difficulties when changing a collection's geometry manager.

The **PICASSO** solution uses slot-value methods to

Name	Function
anchor-gm	controlled stretch and relative positioning
just-pack-gm	full-width menu bars
left-pack-gm	compressed (pushed left) menu bars
linear-gm	linear stretch (useful for bordered objects)
matrix-gm	tabular layout
menu-gm	layout of menu entries
null-gm	default, places objects where they request
packed-gm	perpendicular packing (useful for forms)
root-gm	special manager for root window
rubber-gm	rubber sheet (controlled stretching)
stacked-gm	vertical and horizontal stacks for palettes

Figure 6: Geometry Managers Defined for **PICASSO**

call the appropriate geometry manager. Since each collection has exactly one geometry manager, we include a slot in the collection that holds the name of the geometry manager (i.e., a Lisp symbol). The methods that implement a specific geometry manager discriminate on the value stored in this slot, rather than on the class of the object passed to them. For example, the method that handles repacking a collection is defined as

```
(defmethod  gm-repack ((gm (eql 'my-gm)) self)
          code)
```

This method is called when the first argument is the symbol my-gm. To make it easier to program this way, we add a simple macro to handle passing in the slot-value:

```
(defmacro repack (self)
      '(gm-repack (gm ,self) ,self))
```

Thus, we can call repack as if it were an ordinary method, passing only the collection as an argument, and it will call the correct repack method.

The other difficulty is to allocate storage for the geometry manager to use, since virtual classes are not real classes so they cannot add slots. For geometry managers, the solution is straightforward. All geometry managers are defined to use certain slots that are present in all collections: 1) a children slot that holds a list of child windows for which the geometry manager is responsible (in an order it manages) and 2) a gm-data slot that holds other data including layout hints and cached results. The geometry manager routines are given complete control of this gm-data structure, and they can use it for any purpose.

A second use of slot-value methods in PICASSO is for widget borders and labels. A border describes the graphics that surround a widget to enhance its visual appearance. Many borders are provided including drop-shadows, picture frames, and boxes. A label contains text or an image that identifies the widget. They can be positioned in various locations including to the left, above, or below the widget or in a smaller font in the frame. Figure 7 shows some of the borders and labels provided with PICASSO. Users can define additional borders and labels by naming them and defining appropriate methods.

Labels and borders are implemented using the same technique we used for geometry managers. Since the data structures used by borders and labels are better defined, they are given more detailed slot assignments in-

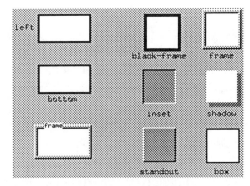

Figure 7: PICASSO Borders and Labels

cluding label-x, label-y, label-position, label-value, border-type, and border-width. When no border or label is desired, there is a small space penalty for these extra slots but no method is executed so the time penalty is insignificant.

There are several benefits to using slot-value methods as an implementation of virtual classes. First, they are easy to implement and extend. For example, a new geometry manager, label, or border can be added by selecting a name and defining a couple of methods. The performance penalty when used is small (i.e., the cost of accessing the slot-value before method discrimination) and the performance penalty when not used is small (i.e., the unused extra space). And, it is easy to change the virtual class of an object by changing the value in the appropriate slot.

With these benefits come some limitations as well. The two biggest limitations are the inability to define slots in virtual classes and the very limited inheritance available. Since virtual classes are not classes, they can only use the slots defined in the classes into which they are mixed. This limitation requires that all classes for a given virtual class must use the same slots, which typically limits this technique to small features implementing different versions of the same attribute. Additionally, the inheritance available for virtual classes is minimal. Since they are based on symbol equality, there is a very strict two-level virtual class tree. At the root is the class t that applies to everything and at the leaves are all of the virtual classes.[3] As a result, virtual classes implemented this way do not work well when there are large amounts of code to be shared among some, but not all, of the variants.

4. Multimethods and Method Combinations

As we have seen, CLOS allows very powerful method constructs that can discriminate on both class membership and equality. This section describes how **PICASSO** used CLOS multimethods and method combinations.

PICASSO has tended to avoid using multimethods due to performance considerations which are discussed in the following section.[4] Multimethods have been used, however, to prototype behaviors that were later implemented in other ways or in some cases abandoned. Two examples are the development of type-sensitive widgets and methods that handle different types of windows.

A feature tested in an early version of **PICASSO** was a type-sensitive widget. This type of widget would display only certain types of values (e.g., integers, strings, or arrays). The widget would change itself into a different widget if it was set to a value that it was unable to display. In this way, a single widget could be created to display a numerical value. If, for some reason, a picture was assigned to that widget, it would automatically change itself into a picture-widget.

Implementing this type of automatic class changing was simplified by writing `setf` methods that discriminated on the type of the value as well as the type of the widget. There would be a method to set meter-widgets to integers and floating point numbers but not to strings. The default method for widgets would then change the class of the widget into one that could display the new value. The performance of multimethods was not a problem in this situation because this operation was executed infrequently and changing classes was already slow. However, we abandoned this idea for a more flexible synthetic gadget.[5]

PICASSO still uses multimethods for a few cases where operations depend on two different widgets or gadgets. In some cases, there is a simple X server call that can perform operations on two X windows (e.g., calculating relative coordinates or positions in the window hierarchy) but does not operate on non-X windows (e.g., gadgets and synthetic gadgets). In these cases, a method is defined that discriminates on the class of both objects. If they are both X windows, the server call is performed. Otherwise, toolkit code is executed to perform the operation.

Multimethods could be replaced in all cases with code that resembles a case structure. Inclusion of multimethods allows programmers to take advantage of the built-in CLOS method dispatching, with its caching and other performance tuning, rather than writing ad hoc, and likely less performance tuned, custom dispatchers.

In CLOS each generic function has primary methods as well as before-, after-, and around-methods. These additional methods layer their execution on top of the primary method. Suppose that we have two classes **super** and **sub** and that a method `foo` has a primary, before-, after-, and around-method on each class. Figure 8 shows the method definitions for class **sub**. The definitions are the same for class **super** except that the formatted print statements read "SUPER" and the primary method does not execute the `call-next-method` call.

When the method `foo` is called on an instance of **sub** the output shown in figure 9 is produced by the `format` calls. In each case where `(call-next-method)` ap-

---

[3] Another possible implementation would create a class for each geometry manager, label or border and place an instance of that class in a slot in the collection or widget. This implementation solves the slot and inheritance problems but is no longer a lightweight implementation. Indeed, it merely adds a list of components to an object, each of which has its own methods, with methods on the holder that invoke methods on the proper component. We initially chose not to employ this implementation but are now experimenting with implementing geometry managers in this fashion. Should this experiment prove successful, we hope to determine criteria for deciding when to use this technique and when to use virtual classes.

[4] In an earlier system we tried to use multimethods to implement event dispatching. A generic dispatch function was defined that took an event and window object and discriminated on both. Besides learning that multimethods were not implemented correctly in the early CLOS implementation we were using, we also quickly realized that method determination for multimethods was too slow for event dispatching. More recent experiments discussed in section 5 show that multimethod dispatching in a native CLOS implementation is only slightly slower than ordinary dispatching. We expect to make greater use of multimethods in the future.

[5] A synthetic gadget contains only data and a list of display parameters. The method `put` is defined on each data type to paint the data onto the screen. Where a text gadget is an object with many slots representing all of the possible functionality for text and windows, a text synthetic gadget contains only a string, a location for painting, a font, and some colors.

```
(defmethod foo ((self sub))
    (format t "Entering SUB Primary Method")
    (call-next-method)
    (format t "Exiting SUB Primary Method"))
(defmethod foo :before ((self sub))
    (format t "SUB Before Method"))
(defmethod foo :after ((self sub))
    (format t "SUB After Method"))
(defmethod foo :around ((self sub))
    (format t "Entering SUB Around Method")
    (call-next-method)
    (format t "Exiting SUB Around Method"))
```

Figure 8: Method Definitions for Class **sub**

pears, not executing that expression would result in skipping forward to the corresponding "Exiting" clause without executing any additional methods in between. For example, if the `foo` around method for **sub** did not execute `call-next-method`, none of the other methods would be called.

Before-methods execute before any primary methods. Before a primary method is executed, *all* before-methods that apply are executed *from most to least specific*. Even if a superclass' primary method is not executed, its before-methods are always executed. Therefore, before-methods should only be used when any possible subclass will also need the same behavior.

In **PICASSO**, before-methods have a natural place in implementing lazy evaluation slots. These slots are typ-

Entering SUB Around Method

Entering SUPER Around Method

SUB Before Method

SUPER Before Method

Entering SUB Primary Method

Entering SUPER Primary Method

Exiting SUPER Primary Method

Exiting SUB Primary Method

SUPER After Method

AUB After Method

Exiting SUPER Around Method

Exiting SUB Around Method

Figure 9: Call Sequence for Method Combinations

ically defined for a class, although they can also be defined for an instance. Lazy evaluation slots check a cache stored in the slot for validity when the slot is accessed. If the cached value is valid, it is returned. If not, the cached value is recomputed. The cache is automatically invalidated when appropriate. It is assumed that there may be primary methods on the slot to properly convert data or perform side effects. This lazy slot behavior is implemented with the following before-method:

```
(defmethod slot-name :before ((self class-name))
    (when   (invalid-p (slot-value self 'slot-name))
            (setf (slot-value self 'slot-name)
                  recomputation-formula)))
```

The body of the method uses the CLOS accessor `slot-value` to avoid recursively calling this method or a `setf` method. This technique is common in before-methods that wish to prepare the data without getting trapped in infinite recursion. This implementation of lazy slots prevents the slot accessors themselves from having to know that the slot is lazy. Instead they can assume that whenever they are called, the correct value is there.

After-methods execute after all primary methods. If one or more primary methods have executed, *all* after-methods are executed *from the least to most specific*. This order is the opposite of the order in which before-methods are executed. Again, all after-methods are executed if any primary method is executed, so they should only be used when any subclass will need the same behavior.

After-methods are used in **PICASSO** to implement side effects that require a fully initialized object. As an example, the `new-instance` method, which is called to initialize a new instance of a class, has an after-method for collections that creates the children objects in the collection. It is more efficient to wait until the collection is properly initialized before creating the children objects, so an after-method is ideal. After-methods are also defined on `new-instance` to perform other side effects such as informing the geometry manager that a new widget has been added to a collection. These side effects are best handled after the object has been properly initialized.

Around-methods wrap behaviors around the rest of the methods. In structure, they are much more like primary methods than before- or after-methods. When a method is invoked, the most specific around-method is called even if there is a more specific primary, before-, or after-method. If an around-method calls `call-next-method` the next most specific around-method is called. If and when the most general around-method calls `call-next-method`, all of the before-methods execute, followed by the most specific primary method and any more general primary methods called by it, and then all of the after-methods are executed. At this point, control returns to the most general around-method and back up the around-methods as each returns.

Around-methods are used in **PICASSO** to prevent primary methods from executing. Section 3 discussed an example in which an instance around-method prevents the primary `setf` method from executing if no change has occurred. Around methods are also useful because, unlike before- and after-methods, they can return values. In some cases, such as the creation and invocation of PO's, around-methods are used to allow values to be correctly returned when they cannot be computed until after all after-methods have executed.

Method combinations have another use when combined with bushy abstract class hierarchies. Proper use of method combinations allows the maximum sharing of code. Using only primary methods, a subclass and superclass have three phases of execution (subclass before `call-next-method`, superclass, subclass after `call-next-method`). Adding before-, after-, and around-methods provide twelve different phases. The method `invoke` for PO's, which calls a PO, is defined in eleven pieces. It handles parameter passing, allocating lexical children, managing the display, and event handling. Figure 10 shows these eleven methods defined for `invoke`. Figure 11 shows the order in which these methods are called when a **PICASSO frame** is called. Recall that the class precedence list for **frame** is **frame, callable-PO, picasso-object**.

Using method combinations to create layered behaviors has benefits and drawbacks. The main benefit is that more code can be implemented once for the class **picasso-object** rather than several times. The biggest drawback is that the implementation is very complicated and requires a clear understanding of the intent of each phase of the method calls. The original implementation of PO's did not use these layered methods. As a result, much of the code that was shared by different PO classes (e.g., notification of parents, invoking contained

Class	Type	Description
picasso-object	before	handles in-use objects, allocates window system resources
picasso-object	primary	processes parameters, allocates local vars, resolves references to external objects
picasso-object	after	notify parent of self, execute setup- and init-code
top-level-po	before	places PO on root window
top-level-po	after	handles mouse warping and exposure
callable-po	primary	processes contained form variables
callable-po	after	invokes contained form
tool	around	handles package search list, calls start frame, starts event loop
dialog	around	positions dialog over caller, starts event loop
form	after	exposes window
frame	around	handles nested calls, starts event loop

Figure 10: Invoke Methods for **PICASSO** Objects

forms, and resource allocation) could not be placed in the superclass methods due to execution order constraints. Consequently, the code was copied into the methods for each PO class which made maintenance difficult. This poor design was so difficult to develop further that we redesigned the PO class hierarchy. By virtue of our prior experience, we were able to see the actions that depended on other actions and developed a

Class	Type	Description
frame	around	check for and conceal existing frame, set invoked frame's parent to tool
picasso-object	before	check to see if frame is in use. allocate X resources for frame
callable-po	primary	no action taken until returned to later
picasso-object	primary	process all variables and parameters, allocate lexical children
callable-po	primary	establish local aliases for form vars.
picasso-object	after	notify lexical parent of call execute setup- and init-code
callable-po	after	invoke form with appropriate args
frame	around	put frame on call-stack and start event-loop.

Figure 11: Invocation of a Frame

cleaner layering of behavior.

Multimethods and method combinations make it possible to write very compact, modular code that takes full advantage of the object system's built-in method dispatcher. However, extensive use of these techniques can result in code which is complex and hard to maintain. Performance, of course, will depend on the implementation of the object system.

5. Discussion

This section discusses the impact CLOS had on the development of **PICASSO** and some performance issues encountered during development.

CLOS made developing **PICASSO** fast and easy. The entire constraint system, including propagation and triggers, was implemented in 350 lines of code. The lazy evaluation slots referred to above were implemented in 50 lines of code. The entire application framework (including all PO's, the lexical environment, and **PICASSO** variables) was implemented in under 2000 lines of code. We estimate that writing the framework and toolkit without CLOS, just in Common Lisp, would require twice as many lines of code. The CLOS features discussed in this paper (i.e., multiple inheritance, instance methods, and method combinations) have saved 5000 to 10,000 lines of code and their use resulted in a cleaner implementation.

For the most part, CLOS has also been a great benefit when adding new features and prototyping changes. Method combinations have made it easy to experiment with new ideas. Multiple inheritance allowed us to implement widgets such as radio-button groups in under 100 lines of code.

With all this saved code and the benefit of the class abstraction, you might infer that CLOS made **PICASSO**'s implementation easier to understand. In fact, the opposite was more often the case. CLOS complicated the system and made it harder for new researchers to make major changes.

Multiple inheritance required each superclass, and almost any class should expect to become a superclass, to be designed to share superclass responsibilities. For example, each method had to invoke `call-next-method` even if the superclass had no next method, since a subclass might inherit this method from two superclasses and `call-next-method` is the way for the second superclass' method to be invoked. Consequently, many methods had to be defined on the class at the top of the hierarchy (i.e., **window**) to serve as placeholders. These methods are required because subclass methods that `call-next-method` generate an error if no method is available.

This problem surfaces in even the simplest example of multiple inheritance. Figure 12 shows a simple multiple inheritance situation where **houseboat** inherits from **house** and from **boat**. A method `clean` is defined on **house** (i.e., clean floors and windows) and on **boat** (i.e., scrape barnacles). Since cleaning a houseboat involves both sets of tasks we want the `clean` method for **houseboat** to call both of the superclass `clean` methods. This cannot be accomplished in CLOS using standard method calls without changing the definitions of `clean` for one or both superclasses and without defining a `clean` method on some root class (e.g., **t**) to handle houses or boats that are not houseboats. This problem stems from the fact that CLOS uses call-next-method to invoke methods both up the tree from the present method and in sibling branches. Since house and boat have no superclasses, and were not designed to exist as co-superclasses, they cannot share any methods.

A possible solution to this would involve providing several standard ways to dispatch methods. Mixins typically work well using the present class-precedence list system. Factored behaviors, however, often would benefit from a system where `call-next-method` actually called *all* of the methods in the superclasses in order. There are certainly other models of method invocation that apply in other circumstances. We expect that CLOS developers will use the metaclass protocol to define some of these behaviors and make them available in in an easy-to-use form.

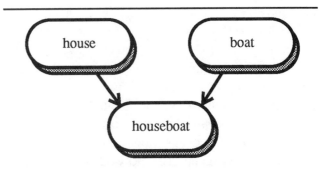

Figure 12: Houseboat Inheritance Hierarchy

Because the metaclass protocol was still under development and because or our own lack of expertise in this area, we chose to work around these difficulties by designing classes to share superclass responsibilities. We found that teaching developers to design clean methods for multiple inheritance took some effort, but good programmers were able to write such methods with a couple of week's practice.

The next problem was that the CLOS model of inheritance does not support or encourage encapsulation. As a result, all behaviors of all superclasses have to be well-understood before writing a new subclass. We discovered that conventional documentation did not address this problem. An interactive, dynamic form of documentation that indicates non-overridden inherited behaviors in the documentation of each child is needed. Moreover, a good development environment should provide an interactive object inspector and class hierarchy browser similar to the tools provided by Genera [12] or SmallTalk [4].

A final difficulty with multiple inheritance is that the class inheritance order matters. While this concept is not difficult to understand, many of our methods are order-dependent and we found that avoiding circular dependencies was often difficult. As a result, method combinations were used to isolate explicitly layered behaviors.

Instance methods presented almost no problems for our developers. While most programmers had not heard of them, they were easy to understand and use. Indeed, instance methods turned out to be the one feature of CLOS that simplified code and made it more compact.

Method combinations, even more than multiple inheritance, made the system harder to understand and modify. The layers of abstraction must be well-understood and conventional documentation was inadequate.

The final serious problem we had using CLOS is ironically problematic with research development. Since CLOS does little to support or encourage encapsulation of superclass features, each detail of the superclass implementation is quite visible to the subclasses. In an existing system, where superclasses towards the root are unlikely to change, this design works well. However, in developing PICASSO we found that major changes were being made to these base classes rather frequently. Most changes to a base class required rewriting code in subclasses that inherited from the class

Image	(Old)	(Devl)	(Run)
Lisp Alone	5MB	n/a	6MB
Lisp + CLOS+CLX	8MB	11MB	7MB
PICASSO	13MB	14MB	10MB
CIMTOOL	15MB	16MB	12MB

Figure 13: Lisp Image Sizes

being changed particularly when the changes involved adding or removing slots and methods. This effect is partly a product of poor object-oriented design, partly unavoidable given the nature of the changes, but partly attributable to CLOS.

The performance of Common Lisp and CLOS continues to be a big concern because the success of a graphical user interface can be determined by the perceived responsiveness of the system. We started our development using a portable implementation of CLOS developed at Xerox (PCL).[1] We have since found that some of our performance considerations have been addressed by native CLOS implementations. Nevertheless, the success of PICASSO is to some extent determined by the performance of Common Lisp and CLOS.

The two major performance concerns are space and time. There is no question that Common Lisp and CLOS cost us a great deal of space. Figure 13 shows the image size for PICASSO in three different Lisp environments. The old environment uses Allegro Common Lisp with PCL and CLX added in separately. The new development environment includes a recent version of Allegro Common Lisp (version 4.0.1) with CLOS and CLX built in. It also includes debugging and profiling tools. The new run-time environment is this development environment without the debugging and profiling tools. All of these measurements were taken on a Sun SPARC-Station 1.[6] The run-time memory demands of PICASSO rarely exceed 16 megabytes which indicates that the

[6] The disk space used is highly dependent on the specific machine architecture and the quality of the compiler. For example, Sun 3 and Sequent Symmetry images of PICASSO are about 25% smaller and DECStation 3100 images are about 25% larger.

system does not grow much when executing.[7]

We recognized that a Lisp system would be larger than a similar system written in C when the project started. For example Windows/4GL [6], a commercial system written in C that uses the X Toolkit and OSF/Motif look and feel, duplicates some of the functionality of **PICASSO** in under 4 megabytes. We estimate that a complete implementation of **PICASSO** in C would result in an image size of 6 to 8 megabytes.

While space is a concern, we see it as a shrinking one. We are experimenting with systems such as Allegro Presto which reduces the application image size by loading infrequently used code on demand at run-time and reduces memory demands for multiple applications by making Lisp code segments reentrant. Eventually, we expect that Lisp vendors will need to provide support for shared libraries to make it practical to run several different Lisp applications on a single workstation.

Runtime performance is largely determined by the time it takes to do a method call. Ironically, the method call time is not a performance bottleneck because method combination lists are cached and a high percentage of methods called are in the cache. The cache reduces the time to call a method to approximately 2.5 times the time required to call a function. Early versions of PCL performed poorly on multimethods, but the latest CLOS implementations are only about 15% slower for multimethod dispatch. Instance methods are about 5% slower than conventional class-based methods.

The biggest performance problem we experienced was with keyword parameters to functions and methods. The Common Lisp keyword mechanism requires that keywords be reparsed for each function called. In particular, every call-next-method reparses the keyword parameters. This performance penalty is substantial because we use many keyword parameters so that applications can selectively override default values (e.g. creating a text widget calls approximately 70 methods with an average of 30 allowable keyword parameters).

We have removed keyword parameters from many run-time critical methods and functions to improve performance, but we still pay a significant overhead on ob-ject creation. A solution to this problem would be an automatic system to normalize methods and method calls. This normalization would define a unique ordering of keyword parameters for any function or generic function. Then, the compilation of a method or method call would automatically rearrange the actual keyword arguments to match this unique ordering. Interpreted methods and method calls would still require keyword parsing but compiled methods and method calls would not. We have not developed such a normalizer but expect that a Lisp implementer will have to do so to stay performance-competitive.

A final performance consideration is the compilation of methods generated at run-time. Triggers, propagation, and some instances of lazy evaluation require that new methods be defined at run-time. Portable implementations of CLOS made it very difficult to compile these methods on the fly. Native implementations provide easier access to the compiler but compilation is still a slow operation. We are working on a background task queue which can compile methods and functions during idle time.

In summary, most of the programming techniques discussed in this paper do not significantly degrade performance. Multiple inheritance could cause problems with method resolution time, but caching of method combination lists minimizes the overhead. Instance methods are a tiny bit slower than class methods but this time is still better than custom dispatching. Method combinations have lowered system performance due to keyword processing costs and the basic overhead of method calls. In addition, the lack of code duplication has caused the size of the **PICASSO** image to shrink as refinements were made to layer behaviors which presumably improved performance.

6. Conclusions

Using CLOS to develop the **PICASSO GUIDE** resulted in faster development, easier prototyping, and more modular and compact code. Taking advantage of CLOS features created complex interactions among classes and methods that makes it hard for a new developer to learn the **PICASSO** implementation and makes certain modifications difficult. The details discussed here are hidden from users who develop and use **PIC-ASSO** applications. And, once a developer has learned the implementation, he or she reaps the benefits of

---

[7] While **PICASSO** does consume memory while running, there is a fair amount of free memory "locked into" the above images because of memory layout strategies that leave gaps when foreign functions and libraries are loaded.

CLOS and is able to accomplish a great deal in a short time.

This paper presents some programming techniques using CLOS that are applicable to other areas. First, instance methods are effective ways of specifying instance-specific behaviors and implementing slot-value methods for lightweight virtual classes. Second, method combinations are an effective way to reduce code duplication by layering behaviors in a cluster of classes. And, mixin classes, when properly designed, can make experimenting with new behaviors easy, and they can make code much easier to read.

Lastly, several areas that need more work were identified. First and foremost is the development of a sophisticated environment for CLOS development. Object systems in general create documentation problems. For a programmer, a tool is needed to browse the class hierarchy and a full code walker is needed to recognize which inherited behaviors are included and which are preempted at a specific place in the code. Work also needs to be done on the performance of Common Lisp and CLOS for CLOS to be competitive with object systems based on C. In addition to speeding up method call time, vendors must develop Lisp systems which can deliver applications that can run in smaller memories. This problem may be a case where individual vendors must part with portability while adhering to the standard to achieve optimal performance.

Acknowledgments

Many people have worked on the design and implementation of PICASSO. David Martin developed the XCL package and the original CLOS abstractions for the X Window System. Donald Chinn, Ken Whaley, and Scott Hauck worked on the early infrastructure and the first version of the toolkit. Scott Luebking extended the toolkit and implemented the first version of the framework. Brian Smith developed much of the present PICASSO toolkit design and implementation, and he developed the CIM facility browser shown in figure 1. Steve Seitz implemented many of the performance enhancements for the toolkit as well as the label and border abstractions, and he prototyped a graphical interface builder. Chung Liu developed many PICASSO widgets and early applications. We also want to thank our early users for their patience and feedback, especially Beverly Becker, who developed a hypermedia system and added hypermedia features to the toolkit.

References

[1] D. Bobrow and G. Kiczales, "Common Lisp Object System Specification", Draft X3 Document 87-001, American National Standards Institute, February 1987.

[2] A. Borning, "The Programming Language Aspects of ThingLab, a Constraint Oriented Simulation Laboratory", *ACM Transactions on Programming Lanaguages and Systems 3*, **4** (Oct.1981), 353-387.

[3] P. R. Calder and M. A. Linton, "Glyphs: Flyweight Objects for User Interfaces", *Proceedings of the ACM SIGGRAPH Symposium on User Interface Software and Technology*, October 1990.

[4] A. Goldberg, *Smalltalk-80: The Interactive Programming Environment*, Addison Wesley, Reading, MA, May 1983.

[5] D. Giuse, "KR: Constraint-Based Knowledge Representation" in *The Garnet Toolkit Reference Manuals: Support for Highly-Interactive, Graphical User Interfaces in Lisp* (B. Myers et. al., ed.). CMU Technical Report CS-90-117, March 1990.

[6] Ingres Corp., *Application Editor Users Guide for Ingres/Windows 4GL*, Ingres Release 6, August 1990.

[7] S. Keene, *Object-Oriented Programming in Common Lisp*, Addison-Wesley, 1988.

[8] L. A. Rowe et. al., "The PICASSO Application Framework", *Electronics Research Lab. Technical Report M90/18*, March 1990.

[9] P. Schank et. al., "PICASSO Reference Manual", *Electronics Research Lab. Technical Report M90/79*, September 1990.

[10] R. W. Scheifler and J. Gettys, "The X Window System", *ACM Transactions on Graphics 5*, **2** (April 1986).

[11] G. L. Steele, *Common Lisp The Language, Second Edition*, Digital Press, 1990.

[12] J. Walker, D. Moon, D. Weinreb and M. McMahon, "The Symbolics Genera Programming Environment", *IEEE Software*, Nov. 1987.

Building Generic User Interface Tools: an Experience with Multiple Inheritance

Nuno Guimarães

AT&T Bell Laboratories, NJ

IST/INESC, Lisbon, Portugal

R.Alves Redol, 9, 6o., 1000 Lisboa

e-mail: nmg@inesc.pt

Abstract

This paper describes the use of a particular object oriented technique, multiple inheritance, and its impact in the construction of generic user interface tools (in C++). Generic user interface tools are defined as user interface components with a high degree of independence from the particular implementation environment. The paper argues that the use of multiple inheritance in the design and implementation of these tools provides additional flexibility. The paper goes further in discussing why the use of single inheritance in this particular context was rejected and what were the major negative implications of that approach.

1 Introduction

The sophistication of the user interfaces in the applications used in current computing environments also means a greater complexity in their design, production and maintenance. Multiple degrees of freedom concerning "look and feel", interaction devices and operating environments require that higher levels of abstraction be provided to the application programmer avoiding, as much as possible, the need for direct interaction with the underlying representation systems. Also, a particular application domain should be supported with a specific set of programming tools, closely related to the abstractions of the domain.

Object oriented programming provides the mechanisms to introduce this abstraction and specialization level. Moreover, user interfaces and object orientation seem to get along very well. One reason is the nature of user interface components, which are easy to classify in terms of behavior, a fundamental step to make object oriented programming useful. On the other hand, user interface components have strong requirements for reusability and extensibility, which makes them a privileged field for the application of the object oriented techniques.

This paper presents some principles and techniques used in the construction of *generic* user interface toolkits, where *generic* means independent from the external environment. These techniques are presented as a case study of multiple inheritance. Multiple inheritance in general, and the facilities provided by C++ in particular, [Stroustrup 85,Ellis 90,Meyer 88] simplify both the production of the code and its later adaptation or tailoring to particular environments. The principle is the combination of classes that define abstract protocols for user interface objects and provide encapsulated implementations for those protocols. This is an instance of the more general problem of separating interface and implementation.

The next section outlines the scope of this work and clarifies what is understood by a *generic* user interface toolkit, its usefulness, and necessity. The following section describes how multiple inheritance was used in the context of this problem. Finally, and addressing the multiple versus single inheritance issue, the use of single inheritance to obtain the same effects is discussed.

OOPSLA'91, pp. 89–96

2 What is a Generic User Interface Toolkit ?

We consider a model for interactive applications where there is a fundamental separation between the user interface, or interactive component, and the computational component. In the user interface component, a fundamental distinction is again considered between *Data* and *View* objects. *Data* objects are manipulated by the computational component and presented to the user through the *Views*. Similarly, *Views* affect *Data* objects as a response to external stimuli.

Applications have a specific domain of concepts. In an object oriented programming language or environment, these concepts are mapped onto abstract data types, or *Data* objects. For representation and interaction purposes, a corresponding set of *Views* is defined. The domains of most applications, however complex they may be, are usually restricted to a limited set of object types. Considering the set of objects necessary to build a *shell*, we have for example *Directory*, *File*, *Mailbox*, and *Clock Data* objects, and *DirectoryView*, *FileView*, *MailboxView* and *ClockView View* objects. Other examples are CAD applications or hypertext [Conklin 87] [1].

User interface toolkits like Xt [McCormack 88], Andrew [Spector 88], or InterViews [Linton 87], are a significant advance in user interface technology, but only provide basic building blocks for the generality of the interfaces, like *buttons*, *scrollbars* or *text windows*. It is up to the application programmer to map the domain concepts onto this set of graphical objects. The result is that, at least conceptually, a new specialized toolkit is designed whenever a new application is produced. To use the database modeling terminology [Borkin 80], current toolkits provide *syntactic* level tools, that are used to build the *semantic* level components of real applications that match the user's conceptual models. *Semantic* level components are closely related with the abstractions of the application domain and, on the other hand, independent from the specific details of the implementation environment. These two characteristics explain why these components are mentioned in this paper as both "domain-specific" and "generic".

The higher level of abstraction provided by a domain-specific user interface toolkit also allows the application to be insulated from the external systems and therefore acquire a higher degree of generality, or *environment independence*. This is particularly important given the variety of input/output devices and tools, and their evolution.

Considering our *shell* example, the *DirectoryView* could be implemented with a traditional graphical object like a "list with selectable items" [2], or with a video image coupled with a voice-recognition based selection mechanism [3]. *Views* are therefore as abstract and domain-specific as the *Data* objects they represent. *Views* provide an additional indirection level between the programmer's object domain and the available user interface tools used for their implementation.

One important idea to retain throughout this paper is that there are several agents participating in the programming process. They are the application programmer, the UI tools programmer and the domain-specific toolkit programmer. Each agent has to accept and use the specifications and implementation tools as they are defined by their designers and builders. In the "real world" , there is no way to access the source code of basic components in order to adapt them to our specific needs.

The objective of the object oriented techniques described next is to maximize the separation between interface and implementation and minimize the changes required to adapt the toolkits to new environments i.e., change the implementation.

The fact that the examples are centered around the *View* concept does not imply that this is the only possible application of these principles. A similar approach could be taken, for example, when considering the addition of "persistence" to the *Data* objects. Just as representation and interaction, persistence is provided by an external stor-

---

[1]This approach was used in the construction of a hypermedia toolkit (*HOT*) described in [Guimaraes 90] and [Puttress 90].

[2]For those akin to user interface programming, an Xt Athena ListWidget, or an InterViews StringBrowser.

[3]This is not a imaginary example, but has actually been implemented for the environment described in [Berkley 90].

age system (a simple file system, a database, an object-oriented environment). An abstract protocol can be defined to handle persistence, and be mapped on the services provided by a particular storage system.

3 Using Multiple Inheritance

Multiple inheritance is the technique used to map between high level components of the generic toolkit and the tools provided by available user interface toolkits. Multiple inheritance is used to combine two classes, one that defines the protocol of the component, and another that provides an implementation. In this section, the principle is outlined first as generically as possible, and then a real example, drawn from the user interface toolkits universe, is provided. The effect of a new implementation is then discussed. Throughout the presentation, the important aspects to observe are the mechanisms used to map between functions of the class that defines the protocol, and functions of the implementation class. This mapping is performed by the class that results of the combination of the two above.

The Principle

The interface of a generic object is defined by an abstract class designated here as the A class. This class is defined to satisfy the internal (domain-specific) requirements. Unless there are some internal operations that the A class has to perform (for example, to be integrated in management system of generic toolkit objects), this class only requires a declaration file. The I class is an implementation class that provides access to a real system. The "real" class R, derived from both A and I, maps internal requirements expressed by A's virtual functions into external facilities offered by I. As described later, I may also impose some behavior in A which is satisfied by R. The technique is shown in fig. 1 [4].

---

[4]The figures presented in the paper are diagrams where the class relations and subobject relations (relating to member functions) are illustrated. The subobject relations do not represent the virtual function tables but the sets of functions

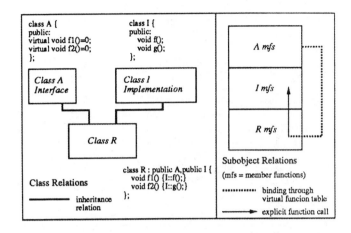

Figure 1: Combining Protocol and Implementation. See also fig.6 in the Appendix

The following facts can be verified, and satisfy our goal of separating interface and implementation.

- A defines exclusively the interface, and has no information at all about implementation.

- R is a concretization of the abstract interface, to which it has to conform.

- The application is completely independent (at source code level) from I. Changes in the implementation do not affect the application.

One of the principles that is important to consider when evaluating this technique and the possible alternatives, is that I classes, the tools used to implement domain-specific classes, are usually provided by class libraries. Thus, only the class declaration is available and naturally, no changes are allowed.

An example

The above technique is illustrated next with a more concrete example, where a *directory view* (*DView*), used in a *shell* application is implemented alternatively, with two different graphical classes, designated *GraphicList* and *GraphicPanel* respectively.

---

defined for each class and the relations between them. The amount of C++ code is minimized to avoid overloading the diagrams, and this code is just meant to provide complementary information. An appendix includes the corresponding C++ code for the readers who prefer the syntactic "view" of the examples.

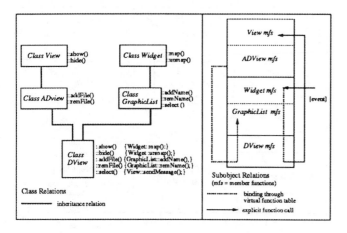

Figure 2: Definition (ADView), a tool (List) and the "real" DView. See also fig.7 in the Appendix

The example presented here is simplified to minimize syntactic overhead, but it closely matches the implementation using a C++ interface to the X toolkit (fig. 2). In the example:

- *View* is a base class for all the representation classes in the generic toolkit. It defines the relations between *Views*, e.g. hierarchy, the relation between *Views* and *Data* objects and the base functionality of a *View*, like *show* and *hide*.

- *Widget* is the base class of the graphical toolkit and defines the basic interface of graphical objects, like *map* and *unmap*. It also enforces a model for the clients of the graphical toolkit, a callback mechanism that is implemented by the *select* member function. This member function is called externally (by the toolkit's run time system) as a result of user actions (events) on the graphic objects. This mechanism introduces an "external" constraint in the generic toolkit architecture.

- *GraphicList* is a class offered by the graphical toolkit. It provides member functions to add or remove names from the list and a *select()* function that is called when the user selects one of the names with the mouse.

- *ADirView* is a fully abstract class that defines the interface to represent a directory. One could argue that since a *View* represents a

Data object, a *update* member function would be sufficient to respond to all changes in the *Data* object. Although this may be true, the fact is that the *updates* in the *Data* objects would have to be decoded by the *View* and the appropriate member function (*add-* or *rem-File*) called internally.

- *DView* is the class that merges interface and implementation. Basic *View* functions are implemented with basic *Widget* functions. *AD-View* specific functions are implemented with *GraphicList*. *DView* also satisfies the need for a callback function suggested by the *GraphicList*. An external callback is converted into an internal message and sent forward, eventually to a *Data* object.

Figure 2 shows how a virtual function defined by the *ADView* interface gets mapped onto a *GraphicList* function and how a call to a *GraphicList* functions triggers a call to a *View* function.

Although the example seems very simplified, experience [Guimaraes 90,Puttress 90] shows that the principle is valid for most cases. A *View* may, of course, be implemented through composition of several graphical objects in which case the *R View* is derived from a composition object. The mapping between internal operations would be more complex, but could be centralized in the *R View* in any case.

The effect of a new implementation

The *DView* could be easily implemented with another graphic object, a *GraphicPanel* that displays icons (fig. 3). The new implementation of a *directory View* only affects the internals if the *DView* class. It can be argued that the new implementation showed here merely changes the graphic class, but uses the same graphical toolkit and therefore the models are kept. In fact, the techniques illustrated here are more obvious when models are consistent across the alternative implementation tools. Given the scope of the example however, a certain degree of commonality is found between existing UI toolkits, concerning visual operations and event handling.

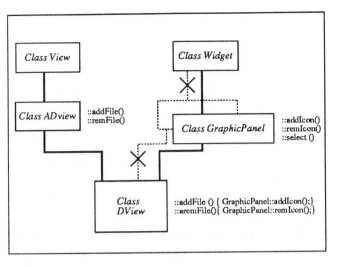

Figure 3: Changing the Implementation of the Directory View. See also fig.8 in the Appendix

4 Why not Single Inheritance ?

The usefulness of multiple inheritance versus the sufficiency of single inheritance has been broadly discussed in recent publications [Carroll 91,Schwarz 91]. This section closely relates to (and benefits from) that discussion.

In general, the problems we face when simulating the above effect with single inheritance derive from the fact that, while with multiple inheritance only one object exists, single inheritance implies the existence of two communicating objects.

The simplest solution of making R ($DView$) derived from I ($GraphicList$) is not feasible since the additional functionality of A ($ADView$), has to be incorporated. The only solution is to either incorporate a I object in R or a pointer for dynamic allocation of that object. To minimize the differences with the multiple inheritance solution, the *member object* `iobj` solution will be used (fig. 4). This solution, composition, is the alternative to multiple inheritance that is usually presented.

External Calls (Callbacks)

A major problem is found when trying to override the *GraphicList* virtual function *select* with a *DView* function (See the question mark in fig 4). Here is where the fact that we are dealing with different objects becomes apparent. The virtual func-

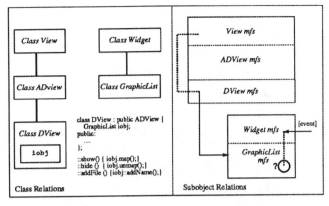

Figure 4: Directory View implementation with Single Inheritance. See also fig.9 in the Appendix

tion tables of *GraphicList* and *DView* are independent and have to be merged "manually" (fig. 5). To solve the problem, the following is required:

- The *GraphicList::select* function has to be overridden by a function of a derived class. This implies the definition of a new class, *GraphicListD* [5].

- The *GraphicListD* object has to know about the *DView* object, in order to call the *DView::select* function. Again, this forces the definition of the *GraphicListD* class containing the address of the *DView* object.

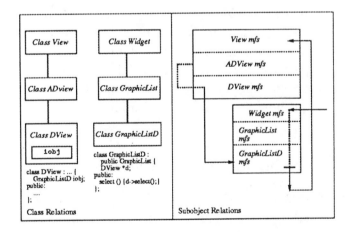

Figure 5: The need for new classes. See also fig.10 in the Appendix

This situation is a real example where the *multiple override criterion* mentioned by Carroll

---

[5] And the `iobj` of *DView* should be a *GraphicListD*.

[Carroll 91] applies. Moreover, the transformation proposed by Schwarz [Schwarz 91] fails because the *select* member function, transferred to *GraphicListD*, refers to a member of a base class of *DView*. Additional members and function definitions are therefore required.

At the programming level, there are now additional requirements for the *DView* constructor, since the *GraphicListD* object has to be informed about where it is contained. A more serious consequence is that a new "interface" has to be built, like a set of "stub routines", to merge *R* and *I* classes. This interface can imply as many classes as graphical objects in a library (which usually means a lot). At the execution level, this solution implies the overhead of an additional function call.

Access Restrictions

One other problem that arises with the single inheritance solution is due to access control. Basically, there is a systematic clash with any *protected* declarations made in any of the two class hierarchies. With the composition solution, any *GraphicList protected* member has to be made *public* to be accessible by *DView*. The same occurs in the opposite direction, i.e., the *protected* declaration in members of *ADView* has to be adjusted to allow calls from *GraphicListD* object. This is a real problem since, given the extensibility requirements of graphical toolkits, it is expectable to find a significant number of *protected* functions, designed for the purpose of further specialization [6].

Changing an implementation

The development of a new implementation of a generic class is localized in the *DView* (*R*) classes if multiple inheritance is used. As seen above, the single inheritance solution implies further modifications, due to the need for "stub" interfaces to the implementation classes.

Other Conflicts

Contrary to the multiple inheritance solution, with single inheritance, the *R* class *is-not-a I* class. Therefore, any type-related functionality that is used by applications has to be modified by the programmer.

One example of this functionality is a simple object I/O mechanism used in *HOT*, where *class objects* are semi-automatically constructed through a set of *cpp* macros. These class objects know how to store and retrieve their corresponding instances and, knowing their upper classes, to call the corresponding methods up through the graph. This mechanism is only based in class relations and therefore there is no need for the programmer to add I/O specific code in the class methods, which he is obliged to do if multiple inheritance is simulated.

5 Conclusions

The construction of domain specific user interface toolkits is a problem where reusability is of extreme importance. Combining domain specific concepts with existing implementation tools is a task that strongly benefits from linguistic support, and multiple inheritance provides a very elegant solution to perform that combination. The result is a more generic set of components, highly independent from the details of the external environment and therefore, easier to program with.

Object oriented techniques can be implemented without object oriented languages [Stroustrup 88], but the extra cost is always paid by the programmer [7]. Analogously, multiple inheritance can be simulated with single inheritance, but it may require auxiliary and redundant coding, affecting understandability and maintenance, and may even break encapsulation decisions made by the builders of the reusable components.

---

[6] A quick look at the header files of the InterViews toolkit is enough to prove this statement.

[7] User interface programmers that have experienced the Xt programming techniques are deeply aware of this fact.

Acknowledgements

This work has been done under a consultancy agreement between the author, a researcher at IST/INESC, Lisbon, Portugal and the Software Techniques Research Department at Bell Labs, Murray Hill, NJ. I would like to thank Paulo Guedes and Manuel Sequeira from INESC, John Puttress, Jon Helfman, Rob Murray and Bill Hopkins from Bell Labs, and William Cook from Apple, for their helpful comments on this paper and ideas.

References

[Berkley 90] D.A. Berkley et J.L. Flanagan. An Experimental Human-Machine Communications Network based on ISDN. *AT&T Technical Journal*, 69(5), October 1990.

[Borkin 80] S.A. Borkin. *Data Models : A Semantic Approach for Database Systems*. The MIT Press, 1980.

[Carroll 91] M. Carroll. Using Multiple Inheritance to Implement Abstract Data Types. *The C++ Report*, 3(4), April 1991.

[Conklin 87] J. Conklin. Hypertext: An Introduction and Survey. *IEEE Computer*, 17–41, September 1987.

[Ellis 90] M. Ellis et B. Stroustrup. *The Annotated C++ Reference Manual*. Addison Wesley, 1990.

[Guimaraes 90] N. Guimaraes. HOT: a Generic Hypermedia Toolkit. Dans *Proceedings of the TOOLS'90 Conference, Paris*, June 1990.

[Linton 87] M. Linton, P. Calder, et J. Vlissides. InterViews: A C++ Graphical Interface Toolkit. Dans *Proceedings of USENIX C++ Workshop , Santa Fe*, November 1987.

[McCormack 88] J. McCormack, P. Asente, et R. Swick. *X Toolkit Intrinsics - C Language Interface*. 1988.

[Meyer 88] Bertrand Meyer. Harnessing Multiple Inheritance. *Journal Object-Oriented Programming*, 48–51, November/December 1988.

[Puttress 90] J.J. Puttress et N. Guimaraes. The Toolkit Approach to Hypermedia. *Proceedings of ECHT'90, Paris*, pages 25–37, Cambridge University Press, November 1990.

[Schwarz 91] J. Schwarz. A Critique of the Skiplist/Associative Array Example. *The C++ Report*, 3(4), April 1991.

[Spector 88] A.Z. Spector et J.H. Howard. *Andrew*. Selected Papers from the Usenix Winter Conference 1988, Dallas, December 1988.

[Stroustrup 85] B. Stroustrup. *The C++ Programming Language*. Addison-Wesley, 1985.

[Stroustrup 88] Bjarne Stroustrup. What Is Object Oriented Programming. *IEEE Software*, May 1988.

Appendix

```
/* Interface -- A.h --*/
class A {
public:
    virtual void f1() = 0;
    virtual void f2() = 0;
};
/* Implementation -- I.h --*/
class I {
public:
    void f();
    void g();
};
/*------ R.h -------*/
#include "A.h"
#include "I.h"

class R : public A, I {
    virtual void f1()  {I::f(); }
    virtual void f2()  {I::g(); }
};
/*---- application ----*/
#include "R.h"

main()  {
R r;
    r.f1();
    r.f2();
};
```

Figure 6: Protocol and Implementation (C++)

```
/*--- Interface : View and ADView */

class View {
public:
    virtual void show() = 0;
    virtual void hide() = 0;
};

class ADView : public View  {
public:
    virtual void addFile(char*) = 0;
    virtual void remFile(char*) = 0;
};

/*--- Implementation : Widget and GraphicList */

class Widget {
public:
    void map   ();
    void unmap ();
};

class GraphicList : public Widget  {
public:
    void addName (char*);
    void remName (char*);
    virtual void select (char*);
};

/*--- Interface + Implementation : DView */

class DView : public ADView, GraphicList {
public:
    virtual void show ();
    virtual void hide ();
    virtual void addFile (char*);
    virtual void remFile (char*);
    virtual void select  (char*);
};

/*--- DView.c ---*/

void DView::show () {
    Widget::map ();
}
void DView::hide () {
    Widget::unmap ();
}
void DView::addFile (char *fn) {
    addName (fn);
}
void DView::remFile (char *fn) {
    remName (fn);
}
void DView::select  (char* s)  {
    View::sendMessage (s);
}
```

Figure 7: The DView definition, a Graphic tool and the implementation (C++)

```
/*--- GraphicPanel.h ---*/
class GraphicPanel : public Widget {
public:
    void addIcon (char*);
    void remIcon (char*);
    virtual void select (char*);
};
/*--- DView.h ---*/
class DView : public ADView, GraphicPanel {
public:
    /* as above */
};
/*--- DView.c ---*/
/* DView::show, ::hide and ::select as above */
void DView::addFile (char *fn) { addIcon (fn); }
void DView::remFile (char *fn) { remIcon (fn); }
```

Figure 8: A new implementation of DView

```
/*--- DView.h ---*/
class DView : public ADView {
    GraphicList  iobj;
public:
    virtual void show ();
    virtual void hide ();
    virtual void addFile (char*);
        ...
};
/*--- DView.c ---*/
void DView::show () { iobj.map   (); }
void DView::hide () { iobj.unmap (); }
void DView::addFile (char *fn) { iobj.addName(fn); }
```

Figure 9: DView with Single Inheritance

```
/*--- GraphicListD.h ---*/
class GraphicListD : public GraphicList {
    DView* d;
public:
    void setParent (DView*);
    virtual void select (char*);
};

/*--- GraphicListD.c ---*/
void GraphicListD::select (char* s) { d->select (s); }
```

Figure 10: The need for new classes

Composite Multimedia and
Active Objects

Simon Gibbs

Centre Universitaire d'Informatique
Université de Genève
12 rue du Lac, Geneva 1207, SWITZERLAND
simon@cui.unige.ch

Abstract

An object-oriented framework for composite multimedia is described. In analogy to constructing complex graphics entities from graphics primitives and geometric transformations, composite multimedia is constructed from multimedia primitives and temporal transformations. Active objects based on real-time processes are proposed as multimedia primitives. Their combination to form composite multimedia and the requisite temporal transformations are illustrated.

1. Introduction

The improving capabilities of multimedia workstations, combined with the development of multimedia recording formats (for example, CD-I and DVI, see [14] for a recent description) is likely to increase the demand for applications involving multimedia. However the development of multimedia applications is presently hampered by two key problems: First, multimedia involves concepts from audio recording, video production, animation, and music – concepts that are novel to many programmers. Second, multimedia operations often involve special hardware, leading to lack of portability and longer development times.

One way of alleviating these two problems is by providing programmers with a high-level programming "framework" [4] for dealing with multimedia. The framework should:

- be based on a simple conceptual model of multimedia functionality, yet one which is general enough to capture the variety of multimedia, including sound, video, music, and animated sequences,

- be easy to use and not require expertise in multimedia technology, yet be open and extensible so that more experienced programmers are not constrained,

- encapsulate hardware dependencies,

- allow complex multimedia effects, for example the synchronization of an audio and video signal, or the juxtaposition of two video signals.

The following describes such a framework and introduces constructs, based on active objects, for multimedia programming. In the next section we discuss just what is multimedia and motivate our model and the use of active objects. Section 3 discusses multimedia primitives and the basic operations they support. Combination of multimedia primitives to form *composite multimedia* is discussed in Section 4, examples of programming with composite multimedia are also given. Finally we review related work and discuss future directions.

2. Objects and Multimedia

The term "multimedia" often appears in descriptions of systems – there are multimedia documents, multimedia interfaces, and multimedia applications. As

OOPSLA'91, pp. 97–112

long as the document, interface, or application deals somehow with multimedia information, the description is viewed as justified. But the question arises, then, as to just what constitutes multimedia information.

One possible view of multimedia information is based on multimedia data types. For example, a multimedia data type CDaudio could consist of all possible audio signals as encoded on a compact disc, i.e., CDaudio values would be sequences of the form sample$_i$ where the data format used by the samples would be specified by the CD recording format. As with other data types, one could then define operations for CDaudio, for example operations dealing with compression, filtering, or concatenation.

An interesting aspect of the data type view is the notion of multimedia data being based on sequences. This appears to hold for multimedia in general (see Table 1). Perhaps this is not surprising since a charac-

Multimedia Data Type	Sequence Of
sound	audio samples
video	video frames
animation	raster frames
music	musical events

Table 1   Multimedia Values as Temporal Sequences.

teristic of multimedia information is its temporal nature, and a sequence of samples is one of the basic representations of a time varying signal.

This suggests the following definition for multimedia data values:

Definition: A *multimedia value*, v, of data type D, is a (finite) sequence d$_i$, where the encoding and interpretation of the d$_i$ are governed by D. In particular D determines how the *presentation* of v (the physical realization of v, within some medi-

um, over some time interval) can be obtained from the d$_i$. Presentation of v takes place at a rate r$_D$, the *data rate* of D.

The above definition is somewhat vague about the meaning of r$_D$. Generally r$_D$ should be viewed as a measure of the "flow" of values of type D. In many cases this rate can be associated with the number of sequence values presented per unit time. For example, CD audio requires some 44 thousand samples per second and NTSC video involves about 30 frames per second. In other cases r$_D$ may indicate an ideal presentation rate – presentation may then take place at a different or varying rate, perhaps with loss of quality. Also there may be data types where the d$_i$ contain explicit timing information. In such cases, although the interval from one d$_i$ to the next will vary, there is likely to be a maximum data rate which can then be associated with r$_D$.

The above definition associates each multimedia value with a lower-level sequence, there are, however, cases where the sequence may not be known *a priori* (i.e., before presentation) or may not be directly accessible by software:

- Presentation may involve synthesis. For example, a pure audio tone might be generated from a sine function rather than from a stored sequence of audio samples.

- We may want to associate a multimedia value with an on-going activity (for instance, a recording session). Here the sequence is not known until the activity has completed.

- Many computer-controllable video products, including VCRs, video disc players, and cameras, have analog inputs or outputs. It is important to support such devices within the framework, so we would like to allow multimedia values which exist only as analog signals. However these signals are not directly accessible by software (i.e., they must be digitized before being processed).

The last case can be accounted for by allowing analog signals as multimedia data types, with the understanding that the underlying d$_i$ are unavailable within a program. Values of these types are software handles;

98

they are used for referring to the inputs and outputs of hardware devices which in turn manipulate the analog signal.

The first two cases involve processes (the sine generator and the recording session) that produce multimedia values. These processes are likely to have their own internal state (e.g., the frequency of the sine generator) and their own operations (e.g., change the frequency, increase the recording volume). To allow programmers to conveniently handle such cases we need a construct which combines the notion of data, behavior *and* process.

An appropriate programming language construct appears to be the *active object* [5][17]. Active objects, like ordinary or *passive* objects, have state (instance variables) and behavior (methods). In addition, an active object may spontaneously perform actions, even if no messages have been sent to the object. There are many ways in which concurrency can be added to an object-oriented programming language in order to support active objects [13]. Here we assume a simple model where objects are *multi-threaded* (i.e., simultaneous invocations of an object's methods do not block). We also assume that synchronization of threads within an object is the responsibility of the programmer.

Using active objects, we can then define multimedia objects as follows:

Definition: A *multimedia object* is an active object which produces and/or consumes multimedia values (of specified types) at their associated data rates.

There are a number of observations we can make from this definition. First, multimedia objects are subject to real-time constraints in that they have to produce or consume data at particular rates. Second, each multimedia object can be viewed as a collection of *ports*. A port has a (multimedia) data type and is used either for input or output. A multimedia object's ports (the number, their data type and direction) would be determined by the class of the object. Third, we can divide multimedia objects into three categories: *sources*, *sinks*, and *filters*. A source produces multimedia values (i.e., has only output ports), a sink consumes values (has only input ports), and a filter both produces and consumes (has both input and output ports).

It will be convenient to use a graphical notation for multimedia objects. We will represent such objects by circles (see Figure 1) with attached boxes for their ports (extruding for output ports and intruding for input ports).

| source | filter | sink |

Figure 1 Multimedia Objects.

We next give some examples of classes of multimedia objects. For each we list the class name, port specification (whether input or output and the associated data type), and give a brief description of what the class's instances do. In general, these classes are *parameterized* by the data types of their input and output ports. In the following port specifications we make use of generic multimedia data types, such as Audio, for sequences of sounds, Video, for analog video signals, and Multimedia, for any multimedia data type. In practice, before instantiating these classes, it would be necessary to bind the ports to specific data types, e.g., CDaudio or NTSC.

AudioIn (output port: Audio)
  Reads an audio input device (for example, an analog to digital converter) and produces an Audio value.

AudioOut (input port: Audio)
  Writes values from its input port to an audio output device (e.g., a digital to analog converter).

AudioFileRead (output port: Audio)
  Produces an Audio value by reading samples stored in a file.

AudioMix (input ports: Audio, Audio;
      output port: Audio)
  Combines (e.g., by averaging or summing) two Audio values to produce a third.

VCR (input port: Video)
  Records a Video value on a video cassette.

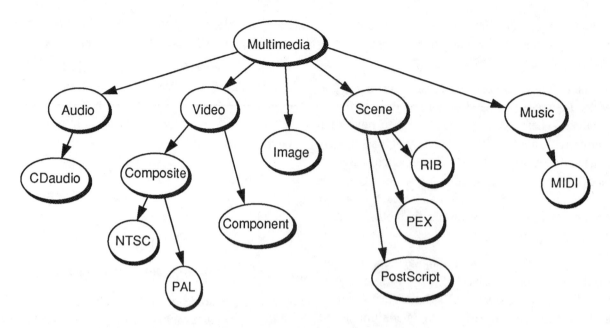

Figure 2 Some Multimedia Data Types.

DVE (input ports: Video, Video; output port: Video)
A DVE (or "digital video effect") combines two Video values to produce a third. Examples are special effects like the wipes and fades commonly seen on television.

Tee (input port: Multimedia; output ports: Multimedia, Multimedia)
Duplicates its input on two output ports.

Perform (input port: Music, output port: Audio)
A Perform object takes from its input port a sequence of musical events (for instance, a MIDI[1] stream) and synthesizes an Audio value.

Render (input port: Scene; output port: Image)
A Render object graphically renders a sequence of scene descriptions (e.g., PEX[2] requests) producing a sequence of images.

FrameBuffer (input port: Image; output port: Video)
A FrameBuffer object converts an image into a video signal.

---

1. MIDI, or *Musical Instrument Digital Interface*, is a standard for communicating with musical devices.

2. PEX is an extension to the X Window System protocol that supports 3d graphics.

3. Multimedia Primitives

Multimedia objects belonging to classes such as those listed above are examples of what we will call *multimedia primitives*. In general a multimedia primitive is a multimedia object which cannot be decomposed into other multimedia objects. Is this section we look at the operations supported by these primitives. In the next section we will look at *composite multimedia*, i.e., objects where such a decomposition is possible.

3.1 Multimedia Hierarchies

Multimedia primitives make use of two hierarchies – a supertype/subtype hierarchy of data types and a class inheritance hierarchy. Figure 2 shows some possible multimedia data types. (It would also be possible to implement multimedia values as passive objects. However, we prefer to retain the data type terminology since it stresses that the internal representation of a multimedia value is not likely to be a matter for the implementor to decide, rather it is likely to be fixed by standard or convention.)

Figure 2 is not intended to be complete but merely to give some indication of the richness of the hierarchy. The division into five high-level subtypes: Audio, Video, Image, Scene and Music (suppose we call them

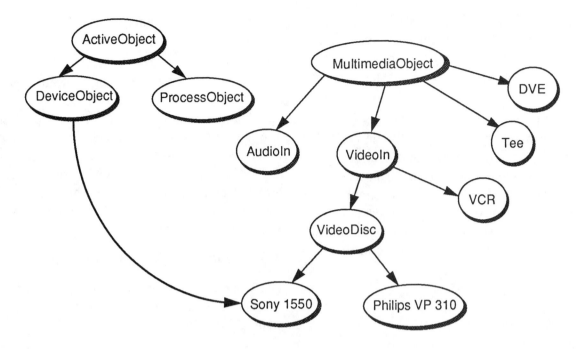

Figure 3   Some Multimedia Object Classes. Concrete multimedia object classes, i.e., those which can be instantiated, inherit from one of DeviceObject or ProcessObject. (Not all such inheritance relationships are shown however.)

base-types) is also somewhat arbitrary and incomplete. Other data types could be added if needed. Some possibilities are static text, static graphics or static images (all sequences of length 1); moving text (e.g., as in a film's credits); or data from specialized acquisition devices (e.g., volume data produced by a CAT scanner). However, the five base-types give a good range and are common enough to be supported on many platforms.

Similarly the multimedia class hierarchy in Figure 3 is also incomplete. Since many of these classes correspond to hardware devices there may be different specializations for different models and manufacturers (illustrated here by the two subclasses of VideoDisc). Another source of variety is the range of filter objects. For example, one product[1] supports over 100 digital video effects; in our framework each of these would correspond to a subclass of DVE. Finally, many of the classes in Figure 3 are parameterized by the multimedia data types of their input and output ports.

---

1. The Video Toaster by NewTek.

3.2 Operations on Multimedia Primitives

Multimedia object classes inherit methods from ActiveObject and MultimediaObject. A partial specification of ActiveObject, written in C++, is:

```
class ActiveObject {
public:
    bool    Start();
    bool    Stop();
    bool    Pause();
    bool    Resume();
};
```

The methods of ActiveObject provide basic activity control for a multimedia object. The two subclasses of ActiveObject, DeviceObject and ProcessObject, differ on how these methods are implemented but do not add additional methods.

The class MultimediaObject introduces a more interesting set of methods. These methods make use of two temporal coordinate systems: *world time* and *object time*. The origin and units of world time are set by the

101

application. The origin would normally be set to coincide with the beginning of multimedia activity. World time would run while the activity is in progress, and be stopped or resumed as the activity is stopped or resumed.

Object time is relative to a multimedia object. In particular, each object can specify the origin of object time with respect to world time and the units used for measuring object time. (Normally these units relate to the data rates of the object's ports.) Furthermore, each object can specify the *orientation* of object time, i.e., whether it flows forward (increases as world time increases) or backwards (decreases as world time increases).

A partial specification for MultimediaObject is:

```
class MultimediaObject {
protected:
        // current value of object time, current
        // scaling factor and current temporal
        // orientation, parent if in a composite
        objectTime      now = 0.0;
        float           scale = 1.0;
        int             orientation = 1;
        CompositeMultimediaObject  parent;
public:
        //
        // temporal coordinates
        //
        objectTime      CurrentObjectTime();
        objectTime      WorldToObject(worldTime);
        worldTime       CurrentWorldTime();
        worldTime       ObjectToWorld(objectTime);
        objectInterval  WorldToObjectI(worldInterval);
        worldInterval   ObjectToWorldI(objectInterval);
        //
        // composition
        //
        void            Translate(worldTime);
        void            Scale(float);
        void            Invert();
        //
        // synchronization
        //
        void            Sync(worldTime);
        worldInterval   SyncInterval();
        worldInterval   SyncTolerance();
        syncMode        SyncMode();
        void            Cue(worldTime);
        void            Jump(worldTime);
        void            Jump(objectTime);
};
```

The methods of MultimediaObject are divided into three groups, those dealing with temporal coordinates, with composition, and with synchronization. The first group contains utilities for converting between the two temporal coordinate systems, these methods are quite simple and will not be discussed further. The composition and synchronization methods are more complex and will be introduced via examples in the following sections.

3.3 Temporal Transformations

The Translate, Scale and Invert methods of MultimediaObject are called *temporal transformations*. Informally, these methods do the following:

> Translate – translates the object in world time.
> Scale – scales the duration of the object.
> Invert – flips the orientation of object time
> between "forward" and "reverse."

To illustrate these operations, suppose we have a VideoDisc object named source#1 which produces a (recorded) Video value on its output port. Convenient units for world and object times could be seconds and frame numbers. If we send the following messages to source#1:

```
Translate(0)    // align the temporal origins
Cue(30.0)       // position the disc at 30 sec.
Scale(0.5)      // scale time by 1/2
Invert()        // invert the disc's orientation
Start()         // start playing
```

the effect would be to play the first 30 seconds of the video disc in reverse at twice the normal rate (i.e., in 15 seconds).

It should be clear that there are many practical limitations on the above methods. In particular:

1. It is not possible to apply Scale or Invert (or Cue) to a "live" source (e.g., a video camera or a microphone).

2. There may be hardware or software limitations on Scale. For instance, video players have a small set, rather than a continuous range, of playback speeds. When Scale is im-

plemented in software, by skipping or interpolating sequence values, again only certain scale factors may be supported.

3. There are limits on the resolution of Translate (and Cue). For example, a video player cannot be cued between frames, an AudioFileRead object can only be cued to sample boundaries.

In general, temporal transformations affect the order and timing of the output of a multimedia object. For an object with no output ports, a sink, these methods can be treated as no-ops.

The effect of temporal transformations can be visualized using *timeline diagrams* of output ports. Figure 4 shows one such diagram for an output port which at time T_B (called the *base time*) starts to produce the sequence $S = d_1, d_2, ..., d_n$. It is useful to denote a timeline by a triple $<T_B, T_L, S>$ where, if D is the data type of the d_i, then $T_L = nr_D$.

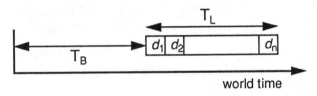

Figure 4   A Timeline Diagram.

The effect on an object's output ports of applying the temporal transformations to the object are illustrated in Figure 5. Using the timeline triples we can express the temporal transformations more concisely:

Translate($<T_B, T_L, S>$, delta) = $<T_B + delta, T_L, S>$
Scale($<T_B, T_L, S>$, s) = $<T_B*s, T_L*s, S'>$
Invert($<T_B, T_L, S>$) = $<T_B, T_L, S''>$

The difficulty in implementing temporal transformations is in producing the new sequences S' and S" required by Scale and Invert. Now for some cases there may be considerable leeway in generating these sequences. For instance, faithfully inverting an Audio sequence is likely to produce meaningless noise. For audio it may be more useful to generate a new sequence, perhaps one whose pitch corresponds to the current scale factor.

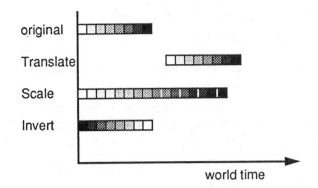

Figure 5   Temporal Transformations.

There are cases though where Scale and Invert produce meaningful information. For instance, we may want to present an image sequence speeded up or in reverse. As a specific example, consider the animation of a bouncing ball. Using multimedia objects, the animation would require a Scene source object, i.e, an object which generates scene descriptions containing the ball. Suppose the object calculates the position of the ball by reading displacement information from a file, and then places an updated scene description on its output port. The basic loop for this object could look something like:

```
while(not EOF) {
        // read displacement from file
        ball.position = ball.position + displacement;
        // put scene description on the output port
}
```

One problem here is that to produce the ith ball position it is necessary to know the $(i-1)^{th}$ position. This makes the Cue operation difficult to implement (but still possible, by scanning the file up to the cue point). The real problem is that if we Invert or Scale this object it will not produce animations of the ball moving backwards or at a scaled velocity.

In general, for a ProcessObject to support temporal transformations, the values produced (on its output ports) must be a function of object time. Invocation of this function can be viewed as *sampling* the object. Note that the sampling rate, which is essentially the data rate of the object's output ports, is constant in world time, but, as measured in object time, varies as the object is scaled.

3.4 Example: "FadeOver" a Filter Object

Let us look at a multimedia object which does perform correctly when temporally transformed. The following is a partial implementation of FadeOver, a filter which gradually switches its output from one input port to another:

```
class FadeOver : public ProcessObject, public
MultimediaObject {
        objectTime      objectDuration = 4.0;
        Port            in1, in2, out;
protected:
        void            Process();
        // this method is defined by subclasses of
        // ProcessObject, when invoked a new
        // process is created and the method
        // body executed concurrently
};

void  FadeOver::Process()
{
        while(now >= 0 && now < objectDuration) {
                Sample(now);
                now += (orientation / scale);
        }
}

void  FadeOver::Sample(objectTime t)
{
        element         val, val1, val2;

        val1 = in1.Read(sizeof(element));
        val2 = in2.Read(sizeof(element));
        val = (t / objectDuration) * val1 +
                ((objectDuration - t) / objectDuration)
                    * val2;
        out.Write(val, sizeof(element));
}
```

The Process method for FadeOver allows for both increasing and decreasing object time, it will function correctly if the object is inverted. Also the method is sensitive to scaling and will vary the object's duration (as measured in world time) appropriately.

4. Composite Multimedia

One reason for the complexity of multimedia information is that it often consists of a richly structured collection of lower-level multimedia components. There are several ways in which this structure may be organized. For instance, *multimedia documents* make use of a hierarchical component structure, while *hypermedia* involves a network structure. While these two forms of organization are certainly useful, they tend to neglect possible temporal relationships between components. A third method of organizing multimedia information, and one that focuses on these relationships, is what we will call *temporal composition*.

4.1 Temporal Composition

The motivation for temporal composition comes from the need to model situations where a number of multimedia components are simultaneously presented. Television and films are two obvious examples, each containing both audible and visual components.

Within our object-oriented framework, we will model composite multimedia through the use of special objects defined as follows:

Definition: A *composite* multimedia object is a multimedia object containing a collection of *component* multimedia objects and a specification of their temporal and configurational relationships.

The two groups of relationships specified by a composite multimedia object are used for different purposes. In particular:

- *temporal relationships* – indicate the synchronization and temporal sequencing of components.

- *configurational relationships* – indicate the connections between the input and output ports of components.

As an example, suppose we want to construct a multimedia composite, c_1, which, when presented, behaves as follows:

> Starting at time t_0 an audio object audio$_1$, and a video object, video$_1$, are presented. At time t_1, a fade starts

from video$_1$ to a second video object, video$_2$. The transition is completed at time t$_2$ and at time t$_3$ both audio$_1$ and video$_2$ are stopped.

Here audio$_1$, video$_1$ and video$_2$ are source objects. To complete the composite, three additional objects are needed: audioOut, an audio sink; videoOut, a video sink; and dve$_1$, a DVE filter for performing the fade from video$_1$ to video$_2$.

The temporal relationships of a composite object are easily depicted with a *composite timeline diagram*. Such a diagram contains one timeline for each output port within the composite. The diagram for the composite c$_1$ is shown in Figure 6.

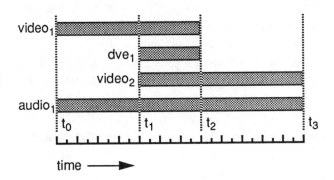

Figure 6 A Composite Timeline.

In constructing a composite timeline, the Translate transformation is used to adjust the positioning of the components; Scale and Invert may also be applied to alter presentation timing. In general, each component's "placement" within the composite is specified by its translation offset, scale, and orientation. This is analogous to how complex graphics objects can be constructed by applying geometric transformations to groups of simpler objects (see Table 2). In graphics,

Graphics	Multimedia
2d or 3d space	1d time
translation	translation
scaling	scaling
rotation	inversion

Table 2 Graphics versus Multimedia.

the sequence of transformations that have been ap-

plied to an object is captured by the object's transformation matrix. Similarly, the sequence of temporal transformations used to place a component within a composite can be described by a 2x2 transformation matrix (if time is expressed in homogeneous coordinates).

Since composites are multimedia objects, it is possible to apply temporal transformations to composites as well as to their components. This allows the construction of *hierarchical composites*. As in graphics modelling, the transformation from object to world coordinates is then calculated by traversing the hierarchy from the node representing the object to the root or "world" node.

A final transformation, the *presentation transformation*, analogous to the viewing transformation in graphics, provides the mapping from world time to *presentation time* – the actual time of the presentation (i.e., the hour of the day, the minute of the hour, etc.). By adjusting this transformation it is possible to dynamically control the presentation, allowing implementation of user-level commands such as "fast forward" or "reverse."

The timeline representation shows the concurrency within a composite due to the superimposition of a number of multimedia *channels* (each horizontal bar in the timeline diagram), it also identifies *transition points*, i.e., times where sources start or stop. For composite c$_1$, there are four channels and four transition points: t$_0$, t$_1$, t$_2$ and t$_3$.

Transition points divide world time into a number of intervals. A composite's configurational relationships specify, for each such interval, the connections between input and output ports of its components. This information can be depicted with a *component network*, where nodes correspond to components of a multimedia composite and edges to port connections. The component network for c$_1$ during the interval [t$_1$, t$_2$] is shown in Figure 7.

4.2 The Class "CompositeMultimedia-Object"

The class CompositeMultimediaObject provides methods for configuring a composite and controlling

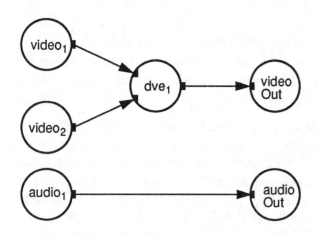

Figure 7 A Component Network (for the interval $[t_1, t_2]$ of Figure 6).

its presentation-time behavior, a partial specification for this class is:

```
class CompositeMultimediaObject :
    public MultimediaObject,
    public ProcessObject
{
    MultimediaObjectSet      components;
    TransitionPointSet       transitions;
    ConnectorSet             connectors;
public:
    //
    // composition
    //
    errCode         AddComponent(...);
    errCode         AddConnection(...);
    bool            IsTopLevel();
    //
    // synchronization
    //
    void            OutOfSync(...);
    void            SlaveTo(MultimediaObject);
};
```

When a composite object is activated (i.e., it has been sent the Start message) it has two major responsibilities: connecting and disconnecting components when transition points are reached, and synchronization of the composite's components.

Regarding port connection, we have not been very specific in describing what ports are and how they may be connected. Connecting ports in our framework is complicated by the fact that there are two ba-

sic categories of multimedia objects: those that are hardware-based (in which case the object is a software handle used to manipulate some external device) and those that are software-based. This means that many communication mechanisms are possible. A particular communication mechanism is abstracted by a *connector* class. Subclasses of MultimediaObject specify, for each port, the connector classes which may be used when connecting the port. The framework presently contains four connector classes: SharedMemoryConnector, BufferedConnector, DelegateConnector, and CableConnector.

A connection is represented by a connector object being attached to two ports. Ports themselves are instances of the Port class. Each Port object has an underlying multimedia data type, a direction, is located on some multimedia object, and may have an attached connector. Methods are provided to read and write data from the port's connector, flush data from the connector, determine the amount of data the connector can accept, and determine how much data is currently queued in the connector. In general these methods simply invoke corresponding methods in the connector.

Port objects are used to enforce valid component networks. For two ports to be connected, they must have the same data type, compatible directions, and allow attachment by connectors of the same class.

When a transition point is reached and a composite object must establish a connection between two ports, its actions will depend on the class of the connector to be used. For CableConnectors the composite cannot actually plug in the cable (unless a computer-controllable switch is available) and so would leave this connection to the user. For the other connector classes, however, the composite can establish the connection.

The second major responsibility of composite objects is synchronization of their components. To be more specific, we define synchronization as follows:

Definition: Two multimedia objects, m_1 and m_2, are *synchronized* to a tolerance Δ_t iff:

$$\text{Abs}(m_1.\text{ObjectToWorld}(m_1.\text{now}) - m_2.\text{ObjectToWorld}(m_2.\text{now})) < \Delta t$$

When a transition point is reached, a composite starts and stops the appropriate components. However once started these components may fall out of synchronization for two reasons. First, a component may not be able to keep up with the rate at which data is provided on its input ports. Second, hardware delays and slight variations in performance may cause objects to drift out of sync (this is often referred to as "jitter", see [12] for instance).

A composite, c, maintains synchronization by attempting to assure:

$$\text{Abs}(c.\text{CurrentWorldTime}() - c_i.\text{CurrentWorldTime}()) < c_i.\text{SyncTolerance}()$$

for each activated component c_i. However, because of the varying nature of components, composites must be flexible and support a variety of synchronization techniques. In the framework, each component has a *synchronization mode* attribute. Depending on the value of this attribute, which can be queried by the method SyncMode, the composite adopts different approaches to synchronization. Presently there are four synchronization modes: NO_SYNC, DEMAND_SYNC, TEST_SYNC, and INTERRUPT_SYNC. The actions a composite takes for a component of each mode can be summarized as follows (see [7] for further details):

NO_SYNC: the composite ignores the component as far as synchronization is concerned.

DEMAND_SYNC: the composite initially queries the component's SyncInterval method which returns a world time value (the inverse of this val-ue is the *sync rate*). When the component is activated, the composite periodically invokes the component's Sync method passing the component the composite's value of current world time.

TEST_SYNC: the composite initially queries the component's SyncInterval and SyncTolerance methods. When the component is activated, the composite periodically queries the component's CurrentWorldTime method and issues a Jump if the component is out of sync.

INTERRUPT_SYNC: the component takes it upon itself to periodically "interrupt" the composite by querying its CurrentWorldTime method. If the component is out of sync with the composite it must take some action. Typically this involves issuing a Jump and/or calling the composite's OutOfSync method.

As an example, consider an audio version of the Unix "talk" program. This could be based on two pairs of composite objects (c_{11} thru c_{22}) as shown in Figure 8.

The problem is to maintain synchronization between AudioIn on one host and AudioOut on the other, that is, we want the delay from when one user speaks until heard by the second user to be less than some threshold. If we assume, as is likely, that AudioIn and AudioOut are essentially pieces of hardware filling and emptying a DMA buffer at some constant rate, then it will be up to AudioToNet and AudioFromNet to maintain synchronization. Suppose that the maximum delay we are prepared to tolerate is 0.25 seconds. Sup-

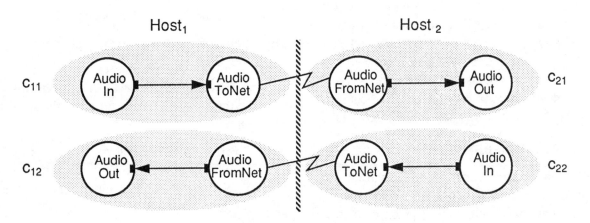

Figure 8 Audio Talk.

pose also that AudioToNet attaches its current world time to each "audio packet" received from AudioIn. Then a possible implementation for the relevant methods of AudioFromNet, using INTERRUPT_SYNC, is:

```
worldInterval AudioFromNet::SyncTolerance()
{
        return 0.25;
}

void  AudioFromNet::Process()
{
        while(TRUE)
                now = Sample(now);
}

objectTime AudioFromNet::Sample(objectTime t)
{
        audioPacket      packet;
        worldInterval    delta;

        // read a packet from a network socket
        delta = parent.CurrentWorldTime()
                   - packet.timeStamp;
        if(delta < SyncTolerance())
                out.Write(packet, sizeof(audioPacket));
        else
                parent.OutOfSync(this, delta);
        return WorldToObject(packet.timeStamp);
}
```

Here note that if AudioFromNet receives data which is too old, the data is thrown away (i.e., not written to the output port) and an OutofSync message is generated. This somewhat drastic since discarding data may produce a perceptible click in the final output. However this can be avoided by writing to the output port a small amount of data which smooths the transition over the skipped packet. Also note that packets received by AudioFromNet that are *ahead* of world time (i.e., delta < 0) are not discarded but passed on to the output port (AudioFromNet will block if the connector attached to this port cannot accept any more data).

4.3 Another Example

As a final and more elaborate example, consider combining interactive 3d graphics with video imagery. Suppose that presentation takes place on a head-mounted stereo display and that the user is wearing an input device which measures head position and orientation (there are commercial user-interface devices which combine both the stereo display and the position/orientation sensor into a single helmet-like package). The problem is to generate 3d imagery which responds to changes in the user's visual perspective and combine this imagery with an appropriately transformed video signal. The video is provided by a source, such as a VCR or video disc and overlaid on a "video surface" appearing in the 3d imagery. For simplicity we assume that the video surface is rectangular (in world coordinates) and of the same aspect ratio as the video signal. However, because of the perspective transformation, the surface may appear skewed. Also the surface may be fully or partially hidden by other surfaces.

The combined video and graphics can be represented by a composite object. This object is not interesting from a timeline perspective since all its components start and stop together. However, the component network is rather complex (see Figure 9) and contains fourteen objects. They are:

head – produces a sequence of head position/orientation values.

model – maintains a 3d scene model, alters the viewing perspective according to deduced eye positions and sends scene descriptions for the left and right eye to its output ports.

rdrL, rdrR – two Render objects. Each accept a scene description, generate an image, and determine the display coordinates of the video surface.

fbufL, fbufR – two FrameBuffer objects.

video - the source of the video signal.

tee - duplicates its input on two output ports.

persL, persR – two DVE objects used to apply a perspective transformation to an input video signal, the transformation is specified by the second input port.

overL, overR – two DVE objects. Each overlays two input video signals to produce a third (some clipping may be done using a technique known as "chroma-keying").

eyeL, eyeR – the final display devices.

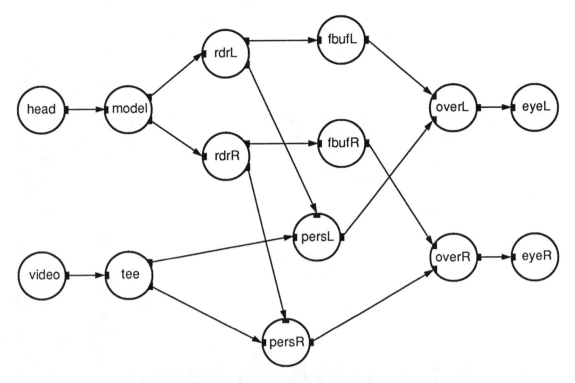

Figure 9 Stereoscopic 3d Graphics with Video Overlays.

Using current technology, most of these objects would be hardware-based, the exceptions being model, rdrL and rdrR. This does not mean, though, that our software structure is redundant. By encapsulating the hardware within subclasses of DeviceObject we gain much flexibility. For example, if we wanted to ignore the video, or ignore stereopsis, we could just form other, simpler, composites. We also gain flexibility from being able to substitute objects. For instance, one might replace the head object by an object which outputs recorded information – this could be useful for debugging or demos. Also, since the composite would then have no live sources, we could apply temporal transformations and reverse or change the speed of presentation.

Furthermore, our framework allows us to address synchronization. In this example there are two synchronization problems. First, the two eyes must be kept synchronized. Second, the display must not lag behind head movements. Eye synchronization could be handled by DEMAND_SYNCing rdrL and rdrR, and having their Sync method switch double buffers (assuming that rendering is done using double buffering).

Head synchronization could be achieved by the model object reducing the data rate from head (perhaps 50 events per second) to the sync rate of Render objects (perhaps 10 frames per second). Finally, the frame update rate for Render objects (which is the same as their sync rate) can be dynamically adjusted and so provide graceful degradation of animation continuity should model complexity increase or computing resources decrease [7].

5. Related Work

Research in multimedia is taking place among many different groups – for instance, user interface designers, database implementors, communication protocol engineers, and workstation builders. There seem to be an abundance of ideas and approaches being discussed, yet few unifying concepts. In this section we describe a few of the ideas and approaches that we feel are closely related to our framework.

The role of component networks was motivated by experience with an audio programming package in-

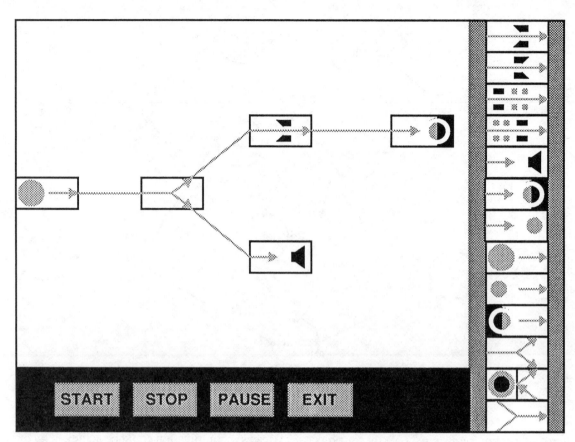

Figure 10   ACE – An Audio Circuit Editor.

tended for a prototype multimedia workstation [8][10]. This workstation contained a number of audio devices which could be connected with software processes to form "audio circuits." ACE, the "audio circuit editor" allowed interactive creation, modification and activation of audio circuits. A screen image from ACE is shown in Figure 10, the right bank is a collection of icons representing different audio devices and processes, the main window shows a circuit which produces an audio data stream from an ADC (analog to digital converter) then tees the stream, one branch going to a DAC (digital to analog converter), the other through a compressor and then to disk. The restriction to audio was a major limitation of ACE. In addition, the underlying audio package used to implement ACE was not object-oriented and could not be readily extended to other devices or other media.

An object-oriented framework for handling digital audio and music is provided by the NeXT Sound Kit and Music Kit [11]. The Sound Kit has two classes: Sound and SoundView. The first is used for actual sound objects and has methods for loading and storing sounds, jects and has methods for loading and storing sounds,

record and playback, editing, and manipulation. The second is for displaying sound data. Sound objects exist in many encodings, but this need not concern an application developer who merely wants to incorporate sound effects. Sound objects are fairly simple and limited in functionality. The Music Kit is more interesting, it is based on the classes Performer, Instrument and Note. Performer and Instrument objects can be connected to form "music networks." A Conductor object coordinates a music network by scheduling the sending of Note objects from Performers to Instruments. The notion of music networks is much like what we have called component networks, also some of the functionality of Conductor objects resembles that of composite objects. However, the Music Kit is specifically for handling music, it shares few concepts with the Sound Kit; it would have to be extended to incorporate multimedia in general, yet it is not clear which parts of its design are specific to music and which parts could be generalized.

Multimedia presentations, we have seen, are constructed by applying temporal transformations to mul-

110

timedia primitives. How these transformations are specified will depend upon the context. Many multimedia authoring systems, for instance, use a timeline representation where temporal transformations can be interactively specified by moving and stretching the timelines. Another approach to constructing complex multimedia presentations is to specify concurrency and synchronization using a "temporal scripting language" [3][6]. For instance, TEMPO [3] provides a set of temporal operators which are used to combine activities – one activity, perhaps the presentation of an audio sequence, can be specified as occurring in parallel, or before, or offset from, a second, visual, activity. A powerful feature of TEMPO is that, provided activities are implemented using a notion of *virtual time* (similar to object time), special effects such as acceleration can be achieved by "filters" which "modulate" virtual time. However, TEMPO does not have a construct similar to component networks so it does not handle activities which interact or communicate with each other.

There has been interest in multimedia within the database community for a number of years, particularly in the storage and retrieval of multimedia documents. Woelk et al. [18] describe extensions to an object-oriented database for handling multimedia input and output. Woelk's model shows the flexibility of treating multimedia as objects but does not treat the problems of composition and synchronization.

More recently a number of authors have proposed multimedia object models which directly address synchronization [9][12][15]. These models take into account device and communication channel characteristics and storage organization. However, the models are used for description and analysis rather than programming – they have yet to be specified within an object-oriented programming language.

6. Conclusion

We have presented an object-oriented framework for multimedia based on a few simple concepts such as ports, sinks and sources. Our hope is that such a framework will make configuring multimedia applications as easy as plugging together modular stereo components.

The framework we have described is not an abstract model, but one that is intended to be implemented and made available to programmers. This, however, is a major task and requires an elaborate hardware platform to fully exercise the model. The platform we have chosen is the NeXTdimension [2] which, in addition to audio processing capabilities, has image compression hardware that allows a video signal to be compressed and stored in real-time. Also NeXTs run the Mach kernel [1]; Mach supports lightweight processes and fast IPC, these features simplify the implementation of active objects and ports. At present we are using C++ to test various parts of the framework, many of the base classes have now been implemented. We are also collecting code for various useful objects – these include a DVE which overlays RGB video with composite (NTSC) video, a 6-degree of freedom trackball, a video disc player, a CD player, and objects for audio recording and playback on a workstation.

In parallel with the framework implementation, we are implementing a trial application which will be used to test the feasibility of complex composites such as shown in Figure 9. We have gathered hardware needed to combine interactive 3d graphics with video. This hardware, which includes a high-performance graphics workstation and a write-once video disc system, is being used to construct a "virtual museum" where a 3d scene of a museum interior is combined with video clips of museum artifacts [16].

Implementation of the framework and trial application is proving an interesting exercise in object-oriented programming. The conceptual model of sources, sinks, ports and connections maps directly into object classes. The implementation makes heavy use of object-oriented techniques such as inheritance and delayed binding. Active objects are essential to the framework, but we have found a fairly simple form of concurrency sufficient.

Future work may focus on two problems. First it would be interesting to develop multimedia objects corresponding to audio and video production equipment – this would also serve as a rigorous test of the framework. Secondly, the conceptual model provides composite multimedia objects but not composite multimedia *values*. It may be possible to integrate composite values, in particular, hypermedia, within the model and then investigate the "loading" and "playing" of hypermedia by composite multimedia objects.

References

[1] Acetta, M., Baron, R., Golub, D., Rashid, R., Tevanian, A., and Young, M. Mach: A New Kernel Foundation for UNIX Development. In *Proc. Summer 1986 USENIX Conf.*, pp. 93-112, July 1986.

[2] Cockroft, G., and Hourvitz, L. NeXTstep: Putting JPEG to Multiple Uses. *Commun. of the ACM 34*, 4 (April 1991), pp. 45.

[3] Dami, L, Fiume, E., Nierstrasz, O. and Tsichritzis, D. Temporal Scripting using TEMPO. In *Active Object Environments*, (ed. D. Tsichritzis) Centre Universitaire d'Informatique, Université de Genève, 1988.

[4] Deutsch, L.P. Design Reuse and Frameworks in the Smalltalk-80 System. In *Software Reusability, Vol. II*, (eds. T.J. Biggerstaff and A.J. Perlis) ACM Press, 57-71, 1989.

[5] Ellis, C. and Gibbs, S. Active Objects: Realities and Possibilities. In *Object-Oriented Concepts, Applications, and Databases*, (eds. W. Kim and F. Lochovsky) Addison-Wesley, 1988.

[6] Fiume, E., Tsichritzis, D., and Dami, L. A Temporal Scripting Language for Object-Oriented Animation. In *Proc. Eurographics' 87*, North-Holland, 1987.

[7] Gibbs, S., Dami, L., and Tsichritzis, D. An Object-Oriented Framework for Multimedia Composition and Synchronisation. *Multimedia – Principles, Systems and Applications*, (ed. L. Kjelldahl) Springer, 1991.

[8] Konstantas, D. and Gibbs, S. Audio Programming: A Framework. (Working paper) Centre Universitaire d'Informatique, Université de Genève, 1987.

[9] Little, T.D.C. and Ghafoor, A. Synchronization and Storage Models for Multimedia Objects. *IEEE Journal on Sel. Areas in Commun. 8*, 3 (April 1990), 413-427.

[10] Naffah, N., White, G., and Gibbs, S. Design Issues of an Intelligent Workstation for the Office, *NCC*, 1986.

[11] *NeXT 1.0 System Reference Manual: Concepts.* NeXT Inc., 1989.

[12] Nicolaou, C. Real-Time Multimedia Communication Systems Architecture. *IEEE Journal on Sel. Areas in Commun. 8*, 3 (April 1990), 391-400.

[13] Papathomas, M. Concurrency Issues in Object-Oriented Programming Languages. In *Object Oriented Development*, (ed. D. Tsichritzis) Centre Universitaire d'Informatique, Université de Genève, 1989.

[14] Press, L. Compuvision or Teleputer? *Commun. of the ACM 33*, 9 (Sept. 1990), 29-36.

[15] Steinmetz, R. Synchronization Properties in Multimedia Systems. *IEEE Journal on Sel. Areas in Commun. 8*, 3 (April 1990), 401-412.

[16] Tsichritzis, D. and Gibbs S. Virtual Museums and Virtual Realities. In *Proc. of the International Conference on Hypermedia and Interactivity in Museums*, 1991.

[17] Wegner, P. Concepts and Paradigms of Object-Oriented Programming. *OOPS Messenger 1*, 1 (Aug. 1990), 7-87.

[18] Woelk, D., Kim, W., and Luther, W. An Object-Oriented Approach to Multimedia Databases. In *Proc. ACM SIGMOD*, 1986, 311-325.

Static Type Checking of Multi-Methods

Rakesh Agrawal   Linda G. DeMichiel   Bruce G. Lindsay

IBM Almaden Research Center
San Jose, California 95120

Abstract

Multi-methods allow method selection to be based on the types of any number of arguments. Languages that currently support multi-methods do not support static type checking. We show how multi-methods can be statically type checked and how information collected at the time of program compilation can be used to make the run-time dispatch of multi-methods more efficient. The results presented can provide the basis for introducing multi-methods in languages with static type checking and for designing new object-oriented paradigms based on multi-methods.

1 Introduction

Most programming languages support the notion of *typed* data. A data type consists of a representation and a set of operations that can be applied to instances of the type. In many object-oriented languages, types are organized in a hierarchy and a *subtype relation* is defined over them. The meaning of this subtype relation usually corresponds to that of *subtype polymorphism*, or *inclusion polymorphism*[4]: A is a subtype of B, A and B not necessarily distinct, exactly when every instance of A is also an instance of B. Operations on the instances of types are defined by *generic functions*, where a generic function corresponds to a set of *methods* and the methods define the type-specific behavior of the generic function. A method is de-

fined for a set of arguments of particular types and can be executed for any objects that are instances of those types or their subtypes. The selection of the method to be executed depends on the types of the actual arguments with which the generic function is invoked. In the presence of subtype polymorphism, this method selection must, in general, occur at run time.

While methods in many object-oriented languages implement multiary operations, in most of these languages, methods are "selfish." That is, there is a single, distinguished argument whose type determines which method is executed when a generic function is called. The remaining arguments are ancillary: they provide values for the method that is selected, but they play no role in method selection itself. Thus, for example, while it is possible in C++ [7] to write a virtual function of the form `float area(shape)`[1] that is dynamically dispatched based on the actual type of `shape` supplied with the function invocation, one cannot write a virtual function of the form `void draw(window, shape)` that is dynamically dispatched based on actual types of both `window` and `shape`.

Multi-methods [3] are a generalization of selfish methods: they allow method selection to be based on the types of all arguments, not just a single argument. Selfish methods can be simulated by multi-methods by associating all but one formal method argument with a most general type. However, in order to simulate multi-methods in a system that does not provide them, the user must resort to awk-

---

[1]The exact syntax is different in C++; we have taken liberty with the syntax to clarify the point.

ward techniques such as currying [5,8].

The integration of multi-methods and statically-typed languages is not well understood. Languages that support multi-methods (e.g., the Common Lisp Object System (CLOS) [2] and its ancestor CommonLoops [3]) do not perform static type checking.

In this paper, we present mechanisms for the static type checking of multi-methods. In addition, we show how these mechanisms allow multi-methods to be more efficiently dispatched at run time. The results presented are intended to provide the basis for introducing multi-methods in statically-typed languages and for designing new object-oriented paradigms based on multi-methods.

The work described here has been performed in the context of Polyglot, a multi-lingual object-oriented database type system that we are designing at the IBM Almaden Research Center. In database type systems, types are persistent and evolving. Type and method definitions come from many sources, such as type library vendors, application developers, and end users. This leads to a separation of processing into three phases:

1. *Type definition*. This phase is akin to schema definition in database parlance. The definitions of types and methods are processed in this phase.

2. *Compilation and type checking*. During program compilation, every generic function invocation is type checked to insure that it cannot result in a run-time type error.

3. *Execution and run-time dispatch*. At run time, appropriate methods are selected for execution on the basis of the actual arguments of the function invocations.

1.1 Organization of the Paper

The organization of this paper is as follows. We formally define the problem of the static type checking of multi-methods in Section 2. The main source of difficulty is the following: Because of subtype polymorphism, there can be more than one method that is applicable for a generic function invocation, and it is not always possible to determine at compile time which method will be executed at run time.[2] Given a generic function invocation, and a set of methods that are applicable for that invocation, a precedence relationship is needed to select the method that in some sense most closely "matches" the invocation. Section 3 discusses various rules for establishing such method precedence. Section 4 describes our methodology for the static type checking of multi-methods. This consists of two steps. First, at the time of method definition, it is insured that the methods of a generic function are mutually consistent. Sufficient conditions for insuring such consistency are given in Section 5. Next, at the time of program compilation, every static function invocation is type checked to determine its validity. This step is described in Section 6. Section 7 discusses the run-time dispatch of multi-methods. We discuss related work in Section 8. Section 9 summarizes the results of our work.

1.2 Notation

In the discussion that follows, we represent the subtype relation by $\preceq$. If $A \preceq B \wedge A \neq B$, we say that A is a *proper subtype* of B and represent this relation by $\prec$. Since the proper subtype relation is a partial order, we can view such a system of types as a directed acyclic graph. There is a path from A to B if and only if A is a subtype of B. If $A \preceq B$, we also say that B is a *supertype* of A.

We will use upper case letters to denote types and the corresponding lower case letters to denote their instances. Thus, we will write a to denote an instance of type A.

We will use upper case letters to denote generic functions. We will denote a particular method m_k of an n-ary generic function M as $m_k(T_k^1, T_k^2, \ldots, T_k^n) \rightarrow R_k$, where T_k^i is the type of the ith formal argument of method m_k, and where R_k is the type of the result. We will sometimes not

---

[2]This problem also exists for languages supporting only selfish methods. The solutions we present apply to such languages as well.

write the result type of such a method. The call to the generic function will be denoted without a subscript on m.

Finally, in our figures, we will draw an arrow from subtype to supertype to denote the subtype relationship.

2 Formal Statement of the Problem

Static type checking in the absence of polymorphism requires that we insure at compile time that every operation receives the proper number of arguments and that these arguments are instances of the proper data types. To allow for subtype polymorphism, this constraint is relaxed in the following way: We assume that it is admissible for a variable or a formal argument of a function to be bound at run time to a value that is an instance of its static type or an instance of any subtype of its static type. However, because instances of subtypes may be substituted for instances of supertypes at run time, the method that is selected for execution at run time for a given generic function invocation may be different from the method that would have been selected were the arguments of the same types as those of the static call. Therefore, for each generic function invocation, we need to be able to determine that there exists some method whose formal argument types are supertypes of the types of the static argument types, that the run-time type of each actual argument will be a subtype of the type of the corresponding static argument, and that the run-time type of the result will be consistent with the context in which it occurs.

In the following, we consider the type checking of expressions of the form

$$r : R \leftarrow f(g(\ldots h(m(\ldots)), \ldots), \ldots), \ldots).$$

In the case in which the result of the generic function invocation is assigned to a variable, the result type of the function invocation must be a subtype of the type of that variable. In the case where the result of the generic function invocation is passed

as an argument to an enclosing function invocation, the result type of the nested function invocation must be acceptable as the type of the corresponding argument of the enclosing function invocation.

Formally, given a generic function M, where M consists of the set of methods $\{m_1, \ldots, m_m\}$,

$$m_1(T_1^1, T_1^2, \ldots, T_1^n) \rightarrow R_1$$
$$\vdots$$
$$m_m(T_m^1, T_m^2, \ldots, T_m^n) \rightarrow R_m$$

and given a static generic function invocation

$$m(T^1, \ldots, T^n)$$

where $T^1, \ldots, T^n$ are the static types of the arguments and are known, the problem is to insure at compile time that the following two conditions hold:

1. There is at least one method of M that can be selected for execution at run time for arguments of types $T^1, \ldots, T^n$.

2. If a method $m_k(T_k^1, T_k^2, \ldots, T_k^n) \rightarrow R_k$ can be selected for execution at run time due to the occurrence of instances of subtypes of any of the static argument types, then:

   a. If the result of the function invocation $m(T^1, \ldots, T^n)$ is assigned to a variable

   $$r : R \leftarrow m(T^1, \ldots, T^n)$$

   then the result type R_k is a subtype of the type R of the receiver r.

   b. If the result of the function invocation $m(T^1, \ldots, T^n)$ is passed as an argument to an enclosing function invocation

   $$\tilde{m}(\tilde{T}^1, \ldots, m(T^1, \ldots, T^n), \ldots, \tilde{T}^p)$$

   then it can be verified that conditions (1) and (2) hold for the static invocation $\tilde{m}(\tilde{T}^1, \ldots, R_k, \ldots, \tilde{T}^p)$.

Condition (1) guarantees that the situation can never arise at run time in which there is no method that is applicable for the actual arguments of the generic function. Condition (2) guarantees that no matter which method is executed, its result will be consistent with the context in which it occurs. If we are able to guarantee that these conditions hold for all generic function invocations, then it is possible to guarantee at compile time that no invocation of a generic function will result in a type error at run time.

To simplify our presentation in the discussion that follows, we assume that all methods of a generic function have the same number of arguments, referred to as the *arity* of the function. This requirement is not necessary provided that each method has a fixed number of arguments, since the methods can be partitioned into equivalence classes by number of arguments. We also assume that no two methods of a generic function are permitted to have identical formal argument types, otherwise it would be impossible to select between them solely on the basis of the argument types of the function invocation. Our discussion is neutral with regard to the issue of whether generic functions are themselves objects or whether a generic function consists solely of a set of methods.

3   Method Applicability and Method Specificity

Because of subtype polymorphism, there can be more than one method that is applicable for a generic function invocation, and it is not possible to determine at compile time exactly which method will be executed at run time.

3.1   Method Applicability and Confusability

Given a generic function invocation, $m(T^1, \ldots, T^n)$, we say that a method $m_k(T_k^1, \ldots, T_k^n)$ is *applicable* for that invocation if and only if $\forall i,\ 1 \le i \le n,\ T^i \preceq T_k^i$.

If two methods are both applicable for some function invocation, we say that they are *confusable*. Formally, methods $m_1(T_1^1, \ldots, T_1^n)$ and $m_2(T_2^1, \ldots, T_2^n)$ are *confusable* if $\forall i,\ 1 \le i \le n$,

there exists a type T^i, such that $T^i \preceq T_1^i \wedge T^i \preceq T_2^i$; otherwise they are *non-confusable*.

Note that confusability is not transitive. Consider the following type hierarchy and the meth-

ods $m_1(A)$, $m_2(B)$, and $m_3(C)$. Methods $m_1(A)$ and $m_2(B)$ are confusable, and methods $m_2(B)$ and $m_3(C)$ are confusable, but methods $m_1(A)$ and $m_3(C)$ are not confusable.

3.2   Method Specificity

In general, more than one method can be applicable for a generic function invocation. Given a set of methods that are applicable for a generic function invocation, a precedence relationship is needed to select the method that in some sense most closely *matches* the invocation. If one method has precedence over another for a given invocation, we say that it is *more specific*.

Given a set of confusable methods, we can identify the following representative mechanisms for determining method specificity, drawing upon the design choices in current object-oriented languages: i) arbitrary global precedence, ii) argument subtype precedence, iii) argument order precedence, iv) global type precedence, v) inheritance order precedence, and vi) arbitrary local precedence.

The first four of these mechanisms are global in that they establish a global precedence relationship over a set of confusable methods. The last two are local in that they allow precedence relationships to be different for instances of different types. These mechanisms are not all equally powerful. We discuss their relative advantages and disadvantages below. Table 1 summarizes their relative power in determining method specificity.

3.2.1   Arbitrary Global Precedence

The user is free to order confusable methods in any way the user pleases.

	single inheritance selfish methods	single inheritance multi-methods	multiple inheritance selfish methods	multiple inheritance multi-methods
arbitrary global precedence	✓	✓	✓	✓
argument subtype precedence	✓			
argument order precedence	✓	✓		
global type precedence	✓	✓	✓	✓
inheritance order precedence	✓	✓	✓	✓
arbitrary local precedence	✓	✓	✓	?

Table 1: Relative power of method precedence orderings

While simple, this approach is undesirable for several reasons. Aside from the burden it imposes on the user, it may permit orderings that violate tacit notions of method specificity, or orderings in which certain methods can never be executed. If the user is not careful, cycles may be created in the precedence relationship.

We are not aware of any language that allows a completely arbitrary global ordering of confusable methods.

3.2.2 Argument Subtype Precedence

The subtype relationships between the corresponding formal argument types of two confusable methods $m_i(T_i^1, T_i^2, \ldots, T_i^n)$ and $m_j(T_j^1, T_j^2, \ldots, T_j^n)$ are used to establish the precedence between those methods. If $\forall k$, $1 \leq k \leq n$, $T_i^k \preceq T_j^k$, and $\exists l$, $1 \leq l \leq n$, such that $T_i^l \prec T_j^l$, we say that m_i and m_j are in an *argument subtype relationship* and that m_i precedes m_j.

Consider, the types A and B, where $B \prec A$, and the confusable methods $m_1(A, A, B)$ and $m_2(A, B, B)$. Since all the formal argument types of m_2 are subtypes of the corresponding formal argument types of m_1 with the second argument type being additionally a proper subtype, m_2 is more specific than m_1.

We show in the appendix that argument subtype precedence is sufficient to establish precedence between confusable methods in a language that supports only single inheritance and selfish method selection.

As an example of such a language, we cite the versions of C++ [12] that predated the introduction of multiple inheritance to that language.

In a single inheritance language with multi-methods, however, argument subtype precedence is not sufficient to order confusable methods. Consider the types A and B, where $B \prec A$, and the confusable methods $m_1(A, B)$ and $m_2(B, A)$. The invocation $m(b, b)$ can be resolved neither to $m_1(A, B)$ nor to $m_2(B, A)$ using only argument subtype precedence.

Argument subtype precedence is likewise not sufficient to order confusable methods in a selfish method language that supports multiple inheritance. Consider the following type hierarchy and the methods $m_1(A)$ and $m_2(B)$. The invoca-

tion $m(c)$ can be resolved neither to $m_1(A)$ nor to $m_2(B)$ using only argument subtype precedence.

3.2.3 Argument Order Precedence

An *argument order* is a total order over the argument positions of the methods of a generic function. It may correspond to the left-to-right ordering of arguments or it may be any permutation of that order. The method $m_i(T_i^1, \ldots, T_i^n)$ precedes the method $m_j(T_j^1, \ldots, T_j^n)$ according to a given argument order if there is some argument position k, $1 \leq k \leq n$, such that $\forall l$, $1 \leq l < k$, $T_i^l = T_j^l$, and $T_i^k \prec T_j^k$.

Consider the types A and B, where $B \prec A$, the confusable methods $m_1(A, B, A, B)$ and $m_2(A, B, B, A)$, and left-to-right argument order. The formal argument types of the two methods differ first in the third position, where the formal argument type of m_2 is a proper subtype of the formal argument type of m_1. Therefore, m_2 is more specific than m_1 according to argument order precedence.

We show in the appendix that argument order precedence is sufficient to establish precedence between confusable methods in a language that supports multi-methods but admits only single inheritance.

In the case of multiple inheritance, confusable methods can have formal argument types that are not in any subtype relationship. Argument order precedence is not sufficient to determine method precedence in this case. Consider again the type hierarchy shown in the figure above and the methods $m_1(C, A)$, $m_2(C, B)$. The invocation $m(c, c)$ can be resolved neither to $m_1(C, A)$ nor to $m_2(C, B)$.

3.2.4 Global Type Precedence

A *global type order* is a partial order α, such that i) if $A \prec B$, then $A \alpha B$, and ii) if there is a type C such that $C \alpha D$ and $C \alpha E$, then either $D \alpha E$ or $E \alpha D$.

Given any two confusable methods $m_i(T_i^1, T_i^2, \ldots, T_i^n)$ and $m_j(T_j^1, T_j^2, \ldots, T_j^n)$, consider their formal argument types in a prespecified order (such as left-to-right) and find the first argument position in which the formal argument types of m_i and m_j differ, say k. Method m_i is more specific than method m_j according to *global type precedence* if and only if $T_i^k \alpha T_j^k$ in the global type ordering.

Consider, again the type hierarchy shown in the figure above and the methods $m_1(C, A)$ and $m_2(C, B)$. If $A \alpha B$, then m_1 is more specific than m_2.

We show in the appendix that global type precedence is sufficient to order confusable methods in a multiple inheritance language with multi-methods.

Note that the global type ordering need not be a total order. For example, consider the following type hierarchy. Types C and D need not be ordered with respect to each other.

3.2.5 *Inheritance Order Precedence*

In a global type ordering, the precedence between two types is required to be the same for all common subtypes of those types. In a local type ordering, on the other hand, the precedence between the supertypes of a type can be freely chosen as long as the precedence relationships defined by their supertypes are not violated. Thus, the precedence between two types need not be the same for all of their common subtypes. The precedence between the supertypes of a type T may be explicitly specified, or it may be inferred from the lexical order in which they occur in the definition of type T.

Unlike the previous mechanisms, where method specificity depends on the types of the formal arguments of the method definitions, *inheritance order precedence* requires method specificity to be determined on the basis of the types of the arguments of the generic function invocation. Given two methods $m_i(T_i^1, T_i^2, \ldots, T_i^n)$ and $m_j(T_j^1, T_j^2, \ldots, T_j^n)$ that are applicable for a generic function invocation $m(T^1, T^2, \ldots, T^n)$, consider their formal arguments in a prespecified order (such as left-to-right) and find the first argument position in which the formal argument types of m_i and m_j differ, say k. If $T_i^k \propto T_j^k$ in the local type ordering of T^k, then m_i is more specific than m_j, and vice versa.

Formally, a *local type ordering for a type C* is a total order $\propto_C$ over C and its supertypes such that if $C \prec A$ and $C \prec B$, then $C \propto_C A$, $C \propto_C B$, and either $A \propto_C B$ or $B \propto_C A$. Furthermore, if $C \prec B$, and if $D \propto_B E$ in the local type ordering for type B, then $D \propto_C E$ in the local type ordering for the type C, and this rule is recursively applied.

For example, consider the following type hierarchy and the methods $m_1(A)$ and $m_2(B)$. We

have that $A \propto_C B$ in the local type ordering for type C and that $B \propto_D A$ in the local type ordering for type D. Method $m_1(A)$ is more specific than method $m_2(B)$ for the invocation $m(c)$, while method $m_2(B)$ is more specific than method $m_1(A)$ for the invocation $m(d)$.

We show in the appendix that inheritance order precedence is sufficient to determine method specificity in a multiple inheritance language with multi-methods.

CLOS is an example of a language that uses inheritance order precedence to determine method specificity.

3.2.6 Arbitrary Local Precedence

C++ allows method precedence to be explicitly specified by the user as part of type definition. We call this mechanism for resolving method specificity *arbitrary local precedence*. For example, consider again the following type hierarchy and the methods

$m_1(A)$ and $m_2(B)$. In C++, it is possible to specify in the definition of type C that method $m_1(A)$ is more specific than method $m_2(B)$, and in the definition of type D that method $m_2(B)$ is more specific than method $m_1(A)$. The invocation $m(c)$ causes $m_1(A)$ to be dispatched, while the invocation $m(d)$ causes $m_2(B)$ to be dispatched.

This approach is feasible in C++ because C++ methods are selfish methods. However, arbitrary local precedence does not appear to generalize cleanly to multi-methods.

4   Static Type Checking of Multi-Methods

Having discussed mechanisms for establishing a method precedence order, we can now state the central result.

Theorem 1 *Multi-methods can be statically type checked as follows:*

1. *Insure that all method definitions are mutually consistent.*

   Two methods $m_i(T_i^1, T_i^2, \ldots, T_i^n) \rightarrow R_i$ and $m_j(T_j^1, T_j^2, \ldots, T_j^n) \rightarrow R_j$ of a generic function M are *mutually consistent* if whenever they are both applicable for arguments of types $T^1, \ldots, T^n$ and m_i is more specific than m_j, then $R_i \preceq R_j$. A generic function is consistent if all of its methods are mutually consistent.

2. *For each static generic function invocation $m(T^1, \ldots, T^n)$, apply the following procedure:*

   a. *Determine that there is at least one method that is applicable for the invocation.*

   b. *Find the definition of the most specific applicable method m_k for the argument types $T^1, \ldots, T^n$.*

   c. *Verify for the method $m_k(T_1^k, \ldots, T_n^k) \rightarrow R_k$ selected in step (2b) that:*

      i. *If the result of the function invocation $m(T^1, \ldots, T^n)$ is assigned to a variable*

      $$r : R \leftarrow m(T^1, \ldots, T^n)$$

      then $R_k \preceq R$.

      ii. *If the result of the function invocation $m(T^1, \ldots, T^n)$ is passed as an argument to an enclosing function invocation*

      $$\tilde{m}(\tilde{T}^1, \ldots, m(T^1, \ldots, T^n), \ldots, \tilde{T}^p)$$

      then step (2) is applied to the static invocation

      $$\tilde{m}(\tilde{T}^1, \ldots, R_k, \ldots, \tilde{T}^p).$$

Step (1) is performed once at method definition time. Step (2) is performed at compile time for each generic function invocation.

Proof: If step (2a) yields a method m_i, we are guaranteed that there will be at least one method of M that can be selected for execution at run time. Let m_k be the most specific applicable method for the static argument types selected in step (2b). If method m_r, different from m_k, is selected at run time, then m_r will be more specific than m_k for the actual argument types, and the definition of method consistency implies that $R_r \preceq R_k$. Since step (2ci) guarantees that $R_k \preceq R$, it follows from the transitivity of the subtype relationship that $R_r \preceq R$ and there cannot be a run-time type error in the case of assignment. The correctness of step (2cii) can be shown by induction on the structure of the expression. ∎

We now discuss mechanisms for achieving steps (1) and (2).

5 Conditions for a Consistent System

Before presenting conditions for insuring that a generic function is consistent, we need the definitions of confusable set, method graph, method precedence graph, result graph, and graph conformance.

A *confusable set* of methods is a maximal set C such that methods m_i and m_j are in C if there are $k \geq 0$ methods m_1, m_2, ..., m_k such that m_i is confusable with m_1, m_1 is confusable with m_2,..., and m_k is confusable with m_j. If a method is not confusable with any other method, it forms a singleton confusable set. The confusable sets over a set of methods M thus disjointly partition M.

A *method graph* for a confusable set is an undirected graph such that

1. For every method m_i in the confusable set, there is a node labeled by that method.
2. There is an edge between the nodes labeled m_i and m_j if and only if m_i and m_j are confusable.

A *method precedence graph* for a confusable set is a directed graph such that

1. For every method m_i in the confusable set, there is a node labeled by that method.

2. There is an arc from node m_i to m_j if and only if m_i and m_j are confusable and m_i is more specific than m_j.

A method precedence graph induces a graph over the result types of the corresponding methods. A *result graph* for a confusable set is a directed graph such that

1. For every result type R_i that is a result type of some method m_i in the confusable set, there is a node labeled by that result type.
2. There is an arc from node R_i to R_j if and only if there is an arc from node m_i to m_j in the method precedence graph.

A directed graph G_1 *conforms* to a directed graph G_2 if for every arc from node i to node j in G_1, there is a path in G_2 from i to j.

5.1 Sufficient Conditions

Theorem 2 *A generic function is consistent if the following two conditions both hold for every confusable set:*

1. *For every edge between two nodes in the method graph, there is at least one arc between those same nodes in the method precedence graph.*
2. *The result graph conforms to the type graph.*

Proof: First, from the maximality of confusable sets, no two methods of a generic function belonging to different confusable sets can be confusable, and hence by definition all such methods are mutually consistent.

For two methods m_i and m_j belonging to the same confusable set, condition (1) guarantees that if they are both applicable for some argument types, then the precedence between them has been established. Condition (2) guarantees that if m_i is more specific than m_j, then the result type of m_i is a subtype of the result type of m_j. ∎

Corollary 1 *A generic function is consistent if every confusable set of this function is a singleton.*

Corollary 2 *All methods in a confusable set of a generic function are mutually consistent if every method has the same result type.*

Theorem 2 implies that if the method precedence graph has a cycle, the methods involved in the cycle must have the same result type for condition (2) to hold. A cycle can arise in the method precedence graph if a local mechanism such as inheritance order precedence is used to resolve method specificity, as is the case in CLOS.

In a system that requires the condition stated in Corollary 1 to hold, many methods can be associated with a given generic function, but at most one method can ever be applicable for any function invocation. Such a system has no need for recourse to run-time discrimination for method selection, since if there is an applicable method for a given static function invocation, it is always unique. It is necessary only to verify at compile time that an applicable method exists and that its result type is consistent with the expression context of the function invocation. Ada is an example of a language that supports *function overloading* in this sense, but not run-time discrimination.

5.2 Verification of Method Consistency

We now present an algorithm for the construction of the method precedence graph of a generic function and the verification of the consistency of its method definitions. The algorithm for this step, *ProcessMethods*, uses three subroutines:

1. *Confusable*: This subroutine determines whether two given methods are confusable.

2. *ComputePrecedence*: This subroutine determines which of two given methods is the more specific.

3. *CheckConsistency*: This subroutine determines whether two given methods are consistent and creates the method precedence graph.

procedure *ProcessMethods*(*generic-function*)
    let m be the number of methods of *generic-function*
    for i **in** 1 **to** m **do**
      for j **in** $i+1$ **to** m **do**
        /* check if m_i and m_j are confusable */
        if *Confusable*(m_i, m_j) **then**
          /* find the relative ordering of m_i and m_j */
          $order := ComputePrecedence(m_i, m_j)$

          /* check if m_i and m_j are consistent */
          if *CheckConsistency*(m_i, m_j, *order*) =
            Inconsistent **then**
              Output("m_i, m_j are inconsistent")
      od
    od

function *Confusable*(m_i, m_j)
    returns {*True, False*}
  let the argument types of m_i be $T_i^1, \ldots, T_i^n$
  let the argument types of m_j be $T_j^1, \ldots, T_j^n$
  for k **in** 1 **to** n **do**
    if T_i^k and T_j^k have no common subtype **then**
      return *False* /* m_i and m_j not confusable */
  od
  return *True* /* m_i and m_j are confusable */

function *ComputePrecedence*(m_i, m_j)
    returns {$\lhd$, $\rhd$, $\diamond$}
  let n be the arity of m_i and m_j
  let the argument types of m_i be $T_i^1, \ldots, T_i^n$
  let the argument types of m_j be $T_j^1, \ldots, T_j^n$
  for k **in** 1 **to** n in the prespecified argument order **do**
    if T_i^k is not the same as T_j^k **then**
      /* this position determines the ordering */
      if $T_i^k < T_j^k$ **then**
        return $\lhd$
      else if $T_j^k < T_i^k$ **then**
        return $\rhd$
      else /* local precedence ordering case */
        return $\diamond$
  od

function *CheckConsistency*(m_i, m_j, *order*)
    returns {*Consistent, Inconsistent*}
  if *order* = $\lhd$ **then** /* m_i more specific than m_j */
    if $R_i \not\preceq R_j$ **then**
      return *Inconsistent*
    else create an arc from m_i to m_j
      in the method precedence graph
  else if *order* = $\rhd$ **then** /* m_j more specific than m_i */
    if $R_j \not\preceq R_i$ **then**
      return *Inconsistent*
    else create an arc from m_j to m_i
  else /* *order* = $\diamond$ */
    /* cannot order m_j and m_i */
    if $R_j \neq R_i$ **then**
      return *Inconsistent*
    else create an arc from m_i to m_j
      and another from m_j to m_i
  return *Consistent*

5.2.1 Remarks

1. Functions *Confusable* and *ComputePrecedence* both examine the formal argument types of the two methods under consideration in some specified order. In an actual implementation, the two subroutines may be merged into one for efficiency. We have not done so in the description above for ease of exposition.

2. The function *ComputePrecedence* is dependent on the mechanism used by the language for determining method specificity. If arbitrary global precedence or arbitrary local precedence is used, the precedence between every two confusable methods is specified by the user. We do not discuss these cases further. In all other cases, the relationships between the types of corresponding formal arguments of confusable methods is used to determine precedence. We define a relationship $<$ on distinct types in the system. For argument subtype precedence and argument order precedence, $<$ is the same as the proper subtype relationship $\prec$. For global type precedence and inheritance order precedence, we define an augmented type graph and define $<$ as any topological sort on this augmented type graph. For global type precedence, the augmented type graph consists of the type graph representing the proper subtype relationship augmented with arcs representing the global type order α. For inheritance order precedence, the augmented type graph consists of the type graph representing the proper subtype relationship augmented with arcs representing all local type orderings α. In the latter case, the augmented type graph may contain cycles, and types in each strongly connected component are coalesced into a virtual node before the topological sort.

3. In *CheckConsistency*, instead of forming a result graph and checking that it conforms to the type graph, we check that $R_i \preceq R_j$ whenever an arc is to be created from m_i to m_j in the method precedence graph. The following lemma guarantees that this procedure is correct:

Lemma 1 *The result graph conforms to the type graph if for every arc from R_i to R_j in the result graph, $R_i \preceq R_j$.*

Proof: Follows from the transitivity of the subtype relationship. ∎

4. Determining whether two methods are confusable requires testing whether corresponding formal argument types have a common subtype. Testing whether the result graph conforms to the type graph also depends on determining whether two types are in a subtype relationship. In order to make subtype relationship tests fast, we maintain a compressed transitive closure of the subtype relationship using the technique described in [1]. An index and a set of ranges are associated with each type. If the index of one type falls into a range of another type, then the first type is a subtype of the second. Furthermore, if any of the ranges associated with two types overlap, then the two types have common subtypes in the overlapping range. Using this technique, we can test subtype relationships in constant time if the type hierarchy is a directed tree (single inheritance). If the type hierarchy is a directed acyclic graph (multiple inheritance), experimental results show that subtype relationships can be tested in essentially constant time[1], and, in the worst case (bipartite graph), in $O(log(n))$ time, where n is the number of types in the system.

5.2.2 Complexity of the Algorithm

ProcessMethods calls functions *Confusable* and *ComputePrecedence* and *CheckConsistency* each $O(m(m+1)/2)$ times, where m is the number of methods of the generic function. Functions *Confusable* and *ComputePrecedence* each require $O(n)$ argument type comparisons, where n is the arity of the generic function. Function *CheckConsistency* requires one subtype test.

5.3 Construction of the Confusable Sets from the Method Precedence Graph

The confusable sets for the generic function correspond to the connected components of the method precedence graph. They can be obtained in time linear in the number of nodes and edges of the method precedence graph by using Tarjan's algorithm[13]. Tarjan's algorithm yields, at the same time, a topological sort of the methods in each confusable set such that if method m_i is more specific than m_j, then method m_i precedes m_j in the sort order. If the method precedence graph contains cycles, Tarjan's algorithm condenses non-trivial strongly connected components (methods involved in cycles) into virtual nodes, which we call *blobs*, and yields a topological sort of the resulting acyclic graph.

6 Checking the Validity of Generic Function Invocations

In the previous section, we discussed the validation of method consistency that is performed at type definition time. We now turn to a discussion of the type checking of generic function invocations that is done at compile time. Recall from Theorem 1 that this requires finding the most specific applicable method for the static argument types and verifying that the result type of this method is consistent with its context.

Finding the most specific applicable method involves two steps:

1. Finding the confusable set in which such a method is contained.

2. Finding the most specific applicable method within that confusable set.

6.1 Finding the Confusable Set

We say that a generic function invocation $m(T^1, \ldots, T^n)$ is *covered by* a confusable set S if there exists a method $m_s \in S$ such that m_s is applicable for m.

Lemma 2 *A generic function invocation $m(T^1, \ldots, T^n)$ is covered by at most one confusable set.*

Proof (by contradiction): Assume that m is covered by two distinct confusable sets, say S_1 and S_2. This implies that there exists a method $m_{s_1} \in S_1$ and a method $m_{s_2} \in S_2$ such that both m_{s_1} and m_{s_2} are applicable for m. This in turn implies that $\forall i$, $1 \leq i \leq n$, $T^i \preceq T^i_{m_{s_1}} \wedge T^i \preceq T^i_{m_{s_2}}$. This, however, implies that m_{s_1} and m_{s_2} are confusable, which contradicts the assumption that S_1 and S_2 are distinct confusable sets. ∎

Before presenting an algorithm for determining the confusable set which covers a generic function invocation, we need a definition and a lemma.

Given a confusable set S for a generic function M of arity n, and an argument position i, $1 \leq i \leq n$, we say that type $\hat{T}$ is an element of $tops(S, i)$ for M if and only if there exists a method $m_j(T^1_j, \ldots, T^n_j) \in S$ such that $\hat{T} = T^i_j$ and there is no method $m_k(T^1_k, \ldots, T^n_k) \in S$ such that $\hat{T} \prec T^i_k$.

Lemma 3 *If a generic function invocation $m(T^1, \ldots, T^n)$ is covered by a confusable set S, then $\forall i$, $1 \leq i \leq n$, $\exists \hat{T}^i | \hat{T}^i \in tops(S, i) \wedge T^i \preceq \hat{T}^i$.*

Proof: If a generic function invocation $m(T^1, \ldots, T^n)$ is covered by a confusable set S, then by definition there exists a method $m(\tilde{T}^1, \ldots, \tilde{T}^n)$ in S such that $\forall i$, $1 \leq i \leq n$, $T^i \preceq \tilde{T}^i$. By definition of *tops*, $\forall i$, $1 \leq i \leq n$, $\exists \hat{T}^i | \hat{T}^i \in tops(S, i) \wedge \tilde{T}^i \preceq \hat{T}^i$. The lemma then follows from the transitivity of the subtype relationship. ∎

Note that this lemma provides a necessary, but not a sufficient condition for a generic function invocation be covered by a confusable set. Consider the following type hierarchy and the methods

$m_1(A, D)$ and $m_2(C, B)$. Now consider the function invocation $m(a, b)$. Clearly there is no applicable method for this invocation, but the condition stated with the lemma is satisfied.

Similarly, it is possible for the *tops* sets of more than one confusable set to satisfy the lemma condition for a given invocation. Consider, for example, the following type hierarchy and the methods $m_1(A_1, A_2)$, $m_2(A_2, A_3)$,

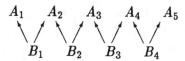

$m_3(A_3, A_4)$, and $m_4(A_1, A_5)$. There are two confusable sets: $CS_1 = \{m_1, m_2, m_3\}$ and $CS_2 = \{m_4\}$. Furthermore, $tops(CS_1, 1) = \{A_1, A_2, A_3\}$, $tops(CS_1, 2) = \{A_2, A_3, A_4\}$, $tops(CS_2, 1) = \{A_1\}$, and $tops(CS_2, 2) = \{A_5\}$. For the function invocation $m(b_1, b_4)$, the tops test is satisfied both by CS_1 and CS_2.

Thus, this lemma can be used to construct an algorithm that can be used to identify the confusable sets in which the most specific applicable method for a given invocation may *potentially* be found. Finding such a set does not guarantee that an applicable method actually exists for the invocation, nor does it guarantee that at most one such set will be found. However, if no such confusable set is found, then it is guaranteed that there is no applicable method.

6.1.1 Algorithm for Constructing Tops Sets

let c be the number of confusable sets
let n be the arity of the generic function
for i **in** 1 **to** c **do**
  let m_i be the number of methods in confusable set i
  for j **in** 1 **to** n **do**
    $tops(S_i, j) = \emptyset$
    for k **in** 1 **to** m_i **do**
      /* T_k^j is the type of the argument of
        method m_k at position j */
      if $\exists T_{S_i} \in tops(S_i, j)$ such that $T_k^j \preceq T_{S_i}$ **then**
        continue with next value of k
      else if $\exists T_{S_i} \in tops(S_i, j)$
        such that $T_{S_i} \preceq T_k^j$ **then**
        /* T_k^j replaces all such $T_{S_i} \in tops(S_i, j)$ */
        $\forall T_{S_i} \in tops(S_i, j)$ such that $T_{S_i} \preceq T_k^j$,

remove T_{S_i} from $tops(S_i, j)$
        add T_k^j to $tops(S_i, j)$
      else /* T_k^j is a new member of $tops(S_i, j)$ */
        add T_k^j to $tops(S_i, j)$
    od
  od
od

The *tops* sets are determined at method definition time. The complexity of this algorithm is linear in the total number of methods of the generic function. For each argument position of every method, the subtype relationship of the type of that formal argument is tested against the members of the corresponding *tops* set. These tests may require $2 \times |tops|$ comparisons.

6.1.2 Algorithm for Finding Confusable Sets for a Function Invocation

We now give the algorithm for finding the confusable sets in which the most specific applicable method for a given generic function invocation $m(T^1, \ldots, T^n)$ may potentially be found.

let c be the number of confusable sets
let n be the arity of the generic function
$confusable\text{-}sets = \emptyset$
for i **in** 1 **to** c **do**
  for j **in** 1 **to** n **do**
    if $\forall T \in tops(S_i, j)\ T^j \npreceq T$ **then**
      /* go to next confusable set */
      continue with next value of i
  od
  /* found a potential confusable set */
  add S_i to $confusable\text{-}sets$
od
return $confusable\text{-}sets$

The complexity of this algorithm is $O(c \times n \times |tops|)$, where $|tops|$ is the size of the largest *tops* set.

If more than one confusable set is identified, the algorithm for finding the most specific method is applied to each such set. Once an applicable method is found, the algorithm can terminate and need not examine other confusable sets because of Lemma 2.

6.2 Finding the Most Specific Applicable Method

We first consider the case where the method precedence graph for the confusable set is acyclic.

As we stated in Section 5.3, a by-product of the algorithm for the construction of confusable sets is a topological sort of the methods in each confusable set such that if method m_i is more specific than m_j then m_i precedes m_j in the sort order.

Given a confusable set and a generic function invocation, the following algorithm finds the most specific applicable method for that invocation, if such a method exists.

1. Examine the methods in the confusable set in the topological sort order.

2. If the method under consideration is applicable for the function invocation, stop; otherwise, continue to the next method.

3. If no applicable method is found, flag the invocation as invalid.

The complexity of this algorithm is $O(m_c \times n)$, where m_c is the number of methods in the confusable set and n is the function arity. The applicability test for a method is linear in number of arguments, and the test for each argument is a subtype relationship test.

We now consider the case where the method precedence graph for the confusable set contains cycles. Recall that this can occur when inheritance order precedence is used to determine method specificity.

As stated in Section 5.3, methods involved in cycles are grouped into virtual nodes, called *blobs*. We obtain a topological sort of the resulting acyclic graph, but do not order methods within blobs.

We again proceed in topological sort order. If the method under consideration is applicable and a non-blob method, it is the most specific applicable method for the given invocation. If the method under consideration is applicable and a blob method, it must be tested for specificity against all remaining applicable methods in the blob. If no applicable blob or non-blob method is found, the invocation is flagged as invalid. The time complexity of this procedure is still $O(m_c \times n)$.

Note that if the most specific applicable method is to be found for the purpose of validating the result type of the generic function invocation, and an applicable blob method has been identified, it is not necessary to examine additional methods in the blob, since as a result of Theorem 2, all methods in a blob are required to have the same result type.

6.3 Validating the Result Type

Once the most specific applicable method for the static function invocation has been found, its result type is checked for consistency with the function invocation context as described in Section 4.

7 Run-time Dispatch

To improve the efficiency of the run-time dispatch of multi-methods, we save information obtained during the type checking of generic function invocations and associate it with these invocations for use at run time. Specifically, when examining the methods in the confusable set at compile time to find the most specific applicable method for a function invocation, we check for each method if it is confusable with the invocation. If it is confusable, it is saved; otherwise, it is discarded. Thus, a subset of the topological ordering is saved with the function invocation.

For example, consider the following type hierarchy and the confusable set consisting of

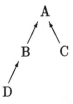

$m_1(A)$, $m_2(B)$, $m_3(C)$, and $m_4(D)$. A valid topological sort of these methods is $\{m_4(D), m_3(C), m_2(B), m_1(A)\}$. Given a static function invocation, $m(b)$, we save a subset of this topological sort, namely $\{m_4(D), m_2(B)\}$, with the invocation. We do not save $m_3(C)$ because it is not confusable with $m(b)$, and $m_1(A)$ is not saved because the search stops as soon as the first applicable method is found.

If the method precedence graph contains blobs, we may still need to examine all methods in these blobs at run time. For example, consider the following type hierarchy. Assume that $B \propto_D C$ in the

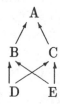

local type ordering for type D and that $C \propto_E B$ in the local type ordering for type E. Consider the confusable set consisting of $m_1(A)$, $m_2(B)$, and $m_3(C)$. Clearly, $m_2(B)$ and $m_3(C)$ are in a blob, and $m_1(A)$ is less specific than both of them. Given a function invocation, $m(a)$, we will need to save the blob consisting of $m_2(B)$ and $m_3(C)$ and examine it at run time because either $m_2(B)$ or $m_3(C)$ might be selected at run time, depending on whether the actual argument is of type D or E respectively.

8   Related Work

The use of multi-method function dispatch appears to have originated with CommonLoops [3]. The Common Lisp Object System (CLOS) [2] supports multi-method dispatch using inheritance order precedence. Type errors are detected at run time when no applicable method can be found for a function invocation.

Lécluse and Richard[10] characterize multi-method dispatch in terms of structural subtyping. Whenever two confusable methods are not ordered by argument subtype precedence, they require that additional methods be defined to insure that a most specific applicable method for any given set of arguments can always be determined by the use of argument subtype precedence alone. They do not discuss algorithms for static type checking or for method dispatch.

Mugridge, et al. [11] discuss multi-method dispatch with static type checking. They describe a method specificity rule that only partially orders the methods of a generic function. They

define the *cover* of a method $m(T^1, \ldots, T^n)$ as the cross-product of all possible argument types: $\{< S^1, S^2, \ldots, S^n > \mid \forall i, S^i \preceq T^i\}$. Method applicability is defined in terms of the non-empty intersection of the covers of the function call and the method definitions. Given a call, applicable methods are found by intersecting corresponding covers. Since the method precedence rule does not totally order methods, if two applicable methods are found that do not have an order defined between them, such a call is declared ambiguous.

Finally, Dussud [6] and Kiczales and Rodriguez [9] describe techniques for efficiently dispatching multi-methods in CLOS. These techniques are based on hashing on the argument types. They select a method from the entire set of methods of the generic function. Because compile-time type checking is absent, the smaller set of potentially applicable methods cannot be used to reduce the run-time search space for method dispatch.

9   Conclusions

Until now, algorithms for the static type-checking of multi-methods with multiple inheritance were unknown.

We have demonstrated the feasibility of static type checking for multi-methods and have shown how the concept of *method confusability* can be used to classify the methods of a generic function.

This classification supports efficient identification of potentially applicable methods in large-scale type systems. The compile-time technique of identifying potentially applicable methods can be used to reduce the run-time search space for method dispatch.

In the course of our development of mechanisms for multi-method type checking, we have identified some language design choices for method specificity and have discussed their impact on the type checking and dispatch of both selfish methods and multi-methods. In particular, the distinctions between global and local method precedence rules and single and multiple inheritance have been shown to significantly affect the complexity of type-checking and method dispatch.

The results presented in this paper can provide the basis for adding multi-methods to existing languages. They can also be used when making choices in designing new object-oriented paradigms.

10   Acknowledgments

We would like to thank Alex Aiken, Laura Haas, Guy Lohman, and Jim Stamos for their helpful comments and suggestions.

11   Appendix

Lemma 4 *In a single inheritance system, if there is a type T such that $T \preceq T_1$ and $T \preceq T_2$, then either $T_1 \preceq T_2$ or $T_2 \preceq T_1$.*

Proof: In a single inheritance system, every type has at most one immediate supertype. ∎

Theorem 3   In a system that supports only single inheritance and selfish method selection, argument subtype precedence is sufficient to establish precedence between confusable methods.

Proof: Consider two confusable methods $m_1(T_1^1, T_1^2, \ldots, T_1^n)$ and $m_2(T_2^1, T_2^2, \ldots, T_2^n)$. Assume without loss of generality that method selection is based on the first argument. Since selfish method selection is used, it must be the case that $T_1^1 \neq T_2^1$. By the definition of confusability, there must be a common subtype of T_1^1 and T_2^1. It follows from Lemma A1 that either $T_1^1 \prec T_2^1$ or $T_2^1 \prec T_1^1$. ∎

Theorem 4   Argument order precedence is sufficient to establish precedence between confusable methods in a system that supports multi-methods but admits only single inheritance.

Proof: If methods $m_1(T_1^1, T_1^2, \ldots, T_1^n)$ and $m_2(T_2^1, T_2^2, \ldots, T_2^n)$ are confusable, then for any given T_1^i, T_2^i there must be a common subtype of T_1^i and T_2^i. In a single inheritance system, it follows from Lemma 4 that either $T_1^i \preceq T_2^i$ or $T_2^i \preceq T_1^i$. Consider the formal argument types of m_1 and m_2 in the specified argument order, and find the first argument position in which the argument types of m_1 and m_2 differ, say k. If $T_1^k \prec T_2^k$, then m_1 is more specific than m_2, and vice versa. ∎

Theorem 5   Global type ordering is sufficient to order confusable methods in a multiple inheritance system with multi-methods.

Proof: Consider   the   corresponding formal argument types of two confusable methods $m_1(T_1^1, T_1^2, \ldots, T_1^n)$ and $m_2(T_2^1, T_2^2, \ldots, T_2^n)$ in the specified argument order, and find the first position in which these types differ, say k. If $T_1^k \, \alpha \, T_2^k$, then m_1 is more specific than m_2, and vice versa. ∎

Theorem 6   Inheritance order precedence is sufficient to determine method specificity in a multiple inheritance system with multi-methods.

Proof: The proof is similar to that of Theorem 5 except that the local type ordering associated with the type of kth argument of the function invocation is used to determine method specificity. ∎

References

[1] Rakesh Agrawal, Alexander Borgida, and H. V. Jagadish. Efficient Management of Transitive Relationships in Large Data and Knowledge Bases. In *Proc. ACM-SIGMOD International Conference on Management of Data*, 1989.

[2] Daniel G. Bobrow, Linda G. DeMichiel, Richard P. Gabriel, Sonya Keene, Gregor Kiczales, and David A. Moon. Common Lisp Object System Specification. *SIGPLAN Notices*, Vol. 23, special issue, Sept. 1988.

[3] Daniel G. Bobrow, Kenneth Kahn, Gregor Kiczales, Larry Masinter, Mark Stefik, and Frank Zdybel. CommonLoops: Merging Lisp and Object-Oriented Programming. In *Proc. Conference on Object-Oriented Programming Systems, Languages, and Applications*, 1986.

[4] Luca Cardelli and Peter Wegner. On Understanding Types, Data Abstraction, and Poly-

morphism. *ACM Computing Surveys*, 17(4), December 1985.

[5] Linda G. DeMichiel and Richard P. Gabriel. The Common Lisp Object System: An Overview. In *Proc. European Conference on Object-Oriented Programming*, 1987.

[6] Patrick H. Dussud, TICLOS: An Implementation of CLOS for the Explorer Family. In *Proc. Conference on Object-Oriented Programming Systems, Languages, and Applications*, 1989.

[7] Margaret A. Ellis and Bjarne Stroustrup. *Annotated C++ Reference Manual*. Addison-Wesley, 1990.

[8] Daniel H. H. Ingalls. A Simple Technique for Handling Multiple Polymorphism. In *Proc. Conference on Object-Oriented Programming Systems, Languages, and Applications*, 1986.

[9] Gregor Kiczales and Luis Rodriguez. Efficient Method Dispatch in PCL. In *Proc. Conference on Lisp and Functional Programming*, 1990.

[10] C. Lécluse and P. Richard. Manipulation of Structured Values in Object-Oriented Databases. In *Proc. Second International Workshop on Database Programming Languages*, 1989.

[11] Warwick B. Mugridge, John Hamer, John G. Hosking. Multi-Methods in a Statically-Typed Programming Language. Report No. 50, Department of Computer Science, University of Auckland, 1991. (To appear in *Proc. European Conference on Object-Oriented Programming*, 1991.)

[12] Bjarne Stroustrup. *The C++ Programming Language*. Addison-Wesley Publishing Co., 1987.

[13] R. Tarjan. Depth-first Search and Linear Graph Algorithms. *SIAM Journal on Computing*, 1(2), 1972.

A Static Type System for Message Passing

Giorgio Ghelli

Dipartimento di Informatica, Università di Pisa,
Corso Italia 40, Italy
ghelli@dipisa.di.unipi.it

Abstract

Much research has been performed with the aim of isolating the basic notions of object-oriented languages and of describing them by basic operators which can be embedded in strongly-typed languages. In this context we define an atomic linguistic construct to capture the notion of message passing, and we define a static and strong type system, based on subtyping, for this construct. Message passing is modelled as the application of an overloaded function, whose behavior is determined only at compile-time on the basis of the class which created a distinguished argument, the object "receiving" the message. By embedding this mechanism in a strongly-typed language with subtyping and abstract data types we can obtain the full functionality of object-oriented languages. We show that this approach is strictly more expressive then the usual interpretation of message passing as selection plus application of a functional record field.

1. Introduction

Object-oriented languages are based on the notions of *objects*, *classes*, *messages/methods* and *inheritance*.

objects are entities with a record-like state, collected in *classes*. A *class* plays both the rôle of an Abstract Data Type (ADT) and of a generator of homogeneous objects; it is defined by specifying: the record type representing the structure of the state of the objects produced, the name of their abstract type, and its *methods*, i.e. the basic functions which can be applied, by *message sending*, to them.

Message sending is the object-oriented version of function call: when a message (a pair <*method name ,args*>) is *sent* to an object *obj*, the "corresponding" method is evaluated, receiving the object *obj* (the *distinguished parameter*) and *args* as parameters. Many different methods in different classes can correspond to a given method name; the one executed depends on the class which created the *distinguished parameter* (this is known as *overloading of method names*). The method associated to a message does not depend on the compile-time type of the receiving object, but on the class which generated the object, so that this meaning can be decided only at run-time (*late binding of method names*). Besides this, the method associated at run-time to a message could even belong to a class defined after the compilation of the code issuing the message call (*dynamic extension of the meaning of method names*).

A new class *NC* can be defined by *inheritance* from an old one *OC* by specifying which fields are added to the structure of the state of the objects of *OC*, which new methods are added, and possibly how the code of some old methods changes; in this case *NC* is called a *subclass* of *OC*.

The high level of reusability of object-oriented software is due to the interplay of all of these four features: overloading, late binding, dynamic extensibility and inheritance.

This work was carried out with the partial support of Selenia, project "Very Large Knowledge Bases", of E.E.C., Esprit B.R.A. 3070 FIDE, and of Italian C.N.R., P.F. "Sistemi informatici e calcolo parallelo".

The embedding of these features into languages with well established semantics and type systems is widely studied, with three objectives: • a formal understanding of object-oriented languages, • the definition of a strong type system for these languages, • the definition of languages enjoying both a strong foundation and the high expressivity and code reusability of object-oriented languages.

Most of these researches are based on the encoding of the mechanisms of object-oriented languages in a strong type system with subtyping (see, e.g. [CarWeg85] [AlbGheOccOrs88] [CanHilOlt88] [Coo89] [CooHilCan90] [Mit90] [Red88] [Ghe91]). An object is represented by a record containing the methods of its class as functional fields; passing a message <*methName*,*params*> to an object *obj* is interpreted as selection and application of that functional field: *(obj.methName)(params)*. This interpretation immediately gives overloading, late binding and dynamical extensibility of methods. In short, field names are overloaded, since a unique field name can be associated with different functions in records produced by different classes. The function contained in a record field does not depend on the record type, but is decided by the function which creates the record, and can be known only at run-time (late binding). Finally, the set of the meanings of a field name can be extended, since it is always possible to define new records where a field name, already used in other records, assumes new meanings; old code accessing this new record will retrieve the new meaning. In this approach class inheritance introduces many type-level complications, since it is modelled by record concatenation, which needs complex type systems in presence of subtyping [CarMit89] [Wan89]. The result is that in these systems either no inheritance is present, like in the seminal work [Car88], either subtyping is heavily limited, like in [CooHilCan90], or both inheritance and subtyping are offered, paying the price of very complex record subtyping rules, like in [Mit90] and in [CarMit89].

The record-based approach presents another well-known technical problem: the interaction of the subtyping rules of the record and function types used to codify objects, has the undesired effect that the argument types of methods redefined in a subclass can be only generalized, rather then specialized (*specializing* means *changing into a subtype*; *generalizing* is the inverse operation). This constraint on the redefinition of method argument types is called *contravariance*.

Contravariance implies immediately that, in the record model, the object receiving the message cannot be seen as a regular argument of the method, since its type is necessarily specialized going from superclasses to subclasses; for this reason the receiving object is not seen as an argument but is accessed by its methods "by recursion" [CarWeg85]. But in turn, this way of accessing the distinguished argument entails new difficulties in the interpretation of inheritance as record concatenation, as discussed in [CooHilCan90] and [Mit90]; the solutions proposed there destroy the simplicity of the record approach.

Besides these technical problems on the distinguished argument, type contravariance is an undesired constraint also for the other method arguments, since experience shows that covariance of argument types is much more common in practice [DanTom88].

The problems above are due to the fact that the record-based approach is not a direct description of the message passing mechanism, but rather an encoding of it. To overcome these difficulties, and to study the object-oriented mechanisms at a more basic level, we introduce a completely different way of viewing objects and message passing.

In our approach inheritance and message passing are modelled, respectively, by the incremental definition and by the application of overloaded functions. The meaning of our overloaded functions can be solved only at compile-time on the basis of the class which created a distinguished argument. Conversely, objects are just entities which can remember the class which created them. This mechanism reflects the kernel of the message passing mechanism, and the record-based approach can be seen just as one "implementation" of this fundamental mechanism.

We define also a strong type system for this mechanism, i.e. a type system such that a well-typed expression cannot raise any run-time failure. Despite late binding, this type system is static: type checking is performed completely at compile-time.

This mechanism models one-half of the object-oriented paradigm, i.e. message passing with late-binding overloading, and inheritance (dynamic extensibility is modelled by the general mechanisms of the host language). The other half of the paradigm is represented by the possibility of encapsulating the state of objects and the implementation of classes. In our approach object-oriented encapsulation can be understood in terms of any general purpose encapsulation mechanism, like abstract data types, modules or existential types (see e.g. [CarWeg85] or [MitPlo85]), since our overloading mechanism can be applied to the functions defined on abstract data types too. This is not true in the record-based approach, where only record field names can be overloaded, while the functions defined on an abstract data type cannot.

To sum up, our model of message passing is more convenient than the traditional record-based one with respect to the following points:

- It allows both covariant and contravariant redefinition of methods in the context of a static and strong type system
- It allows studying simple and multiple inheritance without affecting the subtyping rules
- Non recursive methods can be defined without using recursion

But our construct allows also defining typed languages which are more expressive than traditional object-oriented languages. With respect to method definition, this is showed in the paper through the following example. Let *ColoredPoint* be a subclass of *Point*. In the record model, due to contravariance, a method *equal* comparing two *Point*'s cannot be overloaded to make it able to compare also two *ColoredPoint*'s. In an untyped

object-oriented language this redefinition is allowed, but you cannot explicitly specify what happens when a *Point* and a *ColoredPoint* are compared, and this comparison may even raise a run-time error. In our model the covariant redefinition of the *equal* method is allowed, run-time failures are not possible, and you can even explicitly program how a *Point* is compared with a *ColoredPoint*. Besides this, in our model methods are first class values of the language, which is not true in the record-based model or in the untyped object-oriented languages.

The paper is structured as follows. In §2 we introduce a basic strongly-typed language, a weakly-typed "traditional" object-oriented language and its translation in the record model. In §3 we present our strong type system for late-binding overloading. In §4 we compare our approach with other ones. In §5 we discuss how dynamic extension and encapsulation can be realized. In §6 we draw some conclusions.

2 Basic definitions

2.1 A functional language

This is the syntax of our basic functional language ([a] means a is optional):

Declaration:= **let** *ide* := Val
      | **let** [**rec**] *ide* [:Type] := Val
      | **let** [**rec**] **type** *typeIde* := Type

Val:=   *constant* | *ide* | Declaration; Val
      | **fun** (*ide*:Type,...,*ide*:Type). Val
      | Val(Val,...,Val)
      | **record** *label* := Val,...,*label* := Val **end**
      | Val.*label*
      | **rec** *ide*[:Type]. Val | Val; Val | Val:Type

Type:=   *typeIde* | *basicType* | Type×Type[1]
      | Type→Type
      | **Record** *label* : Type,...,*label* : Type **End**
      | **Rec** *typeIde*. Type

A declaration

---

[1]For simplicity we use product types only to pass parameters

131

"*let ide:=Val* / *let type typeIde := typexpr*"
binds an identifier to a value or to a type in all the
expressions which follow it, in a terminal session or
in this paper. These are constant bindings; updatable
references are also needed in the host language, but
they are not defined here since they are not used in
any example.

"*fun* $(ide_1:Type_1,...,ide_n:Type_n)$. Val" is an
expression which denotes a function:
"$ide_1,...,ide_n$" are the formal parameters,
"$Type_1,...,Type_n$" are the type required for the
actual parameters and "*Val*" is the body of the
function. "$Type_1\times...\times Type_n\rightarrow TypeR$" is the type
of this function if "*TypeR*" is the type of "*Val*".
"*Val(Val,...,Val)*" is function application.

"*record label := Val,...,label := Val end*" is a
record whose type has the form "*Record label :
Type,...,label : Type End*". Record fields can be
selected using the notation "*rec.field*". The order of
labels in records is irrelevant.

"*rec ide. expr*" returns the value of expr evaluated
in an environment where *ide* is recursively bound to
the value which is being built. *let rec ide := expr*
means *let ide := rec ide. expr*, i.e. the identifier *ide*
is recursively bound to the value under construction
(*rec ide. expr*) and remains bound to it after the
construction (*let ide := rec...*; see the example
below):

"*rec typeide. TypeExpr*" returns the value of
TypeExpr evaluated in an environment where
typeide is recursively bound to the type which is
being defined. *let rec type typeide := TypeExpr*
means *let type typeide := Rec typeide. expr* :

```
let rec type Graph :=
    Record  value: Int
        outStar: List of Graph
    End ;
```

```
let loop := rec self:Graph.
    record value:=0,
        outStar:= list of (self)
    end ;
```

```
let rec  loop:Graph :=
    record value:=0,
        outStar:= list of (loop)
    end ;
```

"*Val;Val*" denotes the sequential execution of two
expressions, which returns the result of the second
expression.

If one of the types of "*Val*" is "*Type*" then
"*Val:Type*" is the same expression, but having as
types only "*Type*" and all its supertypes. This
construct is used mainly to avoid ambiguity in the
type of terms with too many types, like the term
denoting an empty list: writing *emptylist: List of Int*
we restrict the type of this empty list to the lists of
integers.

The plugs "*constant*" and "*basicType*" denote a
set of other values, operations and type constructors
which could be useful, like lists (the constructor
List of used above) integers, booleans, pairs etc.

A reflexive and transitive inclusion relation,
subtyping, is defined on types [Car88]. Subtyping
means that if *a:T* and *T* is a subtype of *U* ($T\leq U$),
then *a:U*. The typing and subtyping rules are in the
Appendix A.

2.2 A weakly-typed object-oriented language

We exemplify a weakly-typed object-oriented
language by adding the following *Class* construct,
to declare classes, to our micro functional language.
Notice that the resulting language is *not* our
proposal; the construct below is just aimed to
illustrate some points about message passing in
weakly-typed object-oriented languages:

let ObjType$(x_1:T_1,...,x_n:T_n):=$
            Class <methods> end

The definition above defines a new type *ObjType*
and a function *new[ObjType]*, to generate "objects"
of that type[2]. *<methods>* is a list of bindings
with form

---

[2]In this micro language the state of the object has the same
structure of the input parameters of the creation function; this is
just an irrelevant simplification

$ide(parameters:ParamTypes):=expr:ResultType;$

each of which defines a new function

$ide:ObjType \rightarrow ParamTypes \rightarrow ResultType,$

called "a method of the class *ObjType*"; the distinguished parameter of each method is not explicitly declared, and is called *self*[3]. Classes can be defined "by inheritance" by extending other classes:

let $ChildType(x_{n+1}:T_{n+1},...,x_{n+m}:T_{n+m}):=$
   Class isa $ParentT_1,...,ParentT_l$ <*methods*>
   end

In this case *ChildType* is a subtype of $ParentT_1,...,ParentT_l$, so that any method of a $ParentT_i$ can be applied to values of type *ChildType* too (method inheritance). The creation function **new[ChildType]** requires all the input parameters of the $ParentT_i$'s plus those added in its own definition (state inheritance). If a method is specified both in a $ParentT_i$ and in *ChildType*, then it is overloaded with the new definition; we say that it is *extended*, since it acquires a new *branch* without losing the old ones (we call branches the different definitions supplied for an overloaded method). If a method is defined in more then one $ParentT_i$, but not in *ChildType*, then some *choice rule* of the language selects the inherited definition. *Single inheritance* means that there is just one parent type, so that no choice rule is needed; otherwise we have *multiple inheritance*.

When an overloaded method is applied to an object, a branch is selected depending on the run-time type of the object (the class which created it), which is in general only a subtype of the compile-time type of the expression returning it. E.g., let *Rectangle* and *Circle* be subtypes of *Picture*; in the following function the expression *pic* has compile-time type *Picture*, but if the list *lpics* contains rectangles and circles, then in each run of the *for* loop the *redraw* method of rectangles or of circles is selected:

let redrawAllPictures :=
   fun (lpics: List of Picture).
     for pic **in** lpics **do** redraw(pic);

Solving overloading on the basis of run-time (resp. compile-time) types is called *late* (resp. *early*) *binding*[4]; e.g., imperative languages use early binding for overloaded operators (like, e.g., a "+" operator overloaded on integer and floating point numbers).

The extension of a method affects also already "compiled" method calls: if a new subclass *Square* of *Picture* is added, then the already defined *redrawAllPictures* function will afterwards select the new definition of *redraw* for objects of the class *Square*. This "dynamic extension" is a kind of dynamic binding, which allows changing the meaning of a method identifier by adding new branches for new subtypes. It is related to late binding (solving overloading using the run-time type) from an implementative point of view, since both mechanisms need a run-time binding of method names, but the two notions are different (cf. §5).

The *redrawAllPictures* example suggests how, in object-oriented languages, an application, (e.g. a graphic editor), can be first implemented and packaged, and later on modified simply by adding a subclass (e.g. circles), without modifying or recompiling the existing code, exploiting critically all the four features of inheritance, overloading, late binding and dynamic extensibility.

2.3 The record model for object-oriented languages

The record model is a techinque to understand message passing by translating it into a functional language with rtecors and subtypes. We present the record model through one example. Consider the following declarations, expressed in the weakly-typed object-oriented toy language:

---

[3]In the obiect-oriented jargon, objects "contain" their own methods, and *self* is not a parameter but an auto-reference

[4]This distinction affects only languages with some form of polymorphism, like subtyping, since otherwise the run-time type of a value is just its compile time type

```
let Point(x:Int, y:Int) := Class
  get_x():= x, get_y():= y,
  equal(p:Point) := get_x(self)=get_x(p)
              & get_y(self)=get_y(p)
end;

let ColorPoint(x:Int, y:Int, color:Color) := Class isa
Point
  get_color():= color;
  equal(p:ColorPoint) := get_x(self)=get_x(p)
              & get_y(self)=get_y(p)
              & get_color(self)=get_color(p);
end;
```

In the record model they would be translated as:

```
let rec type Point := Record get_x: Unit → Int,
                  get_y: Unit → Int,
                  equal: Point → Bool
        End;
let newPoint: Int×Int → Point :=
  fun (x:Int, y:Int).
  let state := record x:=x, y:=y end
  in  rec⁵ self.
    record
      get_x:= fun(_:Unit). state.x,
      get_y:= fun(_:Unit). state.y,
      equal:= fun(p:Point). p.get_x()=self.get_x()
                  & p.get_y()=self.get_y()
    end;

let rec type ColorPoint :=
    Record  get_x(y): Unit → Int,
      get_color: Unit → Color
      equal: ColorPoint → Bool
    End;
let newColorPoint: Int×Int×Color → ColorPoint :=
  fun (x:Int, y:Int,color:Color).
  let state := record x:=x, y:=y, color:=color end
  in  rec self  .record
      get_x(y/color):=
                  fun(_:Unit). state.x(.y/.color),
      get_color:= fun(_:Unit). state.color,
```

```
equal:=
    fun(p:ColorPoint).
      p.get_x()=self.get_x()
      & p.get_y()=self.get_y()
      & p.get_color()=self.get_color()
end;
```

Notice that a class definition is expanded into the definition of a record type and of a function which creates new records of that type (the *objects*). The fields of these records correspond just to the messages which can be sent to them, while the state of the object is codified in a local variable shared by these fields, called *state* above (actually this local variable is not needed to translate the toy language, while it is useful in general to model state encapsulation). To get the *x* coordinate of an object *aPoint* the expression *aPoint.get_x()* is used; the implicit argument of the *get_x* method, which would be *aPoint*, is not given explicitly, by writing *aPoint.get_x(aPoint)*, but is accessed by the *get_x* method using the variable *self* which recursively refers to the whole object, *aPoint* in this case. Notice that, intuitively, there is nothing really recursive in trivial functions like *get_x* or *equal* above; we will see that in our model this kind of recursive definitions is avoided.

The example above is a critical one, since *ColorPoint* should be a subtype of *Point*, since it is defined by inheritance from *Point* (in the weakly-typed source code), but it is not a subtype due to the covariant redefinition of the argument type of the equal method[6], and for this reason, in most strongly-typed object-oriented languages, the definition above would not be well-typed; the remaining part of this section is devoted to a better understanding of this problem.

Notice that in the above example the ability of defining classes incrementally (through inheritance), which we find in the source code, is lost in the translation: the type *ColorPoint* and the function *newColorPoint* are fully defined without exploiting the similarities with the preceding two definitions. In

---

[5]Informally, *rec ide. expr* evaluates *expr* binding *ide*, recursively, to *expr* itself (*rec self. record(self)*). *let rec ide :=* *expr* means *let ide := rec ide. expr*.

[6]For subtyping, recursive types are equivalent to their infinite tree expansion; see [AmaCar90] for more details about subtyping and recursive types.

more powerful record models (see e.g. [Mit90]), inheritance is present, and is codified by using record concatenation operators, but other problems then arise.

2.4 Inheritance and subtyping

A subclass *SubC* inherits from *SuperC* when *SubC* is defined by describing how it differs from *SuperC*; a type *T* is a subtype of a type *U* if all the elements of *T* have also type *U*; so subtyping and inheritance are very different notions. However, in strongly-typed object-oriented languages, the type of a subclass is usually required to be a subtype of that of its superclasses, to assure that well-typed methods remain well-typed when are inherited. In fact a method in a superclass with element type *SuperObjType* is type-checked supposing *self:SuperObjType*; when the method is inherited in a subclass with element type *SubObjType*, it should be type-checked another time, under the assumption *self:SubObjType*. This second type-checking can be avoided if *SubObjType* is required to be a subtype of *SuperObjType*, since in this case *self:SubObjType* implies *self:SuperObjType*, which in turn implies the well-typing of the method.

While some important approaches to inheritance and subtyping support a weaker link between the two notions, notably [CanCooHil90] and [Mit90], this linking is a positive feature of object-oriented languages which leads to a better structuring of class definitions.

2.5 Contravariance of method arguments in the record model

In the record model an object type can be a subtype of another one only if the corresponding record types are in the same relation; so, when a record subtype is defined by modifying (by inheritance) a record supertype, the types of the fields which already exist in the supertype, can be only specialized in the subtype. Methods are encoded by functional record fields, and functions can be specialized only by generalizing, and not by specializing, the argument

type (i.e. $T \rightarrow U \leq T' \rightarrow U$ only if $T' \leq T$). For this reason, in the record model, when a method type is redefined in a subclass, its argument type can be only generalized; this is a problem, since in many programming situation specialization would be needed. But contravariance is not just an accidental result of some combination of formal rules, which could be relaxed just by adopting different rules; it is really needed to obtain type-safety in the weakly-typed and record-based approaches, as exemplified below.

Example: due to the covariant specialization of the type of the *other* parameter of the *equal* function in the *ColorPoint* type, *ColorPoint* is not a subtype of *Point*, and if this relation holded, run-time errors could occur:

```
let Point(x,y: Int) := Class
    get_x/y() := x/y;
    equal(p:Point) := get_x(p)=get_x(self)
                    & get_y(p)=get_y(self)
end

let ColorPoint(x,y: Int, color:Color)
    := Class isa Point
        get_color() := color;
        equal(other:ColorPoint) :=
            get_x(other) = get_x(self)
            & get_y(other) = get_y(self)
            & get_color(other) = get_color(self)
end

let one:=new[Point](1,1);
let oneBlue:=new[ColorPoint](1,1,Blue);
equal(oneBlue)(one);  ⇒  ????
```

If *ColorPoint* were a subtype of *Point*, the last application of *equal* would be allowed, the *ColorPoint* equality would be selected by late binding (think to *oneBlue.equal(One)* in the record model) and a *get_color* message would be sent to *one*, resulting in a run-time failure. So this example shows that the contravariance constraint cannot be relaxed in a type safe way without a reconsideration of the run-time semantics of the message passing mechanism, like the one studied in the next section.

3 The proposed type system

In this section we define a static strong type system for late-binding overloading. Late binding overloading allows message passing to be expressed, but is still more expressive; as a result, it allows, in a type safe context, both covariant and contravariant redefinition of method types.

Our overloading mechanism is defined by an operator which allows transforming a regular function in a one-branch overloaded function, an operator to extend an overloaded function by adding new branches to it, and finally by an operation of overloaded function application. Overloaded application selects a branch of the overloaded function, on the basis of the run-time type of a distinguished argument, and then applies that branch to the argument. In §3.1 we give the rules which specify how these constructs are typed, in the case of single inheritance, and which subtyping relation is defined on overloaded function types, and we discuss the compatibility of covariance and contravariance in our model. In §3.2 we generalize this discussion to the case of multiple inheritance, dealing with the conflict resolution rules at a general level. In §3.3 we exemplify our approach. In §3.4 we state some further observations.

3.1 The type rules of overloaded functions

In our model each branch of an overloaded function is associated with an "expected input type" T, which is just the input type of the branch seen as a non-overloaded function. If the run-time type of the argument is exactly one of the "expected input types", the corresponding branch is selected. Otherwise a *choice rule* is invoked, such that in any case the selected input type is a supertype of the run-time argument type; if the set of those *expected input types* which are supertypes of the run-time argument type has a minimum, that minimum is selected. We do not specify how choice rules are defined, but we define which sets of branches can be

put together, with type rules which are "parametric" with respect to the way of specifying choice rules.

With single inheritance, for any run-time argument type, a minimum supertype always exists in the set of the expected input types, so that there is no need of specifying a choice rule. The absence of choice rules, which are also missing in approaches different from single inheritance, simplifies greatly the type rules and the notation, and we now address this. The more general setting, where the minimum supertype is not always defined, is sketched in the next section.

The type of an overloaded function with branches with expected input types A_1, A_2, and A_3, and result types, respectively, B_1, B_2 and B_3 is denoted as $\{A_1 \to B_1, A_2 \to B_2, A_3 \to B_3\}$ or (at the meta-level) as $\{A_i \to B_i\}_{i \in \{1,2,3\}}$.

The first rule below specifies which sets of types can be combined to form a well-formed overloaded type, and implicitly which sets of branches can be combined to form a well-formed overloaded function. Type rules should be read backward; for example the rule below can be read as: "(in the environment Γ) $\{T_i \to U_i\}_{i \in I}$ is a well formed type if a) for any i in I, T_i is a *choice_type* and U_i is a type, and if for any i,j in I if $T_i \leq T_j$ then $U_i \leq U_j$"; Γ is an environment collecting information about the free variables. Well-formed overloaded types are defined by the rule below simply as those types where all the component functional types are "mutually compatible". Mutual compatibility means that if the input types are in the subtyping relation, the output types are related in the same way; we will see in the next section that in case of multiple inheritance the compatibility condition is slightly stronger.

$$(\{\}\text{Form}) \quad \frac{\forall^7 i \in I. \ \Gamma \vdash T_i \ \text{choice\_type}, \ \Gamma \vdash U_i \ \text{type} \quad \forall i,j \in I \ \ \Gamma \vdash T_i \leq T_j \Rightarrow \Gamma \vdash U_i \leq U_j}{\Gamma \vdash \{T_i \to U_i\}_{i \in I} \ \text{type}}$$

The condition $\Gamma \vdash T_i$ *choice_type*, which is not formally specified here, models the fact that in real systems not every type is accepted as an expected input type; however, in our examples below we will

---

[7] This ∀ is a meta-level finite quantification

136

accept any type as a choice type. In object-oriented languages, only object types are accepted as choice types.

The result type of an overloaded function application is determined by applying the • (*choose*) operator to the set of the expected input types of the overloaded function and to the argument type: $\{T_i\}_{i\in I}$•A selects from the set of expected input types $\{T_i\}_{i\in I}$ the type corresponding to the type A. In the case of single inheritance, that type is the minimum supertype of A in $\{T_i\}_{i\in I}$, if it exists; $\{T_i{\rightarrow}U_i\}_{i\in I}$ returns U_i if $\{T_i\}_{i\in I}$•A returns T_i. The condition $\{T_i\}_{i\in I}$ *accepts* A is satisfied when in $\{T_i\}_{i\in I}$ there is a type which corresponds to A; in the case of single inheritance, this means simply that in $\{T_i\}_{i\in I}$ there is one supertype of A. The application of an overloaded function is denoted here as *f•a* to stress the fact that applying an overloaded function is different from applying a regular function, since it involves both a branch selection and a function application.

($\{\}$Elim) $\quad \Gamma \vdash f: \{T_i{\rightarrow}U_i\}_{i\in I} \qquad \Gamma \vdash a{:}A$
$$\frac{\Gamma \vdash \{T_i\}_{i\in I}\text{ accepts }A}{\Gamma \vdash f{\bullet}(a): \{T_i{\rightarrow}U_i\}_{i\in I}{\bullet}A}$$

The same • notation is used at the type and at the value level just to indicate that the same rule is used to choose a type in $\{T_i{\rightarrow}U_i\}_{i\in I}$ at compile-time and to choose a branch in f at run-time. However, the branch of the type which is selected at compile-time could not correspond to the branch of the function which is selected at run-time. In fact we have shown in section 2.2 that the compile-time type of an expression is generally only a supertype of the run-time type of the corresponding value. The compatibility condition $(T_i \leq T_j \Rightarrow \Gamma \vdash U_i \leq U_j)$ of the formation rule assures that in any case the type which is computed at compile-time for the overloaded application is a supertype of the actual run-time type of the result.

An overloaded function is defined by starting from a regular function and adding new type-branch pairs with the + operator; a simpler approach could be obtained by identifying regular functions with one-branch overloaded functions:

($\{\}$Intro) $\quad \dfrac{\Gamma \vdash f{:}T{\rightarrow}U}{\Gamma \vdash \text{overload } f: \{T{\rightarrow}U\}}$

($\{\}$Add) $\quad \Gamma \vdash f: \{T_i{\rightarrow}U_i\}_{i\in I}$
$$\Gamma \vdash g: T_k{\rightarrow}U_k \qquad T_k \notin \{T_i\}_{i\in I}$$
$$\frac{\Gamma \vdash \{T_i{\rightarrow}U_i\}_{i\in I\cup\{k\}}\text{ type}}{\Gamma \vdash f{+}g: \{T_i{\rightarrow}U_i\}_{i\in I\cup\{k\}}}$$

In general, $A{\leq}B$ means that for any context $C[x]$, if any element of type B can substitute x in a type-safe way, then also any element of type A can be inserted in $C[x]$; this implies that if $T_{C[],B}$ (*resp.* $T_{C[],A}$) is the type of the expression obtained by putting an element of type B (*resp. A*) in that context, then $T_{C[],A} \leq T_{C[],B}$. From this definition we have the following general rule (to be read backward, as usual):

($\{\}{\leq}$) $\quad \forall^8 A$ such that $\{V_j\}_{j\in J}$ accepts A .
$$\{T_i\}_{i\in I}\text{ accepts }A\text{ and}$$
$$\frac{\Gamma \vdash \{T_i{\rightarrow}U_i\}_{i\in I}{\bullet}A \leq \{V_j{\rightarrow}W_j\}_{j\in J}{\bullet}A}{\Gamma \vdash \{T_i{\rightarrow}U_i\}_{i\in I} \leq \{V_j{\rightarrow}W_j\}_{j\in J}}$$

Even if this is not apparent, the usual contravariance rule for subtyping can be derived from the rules above. More formally, in Appendix B it is proved that, even in the general case:

$$\Gamma \vdash T'{\leq}T,\ \Gamma \vdash U'{\leq}U \ \Rightarrow\ \Gamma \vdash \{T{\rightarrow}U'\} \leq \{T'{\rightarrow}U\}$$

This observation helps to clarify the fact that our system is a conservative extension of the traditional type systems for subtyping. In our system covariance and contravariance both exist with two neatly different rôles. Covariance is the compatibility constraint to be satisfied when different branches of an overloaded function are put together, used in the rule of type formation, while contravariance is the condition for subtyping, used only in subtyping rules, with no contrast between the two notions. At the end of section 3.3 we will show that the covariance condition does not prevent the contravariant specialization of method argument

137

types.

3.2 Constraints on the set of types of an overloaded function in case of multiple inheritance

In this section we define at a general level which sets of types can be combined to form a well-formed overloaded type, in the general case of multiple inheritance, when choice rules are necessary to select one specific supertype of the run-time argument among the expected input types. This study is general in the sense that we do not commit to any specific mechanism for specifying choice rules.

For generality we suppose that each overloaded function contains its choice rule, which is also a part of its type; this is a heavy formalization which is made here to carry on this discussion at the highest level of generality; by selecting a specific way of defining this choice rule we can model, and compare, some of the known approaches to multiple inheritance. So the type of an overloaded function with a choice rule r is now denoted by $\{A{\rightarrow}T,...,B{\rightarrow}U\}_r$. Instead of detailing how choice rules can be specified, we formalize some constraints on their behaviour, to preserve the property that the compile-time type of any expression is a supertype of the possible run-time types of its values. Since no operation fails if the run-time type of its argument is a subtype of the expected type, this property implies that typed expressions never fail, i.e. that our type system is *strong*.

The well-formedness conditions for an overloaded type are the following ones:

Notation:

$\{T_i\}_{i\in I,s}{\cdot}A$ is the type selected for A by the choice rule s among $\{T_i\}_{i\in I}$

$\{T_i\}_{i\in I,s}$ *accepts* A
means "$\{T_i\}_{i\in I,s}{\cdot}A$ is well defined"

$\{T_i{\rightarrow}T_i\}_{i\in I,s}{\cdot}A=U_j$
is the same as $\{T_i\}_{i\in I,s}{\cdot}A=T_j$

i (internal choice) $\forall T.\ \{T_i\}_{i\in I,s}{\cdot}A\in\{T_i\}_{i\in I}$

ii (nearest choice) $\forall j\in I\ A{\leq}T_j{\leq}\{T_i\}_{i\in I,s}{\cdot}A$
$\Rightarrow\ T_j=\{T_i\}_{i\in I,s}{\cdot}A$

iii (supertype choice) $\forall A.\ \Gamma\vdash A\leq\{T_i\}_{i\in I,s}{\cdot}A$

iv (downward closure)
$\forall A,B.\ \Gamma\vdash A{\leq}B,\ \{T_i\}_{i\in I,s}$ accepts B
$\Rightarrow\ \{T_i\}_{i\in I,s}$ accepts B

v_s[8] (choice covariance)
$\forall A,B.\ \Gamma\vdash A{\leq}B$
$\Rightarrow\ \Gamma\vdash\{T_i{\rightarrow}T_i\}_{i\in I,s}{\cdot}A\leq\{T_i{\rightarrow}T_i\}_{i\in I,s}{\cdot}B$

Conditions i-iii do not need any explanation. Conditions ii specifies that no type in $\{T_i\}_{i\in I}$ can be "nearer" to A than the selected type; it implies that, if a minimum supertype of T exists among $\{T_i\}_{i\in I}$, that minimum is selected. To understand the last two constraints, suppose that A<B (i.e. A≤B and A≠B), that T is a type unrelated to U and that $f:\{A{\rightarrow}T, B{\rightarrow}U\}_r$. Suppose that f is applied as an overloaded function to the value of an expression b whose compile-time type is B, and whose run-time type is A (e.g. b is a formal parameter of type B which is bound to an actual parameter created with type A). Since the compile-time type of b is B, then the compile-time type of $f{\cdot}(b)$ is U. But when f is applied to a value b with run-time type A, the late binding mechanism selects, among the f branches, the piece of code with type $A{\rightarrow}T$, so that the application returns a value with run-time type T, unrelated with its compile-time type U. The rule v_s prevents this kind of problem by forcing the type T to be a subtype of the output type U computed by the compiler, while rule *iv* enforces the condition that for any possible run-time type A corresponding to a compile-time type B the corresponding branch selection is well defined.

To express condition v_s in a more useful way, we define the following preorder on a set τ of expected input types with respect to a choice rule s ($T\sqsubseteq_{s,\tau}U$: read T can be chosen for U by s in τ):

---

[8]The s subscript stands for "strong covariance" since we have also a weaker form of this rule, v_w.

Def.: (subtype choice preorder)

$$T \sqsubseteq_{s,\tau} U \quad \Leftrightarrow_{def} \quad \exists A \leq B: \tau \bullet_s A = T, \; \tau \bullet_s B = U$$

Lemma: $\sqsubseteq_{s,\tau}$ extends $\leq$ on τ; $\sqsubseteq_{s,\tau}$ is reflexive and transitive

Condition v_s can be now expressed as:

v_s (choice covariance for $\{T_i \rightarrow U_i\}_{i \in I,s}$):

$$\forall i,j \in I. \quad \Gamma \vdash T_i \sqsubseteq_{s,\{T_i\}_{i \in I}} T_j \;\Rightarrow\; \Gamma \vdash U_i \leq U_j$$

In systems without multiple inheritance, i-iv are satisfied by the choice rule selecting the minimum expected input supertype of the argument type, and $v_{s(trong)}$ is equivalent to the following requirement, which is weaker than the one needed in the general case:

v_w (type covariance for $s, \{T_i \rightarrow U_i\}_{i \in I,s}$):

$$\forall i,j \in I. \quad \Gamma \vdash T_i \leq T_j \qquad \Rightarrow \Gamma \vdash U_i \leq U_j$$

The five conditions above can be exploited to discuss, with some generality, how choice rules can be specified in the case of multiple inheritance. We do not enter in this discussion, but simply list some of the possibilities:

• When a new choice-type with multiple ancestors is defined, all the overloaded functions defined for a non-empty set of supertypes of this type without a minimum have to be explicitly overloaded for this type. With this constraint condition *ii* specifies completely how the choice is performed, so that no choice rule has to be specified.

• When a new choice-type with multiple ancestors is defined, a linear order is defined on its immediate ancestors. $\tau \bullet A$ always chooses the minimum supertype of A with respect to this order.

• A global linear order is defined on all the choice types; $\tau \bullet A$ always chooses the minimum supertype of A with respect to this order.

• Single inheritance.

By specializing our constraints to the four cases above we obtain the rules specifying what must be checked whenever a new choice type is defined. In this way we can compare in a unique setting different approaches to multiple inheritance, which

is more difficult in the record model.

3.3 An example

We will now exemplify the proposed approach, using just single inheritance for simplicity. For simplicity we suppose that every type can be used as an expected input type, while restricting these types, for example to products of named data types or of abstract data types, would be more usual (named data types are used in [AlbGheOrs91]). We consider again the ColorPoint example of §2.5:

let type P := **Record** x: Int, y: Int **End**;
let eq1: $\{P \times P \rightarrow Bool\}$:=
   overload (**fun** (p,q:P). p.x=q.x & p.y=q.y;

let type CP
   := **Record** x: Int, y: Int, color: Color **End**;

let eq1: $\{P \times P \rightarrow Bool, CP \times CP \rightarrow Bool\}$:=
   eq1
   + (**fun** (p,q:CP). eq1•(p,q) & p.color=q.color);

let eq2: $\{P \times P \rightarrow Bool, CP \times CP \rightarrow Bool,$
        $P \times CP \rightarrow Bool, CP \times P \rightarrow Bool\}$:=
   eq1 + (**fun** (p:P,q:CP).false)
   + (**fun** (p:CP,q:P).false);

let OneRed*(OneBlue)* :=
   record x:=1,y:=1,color:=Red*(Blue)* **end**;
let One := **record** x:=1,y:=1 **end**;

eq1(OneBlue,OneRed) $\rightarrow$ false
   % OneBlue and OneRed are compared as colored
eq1(OneBlue,One) $\rightarrow$ true
   % We can safely compare Points and ColorPoints
eq1(One,OneBlue) $\rightarrow$ true
   % eq1 compares them as Points (One=OneBlue)
eq2(One,OneBlue) $\rightarrow$ false
   % eq2 does not equate colored and uncol. points

eq1 is a safe version of the old *equal* method; it compares a point with a colored point as if they were both points, and never fails, while in §2.5 we have seen that *eq1(OneBlue,One)* would fail, if allowed, in the traditional model. *eq2* shows that we can decide how a point is compared with a colored point (consider them always different (*eq2*), or compare them as uncolored (*eq1*), or consider an uncolored point as a transparent one...). So our general-purpose overloading is both safer and more expressive than the weakly-typed object-oriented overloading, and more expressive than the record model, where *eq1* was ill-typed and *eq2* not expressible.

The possibility of selecting a branch on the basis of more then one parameter is the origin of the expressive power of our approach; the outermost $\rightarrow$ in each element of the overloaded type specifies the examined parameters. For example, consider the two following overloaded types:

$$\{(A \times A) \rightarrow T, (B \times B) \rightarrow T\}_r$$
$$\{A \rightarrow (A \rightarrow T), B \rightarrow (B \rightarrow T)\}_r$$

The first case is the type of an overloaded function which selects the branch on the basis of both arguments, in the second case only the first argument is considered for branch selection. Notice that if $A \leq B$ and B not $\leq A$, only the first type is well formed; so in the second case, where choice is restricted to just one argument, our approach has the same contravariant behaviour of the traditional one. On the other hand the following types are both well formed:

$$\{(A \times A) \rightarrow T, (B \times B) \rightarrow T\}_r$$
$$\{(A \times B) \rightarrow T, (B \times A) \rightarrow T\}_r$$

The first one is the type of a two-parameters functio, where the second parameter is specialized in a covariant way when the first parameter is specialized to type B. The second one is the type of a function where the second parameter is generalized in a contravariant way to type A when the first parameter is specialized to type B. Both types are well-formed, showing that in our approach both covariant and contravariant argument type specialization are allowed.

3.4 Final considerations

Our approach to overloading is very general, but many instances of that approach have unpleasant properties. In object-oriented languages only object types, i.e. named user defined abstract data types, can be used as choice type. But user defined types can acquire new subtypes, when new types are defined, so that well-formed types can lose well-formedness. For example, suppose that two types *Worker* and *Student* are defined, and that an overloaded function *code* of type *{Worker→Int,Student→String}*$_r$ is defined too. The type of *code* is well formed until *Worker* and *Student* have no common subtype. As soon as such a common subtype *TeachingFellow* is defined, the well-formedness of the type of the *code* function would depend on the behaviour of its *r* choice method. We can distinguish three alternative ways to deal with this problem:

- avoiding user defined types: this is an elegant approach, but cannot be used to understand object-oriented languages
- fixing the set of user defined types: also in this case we avoid the problem of evolving type hierarchies, but this approach is effective only to study the type-system of object-oriented languages which are implementated in a compilative way, where the program is read once to collect the type hierarchy and a second time to type-check the methods, and is not useful to study languages which are suitable for an interactive use
- allowing evolving hierarchies: this is the general and most interesting case.

Our general approach encopasses all the three cases above, but is expecially useful to deal with the last case, which is the most interesting and important one.

4 Related researches

4.1 The Canning Cook Mitchell Hill Olthoff approach

Method covariance has been obtained by W. Cook, J. Mitchell and others in the important case when all the arguments have the same type (like in the comparison examples above) [CooHilCan90]

[Mit90]. They use the record model, but they allow the definition of functions which operate not only on all the subtypes of a type, but on a wider set, exploiting their notion of F-bounded quantification [CanCooHilMitOlt89]. Then a subclass can inherit methods even if its type is not a subtype of the superclass, at least in the limited case cited in the second line; so the covariance-contravariance dilemma is faced by breaking the subtyping-inheritance link.

The Cook-Canning-Hill and Mitchell approaches (which are different but share these basic ideas) are much more complex than traditional approaches, since they rely on F-bounded quantification. Moreover, inheritance, which is realized in our model by the overloading "+" operator, is realized in these approaches by using record concatenation, which is not compatible with the standard record subtyping rules. To allow record concatenation, in the Cook-Canning-Hill approach values of a subtype cannot be substituted for values of supertypes everywhere, but only as parameters of functions where this substitution is explicitly allowed; this is a very limited use of the subtyping mechanism. On the other hand the concatenation problem is solved in the Mitchell approach by retaining the usual notion of subtyping, but by exploiting a more complex type system, where record types contain not only some of the labels which *must* be found in the record but also some of the labels which *cannot* be there.

Besides this, these approaches solve just a specific, even if important, case of covariance, and in this case they do not have full subtyping but only inheritance plus that weaker notion of subtyping which is expressed by F-bounded quantification. But this comparison is not fair, since solving a special case of the covariance-contravariance conflict is not the basic aim of the Cook-Canning-Hill and Mitchell approaches, whose fundamental contribution is a clean definition of the operation of inheritance in the record-based model and of its relation with subtyping and with record concatenation.

4.2 Overloading and conjunctive types

A type can be read as a predicate satisfied by its values, e.g., "$f:A \rightarrow B$" means: f is a function which, receiving a parameter satisfying A, does not raise run-time type failures, and its result satisfies B. In this setting, subtyping is implication: $A \leq B$ means that every value satisfying A satisfies also B. Conjunctive types are types which represent the conjunction of the predicates associated to their component types; they have been introduced by Coppo, and have been studied in the context of programming languages by Reynolds (see e.g. [Cop81] [Rey77]). Record types are a kind of conjunctive type: "$r:Record\ l:A\ End$" means "$r.l$ returns a value satisfying A", and "$r:Record\ l_1:A_1,...,l_n:A_n\ end$" is a conjunctive type meaning "$r:Record\ l_1:A_1\ end\ \wedge...\wedge\ r:Record\ l_n:A_n\ end$". Conjunctive types are strictly related to non-trivial subtypes: $(P \wedge Q) \Rightarrow P$ becomes, in the language of types, $\{A \wedge B\} \leq \{A\}$. Our overloaded functions can be read as another special case of conjunctive types, since $f:\{A \rightarrow B, C \rightarrow D\}$ means "$f:A \rightarrow B\ \wedge$ $f:C \rightarrow D$". This link is important mainly from a semantic point of view, since conjunctive type possess a clear semantics based on intersection (or on indexed products, see [BruLon90]), which can be transferred to our overloaded function types.

6 Type safe dynamic extension and encapsulation

Our model supports directly inheritance, overloading and late binding, but does not support dynamic extensibility and encapsulation, which are the other two features of the object-oriented approach. In this section we give a hint about the encoding of these two features.

Dynamic extensibility must be simulated in a strongly-typed language with static binding by exploiting updatable references; a method is modelled as an updatable reference to an overloaded function, and dynamic extension is modelled by updating that reference. This is possible, in a strongly-typed context, since dynamic extension always extends an overloaded function with type $\{T_i \to U_i\}_{i \in I}$ to an overloaded function with type $\{T_i \to U_i\}_{i \in J}$, such that

$$\{T_i \to U_i\}_{i \in J} \leq \{T_i \to U_i\}_{i \in I}.$$

Encapsulation, in our approach, is truly orthogonal to message passing; this is one important result, since breaking down the features of object-oriented languages into orthogonal atomic notions is among the aims of this research. In our approach, encapsulation can be obtained by using any of the well known mechanisms of ADT's, existential types or modules (see [MitPlo85], [CarWeg85]).

Referring to our example, we can encapsulate the type *Point* in a module exporting an abstract version *AbsPoint* of it, together with a creation function and a selector *equal: AbsPoint→Int*. In another module we can do the same with the type *CPoint*, and finally we can collect the two *equal* functions into one overloaded function. This is not possible in the record-based approach (refer to the translation in §2.3), since in that case, once *equal* has been transformed, by a general purpose encapsulation mechanism, from a record field name to a function name, then it is no more possible to overload *equal*. For this reason, in the record-based model, encapsulation cannot be considered orthogonal to message passing.

This is just a very brief discussion about encapsulation; to be more complete we should distinguish encapsulation at least into state encapsulation and method implementation encapsulation, which are actually supported in the record model, and ADT-like encapsulation, i.e. the possibility of specifying that an object type is different from any other, which, in the record model, suffers from the problem highlighted above.

7   Conclusions and directions for future work

We have defined a static and strong type system for late-binding overloaded functions. It can be used to give a strongly-typed model for object-oriented languages which is strictly more expressive than the classical record-based model, and even of the traditional untyped model. We have discussed the origins of the well-known conflict contravariance-covariance and have formally shown that the two notions are not mutually exclusive.

We have left many details to be verified. We should show that, e.g., a notion of state, the "super" operator of object-oriented languages, and mutual recursion among methods, could be all added without problems in our approach. The extension of our mechanism to languages offering parametric polymorphism and existential types, like Fun [CarWeg85], raises many interesting issues.

We should prove decidability of type checking for our type system. The fact that subtyping in this system is not irreflexive, i.e. there exists $U \neq V$ such that $U \leq V$ and $V \leq U$, could constitute a problem [CurGhe91]. It can be solved by introducing a calculus at the type level equating all and only the pairs of types which are mutually subtype-related.

We should define formally operational and denotational semantics for our operators, and then we should give a formal proof of the property of strong typing for our system. The kernel of this proof is the property run-time type≤compile-time type, discussed in the paper, while the remaining part of the work should be routine.

Finally we could design a little object-oriented language around our type system to prove its usability.

References

[AmaCar90]: Amadio R., and L. Cardelli, *"Subtyping Recursive Types"*, DEC-SRC technical report, Palo Alto DEC System Research Center, Ca., USA, 1990.

[AlbGheOccOrs88]: Albano A., G. Ghelli, E. Occhiuto and R. Orsini, *"Galileo Reference Manual Version 2.0"*, Servizio Editoriale Università di Pisa, Italy, 1988.

[AlbGheOrs91]: Albano A., G. Ghelli and R. Orsini, *"Object and Classes for a Database Programming Language"*, Tech. Rep. PFSICP-CNR 5/24, Rome, 1991.

[BruLon90]: Bruce K.B. and G. Longo, *"A Modest Model of Records, Inheritance and Bounded Quantification"*, *Information & Computation*, 87 (1/2), 1990.

[CanHilOlt88]: Canning P.S., W.L. Hill and W. Olthoff, *"A kernel language for object-oriented programming"*, TR. STL-88-21, HP Labs, 1988.

[CanCooHilMitOlt89]: Canning P.S., W.R. Cook, W.L. Hill, J.C. Mitchell and W. Olthoff, "F-bounded polymorphism for object-oriented programming", *Proc. of Conf. on Functional Progr. Languages and Comp. Arch.*, 1989.

[Car88]: Cardelli L., "A Semantics of Multiple Inheritance", *Information & Computation*, 76 (2/3), 1988.

[CarMit89]: Cardelli L. and J.C. Mitchell, "Operations on Records", *Proc. Fifth Intl. Conf. on Mathematical Foundation of Programming Semantics, Tulane Univ.*, New Orleans, 1989.

[CarWeg85]: Cardelli L. and P. Wegner, "On understanding types, data abstraction and polymorphism", *ACM Computing Surveys*, 17 (4), 1985.

[CooHilCan90]: Cook W.R., W.L. Hill and P.S. Canning, "Inheritance is not subtyping", *Proc. of POPL '90*, 1990.

[Cop81]: Coppo M., M. Dezani-Ciancaglini and B. Venneri, "Functional Character of Solvable Terms", *Z. Math. Logik Grundlag Math.*, 27, 1981.

[CurGhe91]: Curien P.L. and G. Ghelli, "Coherence of Subsumption", *Mathematical Foundations of Computer Science*, to appear.

[DanTom88]: Danforth, S. and C. Tomlinson, "Type Theories and Object-Oriented Programming", *ACM Surveys*, 20 (1), 1988.

[Ghe91]: Ghelli G., "Modelling features of object-oriented languages in second order functional languages with subtypes", in *Foundations of Object-Oriented Languages* (G. Rozenberg ed.), Springer-Verlag, Berlin, 1991.

[Mit90]: Mitchell, J., "Toward a typed foundation for method specialization and inheritance", *Proc. of POPL '90*, 1990.

[MitPlo85]: Mitchell J.C. and G.D. Plotkin, "Abstract Types Have Existential Types", *Proc. of POPL '85*, 1985.

[Red88]: Reddy, U.S., "Objects as Closures: Abstract semantics of object-oriented languages", *Proc. of ACM Conf. on Lisp and Functional Programming '88*, 1988.

[Rey77]: Reynolds J.C., "Conjunctive Types and Algol-like Languages", *Proc. of LICS 87*, 1987.

[Wan89]: Wand M., "Type inference for record concatenation and multiple inheritance", *Proc of LICS '89*, pp. 92-97, Asilomar, CA, 1989.

Appendix A: The type rules

Syntax

$$A ::= t \mid A{\to}A \mid A{\times}A'$$
$$\mid \textbf{Rcd}\, l_1{:}A_1,...,l_n{:}A_n \textbf{ End} \mid \{A,...,A\}$$

$$a ::= x \mid \textbf{fun}(x_1{:}A_1,...,x_n{:}A_n).a \mid a(a_1,...,a_n)$$
$$\mid \textbf{rcd}\, l_1{:=}a_1,...,l_n{:=}a_n \textbf{ end} \mid a.l$$
$$\mid \textbf{overload}\, a \mid a + a \mid a{\bullet}(a_1,...,a_n)$$

Environments

(Øenv) $()$ env

($\leq$env) $\dfrac{\Gamma \text{ env} \quad \Gamma \vdash A \text{ type}}{\Gamma, t{\leq}A \quad \text{env}}$

(: env) $\dfrac{\Gamma \text{ env} \quad \Gamma \vdash A \text{ type}}{\Gamma, x{:}A \quad \text{env}}$

Types

(RcdForm) $\dfrac{\forall i.\ \Gamma \vdash A_i \text{ type}}{\Gamma \vdash \textbf{Rcd}\, l_1{:}A_1,...,l_n{:}A_n \textbf{ End type}}$

($\to/\times$Form) $\dfrac{\Gamma \vdash A \text{ type} \quad \Gamma \vdash B \text{ type}}{\Gamma \vdash A{\to}/{\times}\, B \quad \text{type}}$

(ch.Form)

$\forall i{\in}I \qquad\qquad \Gamma \vdash T_i \text{ choice\_type}$

i $\quad \forall A{\in}\text{acc.}\{T_i\}_{i{\in}I,s}.\{T_i\}_{i{\in}I,s}{\bullet}A{\in}\{T_i\}_{i{\in}I}$

ii $\quad \forall A{\in}\text{acc.}\{T_i\}_{i{\in}I,s},\ \forall j{\in}I$
$\qquad A{\leq}T_j{\leq}\{T_i\}_{i{\in}I,s}{\bullet}A. \Rightarrow T_j{=}\{T_i\}_{i{\in}I,s}{\bullet}A$

iii $\quad \forall A{\in}\text{acc.}\{T_i\}_{i{\in}I,s}.\ \Gamma \vdash A \leq \{T_i\}_{i{\in}I,s}{\bullet}A$

iv $\quad \dfrac{\forall B{\in}\text{acc.}\{T_i\}_{i{\in}I,s}.\ \forall A \text{ such that } \Gamma \vdash A{\leq}B.}{A{\in}\text{acc.}\{T_i\}_{i{\in}I,s}}$

$$\overline{\Gamma \vdash s \text{ choice\_for } \{T_i\}_{i{\in}I}}$$

({}Form)

$\forall i,j{\in}I \quad \Gamma \vdash T_i {\neq} T_j$

$\forall i{\in}I \quad \Gamma \vdash U_i \text{ type} \quad \Gamma \vdash s \text{ choice\_for } \{T_i\}_{i{\in}I}$

v $\quad \forall i,j{\in}I \text{ s.t. } \Gamma \vdash T_i \sqsubseteq_{s,\{T_i\}_{i{\in}I}} T_j.\ \Gamma \vdash U_i \leq U_j$

$$\overline{\Gamma \vdash \{T_i{\to}U_i\}_{i{\in}I,s} \text{ type}}$$

Subtypes

(Id$\leq$) $\dfrac{\Gamma \vdash A \text{ type}}{\Gamma \vdash A{\leq}A}$

(Trans$\leq$) $\dfrac{\Gamma \vdash A{\leq}B \quad \Gamma \vdash B{\leq}C}{\Gamma \vdash A{\leq}C}$

($\times{\leq}$) $\dfrac{\Gamma \vdash A \leq A' \quad \Gamma \vdash B \leq B'}{\Gamma \vdash A{\times}B \leq A'{\times}B'}$

(Abs$\leq$) $\dfrac{\Gamma,t{\leq}A,\Gamma' \text{ env} \quad t \text{ not in } \Gamma'\,^9}{\Gamma \vdash t{\leq}A}$

($\to{\leq}$) $\dfrac{\Gamma \vdash A{\leq}A' \quad \Gamma \vdash B{\leq}B'}{\Gamma \vdash A'{\to}B \leq A{\to}B'}$

(Record $\leq$)

$\forall i{:}1,...,n\ \Gamma \vdash A_i {\leq} B_i$

$\dfrac{\forall i{:}n{+}1,...,n{+}m\ \Gamma \vdash A_i \text{ type}}{\begin{array}{l}\Gamma \vdash \textbf{Rcd}\, l_1{:}A_1,...,l_n{:}A_n,m_1{:}A_{n+1},...,l_m{:}A_{n+m} \textbf{ End} \\ \qquad\qquad\qquad \leq \textbf{Rcd}\, l_1{:}B_1,...,l_n{:}B_n \textbf{ End}\end{array}}$

({}$\leq$) $\forall A{\in} \text{accepted}\{V_j\}_{j{\in}J,r}$ then

$\qquad A{\in}\text{acc.}\{T_i\}_{i{\in}I,s}$ and

$$\dfrac{\Gamma \vdash \{T_i{\to}U_i\}_{i{\in}I,s}{\bullet}A \leq \{V_j{\to}W_j\}_{j{\in}J,r}{\bullet}A}{\Gamma \vdash \{T_i{\to}U_i\}_{i{\in}I,s} \leq \{V_j{\to}W_j\}_{j{\in}J,r}}$$

Expressions:

(Var:) $\dfrac{\Gamma, x{:}A, \Gamma' \text{ env} \quad x \text{ is not in } \Gamma'}{\Gamma, x{:}A, \Gamma' \vdash x{:} A}$

(Subsump) $\Gamma \vdash a{:} A \quad \Gamma \vdash A \leq B$

---

[9] A variable t (x) is in Γ if it is present in a left hand side of an element $t \leq A$ $(x : A)$ of the environment.

$$\Gamma \vdash a: B$$

$(\rightarrow \text{Intro}) \quad \dfrac{\Gamma, x_1:A_1,\ldots,x_n:A_n \vdash b: B}{\Gamma \vdash \text{fun}(x_1:A_1,\ldots,x_n:A_n).a: A_1 \times \ldots \times A_n \rightarrow B}$

$(\rightarrow \text{Elim}) \quad \dfrac{\Gamma \vdash f: A_1 \times \ldots \times A_n \rightarrow B \quad \Gamma \vdash a_j:A_j}{\Gamma \vdash f(a_1,\ldots,a_n): B}$

$(\text{RcdIntro}) \quad \dfrac{\forall i:1,\ldots,n \quad \Gamma \vdash a_i:A_i}{\substack{\Gamma \vdash \text{rcd } l_1:=a_1,\ldots,l_n:=a_n \text{ end}: \\ \text{Rcd } l_1:A_1,\ldots,l_n:A_n \text{ End}}}$

$(\text{RcdElim}) \quad \dfrac{\Gamma \vdash r: \text{Rcd } l_1:A_1,\ldots,l_n:A_n \text{ End}}{\Gamma \vdash r.l_i : A_i}$

$(\{\}\text{Intro}) \quad \dfrac{\Gamma \vdash f:T \rightarrow U \quad \Gamma \vdash s \text{ choice\_for } \{T\}}{\Gamma \vdash \text{overload}_s f: \{T \rightarrow U\}_s}$

$(\{\}\text{Add}) \quad \dfrac{\Gamma \vdash f: \{T_i \rightarrow U_i\}_{i \in I,r} \quad \Gamma \vdash g: T_k \rightarrow U_k \quad \Gamma \vdash \{T_i \rightarrow U_i\}_{i \in I \cup \{k\},s} \text{ type}}{\Gamma \vdash f +_s g: \{T_i \rightarrow U_i\}_{i \in I \cup \{k\},s}}$

$(\{\}\text{Elim}) \quad \dfrac{\Gamma \vdash f: \{T_i \rightarrow U_i\}_{i \in I,s} \quad \Gamma \vdash a:A \quad \Gamma \vdash \{T_i\}_{i \in I,s} \text{ accepts } A}{\Gamma \vdash f \bullet_s(a): \{T_i \rightarrow U_i\}_{i \in I,s} \bullet A}$

Appendix B: Compatibility of covariance and contravariance

Suppose that:

$$\Gamma \vdash T' \leq T \quad \Gamma \vdash U' \leq U$$
$$\Gamma \vdash \{T' \rightarrow U\}_r \text{ type} \quad \Gamma \vdash \{T \rightarrow U'\}_s \text{ type}$$

We want to prove that :

$$\Gamma \vdash \{T \rightarrow U'\}_s \leq \{T' \rightarrow U\}_r$$

i.e. that:

$$\forall A \in \text{accepted}\{T'\}_r$$
$$A \in \text{accepted}\{T\}_s, \{T \rightarrow U'\}_s \bullet A \leq \{T' \rightarrow U\}_r \bullet A$$

Proof:

a) Hyp.: $\quad A \in \text{accepted}\{T'\}_r$

b) $\Rightarrow_{i \,(\text{only } T' \in \{T'\})} \quad \{T'\}_r \bullet A = T'$

c) $\Rightarrow \qquad\qquad\qquad \{T' \rightarrow U\}_r \bullet A = U$

$\quad \Rightarrow_{iii,b)} \qquad\qquad A \leq T'$

$\quad \Rightarrow_{T' \leq T} \qquad\qquad A \leq T$

$\quad \Rightarrow_{T \geq A} \qquad\qquad \min\{U \geq A | U \in \{T\}\} = \min\{T\} = T$

d) $\Rightarrow_{ii} \qquad\qquad\quad \{T\}_s \bullet A = T$

e) $\Rightarrow \qquad\qquad\quad \{T \rightarrow U'\}_s \bullet A = U'$

f) $\Rightarrow_{d)} \qquad\qquad\quad A \in \text{accepted}\{T\}_s,$

g) $\Rightarrow_{e), U' \leq U} \qquad \Gamma \vdash \{T \rightarrow U'\}_s \bullet A \leq \{T' \rightarrow U\}_r \bullet A$

a) $\Rightarrow$ f,g):

$$\dfrac{\forall A \in \text{accepted}\{T'\}_r \\ A \in \text{acc.}\{T\}_s \text{ and} \\ \Gamma \vdash \{T \rightarrow U'\}_s \bullet A \leq \{T' \rightarrow U\}_r \bullet A}{\Gamma \vdash \{T \rightarrow U'\}_s \leq \{T' \rightarrow U\}_r}$$

Object-Oriented Type Inference

Jens Palsberg and Michael I. Schwartzbach

palsberg@daimi.aau.dk and mis@daimi.aau.dk

Computer Science Department, Aarhus University
Ny Munkegade, DK-8000 Århus C, Denmark

Abstract

We present a new approach to inferring types in untyped object-oriented programs with inheritance, assignments, and late binding. It guarantees that all messages are understood, annotates the program with type information, allows polymorphic methods, and can be used as the basis of an optimizing compiler. Types are finite sets of classes and subtyping is set inclusion. Using a *trace graph*, our algorithm constructs a set of conditional type constraints and computes the least solution by least fixed-point derivation.

1 Introduction

Untyped object-oriented languages with assignments and late binding allow rapid prototyping because classes inherit implementation and not specification. Late binding, however, can cause programs to be unreliable, unreadable, and inefficient [27]. Type inference may help solve these problems, but so far no proposed inference algorithm has been capable of checking most common, completely untyped programs [9].

We present a new type inference algorithm for a basic object-oriented language with inheritance, assignments, and late binding.

The algorithm guarantees that all messages are understood, annotates the program with type information, allows polymorphic methods, and can be used as the basis of an optimizing compiler. Types are finite sets of classes and subtyping is set inclusion. Given a concrete program, the algorithm constructs a finite graph of type constraints. The program is *typable* if these constraints are solvable. The algorithm then computes the least solution in worst-case exponential time. The graph contains all type information that can be derived from the program without keeping track of nil values or flow analyzing the contents of instance variables. This makes the algorithm capable of checking most common programs; in particular, it allows for polymorphic methods. The algorithm is similar to previous work on type inference [18, 14, 27, 1, 2, 19, 12, 10, 9] in using type constraints, but it differs in handling late binding by *conditional* constraints and in resolving the constraints by least fixed-point derivation rather than unification.

The example language resembles SMALLTALK [8] but avoids metaclasses, blocks, and primitive methods. Instead, it provides explicit **new** and **if-then-else** expressions; classes like **Natural** can be programmed in the language itself.

In the following section we discuss the impacts of late binding on type inference and examine previous work. In later sections we briefly outline the example language, present the type inference algorithm, and show some examples of its capabilities.

2 Late Binding

Late binding means that a message send is dynamically bound to an implementation depending on the class of the receiver. This allows a form of polymorphism which is fundamental in object-oriented programming. It also, however, involves the danger that the class of the receiver does *not* implement a method for the message—the receiver may even be nil. Furthermore, late binding can make the control flow of a program hard to follow and may cause a time-consuming run-time search for an implementation.

It would significantly help an optimizing compiler if, for each message send in a program text, it could infer the following information.

- Can the receiver be nil?

- Can the receiver be an instance of a class which does not implement a method for the message?

- What are the classes of all possible non-nil receivers in any execution of the program?

Note that the available set of classes is induced by the particular program. These observations lead us to the following terminology.

Terminology:

Type: A type is a finite set of classes.

Induced Type: The induced type of an expression in a concrete program is the set of classes of all possible non-nil values to which it may evaluate in any execution of that particular program.

Sound approximation: A sound approximation of the induced type of an expression in a concrete program is a *superset* of the induced type.

Note that a sound approximation tells "the whole truth", but not always "nothing but the truth" about an induced type. Since induced types are generally uncomputable, a compiler must make do with sound approximations. An induced type is a *subtype* of any sound approximation; subtyping is set inclusion. Note also that our notion of type, which we also investigated in [21], differs from those usually used in theoretical studies of types in object-oriented programming [3, 7]; these theories have difficulties with late binding and assignments.

The goals of type inference can now be phrased as follows.

Goals of type inference:

Safety guarantee: A guarantee that any message is sent to either nil or an instance of a class which implements a method for the message; and, given that, also

Type information: A sound approximation of the induced type of any receiver.

Note that we ignore checking whether the receiver is nil; this is a standard data flow analysis problem which can be treated separately.

If a type inference is successful, then the program is *typable*; the error **messageNotUnderstood** will not occur. A compiler can use this to avoid inserting some checks in the code. Furthermore, if the type information of a receiver is a *singleton* set, then the compiler can do early binding of the message to the only possible method; it can even do in-line substitution. Similarly, if the type information is an *empty* set, then the receiver is known to always be nil. Finally, type information obtained about variables and arguments may be used to annotate the program for the benefit of the programmer.

SMALLTALK and other untyped object-oriented languages are traditionally implemented by interpreters. This is ideal for prototyping and exploratory development but often too inefficient and space demanding for real-time applications and embedded systems. What is needed is an optimizing compiler that can be used near the end of the programming phase, to get the required efficiency and a safety guarantee. A compiler which produces good code can be tolerated even it is slow because it will be used much less often than the usual programming environment. Our type inference algorithm can be used as the basis of such an optimizing compiler. Note, though, that both the safety guarantee and the induced types are sensitive to small changes in the program. Hence, separate compilation of classes seems impossible. Typed object-oriented languages such as SIMULA [6]/BETA [15], C++ [26], and EIFFEL [17] allow separate compilation but sacrifice flexibility. The relations between types and implementation are summarized in figure 1.

When programs are:	Their implementation is:
Untyped	Interpretation
Typable	Compilation
Typed	Separate Compilation

Figure 1: Types and implementation.

Graver and Johnson [10, 9], in their type system for SMALLTALK, take an intermediate approach between "untyped" and "typed" in requiring the programmer to specify types for instance variables whereas types of arguments are inferred. Suzuki [27], in his pioneering work on inferring types in SMALLTALK, handles late binding by assuming that each message send may invoke all methods for that message. It turned out, however, that this yields an algorithm which is not capable of checking most common programs.

Both these approaches include a notion of *method type*. Our new type inference algorithm abandons this idea and uses instead the concept of *conditional constraints*, derived from a finite graph. Recently, Hense [11] addressed type inference for a language O'SMALL which is almost identical to our example language. He uses a radically different technique, with type schemes and unification based on work of Rémy [24] and Wand [29]. His paper lists four programs of which his algorithm can type-check only the first three. Our algorithm can type-check all

four, in particular the fourth which is shown in figure 11 in appendix B. Hense uses record types which can be extendible and recursive. This seems to produce less precise typings than our approach, and it is not clear whether the typings would be useful in an optimizing compiler. One problem is that type schemes always correspond to either singletons or infinite sets of monotypes; our finite sets can be more precise. Hense's and ours approaches are similar in neither keeping track of nil values nor flow analyzing the contents of variables. We are currently investigating other possible relations.

Before going into the details of our type inference algorithm we first outline an example language on which to apply it.

3 The Language

Our example language resembles SMALLTALK, see figure 2.

A *program* is a set of classes followed by an expression whose value is the result of executing the program. A *class* can be defined using inheritance and contains instance variables and methods; a *method* is a message selector ($m_{1-} \ldots m_{n-}$) with formal parameters and an expression. The language avoids metaclasses, blocks, and primitive methods. Instead, it provides explicit new and if-then-else expressions (the latter tests if the condition is non-nil). The result of a sequence is the result of the last expression in that sequence. The expression "self class new" yields an instance of the class of self. The expression "E instanceOf ClassId" yields a run-time check for class membership. If the check fails, then the expression evaluates to nil.

The SMALLTALK system is based on some primitive methods, written in assembly language. This dependency on primitives is not necessary, at least not in this theoretical study, because classes such as True, False, Natural, and List can be programmed in the language itself, as shown in appendix A.

```
(Program)     P  ::=  C_1 ... C_n E

(Class)       C  ::=  class ClassId [inherits ClassId]
                      var Id_1 ... Id_k M_1 ... M_n
                      end ClassId

(Method)      M  ::=  method m_1 Id_1 ... m_n Id_n E

(Expression)  E  ::=  Id := E | E m_1 E_1 ... m_n E_n| E ; E | if E then E else E |
                      ClassId new | self class new | E instanceOf ClassId |
                      self | super | Id | nil
```

Figure 2: Syntax of the example language.

4 Type Inference

Our type inference algorithm is based on three fundamental observations.

Observations:

Inheritance: Classes inherit implementation and not specification.

Classes: There are finitely many classes in a program.

Message sends: There are finitely many syntactic message sends in a program.

The first observation leads to separate type inference for a class and its subclasses. Notionally, this is achieved by expanding all classes before doing type inference. This expansion means removing all inheritance by

- Copying the text of a class to its subclasses

- Replacing each message send to **super** by a message send to a renamed version of the inherited method

- Replacing each "self class new" expression by a "ClassId new" expression where ClassId is the enclosing class in the expanded program.

This idea of expansion is inspired by Graver and Johnson [10, 9]; note that the size of the expanded program is at most quadratic in the size of the original.

The second and third observation lead to a finite representation of type information about all executions of the expanded program; this representation is called the *trace graph*. From this graph a finite set of type constraints will be generated. Typability of the program is then solvability of these constraints. Appendix B contains seven example programs which illustrate different aspects of the type inference algorithm, see the overview in figure 3. The program texts are listed together with the corresponding constraints and their least solution, if it exists. Hense's program in figure 11 is the one he gives as a typical example of what he cannot type-check [11]. We invite the reader to consult the appendix while reading this section.

A trace graph contains three kinds of type information.

Three kinds of type information:

Local constraints: Generated from method bodies; contained in nodes.

Connecting constraints: Reflect message sends; attached to edges.

Conditions: Discriminate receivers; attached to edges.

Example program in:	Illustrates:	Can we type it?
Figure 10	Basic type inference	Yes
Figure 11	Hense's program	Yes
Figure 12	A polymorphic method	Yes
Figure 13	A recursive method	Yes
Figure 14	Lack of flow analysis	No
Figure 15	Lack of nil detection	No
Figure 16	A realistic program	Yes

Figure 3: An overview of the example programs.

4.1 Trace Graph Nodes

The *nodes* of the trace graph are obtained from the various methods implemented in the program. Each method yields a number of different nodes: one for each syntactic message send with the corresponding selector. The situation is illustrated in figure 4, where we see the nodes for a method m that is implemented in each of the classes $C_1, C_2, \ldots, C_n$. Thus, the number of nodes in the trace graph will at most be quadratic in the size of the program. There is also a single node for the main expression of the program, which we may think of as a special method without parameters.

Methods do not have types, but they can be provided with type annotations, based on the types of their formal parameters and result. A particular method implementation may be represented by several nodes in the trace graph. This enables it to be assigned several different type annotations—one for each syntactic call. This allows us effectively to obtain method polymorphism through a finite set of method "monotypes".

4.2 Local Constraints

Each node contains a collection of *local constraints* that the types of expressions must satisfy. For each syntactic occurrence of an expression E in the implementation of the method, we regard its type as an unknown variable [[E]]. Exact type information is, of course, uncomputable. In our approach, we will ignore the following two aspects of program executions.

Approximations:

Nil values: It does not keep track of nil values.

Instance variables: It does not flow analyze the contents of instance variables.

The first approximation stems from our discussion of the goals of type inference; the second corresponds to viewing an instance variable as having a single possibly large type, thus leading us to identify the type variables of different occurrences of the same instance variable. In figures 14 and 15 we present two program fragments that are typical for what we cannot type because of these approximations. In both cases the constraints demand the false inclusion {True} ⊆ {Natural}. Suzuki [27] and Hense [11] make the same approximations.

For an expression E, the local constraints are generated from all the phrases in its derivation, according to the rules in figure 5. The idea of generating constraints on type variables from the program syntax is also exploited in [28, 25].

The constraints guarantee safety; only in the cases **4)** and **8)** do the approximations manifest themselves. Notice that the constraints can all be ex-

150

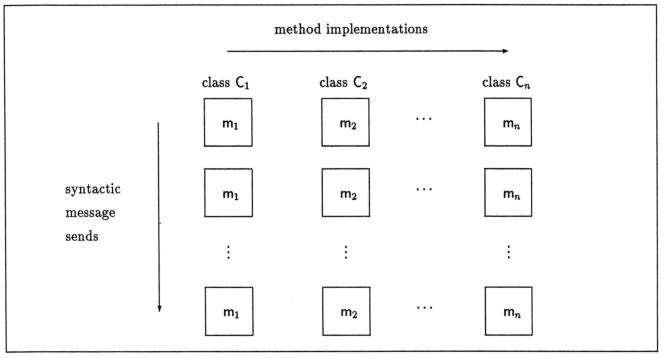

Figure 4: Trace graph nodes.

pressed as inequalities of one of the three forms: "constant $\subseteq$ variable", "variable $\subseteq$ constant", or "variable $\subseteq$ variable"; this will be exploited later.

Each different node employs unique type variables, except that the types of instance variables are common to all nodes corresponding to methods implemented in the same class. A similar idea is used by Graver and Johnson [10, 9].

4.3 Trace Graph Edges

The *edges* of the trace graph will reflect the possible connections between a message send and a method that may implement it. The situation is illustrated in figure 6.

If a node corresponds to a method which contains a message send of the form X m: A, then we have an edge from that sender node to any other receiver node which corresponds to an implementation of a method m. We label this edge with the condition that the message send may be executed, namely $C \in [\![X]\!]$ where C is the class in which the particular

method m is implemented. With the edge we associate the *connecting constraints*, which reflect the relationship between formal and actual parameters and results. This situation generalizes trivially to methods with several parameters. Note that the number of edges is again quadratic in the size of the program.

4.4 Global Constraints

To obtain the *global constraints* for the entire program we combine local and connecting constraints in the manner illustrated in figure 7. This produces *conditional constraints*, where the inequalities need only hold if all the conditions hold. The global constraints are simply the union of the conditional constraints generated by all paths in the graph, originating in the node corresponding to the main expression of the program. This is a finite set, because the graph is finite; as shown later in this section, the size of the constraint set may in (extreme) worst-cases become exponential.

If the set of global constraints has a solution, then

151

	Expression:	Constraint:
1)	Id := E	$[\![\text{Id}]\!] \supseteq [\![\text{E}]\!] \wedge [\![\text{Id} := \text{E}]\!] = [\![\text{E}]\!]$
2)	E m_1 E_1 ... m_n E_n	$[\![\text{E}]\!] \subseteq \{\text{C} \,|\, \text{C implements } m_1 \ldots m_n\}$
3)	E_1 ; E_2	$[\![E_1 ; E_2]\!] = [\![E_2]\!]$
4)	if E_1 then E_2 else E_3	$[\![\text{if } E_1 \text{ then } E_2 \text{ else } E_3]\!] \supseteq [\![E_2]\!] \cup [\![E_3]\!]$
5)	C new	$[\![\text{C new}]\!] = \{\text{C}\}$
6)	E instanceOf C	$[\![\text{E instanceOf C}]\!] = \{\text{C}\}$
7)	self	$[\![\text{self}]\!] = \{\text{the enclosing class}\}$
8)	Id	$[\![\text{Id}]\!] = [\![\text{Id}]\!]$
9)	nil	$[\![\text{nil}]\!] = \{\,\}$

Figure 5: The local constraints.

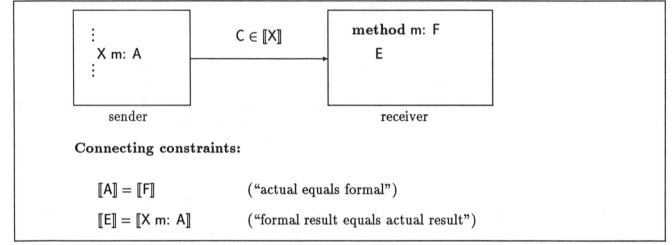

Connecting constraints:

$[\![A]\!] = [\![F]\!]$ ("actual equals formal")

$[\![E]\!] = [\![X \text{ m: A}]\!]$ ("formal result equals actual result")

Figure 6: Trace graph edges.

this provides approximate information about the dynamic behavior of the program.

Consider any execution of the program. While observing this, we can trace the pattern of method executions in the trace graph. Let E be some expression that is evaluated at some point, let $\text{VAL}(\text{E})$ be its value, and let $\text{CLASS}(b)$ be the class of an object b. If L is some solution to the global constraints, then the following result holds.

Soundness Theorem:

If $\text{VAL}(\text{E}) \neq \text{nil}$ then $\text{CLASS}(\text{VAL}(\text{E})) \in L([\![\text{E}]\!])$

It is quite easy to see that this must be true. We sketch a proof by induction in the number of message sends performed during the trace. If this is zero, then we rely on the local constraints alone;

given a dynamic semantics [5, 4, 23, 13] one can easily verify that their satisfaction implies the above property. If we extend a trace with a message send X m: A implemented by a method in a class C, then we can inductively assume that $\text{C} \in L([\![\text{X}]\!])$. But this implies that the local constraints in the node corresponding to the invoked method must hold, since all their conditions now hold and L is a solution. Since the relationship between actual and formal parameters and results is soundly represented by the connecting constraints, which also must hold, the result follows.

Note that an expression E occurring in a method that appears k times in the trace graph has k type variables $[\![\text{E}]\!]_1, [\![\text{E}]\!]_2, \ldots, [\![\text{E}]\!]_k$ in the global constraints. A sound approximation to the induced

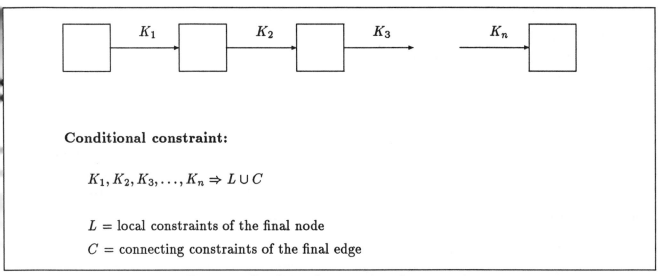

Conditional constraint:

$$K_1, K_2, K_3, \ldots, K_n \Rightarrow L \cup C$$

$L = $ local constraints of the final node

$C = $ connecting constraints of the final edge

Figure 7: Conditional constraints from a path.

type of E is obtained as

$$\bigcup_i L([\![E]\!]_i)$$

Appendix C gives an efficient algorithm to compute the smallest solution of the extracted constraints, or to decide that none exists. The algorithm is at worst quadratic in the size of the constraint set.

The complete type inference algorithm is summarized in figure 8.

4.5 Type Annotations

Finally, we will consider how a solution L of the type constraints can produce a *type annotation* of the program. Such annotations could be provided for the benefit of the programmer.

An instance variable x has only a single associated type variable. The type annotation is simply $L([\![x]\!])$. The programmer then knows an upper bound of the set of classes whose instances may reside in x.

A method has finitely many type annotations, each of which is obtained from a corresponding node in the trace graph. If the method, implemented in the class C, is

Input:	A program in the example language.
Output:	Either: a safety guarantee and type information about all expressions; or: "unable to type the program".
1)	Expand all classes.
2)	Construct the trace graph of the expanded program.
3)	Extract a set of type constraints from the trace graph.
4)	Compute the least solution of the set of type constraints. If such a solution exists, then output it as the wanted type information, together with a safety guarantee; otherwise, output "unable to type the program".

Figure 8: Summary of the type inference algorithm.

$$\textbf{method } m_1\text{: } F_1 \; m_2\text{: } F_2 \ldots m_n\text{: } F_n$$
$$E$$

then each type annotation is of the form

$$\{C\} \times L([\![F_1]\!]) \times \cdots \times L([\![F_n]\!]) \to L([\![E]\!])$$

The programmer then knows the various manners in which this method may be used.

A constraint solution contains more type information about methods than the method types used by Suzuki. Consider for example the polymorphic identity function in figure 12. Our technique yields both of the method type annotations

$$\text{id} : \{C\} \times \{\text{True}\} \rightarrow \{\text{True}\}$$
$$\text{id} : \{C\} \times \{\text{Natural}\} \rightarrow \{\text{Natural}\}$$

whereas the method type using Suzuki's framework is

$$\text{id} : \{C\} \times \{\text{True}, \text{Natural}\} \rightarrow \{\text{True}, \text{Natural}\}$$

which would allow neither the succ nor the isTrue message send, and, hence, would lead to rejection of the program.

4.6 An Exponential Worst-Case

The examples in appendix B show several cases where the constraint set is quite small, in fact linear in the size of the program. While this will often be the situation, the theoretical worst-case allows the constraint set to become exponential in the size of the program. The running time of the inference algorithm depends primarily on the topology of the trace graph.

In figure 9 is shown a program and a sketch of its trace graph. The induced constraint set will be exponential since the graph has exponentially many different paths. Among the constraints will be a family whose conditions are similar to the words of the regular language

$$(\text{CCC} + \text{DCC})^{\frac{n}{3}}$$

the size of which is clearly exponential in n.

Note that this situation is similar to that of type inference in ML, which is also worst-case exponential but very useful in practice. The above scenario is in fact not unlike the one presented in [16] to illustrate exponential running times in ML. Another similarity is that both algorithms generate a potentially exponential constraint set that is always solved in polynomial time.

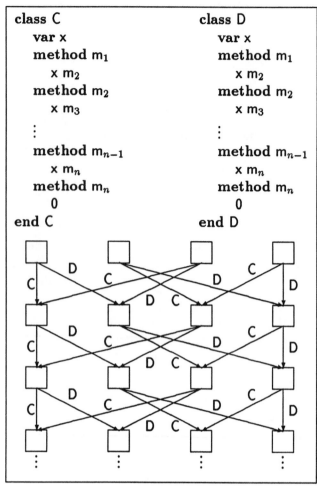

Figure 9: A worst-case program.

5 Conclusion

Our type inference algorithm is sound and can handle most common programs. It is also conceptually simple: a set of uniform type constraints is constructed and solved by fixed-point derivation. It can be further improved by an orthogonal effort in data flow analysis.

The underlying type system is simple: types are finite sets of classes and subtyping is set inclusion.

An implementation of the type inference algorithm is currently being undertaken. Future work includes extending this into an optimizing compiler. The inference algorithm should be easy to modify to work for full SMALLTALK, because metaclasses are simply classes, blocks can be treated as objects with a single method, and primitive methods can be handled by stating the constraints that the machine code must satisfy. Another challenge is to extend the algorithm to produce type annotations together with type substitution, see [20, 22, 21].

Appendix A: Basic classes

```
class Object
end Object

class True
    method isTrue
        Object new
end True

class False
    method isTrue
        nil
end False
```

Henceforth, we abbreviate "True new" as "true", and "False new" as "false".

```
class Natural
    var rep
    method isZero
        if rep then false else true
    method succ
        (Natural new) update: self
    method update: x
        rep := x; self
    method pred
        if (self isZero) isTrue then self else rep
    method less: i
        if (i isZero) isTrue
        then false
        else if (self isZero) isTrue then true
        else (self pred) less: (i pred)
end Natural
```

Henceforth, we abbreviate "Natural new" as "0", and, recursively, "*n* succ" as "*n* + 1".

```
class List
    var head, tail
    method setHead: h setTail: t
        head := h; tail := t
    method cons: x
        (self class new) setHead: x setTail: self
    method isEmpty
        if head then false else true
    method car
        head
    method cdr
        tail
    method append: aList
        if (self isEmpty) isTrue
        then aList
        else (tail append: aList) cons: head
    method insert: x
        if (self isEmpty) isTrue
        then self cons: x
        else
            if (head less: x) isTrue
            then self cons: x
            else (tail insert: x) cons: head
    method sort
        if (self isEmpty) isTrue then self
        else (tail sort) insert: head
    method merge: aList
        if (self isEmpty) isTrue
        then aList
        else
            if (head less: (aList car)) isTrue
            then (tail merge: aList) cons: head
            else (self merge: (aList cdr)) cons: (aList car)
end List

class Comparable
    var key
    method getKey
        key
    method setKey: k
        key := k
    method less: c
        key less: (c getKey)
end Comparable
```

Appendix B: Example Programs

```
class A
    method f
        7
end A
class B
    method f
        true
end B
x := A new; (x f) succ
```

Constraints:

$[\![A\ new]\!] = \{A\}$
$[\![x]\!] \supseteq [\![A\ new]\!]$
$[\![x := A\ new]\!] = [\![A\ new]\!]$
$[\![x]\!] \subseteq \{A, B\}$
$A \in [\![x]\!] \Rightarrow [\![x\ f]\!] = [\![7]\!]$
$A \in [\![x]\!] \Rightarrow [\![7]\!] = \{Natural\}$
$B \in [\![x]\!] \Rightarrow [\![x\ f]\!] = [\![true]\!]$
$B \in [\![x]\!] \Rightarrow [\![true]\!] = \{True\}$
$[\![x\ f]\!] \subseteq \{Natural\}$
$Natural \in [\![x\ f]\!] \Rightarrow [\![(x\ f)\ succ]\!] = \{Natural\}$
$[\![x := A\ new; (x\ f)\ succ]\!] = [\![(x\ f)\ succ]\!]$

Smallest Solution:

$[\![x]\!] = [\![A\ new]\!] = [\![x := A\ new]\!] = \{A\}$
$[\![x\ f]\!] = [\![(x\ f)\ succ]\!] =$
$[\![x := A\ new; (x\ f)\ succ]\!] = [\![7]\!] = \{Natural\}$
$[\![true]\!] = \{True\}$

Trace graph sketch:

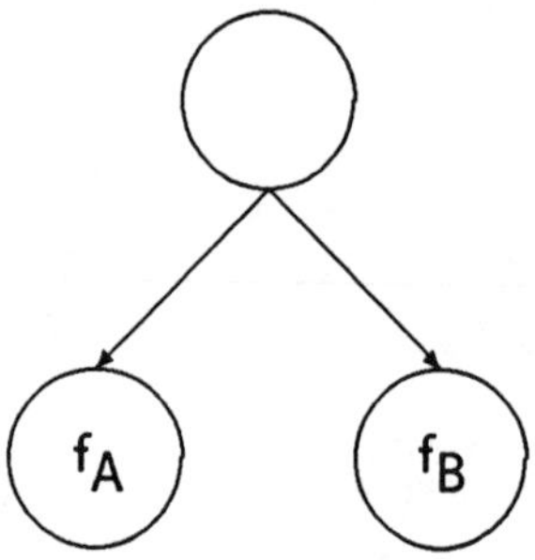

Figure 10: Conditions at work.

```
class A
    method m
        0
end A
class B inherits A
    method n
        0
end B
a := A new;
b := B new;
a := b;
a m
```

Constraints:

$[\![A\ new]\!] = \{A\}$
$[\![a]\!] \supseteq [\![A\ new]\!]$
$[\![B\ new]\!] = \{B\}$
$[\![b]\!] \supseteq [\![B\ new]\!]$
$[\![a]\!] \supseteq [\![b]\!]$
$[\![a]\!] \subseteq \{A, B\}$
$A \in [\![a]\!] \Rightarrow [\![a\ m]\!] = [\![0]\!]$
$B \in [\![a]\!] \Rightarrow [\![a\ m]\!] = [\![0]\!]$
$[\![0]\!] = \{Natural\}$
$\vdots$

Smallest Solution:

$[\![a]\!] = \{A, B\}$
$[\![b]\!] = \{B\}$
$[\![a\ m]\!] = \{Natural\}$
$[\![A\ new]\!] = \{A\}$
$[\![B\ new]\!] = \{B\}$
$\vdots$

Trace graph sketch:

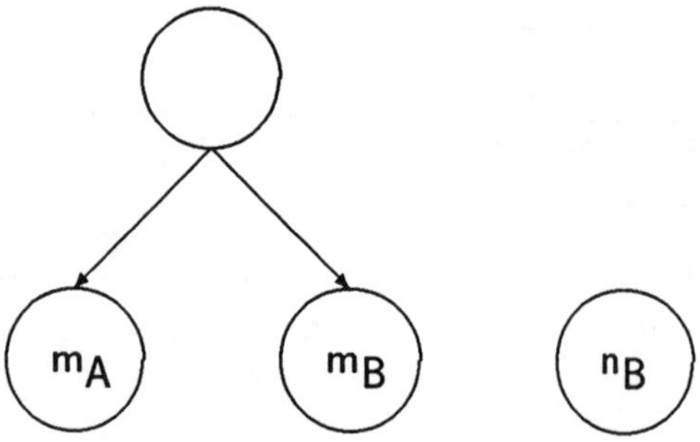

Figure 11: Hense's program.

```
class C
    method id: x
        x
end C
((C new) id: 7) succ;
((C new) id: true) isTrue
```

Constraints:

$\llbracket C\ new\rrbracket_1 = \{C\}$
$\llbracket C\ new\rrbracket_1 \subseteq \{C\}$
$C \in \llbracket C\ new\rrbracket_1 \Rightarrow \llbracket 7\rrbracket = \llbracket x\rrbracket_1$
$C \in \llbracket C\ new\rrbracket_1 \Rightarrow \llbracket x\rrbracket_1 = \llbracket (C\ new)\ id:\ 7\rrbracket$
$\llbracket 7\rrbracket = \{Natural\}$
$\llbracket (C\ new)\ id:\ 7\rrbracket \subseteq \{Natural\}$
$Natural \in \llbracket (C\ new)\ id:\ 7\rrbracket \Rightarrow \{Natural\} = \llbracket ((C\ new)\ id:\ 7)\ succ\rrbracket$
$\llbracket C\ new\rrbracket_2 = \{C\}$
$\llbracket C\ new\rrbracket_2 \subseteq \{C\}$
$C \in \llbracket C\ new\rrbracket_2 \Rightarrow \llbracket true\rrbracket = \llbracket x\rrbracket_2$
$C \in \llbracket C\ new\rrbracket_2 \Rightarrow \llbracket x\rrbracket_2 = \llbracket (C\ new)\ id:\ true\rrbracket$
$\llbracket true\rrbracket = \{True\}$
$\llbracket (C\ new)\ id:\ true\rrbracket \subseteq \{True, False\}$
$True \in \llbracket (C\ new)\ id:\ true\rrbracket \Rightarrow \{Object\} = \llbracket ((C\ new)\ id:\ true)\ isTrue\rrbracket$
$False \in \llbracket (C\ new)\ id:\ true\rrbracket \Rightarrow \{\} = \llbracket ((C\ new)\ id:\ true)\ isTrue\rrbracket$

Smallest Solution:

$\llbracket C\ new\rrbracket_1 = \llbracket C\ new\rrbracket_2 = \{C\}$
$\llbracket 7\rrbracket = \llbracket x\rrbracket_1 = \llbracket (C\ new)\ id:\ 7\rrbracket = \llbracket ((C\ new)\ id:\ 7)\ succ\rrbracket = \{Natural\}$
$\llbracket true\rrbracket = \llbracket x\rrbracket_2 = \llbracket (C\ new)\ id:\ true\rrbracket = \{True\}$
$\llbracket ((C\ new)\ id:\ true)\ isTrue\rrbracket = \{Object\}$

Trace graph sketch:

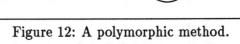

Figure 12: A polymorphic method.
```
157
```

```
class D
    method f: x
        if x then self f: x else nil
end D
(D new) f: nil
```

Constraints:

$[\![D\ new]\!] = \{D\}$

$[\![D\ new]\!] \subseteq \{D\}$

$D \in [\![D\ new]\!] \Rightarrow [\![nil]\!] = [\![x]\!]_1$

$D \in [\![D\ new]\!] \Rightarrow [\![if\ x\ then\ self\ f:\ x\ else\ nil]\!]_1 = [\![(D\ new)\ f:\ nil]\!]$

$D \in [\![D\ new]\!] \Rightarrow [\![if\ x\ then\ self\ f:\ x\ else\ nil]\!]_1 \supseteq [\![self\ f:\ x]\!]_1 \cup [\![nil]\!]_1$

$D \in [\![D\ new]\!] \Rightarrow [\![nil]\!]_1 = \{\}$

$D \in [\![D\ new]\!] \Rightarrow [\![self]\!]_1 = \{D\}$

$D \in [\![D\ new]\!] \Rightarrow [\![self]\!]_1 \subseteq \{D\}$

$D \in [\![D\ new]\!], D \in [\![self]\!]_1 \Rightarrow [\![x]\!]_1 = [\![x]\!]_2$

$D \in [\![D\ new]\!], D \in [\![self]\!]_1 \Rightarrow [\![if\ x\ then\ self\ f:\ x\ else\ nil]\!]_2 = [\![self\ f:\ x]\!]_1$

$D \in [\![D\ new]\!], D \in [\![self]\!]_1 \Rightarrow [\![if\ x\ then\ self\ f:\ x\ else\ nil]\!]_2 \supseteq [\![self\ f:\ x]\!]_2 \cup [\![nil]\!]_2$

$D \in [\![D\ new]\!], D \in [\![self]\!]_1 \Rightarrow [\![nil]\!]_2 = \{\}$

$D \in [\![D\ new]\!], D \in [\![self]\!]_1 \Rightarrow [\![self]\!]_2 = \{D\}$

$D \in [\![D\ new]\!], D \in [\![self]\!]_1 \Rightarrow [\![self]\!]_2 \subseteq \{D\}$

$D \in [\![D\ new]\!], D \in [\![self]\!]_1, D \in [\![self]\!]_2 \Rightarrow [\![x]\!]_2 = [\![x]\!]_2$

$D \in [\![D\ new]\!], D \in [\![self]\!]_1, D \in [\![self]\!]_2 \Rightarrow [\![if\ x\ then\ self\ f:\ x\ else\ nil]\!]_2 = [\![self\ f:\ x]\!]_2$

$[\![nil]\!] = \{\}$

Smallest Solution:

$[\![D\ new]\!] = [\![self]\!]_1 = [\![self]\!]_2 = \{D\}$

$[\![nil]\!] = [\![x]\!]_1 = [\![nil]\!]_1 = [\![if\ x\ then\ self\ f:\ x\ else\ nil]\!]_1 = [\![self\ f:\ x]\!]_1 =$
$[\![(D\ new)\ f:\ nil]\!]_1 = [\![x]\!]_2 = [\![nil]\!]_2 = [\![if\ x\ then\ self\ f:\ x\ else\ nil]\!]_2 =$
$[\![self\ f:\ x]\!]_2 = [\![(D\ new)\ f:\ nil]\!]_2 = \{\}$

Trace graph sketch:

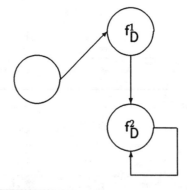

Figure 13: A recursive method.

```
x := 7;
x succ;
x := true;
x isTrue
```
Constraints:

$\llbracket x \rrbracket \supseteq \llbracket 7 \rrbracket$
$\llbracket 7 \rrbracket = \{\text{Natural}\}$
$\llbracket x \rrbracket \subseteq \{\text{Natural}\}$
$\llbracket x \rrbracket \supseteq \llbracket \text{true} \rrbracket$
$\llbracket \text{true} \rrbracket = \{\text{True}\}$
$\llbracket x \rrbracket \subseteq \{\text{True}, \text{False}\}$
$\vdots$

Figure 14: A safe program rejected.

```
(if nil then true else 7) succ
```
Constraints:

$\llbracket \text{if nil then true else } 7 \rrbracket \subseteq \{\text{Natural}\}$
$\llbracket \text{if nil then true else } 7 \rrbracket \supseteq \llbracket \text{true} \rrbracket \cup \llbracket 7 \rrbracket$
$\llbracket \text{true} \rrbracket = \{\text{True}\}$
$\llbracket 7 \rrbracket = \{\text{Natural}\}$
$\vdots$

Figure 15: Another safe program rejected.

```
class Student inherits Comparable
   ...
end Student
class ComparableList inherits List
   method studentCount
      if (self isEmpty) isTrue
      then 0
      else
         if (self car) instanceOf Student
         then ((self cdr) studentCount) succ
         else (self cdr) studentCount
end ComparableList
```

Figure 16: An example program.

Appendix C: Solving Systems of Conditional Inequalities

This appendix shows how to solve a finite system of conditional inequalities in quadratic time.

Definition C.1: A *CI-system* consists of

- a finite set $\mathcal{A}$ of *atoms*.

- a finite set $\{\alpha_i\}$ of *variables*.

- a finite set of *conditional inequalities* of the form
$$C_1, C_2, \ldots, C_k \Rightarrow Q$$
Each C_i is a *condition* of the form $a \in \alpha_j$, where $a \in \mathcal{A}$ is an atom, and Q is an *inequality* of one of the following forms
$$\begin{aligned} A &\subseteq \alpha_i \\ \alpha_i &\subseteq A \\ \alpha_i &\subseteq \alpha_j \end{aligned}$$
where $A \subseteq \mathcal{A}$ is a set of atoms.

A *solution* L of the system assigns to each variable α_i a set $L(\alpha_i) \subseteq \mathcal{A}$ such that all the conditional inequalities are satisfied. □

In our application, $\mathcal{A}$ models the set of classes occurring in a concrete program.

Lemma C.2: Solutions are closed under intersection. Hence, if a CI-system has solutions, then it has a unique minimal one.
Proof: Consider any conditional inequality of the form $C_1, C_2, \ldots, C_k \Rightarrow Q$, and let $\{L_i\}$ be all solutions. We shall show that $\cap_i L_i$ is a solution. If a condition $a \in \cap_i L_i(\alpha_j)$ is true, then so is all of $a \in L_i(\alpha_j)$. Hence, if all the conditions of Q are true in $\cap_i L_i$, then they are true in each L_i; furthermore, since they are solutions, Q is also true in each L_i. Since, in general, $A_k \subseteq B_k$ implies $\cap_k A_k \subseteq \cap_k B_k$, it follows that $\cap_i L_i$ is a solution. Hence, if there are any solutions, then $\cap_i L_i$ is the unique smallest one. □

Definition C.3: Let $\mathcal{C}$ be a CI-system with atoms

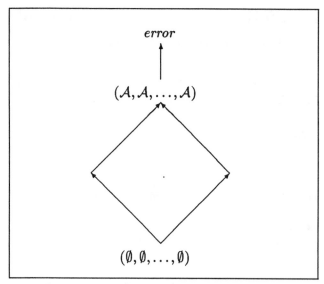

Figure 17: The lattice of assignments.

$\mathcal{A}$ and n distinct variables. An *assignment* is an element of $(2^{\mathcal{A}})^n \cup \{error\}$ ordered as a lattice, see figure 17. If different from *error*, then it assigns a set of atoms to each variable. If V is an assignment, then $\tilde{\mathcal{C}}(V)$ is a new assignment, defined as follows. If $V = error$, then $\tilde{\mathcal{C}}(V) = error$. An inequality is *enabled* if all of its conditions are true under V. If for any enabled inequality of the form $\alpha_i \subseteq A$ we do *not* have $V(\alpha_i) \subseteq A$, then $\tilde{\mathcal{C}}(V) = error$; otherwise, $\tilde{\mathcal{C}}(V)$ is the smallest pointwise extension of V such that

- for every enabled inequality of the form $A \subseteq \alpha_j$ we have $A \subseteq \tilde{\mathcal{C}}(V)(\alpha_j)$.

- for every enabled inequality of the form $\alpha_i \subseteq \alpha_j$ we have $V(\alpha_i) \subseteq \tilde{\mathcal{C}}(V)(\alpha_j)$.

Clearly, $\tilde{\mathcal{C}}$ is monotonic in the above lattice. $\square$

Lemma C.4: An assignment $L \neq error$ is a solution of a CI-system $\mathcal{C}$ *iff* $L = \tilde{\mathcal{C}}(L)$. If $\mathcal{C}$ has no solutions, then *error* is the smallest fixed-point of $\tilde{\mathcal{C}}$.

Proof: If L is a solution of $\mathcal{C}$, then clearly $\tilde{\mathcal{C}}$ will not equal *error* and cannot extend L; hence, L is a fixed-point. Conversely, if L is a fixed-point of $\tilde{\mathcal{C}}$, then all the enabled inequalities must hold. If

there are no solutions, then there can be no fixed-point below *error*. Since *error* is by definition a fixed-point, the result follows. $\square$

This means that to find the smallest solution, or to decide that none exists, we need only compute the least fixed-point of $\tilde{\mathcal{C}}$.

Lemma C.5: For any CI-system $\mathcal{C}$, the least fixed-point of $\tilde{\mathcal{C}}$ is equal to

$$\lim_{k \to \infty} \tilde{\mathcal{C}}^k(\emptyset, \emptyset, \ldots, \emptyset)$$

Proof: This is a standard result about monotonic functions on complete lattices. $\square$

Lemma C.6: Let n be the number of *different* conditions in a CI-system $\mathcal{C}$. Then

$$\lim_{k \to \infty} \tilde{\mathcal{C}}^k(\emptyset, \emptyset, \ldots, \emptyset) = \tilde{\mathcal{C}}^{n+1}(\emptyset, \emptyset, \ldots, \emptyset)$$

Proof: When no more conditions are enabled, then the fixed-point is obtained by a single application. Once a condition is enabled in an assignment, it will remain enabled in all larger assignments. It follows that after n iterations no new conditions can be enabled; hence, the fixed-point is obtained in at most $n + 1$ iterations. $\square$

Lemma C.7: The smallest solution to any CI-system, or the decision that none exists, can be obtained in quadratic time.

Proof: This follows from the previous lemmas. $\square$

References

[1] Alan H. Borning and Daniel H. H. Ingalls. A type declaration and inference system for Smalltalk. In *Ninth Symposium on Principles of Programming Languages*, pages 133–141. ACM Press, January 1982.

[2] L. Cardelli. A semantics of multiple inheritance. In G. Kahn, D. MacQueen, and Gordon Plotkin, editors, *Semantics of Data Types*, pages 51–68. Springer-Verlag (*LNCS* 173), 1984.

[3] L. Cardelli and P. Wegner. On understanding types, data abstraction, and polymorphism. *ACM Computing Surveys*, 17(4), December 1985.

[4] W. R. Cook. *A Denotational Semantics of Inheritance.* PhD thesis, Brown University, 1989.

[5] William Cook and Jens Palsberg. A denotational semantics of inheritance and its correctness. In *Proc. OOPSLA'89, ACM SIGPLAN Fourth Annual Conference on Object-Oriented Programming Systems, Languages and Applications*, 1989. To appear in Information and Computation.

[6] O. J. Dahl, B. Myhrhaug, and K. Nygaard. Simula 67 common base language. Technical report, Norwegian Computing Center, Oslo, Norway, 1968.

[7] Scott Danforth and Chris Tomlinson. Type theories and object-oriented programming. *ACM Computing Surveys*, 20(1), March 1988.

[8] A. Goldberg and D. Robson. *Smalltalk-80—The Language and its Implementation.* Addison-Wesley, 1983.

[9] Justin O. Graver and Ralph E. Johnson. A type system for Smalltalk. In *Seventeenth Symposium on Principles of Programming Languages*, pages 136–150. ACM Press, January 1990.

[10] Justin Owen Graver. *Type-Checking and Type-Inference for Object-Oriented Programming Languages.* PhD thesis, Department of Computer Science, University of Illinois at Urbana-Champaign, August 1989. UIUCD-R-89-1539.

[11] Andreas V. Hense. Polymorphic type inference for a simple object oriented programming language with state. Technical Report Tech. Bericht Nr. A 20/90, Universität des Saarlandes, 1990.

[12] R. E. Johnson. Type-checking Smalltalk. In *Proc. OOPSLA'86, Object-Oriented Programming Systems, Languages and Applications.* Sigplan Notices, 21(11), November 1986.

[13] S. Kamin. Inheritance in Smalltalk-80: A denotational definition. In *Fifteenth Symposium on Principles of Programming Languages*, pages 80–87. ACM Press, January 1988.

[14] Marc A. Kaplan and Jeffrey D. Ullman. A general scheme for the automatic inference of variable types. In *Fifth Symposium on Principles of Programming Languages*, pages 60–75. ACM Press, January 1978.

[15] B. B. Kristensen, O. L. Madsen, B. Møller-Pedersen, and K. Nygaard. The BETA programming language. In B. Shriver and P. Wegner, editors, *Research Directions in Object-Oriented Programming*, pages 7–48. MIT Press, 1987.

[16] H. G. Mairson. Decidability of ML typing is complete for deterministic exponential time. In *Seventeenth Symposium on Principles of Programming Languages.* ACM Press, January 1990.

[17] Bertrand Meyer. *Object-Oriented Software Construction.* Prentice-Hall, Englewood Cliffs, NJ, 1988.

[18] Robin Milner. A theory of type polymorphism in programming. *Journal of Computer and System Sciences*, 17, 1978.

[19] Prateek Mishra and Uday S. Reddy. Declaration-free type checking. In *Twelfth Symposium on Principles of Programming Languages*, pages 7–21. ACM Press, January 1985.

[20] Jens Palsberg and Michael I. Schwartzbach. Type substitution for object-oriented programming. In *Proc. OOPSLA/ECOOP'90, ACM SIGPLAN Fifth Annual Conference on Object-Oriented Programming Systems, Languages and Applications; European Conference on Object-Oriented Programming*, 1990.

[21] Jens Palsberg and Michael I. Schwartzbach. Static typing for object-oriented programming. Computer Science Department, Aarhus University. PB-355. Submitted for publication, 1991.

[22] Jens Palsberg and Michael I. Schwartzbach. What is type-safe code reuse? In *Proc. ECOOP'91, Fifth European Conference on Object-Oriented Programming*, 1991.

[23] U. S. Reddy. Objects as closures: Abstract semantics of object-oriented languages. In *Proc. ACM Conference on Lisp and Functional Programming*, pages 289–297. ACM, 1988.

[24] Didier Rémy. Typechecking records and variants in a natural extension of ML. In *Sixteenth Symposium on Principles of Programming Languages*, pages 77–88. ACM Press, January 1989.

[25] Michael I. Schwartzbach. Type inference with inequalities. In *Proc. TAPSOFT'91.* Springer-Verlag (*LNCS* 493), 1991.

[26] B. Stroustrup. *The C++ Programming Language.* Addison-Wesley, 1986.

[27] Norihisa Suzuki. Inferring types in Smalltalk. In *Eighth Symposium on Principles of Programming Languages*, pages 187–199. ACM Press, January 1981.

[28] Mitchell Wand. A simple algorithm and proof for type inference. *Fundamentae Informaticae*, X:115–122, 1987.

[29] Mitchell Wand. Type inference for record concatenation and multiple inheritance. In *LICS'89, Fourth Annual Symposium on Logic in Computer Science*, 1989.

Can Structured Methods be Objectified?
(PANEL)

Kent Beck, *MasPar Computer Corp. and First Class Software*, (moderator)
Grady Booch, *Rational*
Peter Coad, *Object International*
Meilir Page-Jones, *Wayland Systems*
Paul Ward, *System Development Concepts*

The first decision encountered when applying formal methods to the analysis and design of object-oriented programs is whether to use an adaptation of a structured method which includes object-oriented concepts or to use one of the new methods based purely on objects. The panelists are the prime movers in creating and disemminating these two approaches. They have been asked to address two questions: what is the effect of their approach on experienced analysts and designers who are learning objects and what is the effect on experienced object-oriented analysts and designers who are putting the method into daily use. The discussion will illuminate the issues involved in making the decision of which analysis or design technique to use.

Issues in Moving from C to C++
(PANEL)

David R. Reed, *Saber Software Inc.*, (moderator)
Marty Cagan, *Interactive Development Environments*
Ted Goldstein, *Sun Laboratories*
Barbara Moo, *AT&T*

Background

C++ is rapidly emerging as the most widely used object oriented language. One major reason is that C++ is derived from the popular C programming language. Because C++ is considered the successor to C, C programmers wanting the benefits of the object oriented paradigm look to C++ as a logical step toward object oriented programming.

This panel will focus on the issues in moving from C to C++ and will try to present different points of view on how the C programmer should make the transition. Simply stated, one view promotes an incremental style in adapting both the language and the paradigm, the other more radical teaching, takes the view that the C programmer must adopt both a new paradigm and language at the onset.

Other related topics include:

- To what extent can existing systems be extended and enhanced using object-oriented programming techniques, and what are the issues involved and the solutions available.

- Many existing C programs were designed and modeled using conventional structured design techniques. What are the issues relating to front-end design of systems written in a mix of C and C++.

- Does using technologies associated with C++ such as object-oriented database technology require extensive knowledge of the object-oriented paradigm.

- Is it practical to start a new project using C++ simply as a better C, and then gradually employ object-oriented programming techniques as the project progresses? What would be the impact of this learn-as-you-go approach on program quality and team productivity.

The panel will be made up of both end users and technology providers that have experience in making the transition from C to C++, some with a particular focus such as front-end design methodologies.

Marty Cagan

At IDE we build integrated environments to support both C and C++ development, as well as combinations of the two. Like ourselves, many of our customers have been migrating from C to C++.

The migration from structured development to object-oriented development presents several interesting issues from the perspective of design support environments. A long-standing limitation of structured development has been the gap between the various levels of specification and implementation. Object-oriented development holds the promise of reducing this gap by providing a smooth transformation between specification and implementation.

The question then arises as to the best way for an organization to move from a structured development process to an object-oriented one. At this panel we will discuss experiences of groups that have moved to object-oriented design and implementation, but have remained with structured analysis, groups that have moved to object-oriented analysis methods yet remained with conventional structured design and implementation languages, and groups that have moved completely to object-oriented analysis, design and implementation.

Barbara Moo

The path to Object Oriented Happiness: Immediate or Gradual?

My position is based on the experiences of AT&T R&D projects using C++ and Object Oriented Programming over the past 5 years. The issues in moving to OOP are primarily learning curve issues: how to design and think about problems in a new way.

It is much harder to convince a skeptical development manager to try a new technology if they have to start off with a large investment before seeing any return. C++ allows us to "learn while doing"; we can capitalize on the large investment we already have in C knowledge and gradually evolve systems and people to use the data abstraction and OOP facilities of the language to dramatically improve productivity. Our approach:

- In the first release, keep it simple, using the "better C" facilities of C++. Senior members of the team define and implement a few central data abstractions that model the application for use by all on the project.

- In subsequent releases more opportunities for class design will be clearer and opportunities for reuse and inheritance from the original classes will present themselves.

The first release gets staff comfortable with the language and with concentrating on the data and builds both a human and a code base for more aggressive application of the technology in later releases. Also, management confidence is increased since even the first release shows benefits from stronger type checking and modest reuse benefits.

This process has been successfully applied to projects ranging in size up to 70 developers. The benefits of the approach:

- lower risk in taking in a new technology

- training gets spread across a release rather than being concentrated up front

- learning, we find, is more effective if coordinated with practice

- gives time for local experts to evolve

The benefit of spreading out the learning costs is especially important when migrating larger projects to a new technology. We have had some successes with the direct leap approach as well. These tend to come on small (1 - 5 in staff size) projects without rigorous schedule constraints. These projects, because they are small, can learn as a group, and because they are not over constrained with deadlines can afford to change design as learning progresses. This is infeasible both for communication reasons and for schedule on larger projects.

Ted Goldstein

Once upon a time, the "Software crisis" was the backlog in application development by the corporate MIS department. Structured programming and artificial intelligence was the solution proposed to solve this first software crisis. Complex systems such as user interfaces, databases, and network services have brought about a new crisis of ever more interrelated and complex software. Recently, object-oriented programming has been proposed as the solution to both crises.

Unfortunately, object-oriented programming is not a panacea. There is considerable risk involved in making any technology transition, and object-oriented technology is no exception. A similar situation occurred during the 1980's to AI programming. Many promises made, but few were kept. In the early '80's, artificial intelligence was supposed to solve the "software crisis". Reality set in and many problems turned out to be harder than expected. People became disillusioned and even those AI techniques which had validity were dismissed. This had led to the current state of an "AI winter."

There are a number of issues involving languages, systems, and libraries which could easily bring on "an object-oriented winter." It is important for managers and practitioners of object-oriented programming to recognize exactly what the technology can accomplish. Myths concerning productivity improvement, language choice, dynamic versus statically typed languages, performance results, and testing must be countered with the reality of experience in object-oriented programming. The reality behind object-oriented programming is more about making a commitment to well designed software, and making the capital investment in training and tools to accomplish the goal of software quality and overcome the software crisis.

Formal Techniques for OO Software Development (PANEL)

Dennis de Champeaux, *HP-Lab Palo Alto*, (moderator)
Pierre America, *Philips Research Laboratories*
Derek Coleman, *HP-Lab Bristol*
Roger Duke, *University of Queensland*
Doug Lea, *Syracuse University & SUNY-Oswego*
Gary Leavens, *Iowa State University*

Co-organizer: **Fiona Hayes**, *HP-Lab Bristol*

Background

In this panel, we discuss the relevance of formal techniques for applying object-orientation.

The object-oriented paradigm is currently broadened from the programming realm to cover the full development life cycle, including (domain) analysis and design.

These extensions are driven by the demands of large system development. Delivering huge OO software systems routinely and cost effectively is a significant challenge. To quote Ed Yourdon: "A system composed of 100,000 lines of C++ is not to be sneezed at, but we don't have that much trouble developing 100,000 lines of COBOL today. The real test of OOP will come when systems of 1 to 10 million lines of code are developed."

Scaling up seems to require increasing the precision of the semantics of the languages/ notations used by a team.

Large, mission critical projects may have to demonstrate that a target system satisfies its specifications provably. This suggests having, at least, formal semantics for the specification language.

When a target system contains an abundance of parallelism, we face the problem of validation. Errors can be nearly impossible to duplicate in a concurrent setting. Transformations that preserve meaning can assist the validation. They require precise semantics in their domain of operation.

Relational databases are well understood. They can be accessed out of "any" programming language. OO database vendors wants to offer the same service. Relational database theory is soundly grounded in mathematical theories like the (tuple) relational calculus. Similar formal foundations may be required for objects.

Can formal techniques play a role to solve the above mentioned issues? The panel will contrast short term feasibility and relevance against what to expect in the medium and longer term.

To help focus the discussion, we look at the following specific topics:

- Will using OO throughout the life cycle increase the level of formality in comparison to what has been achieved in the structured paradigm?

OOPSLA'91

- Will formal techniques in OO make the testing/ validation/ verification of a target system against its requirements easier by orders of magnitude in comparison with current practice?

- Will formal techniques facilitate the development of sizable libraries (at the conceptual, design and code level)? If so, can we expect massive reuse, and thus a speed up of the development process by orders of magnitude?

Pierre America

Object-oriented programming has originally developed without a strong basis in mathematical formalism. For many people it even seemed to offer a solution to the software crisis without the need for all that complicated math. However, recently there is a rapidly increasing interest in applying formal techniques to object-oriented programming.

There are several ways in which formal techniques could help in object-oriented software development:

- Describing the basic concepts of our languages and systems in a formal, mathematical way can dramatically enhance our understanding of them and in such a way lead to better languages and systems. This applies particularly to databases, parallelism, typing, and support for the early phases of development (e.g., requirements specification). Here it is not necessary that the individual programmer has detailed knowledge of all applicable formal techniques, but that the designers of the language or model take them into account, thus coming up with a better environment for the programmer to work in.

- Formal techniques can support the development of methods for software development, which can then be taught to the programmers in a less formal, but nevertheless rigorous way. This is what happened to high school mathematics, but also to well-known techniques such

as pre- and postconditions and invariants.

- In order to be able to reuse software components, it is necessary to describe what exactly they do, without referring to the code (which is often intentionally unavailable). Formal specifications have definite advantage over natural language here because they are unambiguous (I know about 50 different things that could each be called a 'stack') and because they can be processed by a machine (which opens perspectives for automatic search in component libraries, for example). Even if the actual specifications used are not (completely) formal, formal techniques could help us to develop a framework for specifying components independently of the code that implements them.

- Finally, there is of course the possibility of full formal verification of critical software. It will certainly still take a long time before this is a routine matter, but to a limited extent these techniques can already be used now. However, I think that this aspect has been overemphasized in research on formal techniques.

While the potential is clearly present, a lot of problems still have to be solved before the above possibilities can be exploited fully. Some of these problems are specific for object-oriented programming (for example, the semantic treatment of inheritance), but others have been around for a long time and either have been shied away from (e.g., formal description of dynamically changing pointer structures) or have proved to be so difficult that even after decades of active research there is no final solution yet (e.g., specification and verification of concurrent systems). Therefore there is no hope that formal techniques will shortly lead to a revolution in the software development process, but I am sure that they will make all the difference in the long run. Nevertheless, experience in my company shows that even on a short term, the right use of formal techniques supported by the right tools can make a substantial contribution to the speed and accuracy of the development process. And that is what it is all about: formality is not a goal in itself, but it is only useful as a means towards more efficient and more reliable software development.

Derek Coleman

Motto: What's Formal Methods got to do with Object-oriented Development?

The success of the object-oriented approach has gained much attention during the last decade. However the success is at the level of small team developments. Industry has learned the hard way that large scale efforts are not straightforward. We are beginning to remember what we used to know! The laws of software engineering still hold - software development must be a systematic and managed process. **Objects are not a panacea.**

Yourdon's test[1] is a measure of the problem that faces the new paradigm. One of the responses is the upsurge in interest in object-oriented analysis and design and CASE tools. Currently there is a deluge of object-oriented analysis and design methods and CASE tools.

A method is essentially a set of notations together with a strategy, and heuristics, for deploying them. The best of the new methods have effective strategies and contain useful heuristics, but they are characterized by too much emphasis on naturalness of expression and intuition. When it comes to notations *ad-hoc*-ery is the order of the day. Everybody's powerful feature is included and every difficult issue is ignored. Whichever method you choose, you can be sure that the models that you develop are built on sand and hence any supporting tool can be little more than a diagram editor.

In order to measure up to Yourdon's test, develop safety-critical software, or write large concurrent software, the methods must use *notations that have a semantics*. This is where **formal methods are relevant**. Despite the name, formal methods has relatively little to say about methods - it is all about formal notations. The notations are wide and varied. Specification languages like Z, VDM

---

[1] Can we build object-oriented systems that are composed of millions of lines of code?

and HP-SL provide precise and abstract descriptions of software. Algebraic languages like OBJ and Axis show how modularity and executability can be combined to provide design time prototyping and testing. Higher order logic specification languages, like HOL, have proved effective in verifying designs.

I believe that if formal notations were incorporated into object-oriented methods then we could expect:

- Improved analysis and design methods that produce coherent models capable of being validated against requirements.

- Rigorous object-oriented methods of development for use on safety-critical applications.

- Object-oriented CASE tools which can check the semantics of models.

The panel statement asks whether using the object-oriented approach throughout the life cyle will increase the level of formality? No, it will not. Structured methods have not led to the introduction of formal methods. It will require a conscious effort to combine the naturalness of objects with the precision of formality in order to improve the quality of object-oriented techniques. Until such a fusion takes place I am pessimistic about the prospects for large-scale object-oriented software development.

Roger Duke

Object orientation can be viewed as a natural progression in the trend towards increased formality in software design. Issues like reusability, inheritance and subtyping that are integral to object orientation encourage the sound formal design of systems, and it can be argued that it is precisely because of this that object orientation is becoming so important.

But are we now in a position where the development, production and maintenance of software systems can be considered an engineering discipline?

Is the term *Software Engineering* an accurate reflection of our discipline, or merely some fraudulent misnomer?

Although system design is central in any formal development, it is only part of the story: methods for formal specification and verification need to be combined with object-oriented design, and the whole structure integrated within a sound refinement theory. At present we have a collection of somewhat disjoint theoretical results. A major problem that remains is the weaving of these results into a unified, cohesive and *practical* engineering discipline that is formally based.

There is good evidence that the object-oriented paradigm can suggest to us how to proceed.

- Object-oriented specification techniques are being developed. Central to this development is the realization that specification can be strengthened by incorporating aspects of object-oriented design, quite contrary to the conventional wisdom that separation of concerns demands that the issues be divorced.

- Refinement within object-oriented systems can be related to subtyping and realized by (restricted) inheritance, i.e. inheritance itself suggests a possible approach to refinement.

- As object-oriented systems are constructed by composing underlying objects, this compositional structure strongly suggests how verification proofs could also be structured.

Hence the prognosis is good. For those willing to dream of a future Utopia there is every reason to believe that object orientation can be combined with other formal methods to produce techniques that will dramatically assist the software engineer throughout the software-cycle.

For those more concerned with taking stock of where we are at the present time, we already have a collection of (somewhat incomplete) formal object-oriented techniques that, even although far from perfect, can nevertheless help us to construct more reliable software systems whose behavior can be predicated and guaranteed with some certainty.

Should we be using these formal techniques? Given the increasing importance of software correctness and reliability we're damn fools if we don't.

Doug Lea

People have grounds to be naively optimistic about the prospects for coupling formal methods with OO design and programming.

Many everyday aspects of OOD/OOP represent "informal formal methods", that are analogous to those found in various formal specification systems. These include the use of abstract classes to declare behavior in an implementation-independent fashion, the use of inheritance to indicate subtype relations, and reliance on well-understood abstractions like Sets, Sequences, and Maps.

The effects of such practices may be enhanced by the creation of formal methods that extend the semantic power of these aspects of OOD/OOP, by supporting the expression of predicate-based constraints, axioms, and invariants that allow fuller specification of behavior than is now possible in most common OO languages. Languages and support tools need to evolve to accommodate behavioral specification constructs that are, ideally, as natural and successful as the OO constructs and practices they extend and modify.

Use of formal methods need not be separated from ordinary successful OO software development activities. Efforts to integrate stronger specification methods into OO languages themselves, even when this results in loss of expressiveness and/or verifiability are more likely to be *used* in everyday development than are isolated formalisms.

While verification is an important aspect of formal approaches to software development, automated verification of OO software consisting of the kinds of mutable, aliased, and/or concurrent objects commonly found in OO programs remains a distant goal. However, researchers and practitioners in non-OO contexts have found that the use of formal methods by designers and programmers improves reliability, testability, and productivity, because of the precision and completeness of requirement and design specifications formal methods encourage. It does not seem farfetched to believe that the same will hold true for OO formal methods, which already tend to outperform structured methods on these qualities.

While formal methods themselves will not automatically cause greater reuse, their pragmatic role in increasing "consumer confidence" is an important ingredient in making good on the promise of OO methods to result in massive reuse and productivity improvements. In order to use off-the-shelf components with confidence, clients require detailed semantic specifications of the components, optimally along with evidence that implementations meet those specifications. This, in turn has the positive effect of enhancing the well-specifiedness of large systems that use many such components.

Gary Leavens

Formal techniques can aid in the development of high quality application frameworks and libraries of reusable modules (such as classes). It is a mistake to concentrate on getting more code faster, because poorly designed, bug-ridden code will not be reused. If you accept the premise that quality is essential for reuse, then you are led inexorably to formal techniques. Quality software is well documented, easy to understand, etc. The more careful you try to be about such aspects of software, the more you will use formal techniques.

For example, to develop a reusable application framework, you should reuse it yourself. Hence you are constantly playing both developer and client. Specifications that say what properties of software a client can rely on are crucial for keeping these roles straight. You must be sure to program client code from these specifications, so that you do not use your developer's knowledge as a client. A formal verification can guarantee, for example, that client code only relies on a method's specification, not its implementation details. Informal techniques are too easily supplemented by your intuition as a developer.

Object-oriented design makes consistent use of abstraction. Data abstraction helps you separate implementation from observable behavior. Supertype abstraction, letting supertypes stand for their subtypes, helps you separate interesting behavior from non-interesting behavior. These kinds of abstraction by specification are useful not only in programs but also in formal specification, verification, design, and testing. For example, you can verify the effect of a message send, based on the specification of the receiving expression's static type, without knowing the receiving object's dynamic type or what class implements it. That is, you use data abstraction to ignore implementation detail, and supertype abstraction to ignore some of the observable behavior of subtypes.

In design, you can use subtyping as a more general version of data type refinement. You can create a subtype to embody a design decision, and to limit the parts of a design that depend on that decision. You can also use subtype relationships to organize the types in a framework or library in a way that is suited to verifiers and clients, since subtype relationships are based on observable behavior. Tests can also be organized in layers based on subtype relationships, since tests for a subtype can inherit tests from a supertype's test suite.

The real problem in validating software against requirements is finding the "right" requirements, since one cannot formally validate software against informal requirements. Exploratory programming has been useful when requirements are fuzzy, but it can be expensive to construct a prototype and throw it away. A better way to find the right requirements would be exploratory specification. In exploratory specification, you would formally specify fuzzy aspects of the system as many times as needed to firm up the requirements. Then you could prototype just those aspects of the system.

Coherent Models for Object-Oriented Analysis

Fiona Hayes, Derek Coleman

Hewlett Packard Laboratories,
Bristol BS12 6QZ, UK.
e-mail: dc@hplb.hpl.hp.com, fmh@hplb.hpl.hp.com.
tel: +44 272 799910, fax: +44 272 228003.

Abstract

Analysis is intended for the formulation and communication of domain descriptions. Consequently, the notations used must be intuitive, expressive and precise. Current object-oriented analysis techniques satisfy the first two goals. However, they are informal and rely on domain knowledge for establishing semantics and consistency.

In this paper, we present a set of formally based coherent models extending current informal techniques. The models have a precise semantics and they constitute a consistent description technique for domain analysis.

Each model is described and its role in the analysis process discussed. Consistency checking between models is demonstrated. The ideas are illustrated using a simple drawing application example.

1 Introduction

Experience of the industrial use of object-oriented technology indicates that a disciplined software process is the essential factor determining success [4]. Key components of a software process are systematic analysis and design techniques and recently a number of object-oriented analysis and design techniques have been developed [11],[3],[12]. The techniques are similar since they use entity-relationship models, state machines and data flow diagrams to build different views of the problem domain, or software in the case of design.

In this paper we concentrate on object-oriented analysis. Analysis is intended to facilitate the formulation and communication of object-oriented descriptions of the problem domain. It is clearly important that the notations used be powerful enough to ensure that the analyst does not have to "fight" them.

If power of expression, alone, were a sufficient criterion for judging an analysis notation then natural language would suffice. However analysis models must foster *precise* communication about complex domains. Consequently the notations should be :-

Unambiguous A model should have a single discernible meaning. Ambiguity leads to confusion and can cause the "wrong" problem being analysed and solved.

Abstract A model should not be cluttered with unnecessary detail that can prejudice the design and implementation phases.

Consistent It should be possible to check if different models of the same system conflict. Inconsistency causes the same problems as ambiguity.

The process and notations used by a method should assist in the production of a *coherent* set of models which constitute a reasoned and a convincing description of the problem domain. The objective of this paper is to show how a current analysis method can be improved to more nearly meet this goal.

OOPSLA'91, pp. 171–183

The next section introduces the models used in object-oriented analysis. Section three shows how the informal analysis models can be made more coherent. The paper concludes with a short discussion of the results.

2 Object-oriented Analysis

In this section we discuss the models that are produced during object-oriented analysis. We have chosen to follow the approach advocated in the recent book by Rumbaugh et al [11]. The book gives a clear definition of a process, and associated models, which is similar to a number of other, less well-documented, methods. In order to help the explanation we use a simple example based on a real problem. The reader should bear in mind that *the problem is intended to illustrate the models produced during analysis rather than the process of analysis as applied to a real world problem.*

2.1 Problem Statement

The aim is to analyse a simple drawing application which allows the user to draw lines and boxes and move them.

A Diagram is a graph composed of rectangular *boxes* of different sizes situated in different positions on a screen and of *lines*. A line may be *attached* to at most two boxes but cannot be attached to the same box twice. A set of boxes is *connected* if there is a path between them. To simplify the problem we require that each connected sub-graph must be acyclic. Lines can optionally have a colour or be dashed - but not both.

The user should be able to create new lines and new boxes, attach a line to a box, move a box together with all its attached lines and connected boxes.

2.2 Analysis Models

Rumbaugh uses three kinds of model, each of which, captures a different aspect of the system. The *functional model* captures what happens, the *dynamic model* captures how and when it happens and the *object model* captures the object structure to which it happens. We now briefly review these models with reference to the problem.

2.3 Object Model

An *object model* uses a form of Entity-Relationship diagram to capture static structure by showing the object classes in a system and the relationships between them.

Class entities may have attributes, which are the data values (i.e. non-object values) held by the objects. The instances of each class have unique identifiers, which are left implicit and are not shown. A relationship between n classes defines sets of n-tuples, each n-tuple containing the identifiers of a set of related objects. An instance of a relationship is called a *link*.

Relationships are shown by lines drawn between entities. The number of participants in a relationship can be specified. An empty circle indicates zero or one participants; a filled circle denotes zero or more. The default representation, no circle, indicates exactly one participant.

Specialisation is an inheritance relationship between classes. A subclass is a specialisation of a superclass, if it participates in all the relationships of the superclass and has all the attributes of the superclass. A subclass may have extra attributes and/or participate in relationships distinct from those of the superclass. The notation for specialisation is a triangle connecting a superclass to its subclass.

Figure 1 shows the object model for the example problem. Box and Line are classes[1], attached and connected are relationships. The Box class has attributes, viz posn, height and width, and the Line class has attributes posn and length. Coloured_Line and Dashed_Line are classes which inherit from Line; each has an additional attribute.

A line can be optionally attached to at most two

---

[1] We use the convention that class names start with a an upper case letter and instances of that class have the same spelling except that they start with a lower case letter

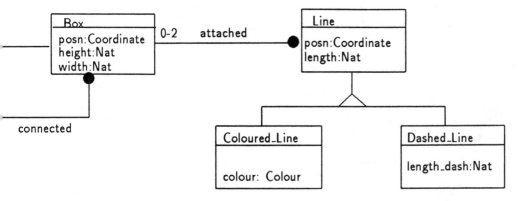

Figure 1: The Object Model for the Drawing Problem

boxes, and a box can be optionally connected to zero or more boxes. There is a consistency relationship between the connected relation and the attached relation, i.e. boxes cannot be connected unless there is a sequence of lines joining them. This can be stated by adding invariant conditions to the object model.

2.4 Dynamic Model

The Dynamic Model is concerned with temporal behaviour and uses extended finite state machines to specify the behaviour of classes. The state of a machine is an abstraction of attributes values and links of an object. State machines have an event model of communication. An event is a named, one-way, instantaneous unit of communication that may have data associated with it. On receiving an event a machine may change state, output another event and/or perform an action. An action is an instantaneous operation which updates the values of attributes or links.

Figure 2 shows a Mealy state machine for the Box class. There is only one state, ready. A box object responds to two events, **move** and **attachline(l)**. The move event is invoked by the user, its effect is to output move events to all attached line objects and connected box objects. Attachline(l) adds l to the attached link.

A pragmatic problem with state machines is that they do not scale-up well because of the combinatorial explosion in the growth in the number of states.

Using Harel's Statechart notation [7], diagrams can be structured by nesting diagrams to denote the "OR" combination of states and the parallel combination diagrams to denote the "AND" combination of states. .

The Line class state machine diagram in Figure 3 illustrates the nesting of diagrams. A line is always willing to respond to a move event by updating its posn attribute. The ready state comprises the "OR" combination of detached, attached_one and attached_two. A line can only receive two attachtobox events, thereafter all attachtobox events have no effect. Attachtobox(b) adds the box to the attached link and sends an attach(self) message to the box b.

2.5 Functional Model

The functional model shows system behaviour rather than the behaviour of individual objects. In Rumbaugh, data flow diagrams [10], DFDs, are used for this purpose. A DFD is a graph showing the flow of data values from their sources, through processes that transform them, to their destination. A DFD does not show control information, such as the time at which processes are executed or the decisions among dynamic paths.

A DFD contains *processes* (ellipses) that transform data, *data flows* (arcs) that move data, *data stores* (pairs of parallel lines) which are passive stores, and *actors* (rectangles) that produce and consume data at the boundaries of the system. Al-

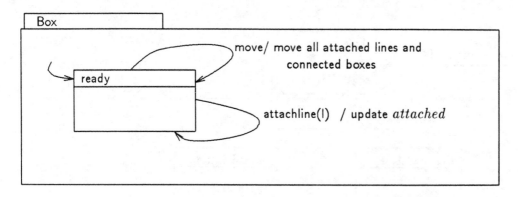

Figure 2: State Machine for the Box Class

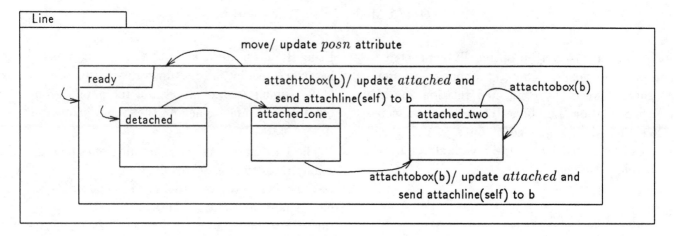

Figure 3: State Machine for the Line Class

though our simple example does not show it, DFDs can be hierarchically structured, each process being decomposed into a DFD of a sub-processes. The bottom level of primitive processes are specified using natural language, pseudo-code, decision tables or some other means.

Figure 4 specifies the behaviour of the system level Move Box operation. It shows that the computation is accomplished by moving the original box and then by moving each of its attached lines. This may recursively reveal further boxes to be moved i.e. those to which the line is attached. The process continues until all leaf boxes have been moved. The data stores, boxes and lines, hold box and line values. The data store, position change, is used to remember the required change of position, Δposn.

2.6 Process of Analysis

The construction of the models is part of the process of carrying out an analysis. The models form the results of the analysis. Rumbaugh suggests that the process be broken into a number of steps:-

1. Develop a natural language description of problem.

2. Build an object model together with a data dictionary of classes, relationships and attributes.

3. Build a dynamic model together with diagrams showing examples of how events flow through the system in response to system operations.

4. Build a functional model together with any constraints that may apply between objects.

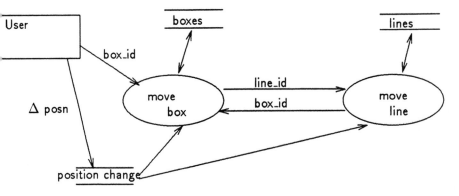

Figure 4: DFD for the Move Box operation

5. Iterate through the steps looking for missing classes, relationships, attributes, events etc.

Analysis is not a mechanical process and the steps cannot always be carried out in a rigid sequence. Model building usually reveals ambiguities, misconceptions and omissions in the problem statement which have to be resolved by communicating with the customer and revisiting some of the steps.

3 Coherent Analysis Models

In this section we look at the notations and process of object-oriented analysis from the viewpoint of ambiguity, abstractness and consistency.

The E-R notation used to express object models has a formal semantics [6] and is unambiguous and abstract. The state machine and DFD notations are less formal and prone to ambiguity since they rely on natural language to define basic concepts, e.g. actions in the dynamic model and processes in the functional model.

There is a further problem with the state-machine notation. Each state-machine defines the behaviour of individual objects. However, because no inter-machine communication primitive is defined, the behaviour of an interacting community of objects cannot be discerned. This makes it impossible to check that the dynamic model is consistent with the functional model.

DFDs are an inappropriate choice for the functional model since the flow of data through processes partially determines an order of computation. This leads Rumbaugh to have contradictory requirements for the functional model. Its prime purpose is to show how output values are derived from input values, without regard for the order in which the values are computed. However it is also required that the functional model relate to the object model by making the bottom-level processes of the DFD correspond to operations on objects. Clearly any DFD that shows object behaviour is prescribing, at least in part, a particular computation rather than specifying system behaviour.

The net effect is that the analysis models do not form a coherent set of descriptions. They can be ambiguous and it is not possible to properly address consistency between models. To rectify these problems we have to give the models a more formal footing and, in the case of the functional model, make it more abstract. In the next section we introduce some simple mathematical notation necessary for formalising the models.

3.1 Mathematical Notation

The key to improving the precision of analysis lies in providing a mathematical basis for the models used. To do this we use a many sorted predicate logic with built in types, like natural and char, and type constructors like those found in formal specification languages[2].

---

[2] Our type system, logic and concrete syntax are based on HP-SL [1], a derivative of VDM [8].

- [[*N1*: *F1* , *N2* : *F2* , ..]] which forms records with fields named *N1,N2*.. of types *F1,F2*..

- **seq of** *E* - finite ordered collections of *E* values

- **set of** *E* - finite sets of *E* values,

- **map** *D* **to** *R* - finite map from domain type, *D*, to range type *R*,

- **compose** *x* **of** *T1* | **compose** *y* **of** *T2* - which creates a disjoint union type by taking the union of values from type *T1* tagged by *x* and values of type *T2* tagged by *y*.

We allow *abstract types* whose values are distinct from any other types and whose properties are determined implicitly by the functions defined on that type. As an example of the use of types, we can define a very simple record type for a Person.

$$\textbf{type Person} \quad \triangleq \quad [\![\text{ name : } \textbf{seq of } \text{Char,}$$
$$\text{address: Address\_type,}$$
$$\text{age : Nat }]\!]$$

where Address_type is an abstract type whose properties have yet to be determined.

The next sections look at more precise analysis models and how they can be checked for consistency.

3.2 Object Structure Model

In this section, the *Object Structure Model* is introduced, in order to form a link between the object model and both the dynamic and the functional models. It is used to provide traceability and consistency checking.

The object structure model is a reified version of the object model in which the relationships have been instantiated as explicit "pointer" attributes between related objects. It can be derived systematically from the object model but we omit the rules for reasons of space. In essence each class, C, of the object model becomes a record type containing a

- self: C_id, the object instance identifier,

- att : Att_type, for each attribute, att, of the class,

- R : **set of** D_id, for each binary relationship R: C × D.

The rules also cover general relationships and inheritance but these details are not considered here. Strong typing is modelled by using disjoint union types. Ignoring the subclasses of Line, the Object model in Figure 1 maps to the object structure model shown in Figure 5.

The object structure model, **type** System, is a simple concrete realisation of the object model. It is an object structured description of the entire state space of the system. Any configuration of lines and boxes can be described as a value of the **type** System.

3.3 Functional Model

The functional model must capture the meaning of the system level operations invoked by the environment. In the informal model, DFDs are used. However, as we discussed earlier, they have a number of problems. They are operational descriptions that show flow of data through a computation, rather than specify the effect of a computation. They are imprecise because they rely on informal process descriptions and their relationship with the other models is not clearly defined.

To overcome these problems we dispense with DFDs and specify the system level operations by pre-post condition specifications over the object structure model. The resulting specifications are *declarative* because they do not reference how the operations are to be computed. They are formal and also link with the other models through the use of the object structure model. As an example consider the **Move** a box operation.

3.3.1 Move a Box

The system operation **Move** moves a box, together with its attached lines and connected boxes to a new position. The DFD for this was given in Section 2.5. In the revised form of functional model,

```
type Box  ≜  ⟦self : Box_id,
               posn : Coordinate,
               width : Nat,
               height : Nat,
               attached : set of Line_id,
               connected : set of Box_id ⟧
type Line ≜  ⟦self : Line_id,
               posn : Coordinate,
               length : Nat,
               attached : set of Box_id ⟧
type Object ≜  compose box of Box | compose line of Line
type Obj_id ≜  compose box_id of Box_id | compose line_id of Line_id
type System ≜  map Obj_id to Object
```

Figure 5: Object Structure Model for the Drawing Problem

system level operations are defined declaratively in terms of the object structure model using pre-post conditions. Informally, Move, can be specified by

operation:
Move(bx_id: Box_id , diffpos: Coordinate)
pre
bx_id must be a valid box identifier
post
Move bx_id and all its connected boxes, together with all attached lines to the new position;
No other changes.

However, pre-post conditions can be used at varying levels of formality and a more formal specification is given in Figure 6. Refering to Figure 6, the identifier, sys, is of type System, the object structure model type. The connected_set contains all the objects to be moved. Movement occurs by overwriting the attribute, posn, of all the objects. Objects in the complement of connected_set are not changed as stated by the auxiliary predicate, remainder_unchanged. The auxiliary predicate, no_new_objects ensures that objects are neither created nor deleted. The definitions of both these simple predicates are omitted.

The next section uses the object structure model to define the dynamic model.

3.4 Dynamic Model

The dynamic model specifies how objects dynamically interact to provide the behaviour described by the functional model. In Section 2.4 each class is described as a state machine which communicates with other state machines by sending and receiving events.

A problem with the informal model is that it uses natural language which precludes showing that the dynamic model satisfies the functional model. Also, the lack of a defined communication primitive between machines means that overall system behaviour cannot be deduced from the behaviour of individual objects.

These problems are overcome by using the Objectchart notation, which may be regarded as a formal version of the state machines used in the informal model. An Objectchart[2],[5], for a class is an extended finite state machine presented as a Harel statechart. The effect of events on local attributes

---

operation: Move(bx_id: Box_id , diffpos: Coordinate)
ext wr sys: System *;; the global writeable state for this operation*
pre in_system(sys, bx_id)
post   **let val** connected_boxes = connected(sys[bx_id]) ∪ {bx_id}
              val attached_lines = dunion ({ attached(sys[bx_id]) | bx_id ∈ connected_boxes})
              val connected_set = connected_boxes ∪ attached_lines
      in
          ∀ obj_id ∈ connected_set.
             let val obj = sys[obj_id] **in**
                sys′[obj_id] = obj † ⟦posn = posn(obj) + diffpos⟧
             endlet
          ∧ remainder_unchanged(connected_set, sys, sys′) ∧
          no_new_objects(sys,sys′)
        endlet

Note that a primed variable, as in sys′, indicates final values and unprimed variables indicate initial values, sys[bx_id] is the value of the map sys at bx_id, † is record field overwrite and dunion is distributed union.

Figure 6: Formal Specification of Move Operation

is defined using pre-post condition specifications. Global effects are defined using synchronous event communication between objects.

The object structure model determines the attributes in each Objectchart description. Thus the Objectchart for a class C has the attributes defined for class C in the object structure model. Use of the object structure model, in both the functional and dynamic models, means that it is possible to show consistency.

3.4.1 Objectchart for Box

The informal state machine for Box given in figure 2 should be compared with the Objectchart given in figure 7. It can be seen that three new events have been added; **connect(b)**, **add_to_connected(boxes)** and **change_position(p)**. Note that the attributes for Box, as defined in the object structure model, are shown in the bottom right corner of the Objectchart.

The following specification shows that the move event causes change_position to be sent to each of the boxes in connected.

pre true
move(p:Coordinate)/{b.change_position(p:Coordinate
| b ∈ connected ∪ { self }}
post {}

All attributes of the Box are unchanged as indicated by the empty post condition[3]. Any box receiving a change_position event updates its posn attribute and sends a move event to all its attached lines.

pre true
change_position(p:Coordinate)/{l.move(p:Coordinate
| l ∈ attached}
post posn′ = posn + p

The Objectchart specification reveals a flaw in the informal model (figure 2). In that machine a move sends move events to all connected boxes. However this causes a race situation because each recipient box will send out **move** to all connected boxes, including the the original sender. The

---
[3]Objectcharts uses a frame condition that any attribute that is not mentioned in a post condition is unchanged by that event.

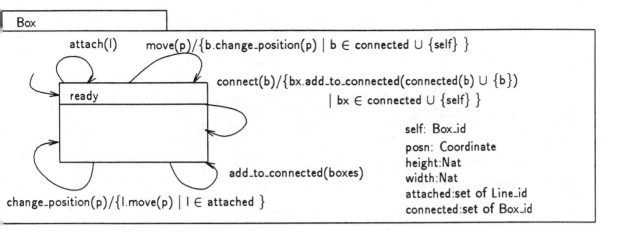

Figure 7: Objectchart for Box Class

change_position event is introduced into the state machine to overcome this problem. We omit the reasoning for introducing the other two new events, connect and add_to_connected. The need for them is apparent if how objects interact to provide system behaviour is considered.

The specifications of the other events are omitted.

3.4.2 Objectchart for Line

The Objectchart for Line has the same structure as the informal model (figure 3). It should be noted that the attribute corresponding to attached relation has been changed from a **set** to a **seq** of Box_id. This simplifies the specification as it allows the endpoints of the line to distinguished. It must be reflected back in the object structure model on the next iteration through the analysis process.

The move event received from a box just updates posn. Since it does not communicate with the attached Boxes, no race condition is generated.

> **pre** true
> move(p:Coordinate)
> **post** posn$'$ = posn + p

Up to two attach events are permissible for a detached line, after that they are ignored. The first updates the attached sequence for the line and outputs an attach to the box to which it has just been attached.

> **pre** true
> attach(b:Box_id)/b.attach(self)
> **post attached$'$** = <<b>> *where* <<b>> *is*
> *the single element sequence*

When the boxes are not connected, the second attach event updates the line's attached information and sends events to both "attached" boxes that they have been connected.

> **pre** b $\notin$ connected(first(attached))
> attach(b:Box_id)/(b.connect(first(attached))).
> (first(attached).connect(b))
> **post attached$'$** = append(attached, <<b>>)

If the boxes are already connected, the second attach is ignored.

The representation of attached as a sequence makes it straight forward to record the distinction between the first and second boxes to be attached to the line. Without this, race conditions may arise when updating the connected boxes' information.

The use of Objectcharts allows the dynamic model to be made more precise and thus can reveal errors in the interactions between objects. Of particular importance is the ability to reason about potential race and deadlock conditions. The next section shows how to establish consistency between different models produced during the analysis process.

179

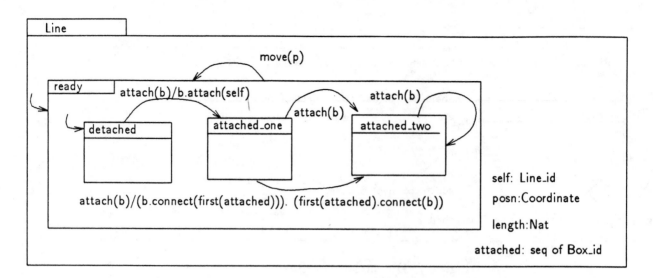

Figure 8: Objectchart for Line

3.5 Consistency between Models

In this section, we consider how consistency between the definition of operations in the functional model and dynamic model can be determined. As both models are expressed using the data domains of the object structure model and by pre-post condition specifications, there is a logical framework for consistency checking.

Operations in the functional model are defined declaratively in terms of their effect on the data types of the object model. The dynamic model implicitly defines system behaviour in terms of event traces, i.e. the sequences of events that flow between objects. Given the start state of the system, the effect of a trace can be computed from the Objectchart definitions. The task is to show that the event traces implement the declarative specifications of the functional model.

For the dynamic model to implement the functional model, each event trace must guarantee to bring about at least the effect of the functional specification, i.e. *the post-condition of the event trace must imply the post-condition of the functional definition.*

Additionally, each event trace must be able to occur in at least as many circumstances as the functional specification allows, i.e. *the pre-condition of the functional models must imply the pre-condition*

of the event trace.

For event traces, *that do not involve mutual messaging*, the post condition of the event trace is the AND-conjunction of the post conditions of each event in the trace. This is because the effect of each event as defined by its Objectchart post-condition is defined on the local state of only one object.

As an example, consider the effect of the operation, Move(b1,p) on a configuration of two connected boxes **b1** and **b2** with lines **l1**, **l2** and **l3** in figure 9.

A resulting trace is:-

$$\text{b1.move(p)} \quad \text{b1.change\_position(p)} \quad \text{b2.change\_position(p)}$$
$$\text{l1.move(p)} \quad \text{l2.move(p)} \quad \text{l3.move(p)}$$

The pre-condition of the functional model, b1 is a valid box_id, trivially implies the pre-condition of the trace, true. The post-condition of the trace is

$$\text{post}_{trace} =_{def}$$
$$\text{post}_{b1.\text{move}(p)} \wedge \text{post}_{b1.\text{change\_position}(p)} \wedge$$
$$\text{post}_{b2.\text{change\_position}(p)} \wedge \text{post}_{l1.\text{move}(p)} \wedge$$
$$\text{post}_{l2.\text{move}(p)} \wedge \text{post}_{l3.\text{move}(p)}$$
$$=_{def}$$
$$\text{b1.posn'} = \text{b1.posn} + \text{p} \wedge$$
$$\text{b2.posn'} = \text{b2.posn} + \text{p} \wedge$$
$$\text{l.posn'} = \text{l.posn} + \text{p} \; \forall \; \text{l} \in \{ \text{l1, l2, l3} \}$$

The post condition for **Move(b1,p)** defined by the functional model is

180

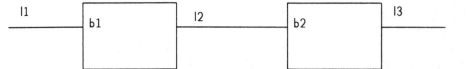

Figure 9: The Example Configuration

$$\text{post}_{func} =_{def} \text{posn}' = \text{posn(obj)} + p$$
$$\forall\ \text{obj} \in \text{connected}$$

where **connected** is the set {b1,b2,l1,l2,l3}.

Since these post conditions are equivalent it follows that, in this example, the dynamic and functional models are consistent. Proof in the general case is by induction over the object structure model.

In practice, proof is totally impractical. Thus we do not expect the analyst to prove consistency between models in the general case. Informal reasoning about judiciously selected examples has to be sufficient. The important point is that having a formal basis for analysis models opens the question of consistency to inspection.

3.6 Process

The introduction of more precision into the analysis models requires that the analysis process be modified. We favour a different process from that presented in Section 2.6.

1. Develop a natural language description of problem.

2. Build an object model together with a data dictionary of classes, relationships and attributes. Check completeness by stating consistency conditions between relations.

3. Derive an object structure model from the object model.

4. Use the object structure model to define a declarative functional model.

5. Use the object structure model to define a dynamic model together with diagrams showing examples of how events flow through the system in response to system operations.

6. State reasoned arguments, and test case event flows, to show that the dynamic model and functional model are consistent.

7. Iterate through the steps looking for missing classes, relationships, attributes, events etc.

Apart from the introduction of more formality, this process suggests that the functional model be constructed before the dynamic model. This is because it only makes sense to start the "programming" inherent in dynamic modelling when the system functionality has been defined. This ordering helps protect dynamic modelling from unnecessary perturbations due to requirements change. Even in trivial systems, like the example problem, minor changes to requirements can totally invalidate a dynamic model. As an example, the reader is asked to contemplate the effect on the dynamic model of the "minor" requirements change that no two boxes may overlap[4].

4 Conclusion

In this paper we have considered how object-oriented analysis models can be made more coherent. We have modified the informal models and produced four precise models which work together. This adds to the value of an analysis by reducing duplication, and avoiding ambiguity and inconsistency. The formal foundation also means that object-oriented analysis techniques may be usable in application domains, such as the safety-critical

---

[4]This effect is to make all box moves provisional until it has been ascertained that the move can be completed without causing an overlap

area, where formal methods is being vigorously pursued and may even be mandated ([9]).

Formal models have benefits when seen from the CASE perspective. Current analysis models lack precise semantic descriptions, consequently there is a severe limitation on the extent to which tools can provide semantic processing. The introduction of formality opens up the possibility semantic checking and simulation. The fact that the models can be linked through the object structure model also allows for the possibility of the closer integration of analysis tools. This fits well with the development of open integration platforms for CASE tools.

5 Acknowledgements

The authors readily acknowledge the contribution of their colleagues Patrick Arnold, Stephanie Bodoff and Helena Gilchrist to this paper. Thanks are also due to Dennis de Champeaux and Stephen Bear for many illuminating discussions on the nature of object-oriented analysis and design. We also wish to acknowledge the valuable contribution to this paper made by Matthieu Goutet, from the University of Paris-Sud.

References

[1] S. Bear. An Overview of HP-SL. In *Proceedings of VDM 91*, Noordwijkerhout, Netherlands, October 1991.

[2] S. Bear, D. Coleman, F. Hayes, and P. Allen. Graphical specification of object-oriented systems. In *ACM OOPSLA ECOOP '90 Conference Proceedings*, pages 28–37, Ottawa, Canada, October 1990.

[3] P. Coad and E. Yourdon. *Object-Oriented Analysis*. Yourdon Press, New York, NY (USA), 1990.

[4] D. Coleman and F. Hayes. Lessons from Hewlett-Packard's experience of using object-oriented technology. In *Proceedings of TOOLS 4*, pages 327–333, Paris, March 1991.

[5] D. Coleman, F. Hayes, and S. Bear. Introducing objectcharts or how to use statecharts in object-oriented design. *IEEE Transactions in Software Engineering*, to appear.

[6] A. Furtado and E. Neuhold. *Formal Techniques for Data Base Design*. Springer-Verlag, 1986.

[7] D. Harel. Statecharts: A visual formalism for complex systems. *Science of Computer Programming*, 8:231–274, 1987.

[8] C.B. Jones. *Systematic Software Development Using VDM*. Prentice-Hall, second edition, 1990.

[9] UK MoD. *Requirements for the Procurement of Safety Critical Software in Defence Equipment*. MoD Directorate of Standardisation, Kentigern House, 65 Brown Street, Glasgow G2 8EX, May 1989. Draft Defence Standard 0055.

[10] M. Page-Jones. *The Practical Guide to Structured Systems Design*. Yourdon Press, New York, NY (USA), 1980.

[11] J. Rumbaugh, M. Blaha, W. Premerlani, F. Eddy, and W. Lorensen. *Object-Oriented Modeling and Design*. Prentice Hall, Englewood Cliffs, NJ (USA), 1991.

[12] S. Shlaer and S.J. Mellor. *Object-Oriented Systems Analysis: Modeling the World in Data*. Prentice-Hall, 1988.

An Empirical Study of the Object-Oriented Paradigm and Software Reuse

John A. Lewis   Sallie M. Henry   Dennis G. Kafura

(Department of Computer Science)

and

Robert S. Schulman

(Department of Statistics)

Virginia Tech

Blacksburg, Virginia   24060

Internet: lewis@vtopus.cs.vt.edu

ABSTRACT

While little or no empirical validation exists for many of software engineering's basic assumptions, the need for scientific experimentation remains clear. Several assumptions are made about the factors affecting software reuse, and in particular, the role of the object-oriented paradigm. This paper describes the preliminary results of a controlled experiment designed to evaluate the impact of the object-oriented paradigm on software reuse. The experiment concludes that (1) the object-oriented paradigm substantially improves productivity, although a significant part of this improvement is due to the effect of reuse, (2) reuse without regard to language paradigm improves productivity, (3) language differences are far more important when programmers reuse than when they do not, and (4) the object-oriented paradigm has a particular affinity to reuse.

1. Introduction

The use of precise, repeatable experiments to validate any claim is the hallmark of a mature scientific or engineering discipline. Far too often, claims made by software engineers remain unsubstantiated because they are inherently difficult to validate or because their intuitive appeal seems to dismiss the need for scientific confirmation.

The effects of the object-oriented paradigm on software reuse is one area which begs further empirical investigation. While the characteristics of the object-oriented approach and the qualities which support successful reuse seem to complement each other, little empirical evidence has been given to support this relationship.

Studies related to software reuse are important because of the key role reuse assumes in improving software productivity. Brooks asserts that while no single development will

OOPSLA'91, pp. 184–196

result in an order-of-magnitude increase in productivity, software reuse is an area where the greatest results can be achieved because reuse addresses the "essence", as opposed to the "accidents," of the development problem [BROF87]. However, reusable software is not being exploited to its full potential. According to Freeman, the state-of-the-practice of reuse in the United States is embarrassing [FREP87]. On an evolutionary scale, he puts reuse technology in an awakening stage, slowly approaching an early utilization period. Developers and users of potentially reusable products are unnecessarily hampered because they lack specific knowledge concerning the factors which influence software reusability.

Studies of the object-oriented paradigm are important because, according to Biggerstaff's framework of software reuse [BIGT87], the object-oriented paradigm has a good balance between power and generality. In his framework, procedural based solutions are also depicted having a good balance, but are considered less effective than object-oriented solutions. The fundamental characteristics of the object-oriented paradigm seem to complement the needs of the reusing developer. Encapsulation capabilities create self-contained objects which are easily incorporated into a new design [KERB84]. The data-based decomposition of objects, resulting in class-hierarchies and inheritance, promotes reuse far more than the top-down approach which promotes "one-of-a-kind" development [MEYB87]. Greater abstraction is the key to to greater reusability, and object-based languages provide abstraction far

better than procedural languages [WEGP83].

Tracz makes several points which tend to support the use of the object-oriented paradigm to promote successful reuse [TRAW88]. For instance, special tools are not employed in current successful software reuse situations and are not the answer to the problem. Reuse success comes from formalizations of process and product, which an object-oriented environment creates. Furthermore, unplanned software reuse is costly. Software must be designed for reuse, with an emphasis on interface and modularization. The object-oriented paradigm stresses these characteristics. However, Tracz admits that no language, including an object-oriented one, will solve the the reuse problem inherently.

While the reuse potential of the object-oriented paradigm has been promoted, little scientific experimentation has been conducted to confirm this expectation. The research described in this paper provides a comparison of a standard procedural approach to that of the object-oriented techniques. A controlled experiment was designed and executed in order to measure the relative affects of a procedural language and an object-oriented language in terms of software reuse.

Similar experiments have been successful in making comparisons of the object-oriented and procedural approaches relative to other aspects of software development. One study determined that the object-oriented paradigm is quantitatively more beneficial than a procedural approach in terms of software maintenance [HENS90]. An interesting point made in that research is that subjects viewed the object-oriented techniques as more difficult to accomplish, even though all objective data supported the hypothesis that using it resulted in fewer maintenance tasks and reduced maintenance effort. This result clearly illustrates the danger of relying only on anecdotal evidence to assess software engineering technology.

The goal of the experiment described in this paper is to answer the following questions with respect to the impact of the object-oriented paradigm vs. the procedural paradigm on the successful reuse of software components:

1) Does the object-oriented paradigm promote higher productivity than the procedural paradigm?

2) Does reuse promote higher productivity than no reuse?

3) Does the object-oriented paradigm promote higher productivity than the procedural paradigm when programmers do not reuse?

4) Does the object-oriented paradigm promote higher productivity than the procedural paradigm when programmers reuse?

5) Does the object-oriented paradigm provide incentives to reuse above those of the procedural paradigm?

The experimental design was constructed

with these questions in mind. We define productivity as the inverse of the effort expended to produce a specific software product. Effort is measured in several quantifiable ways. We hypothesize that both reuse and the object-oriented paradigm are important factors in the software development effort.

The next section describes the design of the experiment and discusses the specifications of the tasks performed. Section 3 defines the data collected and the statistical analysis performed. Section 4 draws conclusions from the analysis, specifically addressing the questions presented above. Finally, Section 5 summarizes the experimental results and discusses future work in this area.

2. Experimental Design

Some reuse experiments employ hypothetical, question-and-answer situations where the subjects do not actually perform all the various tasks inherent in the reuse process. The authors believe, however, that to accurately determine influential factors, the experimental subjects must perform all of the following tasks: evaluating potentially reusable products, adapting them to the new situation, and integrating them into a functionally complete product. It is important to create, as accurately as possible, a representative situation while maintaining a valid experimental design [CURB80].

The experiment described in this paper is based on a target system developed by each of a set of senior-level software engineering students. The use of students as subjects, while sometimes considered unrealistic, is justified in this case due to two overriding considerations. First, empirical evidence by Boehm-Davis indicates that students are equal to professionals in many quantifiable measures, including their approach to developing software [BOED84]. Although new techniques are learned and further refinement does occur, a programmer's basic approach and development habits are formed quite early in their professional development. Second, given the amount of control necessary to execute this experiment, students are the only viable alternative. The efficacy of students as subjects is supported for within-subject experiments by Brooks [BROR80].

The subjects in this experiment developed a specified target system. The system specification is couched in the guise of computerizing a fictional company and is separated into two tasks. The specific functions making up the system were abstracted from the commercial software development experience of the first author. They involve a variety of programming techniques including data management, numerical processing, and graphics.

Previous research investigating the factors affecting software reuse have concentrated on two issues: 1) the impact of software engineering characteristics of code components, such as readability, structured code, etc., and 2) the techniques used to find appropriate code components from a set of possible candidates. Neither of these issues are

the focus of this study. Code quality was allowed to vary only within the controlled confines of "adequate" testing and software engineering standards. All completed projects were verified to meet a set of requirements concerning documentation, code quality, and functional correctness. Furthermore, subjects were given no special tools for searching or identifying candidate components. It is assumed that any assistance in this area would only improve the reuse results. This study focuses on language issues, specifically the comparison of the object-oriented paradigm to the procedural approach with respect to reuse of previously developed components.

In the experiment, reusable code components were made available to the subjects implementing the target system. To affect further control, the code component sets were specifically generated for this study. Therefore, the research consists of two phases. The first phase was preparatory, in which potentially reusable components were designed and implemented. The experiment was executed in the second phase, in which the target system was developed by a set of subjects, who are unrelated to the programmers who designed and implemented the reusable components. These two phases are described in the following sections.

2.1 Phase 1: Component Development

Two sets of potentially reusable components were created during phase one. One set was implemented in a procedural based language, Pascal, and the other in an object-oriented language, C++. The choice of languages was not arbitrary. We deliberately chose not to use C as the procedural programming language to make as clear a distinction as possible between the object-oriented approach and the procedural approach. Since C is basically a subset of C++, we feared the similarities of the two languages might cloud that distinction. C++ was chosen over Smalltalk because we believed the powerful programming environment of Smalltalk, not available to a Pascal programmer, might jeopardize the comparison. Finally, both C++ and Pascal emphasize strong typing, thus controlling another possible source of variation.

Both component sets were implemented on Apple Macintosh II's running A/UX. They were designed to be functionally equivalent, though design and coding techniques naturally vary. Equivalence was guaranteed by ensuring that all code met the same fundamental functional and error-handling requirements. Furthermore, all developed code passed the same level of testing thoroughness.

Knowing the requirements of the target system to be implemented in the second phase, each component was designed to have a specific level of applicability. The levels of reuse can be described as:

1) completely reusable,
2) reusable with slight revision (< 25%),
3) reusable with major revision (> 25%), and
4) not applicable for reuse.

With respect to the target system, the component sets were designed to contain elements from each reuse level. The 25% marks of levels 2 and 3 are only intuitive guidelines and refer to the amount of code that must be added, deleted and modified to create a component that meets the target system's requirements. Providing components which span a wide range of applicability ensures a realistic, diverse collection from which subjects evaluate and choose components.

2.2 Phase 2: Project Implementation

Using the two sets of components, independent subjects were assigned the task of implementing the target project. The subjects were divided into four groups, pictured as cells in Figure 1. Half the subjects implemented the project in Pascal, the other half in C++. Furthermore, a portion of the students from each language were not allowed to reuse at all, while the others were encouraged to reuse. The "no reuse" groups serve as control groups.

No Reuse Procedural	Reuse Procedural
No Reuse Object-Oriented	Reuse Object-Oriented

Figure 1: Subject group breakdown.

Twenty-one subjects were distributed unevenly across the groups. The uneven distribution of subjects was factored into the statistical analysis. The subjects were divided into the groups randomly, but were statistically blocked across their computer science grade point averages. This blocking was an effort to reduce variability within each group. An anova test comparing the grade point averages of subjects showed no significant differences between groups ($p < 0.9795$).

The functional requirements of the system are divided into two equal tasks concerned with "employee management" and "business management." Employee management functions deal with processes such as an employee database, payroll, security control, and cost center management. Business management functions are concerned with the details of shop floor control, quality control testing, warehouse management, and customer interactions.

Although the two tasks focus on different aspects of running a business, they were designed to be comparable in computational complexity. Both are divided into seven subtasks, each of which has a counterpart in the other task designed to require approximately the same amount of effort to develop. Since preliminary analyses showed that the results are not affected by the difference between the two tasks, this factor was ignored in subsequent analysis, thereby increasing statistical power in addressing the questions of primary interest. To further control this aspect of the experiment, half of the subjects designed and implemented the employee management task first, while the other half of the subjects designed and implemented the business management task first. Then each half switched, resulting in both system tasks being developed by each subject. This organization offsets any learning benefit of doing a particular task first. An introductory material section was provided with information both groups need to perform their respective tasks.

3. Data Analysis

Given a feasible and well-controlled experimental design, the rigorous analysis of data collected during the experiment determines the conclusions that can be made about the hypotheses. In this experiment, the goal is to determine which groups from Figure 1, on average, had a significantly different productivity rate than others.

The data collected during the experiment measures the productivity of a subject in implementing the target system. Productivity and effort are considered to have an inverse relationship. Therefore, the less effort expended by a subject to satisfy the requirements of one task, the higher the productivity of that subject. The measurements of effort, and therefore of productivity, are:

<u>Main productivity measures</u>

- **Runs** - The number of runs made during system development and testing,
- **RTE** - The number of run time errors discovered during system development and testing, and
- **Time** - The time (in minutes) to fix all run time errors,

189

<u>Secondary productivity measures</u>

- **Edits** - The number of edits performed during system development and testing, and
- **Syn.** - The number of syntax errors made during system development and testing.

Since each subject implemented the same tasks, a comparison of data across subjects yields a relative measure of the effort used to develop a task. A subject with a high value for a given measure is considered less productive than a subject with a low value.

Multiple productivity variables are used to obtain a complete picture of the development process. The Runs, RTE and Time variables, given their significance to the development process, are considered the main variables of interest. The Edits and Syntax Errors variables are gathered for completeness, but are given less emphasis. To reduce the overhead of the data collection, some measures that might have been of interest, such as total development time, were not collected.

Data was collected by the subjects using tally sheets. To assure the data's validity, subjects were informed that their names would not be associated with these data, and that the values themselves would have no bearing on their course evaluation. They were also told that a negative impact on their course evaluation would occur if they did not record their development information honestly and completely. The tally sheets were coded such that no subject name was ever connected to particular data.

The group means for each productivity variable are depicted graphically in Figure 2. These charts give a rough indication of how the groups compare although statistical analyses are employed to verify perceived differences. In each analysis, a difference in means was considered significant if the p-value for the test was less than 5% ($p < 0.05$), which is an accepted norm. Since our research questions all predict the direction of difference, all tests were performed in a one-sided manner.

Initial analysis of the task factor determined that the difference between the two tasks played no role in influencing any of the productivity variables (all p-values for task effects were ≥ 0.2073). In other words, the two tasks were determined to be equally difficult. The lack of difference is attributed to the careful design of task specifications and the blocking of subjects across grade point average. Therefore, all further analyses ignore the task factor, effectively creating 42 observations on which to perform the tests, which gives them more statistical power.

4. Experimental Results

This section draws conclusions from the analysis performed on the productivity data. In general, the hypotheses suggested at the beginning of this paper are supported, with some notable exceptions.

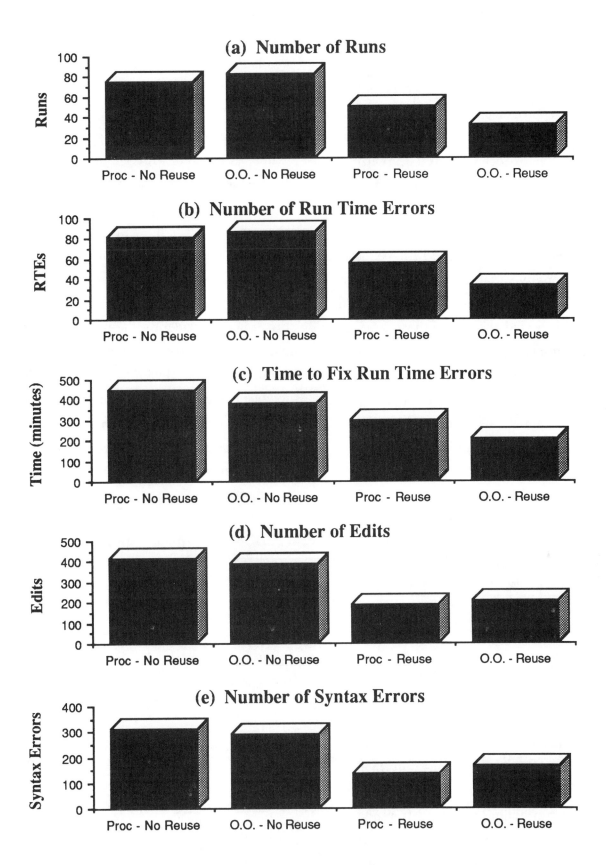

Figure 2. Group means for each production variable.

The experimental questions posed in Section 1 will be used as a framework for discussion of the statistical analysis. Each question will be addressed separately, giving the results of the appropriate analysis.

1) Does the object-oriented paradigm promote higher productivity than the procedural paradigm?

The third column in Table 1 list the means of the productivity variables calculated from all subjects using the procedural language, including subjects who reused as well as those who did not. The fourth column shows similar means for subjects in the object-oriented categories. Our hypothesis is that the values for the object-oriented paradigm will be lower than those of the procedural paradigm, indicating a higher productivity for the object-oriented subjects.

| | Significant? | p-value | Means | |
			Procedural	O-O
Runs	Yes	0.0066	59.27	47.50
RTE	Yes	0.0078	65.00	50.20
Time	Yes	0.0104	354.41	261.70
Edits	No	0.3469	271.55	263.65
Syn.	No	0.8675	183.67	202.40

Table 1. Language Main Effect

For each productivity variable, a p-value was computed for the difference between the means. The p-value is the probability that the difference could have been obtained by chance, rather than reflecting a true difference in productivity. Following conventional criteria, a difference is deemed statistically significant if its p-value is less than 0.05. In such cases, it is extremely unlikely that the difference in means is due to chance, and we conclude that productivity was indeed higher for subjects using the object-oriented paradigm.

The three main productivity variables (Runs, RTE and Time) show a significant difference between the means, favoring the object-oriented paradigm. In addition, the object-oriented mean for the Edit variable was also lower than the procedural mean, although not to a significant degree. The means on the Syntax Errors variable did not differ in the predicted direction. Considering the nature of the Edits and Syntax Errors variables, the lack of significance is attributed to the subjects lack of practice using the object-oriented language. The results of the analysis on the main variables indicate that the object-oriented paradigm does promote higher productivity than the procedural paradigm.

2) Does reuse promote higher productivity than no reuse?

From the results in Table 2, the answer to this question is clearly yes. The means in the third column of Table 2 are calculated for all subjects who did not reuse, regardless of the

| | Significant? | p-value | Means | |
			No Reuse	All Reuse
Runs	Yes	0.0001	78.71	41.14
RTE	Yes	0.0001	83.79	45.04
Time	Yes	0.0001	420.07	255.36
Edits	Yes	0.0001	405.71	198.82
Syn.	Yes	0.0001	302.14	150.92

Table 2. Reuse Main Effect

language used. Likewise, the fourth column shows means for all subjects who did reuse. Our hypothesis is that the means will be lower for the reuse groups, indicating a higher productivity for the subjects who were encouraged to reuse. This hypothesis is strongly supported by all variables.

	Significant?	p-value	Means	
			Procedural No Reuse	Procedural All Reuse
Runs	Yes	0.0001	75.38	50.07
RTE	Yes	0.0008	81.25	55.71
Time	Yes	0.0047	446.38	301.86
Edits	Yes	0.0001	416.00	189.00
Syn.	Yes	0.0001	311.00	137.14

Table 3. Procedural (No Reuse vs. Reuse)

	Significant?	p-value	Means	
			O - O No Reuse	O - O All Reuse
Runs	Yes	0.0001	83.17	32.21
RTE	Yes	0.0001	87.17	34.36
Time	Yes	0.0017	385.00	208.86
Edits	Yes	0.0001	392.00	208.64
Syn.	Yes	0.0001	290.33	164.71

Table 4. Object-Oriented (No Reuse vs. Reuse)

This result is further supported by the charts in Tables 3 and 4, which view the data across the reuse factor, but consider each language separately. Table 3 shows the means for the procedural groups with respect to reuse, and Table 4 shows the means for the object-oriented groups with respect to reuse. In both analyses, all variables showed a significant difference in the hypothesized direction.

3) Does the object-oriented paradigm promote higher productivity than the procedural paradigm when programmers do not reuse?

The means listed in Table 5 are calculated for subjects who did not reuse. The third column represents subjects using the procedural language, and the forth column represents subjects using the object-oriented language. Our hypothesis is that the object-oriented values will be lower than the procedural values. Surprisingly, none of the variables indicate a significant difference.

Interestingly, the group means do not consistently favor one language or the other. The means for the object-oriented groups are lower for Time, Edits, and Syntax Errors, but the means for the procedural groups are lower for Runs and RTEs. According to this analysis, we must conclude that when reuse is not a factor, the object-oriented paradigm does not promote higher productivity. In other words, in the absence of reusable components, either language works equally well.

	Significant?	p-value	Means	
			Procedural No Reuse	O - O No Reuse
Runs	No	0.8909	75.38	83.17
RTE	No	0.7506	81.25	87.17
Time	No	0.1607	446.38	385.00
Edits	No	0.2360	416.00	392.00
Syn.	No	0.1733	311.00	290.33

Table 5. No Reuse (Procedural vs. Object-Oriented)

4) **Does the object-oriented paradigm promote higher productivity than the procedural paradigm when programmers reuse?**

Given the answers to the first and third questions, the answer to this question should logically be yes. The results in Table 6 confirm this for the three main productivity variables. The means listed are for subjects who did reuse, with the third column representing subjects using the procedural paradigm and the forth column representing subjects using the object-oriented paradigm. Once again, our hypothesis favors the object-oriented paradigm.

| | Significant? | p-value | Means | |
			Procedural All Reuse	O-O All Reuse
Runs	Yes	0.0001	50.07	32.21
RTE	Yes	0.0005	55.71	34.36
Time	Yes	0.0153	301.86	208.86
Edits	No	0.8380	189.00	208.64
Syn.	No	0.9767	137.14	164.71

Table 6. Reuse (Procedural vs. Object-Oriented)

Variables Runs, RTE and Time all proved significant with means favoring the object-oriented group, but the Edits and Syntax Errors variables did not differ in the hypothesized direction. Given the importance of the main productivity variables, we can conclude that the object-oriented paradigm does promote higher productivity than the procedural paradigm when reuse in employed. Note that most of the support given to the first question comes from differences between the groups which were encouraged to reuse.

5) **Does the object-oriented paradigm provide incentives to reuse above those of the procedural paradigm?**

As shown by the results in Tables 3 and 4, reuse improved productivity over non-reuse for both the procedural and object-oriented paradigms. The fifth question asks whether the *extent* of improvement is comparable for the two language paradigms. Our hypothesis is that the improvement due to reuse will be greater for the subjects using the object-oriented paradigm than those using the procedural paradigm, indicating that the object-oriented paradigm is particularly suited to reuse.

The third column in Table 7 shows for each variable the difference between the mean of the procedural non-reuse group and the mean of the procedural reuse group. This is a measure of the amount of improvement in productivity due to reuse -- the large the difference, the greater the increase in productivity. The forth column show comparable mean differences for the object-oriented groups. Therefore, our hypothesis predicts that values in the fourth column should be greater than those in the third column.

| | Significant? | p-value | Mean Differences | |
			Procedural NR - R	O-O NR - R
Runs	Yes	0.0009	25.31	50.96
RTE	Yes	0.0062	25.54	52.81
Time	No	0.3176	144.52	176.14
Edits	No	0.8753	227.00	183.36
Syn.	No	0.9716	173.86	125.62

Table 7. Interaction (Extent of Improvement)

On the Runs and RTE variables, the increase in productivity due to reuse was greater for the object-oriented paradigm than for the procedural paradigm. The same pattern occurred on the Time variable, although the difference in means was not large enough to be statistically significant. Once again, contrary to the main productivity variables, the Edits and Syntax Errors variables seem to oppose the hypothesis. Given that two of the three main measures of productivity (Runs and RTE) show significant differences in the hypothesized direction, and that the third main variable (Time) favored the same direction, we conclude that there is a significant difference between the extent of improvement due to reuse across the two language paradigms. In other words, the results show that the object-oriented paradigm demonstrates a particular affinity to the reuse process.

5. Summary and Future Work

The experiment in this paper has shown:

(1) The object-oriented paradigm substantially improves productivity, although a significant part of this improvement is due to the effect of reuse (questions 1, 3 and 4),

(2) Software reuse improves productivity no matter which language paradigm is used (question 2),

(3) Language differences are far more important when programmers reuse than when they do not (questions 3 and 4), and

(4) The object-oriented paradigm has a particular affinity to the reuse process (question 5).

Although we did not demonstrate that the object-oriented paradigm promotes productivity when reuse is not a factor, the development efforts using either language paradigm were not significantly different. Furthermore, given the reuse potential demonstrated by the object-oriented paradigm, greater benefits can be achieved by using the object-oriented paradigm than by using a procedural approach.

An important facet of the experimental method is that the results are repeatable. Experiments similar to the one described in this paper should be conducted to verify the results of this experiment. In particular, the secondary variables of Edits and Syntax Errors did not always support the analysis of the main variables, even when intuition says they should. This tendency deserves further investigation.

Other experiments should be conducted which independently investigate the two main elements of this research: software reuse and the object-oriented paradigm. The factors which affect software reuse are many and varied. Similar experiments can be designed to determine the impact of human factors, code characteristics, and other language differences.

The object-oriented paradigm contains a wealth of possible benefits that have yet to be proven empirically. Claims that associate the object-oriented approach with improved design, less and easier maintenance, and higher reliability when compared to its procedural counterpart demand further investigation. Experience reports alone, while useful, are not enough to validate the assumptions that are associated with the object-oriented paradigm. Experimental research into these areas is necessary to provide a solid base to support the theories that shape state-of-the-art software production.

References

[BIGT87] Biggerstaff, T., Richter, C., "Reusability Framework, Assessment, and Directions," IEEE Software, March 1987, pp. 41-49.

[BROF87] Brooks, F.P., "No Silver Bullet: Essence and Accidents of Software Engineering," Computer, April 1987, pp. 10-19.

[BOED84] Boehm-Davis, D., Ross, L., "Approaches to Structuring the Software Development Process," International Journal of Man-Machine Systems, (to appear 1991).

[BROR80] Brooks, R., "Studying Programmer Behavior Experimentally: The Problems of Proper Methodology," Communications of the ACM, 1980, Volume 23, Number 4, pp. 207-213.

[CURB80] Curtis, B., "Measurement and Experimentation in Software Engineering," Proceedings of the IEEE, 1980, Volume 68, Number 9, pp. 1144-1157.

[FREP87] Freeman, P., "A Perspective on Reusability," Software Reusability, Computer Society Press of the IEEE, 1987, pp. 2-8.

[HENS90] Henry, S.M., Humphrey, M., Lewis, J.A., "Evaluation of the Maintainability of Object-Oriented Software," Proceedings of the Conference on Computer and Communication Systems, Volume 1, Hong Kong, September 1990, pp. 404-409.

[KERB84] Kernighan, B.W., "The Unix System and Software Reusability," IEEE Transactions on Software Engineering, September 1984, pp. 513-518.

[MEYB87] Meyer, B., "Reusability: The Case for Object-Oriented Design," IEEE Software, March 1987, pp. 50-64.

[TRAW88] Tracz, W., "Software Reuse Myths," ACM SIGSOFT Software Engineering Notes, January 1988, pp. 17-21.

[WEGP83] Wegner, P., "Varieties of Reusability," ITT Proceedings of the Workshop on Reusability in Programming, 1983, pp. 30-44.

TOWARDS A METRICS SUITE FOR OBJECT ORIENTED DESIGN

Shyam R. Chidamber
Chris F. Kemerer

Sloan School of Management
Massachusetts Institute of Technology
Cambridge, MA 02139

ABSTRACT

While software metrics are a generally desirable feature in the software management functions of project planning and project evaluation, they are of especial importance with a new technology such as the object-oriented approach. This is due to the significant need to train software engineers in generally accepted object-oriented principles. This paper presents theoretical work that builds a suite of metrics for object-oriented design. In particular, these metrics are based upon measurement theory and are informed by the insights of experienced object-oriented software developers. The proposed metrics are formally evaluated against a widely-accepted list of software metric evaluation criteria.

I. INTRODUCTION

In order for object-oriented software production to fulfill its promise in moving software development and maintenance from the current 'craft' environment into something more closely resembling conventional engineering, it will require measures or *metrics* of the process. While software metrics are a generally desirable feature in the software management functions of project planning and project evaluation, they are of especial importance with a new technology such as the object-oriented approach.

This is due to the significant need to train current and new software engineers in generally accepted object-oriented principles. This paper presents theoretical work that builds a suite of metrics for object-oriented design (OOD). In particular, these metrics are based upon *measurement theory* and are informed by the insights of experienced object-oriented software developers. The proposed metrics are evaluated against a widely-accepted list of seven software metric evaluation criteria, and the formal results of this evaluation are presented. Development and validation of software metrics is expected to provide a number of practical benefits. In general, techniques that provide measures of the size and of the complexity of a software system can be used to aid management in:

- estimating the cost and schedule of future projects,
- evaluating the productivity impacts of new tools and techniques,
- establishing productivity trends over time,
- improving software quality,
- forecasting future staffing needs, and
- anticipating and reducing future maintenance requirements.

More specifically, given the relative newness of the OO approach, metrics oriented towards OO can aid in evaluating the degree of object orientation of an implementation as a learning tool for staff members who are new to the approach. In addition, they may also eventually be useful

OOPSLA'91, pp. 197–211

objective criteria in setting design standards for an organization.

This paper is organized as follows. Section II presents a very brief summary of the need for research in this area. Section III describes the theory underlying the approach taken. Section IV presents the proposed metrics, and Section V presents Weyuker's list of software metric evaluation criteria [Weyuker, 1988]. Section VI contains the results of the evaluation of the proposed metrics, and some concluding remarks are presented in Section VII.

II. RESEARCH PROBLEM

There are two types of criticisms that can be applied to current software metrics. The first category are those criticisms that are leveled at conventional software metrics as they are applied to conventional, non-OO software design and development. These metrics are generally criticized for being without solid theoretical bases[1] and for failing to display what might be termed normal predictable behavior [Weyuker, 1988].

The second category is more specific to OO design and development. The OO approach centers around modeling the real world in terms of its objects, which is in stark contrast to older, more traditional approaches that emphasize a function-oriented view that separated data and procedures. Given the fundamentally different notions inherent in these two views, it is not surprising to find that software metrics developed with traditional methods in mind do not direct themselves to notions such as classes, inheritance, encapsulation and message passing. Therefore, given that current software metrics are subject to some general criticism and are easily seen as not supporting key OO concepts, it seems appropriate to develop a set, or suite of new metrics especially designed to measure unique aspects of the OO approach.

---

[1]For example, see [Vessey and Weber, 1984] and [Kearney, *et al.*, 1986].

Some early work has recognized the shortcomings of existing metrics and the need for new metrics especially designed for OO. Some proposals are set out by Morris, although they are empirically suggested rather than theoretically driven [1988]. Pfleeger also suggests the need for new measures, and uses counts of objects and methods to develop and test a cost estimation model for OO development [Pfleeger, 1989; Pfleeger and Palmer, 1990]. Moreau and Dominick suggest three metrics for OO graphical information systems, but do not provide formal, testable definitions [1989]. In contrast, Lieberherr and his colleagues present a well-articulated, formal approach in documenting the Law of Demeter™ [1988].

Given the extant software metrics literature, the approach taken here is to develop theoretically-driven metrics that can be shown to offer desirable properties, and then choose the most promising candidates for future empirical study. This paper is an initial presentation of six candidate metrics specifically developed for measuring elements contributing to the size and complexity of object-oriented design. Since object design is considered to be a unique aspect of OOD, the proposed metrics directly address this task. The metrics are constructed with a firm basis in theoretical concepts in measurement, while capturing empirical notions of software complexity.

III. THEORY BASED METRICS FOR OOD

Booch (1986) defines object oriented design to be the process of identifying objects and their attributes, identifying operations suffered by and required of each object and establishing interfaces between objects. Design of classes involves three steps: 1) definition of objects, 2) attributes of objects and 3) communication between objects. Methods design involves defining procedures which implement the attributes and operations suffered by objects. Class design is therefore at a higher level of abstraction than the traditional data/procedures approach (which is closer to methods design). It is the task of class design that makes OOD different than data/procedure design [Taylor & Hecht, 1990]. The reader is referred to works by Deutsch, *et al.* [1983], Meyer [1988], Page, *et al.* [1989], Parnas, *et al.* [1986], Seidewitz and Stark [1986] and others for an introduction to the fundamental concepts and terminology of object-oriented design.

Figure 1 shows the fundamental elements of object oriented design as outlined by Booch [1986].

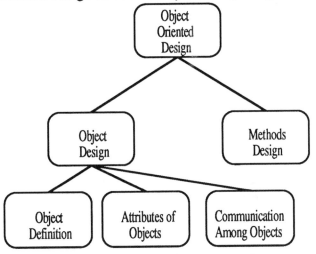

Figure 1: Elements of Object Oriented Design

Measurement theory base

A design can be viewed as a relational system, consisting of object elements, empirical relations and binary operations that can be performed on the object elements.

Notationally: design $P \equiv (A, R_1... R_n, O_1...O_m)$
where
A is a set of object elements
$R_1...R_n$ are *empirical* relations on object elements
A (e.g, bigger than, smaller than, etc)
$O_1...O_m$ are *binary* operations (e.g., concatenation)

A useful way to conceptualize empirical relations on a set of object elements in this context is to consider the measurement of complexity. A designer has ideas about the complexity of different objects, as to which object is more complex than another. This idea is defined as a *viewpoint*. The notion of a viewpoint was originally introduced to describe evaluation measures for information retrieval systems and is applied here to capture designer views [Cherniavsky, 1971]. An empirical relation is the embodiment of a viewpoint.

A viewpoint is a binary relation $.\geq$ defined on the set P. For P, P', P" $\in$ set P , the following axioms must hold:

$$P .\geq P \qquad \text{(reflexivity)}$$
$$P .\geq P' \text{ or } P' .\geq P \qquad \text{(completeness)}$$
$$P .\geq P', P' .\geq P" => P .\geq P" \qquad \text{(transitivity)}$$

i.e., a viewpoint must be of weak order [Zuse, 1987].

To be able to measure something about a object design, the *empirical relational system* as defined above needs to be transformed to a *formal relational system* [Roberts, 1979]. Therefore, let a formal relational system Q be defined as follows:

$$Q \equiv (C, S_1... S_n, b_1... b_m)$$

C is a set of elements (e.g., real numbers)
$S_1... S_n$ are *formal* relations on C (e.g., >, <, =)
$b_1... b_m$ are *binary* operations (e.g., +,-,*)

This is accomplished by a metric μ which maps an empirical system P to a formal system Q. For every element a $\in$ P, $\mu(a) \in Q$.

Definitions

The ontological basis principles proposed by Bunge in his "Treatise on Basic Philosophy" forms the basis of the concept of objects [Bunge, 1977]. Consistent with this ontology, objects are defined independent of implementation considerations and encompass the notions of encapsulation, independence and inheritance. According to this ontology, the world is viewed as composed of things, referred to as *substantial individuals* ,and concepts. The key notion is that substantial individuals possess *properties*. A property is a feature that a substantial individual possesses inherently. An observer can assign features to an individual, these are attributes and not properties. All substantial individuals possess a finite set of properties. "There are no bare individuals except in our imagination" [Bunge, 1979].

Some of the attributes of an individual will reflect its properties. Indeed, properties are recognized only through attributes. A known property must have at least one attribute representing it. Properties do not exist on their own but are "attached" to individuals. On the other hand, individuals are not bundles of properties. A substantial individual and its properties collectively constitute an *object* [Wand, 1987; Wand and Weber, 1990].

An object can be represented in the following manner:

$X = <x, p(x)>$ where x is the substantial individual and $p(x)$ is the finite collection of its properties.

x can be considered to be the token or name by which the individual is represented in a system. In object oriented terminology, the instance variables together with its methods are the properties of the object [Banerjee, *et al.*, 1987].

Coupling
Two things are coupled if and only if at least one of them "acts upon" the other [Wand, 1990]. X is said to act upon Y if the history of Y is affected by X, where history is defined as the chronologically ordered states that a thing traverses in time.

let $X = <x, p(x)>$ and $Y = <y, p(y)>$ be two objects.

$p(x) = \{ S_X \} \cup \{ I_X \}$
$p(y) = \{ S_Y \} \cup \{ I_Y \}$

where $\{ S_i \}$ is the set of methods and $\{ I_i \}$ is the set of instance variables of object *i*.

Using the above definition of coupling, any action by $\{S_X\}$ on $\{S_Y\}$ or $\{I_Y\}$ constitutes coupling, as does any action by $\{S_Y\}$ on $\{S_X\}$ or $\{I_Y\}$. Therefore, any evidence of a method of one object using methods or instance variables of another object constitutes coupling. This is consistent with the law of Demeter™ [Lieberherr, *et al.*, 1988]. In order to promote encapsulation of objects it is generally considered good practice to reduce coupling between objects.

Cohesion
Bunge [1977] defines *similarity* $\sigma()$ of two objects to be the intersection of the sets of properties of the two objects:

$$\sigma(X, Y) = p(x) \cap p(y)$$

Following this general principle of defining similarity in terms of sets, the degree of similarity of the methods within the object can be defined to be the intersection of the sets of instance variables that are used by the methods. It should be clearly understood that instance variables are not properties of methods, but it makes intuitive sense that methods that operate on the same instance variables have some degree of similarity.

$$\sigma(M_1, M_2...M_n) = \{ M_1 \} \cap \{ M_2 \} \cap \{ M_3 \} ... \{ M_n \}$$

where $\sigma() =$ degree of similarity and $\{ M_i \} =$ set of instance variables used by method M_i.

The degree of similarity of methods relates both to the conventional notion of cohesion in software engineering, (i.e., keeping related things together) as well as encapsulation of objects, that is, the bundling of methods and instance variables in an object. Cohesion of methods can be defined to be the *degree of similarity* of methods. The higher the degree of similarity of methods, the greater the cohesiveness of the methods and the higher the degree of encapsulation of the object.

Complexity of an object

Bunge defines complexity of an individual to be the "numerosity of its composition", implying that a complex individual has a large number of properties. Using this definition as a base, the complexity of an object can be defined to be the cardinality of its set of properties.

Complexity of $<x, p(x)> = |p(x)|$, where $|p(x)|$ is the cardinality of $p(x)$.

Scope of Properties

The scope of a property P in J (a set of objects) is the subset G (P; J) of objects possessing the property.

$G(P; J) = \{ x | x \in J \text{ and } P \in p(x) \}$, where $p(x)$ is the set of all properties of all $x \in J$.

Wand defines a class on the basis of the notion of scope [1987]. A class P with respect to a property set p is the set of all objects possessing all properties in p.

$C(p; J) = \cap_{\text{all } P} \{ G(P) | P \in p(x) \}$

The inheritance hierarchy is a tree structure with classes as nodes, leaves and a root. Two useful concepts which relate to the inheritance hierarchy can be defined. They are *depth of inheritance* of a class and the *number of children* of a class.

Depth of Inheritance = height of the class in the inheritance tree

The height of a node of a tree refers to the length of the longest path from the node to the root of the tree.

Number of Children = Number of immediate descendents of the class

Both these concepts relate to the notion of scope of properties. i.e., how far does the influence of a property extend? The number of children and depth of inheritance collectively indicate the genealogy of a class. Depth of inheritance indicates the extent to which the class is influenced by the properties of its ancestors and number of children indicates the potential impact on descendents.

Methods as measures of communication

In the object oriented approach, objects can communicate only through message passing. A message can cause an object to "behave" in a particular manner by invoking a particular method. Methods can be viewed as definitions of responses to possible messages [Banerjee, *et al.*, 1987]. It is reasonable therefore to define a *response set* for an object in the following manner:

Response set of an object $\equiv$ {set of all methods that can be invoked in response to a message to the object}

Note that this set will include methods outside the object as well, since methods within the object may call methods from other objects. The response set will be finite, since the properties of an object are finite and there are a finite number of objects in a design.

IV. THE CANDIDATE METRICS

The candidate metrics outlined in this section were developed over a period of several months. This was done in conjunction with a team of software engineers in an organization which has used OOD in a number of different projects over the past four years. Though the primary development language for all projects at this site was C++, the aim was to propose metrics that are not language specific. The viewpoints presented under each metric reflect the object oriented design experiences of many of the engineers, and are presented here to convey the intuition behind each of the metrics.

Metric 1: Weighted Methods Per Class (WMC)

Definition:
Consider a Class C_1, with methods $M_1,... M_n$. Let $c_1,... c_n$ be the static complexity of the methods. Then

$$WMC = \sum_{i=1}^{n} c_i.$$

If all static complexities are considered to be unity, $WMC = n$, the number of methods.

Theoretical basis:
WMC relates directly to the definition of complexity of an object, since methods are properties of objects and complexity of an object is determined by the cardinality of its set of properties. The number of methods is, therefore, a measure of object definition as well as being attributes of an object, since attributes correspond to properties.

Viewpoints:
The number of methods and the complexity of methods involved is an indicator of how much time and effort is required to develop and maintain the object.

The larger the number of methods in an object, the greater the potential impact on children, since children will inherit all the methods defined in the object.

Objects with large numbers of methods are likely to be more application specific, limiting the possibility of reuse.

Metric 2: Depth of Inheritance Tree (DIT)

Definition:
Depth of inheritance of the class is the DIT metric for the class.

Theoretical basis:
DIT relates to the notion of scope of properties. DIT is a measure of how many ancestor classes can potentially affect this class.

Viewpoints:
The deeper a class is in the hierarchy, the greater the number of methods it is likely to inherit, making it more complex.

Deeper trees constitute greater design complexity, since more methods and classes are involved.

It is useful to have a measure of how deep a particular class is in the hierarchy so that the class can be designed with reuse of inherited methods.

Metric 3: Number of children (NOC)

Definition:
NOC = number of immediate sub-classes subordinated to a class in the class hierarchy.

Theoretical basis:
NOC relates to the notion of scope of properties. It is a measure of how many sub-classes are going to inherit the methods of the parent class.

Viewpoints:
Generally it is better to have depth than breadth in the class hierarchy, since it promotes reuse of methods through inheritance.

It is not good practice for all classes to have a standard number of sub-classes. Classes higher up in the hierarchy should have more sub-classes than classes lower in the hierarchy.

The number of children gives an idea of the potential influence a class has on the design. If a class has a large number of children, it may require more testing of the methods in that class.

Metric 4: Coupling between objects (CBO)

Definition:
CBO for a class is a count of the number of non-inheritance related couples with other classes.

Theoretical basis:
CBO relates to the notion that an object is coupled to another object if two objects act upon each other, i.e., methods of one use methods or instance variables of another. This is consistent with traditional definitions of coupling as "measure of the degree of interdependence between modules" [Pressman, 1987].

Viewpoints:
Excessive coupling between objects outside of the inheritance hierarchy is detrimental to modular design and prevents reuse. The more independent an object is, the easier it is to reuse it in another application.

Coupling is not associative, i.e., if A is coupled to B and B is coupled to C, this does not imply that C is coupled to A.

In order to improve modularity and promote encapsulation, inter-object couples should be kept to a minimum. The larger the number of couples, the higher the sensitivity to changes in other parts of the design and therefore maintenance is more difficult.

A measure of coupling is useful to determine how complex the testing of various parts of a design are likely to be. The higher the inter-object coupling, the more rigorous the testing needs to be.

Metric 5: Response For a Class (RFC)

Definition:
RFC = | RS | where RS is the response set for the class.

Theoretical basis:
The response set for the class can be expressed as:

$$RS = \{ M_i \} \cup_{all\ n} \{ R_i \}$$
where M_i = all methods in the class
and $\{ R_i \}$ = set of methods called by M_i

The response set is a set of methods available to the object and its cardinality is a measure of the attributes of an object. Since it specifically includes methods called from outside the object, it is also a measure of communication between objects.

Viewpoints:
If a large number of methods can be invoked in response to a message, the testing and debugging of the object becomes more complicated.

The larger the number of methods that can be invoked from an object, the greater the complexity of the object.

The larger the number of possible methods that can be invoked from outside the class, greater the level of understanding required on the part of the tester.

A worst case value for possible responses will assist in appropriate allocation of testing time.

Metric 6: Lack of Cohesion in Methods (LCOM)

Definition:
Consider a Class C_1 with methods $M_1, M_2...$, M_n. Let $\{I_i\}$ = set of instance variables used by method M_i. There are *n* such sets $\{I_1\},... \{I_n\}$.

LCOM = The number of disjoint sets formed by the intersection of the *n* sets.

Theoretical basis:
This uses the notion of degree of similarity of methods. The degree of similarity for the methods in class C_1 is given by:

$$\sigma() = \{I_1\} \cap \{I_2\}... \cap \{I_n\}$$

If there are no common instance variables, the degree of similarity is zero. However, this does not distinguish between the case where each of the methods operates on unique sets of instance variables and the case where only one method operates on a unique set of variables. The number of disjoint sets provides a measure for the disparate nature of methods in the class. Fewer disjoint sets implies greater similarity of methods. LCOM is intimately tied to the instance variables and methods of an object, and therefore is a measure of the attributes of an object.

Viewpoints:
Cohesiveness of methods within a class is desirable, since it promotes encapsulation of objects.

Lack of cohesion implies classes should probably be split into two or more sub-classes.

Any measure of disparateness of methods helps identify flaws in the design of classes.

Low cohesion increases complexity, thereby increasing the likelihood of errors during the development process.

Summary

The table below summarizes the six metrics in relation to the elements of OOD shown in figure 1.

Metric	Object Definition	Object Attributes	Object Commun-ication
WMC	✔	✔	
DIT	✔		
NOC	✔		
RFC		✔	✔
CBO			✔
LCOM		✔	

Table 1: Mapping of Metrics to OOD Elements

IV. METRICS EVALUATION PROPERTY LIST

Weyuker has developed a list of desiderata for software metrics, and has evaluated a number of existing software metrics using these properties [Weyuker, 1988]. These properties are repeated below.

Property 1: Non-coarseness
Given an object P and a metric μ another object Q can always be found such that:
$\mu(P) \neq \mu(Q)$.

This implies that every object cannot have the same value for a metric, otherwise it has lost its value as a measurement.

Property 2: Non-uniqueness (notion of equivalence)
There can exist distinct objects P and Q such that $\mu(P) = \mu(Q)$. This implies that two objects can have the same metric value, i.e. the two objects are equally complex.

Property 3: Permutation is significant
There exist objects P and Q such that if P is a permutation of Q (i.e., elements in P are simply a different ordering of the elements of Q) then $\mu(P) \neq \mu(Q)$.

Property 4: Implementation not function is important
Suppose there are two object designs P and Q which perform the same function, this does not imply that $\mu(P) = \mu(Q)$. The intuition behind Property 4 is that even though two object designs perform the same function, the details of the implementation matter in determining the object design's metric.

Property 5: Monotonicity
For all objects P and Q, the following must hold:
$\mu(P) \leq \mu(P+Q)$
$\mu(Q) \leq \mu(P+Q)$
where $P + Q$ implies concatenation of P and Q. This implies that objects are minimally zero, and therefore that the combination of two objects can never be less than either of the component objects.

Property 6: Non-equivalence of interaction
Given $\exists$ P, $\exists$ Q, $\exists$ R,
$\mu(P) = \mu(Q)$ does not imply that $\mu(P+R) = \mu(Q+R)$.

This implies that interaction between P and R can be different than interaction between Q and R.

Property 7: Interaction increases complexity
$\exists$ P and Q such that:
$$\mu(P) + \mu(Q) \leq \mu(P+Q)$$
The idea is that interaction between objects will tend to increase complexity.

V. RESULTS: PROPERTIES OF THE CANDIDATE METRICS

A design goal for all six metrics is their use in analysis of object oriented designs independent of the programming language.in which the application is written. However, there are some basic assumptions made regarding the distribution of objects, methods and instance variables in the discussions for each of the metric properties.

Assumption 1:
Let X_i = The number of methods in a given class i.
 Y_i = The number of methods called from a given method i.
 Z_i = The number of instance variables used by a method i.
 C_i = The number of couplings between a given object i and all other objects.

X_i, Y_i, Z_i, C_i are discrete random variables each characterized by some general distribution function. Further, all the X_is are independent and identically distributed. The same is true for all the Y_is, Z_is and C_is.
Assumption 2: $X_i \geq 1$ i.e., each class contains one or more methods.
Assumption 3: Two classes can have identical methods, in the sense that combination of the two classes into one class would result in one of the methods being redundant.
Assumption 4: The inheritance tree is "full" i.e., there is a root, several intermediate nodes which have siblings, and leaves. The tree is not balanced, i.e., each node does not necessarily have the same number of children.

These assumptions while believed to be reasonable, are of course subject to future empirical test.

Metric 1: Weighted Methods Per Class (WMC)

Let X_p = number of methods in class P and X_q = number of methods in class Q.
Let y = probability $X_p \neq X_q$, and (1 - y) = probability $X_p = X_q$

As $0 < P < 1$ from assumption 1, there is a finite probability that $\exists$ a Q such that $\mu(P) \neq \mu(Q)$, therefore property 1 is satisfied. Similarly, $0 < 1 - y < 1$, there is a finite probability that $\exists$ a Q such that $\mu(P) = \mu(Q)$. Therefore property 2 is satisfied. Permutation of elements inside the object does not alter the number of methods of the object. Therefore Property 3 is not satisfied. The function of the object does not define the number of methods in a class. The choice of methods is an implementation decision, therefore Property 4 is satisfied.
 Let $\mu(P) = n_p$ and $\mu(Q) = n_q$, then $\mu(P+Q) = n_p + n_q$. Clearly, $\mu(P+Q) \geq \mu(P)$ and $\mu(P+Q) \geq \mu(Q)$, thereby satisfying property 5. Now, let $\mu(P) = n$, $\mu(Q) = n$, $\exists$ an object R such that it has a number of methods ∂ in common with Q but no methods in common with P. Let $\mu(R) = r$.
$$\mu(P+R) = n + r$$
$$\mu(Q+R) = n + r - \partial$$
therefore $\mu(P+Q) \neq \mu(Q+R)$ and property 6 is satisfied. For any two objects P and Q, $\mu(P+Q) = n_p + n_q - \partial$, where n_p is the number of methods in P, n_q is number of methods in Q and P and Q have ∂ methods in common.
Clearly, $n_p + n_q - \partial \leq n_p + n_q$ for all P and Q.
i.e., $\mu(P+Q) \leq \mu(P) + \mu(Q)$ for all P and Q.
Therefore Property 7 is not satisfied.

Metric 2: Depth of Inheritance Tree (DIT)

Per assumption 4, every tree has a root and leaves. The depth of inheritance of a leaf is always greater than the root. Therefore, property 1 is satisfied. Also, since every tree has at least some nodes with siblings, there will always exist at least two objects with the same depth of inheritance, i.e., property 2 is satisfied. Permutation of the elements within an object does not alter the position of the object in the inheritance tree, and therefore property 3 is not satisfied. Implementation of an object involves choosing what properties the object must inherit in order to perform its function. In other words, depth of inheritance is implementation dependent, and property 4 is satisfied.

When any two objects P & Q are combined, there are three possible cases:
i) when one is a child of the other:

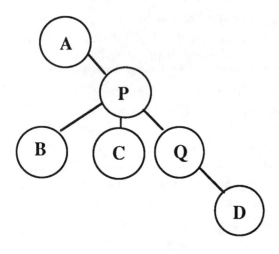

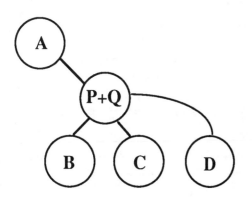

In this case, $\mu(P) = n$, $\mu(Q) = n + 1$, but $\mu(P+Q) = n$, i.e. $\mu(P+Q) < \mu(Q)$. Property 5 is not satisfied.

Case ii) P & Q are siblings

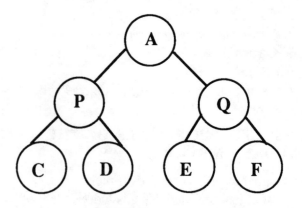

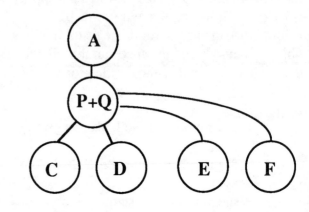

In this case, $\mu(P) = \mu(Q) = n$ and $\mu(P+Q) = n$, i.e. Property 5 is satisfied.

Case iii) P & Q are not directly connected.

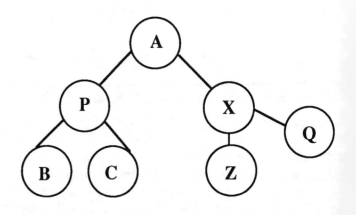

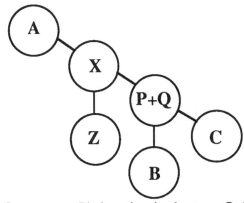

If P+Q moves to P's location in the tree, Q does cannot inherit methods from C, however if P+Q moves to Q's location, P maintains its inheritance. Therefore, P+Q will be in Q's old location. In this case, $\mu(P) = x$, $\mu(y)$ and $y > x$. $\mu(P+Q) = y$, i.e., $\mu(P+Q) > \mu(P)$ and $\mu(P+Q) = \mu(Q)$ and property 5 is satisfied. Since $\mu(P+Q) \geq \mu(P)$ is not satisfied for all possible cases, Property 5 is not satisfied. Let P and Q be siblings, i.e. $\mu(P) = \mu(Q) = n$, and let R be a child of P. Then $\mu(P+R) = n$ and $\mu(Q+R) = n + 1$. i.e. $\mu(P+R)$ is not equal to $\mu(Q+R)$. Property 6 is satisfied. For any two objects P & Q, $\mu(P+Q) = \mu(P)$ or $= \mu(Q)$. Therefore, $\mu(P+Q) \leq \mu(P) + \mu(Q)$ i.e. Property 7 is not satisfied.

Metric 3: Number Of Children (NOC)

Let P and R be leaves, $\mu(P) = \mu(R) = 0$, let Q be the root $\mu(Q) > 0$. $\mu(P) \neq \mu(Q)$ therefore property 1 is satisfied. Since $\mu(R) = \mu(P)$, Property 2 is also satisfied. Permutation of elements within an object does not change the number of children of that object, therefore Property 3 is not satisfied. Implementation of an object involves decisions on the scope of the methods declared within the object, i.e, the sub-classing for the object. The number of sub-classes is therefore dependent upon implementation of the object. Therefore, property 4 is satisfied. Let P and Q be two objects with n_p and n_q sub-classes respectively (i.e., $\mu(P) = n_p$ and $\mu(Q) = n_q$). Combining P and Q, will yield a single object with $n_p + n_q - \partial$ sub-classes, where ∂ is the number of children P and Q have in common. Clearly, ∂ is 0 if either n_p or n_q is 0.

Now, $n_p + n_q - \partial \geq n_p$ and $n_p + n_q - \partial \geq n_q$. This can be written as:
$\mu(P+Q) \geq \mu(P)$ and $\mu(P+Q) \geq \mu(Q)$ for all P and all Q.
Therefore, Property 5 is satisfied. Let P and Q each have n children and R be a child of P which has r children. $\mu(P) = n = \mu(Q)$. The object obtained by combining P and R will have $(n-1) + r$ children, whereas an object obtained by combining Q and R will have $n + r$ children, which means that $\mu(P+R) \neq \mu(Q+R)$. Therefore property 6 is satisfied.
Given any two objects P and Q with n_p and n_q children respectively, the following relationship holds:
$\mu(P) = n_p$ and $\mu(Q) = n_q$.
$\mu(P+Q) = n_p + n_q - \partial$
where ∂ is the number of common children.
Therefore, $\mu(P+Q) \leq \mu(P) + \mu(Q)$ for all P and Q. Property 7 is not satisfied.

Metric 4: Response for a Class (RFC)

Let X_p = RFC for class P
     X_q = RFC for class Q.
Let y = probability $X_p \neq X_q$, $(1 - y)$ = probability $X_p = X_q$
$X_p = F(Y_i)$ and $X_q = F(Y_j)$ i.e., X_p is some function of the number of methods called by a method in class P. Now, F() is monotonic in Y, since the response set can only increase as the number of methods called increases. Y_i and Y_j are independent identically distributed discrete random variables, as per assumption 1. Therefore, $F(Y_i)$ and $F(Y_j)$ are also discrete random variables that are i.i.d. Therefore, there is a finite probability that $\exists$ a Q such that $\mu(P) \neq \mu(Q)$ resulting in property 1 being satisfied. Also as $0 < 1 - y < 1$ there is a finite probability that $\exists$ a Q such that $\mu(P) = \mu(Q)$, therefore property 2 is satisfied. Permutation of elements within an object does not change the number of methods called by that object, and therefore property 3 is not satisfied. Implementation of an object involves decision about the methods that need to be called and therefore Property 4 is satisfied. Let P and Q be two classes with RFC of P = n_p and RFC of Q =

n_q. If these two classes are combined to form one class, the response for that class will be the larger of the two RFC values for P and Q $\Rightarrow \mu (P+Q) = Max(n_p, n_q)$. Clearly, $Max(n_p,n_q) \geq n_p$ and $Max(n_p,n_q) \geq n_q$ for all possible P and Q. $\mu(P+Q) \geq \mu(P)$ and $\geq \mu(Q)$ for all P and Q. Therefore, property 5 is satisfied. Let P, Q and R be three classes such that, $\mu(P) = \mu(Q) = n$ and $\mu(R) = r$. Then $\mu(P+Q) = Max(n,r)$ and $\mu(Q+R) + Max(n,r)$. i.e., $\mu(P+Q) = \mu(R+Q)$. Therefore property 6 is not satisfied. For any two classes P and Q, $\mu(P+Q) = Max(\mu(P), \mu(Q))$. Clearly, $Max(\mu(P), \mu(Q)) \leq \mu(P) + \mu(Q)$ which means that Property 7 is not satisfied.

Metric 5: Lack Of Cohesion Of Methods (LCOM)

Let X_p = LCOM for class P
$\quad X_q$ = LCOM for class Q.
Let y = probability $X_p \neq X_q$, (1 - y) = probability $X_p = X_q$
$X_p = F(Y_i)$ and $X_q = F(Y_j)$ i.e., X_p is some function of the number of instance variables used by a method in class P. Now, F() is monotonic in Y, since the LCOM can only decrease as the number of instance variables used increases. Y_i and Y_j are independent identically distributed discrete random variables, as per assumption 1. Therefore, $F(Y_i)$ and $F(Y_j)$ are also discrete random variables that are i.i.d. therefore property 1 is satisfied. Also as $0 < 1 - y < 1$. then there is a finite probability that $\exists$ a Q such that $\mu(P) = \mu(Q)$, therefore property 2 is satisfied. Permutation of the elements of an object does not alter the set of methods called from that object, consequently not changing the value of LCOM. Therefore, property 3 is not satisfied. The LCOM value depends on the construction of methods, which is implementation dependent, making LCOM also implementation dependent and satisfying property 4. Let P and Q be any two objects with $\mu(P) = n_p$ and $\mu(Q) = n_q$. Combining these two objects can potentially reduce the number of disjoint sets. i.e., $\mu(P+Q) = n_p + n_q - \partial$ where ∂ is the number of disjoint sets reduced due to the combination of P and Q. The reduction ∂ is some function of the particular sets

of instance variables of the two objects P and Q. Now, $n_p \geq \partial$ and $n_q \geq \partial$ since the reduction in sets obviously cannot be greater than the number of original sets. Therefore, the following result holds:
$n_p + n_q - \partial \geq n_p$ for all P and Q and
$n_p + n_q - \partial \geq n_q$ for all P and Q.
Property 5 is satisfied.
Let P and Q be two objects such that $\mu(P) = \mu(Q) = n$, and let R be another object with $\mu(R) = r$.
$\mu(P+Q) = n + r - \partial$, similarly
$\mu(Q+R) = n + r - ß$
Given that ∂ and ß are not functions of n, they need not be equal. i.e., $\mu(P+R) \neq \mu(Q+R)$, satisfying property 6. For any two objects P and Q, $\mu(P+Q) = n_p + n_q - \partial$. i.e.,
$\mu(P+Q) = \mu(P) + \mu(Q) - \partial$ which implies that $\mu(P+Q) \leq \mu(P) + \mu(Q)$ for all P and Q.
Therefore property 7 is not satisfied.

Metric 6: Coupling Between Objects (CBO)

As per assumption 1, there exist objects P, Q and R such that $\mu(P) \neq \mu(Q)$ and $\mu(P) = \mu(R)$ satisfying properties 1 and 2. Permutation of the elements inside an object does not change the number of inter-object couples, therefore property 3 is not satisfied. Inter-object coupling occurs when methods of one object use methods or instance variables of another object, i.e., coupling depends on the construction of methods. Therefore property 4 is satisfied. Let P and Q be any two objects with $\mu(P) = n_p$ and $\mu(Q) = n_q$. If P and Q are combined, the resulting object will have $n_p + n_q - \partial$ couples, where ∂ is the number of couples reduced due to the combination. That is $\mu(P+Q) = n_p + n_q - \partial$, where ∂ is some function of the methods of P and Q. Clearly, $n_p - \partial \geq 0$ and $n_q - \partial \geq 0$ since the reduction in couples cannot be greater than the original number of couples. Therefore,
$n_p + n_q - \partial \geq n_p$ for all P and Q and
$n_p + n_q - \partial \geq n_q$ for all P and Q
i.e., $\mu(P+Q) \geq \mu(P)$ and $\mu(P+Q) \geq \mu(Q)$ for all P and Q. Thus, property 5 is satisfied. Let P and Q

be two objects such that $\mu(P) = \mu(Q) = n$, and let R be another object with $\mu(R) = r$.

$\mu(P+Q) = n + r - \partial$, similarly

$\mu(Q+R) = n + r - \beta$

Given that ∂ and β are not functions of n, they need not be equal, i.e., $\mu(P+R)$ is not equal to $\mu(Q+R)$, satisfying property 6. For any two objects P and Q, $\mu(P+Q) = n_p + n_q - \partial$.

$\mu(P+Q) = \mu(P) + \mu(Q) - \partial$ which implies that

$\mu(P+Q) \leq \mu(P) + \mu(Q)$ for all P and Q.

Therefore property 7 is not satisfied.

Summary of results

All six metrics fail to meet property 3, suggesting that perhaps permutation of elements within an object is not significant. The intuition behind this is that measurements on class design should not depend on ordering of elements within it, unlike program bodies where permutation of elements should yield different measurements reflecting the nesting of if-then-else blocks.

The rationale behind property 7 according to Weyuker is to "allow for the possibility of increased complexity due to potential interaction" [Weyuker, 1988]. All six metrics fail to meet this, suggesting that perhaps this is not applicable to object oriented designs. This also raises the issue that complexity could increase, not reduce as a design is broken into more objects. Further research in this area is needed to clarify this issue.

The RFC metric fails to satisfy property 6 and the DIT metric fails to satisfy property 5. These deficiencies are a result of the definition of the two metrics and further refinements will be required to satisfy these properties. It is worth pointing out that Harrison [1988] and Zuse [1991] have criticized the non-equivalence of interaction property (property 6) and note that this property may not be widely applicable. Also, the DIT metric, as shown earlier does not satisfy the monotonicity property (property 5) only in the case of combining two objects in different parts of the tree, which empirical research may demonstrate to be a rare occurrence. Table 2 presents a summary of the metrics properties.

Summary of Results

METRIC	P1	P2	P3	P4	P5	P6	P7
WMC	Yes	Yes	NO	Yes	Yes	Yes	NO
DIT	Yes	Yes	NO	Yes	NO	Yes	NO
NOC	Yes	Yes	NO	Yes	Yes	Yes	NO
RFC	Yes	Yes	NO	Yes	Yes	NO	NO
LCOM	Yes	Yes	NO	Yes	Yes	Yes	NO
CBO	Yes	Yes	NO	Yes	Yes	Yes	NO

Table 2: Summary of Metrics Properties

VI. CONCLUDING REMARKS

This research has developed a new set of software metrics for OO design. These metrics are based in measurement theory, and also reflect the viewpoints of experienced OO software developers. In evaluating these metrics against a set of standard criteria, they are found to both (a) perform relatively well, and (b) suggest some ways in which the OO approach may differ in terms of desirable or necessary design features from more traditional approaches. Clearly some future research designed both to extend the current proposed metric set and to further investigate these apparent differences seems warranted.

In particular, this set of six proposed metrics is presented as a first attempt at development of formal metrics for OOD. They are unlikely to be comprehensive, and further work could result in additions, changes and possible deletions from this suite. However, at a minimum, this proposal should lay the groundwork for a formal language with which to describe metrics for OOD. In addition, these metrics may also serve as a generalized solution for other researchers to rely on when seeking to develop specialized metrics for particular purposes or customized environments.

Currently planned empirical research will attempt to validate these candidate metrics by measuring them on actual systems. In particular, a three-phased approach is planned. In Phase I, the metrics will be measured on a single pilot system. After this pilot test, Phase II will consist of calculating the metrics for multiple systems and simultaneously collecting some previously established metrics for purposes of comparison. These previously existing metrics could include such well-known measures as source lines of code, function points, cyclomatic complexity, software science metrics, and fan-in/fan-out. Finally, Phase III of the research will involve collecting performance data on multiple projects in order to determine the relative efficacy of these metrics in predicting managerially relevant performance indicators.

It is often noted that OO may hold some of the solutions to the software crisis. Further research in moving OO development management towards a strong theoretical base should provide a basis for significant future progress.

REFERENCES

Abbot, R. J. (1987). "Knowledge Abstraction," *Communications of the ACM*, 30, 664-671.

Banerjee, J., *et al.* (1987). "Data Model Issues for Object Oriented Applications," *ACM Transactions on Office Information Systems*, 5, January, 3-26.

Booch, G. (1986). "Object Oriented Development," *IEEE Transactions on Software Engineering*, SE-12, February, 211-221.

Bunge, M. (1977). *Treatise on Basic Philosophy : Ontology I : The Furniture of the World.* Boston, Riedel.

Bunge, M. (1979). *Treatise on Basic Philosophy : Ontology II : The World of Systems.* Boston, Riedel.

Cherniavsky, V. and D. G. Lakhuty (1971). "On The Problem of Information System Evaluation," *Automatic Documentation and Mathematical Linguistics*, 4, 9-26.

Cunningham, W. and K. Beck (1987). "Constructing Abstractions for Object Oriented Applications", Computer Research Laboratory, Textronix Inc. Technical Report CR-87-25, 1987.

Deutsch, P. and A. Schiffman (1983). "An Efficient Implementation of the Smalltalk-80 System," *Conference record of the Tenth Annual ACM Symposium on the Principles of Programming Languages.*

Fenton, N. and A. Melton (1990). "Deriving Structurally Based Software Measures," *Journal of Systems and Software*, 12, 177-187.

Harrison, W. (1988). "Software Science and Weyuker's Fifth Property", University of Portland Computer Science Department Internal Report 1988.

Hecht, A. and D. Taylor (1990). "Using CASE for Object Oriented Design with C++," *Computer Language*, 7, November, Miller Freeman Publications, San Francisco, CA.

Kearney, J. K., *et al.* (1986). "Software Complexity Measurement," *Communications of the ACM*, 29 (11), 1044-1050.

Lieberherr, K., *et al.* (1988). "Object Oriented Programming : An Objective Sense of Style," *Third Annual ACM Conference on Object Oriented*

Meyer, B. (1988). *Object Oriented Software Construction (Series in Computer Science)*. New York, Prentice Hall International.

Moreau, D. R. and W. D. Dominick (1989). "Object Oriented Graphical Information Systems: Research Plan and Evaluation Metrics," *Journal of Systems and Software*, 10, 23-28.

Morris, K., (1988). *Metrics for Object Oriented Software Development,* unpublished Masters Thesis, M.I.T., Cambridge, MA.

Page, T., et al. (1989). "An Object Oriented Modelling Environment," *Proceedings of the Fourth Annual ACM Conference on Object Oriented Programming Systems, Languages and Applications (OOPSLA).*

Parnas, D. L., et al. (1986). Enhancing Reusability with Information Hiding. *Tutorial: Software Reusability*. P. Freeman, Ed., New York, IEEE Press. 83-90.

Peterson, G. E. (1987). *Tutorial: Object Oriented Computing*. IEEE Computer Society Press.

Pfleeger, S. L. (1989). "A Model of Cost and Productivity for Object Oriented Development", Contel Technology Center Technical Report.

Pfleeger, S. L. and J. D. Palmer (1990). "Software Estimation for Object Oriented Systems," *Fall International Function Point Users Group Conference*. San Antonio, Texas, October 1-4, 181-196.

Pressman, R. S. (1987). *Software Engineering: A Practioner's Approach*. New York, McGraw Hill.

Roberts, F. (1979). *Encyclopedia of Mathematics and its Applications*. Addison Wellesley Publishing Company.

Seidewitz, E. and M. Stark (1986). "Towards a General Object Oriented Software Development Methodology," *First International Conference on the ADA Programming Language Applications for the NASA Space Station*. D.4.6.1-D4.6.14.

Vessey, I. and R. Weber (1984). "Research on Structured Programming: An Empiricist's Evaluation," *IEEE Transactions on Software Engineering*, SE-10 (4), 394-407.

Wand, Y. and R. Weber (1990). "An Ontological Model of an Information System," *IEEE Transactions on Software Engineering*, 16, N 11, November, 1282-1292.

Wand, Y. (1987). A Proposal for a Formal Model of Objects. *Research Directions in Object Oriented Programming*. Ed., Cambridge, MA, M.I.T. Press. 537-559.

Weyuker, E. (1988). "Evaluating Software Complexity Measures," *IEEE Transactions on Software Engineering*, 14, No 9, September, 1357-1365.

Wybolt, N. (1990). "Experiences with C++ and Object Oriented Software Development," *USENIX Association C++ Conference Proceedings*. San Francisco, CA.

Zuse, H. (1991). *Software Complexity: Measures and Methods*. New York, Walter de Grutyer.

Zuse, H. and P. Bollman (1987). "Using Measurement Theory to Describe the Properties and Scales of Static Software Complexity Metrics", I.B.M. Research Center Technical Report RC 13504, August.

211

Communication as Fair Distribution of Knowledge

Jean-Marc Andreoli and **Remo Pareschi**

ECRC, Arabellastrasse 17
D-8000 Munich 81, Germany
{jeanmarc,remo}@ecrc.de

Abstract

We introduce an abstract form of interobject communication for object-oriented concurrent programming based on the proof theory of Linear Logic, a logic introduced to provide a theoretical basis for the study of concurrency. Such a form of communication, which we call forum-based communication, can be seen as a refinement of blackboard-based communication in terms of a more local notion of resource consumption. Forum-based communication is introduced as part of a new computational model for the object-oriented concurrent programming language *LO*, presented at last year OOPSLA/ECOOP (1990), which exploits the proof-theory of Linear Logic also to achieve a powerful form of knowledge-sharing.

1   Introduction

The programming language *LO* (for Linear Objects) [6, 4, 3] has been designed to supply a logical framework for object-oriented concurrent programming, with the purpose of rigorously accounting for its various aspects (concurrent communication, knowledge sharing, object creation, object termination etc.) in terms of the proof-theoretic behav-

ior of logical connectives, thus making very simple and completely abstract the operational semantics of the system; its formal background is given by Linear Logic [11], a logic introduced by Jean-Yves Girard to provide a theoretical basis for the study of concurrency. *LO*'s view of active, concurrent objects as structured entities capable of sharing knowledge has on the other hand been illustrated in [4] in terms of a sociological metaphor: objects can be thought of as complex organizations which inherit the problem solving capabilities of their suborganizations. Procedural knowledge is correspondingly encoded by specifying state transitions (*methods*) of the form

$$C_1 \,\wp\, \ldots \,\wp\, C_n \,\circ\!\!-\, Body.$$

where each C_i is an atomic logical formula. The logical (proof-theoretic) interpretation of methods hinges on the identification of objects, and of systems of objects, with proof trees and goes as follows: if, in constructing a proof tree in the Linear Logic calculus of sequents, we have reached an open node containing, among others, components $C_1 \ldots C_n$, then expand this node into another node obtained by replacing $C_1 \ldots C_n$ with the contents specified in *Body*, and leaving the remaining components untouched; this may lead to the creation of other nodes, or to a stop in the evolution of that branch of the proof, depending on the logical nature of the information provided by *Body*. The sociological interpretation goes instead as follows: if an organization contains in its current state a suborganization whose member elements

OOPSLA'91, pp. 212–229

are $C_1 \ldots C_n$ then let the given suborganization perform the task specified in *Body*, thus changing its own state and, consequently, that of the whole organization. According to both the logical and the sociological interpretation, objects evolve by explicitly performing actions: elements in the current state of affair may irreversibly disappear, to be replaced by new ones. On the sociological side this, and nothing else, could have been expected; but, on the logical side, such a capability to deductively deal with change in open worlds of independently coexisting entities specifically exploits the fact that Linear Logic accounts not just for truth, but also for the complementary notion of action, which had been instead neglected in more traditional logical developments. Thus, logic and sociology agree to each other, the first one giving us a rigorously defined abstract operational semantics for the language, and the other an anthropomorphic view of it which fits well within the tradition of object-oriented programming.

LO's organizational approach to knowledge sharing can be viewed as a form of *intraobject* communication, with objects acting as structured entities: for the capability of a subobject to handle a certain task is transmitted to the entire object in terms of the operational semantics of method triggering. We have argued that this form of inheritance does not suffer from the computational drawbacks of dynamic approaches to knowledge sharing like *delegation* [18], since it avoids the proliferation of delegate objects, which act as "bureaucrats" whose only purpose is delivering requests for tasks someone else is going to do; on the other hand, none of the malleability of delegation is lost, as *LO*'s objects have a completely flexible structure, where new types of components can be added at run time, while other ones may altogether disappear; nor does this entail populating our universe with anything more but simple "individuals" and their aggregations — abstract in its operational semantics, *LO* is quite concrete in its ontology: no notion of class is introduced, and the object-subobject relationship suffices to achieve inheritance (this can be contrasted with the class-superclass relationship characterizing class-based languages)[1].

However, another equally crucial and primary form of communication characterizes object-oriented concurrent programming: *interobject* communication, where separate entities exchange information, whether they be structured or not. This is the basic ingredient for object-based concurrency, particularly in languages of the Actor family [2], of which *LO* is an offspring on the side of its logic programming branch [27]; communication of such kind reduces procedure calls to exchanges of messages between objects, thus leading to a completely decentralized and truly concurrent model of computation. The computational model for *LO* presented in [6, 4, 3] has dealt with interobject communication simply by importing the technique of "shared logical variables" directly from concurrent logic programming languages based on Horn logic, like Concurrent Prolog [26], Parlog [12] and GHC [29]. However, such a solution is to be considered as temporary and not completely satisfactory mainly for the following (strictly related) reasons:

(*i*) It is committed to a specific implementation choice (the use of unification of logical variables in order to achieve communication) and thus defies *LO*'s effort towards a completely abstract operational semantics, which can be supported by different kinds of implementations and architectures.

(*ii*) It burdens the programmer with the task of dealing her/himself with problems related to stream-based communication, like stream-merging in many-to-one communication.

(*iii*) Although intraobject and interobject communication appear as conceptually dual, they are not so at the operational level: the intraobject case is accounted for in terms of proof construction, while unification handles the interobject case. The situation would become quite

---

[1]Obviously, we view classes and aggregations of individuals as quite different entities: the former are abstractions on individuals, the other are simply obtained by putting together simpler individuals to obtain more complex (composite) ones.

213

more pleasant by making proof construction capable of handling both cases; it would also be quite more in the spirit of Linear Logic, which is based on a system of dualities of logical operators.

In this paper, we provide a computational model for *LO* which refines the one described in the previous papers precisely by making proof construction responsible both for intraobject and interobject communication. In such a new model, proof construction is going to be seen as a *bidirectional* process, where, by starting from a *partially* defined initial node, we both go ahead in building the branches of the proof-tree and in further specifying its initial node. Thus, perhaps not surprisingly, dual communication concepts can both be accounted for via a fully symmetric approach to proof construction. This is obtained by permitting partially specified nodes to be instantiated upon the triggering of methods, which are now written as

$$C_1 \,\otimes\, \ldots \,\otimes\, C_i \,\otimes\, {}^{\wedge}C_{i+1} \,\otimes\, \ldots \,\otimes\, {}^{\wedge}C_n \,\circ\!\!-\, Body.$$

Here, the components ${}^{\wedge}C_{i+1}, \ldots, {}^{\wedge}C_n$ (if any) are added to the unspecified part of the node once the method is triggered, while the components $C_1, \ldots, C_i$ must be found already there. But the unspecified part of any node gets percolated from the unspecified part of the initial node, and is therefore shared by all objects; consequently, whenever the triggering of a method by an object makes new components to be added to the unspecified part of the node, then these components are propagated back to the root of the proof tree and can in turn be used by other objects. To stick to the organizational metaphor, we can think of the unspecified part of the initial node as a kind of *discussion forum*: this is a suborganization shared by all organizations, through which they exchange information between each other. From the point of view of proof construction, whenever information is exchanged, we make progress in building the proof tree in the direction of the root; on the other hand, making progress towards the leaves along a certain

branch of the proof tree has to do with information which is strictly local to the object identified with the given branch, thus accounting for intraobject communication.

Now, communication in a forum is characterized by two basic kinds of speech acts:

- the act of the speaker's addressing one specific hearer, in front of the remaining part of the audience (*specific communication*);

- the act of the speaker's addressing the whole audience (*generic communication*).

In both cases, communication is achieved through a shared communication medium, even when it is specific; moreover, generic communication is always *fair*, in the sense that no receiver can limit only to her/himself the use of a message which is meant for the whole community. As we shall see, our approach to forum-based interobject communication will support both specific and generic communication, and will maintain the fairness of generic communication. But we shall also ensure the *safeness* and the *privacy* of specific communication, by providing a clean way of generating private names to be used as mail addresses labeling messages which have to be specifically addressed, so that the capability to read one of such messages requires acquaintance of the corresponding mail address; alternatively, from the point of view of the speaker/hearer relationship, we can think of such private names as "interpretation keys", whose acquaintance unlocks the meanings of the messages with which they are associated. Furthermore, we shall characterize the relationship between such a novel form of communication and the well-established blackboard-based communication (see for instance [10]): as it will be shown, forum-based communication can both be viewed as a logical version of blackboard-based communication and also as an operational refinement of it in the sense of being endowed with a more local notion of resource consumption (corresponding to the property of fairness of generic communication) which makes it fully adequate for distributed computing.

We shall also compare our approach to communication with the one adopted for Concurrent Constraint Logic Programming (CCLP) languages described in [24, 15]; indeed, both approaches implement a logic-based form of fair generic communication, and appear as complementing each other in the following sense: in the case of forums the items of information can be removed from the "visual field" of agents (i.e., once accessed they are actually consumed, albeit just within the local scope of the accessing agent); in the case of CCLP languages, items of information are instead permanently stored for all agents.

The remaining part of this paper is organized as follows: Section 2 will give a description of the new computational model of *LO* leading to forum-based communication, and will formally characterize it both in terms of an operational (proof-theoretic) semantics and a model-theoretic semantics; Section 3 will describe two applications of this new model of computation, the first one of which (a graphical application) will be characterized by specific communication, while the other (a concurrent chart parser) will be characterized by generic communication and will provide us with an instance of a highly general methodology for distributed problem solving; Section 4 will compare our approach with related work, and Section 5 will give a brief overview of ongoing directions of research.

2 Description of the Language *LO*

2.1 Formulae, Sequents, Proofs

The syntax of the language *LO* uses three connectives of Linear Logic: "par" (written γ), "with" (written $\&$), and "top" (written $\top$). We also make use of the Linear implication (written $\circ\!-$) which can be defined in terms of the other connectives of Linear Logic. Two classes of Linear formulae, namely "goals" G and "methods" M, are built recursively from the class A of atomic formulae (i.e. simple terms possibly containing variables), as follows:

$$G = A \mid G \gamma G \mid \top \mid G \& G$$
$$M = A \circ\!- G \mid A \gamma M$$

A "program" is a set of methods and a "context" is a multiset of *ground* goals (i.e. containing no free variables). An *LO* "sequent" is a pair written $\mathcal{P} \vdash \mathcal{C}$ where $\mathcal{P}$ is a program and $\mathcal{C}$ is a context.

2.1.1 Definition of the Inference Figures for *LO*

A proof is a tree structure whose nodes are labeled with sequents. By convention, a proof tree is graphically represented with its root at the bottom and growing upward. Its branches are obtained as instances of the inference figures of the following sequent system, which defines *LO*'s operational semantics.

- Decomposition

$$[\gamma] \frac{\mathcal{P} \vdash \mathcal{C}, G_1, G_2}{\mathcal{P} \vdash \mathcal{C}, G_1 \gamma G_2} \qquad [\top] \frac{}{\mathcal{P} \vdash \mathcal{C}, \top}$$

$$[\&] \frac{\mathcal{P} \vdash \mathcal{C}, G_1 \qquad \mathcal{P} \vdash \mathcal{C}, G_2}{\mathcal{P} \vdash \mathcal{C}, G_1 \& G_2}$$

- Propagation

$$[\circ\!-] \frac{\mathcal{P} \vdash \mathcal{C}, G}{\mathcal{P} \vdash \mathcal{C}, A_1, \ldots, A_n}$$

$$\text{if } (A_1 \gamma \cdots \gamma A_n \circ\!- G) \in [\mathcal{P}]$$

In these figures, $\mathcal{P}$ and $\mathcal{C}$ denote, respectively, a program and a context. G, G_1, G_2 denote ground goals and the expression $\mathcal{C}, G$ denotes the context obtained as the multiset union of $\mathcal{C}$ and the singleton G.

In the propagation inference figure $[\circ\!-]$, we take $[\mathcal{P}]$ to be the set of all the ground instances of the methods in $\mathcal{P}$. The letters $A_1, \ldots, A_n$ denote ground atoms. Thus, the context in the lower sequent contains (in the sense of multiset inclusion) a submultiset of atoms which matches exactly the head of a ground instance of a method from the program. The upper sequent is obtained by *replacing* in the lower sequent this submultiset with the body of the selected instance of method (i.e. a ground goal).

Notice that, by definition, the elements of a multiset are not ordered. Therefore, the order of the atoms in the head of a method is not relevant.

2.1.2 Operational Interpretation of the Inference Figures

Read bottom-up, a proof gives a static representation (a "snapshot") of the overall dynamic evolution of a system of objects viewed as active processes (agents). Each sequent at the node of a proof-tree encodes the state of an object at a given time. The branches of the proof-tree represent object state transitions.

Thus, the sequent system of *LO* can be interpreted as a general specification of a set of valid object state transitions: the lower sequent in each inference figure is the input state of a valid transition, whose output states (if any) are the upper sequents.

- Inference figure [⊤], which has no upper sequents, encodes a transition without output states. In other words, it allows termination of objects.

- Inference figure [&] has two upper sequents which share a part of their context. Thus, the two output states of this transition can be viewed as clones, that is, as independent entities with a similar structure. In other words, the connective & allows creation of objects by cloning.

- Inference figure [⅋] aggregates, within the same object, two different components. It allows construction of object states with multiple elements, which lies at the basis of the object/subobject relationship in *LO*.

- Inference figure [∘−] allows the transformation of an aggregation of components (a subobject) within an object.

Notice that, for each transition, the program (left-hand side of the sequents) never changes while the context (right-hand side) is always modified (at least one formula is replaced by another). In other words, the program contains the unrestricted resources of the object, that is, those which can be reused as many times as needed, while any element from the context is a restricted resource, which disappears once used.

LO proofs are characterized by two levels of concurrency: *AND*-concurrency, involving processes evolving on different branches of the proof; and *OR*-concurrency, involving different subprocesses aggregated within a single process, evolving on a single branch. These two forms of concurrency correspond to the two forms of communication which, in the introduction, we have called, respectively, interobject and intraobject communication. The terminology for *AND/OR*-concurrency has been chosen to make a direct connection with Linear Logic, where the connective & responsible for *AND*-concurrency is the (additive) conjunction whereas the connective ⅋ responsible for *OR*-concurrency is the (multiplicative) disjunction.

2.2 Computational Model

In this paper, we keep the basic computational mechanism already proposed in previous papers, which can be summarized as follows:

> **Computation = Proof Search**

The important novelty here is in the specification of the class of proofs to be searched, called the target proofs, associated with a given query.

2.2.1 Contextual Proof Search

A query is a pair consisting of a program $\mathcal{P}$ and a ground goal G. Target proofs are then defined as follows:

Definition 1 *A target proof is an LO-proof such that its root is a sequent of the form $\mathcal{P} \vdash \mathcal{C}, G$, where $\mathcal{C}$ is a context (also called an answer context for the query).*

In other words, proofs are searched in such a way that the context of their root node may *properly contain* the query goal. This new model of

216

computation can be used within the two different paradigms of transformational and reactive programming [13].

- In the "transformational" paradigm, the systems reads an input, processes it and produces an output. The input is here the initial query and the output is any possible answer context $\mathcal{C}$. The elements of $\mathcal{C}$ can be viewed as constraints and thus, a query can be interpreted as "find a set of constraints from which a given formula is derivable".

- In the "reactive" paradigm, several agents interact together by exchanging messages. There is no notion of input and output in this case; the initial query is used only for the purpose of bringing into life certain agents. The answer context $\mathcal{C}$ acts as a medium of communication between agents. $\mathcal{C}$ is initially unspecified but each agent can read and write in it during a state transition; each time an agent writes in $\mathcal{C}$, the written formula is automatically propagated to all the other agents. This kind of communication we call *forum-based communication*, by viewing a sender agent as a speaker talking in front of an audience gathered in a forum.

In this paper, we focus on the second paradigm, where the answer context is used as a communication medium.

2.2.2 Example

Consider the following propositional *LO* program $\mathcal{P}$:

$$p \,\invamp\, a \multimap r.$$
$$q \,\invamp\, a \,\invamp\, b \multimap \top.$$
$$r \,\invamp\, b \multimap \top.$$

The following proof Π (where the program $\mathcal{P}$ is omitted from the left hand side of the sequents) is a possible target proof for the query $\langle \mathcal{P} \,;\, p \,\&\, q \rangle$.

$$\Pi \;=\; [\&] \;\cfrac{[\multimap] \;\cfrac{[\top] \;\cfrac{}{\vdash \top}}{\vdash b, r} }{\vdash b, a, p} \qquad [\multimap] \;\cfrac{[\top] \;\cfrac{}{\vdash \top}}{\vdash b, a, q}}{\vdash b, a, \;\; p \,\&\, q}$$

Thus, the multiset b, a is an answer context for the query above. Let us go into the details of a possible construction of Π. Initially, the search tree is reduced to a single node

$$\Pi_0 \;=\; \vdash \mathcal{C}, \; p \,\&\, q$$

where $\mathcal{C}$ is a still unspecified context.

1. Inference figure $[\&]$ applies to the single node of Π_0 and expands it to

$$\Pi_1 \;=\; [\&] \;\cfrac{\vdash \mathcal{C}, p \quad \vdash \mathcal{C}, q}{\vdash \mathcal{C}, \; p \,\&\, q}$$

2. At this point, no inference figure applies without making some assumption on the content of $\mathcal{C}$. For example, if we assume that $\mathcal{C}$ contains a (i.e. $\mathcal{C} = \mathcal{C}', a$), then the first method of $\mathcal{P}$ applies to the leftmost leaf of Π_1 (inference figure $[\multimap]$), and yields

$$\Pi_2 \;=\; [\&] \;\cfrac{[\multimap] \;\cfrac{\vdash \mathcal{C}', r}{\vdash \mathcal{C}', a, p} \quad \vdash \mathcal{C}', a, q}{\vdash \mathcal{C}', a, \;\; p \,\&\, q}$$

3. To continue, we need further assumptions on $\mathcal{C}$. For example, if we assume that $\mathcal{C}'$ contains b (i.e. $\mathcal{C}' = \mathcal{C}'', b$), then the second method of $\mathcal{P}$ applies to the rightmost leaf of Π_2 (inference figures $[\multimap]$, and then $[\top]$), and yields

$$\Pi_3 \;=\; [\&] \;\cfrac{[\multimap] \;\cfrac{\vdash \mathcal{C}'', b, r}{\vdash \mathcal{C}'', b, a, p} \quad [\multimap] \;\cfrac{[\top] \;\cfrac{}{\vdash \mathcal{C}'', \top}}{\vdash \mathcal{C}'', b, a, q}}{\vdash \mathcal{C}'', b, a, \;\; p \,\&\, q}$$

4. Now, the third method of $\mathcal{P}$ applies to the leftmost leaf of Π_3, and yields

$$\Pi_4 \;=\; [\&] \;\cfrac{[\multimap] \;\cfrac{[\multimap] \;\cfrac{[\top] \;\cfrac{}{\vdash \mathcal{C}'', \top}}{\vdash \mathcal{C}'', b, r}}{\vdash \mathcal{C}'', b, a, p} \quad [\multimap] \;\cfrac{[\top] \;\cfrac{}{\vdash \mathcal{C}'', \top}}{\vdash \mathcal{C}'', b, a, q}}{\vdash \mathcal{C}'', b, a, \;\; p \,\&\, q}$$

5. Finally, Π is identified as the instance of Π_4 in which $\mathcal{C}''$ is the empty multiset.

Of course this construction is far from being the only possible one. At each step, we have made several decisions, some of which were arbitrary. Hence the need to define a control strategy.

2.3 Proof Search Control

2.3.1 The "tell" marker

A large amount of non-determinism in proof search is eliminated by the following result, which identifies a complete subset of *LO*-proofs, so that the search procedure can be restricted to proofs in this subset.

Theorem 1 *A sequent $\mathcal{P} \vdash \mathcal{C}$ is derivable in LO if and only if it has a "focusing" proof, i.e. one in which the bottom context in each occurrence of the propagation inference figure [∘−] contains only atoms.*

This result is a special case of a more general theorem for full Linear Logic (called the "focusing" theorem), stated in [3], and which is in fact stronger: if any of the decomposition inference figures ([⊤], [&] or [⅋]) applies at one node of the proof, then it can deterministically be applied immediately. Therefore, as long as the current context contains a non-atomic goal, the proof search procedure can be made completely deterministic.

However, once the context contains only atoms, and it is therefore time for the propagation inference figure [∘−] to be applied, we are faced with a non-deterministic choice which we would like to control. Here the crucial problem is that of selecting an appropriate method from the program. By adopting a blind search strategy, any method could be triggered: for, as long as no restriction is put on the context, it would always be possible to assume that the method's head is entirely contained in the yet unspecified part of the context. We introduce therefore a pragmatic tool which gives the user control on such assumptions. Let $^\wedge$ be a special symbol, called the "tell" marker, which can be used to prefix any atom in the head of a method. Thus, the first method of program $\mathcal{P}$ of Section 2.2.2 could be marked as follows:

$$p \mathbin{⅋} {}^{\wedge}a \circ\!\!- r$$

This means that, to apply this method, the atom p (unmarked) must be found in the *already specified* part of the context, while the atom a (marked)

must be assumed in the *still unspecified* part of the context. Of course, when triggering the method, both the marked and the unmarked atoms of the head (here p, a) are replaced by the body of the method (here, r alone). Thus, the head of each method is split into two groups of atoms: those (unmarked) which are asked from the context (i.e. from its already specified part) and those (marked) which are told to the context (i.e. to its still unspecified part).

Now consider the program $\mathcal{P}$ of Section 2.2.2 with the following marking:

$$p \mathbin{⅋} {}^{\wedge}a \circ\!\!- r.$$
$$q \mathbin{⅋} a \mathbin{⅋} {}^{\wedge}b \circ\!\!- \top.$$
$$r \mathbin{⅋} b \circ\!\!- \top.$$

It is easy to check that the proof construction described in Section 2.2.2 is the only possible one with respect to the marking above.

The interactions between the two branches created at step 1 in the search illustrates the communication mechanism obtained by this use of the markings in the head of the methods: first the left branch sends a message a to the right branch (step 2); then the right branch receives this message a, sends a message b to the left branch and terminates (step 3). Finally, the left branch receives the message b and terminates (step 4). In both send and receive operations, the message is locally consumed by the concerned agent and disappears from its scope, but not from the scope of the other agent(s). There lies the fundamental difference between our forum-based communication and blackboard-based systems (like Linda [10], for instance), where, once an agent consumes a resource, it takes it away globally also for all the other agents. Similarly, the "forum based" communication mechanism differs from the one available in the CCLP languages described in [24, 15], where "told" constraints are never removed from the local "visual field" of an agent.

Clearly, communication of this kind directly depends on the possibility of suspending and resuming computation. Indeed, notice that after step 1, no method applies to the right branch. However, no failure occurs because of this. Instead computation on the right branch gets suspended; resuming it must wait for the transition on the left branch (step 2) to produce the atom (a) needed to trigger a method on the right branch. Thus, in LO's proof theory, the closed-world notion of *failure* characterizing traditional logic programming languages is replaced by the open-world one of *suspension*. Deadlocks may follow from the situation of suspension of all proof processes.

2.3.2 Information Hiding via Variable Instantiation

It has been shown above that the use of the tell marker $\wedge$ provides a form of control on the choice of methods. But, once a method has been selected, another kind of choice is required, in determining an instantiation for the variables of the selected method (this problem did not appear in previous examples since the methods contained no variables). Unification is the traditional solution for this problem; however, we opt here for another mechanism, which suits better the proposed computational model. It can be summarized as follows:

- Instantiation of variables occurring in the unmarked atoms of the head is effected by simple pattern matching with the corresponding atoms in the context.

- All the other variables of the method are instantiated with distinct "new" constants, that is, constants which do not appear in the portion of the proof built so far.

Assume for instance that we have a branch of the proof where the current context is given by

$$\mathcal{C} \, , \, p(a) \, , \, q \, , \, r$$

where $\mathcal{C}$ is the still unspecified part of the context, and we want to apply the following method[2].

$$p(X) \,\mathbin{\rotatebox[origin=c]{180}{\&}}\, q \,\mathbin{\rotatebox[origin=c]{180}{\&}}\, {}^{\wedge}s(X,Y) \circ\!\!-\, t(Y)$$

This is possible since the unmarked atoms of the head, namely $p(X), q$, match a submultiset of the

already known part of the context, namely $p(a), q$. This matching instantiates the variable X to a. The (only) other variable, Y, is instantiated with some arbitrary new constant, say c. Now, the method is fully instantiated and can be triggered by assuming that the atom $s(a, c)$ is in $\mathcal{C}$ (since this atom is prefixed with the tell marker). Thus $\mathcal{C} = s(a, c), \mathcal{C}'$, and a new node can be added to the proof:

$$[\circ\!\!-] \, \frac{\vdash \mathcal{C}', r, t(c)}{\vdash \mathcal{C}', s(a,c), p(a), q, r}$$

This mechanism for variable instantiation provides a clean way to generate new unique identifiers. Such identifiers can then be used as mail addresses for messages to be sent in the specific mode. The fact that each mail address thus created is bound to be different from any other previously or subsequently created ensures the safeness and privacy of specific communication; information items labeled with a given mail address will be hidden from those potential receivers unacquainted with it[3].

2.4   Phase Semantics

It has been shown in [3] that LO's sequent system is sound and complete wrt Linear Logic. More precisely,

Theorem 2 *A sequent $\mathcal{P} \vdash \mathcal{C}$ is derivable in LO if and only if the sequent $\vdash (!\bar{\mathcal{P}})^{\perp}, \mathcal{C}$ is derivable in Linear Logic, where $\bar{\mathcal{P}}$ is the conjunction (&) of the methods of $\mathcal{P}$ (universally quantified) and ! is the Linear modality "of-course".*

Notice the use of the modality ! to prefix the program $\mathcal{P}$ in its Linear Logic version; this explicitly marks the elements of the program (the methods) as unrestricted resources, which can be used as

---

[2]We follow the convention of starting variable identifiers with an uppercase letter.

[3]Identifiers of this kind are related to the *eigenvariables* used in proof theory to introduce fresh constants in the proof; eigenvariables have been recently proposed in [21] as a way of adding information hiding to logic programming. The difference is that eigenvariables have just "forward" and, therefore, local scope on the branch of the proof where they are introduced; by contrast our newly created identifiers are propagated back to the root of the proof tree, so they have global scope.

many times as needed, whereas the elements of the context $\mathcal{C}$ (the goals) are instead bounded resources which can be used just once.

Theorem 2 above shows in proof-theoretic terms that LO is a fragment of Linear Logic. But there is also a model-theoretic characterization of this fact, based on the "Phase Semantics" proposed in [11] as an interpretation of Linear Logic; such a characterization applies to the computational model presented here in a particularly perspicuous manner.

Take a phase model $\mathcal{M}$ to be a given set of "phases"; the denotation of a formula F in $\mathcal{M}$, written $\lceil F \rceil_{\mathcal{M}}$, is a "fact" of $\mathcal{M}$, i.e. a subset of the set of phases verifying certain properties[4]. Intuitively, the phases can be viewed as *actions*, and the denotation of F is the set of actions which must alternatively be performed so as to make F true. This provides a constructive, dynamic notion of truth, which can be contrasted with the non-constructive, static truth of Boolean semantics.

Denotations of formulae in phase models satisfy two nice properties, shared with Boolean semantics:

- Compositionality:
  The denotation of a complex (non-atomic) formula depends solely on the denotations of its components; thus, e.g.

$$\lceil F \,\&\, G \rceil = \lceil F \rceil \cap \lceil G \rceil$$
$$\lceil F \,⅋\, G \rceil = (\lceil F \rceil^{\perp} \circ \lceil G \rceil^{\perp})^{\perp}$$

  where $\circ$ and $^{\perp}$ are operators of the phase model[5].

- Soundness and completeness of the proof system:
  A formula is provable if and only if it holds in all models; i.e.

$$\vdash F \text{ if and only if for all } \mathcal{M}, \ \mathcal{M} \models F$$

  $\vdash$ is the provability relation of Linear Logic and $\mathcal{M} \models F$ means that the empty phase belongs to the denotation of F in $\mathcal{M}$.

---

[4]See [11] for the exact definitions.
[5]See [11] for the exact definitions.

However, the Phase Semantics has another pleasant feature which does not hold in the Boolean case: there is a "canonical" phase model[6] $\mathcal{M}_o$ in which the following property holds.

$$\vdash F \text{ if and only if } \mathcal{M}_o \models F$$

Such a canonical model can be directly connected to the computational model proposed here, since computing a query Q can be viewed as building its denotation $\lceil Q \rceil_{\mathcal{M}_o}$ in the canonical model, by enumerating the elements (phases) of the set $\lceil Q \rceil_{\mathcal{M}_o}$. More precisely, in the canonical model $\mathcal{M}_o$, the phases are the multisets Γ of formulae of Linear Logic, and the denotation of a formula F is given by

$$\lceil F \rceil_{\mathcal{M}_o} \overset{\text{def}}{=} \{\Gamma \ / \ \vdash \Gamma, F\}$$

Now, notice that given an LO query $\langle \mathcal{P}; G \rangle$, the computational model proposed in the previous section precisely attempts to enumerate the elements of $\lceil (!\mathcal{P}) \multimap G \rceil_{\mathcal{M}_o}$. Indeed, for any answer context $\mathcal{C}$ to the query, the following three equivalent properties hold:

(i) $\mathcal{P} \vdash \mathcal{C}, G$ is derivable in LO (by Definition 1 of an answer context).

(ii) $\vdash (!\bar{\mathcal{P}})^{\perp}, \mathcal{C}, G$ is derivable in Linear Logic (from *(i)*, by application of Theorem 2).

(iii) $\vdash \mathcal{C}, (!\bar{\mathcal{P}}) \multimap G$ and hence $\mathcal{C} \in \lceil (!\bar{\mathcal{P}}) \multimap G \rceil_{\mathcal{M}_o}$ (from *(ii)* by definition of the Linear implication $\multimap$ and of the canonical denotation).

As a matter of fact, the proof search procedure described in the previous section can only generate atomic phases (i.e. containing only atoms). If the control strategy induced by the use of the tell marker $^\wedge$ were ignored, i.e. if all the possible markings and all the possible variable instantiations were allowed for all the program methods, then all the atomic phases of $\lceil (!\bar{\mathcal{P}}) \multimap G \rceil_{\mathcal{M}_o}$ would be generated by exploring all the alternatives at each non-deterministic choice in the procedure (with a backtrack mechanism, for instance). This complements

---

[6]See [11] for the exact definitions.

the soundness result given by $(i) - (iii)$ above with a completeness result of our operational search procedure with respect to the Phase Semantics. From a practical point of view, completeness and computational tractability are however incompatible: by imposing one specific marking upon the methods, the programmer enforces the order in which the atomic phases of $\lceil (!\bar{\mathcal{P}}) \multimap G \rceil_{\mathcal{M}_o}$ are enumerated, but, at the same time, enables possible situations of deadlock which preclude some atomic phases ever to be constructed.

3 Applications

We illustrate the expressiveness of the computational model described above by two simple applications. The first one (Section 3.1) gives an example of specific communication, and the second one (Section 3.2) an example of generic communication. From now on we replace the logical symbols $\otimes$, $\&$, $\top$ and $\circ\!\!-$ with, respectively, keyboard typable symbols @, &, #t and <>-, which are used in the actual implementation of LO.

3.1 Specific Communication: Computer Graphics

We describe here a simple graphical application for manipulating geometrical drawings on a 2-Dimensional display. This example is a modification of the one given in [4], where it was used to illustrate LO's approach to knowledge sharing in terms of intraobject communication, while streams were used for interobject communication; here, we replace streams with the use of the forum as a communication medium, and we stress aspects of interobject communication. The evolution of the system of agents is modeled by the construction of a proof tree as in Section 2.2.2.

There are three kinds of communicating agents: the user (of the drawings), the drawings and the display device. Hence, the query which brings into life such agents is given by the goal

```
user & drawings & display.
```

together with a program containing methods executable by these three agents. The unspecified context which is incrementally specified by searching a target proof for the query acts as the forum for communication between agents. Communication here is specific, in that it will involve one agent specifically addressing other agents by posting to their mail addresses.

We focus here on the behavior of the *drawing* agents. At the moment of its creation, a drawing is represented as a context containing the following components:

```
drawing , noshape , id(S) , center(O)
```

S is an identifier used as a mail address for the drawing for the purpose of sending messages to it. O is a point of the screen, encoded in the form of a pair of coordinates, specifying the center of the drawing. Initially, we only need one single prototype drawing, with mail address proto; such a prototype, located at the center of the screen, is initialized by expanding the drawings agent in the query, and can be later cloned to create new drawings. Expansion of the drawings top-level agent is obtained via the following method:

```
drawings <>- drawing @ noshape @
             id(proto) @ center(m(0,0)).
```

Cloning is triggered upon reception of a message dup/2 (with 2 arguments) told to the forum by, say, the user agent: the first argument and the second argument of this message are, respectively, the mail address of the drawing we clone from and the mail address of the newly cloned drawing. Immediately after cloning, the two drawings differ only by their mail addresses; however, from now on, they follow completely independent evolutions. This is achieved by the following cloning method for drawings, which exploits crucially the connective &, like all methods dealing with creations of new agents:

```
drawing @ id(S) @ dup(S,S1) @ ^ack(S) <>-
        drawing @ (id(S) & id(S1)).
```

The sender of the dup/2 message can ensure uniqueness of the mail address of the new drawing by using the mechanism for generating new identifiers described in Section 2.3.2. Notice also how the atom `ack(S)` is sent back to the forum as a message acknowledging that the requested creation has taken place. This is because, in this application, the order in which messages are processed is important: for instance, cloning or printing an object before or after moving it leads to two different results. Acknowledgement messages take a very simple form in this application, as we assume that there is only one single sender that needs to be acknowledged (the user); in a situation where multiple senders need to be acknowledged, such messages should contain not just the address of the acknowledging agent, but also the "return" address of the original sender, to ensure that they are properly delivered.

Once created by cloning, each drawing agent can be modified. For example, to move a drawing (by a specified amount D) we have the following method.

```
drawing @ id(S) @ center(O) @
    move(S,D) @ ^ack(S) <>-
        drawing @ id(S) @ center(O+D).
```

The prototype drawing `proto` has no specific shape, and, therefore, neither have its clones at the time of their creation. Giving shape to such formless entities involves using a method like the following one, which constrains a drawing to be a square with sides of length `A`.

```
drawing @ noshape @ id(S) @
    make_square(S,A) @ ^ack(S) <>-
        drawing @ square @
        id(S) @ side(A).
```

Printing a square is done via the following method.

```
square @ side(A) @ center(O) @ id(S) @
    print(S) @ ^ack(S) @
    ^line(M1,M2) @ ^line(M2,M3) @
    ^line(M3,M4) @ ^line(M4,M1) <>-
        square @ side(A) @
        center(O) @ id(S).
```

The points `M1,M2,M3,M4` are the four vertices of the square. They must be computed from the center O and side `A` of the square (for clarity, this computation is omitted here). The four messages `line/2` sent upon triggering of this method correspond to graphical commands to print the four edges of the square and are meant for the `display` agent. Notice that there is no need for the messages to this agent to be ordered (we assume here for simplicity sake that the `display` agent consumes only `line/2` messages, and the order in which lines are printed is irrelevant). Therefore, a drawing object does not need to wait for an acknowledgement to such messages to pursue its activity.

The flow of information is represented in Fig. 1. Agents are represented in square boxes and messages in round boxes (only their topmost functor is displayed). An arrow from an agent to a message (resp. from a message to an agent) means that the agent produces (resp. consumes) the message.

The example of this section illustrates the synchronization mechanism based on a send/acknowledge protocol between agents sharing a common communication medium, the forum. This communication mechanism is more flexible than the usual stream-based one, in that it saves the programmer from the burden involved in stream manipulations (stream merging, explicit interobject connections, etc.).

3.2 Generic Communication: Concurrent Chart Parsing

The example we provide here is a particularly interesting case of distributed problem solving which illustrates well the use of local resource consumption in generic communication. The problem we address specifically is concurrent parsing, a topic which has attracted the interest of several researchers in the object-oriented programming community [23, 30]; on the other hand the problem-solving technique we employ here can be fruitfully generalized to more complex examples, like distributed expert systems operating on highly complex domains, where different experts are required to work independently on shared data, feeding back

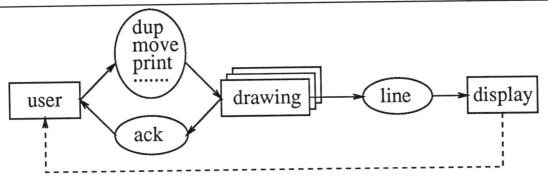

Figure 1: The flow of information

different outputs which all need to be taken in consideration for the final solution of a given problem.

The program we describe amounts to a concurrent implementation of the Earley's algorithm for context-free parsing [9] and draws much in the spirit of the active chart parsing methodology [16], where incomplete phrasal subtrees are viewed as agents consuming already completed elements to produce other (complete or incomplete) subtrees. However, in our case even the rules of the grammar and the entries of the lexicon act as independent units directly partaking in the computation. Moreover, as distinct from the usual sequential formulations of chart parsing, here no superimposed scheduler is in charge of the task of feeding incomplete subtrees with complete ones; instead, incomplete elements behave as truly active decentralized computational units which get their information from the forum, where finished subtrees are told as soon as they have been found. But we must preserve the fact that, once a subtree is completed, this information must be broadcast to *all* the active agents which can make use of it; indeed, in the case of ambiguous grammars, the number of such agents may be greater than one, thus leading to different parses for the same string. Local consumption neatly deals with this problem.

3.2.1 The Program

We view parsing as being performed by four top-level agents, a string scanner, a grammar, a dictionary and a creator of new subtrees. This is expressed by the following method, which contains in its head a single literal parse(I,S), where I is the input string and S is the symbol of the grammar defining the set of strings with respect to which we want to test membership of I.

```
parse(Input,Symbol) <>-
    grammar & dictionary &
    scanner(Input,Symbol) & create_tree.
```

The *scanner* agent, defined in the methods in Fig. 2, performs the two following actions:

- It keeps popping words from the input and producing pos(N) and word(W,N) messages where

  - a pos(N) message supplies the information that position N has been reached in the input;
  - a word(W,N) message supplies the information that there is a word W between positions N and N+1 in the input.

Positions are encoded as integers in the "successor" notation.

- Upon reaching the end of the input string, it sends a seek(0,S) message, where S is the targeted grammar symbol, and then reduces itself into an agent whose sole task is that of retrieving answers. This is simply done by waiting for trees covering the whole input string with

```
scanner(I,S) <>-
        scan(I,0) @ target(S).

scan([W|I],N) @ ^pos(N) @ ^word(W,N) <>-
        scan(I,s(N)).

scan([],N) @ target(S) @ ^seek(0,S) <>-
        wait(N,S).

wait(N,S) @ ctree(0,N,S,T) @ ^answer(T) <>-
        wait(N,S).
```

Figure 2: Methods for scanning

```
grammar <>-
    s ==> [np,vp] &
    np ==> [det,n] &
    np ==> [pn] &
    np ==> [np,pp] &
    vp ==> [tv,np] &
    vp ==> [vp,pp] &
    pp ==> [prep,np].
```

```
dictionary <>-
        entry(a,det) &
        entry(robot,n) &
        entry(telescope,n) &
        entry(terry,pn) &
        entry(saw,tv) &
        entry(with,prep).
```

Figure 3: A grammar and a dictionary

```
entry(W,S) @ word(W,N) @ ^ctree(N,s(N),S,S-W) <>-
        entry(W,S).

(S ==> Ss) @ seek(N,S) @ pos(N) @ ^new(N,N,S,Ss,S) <>-
        (S ==> Ss).
```

Figure 4: Methods for lexical entries and rules

```
create_tree @ new(M,N,S,[],T) @ ^ctree(M,N,S,T) <>-
        create_tree @ ctree(M,N,S,T).

create_tree @ new(M,N,S,[S1|Ss],T) @ ^seek(N,S1) <>-
        create_tree & itree(M,N,S,S1,Ss,T).

itree(M,N,S,S1,Ss,T) @ ctree(N,P,S1,T1) @ ^new(M,P,S,Ss,T-T1) <>-
        itree(M,N,S,S1,Ss,T).
```

Figure 5: Creation and completion of trees

224

symbol S to appear in the forum; the structure T with which any of such trees has been represented is then explicitly added as an answer.

The *grammar* and the *dictionary* agent expand, respectively, into a set of grammatical rules and of lexical entries, each originating a different agent; a sample dictionary and grammar[7] are given in Fig. 3. Notice that the grammar is an ambiguous one. The behavior of lexical entries and rule agents is defined in terms of the methods in Fig. 4. Lexical entry agents accept as messages words with which they match and send back corresponding *complete* preterminal trees, labeling the given word with a preterminal symbol. On the other hand, rule agents consume seek(N,S) messages *together* with pos(N) messages, if the sought grammar symbol S corresponds to their own left-hand side symbol; in this case, they issue back a message for the creation of a new agent encoding an *incomplete* (empty) tree. Crucial is here the fact that the consumption by rule agents of seek/2 messages must be concomitant with the consumption of matching (in the sense of being characterized by the same integer argument) pos/1 messages; indeed, this correctly ensures that a rule agent can produce no more than one empty incomplete tree for any position of the input string, given that, for any N, it will be able to consume no more than one pos(N) message. In this way, we prevent the possibility of infinite loops of the left-recursive kind deriving from rules like the fourth and the sixth one in the grammar of Fig. 3; furthermore, we block the possibility of redundant analyses. This will be illustrated in describing a sample run of the parser further on in this section.

Creating and completing new trees is accounted for in terms of the methods in Fig. 5. The top-level create_tree agent consumes messages of the form new(M,N,S,Ss,T) where M and N are, respectively, the two string positions spanned by the new tree to be created, S is the root of the tree, Ss is a list of symbols corresponding to the roots of the complete subtrees which are still needed in order to make this

---

[7]The symbol ==> appearing in the grammar rules is not a primitive of *LO* but simply a convenient infix notation for a binary term constructor.

tree complete, and T is the representation associated with the tree itself. It then deterministically chooses between the following two actions:

- in case the list Ss is empty, it sends a message ctree(M,N,S,T) to signal that a complete tree with root S and representation T has been found between positions M and N;

- in case the list Ss is of the form [S1|Ss1], it sends a message of the form seek(N,S1) and then creates an incomplete tree agent of the form itree(M,N,S,S1,Ss1,T).

As for incomplete tree agents of the form itree(M,N,S,S1,Ss,T), they consume complete trees of the form ctree(N,P,S1,T1) to produce messages of the form new(M,P,S,Ss,T-T1). Thus, requests for the creation of new trees can come either from rule agents as answers to seek/2 messages, or from incomplete tree agents; in the former case such requests can be thought of as leading to the formulation of further hypotheses which need to be verified in order to satisfy a certain initial hypothesis (this is known as step of *prediction* in the usual formulations of the Earley algorithm), while in the second case they follow from having progressed "one step" in the verification of a certain hypothesis (this is known as a step of *completion*). Fig. 6 shows the flow of information among the agents. The convention are the same as in the previous section (Fig. 1), except that we also make use of a thicker arrow to explicitly connect the create_tree agent with the agents it creates.

3.2.2 A Sample Run

Let us now briefly consider a sample run of the parser. Assuming the grammar and the lexicon in Fig. 3, consider the goal

```
?- parse(
    [terry,saw,a,robot,with,a,telescope],
    s)
```

After running the parser, the following two answers, corresponding to the two parses of the input sentence, will be found in the global context.

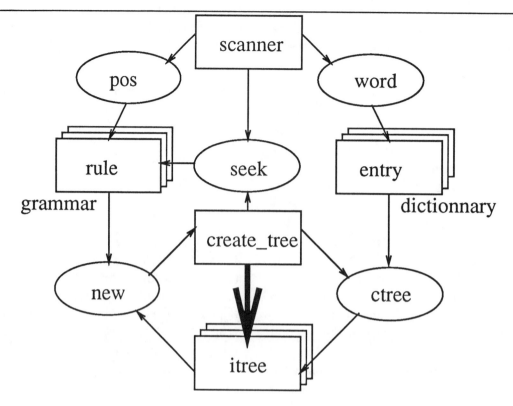

Figure 6: The flow of information

```
answer(
    s-(np-(pn-terry))
    -(vp-(tv-saw)
        -(np-(np-(det-a)-(n-robot))
            -(pp-(prep-with)
                -(np-(det-a)
                    -(n-telescope)))))).

answer(
    s-(np-(pn-terry))
    -(vp-(vp-(tv-saw)
            -(np-(det-a)-(n-robot)))
        -(pp-(prep-with)
            -(np-(det-a)
                -(n-telescope)))))).
```

These two answers originate from the fact that the same complete trees can be consumed by several agents encoding different incomplete trees; specifically, the agents encoded as

```
itree(1,2,vp,np,[],vp-(tv-saw))
```

```
itree(2,2,np,np,[pp],np)
```

will both consume the complete tree

```
ctree(2,4,np,(np-(det-a)-(n-robot)))
```

Furthermore, the agents encoded as

```
itree(1,4,vp,pp,[],
    (vp-(vp-(tv-saw)
        -(np-(det-a)-(n-robot))))))
```

```
itree(2,4,np,pp,[],
    (np-(np-(det-a)-(n-robot))))
```

will both consume the complete tree

```
ctree(4,7,pp,
    (pp-(prep-with)
        -(np-(det-a)-(n-telescope))))
```

As a consequence, we end up with two different analyses for the substring *saw a robot with a telescope*. On the other hand, notice that the rules whose left-hand side symbol is np will receive in the course of parsing more than one seek(2,np) message to create empty trees with root np and starting position 2; however, any of such rules will never create more than one of such trees, as seek/2 messages must be consumed together with matching pos/1 messages, and any rule will be able to consume at most one pos(2) message. Thus, both redundant analyses and infinite loops deriving from left-recursion are in this way avoided. This approach to enforcing redundancy checking is quite simple and elegant and comes natural in a decentralized, object-oriented style of programming; it can be contrasted with the more usual way of enforcing it, which is obtained by explicitly comparing newly created trees with previously existing ones.

3.2.3 Summary

We can summarize the salient points of this implementation of a chart parser as follows:

- with respect to sequential implementations, we do not need to take care of specifying a scheduler which handles the feeding of incomplete trees with complete ones;

- with respect to concurrent, stream-based implementations (see for instance [28]) we do not need to bother about the merging of streams of messages coming from different producers;

- with respect to what would be possible in standard blackboard-based communication, we exploit the specific feature of local consumption characterizing forum-based communication, which allows different agents to feed themselves on the same input to produce different outputs.

This produces a concise, "conceptual" style of programming, with little burden on requirements which do not come from the problem itself, but are instead imposed by particular implementation choices. Since the Earley algorithm is an instance

of the technique of *dynamic programming*, this approach can be generalized to other examples of dynamic programming, as shown in [5].

4   Related Work

We have seen how forum-based communication, which lies at the basis of the computational model for *LO* presented here, provides a refinement of blackboard-based communication [10] in terms of local consumption. Proposals for a more local form of blackboard-based communication were also presented in [19] in a non-logical setting, sharing our same intent of making use of blackboards in the context of object-oriented programming. [7] provides instead a logical version of blackboard-based communication in its standard global interpretation.

LO can also be seen as an instance of Concurrent Constraint Programming [25], the programming paradigm towards which the concurrent branch of logic programming languages is naturally evolving. (In a nutshell, we can think of Concurrent Constraint Programming as what becomes of logic programming once it is stripped of its obsolete commitments to Classical Logic, minimal Herbrand models, closed-world assumption etc., and computation is explicitly viewed as the interaction of logical agents refining an initial amount of information by incrementally adding new chunks of information, i.e. *constraints*.) Indeed, *LO* can be considered as a Concurrent Constraint language with agents whose point of view of the outside world changes over time: once an agent has seen a piece of the outside landscape (the forum) then it will not see it anymore, unless it copies it explicitly into its own "local" landscape. This can be contrasted with the Concurrent Constraint Logic Programming languages described in [24, 15], where agents never change their point of view with respect to the outside world (the store of constraints). These two ways of implementing concurrent agents clearly complement each other, as they cover different aspects of concurrent problem solving. Merging of the two approaches in a Linear Logic setting could be possible by permitting permanent elements to be added to the forum; such elements would be distinguished from the non-permanent ones in the fact of being marked by Linear Logic modalities which give them explicitly the status of unrestricted resources.

Linear Logic has been exploited to account for concurrency also in [1, 17]; however, the background there is functional programming, instead of logic programming. [14] exploits the intuitionistic (sequential) version of Linear Logic to refine the control mechanisms of sequential logic programs. [20] describes a general framework for "rewriting logics", suitable for accounting for change in a concurrent programming context. [22] approaches the problem of locality of interaction among concurrent subsystems from the point of view of process algebras.

5 Open Problems

Our main effort is currently in the direction of finding an efficient execution model for the language. Indeed, from a practical point of view, *LO* offers challenging but reasonably solvable implementation issues. We currently have a toy interpreter for the language, written in Prolog (with coroutining facilities to simulate concurrency). Selection and access to the methods is one of the main bottleneck of the interpreter; implementations technique used in production systems are currently being explored to overcome this problem [8]. We also think of a compilation process, based on a type-inference mechanism, which would avoid the accumulation of useless messages in object states (a garbage collector could complete the job at runtime). The ultimate compiler should be able to detect cases of specific communication (one-to-one) and implement it as such, that is, without propagating a specifically sent message to the whole forum in such a case, but sending it directly to the intended receiver. Intermediate cases between specific and generic communication, for instance when an object addresses a certain group of objects, could also be given a special treatment.

Acknowledgement

We are grateful to Gerard Comyn and Alexander Herold for helpful comments on this paper. We also thank Nabiel Elshiewy for helpful discussions.

References

[1] S. Abramsky. Computational interpretations of linear logic. Technical report, DOC, Imperial College, London, U.K., 1990.

[2] G. Agha and C. Hewitt. Actors: a conceptual foundation for concurrent object-oriented programming. In B. Shriver and P. Wegner, editors, *Research Directions in Object-Oriented Programming*. MIT Press, 1987.

[3] J.M. Andreoli. Proposition pour une synthèse des paradigmes de la programmation logique et de la programmation par objets, 1990. Thèse d'Informatique de l'Université de Paris VI (Paris, France).

[4] J.M. Andreoli and R. Pareschi. LO and behold! concurrent structured processes. In *Proc. of OOPSLA/ECOOP'90*, Ottawa, Canada, 1990.

[5] J.M. Andreoli and R. Pareschi. Dynamic programming as multi-agent programming, 1991. *ECOOP'91* workshop on Object-based concurrent computing.

[6] J.M. Andreoli and R. Pareschi. Linear objects: Logical processes with built-in inheritance. *New Generation Computing*, To appear, 1991. (Special issue, Selected papers from ICLP'90).

[7] A. Brogi and P. Ciancarini. The concurrent language shared prolog. *ACM Transactions on Programming Languages and Systems*, To appear, 1991.

[8] M. Clemente. Forthcoming Ms Thesis, TU München.

[9] J. Earley. An efficient context-free parsing algorithm. *Communications of the ACM*, 13(2), 1970.

[10] D. Gelernter. Generative communication in linda. *ACM Transactions on Programming Languages and Systems*, 7, 1985.

[11] J.Y. Girard. Linear logic. *Theoretical Computer Science*, 50, 1987.

[12] S. Gregory. *Parallel Logic Programming in Parlog*. Addison-Wesley, 1987.

[13] D. Harel and A. Pnueli. On the development of reactive systems. In K.R. Apt, editor, *Logic and Models of Concurrent Systems*. Springer Verlag, 1985.

[14] J.S Hodas and D. Miller. Logic programming in a fragment of intuitionistic linear logic. In *Proc. of LICS'91*, 1991. To appear.

[15] K. Kahn and V.A. Saraswat. Actors as a special case of concurrent constraint logic programming. In *Proc. of OOPSLA/ECOOP'90*, Ottawa, Canada, 1990.

[16] M. Kay. Algorithm schemata and data structure in syntactic processing. Technical report, Xerox Parc, Palo Alto, U.S.A., 1980.

[17] Y. Lafont. Interaction nets. In *Proc. of 17th ACM Symposium on Principles of Programming Languages*, San Francisco, U.S.A., 1990.

[18] H. Lieberman. Concurrent object oriented programming in ACT1. In A. Yonezawa and M. Tokoro, editors, *Object Oriented Concurrent Programming*. MIT Press, 1987.

[19] A. Matsuoka and S. Kawai. Using tuple space communication in distributed object oriented languages. In *Proc. of OOPSLA'88*, San Diego, U.S.A., 1988.

[20] J. Meseguer. A logical theory of concurrent objects. In *Proc. of OOPSLA/ECOOP'90*, 1990.

[21] D. Miller. Lexical scoping as universal quantification. In *Proc. of the 6th International Conference on Logic Programming*, Lisboa, Portugal, 1989.

[22] L. Monteiro and F.C.N. Pereira. A sheaf-theoretic model of concurrency. Technical report, CSLI, Menlo Park, U.S.A., 1986.

[23] C. Numaoka and M. Tokoro. A decentralized parsing method using communicating multiple concurrent objects. In *Proc. of 2nd International Conference of Technology of Object Oriented Languages and Systems*, Paris, France, 1990.

[24] V.A. Saraswat. *Concurrent Constraint Programming Languages*. PhD thesis, Carnegie-Mellon University, Pittsburg, U.S.A., 1989.

[25] V.A. Saraswat, M. Rinard, and P. Panangaden. Semantic foundations of concurrent constraint programming. Technical report, Xerox Parc, Palo Alto, U.S.A., 1990.

[26] E. Shapiro. A subset of concurrent prolog and its interpreter. Technical report, Institute for New Generation Computer Technology, Tokyo, Japan, 1983.

[27] E. Shapiro. The family of concurrent logic programming languages. Technical report, The Weizmann Institute of Science, Rehovot, Israel, 1989.

[28] R. Trehan and P.F. Wilk. A parallel chart-parser for the commited choice logic languages. In *Proc. of the 5th International Conference on Logic Programming*, Seattle, U.S.A., 1988.

[29] K. Ueda. *Guarded Horn Clauses*. PhD thesis, Dept of Information Engineering, University of Tokyo, Japan, 1986.

[30] A. Yonezawa and I. Ohsawa. Object-oriented parallel parsing for context-free gramars. In *Proc. of COLING'88*, Budapest, Hungary, 1988.

The Kala[1] Basket
A Semantic Primitive Unifying Object Transactions, Access Control, Versions, and Configurations

SERGIU S. SIMMEL
Samsung Software America, Inc.[2]

IVAN GODARD
Penobscot Research Center, Inc.[3]

ABSTRACT

Kala is an untyped persistent store for practical object-based systems, such as OODBMS, OMS, and object-oriented languages with persistence. **Baskets** are dynamic groupings of immutable data elements managed by Kala. Baskets synthesize transaction, configuration management, and access control semantics, and thus offer a platform for implementing arbitrary such models. In this article we introduce Kala baskets, their design motivations and goals. We then explain Kala's basket mechanism in some detail. Finally, we offer a few examples of how baskets are used to implement features of arbitrary transaction, configuration, and access models.

1. INTRODUCTION

Kala [6] [7] is a low-level untyped storage management system. Kala is positioned below the line marking the decomposition of objects into untyped data. It implements the semantics of robust, distributed, secure, changing, and shareable persistent data. Layers built upon the Kala platform can implement the semantics of objects with the same properties.

Kala employs **baskets**, a single unifying mechanism that supports higher-level notions such as transactions, configurations, versions, access groups, etc. Baskets are non-partitioning groupings of immutable data elements. Their semantics allows wide versatility of above-Kala concepts while preserving economy of means at Kala's level. In particular, Kala baskets support the implementation of most useful transaction, access, grouping, and change models. They support arbitrary models in these domains, rather than imposing a specific model.

Kala manages the storage of and access to data of arbitrary size. It effects the transfer of data between main (volatile) and secondary (persistent) memory, and manages the store on a variety of hardware. All access to a stored data elements is done via baskets.

Kala incorporates functionality not ordinarily associated with this low-level architectural component, without the disadvantages of a monolithic architecture or sluggish performance. Kala satisfies all of TI's Open OODB's Transactional Store Module's requirements [10]. Kala implements many of the Object Services within the O.M.G. Reference Model [9].

2. MOTIVATION

Object persistence is becoming a desideratum for most practical object-based and object-oriented systems. Craig Thompson et.al. makes the case for modular object systems [10] by identifying orthogonal design dimensions and associating them with

---

[1] Kala is a Trademark of Penobscot Research Center, Inc.
[2] Author presently with Oberon Software, Inc., One Memorial Drive, Cambridge, Massachusetts 02142, 617-494-0990, simmel@oberon.com
[3] Author presently with Star Semiconductor, Inc., 25 Independence Drive, Warren, New Jersey, 07059, 908-647-9400.

modules. Support for persistence has been concentrated in one module of object systems' architecture, usually termed **persistent store** or **storage system**.

Modularity is one force driving the design process. Another is the attempt to discover *commonality* among various functions once thought of as belonging to distinct dimensions. After identifying the common features, the once multiple modules collapse (at least in part) into a common one. To achieve light-weight, compact, and efficient designs, one must maintain a delicate balance between modularity and commonality.

Kala achieves this balance by providing the basket mechanism as a primitive facility from which other facilities supporting the conventional notions of Transaction, Configuration, Version, and Access Control may be built. Kala baskets do not impose specific models of these facilities, but rather allow for a wide range of variation. This represents an application of the general design principle of *composability*, by which well chosen primitives with minimal interaction may be composed to provide more specialized facilities.

Traditional database theory typically defines a **Transaction** as a single execution of a program section [12]. Transactions are viewed as sequences of actions taken during execution[4]. Research and commercial object oriented systems, including object-oriented DBMSs, maintain this definition, regardless of the supported transaction models. As transactions have become central to the database field, the transaction typology has correspondingly grown to accommodate very diverse application requirements. For example, Chung C. Wang lists 11 classification dimensions (parameters) in his survey of transaction models [13].

Access control has traditionally been provided for by file systems and DBMSs, as motivated by protection and security needs. The traditional comprehensive solution to the access specification and control problem has employed access control lists (ACLs), such as in the Aegis operating system. A simpler but widespread commercial solution is Unix, which has a user - group - world hierarchy. These and other

schemes have been plagued by scaleability and inflexibility problems.

Configurations represent views over a database of *versioned objects*. Configuration supporting mechanisms have both exploratory use (for example, in studying aggregation mechanisms in object bases, such as worlds [14]) and practical use (for example, in controlling change in project software bases [4]). They have been studied and implemented mostly in isolated, application domain specific areas, such as software engineering and document management environments.

Kala's design extracts the following common notions from the above requirement domains, and embodies them in the basket mechanism:

- **Sets of Instances**. All these concepts are set oriented notions. A transaction can be viewed as a set of new class instances created during a single execution of a program section. Controlling access to objects can be viewed as allowing an agent to access a certain set of objects. A configuration is simply a set of object versions which are combined into an instance of one or more composite objects.

- **Set Calculus**. In each of these cases the sets are combined in ways that involve network- and often tree-organized set groups. Transactions are often grouped in tree-like fashion (nested). Transaction operations such as *commit* and *fail* are very common. Access sets are often arranged in tree-like fashion (user, group, etc.), and operations such as *expose* and *hide* are very useful. Configurations are often organized in trees and DAGs to model linear and branching evolution over time. Operations such as *merge* are central.

- **Dynamic Nature**. Each concept models a dynamically changing reality. Transactions, including long ones, continuously change as newly created objects are added during the execution of the program section. Protection and security needs change very often. Configurations are subject to substantial change until frozen for archiving purposes.

- **Visibility Control**. Each concept is a solution to a different facet of the visibility problem. Transactions control visibility of change. Access control deals with visibility of objects. Configura-

---

[4] The term itself suggests this view: 'trans-action' means "across actions".

tions control visibility of the state of composite objects. Versions control visibility of object history.

In addition, in each of the three domains:

- **Transience and Persistence**. All notions are germane to both transient and persistent objects. Also, transactions, access control groups, and configurations themselves can usefully be either transient or persistent.
- **Datum Orientation**. Although each notion is pertinent to object-based systems, they are certainly not specific or bound to systems designed or implemented within this paradigm. For instance, these notions do also relate to lower level raw data.

These observations have encouraged us to seek a unique mechanism to model and implement the common features in the context of a low-level storage system. Their distillation led to the design of Kala's basket mechanism.

3. DESIGN GOALS

The following have guided us throughout the design and implementation process:

- **Commonality**. Capture as many of the common traits of all higher-level concepts as can be identified. We believe that an expressive and more general low-level subsystem enhances the likelihood that the entire object-based system will be lighter and more compact.
- **Simplicity**. Make Kala's interface with the other subsystems as simple (i.e., the lowest number of interface concepts) as possible. Not only does this enhance Kala's usability, but it has a positive effect on its own design and implementation.
- **Feasibility**. The design should be implementable in an industrial-strength fashion. There is widespread agreement that compactness, maintainability, ease of use, and performance are desirable qualities.
- **Primitiveness**. Keep functions that can be practically derived out of this subsystem. Keeping the abstraction level boundaries clean has important beneficial effects on both Kala's and the entire object system's design and implementation.

This requires a crisp, rigorous definition of Kala's level of abstraction. Such a definition makes the decisions about which side of this boundary a certain function belongs consistently possible.

Although the design goals above were primary throughout this work, there are two other requirements which we have always considered central and overriding:

- **Performance**. Build Kala to be a highly performing module, both in space and time.
- **Security**. Build Kala to introduce no more security holes than already exist in the host operating system.

4. BRIEF KALA OVERVIEW

Kala's data model is simple and largely untyped. Kala manages data elements of arbitrary size consisting of bits and embedded references. These data elements are termed *monads*. Monad references are essentially pointers *into* other monads. The salient feature here is that monads are *immutable*. Once created, a monad can never be deleted or modified. It may become inaccessible[5] (if it does Kala will recover its physically allocated resources), but the monad's identity is never discarded.

Monads are universally and uniquely identified by *monad identifiers*, or *mids*. A mid is a Kala-supplied abstract data type (ADT). *Each mid is guaranteed to be unique at all times and all places*. Mids are *never* reused, and thus guaranteed to be universally unique if created unique. Kala insures uniqueness by using a Kala store (cf. §7) creation time based scheme for generating ids, thus reducing the risk of inadvertent creation of duplicate ids to negligible levels.

Monads are persistent. Although we casually talk about *loading* a monad, what we actually mean is that we "create a copy of a monad's value in volatile memory." Informally, the model is that of a persistent store from which we can get copies of values into volatile memory, and within which we can create new values. Since monads are immutable, there

---

[5] A monad can become inaccessible when the last reference to it is dropped, and the Kala server (cf. §7) which manages the monad is made aware of this event.

is no "storing" a monad. We can only *create* a new monad.

Monads are statically grouped into *kin*. Each monad belongs to some kin, and the membership is assigned at the monad's creation. Kin membership is *static*; it can never be changed or revoked. Once created as a member of a certain kin, a monad can never be made a member of any other kin. Kin are *abstract* groupings of monads; there is no representation of a kin held or managed by Kala. A monad's kin membership is determinable using its mid.

Kin are used to group monads which implement semantically-related higher level entities. However, Kala is totally unaware of any such semantic relation; it only preserves the grouping. For example, kin can be used to group together all versions of the same entity. Section 10.1 provides a further details on the uses for the kin mechanism.

There are two ways to access monads. One is through references from other monads. A monad can contain any number of references. Each reference "points" into another monad, that is to a monad plus a numeric offset measured in bits. References in Kala storage have sophisticated but compact representations. In main memory, references are represented as ordinary machine pointers. Once in main memory, accessing a monad through another monad's reference amounts to dereferencing a pointer - no function call required.

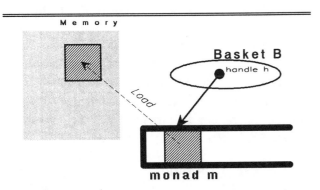

Figure 1: Loading a monad into volatile memory

Alternatively, monads can be accessed through *handles*. A handle is a Kala abstraction representing a path to a monad. Handles exist only in groupings termed *baskets*. A basket is thus a (possibly empty)

set of handles. Handles can only be found in baskets.

Figure 1 illustrates these basic concepts with a simple example showing a monad **m** (in the persistent store on the disk) referenced by a handle **h** in a basket **B**. Loading the monad means creating a copy of its data in volatile memory. The memory copy can now be used by the application in whatever way it desires, including modifying it. The monad, however, cannot be modified: it is immutable.

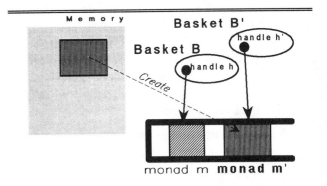

Figure 2: Creating a new monad

When changes to the volatile memory copy need be saved to the persistent store, a new monad **m'** is created. Figure 2 shows the new monad being created with the changed memory data as its value. A new handle **h'** has also been created in basket **B'** to refer to it.

5. KALA BASKETS

The basket is one of Kala's central externalized concepts. It has fairly rich semantics, and it intimately interacts with Kala's other externalized concepts.

5.1. Baskets as a Grouping Device

In contrast with kin, which are static and abstract groupings of monads, baskets are dynamic and concrete groupings. The *dynamic* nature of baskets means that a basket's composition can be changed at any time. Handles can be explicitly deleted from a basket: **void DeleteHandles(handles)** removes a specified set of handles in one or more baskets, and may indeed leave some of the baskets empty. Handles can be explicitly moved from one basket to another: `void MoveHandles(handles, baskets)` moves a specified set of handles from several baskets to other baskets.

In addition, copies of handles can also be made and placed in other baskets: `void CopyHandles (handles, baskets)` makes copies of a specified set of handles, and places them into other baskets.

Baskets are *concrete* in that Kala maintains representations of them. Baskets are identifiable and can be manipulated using Kala's programmatic interface. All operations which change the contents of one or more baskets are atomic and (optionally) persistent.

5.2. Basket Composition

A basket contains zero or more handles. Its composition can be queried: the `ResolveHandles` operation can be used to query a basket for its handles. Baskets may contain any combination of handles with one quintessential constraint, termed *Kala's Central Dogma*: *In any basket at any time there cannot be more than one handle to akin[6] monads.*

This constraint is strictly enforced by Kala. It determines basket semantics, and controls the use of monads, kin, and baskets by other subsystems. The Central Dogma provides Kala's general usefulness, as should become apparent throughout the remainder of this paper.

Handles are inserted in baskets during the process of creating a new monad, or moving or copying a handle from a different basket. One immediate corollary to the Central Dogma is that whenever a new handle must be inserted into a basket and an akin handle already exists in that basket, the existing handle must be immediately and atomically discarded and replaced with the new one. This process is termed *supplanting*.

Figure 3 shows an example of a Kala store containing several monads of various kin. All akin monads are depicted as rectangles with the same fill pat-

tern. For example, monads **m2**, **m4**, **m7**, and **m8** are all of the same kin. The example shows a few common situations. Basket **B3** is empty, while baskets **B1**, **B2**, and **B4** contain handles. Among the handles shown, there are two pointing to the same monad **m1**: one in basket **B1** and the other in **B4**. There are no handles pointing to monads **m4** and **m7**. This example certainly satisfies the Central Dogma.

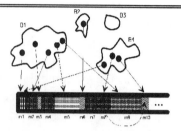

Figure3: Baskets as Groups of Handles to Monads

In addition, the figure shows a reference in monad **m8** pointing into monad **m10**, that is at some offset within **m10**'s bits.

5.3. Basket Identification

At each point during its execution, a Kala application may be using several baskets to access (e.g., load or create) various monads of interest. Each basket is identified using a Kala generated and maintained identifier. Like all Kala's identifiers (e.g., monad identifiers, kin identifiers), *basket identifiers* (or *bids*) are guaranteed to be universally unique. A bid is assigned by Kala to each basket upon creation; `bid NewBasket(void)` creates a new basket, and supplies its identifier to the caller.

The Kala bid is in fact a Kala-supplied ADT. Instance operations are provided, such as the `bool EqualBid (bid,bid)` test for equality.

5.4. Basket Grouping

Monads are accessed by the application software via handles in baskets. At any point there may be several baskets used by the application code to access the data stored in monads. As a set of handles, each basket defines a *scope* for references to the values held in the corresponding monads. Using

---

[6] Two or more monads are said to be *akin* if they belong to the same kin. The term extends to handles as well.

askets to define scope leads to the idea of scope nesting, similar to that in programming languages or transaction models. Nested scopes are naturally represented as ordered lists. Going from inner scopes towards outer scopes corresponds to searching down such a list.

In Kala, an ordered list of baskets is an externalized object termed the **Basket Search List** (or **BSL**). Kala currently maintains one BSL for each Kala application client (see §7). Its contents is totally under the application code's control; **void BasketSearchList (rowBid)** updates the BSL by replacing it with the provided ordered list of baskets, all identified by their bids.

There are five ways to affect the contents of the BSL. One is by redefining it, as shown above. Secondly, Kala places the basket created with **bid NewBasket(void)** into the BSL according to a well defined rule.

The third operation affecting the BSL permits multiple cooperating Kala-client processes to share baskets; **void ProvideBasket(bid, kalaClient)** makes an extant basket available to another Kala client (cf. §7). The affected BSL in this case is that of the target Kala client. The basket to be shared is identified by its bid, which is a unique identifier and is thus exportable beyond a client's boundaries. The target Kala client is identified by whatever the operating environment provides to securely identify other clients.

As expected, **void DeleteBasket(bid)** removes a basket from the BSL of the executing application. If no other application is using this basket and the basket is not persistent, Kala will recover its resources. Finally, accessing a persistent basket or a basket snapshot (cf. §6) also inserts it into the BSL, for convenience.

5.5. Addressing Handles

A handle is fully specified by supplying the bid of a basket containing it and the mid of the monad referred to by the handle. This method is precise, but not very convenient. Kala provides the ability to incompletely specify a handle using a set of rules to resolve the specification to zero, one, or many handles. The specification is termed a **handle address**, and the process **resolving an address**.

Kala provides several methods to express a handle address, called **addressing modes**. In all modes, each handle address has two components: identity and scope. The **identity** component of a handle address specifies _what_ monad(s) we are looking for:

- a specific monad, of a known mid,
- monad(s) in a specific kin, of a known kid,
- monad(s) in any kin,
- every monad with a handle in a specific basket, or
- monad in a new kin, of which the first monad is to be created.

The **scope** component of a handle address specifies _where_ Kala should look for the monad(s):

- a specific basket, of a known bid, or
- any of the baskets in the BSL, searched in order.

In addition, handle addresses can be either **single-valued** (their resolution contains zero or one handle) or **multi-valued** (their resolution contains zero or more handles).

For example, the simplest addressing mode is **{mid,bid}**. It specifies a specific monad in a specific basket. If a handle to monad **mid** exists in basket **bid**, then the address resolves to it. Otherwise, it resolves to no handle.

{kid,firstFound} specifies a monad of a given kin to be searched for in the BSL. If a handle to a monad in kin **kid** is found by orderly searching through the baskets currently in the BSL, the address resolves to that handle. Otherwise, it resolves to no handle.

{everyKid,bid} is a multi-valued address specifying all monads with handles in a given basket. Note that the resolution will never contain akin monads, due to Kala's Central Dogma. The resolution however may be an empty set. If basket **bid** is not an accessed basket for the issuing client, an exception is raised.

Finally, **{kid,allFound}** is also a multi-valued address specifying all monads in a given kin which have handles in any of the baskets currently in the BSL. The address resolves to the unordered set of these handles. If no handle is found, the resolution is empty.

6. PERSISTENCE

So far, baskets have been introduced with no mention of their lifetime. A basket can be either transient or persistent. When newly created, a basket is *transient*; it will disappear as soon as the creating Kala client disappears. Since Kala identifiers are universally unique, a basket's identifier will never be reused.

There are two persistence regimes for baskets: basket snapshots and recoverable baskets.

6.1. Basket Snapshots

As the name suggests, a ***basket snapshot*** is the persistent image of a Kala basket object, taken at a certain instance of time. Basket snapshots are not persistent baskets. A basket snapshot just holds a basket state persistently.

A basket snapshot is held in a monad, and behaves like a regular monad. It is created by `mid CreateBasketSnapshot(kid, bid1, bid2)`, which creates a snapshot for a basket identified by `bid2` in a monad of kin `kid`, and creates a handle to that monad in the basket `bid1`. The snapshot reflects the state of the `bid2` basket at the time the method is executed (Kala servers are conceptually single-threaded; although operation requests are queued up, the execution of each method is atomic).

Basket snapshots are used to supply initial values to newly created baskets. `bid AccessBasket(kid, bid)` creates a new basket whose initial contents are the handles in the snapshot addressed through the `{kid, bid} handle`. This is in contrast with `bid NewBasket(void)`, which creates an empty basket.

6.2. Recoverable Baskets

Recoverable baskets are truly persistent baskets, in that they outlive the Kala client that created them. A transient basket can be made recoverable; `mid MakeBasketRecoverable(kid, bid1, bid2)` makes the basket `bid2` recoverable. In order for the basket to be accessible to other or subsequent applications, a handle to it is created in basket `bid1`. From now on, the handle looks like any other handle to a monad of kin `kid`. But this is a "special" kind of monad: upon accessing it with `bid AccessBasket(kid, bid)` it becomes available to this or any other Kala client at any time. All applications that access this monad share the persistent basket.

Any change to a recoverable basket, such as creating a new handle or moving a handle into the basket, is persistently recorded. The state of a recoverable basket is restored after any unexpected termination of the Kala client or server, short of media damage[7]. The recovery is done automatically upon Kala server restart.

7. SHARING

Kala's execution architecture is comprised of an arbitrary number of servers and clients running on a computer network. Each ***Kala server*** executes the same Kala server code, and manages a single Kala storing area, termed ***Kala store***. A server and its store form a unit, termed ***Kala installation***.

Each ***Kala client*** executes the application's code, linked with the same ***Kala client library*** code. A Kala client can be attached to one or more Kala servers. There is a default Kala server to which a client attaches upon issuing its first Kala service request. Each Kala server may communicate with several other Kala servers. Kala servers can fetch values stored in any accessible Kala store on behalf of each of their clients by making requests to the appropriate Kala server. This maintains the illusion that a client is served by only one single Kala server, while in reality many other servers may be involved.

The totality of all Kala stores existing at a certain time at any place, whether accessible or not, forms ***The Kala Monadbase***. There is only one such entity, although only portions of it may be accessible to a client at any time. The universality and uniqueness of all Kala identifiers such as mids and bids supports the universal uniqueness of the Monadbase. The Kala Monadbase is implemented as an ever growing set of Kala stores, each established in a separate Kala installation.

---

[7] Dealing with recoverablity after media damage is left to the subsystem "under" Kala, such as mirrored disks and disk drivers.

Kala clients can share baskets. There are two basket sharing regimes: provided baskets and persistent baskets.

7.1. Sharing through Providing Baskets

Two or more concurrently executing Kala clients can share a basket by having one client provide the basket to another through the **void ProvideBasket (bid, kalaClient)** operation. Once the target Kala client has the basket, it can "provide" it to any other Kala client for which it has valid identification. Provided baskets can be transient or persistent.

The Provide Basket mechanism has a shared memory semantics. The shared memory structure (the shared basket) exists however only in the Kala server's memory, and is accessed soley through Kala's programmatic interface.

7.2. Sharing Persistent Baskets

The second way to share a basket is to have multiple Kala clients access a recoverable basket (cf. §6.2) from the monad which holds its state. Since the basket is persistent, it can be shared among Kala clients which don't necessarily execute concurrently. Note that in order to share a recoverable basket, each Kala client must have access to a handle to the monad that holds its state. Each client may access the recoverable basket through its own private handle, or more likely through the same handle in yet another shared basket. Thus, to be shareable is a transitive relation: if a basket is shareable, all persistent baskets which have handles in this basket are shareable, too.

When shared among concurrently executing Kala clients, any change performed by any one client is made instantaneously visible to all other clients who had accessed the basket. This is true not only in a single-server configuration, but in the more common multi-server configurations. Basket objects are maintained on the Kala server side, but they are not distributed objects: a single basket is represented by a Kala-internal basket object held in one single server at a time. The inter-server communications establish client-server relationships between the server owner of a shared basket and all clients and other servers that share it.

8. LOCKING

Since baskets, and hence monads, can be shared among clients, Kala supports the notion of locking as a means to prevent unwanted modifications, and to insure serializability.

Since monads are immutable entities, locking a monad is a senseless operation. However, basket contents are mutable, so Kala allows one to *freeze* and correspondingly *thaw* handles. *Freezing a handle in a basket* means disallowing any operation concerning that handle: its creation (if the handle has not been created yet), its removal, its replacing with another akin handle, its move into that basket, etc.

A *freezer* is a Kala maintained object used to tag such handles when they are frozen. Like monads, baskets, and kin, freezers are identified by *freezer identifiers* (or *fids*), which are also universally unique. **void FreezeHandle(mid, bid, fid)** freezes the handle of a monad or kin in a basket, and tags it with the freezer. A freezer may tag many frozen handles.

Kala supports two freezing/thawing regimes. The first regime requires explicit thawing; a handle frozen by **FreezeHandle** needs be thawed by **void ThawHandle(mid, bid)**. A Kala client can thaw a handle as long as it possesses the freezer the handle was tagged with at freezing time.

This regime is used to implement "long transactions" and check-in / check-out strategies (cf. §10.5). It was designed to support such "ownership" notions, and thus it is oriented towards longer term cycles, and survives system crashes.

In contrast, the second regime was designed with transient lock-up in mind. It supports a request/grant freezing strategy. This allows freezing requests to be placed, queued up by Kala, and granted automatically as previously granted freezes for the same handles either expire or are explicitly thawed. The **void FreezeKinInBasket (kid, bid, fid, duration1, duration2)** operation allows one to request that the handle to a monad of kin **kid** in basket **bid** be eventually frozen, and labelled with freezer **fid**. Once granted, the freeze will expire after **duration1**. The request itself will expire after **duration2** .

Note that freezing is not associated with a handle to a specific monad, but to any handle to a monad of a specific kin in a basket. Thus, the handle does not even have to exist in the specified basket. If it does, then the request is for it to be eventually frozen. If it doesn't, then the request refers to this "handle placeholder" meaning that no handle to a monad of the kin **kid** can be inserted into that basket until the thaw occurs, either by time-out or explicitly by **void ThawKinInBasket(kid, bid)** .

Unlike the first regime, this freezing does not survive system crashes, and is automatically thawed during recovery.

9. BASKETS AND TRANSACTIONS

Basket is the primitive mechanism for implementing the higher level notion of transaction. In this section we will briefly explore the possible design space of a Kala-using module which implements some transaction model. We will start with a very simple transaction model: the conventional OLTP transactions. We will then briefly explore more modern transaction models.

9.1. Simple Transactions

Let's assume that a portion of the Kala monadbase represents a database of items. Each item **e** in the database is represented by a kin **k**. A monad of that kin represents a specific state of that item. For each kin (and item) there is a handle **h** in a unique, shared-by-all-users basket $\mathcal{P}$ (for "public"). Handle **h** points to the monad which represents the current public value of that item. Thus each item **e** can be accessed by accessing the monad **m** of its corresponding kin **k** for which there exists a handle **h** in $\mathcal{P}$.

A transaction **T** is represented by a basket **B**. Starting a new transaction corresponds to creating a new, empty, transient basket. Each of **T**'s actions (or schedule, cf. [12]) creating new items or updating existing ones is represented as an action (a call to a Kala function) which creates a new handle in **B** to a new monad. Each application's BSL has either one

or two baskets. If the application executes within a transaction **T**, its BSL ≡ {**B**, $\mathcal{P}$}. If the application executes outside any transaction, its BSL ≡ {$\mathcal{P}$}.

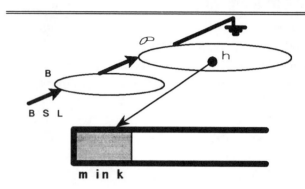

Figure 4: Loading an Item initially

The application code must call Kala's Load operation to attempting to access an item from the database. The handle is addressed using the **{kid, firstFound}** addressing mode. If this is the first time that item is accessed by this client, the address resolves to the handle **h** in $\mathcal{P}$, for there is no handle to any monad of that kin in **B**. Figure 4 illustrates this case.

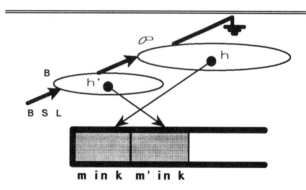

Figure 5: Updating the Item within a Transaction

After the item is processed in memory, its new state must be saved on disk. This corresponds to creating a new Kala monad **m'** akin to the original one. But since this update is done within the transaction **T**, the handle **h'** to the new monad is created in **B**. Since there was no handle to a monad of this kin in **B**, this handle has nothing to supplant. The result is shown in Figure 5.

238

From this point on, within the transaction **T**, any attempt on the part of this Kala client to re-load the item will result in (conceptually) loading the monad to which the handle in **B** points. On the other hand, any other Kala client that desires to access the item from the database will load **m**, because **B** is not shared, and it can only see **h**.

9.2. Transaction Commit, Undo, and Redo

After loading and updating several items as part of our transaction **T**, the Kala application reaches a point where it must decide whether to make all these updates visible to the rest of the world or not. In other words, commit **T** or fail it, thus undoing all the changes.

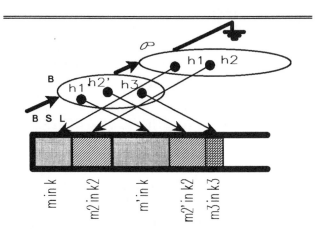

Figure 6: After a series of creates & updates

Let's assume that the application updated two items represented by kin **k1** and **k2**, and created a new item, represented by kin **k3**. The state after these modifications of the database is shown in Figure 6.

Committing the transaction **T** represented in this simple model by the Kala basket **B** corresponds to moving all the handles in **B** over to $\mathcal{P}$. To satisfy Kala's Central Dogma (cf. §5.2), handles **h1** and **h1'** cannot coexist in $\mathcal{P}$. Thus, **h1'** supplants **h1**. A similar situation is encountered with **h2** and **h2'**, and **h2'** supplants **h2**. **h3** however does not encounter any other akin handle, and it is just moved to $\mathcal{P}$. The situation after transaction commit is shown in Figure 7.

In summary, a committing a transaction results to the following Kala call:

    MoveHandle(everyKin, tactionBas-
    ket, publicBasket);

where **tactionBasket** is the basket representing the transaction.

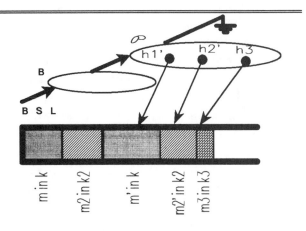

Figure 7: After transaction commit

Alternatively, if the decision is to fail the transaction and undo all the modifications to the database, merely remove all the handles in **B**, thus bringing the state of the database like it was in Figure 4[8]. Kala will soon deallocate the values in the Kala store for which there is no handle in any basket.

Redoing a transaction is again trivial: remove all the handles in **B**, and then perform the sequence of actions in the transaction once again. New monads will be generated, and the redone transaction can finally be committed, failed, or redone once again.

9.3. Nested and Long Transactions

The simple model presented in the previous sections can be extended to a full *nested transaction* model by allowing transaction-representing baskets to be placed in ordered lists, the BSLs. Any Transaction Module built above Kala baskets imposes a certain transaction model by the manner in which it administers a client's BSL. For example, suppose any time a new transaction is started, the implement-

---

[8] In reality, failing a transaction is more properly represented by moving all the handles to a "special" basket named the Failed basket. This method allows for a one-level undo facility even for transaction failing.

ing basket is placed at the beginning of the BSL, and each time a transaction is committed, the handles in the basket representing that transaction are moved to the basket next on the BSL. Then, the implemented semantics is that of nested transactions. Similarly, other multiple transaction model can be built with an appropriate structure of baskets.

A BSL represents a path from a transaction to the root of all transactions. Although Kala does not impose any such root, it offers a convenient default through the *Public Basket*, a basket created by default during the process of initialization of any Kala installation, and automatically provided to every application which attaches to that server.

The ability to maintain persistent baskets and freezers offers support for *long transactions* in a straightforward manner. The basket which represents the long transaction is made recoverable (cf. §6.2). The transaction will exist as long as there is a handle to a monad containing the state of this recoverable basket. A new Kala client process can use the transaction by accessing this monad, creating a basket in its environment, placing it on its BSL, and then using it to place handles pointing to newly created values. The first three steps are all done by Kala's **AccessBasket** operation.

The BSL itself can be made persistent by saving its state into a monad and restoring it back. Thus the transaction nesting itself can be preserved across clients' executions. Kala provides convenient primitives for storing the BSL's data structure (a linked list of basket identifiers) in a monad.

Further details on Kala's support for modern transaction models are to be found in [8].

9.4. Check-in / Check-out

The presence of long transactions in conjunction with handle freezing makes the implementation of check-in / check-out models straightforward. Let's assume for simplicity that the object versions subject to check-out are implemented by monads with handles in some shared basket, such as P in figure 4^9.

A check-out operation on the versioned object represented by kin **k** corresponds to freezing the handle **h** in P. The freezing is done with a persistent freezer, so that the handle remains frozen after the freezing process exits.

While this and other handles are frozen, all updates to the versioned objects are done into an "inner" transaction, implemented as a persistent basket **B** located in the BSL before P. This strategy makes the updates "local". **B** implements a long transaction. For example, a new object version for our versioned object is represented by monad **m'** with a handle **h'** in **B** (cf. figure 5).

The versioned objects may be checked-in all at once or in arbitrary groups. If the former is preferred, a call such as **MoveHandles(B, P)** followed by thawing the handles in P is all that is needed. Single check-in (for example, on versioned object represented by kin **k**) is implemented by doing a **MoveHandle(k, B, P)**, followed by a **ThawHandle(k, P, aFid)**.

10. BASKETS AND CONFIGURATIONS

Configurations are software objects used to organize the evolution of complex systems, such as software during program development [11][3]. In this section, we briefly illustrate Kala's support for three fundamental organizational aspects supported by software configuration management (SCM), and in particular the use of baskets in supporting software composition. Finally, the support for the check-in/check-out model is also illustrated.

Gustavsson [3] distinguishes three organizational dimensions SCM systems need to support: evolution, membership, and composition. He argues for their complete orthogonality. Kala supports all three dimensions in a straightforward manner, and guarantees their orthogonality.

10.1. Evolution

Objects are organized along the *evolution* dimension to record their change over time. The motivation is both referential (we should be able to inspect

---

9 In the more common case, the "environment" is constructed by assembling several shared baskets by placing them in the application's BSL. Their order determines which object vesions for each versioned

objects will be visible when the access is done using the {kid, firstFound} addressing mode.

older versions of an object) and restoration oriented (we should be able to restore older versions into current use). Conventional tools like RCS or sccs implement such organizations.

Although Kala does not impose any particular versioning model, it supports versioning through the kin mechanism. *Versioned objects* correspond to kin, while an individual *object version* corresponds to a monad of that kin. *Version group objects* are objects that organize other objects by evolution. A version group object is implemented as a monad containing both references to the monads, all of the same kin, representing various object versions, as well as change relation information (e.g., the evolution tree or graph, or portions thereof). Version group objects can be versioned, too.

The versioned object -> version group object map is not a one-to-one relation, due to the distributed and separable nature of The Kala Monadbase. Any Kala installation can be easily separated from others (for example, by partitioning the network or by removing the diskette that holds the Kala store), and thus new object versions may be independently generated. The universal uniqueness of Kala's mids guarantees that akin version group objects can indeed be merged without ambiguity.

A particular versioning model, implemented through the structure of and operations around version group objects, is the domain of a software layer above Kala. This reflects the higher level semantic nature of such models.

10.2. Membership

Objects are organized along the *membership* dimension to express semantic relationships among them. This is mainly motivated by the complexity of common software repositories. This organization is conventionally supported by file systems (e.g., the Unix' directory, the Macintosh Finder's folder) and software environment tools (e.g., DSEE's library, NSE's component).

Since organization along this dimension reflects higher level semantics, *directory objects* are implemented by a layer above Kala. The directory facility implements a function from names to identifiers, mapping human-oriented names of arbitrary syntax

(e.g., textual, iconic) to software-oriented identifiers (e.g., kids, mids). A directory is implemented as a data structure containing references into baskets, and it is stored as one or many monads, typically grouped into a single basket for convenience and economy.

10.3. Composition

Objects are organized by *composition* to express compound software entities, such as modules and subsystems, and to construct derived objects, such as executables, libraries, formatted help text, and published manuals. This organization is supported by conventional software building tools (e.g., Unix' make, DSEE's builder).

Configuration objects are implemented as Kala baskets containing handles to the monads which represent the object versions. Configurations can be stored as recoverable baskets or basket snapshots. The builder tool accesses the needed source fragments exclusively through the configuration (corresponding to accessing a kin via a specific basket), guaranteeing that the correct object version will be used.

Archival configurations (i.e. configurations that reflect historical states of a released product, which are to be protected against any further change) are accomplished by freezing the entire basket and keeping the freezer very private (e.g., accessible only by some administrator or by nobody). Alternatively, a single basket can represent the "current" configuration, and basket snapshots can be used to represent archival configurations.

Floating configurations (i.e. configurations which are fixed as to what versioned objects they contain, but not as to what object versions are used) can be represented using baskets with indirect handles. An *indirect handle*[10] is a handle to yet another handle whose resolution leads to the desired monad. A *static indirect handle* is an indirect where the basket containing its target handle was bound at its creation. To represent a configuration to the "latest version" of some or all of its constituent

---

[10] Indirect and thunk handles are two kinds of handles which enrich Kala's expressive power. Additional kinds of handles are treated in detail in [6].

objects, or to "Bill's version" of some or all of its objects, one uses baskets containing static indirects for each of the objects the "latest version" or "Bill's version" contains. The target baskets of these indirects represent the "latest" or "Bill's" working context.

Computed configurations (i.e. configurations whose version object membership is determined, but where some or all object versions are computed "on the fly") are represented using baskets with thunk handles. A *thunk handle* is a handle to a monad whose value can be computed at load time. Both indirects and handles are explained in detail in [6].

10.4. A Simple Example

Let's take two versioned objects **VO1** and **VO2** (see figure 8). Version Group Object **VGO1** represents the evolution of **VO1**, while **VGO2** represents **VO2**'s evolution. **VGO1** is distributed; it is represented as two monads: **VGO1a** and **VGO1b**. This means that at a certain point, versions of **VO1** were generated from an object version passed to a server that was subsequently disconnected. **VGO2** is not distributed; it contains **VO2**'s entire history. The icons representing the version group objects show possible structuring of their versions in trees.

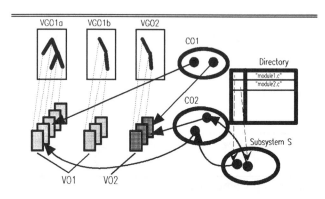

Figure 8: Simple example of Configuration Representations

Two configurations are illustrated in the figure: **CO1** and **CO2**. They are both represented by baskets. **CO1** presents the world as containing **VO1**'s third version and **VO2**'s third version. **CO2** presents the world as containing **VO1**'s second version and **VO2**'s third version.

Finally, a section of a dictionary data structure shows mappings between the strings "**module1.c**" and "**module2.c**", and the two versioned objects. This mapping is done via a basket containing two indirect handles. The figure shows a situation where the indirects are all resolved with handles in the **CO2** basket. At a later time, the resolution may be changed to use **CO1** instead. Switching configurations presents a different view on the software repository.

11. BASKETS AND ACCESS CONTROL

Access control is the mechanism used by data and object management systems to prevent unauthorized access to the managed data and objects. In this section, we briefly illustrate Kala's support for controlling access to persistent data.

11.1. Allowing Access

Although a monad's value can be proximately accessed either via a handle or via a reference from another monad, its ultimate accessibility by a Kala client is determined by the presence or absence of a handle to it in a transitively accessible basket. In other words, *a monad is accessible by a client iff the client has at least one basket containing a handle to that monad or transitively to a monad which refers to it*. This accessibility rule leads to the idea of controlling monad accessibility by controlling the baskets accessible to a client.

Upon attaching to a Kala installation, a client spontaneously receives several baskets in its space. These baskets are placed on its BSL in a certain order. The set of initial baskets are determined in part automatically, and in part by the Kala installation administrator.

The baskets in the initial *accessed basket set* represent entry points into an accessibility graph. The client can extend its accessed basket set by transitively accessing persistent baskets which have handles in the currently accessed baskets. The totality of baskets that can be transitively accessed in this fashion is termed the *accessible basket set*.

The Monadbase's persistent baskets can be viewed as organized in a dependency graph. Access control is thus realized by partitioning this graph, and offering each client an initial accessed basket set containing only baskets in permissible partitions. Kala's administrative interface provides operations for associating the operating environment's identification notions with initial accessible basket sets. There are also default provisions for a small set of baskets to account for very general notions, such as the Public Basket (analogous to **/tmp** in Unix practice), or the User Basket (analogous to **~user** in Unix practice).

The accessed basket set is also dynamically augmentable through the basket providing mechanism (cf. §7.1).

This access management method avoids the use of conventional access control lists, which are known to be cumbersome and inflexible. The general graph nature of basket references permits arbitrary access control structures with low overhead.

11.2. Preventing Access

All Kala managed entities, such as monads, freezers, kin, and baskets, are specified by their identifiers, such as mids, fids, kids, and bids. The Kala server keeps track of all identifiers known by each of its attached clients. A Kala client which supplies a fabricated bit pattern as an identifier can never obtain access of a monad or basket which couldn't have been accessible otherwise. *Kala identifiers are unforgeable.* Consequently, unless a client can obtain an identifier through "legal" means, it can never access a basket or a monad[11].

12. IMPLEMENTATION

Every client access to a monad must go through one or more baskets to determine the monad's identity and to verify its accessibility. Consequently, the basket implementation has an extraordinary impact on Kala's performance. The implementation today reflects the evolution of increasingly sophisticated data structures and algorithms. In the present Kala 2.0 implementation, basket overhead has been reduced to a trivial part of the i/o and data copy costs inherent in any data movement. In effect, the basket mechanism and the functionality it presents are free to the user.

12.1. Requirements

This zero cost has been achieved by careful examination of and accommodation to the following characteristics of basket usage:

- *Basket volume* varies widely. Most baskets remain empty[12], and are discarded without ever containing any handles. Most of the remaining baskets are used to implement some transaction model and will hold less than a dozen handles, and will be empty when discarded. The remaining small fraction are persistent baskets. They will hold from tens to tens of millions of handles.
- There is a high *locality of reference* to handles, both within and across applications and transactions. Most handles will be for monads created by the installation which also holds the basket containing the handle, as will the bulk of those monads. Most handles will never be frozen. Many kin have only a single monad ever created of that kin.
- *Lookup* within a basket is by kin (cf. Kala's Central Dogma). However, the ensuing fetch from disk requires information which is unique to the particular monad, not per kin. In addition, handles for the same monad can appear simultaneously in many baskets. Replicating per-monad information in each handle would be expensive, and present problems for consistency maintenance when some baskets exist as snapshots.
- While Kala's *multi-threading* may overlap regular disk and communications packet i/o with server processing, it cannot overlap with i/o resulting from page faults.

12.2. Implementation Outline

The basket implementation collects all per-monad information for every monad resident in a Kala installation into a single per-server object, termed the ***Kala Map***. The per-monad Kala Map information includes reference counts, disk addresses, kin

---

[11] Kala does not attempt to compensate for any security loopholes the operating system or the hardware may already have. Thus, forceful and knowledgeable intrusions into Kala server process memory can lead to security breaches.

[12]Certain baskets are spontaneously generated by the system at each application's start, for convenience. Most of them never get used by most executions, and thus remain empty.

identity — all searchable by mid. The Kala Map implements a mid-to-kid function.

Baskets, on the other hand, implement a kid-to-mid function. The basket handles contain only mid, kid, and freezing information. The kin membership of a monad is static at creation, and freezing status is per-basket and can change only in accessed and application-referenced baskets. Consequently, no information can change in a basket snapshot, and there are thus no consistency maintenance problems.

A kin-based request results in the examination of one or more baskets. The resulting mid is then applied to the Kala Map to yield a disk address or other monad attribute. Basket searches by mid first use the Kala Map to get the corresponding kid, followed by normal kid-based basket searches and a check to confirm that the handles found are for the desired mid.

Kala's implementation was carried out under the assumption that memory is cheap, but page faults are expensive. This led to an emphasis on reducing the size of key data structures, particularly the Kala Map and the baskets. Many baskets have their size reduced to the ultimate: they are not there at all. Dynamically created transient baskets, such as the "process" and "failed" baskets which appear spontaneously when an application attaches to a Kala server, are not physically created until the first handle is inserted.

While most baskets that actually have contents will have very few handles during their lifetimes, most handles will reside in a small number of very large baskets. This dichotomy is addressed by actually providing two different implementations of baskets: one is optimized for low access overhead to small baskets, and the other for efficient reference to large baskets. Baskets are first created with the first implementation, and are automatically converted to the second after as they grow in size.

Small baskets are organized as linearly linked lists of hash tables, initially quite small (10 entries). When insertions bring the top table to about 70% full, a new larger table is created and linked to the front of the list. Search is from the front of the list, probing in each table in turn. If a search locates a handle in a table not at the front, the handle is pro-moted to the front table. This process, along with deletions, gradually empties the rear tables, which are periodically consolidated with adjacent tables to constrain the list length. Due to locality of reference, most handles are found in the front tables, which thereby tend to stay in the server's memory working set, and thus page faults are rare.

Large baskets are implemented as quasi-balanced n-ary trees of tables. The search is globally recursive, and binary within a table. Table size and alignment are set to the underlying architecture's memory page size and alignment. The expectation is that the root and the first layer of tables will remain resident in a server's memory (around 0.5 megabyte for typical page sizes). Thus, a single page fault will return a desired handle from a basket containing up to 10 million handles. In addition, special techniques can commonly determine without actual search that the desired handle cannot be in the basket, making it unnecessary to waste page faults in large baskets when more than a single basket is to be checked.

12.3. Further Optimizations

In the general case, a single handle occupies 24 bytes: three 8-byte identifiers for the monad, kin, and freezer. In reality, the implementation replicates the data structure three times at different sizes to exploit regularities in the usage patterns.

First, since handles are rarely frozen, the fid field is generally unnecessary. Secondly, since most kin and monads are created by the server which also maintains the basket, the portions of the mid and kid which identify the creating servers are also often not necessary. Lastly, since most kin only get one monad of that kin, Kala gives the first monad in the kin a mid which is bitwise the same as its kin's kid. Thus, it is often unnecessary to record both the kid and the mid.

The combination of the three special cases above leads to a tripartite data structure for a basket: one with 24-byte entries, one with 8-byte entries, and one with 4-byte entries. The remaining possibilities have not appeared to be common enough to warrant complicating the already complex structure maintenance algorithms.

12.4. Results

Space limitations of this article prevent a discussion of Kala's space and time performance results; this topic is discussed at length in [2]. Timing measurements for the large (200,000 parts) Cattell database [1] show that basket operations consume less than 5% of total processor time. This and other benchmarks have shown that Kala's time performance is determined entirely by disk and network bandwidths.

For the same benchmark database, the basket information occupies about 80 kilobytes, compared to the 20 megabytes occupied by the 200,000 parts themselves.

13. CONCLUSIONS

Baskets have proven to be a very versatile and at the same time economical mechanism. Their implementation within a low-level architectural component offers object-based systems a wide range of options to address transactions, access control, and configuration management in a simple, uniform manner. Baskets can also be used to model dynamic multi-level defaulting mechanisms (e.g., for user profiles), as well as static and dynamic scoping in programming languages with persistence.

BIBLIOGRAPHY

[1]   Cattell, R.G.G. and Skeen, J., *Engineering Database Benchmark*, Sun Microsystems Report, April 1990.

[2]   Godard, Ivan and Simmel, Sergiu S., *Kala's Space and Time Performance*, in progress.

[3]   Gustavsson, Anders, *Software Configuration Management in an Integrated Environment*, Lund University Report LU-CS-TR:90-52, Malmo, Sweden.

[4]   Leblang, D., Chase, R., and McLean, G., *The DOMAIN Software Engineering Environment for Large Scale Development Efforts*, 1st Int'l Conference on Computer Workstations, 1985.

[5]   Moss, J. Eliot B., *Design of the Mneme Persistent Object Store*, ACM Transactions on Information Systems, 1990.

[6]   Simmel, Sergiu S., *Kala - Main Concepts*, Samsung Software America, Inc. and Penobscot Research Center, Inc. Report, version 1.00, June 1990.

[7]   Simmel, Sergiu S., *Kala - Interface Reference*, Samsung Software America, Inc. and Penobscot Research Center, Inc. Report, version 1.00, August 1990.

[8]   Simmel, Sergiu S., and Godard, Ivan, *Kala's Support for Transaction Models*, in progress.

[9]   Soley, Richard Mark (ed.), *Object Management Architecture Guide*, Object Management Group, O.M.G. TC Document 90.9.1, Version 1.0, 1 November, 1990.

[10]   Thompson, Craig et.al., *Open Architecture for Object-oriented Database Systems*, Texas Instruments Incorporated, Technical Report #89-12-01(2), 1989.

[11]   Tichy, Walter, *Tools for Software Configuration Management*, Int'l Workshop on Software Version and Configuration Control, 1988 Grassau, West Germany.

[12]   Ullman, Jeffrey D., *Principles of Database Systems*, Computer Science Press, 1982.

[13]   Wang, Chung C., *A Strawman Reference Model in Transaction Processing for an Object Oriented Database*, Texas Instruments Incorporated Report, 1990.

[14]   Wile, David S. & Dennis G. Allard, *Worlds: Aggregates for Object Bases*, USC/Information Sciences Institute, 1988.

APPENDIX

The following is a selection of relevant declarations from Kala's main ANSI C application programmatic interface (API), given here to illustrate the nature of the interface, rather than to specify it. Due to space limitations as well as their implementation dependent nature, the typedef declarations were left out.

```
bid AccessBasket(mid, bid);
              /* Causes the basket monad at <mid, bid> to be
              loaded and returns its bid . */

rowBid Baskets(bid);
              /* Returns a row of all basket ids corresponding to the
              supplied bid, in search order for multi-basket bids. */

void BasketSearchList(rowBid);
              /* Replaces the default basket search list with the bas-
              kets in the row. */

void CopyHandle(mid, bid, bid);
              /* Atomically copies the handle(s) at <mid, bid> to the
              specified basket . */

rowMonadSpec CopyHandles(rowMonadSpec,
          rowBid);
              /* Atomically copies the handles at rowMonadSpec to
              the corresponding baskets and returns the resolutions
              of the destinations. */

pointer CreateBasketSnapshot(kid, bid,
          bid);
              /* Creates the basket named bid as a monad and a
              handle to it at <kid, bid>, and returns the mid.*/
```

```
mid CreateDatum(kid, bid, setAddress,
    rowRefPointer, range);
                        /* Creates a monad and a handle to it at <kid, bid>
                        whose value is the contents of memory described by
                        the setAddress, containing pointers as described by the
                        rowRefPointer, which must point to other monad values
                        in memory defined by either previous Creates or
                        Defines. If there already is a handle at <kid, bid>, that
                        handle is replaced. */


void DeleteBasket(bid);
                        /* Removes the basket from all search lists. */


#define DeleteHandle(mid, bid) \
  MoveHandle(mid, bid, noBasket)
                        /* Discards Kala's knowledge of the handle(s) at <mid,
                        bid>. */


#define DeleteHandles(rowMonadSpec) \
  MoveHandles(rowMonadSpec, Only(&noBasket, bid))
                        /* Discards Kala's knowledge of these handles. */


void FreezeBasket(bid, fid);
                        /* Freezes the basket(s) from further change of any
                        sort until explicitly unfrozen, using fid as the key. */


void FreezeHandle(mid, bid, fid);
                        /* Freezes the described handles in their baskets from
                        further change of any sort until explicitly unfrozen,
                        using fid as the key. */


rowMonadSpec FreezeHandles(rowMonadSpec,
                rowFid);
                        /* Freezes the described handles in their baskets from
                        further change of any sort until explicitly unfrozen,
                        using the corresponding fids as keys. */


void FreezeKinInBasket(kid, bid, fid,
                duration, duration);
                        /* Locks the basket at (kid, bid) from stores by other
                        processes in the indicated kin. Raises exception
                        LockNotGranted if the freeze cannot be granted before
                        the first duration elapse; Raises exception
                        TimedOutLock if ThawHandle for the same <kid, bid>
                        is not executed before the second duration elapses
                        after the grant. All freezes granted or pending are
                        removed when the caller exits. */


fid FrozenBasket(bid);
                        /* Returns the fid which is the freezing key for the bas-
                        ket, or thawed if not frozen. */


fid FrozenHandle(mid, bid);
                        /* Returns the fid which is the freezing key for the
                        described handle, or thawed if not frozen */
```

```
void Load(mid, bid, transitivity,
            allocator);
                        /* Copies the value of the monad at <mid, bid> to
                        application memory. If the monad was originally
                        Created from a single contiguous piece of memory then
                        the Loaded image will have the same structure.. */


monadSpec MakeBasketRecoverable(kid, bid,
                bid);
                        /* Flags bid as recoverable, and stores a reference to it
                        at <kid, bid>, returning the new mid */


void MoveHandle(mid, bid, bid);
                        /* Performs the CopyMonad operation, and also in the
                        same atomic operation removes the handle from its
                        former basket. */


rowMonadSpec MoveHandles(rowMonadSpec,
                rowBid);
                        /* Performs the CopyMonads operation, and also in the
                        same atomic operation removes the handles from their
                        former baskets. */


bid NewBasket(void);
                        /* Creates a basket, enters it on the BSL, and returns
                        its id. Does not monadize it (see MakeBasket- Recov-
                        erable) .*/


fid NewFreezer(void);
                        /* Generates a new unique freezer and adds it to the
                        freezer list. */


void ProvideBasket(bid, identity);
                        /* Adds that basket to the BSL of the client using that
                        identity. */


rowMonadSpec ResolveHandle(mid, bid);
                        /* Atomically returns the resolutions of the  <mid, bid>.
                        address*/


rowMonadSpec ResolveHandles
                (rowMonadSpec);
                        /* Atomically returns the resolutions of the rowMonad-
                        Spec addresses. */


#define ThawBasket(mid, bid) \
  FreezeBasket(mid, bid, thawed)

#define ThawHandle(mid, bid) \
  FreezeHandle(mid, bid, thawed)

#define ThawHandles(rowMonadSpec) \
  FreezeHandles(rowMonadSpec, nilRow)

void ThawKinInBasket(kid, bid);
                        /* Unlocks a previously granted FreezeKinInBasket .*/
```

An Extensible Kernel Object Management System

Rahim Yaseen, Stanley Y.W. Su and Herman Lam

Database Systems Research and Development Center
Department of Computer and Information Sciences
Department of Electrical Engineering
CSE 470, University of Florida
Gainesville, FL32611.
rmy@trout.cis.ufl.edu

Abstract

Traditional monolithic database system architectures have been found to be inadequate for supporting end-user data modeling paradigms needed in complex application domains. Instead, database system architectures which are open, multi-layered, and extensible must be developed. In this paper, we explore the concept of a multi-layer, extensible architecture for building new generation knowledge/data base systems. A Kernel Object Management System (KOMS) which serves as an intermediate layer in a multi-layer architecture is described. The aim is to build a generalized and extensible system which can be (a)upwardly extended into a high-level, end-user, semantic model and (b)downwardly extended to interface with various storage systems. To satisfy the generic or kernel requirement, the system uses an eXtensible Kernel Object Model (XKOM) which consists of a set of generalized or core object modeling constructs. *Model Extensibility* is facilitated by reflexively modeling the constructs of XKOM as objects, classes and associations. An object-based specification and implementation of the system architecture is used to achieve *System Extensibility*. By modifying and extending these model and system schemata, the model and system can be tailored or customized to suit various application domains. Various implementation issues and techniques related to the development of KOMS are also described.

1 Introduction

In recent years, the growing demand for database technology by advanced application domains (e.g. CAD/CAM, CASE, VLSI, etc.) coupled with the inadequacy of traditional (i.e. relational, network, hierarchical) data models to support such applications has prompted the development of advanced data modeling paradigms. Several semantic and object-oriented data models, specialized modeling constructs, languages, and systems [AND87, BAN87, COP84, DIT86, FIS87, HAM81, HULL87, LEC88, LOO86, SHI81, SU89, ZAN83], have been proposed. An important issue is defining and developing a suitable knowledge/data base system to support these diverse applications and data models.

Traditionally, database management systems have been built as monolithic systems. Such systems are monolithic in the sense that the system is developed based on some original specifications (e.g. a specific data model or language), and cannot accommodate any change in the original specifications easily. For example, System R [AST76] provides two layers: a lower layer (RSS) to provide storage management and an upper layer (RDS) which is a monolithic implementation of a specific (relational) model. A monolithic upper or lower layer is still not conducive to functional extensions, and such an architecture is inadequate for advanced applications.

To address the limitations of traditional database systems, and to support advanced

OOPSLA'91, pp. 247–263

applications, a new class of database systems called *object-oriented database systems* have evolved. Systems such as Orion[BAN87], Gemstone[MAI86a], Vbase[AND87], Iris[FIS87], etc., have mainly focussed on developing a specific system based on a specific high-level object-oriented data model. These models and systems cater to advanced applications by offering enhanced functionalities. However, such systems are model-specific, and have not been developed with extensibility as a key goal. Thus, such systems cannot easily handle a change in their original specifications that an advanced or emerging application may require. This implies that an application must be forced to use the model and system even if the model or system does not match the application requirements.

Based on the premise that emerging applications have dynamic requirements, several systems such as Exodus[CAR86b], Postgres[STO86], Starburst[SCH86], and Genesis[BAT88] have been at the forefront of a class of systems known as *extensible database systems*. Postgres and Starburst aim to provide a complete extensible database system for all applications within a relational framework. Exodus and Genesis have taken a "toolkit" approach in which a customized system is generated for each application. Genesis is based on the Unifying Model (a variant of the network model) and uses a strict framework of building blocks to achieve layering and extensibility. Exodus is an object-based system which provides a set of fixed components plus a collection of tools for building system components. Although having similar goals, each system uses a different approach to achieve extensibility.

With increasing complexity of application domains, and the multitude of end-user data modeling constructs, it is clear that monolithic database architectures are inadequate to support the diverse needs of advanced application domains. On the one hand, it is not feasible for a single (fixed) data model and system to support all applications. Even in object-oriented database systems, a single system has not emerged (unlike the relational model) since there is no consensus [ATK89] on which object model is the "right" model. On the other hand, due to excessive monetary cost and development time, it is not feasible to develop many customized systems for many specialized models and different application domains. A viable alternative is to have a kernel or generalized database system that can be extended or evolved to support specialized models and application domains.

We are currently exploring such an option by pursuing the concept of an open, extensible, and multi-layer knowledge/data base system architecture. Our approach builds upon an integration of the object-oriented and extensible system approaches described above. The system under development, OSAM*.KBMS/X, is targeted to be a knowledge base management system that integrates the notion of data (objects), methods, queries, and rules in a single extensible object-oriented environment. The layered architecture of OSAM*.KBMS/X is shown in Fig 1.

Our goals also parallel those of the Darmstadt Kernel System [PAU87] and O_2[VEL89]. In both these systems, a layered approach is taken and efforts are made to be canonical. The Darmstadt Kernel System takes a kernel and extensible approach but their kernel is more oriented toward a storage kernel whereas our kernel is oriented towards an intermediate layer. O_2 is targeted as a layered object-oriented system with not much emphasis on extensibility. Although these systems have similar goals, the overall approach that we take and the mechanisms that we propose for extensibility are considerably different from these systems.

In this paper, we describe a Kernel Object Management System (KOMS) which serves as an intermediate layer in the multi-layer architecture of OSAM*.KBMS/X. This intermediate layer is built on top of an underlying storage layer and is used to manage kernel objects – objects whose abstractions are described by an eXtensible Kernel Object Model (XKOM). The objectives of this approach are as follows. Firstly, to develop a Kernel Object Management System (KOMS), which can be extended (upwards) to support different object-oriented models to be used by different applications. Secondly, to serve as an intermediate layer which provides upper layers with a common inter-

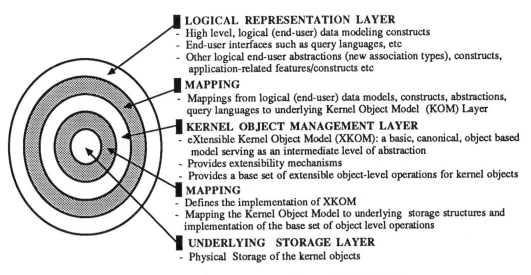

LOGICAL REPRESENTATION LAYER
- High level, logical (end-user) data modeling constructs
- End-user interfaces such as query languages, etc
- Other logical end-user abstractions (new association types), constructs,
  application-related features/constructs etc

MAPPING
- Mappings from logical (end-user) data models, constructs, abstractions,
  query languages to underlying Kernel Object Model (KOM) Layer

KERNEL OBJECT MANAGEMENT LAYER
- eXtensible Kernel Object Model (XKOM): a basic, canonical, object based
  model serving as an intermediate level of abstraction
- Provides extensibility mechanisms
- Provides a base set of extensible object-level operations for kernel objects

MAPPING
- Defines the implementation of XKOM
- Mapping the Kernel Object Model to underlying storage structures and
  implementation of the base set of object level operations

UNDERLYING STORAGE LAYER
- Physical Storage of the kernel objects

Figure 1: The Layered Architecture of OSAM*.KBMS/X

face to different underlying storage layers. Thirdly, to provide an interface comprising of a set of basic yet semantically meaningful operators for processing objects and object references (links). Such operators are to be used by clients of the KOMS such as the query processor, rule processor, transaction manager, etc.

KOMS has been designed and implemented to support an eXtensible Kernel Object Model (XKOM). XKOM consists of a set of generalized or core object modeling constructs. Based on these constructs, we extract a generic, uniform, and semantically meaningful model of storage for kernel objects. To support XKOM, a storage strategy based on a natural distribution of object instances along class boundaries is used. In order to provide strong support for associations or relationships among object classes, KOMS provides comprehensive support for object references or links. Based on these features, a basic set of object manipulation operators have been defined, and algorithms for their processing have been developed.

We note that KOMS differs from object managers proposed in [CHO85, CAR86a, SKA86, VEL89]. Many of these object managers are more appropriately called storage managers primarily because the structural representation of an object at this level is a low-level (storage) representation (e.g. files, records). Furthermore, operators at this level provide a low-level interface (such as get/put, read/write), based on this storage level representation. Ideally, a storage layer must deal only

with abstractions and issues that are relevant to the storage level. Consequently, storage managers should *not* include functionalities such as high-level object representations, high-level operators, and set-oriented retrievals, but rather provide adequate support for such functionalities. Instead, management of objects at a higher level of abstraction should be carried out in a layer above the storage layer – it is this layer that KOMS caters to.

Extensibility is an important feature of the system. Model Extensibility or data model extensions are facilitated by using the concept of *model reflexivity*. In model reflexivity, a data model is used to model itself resulting in a set of meta-classes which represent data model constructs such as classes, associations, identity, rules, methods, etc., as first class objects. Data model extensions are realized by modifying this set of meta-classes. System Extensibility or extensions to the software architecture of the system are facilitated by explicitly modeling system components as objects, classes, and associations. Similar to data model extensions, system components can be modified or extended by manipulating the classes and objects that represent components of the system architecture. The system is developed as an open, modular, and extensible architecture with well-defined interfaces.

KOMS has been implemented using the C++ programming language [STR86] and the ONTOS object server [ONT90] as the underlying storage layer. However, in the design and implementation of KOMS, we have made a conscious attempt to define the intermediate layer with a view to interfacing to a generic underlying storage layer, having get/put or read/write semantics.

This paper is organized as follows. In Section 2, the eXtensible Kernel Object Model (XKOM) is presented. We describe design requirements, basic modeling constructs, a distributed model of storage for kernel objects, and mechanisms for achieving data model extensions. Issues relating to the processing of kernel objects are discussed in Section 3, and a set of high-level operators that constitute the interface are presented. Section 4 describes the implementation of the system, and illustrates the notion of system extensibility. Section 5 presents a conclusion and discussion on future work.

2 An Extensible Kernel Object Model (XKOM)

2.1 Data Model Requirements

1. Core or Kernel Requirement: The data model must support a set of core data modeling constructs common to existing high-level semantic and/or object-oriented data models. These include the notions of *objects, classes, instances, identity, and associations (attributes)*.

2. Extensibility Requirement: The data model should be *extensible*. It should allow additional data model constructs to be "plugged" in thereby extending the set of core constructs to support higher level data model constructs.

2.2 Basic Modeling Constructs

The set of basic data modeling constructs that comprise XKOM are identified and presented below. A deliberate attempt has been made to identify constructs that are neither semantically too specialized nor too primitive. We will use an example schema shown in Fig. 2 to illustrate these basic model constructs.

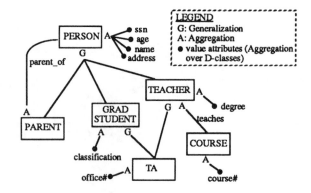

Figure 2: An example application schema

2.2.1 Objects, Instances, and Classes

A kernel *object* is the basic unit that models the abstract representation of any entity. A kernel *class* is an abstraction that describes the structural and behavioral semantics of a set of like objects. A kernel *instance* is the representation of a kernel object in a particular class. A kernel object may participate in (belong to) more than one class. Thus, the structural and behavioral properties of a single kernel object are distributed across as many classes as it belongs to, and an object has an instance in every class it belongs to. Effectively, a kernel object is a *union* of all its instances. This distributed view of objects is used to support the notion of generalization and inheritance.

A kernel object may be self-named or system-named. A self-named object, e.g. the integer 3, is an object whose value is the only means of referencing it. A system-named object is one to which the system assigns a globally unique identifier. Such objects are used to model real world entities: physical objects (e.g. a person), abstract concepts (e.g. a company), relationships (e.g. marriages), or events (e.g. earthquakes). Self-named objects are usually embedded as part of system-named objects.

An important concept that must be supported is the notion of different types of classes corresponding to different types of objects. Two kinds of classes are included in the set of core concepts to be supported: Entity classes (E-classes) and Domain classes (D-classes). Instances of E-classes are independently accessible objects, i.e. system-named objects. D-classes serve mainly as type definitions for domains of values, and instances of D-classes are self-naming objects which are not stored as persistent instances. E-classes have an associated set of persistent instances.

In the example schema shown in Fig. 2, entities such as persons, courses are represented as E-classes, whereas domains of values such as age, ssn, course#, are represented as D-classes. Also, the structural and behavioral properties of an object corresponding to a TA (Teaching Assistant) are distributed across four classes (Person, Teacher, Grad Student, and TA) with the object having a corresponding instance in each class.

2.2.2 Identity

A strong notion of identity, based on tagged surrogates is used for system-named objects. Our reasons for using surrogates rather than disk addresses are discussed in Section 2.4 which deals with the implementation issues of identity and identity-address mappings. Two forms of identity, namely object identity and instance identity, are proposed.

object identity $\langle oid \rangle$: a unique p-bit integer assigned to each system-named object

instance identity $\langle iid \rangle$: a (p+p) bit integer used to identify the instantiation of a specific object in a particular class.

Thus, *instance identity* $\langle iid \rangle = \langle cid \rangle \langle oid \rangle$ where,

class identity $\langle cid \rangle$: a unique p-bit integer assigned to each class in the system

2.2.3 Associations

In data modeling, an important concept is the notion of associations or relationships among classes[SU89] and the corresponding associations among instances. XKOM supports the notion of *associations* among classes.

Two basic types of associations, namely Aggregation and Generalization [SMI77] are included in the core set of concepts to be supported.

Generalization (G): captures the super-sub class relationships among classes. Unlike in programming languages, in database systems it is important to consider the extension of a class: the set of persistent instances of the class. Consequently, the set-subset relationship among instances of super-sub classes must also be considered. The example schema illustrates such a G-hierarchy whereby a person can be a teacher and a parent.

Aggregation (A): defines a directed structural relationship between a defining class and a constituent class. It represents a named mapping from one class (the defining class) to any other class in the system. Aggregation associations are used to describe the structure of a class in terms of other classes. Again, since extension is important, such associations define the structure of an instance in relation to instances of other classes. In object-oriented terminology, aggregation associations are also referred to as attributes or instance variables. The example schema illustrates aggregation associations such as that between Person and ssn, and that between Teacher and Course.

All model level associations are internally implemented as either value attributes or object reference attributes, and this aspect is described in Section 2.3.2.

2.3 Storage Model

In KOMS, an important issue is a generalized mapping to the underlying storage layer. To facilitate such a mapping, a well-defined model of storage for kernel objects is used as a basis. Issues relating to such a storage representation are presented below.

2.3.1 Static Storage Model vs Distributed Storage Model

In implementing the structural aspects of XKOM, the storage and processing of objects in a generalization or super-sub class hierarchy is an important consideration. This determines how inherited attributes are stored and processed.

We considered two possible strategies for objects in a Generalization (G) hierarchy; a Static Storage Model (SSM), and a Distributed Storage Model (DSM). These strategies are illustrated in Fig. 3. In SSM, an object physically exists in exactly one class of the class hierarchy. Here, an object is "pushed" to the lowest class it belongs to in the hierarchy, and each object stores direct attributes

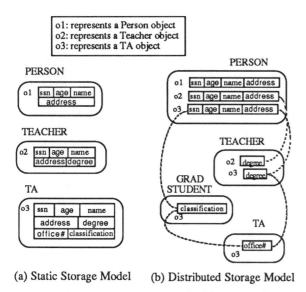

figure caption

PERSON

TEACHER

TA

(a) Static Storage Model

PERSON

TEACHER

GRAD STUDENT

TA

(b) Distributed Storage Model

Figure 3: Models of storage

of that class, and also stores statically inherited attributes from all superclasses. Thus, for example, a Teacher object contains storage slots or fields for direct attributes (degree, salary), and for inherited attributes (name, ssn). In DSM, the structural properties of an object are physically distributed into as many classes as it belongs. An instance is thus the corresponding partition of an object in a given class. Each instance only stores the attributes defined for that class. Thus, for example, a Teacher object has a representation (instance) in the Teacher class and a representation (instance) in the Person class, as well. A dotted line shows that they represent the same object.

The main advantage of SSM is that since all the attributes (direct and inherited) are clustered together, creation, update, and deletion of objects is straightforward and efficient. For retrieving all attributes of a given object, this approach is fast. In SSM, a main disadvantage is that scan-based access is inefficient, and indexing is complicated. For example, retrieving all persons whose age > 50, is not very efficient. This requires scanning all objects in the class Person, and all objects in all subclasses of Person. Similarly, indexing becomes complicated, requiring strategies such as class hierarchy indexes [KIM89, MAI86b]. A more serious shortcoming is the inability to represent an object that spans more than one branch of a hierarchy.

For example, the case where a person is a parent *and* a teacher cannot be handled.

For DSM, the main advantages are faster access for scan based access (e.g. selection), and the ability to represent the instantiation of an object across many classes (including the case where the object spans more than one branch of the generalization hierarchy). Both these factors are important in database applications, and thus we opted for using DSM. The DSM approach also allows instances to be clustered on a class basis (all instances of a class clustered together) or on a class hierarchy basis (all distributed instances of an object clustered together). In SSM, the latter technique is built in, and cannot be changed. The main disadvantage in DSM is the added complexity and overhead in creating, updating, and deleting an object that is partitioned. The cost of inserts, updates, and deletes is higher than SSM, but can be minimized by using class hierarchy clustering techniques.

2.3.2 Storage structure of a generic instance

The storage structure of a generic instance based upon DSM is shown in Fig. 4. A storage instance contains two types of attributes or fields; descriptive data attributes (value fields) and association attributes (object reference fields). Using these two types of attributes or fields allows for the uniform representation of all objects. Complex/composite objects can be represented using a combination of value and reference fields. Large uninterpreted objects can be represented using a value field called "raw" (i.e. "blobs"). Complex data types can be similarly represented using value fields.

Value Fields

Value fields are used to store primitive data types (e.g. integer, string) or D-class objects (e.g. user-defined data types)

The primitive data types that are currently supported are integers, floating point numbers, characters, and strings. It is planned to add two more primitive data types, called short_raw, and

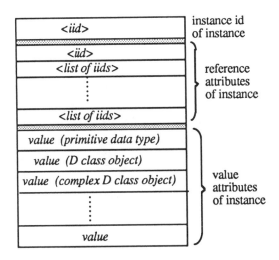

<iid>	instance id of instance
<iid>	
<list of iids>	reference attributes of instance
⋮	
<list of iids>	
value (primitive data type)	
value (D class object)	
value (complex D class object)	value attributes of instance
⋮	
value	

Figure 4: Stucture of a generic storage instance

long_raw, to accommodate user defined data types, and values that represent large/small unstructured objects (e.g. bitmaps). Short_raw represents a short (<1 block) uninterpreted sequence of bytes, and long_raw represents a large uninterpreted sequence of bytes. Management of long_raw would require techniques such as those proposed by Exodus [CAR86a] and WiSS [CHO85] (the long field manager). Also, complex D-class objects (e.g. user-defined data types) would be stored as uninterpreted bytes and are interpreted by the Type Management Module of the Kernel System.

Object Reference Fields

Object reference fields are used to support the notion of links between object instances. We implement object references via identity reference, i.e., an instance stores the identity (surrogate) of the instance it refers to. Motivation and justification of this decision is presented in Section 2.5. An object reference field is specified either as IID or as IID-ARRAY. The former supports 1:1 references and the latter supports 1:m references. Note that every instance stores its own identity using an IID field, as well.

2.4 Identity and Identity-Address mappings

While it has been argued that logical disk addresses can provide a high performance mechanism

for implementing identity, we use surrogates in order to insulate the upper layers from having to know the address formats used by storage managers. This provides data independence and allows modules in upper layers such as query processors, to be developed in a manner that easily accommodates the substitution or replacement of the storage layer. For the same reasons, object references are implemented as identity references. System-defined surrogates can provide the highly desirable features of uniqueness, immutability, and the ability of the system to define surrogates in any specialized format. In contrast, if disk addresses are used, identity is no longer immutable and disk garbage collection becomes a serious problem when objects are moved around on disk. An in-depth study of these aspects can be found in [KHO86].

The main argument against using surrogates as identity is that it involves a performance penalty due to the use of an object table to perform identity-address mappings. While this is a valid argument, we believe that surrogates serve an important purpose and instead better techniques for performing fast lookups must be developed. To perform faster lookups, the following techniques are utilized.

a. specialized formats for identity: Currently, the system uses 32 bit identifiers that are generated using a counter or the system clock. To improve the hashing performance of an object lookup, a skewing technique may be used to shuffle the positions of the identifier bits by a predefined transformation to produce another 32 bit identifier having better hash characteristics.

b. partitioned object tables: Partitioned object tables are used, with each class maintaining a partition to perform identity-address mappings for that class. The smaller size of the partition implies a faster lookup.

c. main memory object tables: Currently, if any class is referenced or an object of a class is accessed, the entire object table partition corresponding to that class is staged in memory to provide faster lookups.

2.5 Object References

In KOMS, object references are implemented as identity references. In main memory systems such as programming languages, object references are achieved through virtual memory pointers since there is no persistence. In persistent systems, either disk pointers or identity can be used to implement references. If disk pointers are used, a given application must ensure that disk pointers are correctly transformed to virtual memory pointers and vice versa. This requires techniques such as "pointer swizzling" and dual/three-way pointers. Again, to achieve data independence we use identity references.

When access to the referenced object is required, a simple lookup operator (#) is used to return the virtual memory pointer (this lookup is done once, at the beginning). The lookup operator(#) provides transparent object access: if the object is already present in main memory, the corresponding virtual memory pointer is returned, otherwise the object is retrieved from disk, and the virtual memory pointer returned. The application deals only with identity and memory pointers. It *never* sees the disk pointers, and thus does not have to keep track of disk pointers. This is shown below;

```
IID x;   /* x represents an iid */
OBJECT* y;   /* y is a virtual memory pointer */
x = select (Person, ssn = 111222333);
    /* set x to the iid of a given person */
y = #x ;
    /* y is now the virtual memory pointer of x */
```

2.6 Class System

Model reflexivity is the concept of using a given model to model itself. In this section, we present the model meta-class system: a set of meta-classes which results when a data model is used to explicitly model itself. This class system provides a specification and implementation of the data model constructs, and can be used as a powerful mechanism for achieving extensibility and parameterization. We use the term meta-class to refer to a class which is used to define model or system semantics.

Internally, there is no distinction between a class and a meta-class.

A simplified version (without many details) of these model meta-classes is shown in Fig. 5. Model constructs such as classes, associations, methods, and rules are treated as first class objects. Objects in the meta-class CLASS represent class objects, including application classes, system classes or meta-classes. Similarly, objects in the meta-class ASSOCIATION represent associations or relationships between classes, including relationships such as generalization, aggregation or any other association type. Each association has a defining class (the class that defines the relationship) and one or more constituent classes (the classes over which the relationship is defined). In binary relationships, an association has a single constituent class whereas in n-ary relationships, an association has multiple constituent classes. Objects in the meta-class METHOD represent method objects and objects in the meta-class RULE represent rule objects. The root of this class hierarchy is the class OBJECT, which indicates that everything in the model is an object. The meta-classes E-CLASS OBJECT and D-CLASS OBJECT, represent the fact that every object in the model is either a system-named object or a self-named object. The class CLASS is sub-classed into classes E-CLASS and D-CLASS to represent class objects corresponding to E-classes and D-classes respectively. Similarly, the class ASSOCIATION is sub-classed into classes GENERALIZATION and AGGREGATION to represent association objects corresponding to the two types of associations, namely, Generalization and Aggregation. Other association types can be added to the model by creating subclasses of the class ASSOCIATION and/or any of its subclasses.

The meta-class CLASS is an important meta-class, and is described further. It represents the concept of a class in the data model. Every class has a className, a classID, a set of Associations, a set of Methods, and a set of Rules. The set of Associations associated with a class can include G-associations, A-associations or any other form of Association. For example, if the data model allows a class to have more than one superclass

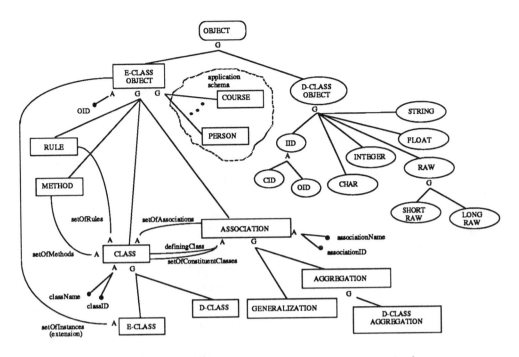

Figure 5: Modeling the model (Model Reflexivity)

(i.e. multiple inheritance), then this is reflected in the model meta-schema by this class participating in G-associations with all its superclasses. Other meta-classes can be similarly described.

When using the model to model itself, a *bootstrap* process is required to initially populate the model schema with information of the model itself. To bootstrap the meta-class CLASS, the meta-class CLASS must be first defined, and the first object that must be instantiated in this class is the object that represents the meta-class CLASS itself. This is the first object in the system. For the sake of clarity, we will term this first object as the CLASS-object. The CLASS-object is the only object in the system whose class-id is identical to its object-id; the instance-id is thus a concatenation of two 32 bit integers, both of which have the same value. In the model of the model, the attribute called SetOfInstances defined for E-CLASS, represents the fact that all E Classes have an extension. The meta-class CLASS is also an E-class, since instances of class CLASS represent system-named objects. Hence, CLASS-object must also instantiate the meta-class E-CLASS. The extension of the meta-class CLASS is represented by the setOfInstances attribute of the instance in E-CLASS corresponding to the CLASS-object. Thus, if we it-

erate the extension of the meta-class CLASS, we would get all classes in the system. The bootstrap process proceeds by setting up the class hierarchy that defines the model, setting up the first object of class CLASS, and then instantiating meta-classes such as CLASS, ASSOCIATION, etc., with all necessary objects that describe the model itself (i.e. classes and associations that describe the model). Once this is done, the model is ready for use by an application.

An initial version of this model meta-architecture has been completed. A bootstrap process has been defined in which the C++ programming language is used to perform bootstrapping. The meta-classes METHOD and RULE have not yet been implemented, and are currently under investigation. The meta-model schema component that deals with user-defined complex data types (e.g. matrices) has not been investigated as yet.

2.7 Model Extensibility

One requirement for the Kernel Object Management System is that the layer it represents be extensible upwards to support different application domains and data models. Model Extensibility encompasses data model extensions such as various forms of inheritance, abstract data types, parameterized classes, user-defined class and association types, etc.

Model Extensibility is achieved by modifying the model meta-classes: the model meta-class system serves not only as a specification of the user data model constructs but also as a basis for the implementation of such constructs. Methods (functions) and/or rules defined in the meta-classes are used to implement data model constructs. We illustrate some scenarios with respect to Fig. 5. For example, modifying the specification and implementation of the meta-class CLASS causes the semantics of a class in the data model to change. Consider the case where the meta-class CLASS does not have the attributes setOfRules and setOfMethods. This implies a model that is structurally object-oriented but not behaviorally object-oriented [DIT86]. Additionally, if the setOfAssociations attribute of CLASS is constrained to only contain objects from D-CLASS AGGREGATION, this implies a model that has no Generalization or E-class Aggregation associations (e.g. the relational model). Similarly, appropriate constraints on the setOfAssociations attribute can determine whether a class has one or more superclasses, i.e. single or multiple inheritance.

Two aspects of such model extensibility are of main interest to us, namely, *class extensibility*, and *association extensibility*. We also note that another important consequence (actually, a side-effect) of modeling the model is that it automatically provides a basis or schema for the data dictionary (catalog). In this case, the data dictionary maintains not only meta-information of the application, but also of the data model and system architecture. Thus, the model itself, the meta-data, and application are all uniformly represented as objects using the o-o paradigm.

Class and Association Extensibility

Class Extensibility is a form of extensibility whereby a model can be extended to provide new types or categories of classes. Similarly, Association Extensibility is a form of extensibility whereby a model can be extended to provide new types or

categories of associations or relationships among classes. To provide such extensibility, we exploit the parameterization of classes and associations at a meta level.

To illustrate class extensibility, consider the two basic types or categories of classes in XKOM: E-classes and D-classes. One important distinction is that E-classes explicitly store an extension. Consequently, operations such as select (described in Section 3), can be defined and implemented in the (meta) class E-CLASS. If a class called Person is defined as a subclass of E-CLASS OBJECT, then the class Person inherits methods that apply to all E-class objects. However, methods defined in E-CLASS apply to the Person class object (the object representing the class Person), since the Person class object is an instance of the class E-CLASS. Thus, it is possible to send a message called select to the instance of E-CLASS that represents the Person class. Class Extensibility is carried out as follows. If a new class type called X is required, then XCLASS OBJECT is defined as a subclass of Object, and XCLASS is defined as a subclass of CLASS. The semantics of X classes are described by defining XCLASS in an appropriate manner. Existing class types (e.g. E-class, D-class) may also be extended by sub-classing the meta-classes corresponding to such existing class types.

Similarly, we illustrate the notion of Association Extensibility. In [SMI77], Aggregation and Generalization, have been recognized as fundamental types of relationships or associations. For Aggregation and Generalization, the explicit modeling of such association types is illustrated in Fig. 5. Similar to class extensibility, it is possible to add a new association type or extend an existing association type by sub-classing. Thus, the model can be extended by defining customized association or relationship types to fit a particular domain.

Our experience with such meta-classes indicates that specifying customized semantics is easily facilitated by specifying constraints or rules in these meta-classes. These constraints may govern the processing of object instances belonging to particular class types and object references corresponding to specific association types. Thus, we plan to explore the specification of high-level declarative rules for expressing extended semantics in order to achieve model extensibility. Such rules will be defined for meta classes such as CLASS, E-CLASS, ASSOCIATION, AGGREGATION and other classes representing class and association types.

3 Object Processing

3.1 Processing Requirements

The processing requirements of KOMS are primarily based on the needs of client modules such as query and rule processors, transaction managers, etc., in the upper layers. To support such client processing needs, KOMS must support *set-oriented* processing, *association-based* processing and *value-based* processing.

3.2 Processing Issues

In database applications, as evidenced by the nature of database query languages, a key requirement is set-oriented processing. As such, KOMS provides a well-defined and generic interface to clients in the upper layers in the form of a set of kernel object operations. These basic, semantically meaningful, and *set-oriented* operators are based on the small set of core object model constructs described previously, and are used to perform inserts, updates, deletes and retrievals on kernel objects.

In KOMS, the interface serves as access methods which (1) are at the class level (operations involve the set of objects belonging to a single class), (2) at most, require a single scan, and (3) are set-oriented. We expect operations that span multiple classes to be carried out by access methods in the clients of KOMS. The implementation of the interface uses the underlying model of storage objects described in Section 2.3, and has been carried out with a view towards extensibility, i.e. the addition of extra operators to the basic set provided. For retrievals, two important form of access are provided: *association-based access*, and *value-based access*.

3.2.1 Association-based access

A key feature in object-oriented databases (unlike in relational systems), is the notion of association queries. Such queries compute patterns of associations or relationships among instances of object classes.

Consider the following query;

*Teacher * Course*

This query computes all objects of class Teacher that are associated with (i.e. related to) objects of class Course. The star (∗) indicates "associated with" This requires KOMS to iterate the set of kernel objects of class Person, and determine all object references to class Course. Such processing is set-oriented, and requires a single scan of the instances of a class.

KOMS incorporates access methods (structures, indexes and algorithms) to support such association-based access. The following factors have been a consideration: (a) the processing of object references is set-oriented, (b) the nature of the processing is navigational, and (c) inverse object references may be required and must be optimized.

In this respect, KOMS offers a functionality that is different from that of many other existing object-based systems. Also provided is the capability of determining non-associations, i.e. objects of one class that are not associated with objects of another class. In comparison with relational systems, a join-operation is a value-based match on specific columns. Unlike relational systems, associations can be considered as a set of pre-joins (links) which for a given class can be accessed in a single scan since links are explicitly stored. For the same reason, it is also possible to compute non-associations easily and efficiently. Our work on a pattern based query language (OQL) and a pattern-based constraint language illustrating the use of association-based processing can be found in [ALA89, SU91].

3.2.2 Value-based access

In object-oriented databases it is also necessary to perform value based processing on descriptive data attributes or value fields of objects. This includes processing of complex data types such as matrices.

Consider the following query;

$Teacher[select - cond] * Course$

This query illustrates a combination of value-based access and association-based access. It computes all instances in the class Teacher satisfying a selection condition (placed on the value fields of teacher instances) which are associated with instances of class Course. The value-based access refers to the ability to determine which instances of the class Teacher satisfy the value based selection condition. If the condition is $[age = 35]$, a point access is desired and a scan may be necessary if there is no index on age. If the condition is $[age > 35]$, a partial scan may be required. For more complex selection conditions such as $[age > 35$ AND $degree = "Ph.D"]$, an index (if available) must be considered or full scans must be performed. Thus, *direct access, partial scans or full scans* are needed to support value-based processing. Traditional notions of indexing, and sorting can be used.

3.3 Interface

The set of operations that comprise the interface of KOMS can be broadly classified into five categories: create, insert, update, delete, and retrieve. Currently, all retrieve operations are set-oriented, while the others are specified either as instance-level or object-level operations. Operations at the instance level simply deal with the semantics of a single instance within a given class, while those at the object level deal with the semantics of an object whose instances are distributed across a generalization hierarchy or class lattice.

3.3.1 Syntax and informal description of operators

Category #1: Create

1. *create_Object ():* Creates a new oid. This operation is called when a new object is created, invokes the necessary identity management routines, and returns a new oid.

Category #2: Insert

2. *insert_Instance (⟨class⟩, ⟨oid⟩, ⟨arg-list⟩):* Inserts an instance of object ⟨oid⟩ into a class ⟨class⟩. The operation inserts the instance into the Object Table partition of the given class, sets the value fields of the instance, sets the association attributes, and finally, inserts the instance in the database. An argument list ⟨arg-list⟩ specifies association and value attributes as ⟨name-value⟩ pairs. Unlike insert_Object, the argument list cannot specify any inherited attributes. Association attributes (except G) are specified by using oids as values. G-association attributes cannot be specified, since these attributes are automatically maintained by the system as it enforces the partitioning of the object along class boundaries.

3. *insert_Object (⟨class⟩, ⟨oid⟩, ⟨arg-list⟩):* Inserts an instance of object ⟨oid⟩ into a class ⟨class⟩, and corresponding instances into all appropriate classes in the superclass hierarchy of the class ⟨class⟩. This operation is used when inserting an object for the first time in a class hierarchy or lattice, and when inserting an existing object in another branch or a lower level of the class hierarchy. Starting with the given class ⟨class⟩, the operation recursively navigates up each branch of the super-class hierarchy and invokes the insert_Instance operation for each class in the hierarchy, beginning from the top-most level reached down to the given class. The algorithm corresponding to this operation implements the partitioning of the structural properties of an object along class boundaries. The argument list specifies association and value attributes as ⟨name-value⟩ pairs, including inherited attributes.

Category #3: Update

4. *update_Instance (⟨class⟩, ⟨oid⟩, ⟨arg-list⟩):* Updates attributes of the instance of object ⟨oid⟩ in class ⟨class⟩. An argument list ⟨arg-list⟩ specifies attributes to be updated. The ⟨arg-list⟩ contains (direct) attributes from the specified class only (no inherited attributes), and association attributes (except G) may be specified.

5. *update_Object (⟨class⟩, ⟨oid⟩, ⟨arg-list⟩)*: Updates attributes of the instance of object ⟨oid⟩ in the given class ⟨class⟩ and of any instance of ⟨oid⟩ in the super-class hierarchy of ⟨class⟩. Starting with the given class, the operation determines which instances of the specified object in the superclass hierarchy of the given class are to be updated. Then, update_Instance operation is invoked (with the appropriate argument list) in all classes containing instances that are to be updated. The argument list ⟨arg-list⟩ specifies attributes to be updated. The ⟨arg-list⟩ may contain inherited attributes, and association attributes (except G) are also allowed.

6. *associate (⟨class1⟩, ⟨oid⟩, ⟨class2⟩, ⟨oid-list⟩, ⟨assoc-name⟩)*: Associates the instance of object ⟨oid⟩ in class ⟨class1⟩ with instances of objects ⟨oid-list⟩ of class ⟨class2⟩. This operation serves as a mechanism to set or update the association or object reference attribute of a kernel object. It ensures that when objects are associated, two-way(inverse) binary associations (or links) are created. The ⟨assoc-name⟩ specifies the name of the schema level association from ⟨class1⟩ to ⟨class2⟩.

7. *dissociate (⟨class1⟩, ⟨oid⟩, ⟨class2⟩, ⟨oid-list⟩, ⟨assoc-name⟩)*: Dissociates (unlinks) the association that exists between the instance of object ⟨oid⟩ in class ⟨class1⟩ to the instances of objects ⟨oid-list⟩ of class ⟨class2⟩. This operator ensures that when objects are dissociated, the binary, two-way(inverse) association between objects is updated accordingly. The ⟨assoc-name⟩ specifies the name of the schema level association from ⟨class1⟩ to ⟨class2⟩.

Category #4: Delete

8. *delete_Instance (⟨class⟩, ⟨oid⟩)*: Deletes the instance of object ⟨oid⟩ in the class ⟨class⟩. The operation unlinks this object instance from all other object instances, removes the entry corresponding to this instance in the object table segment of the given class, and then removes the the instance removed from the

database.

9. *delete_Object (⟨class⟩, ⟨oid⟩)*: Deletes all instances of a given object ⟨oid⟩ in the given class ⟨class⟩ and in all classes in the subclass hierarchy of class ⟨class⟩. This operation is used to remove all instances of an object starting at a specified level and below in the class hierarchy. If an object has a single root class, and this operation is invoked at the root class, the net effect is the removal of all instances of the given object. The operation determines the subclass hierarchy rooted at the given class, and invokes the delete_Instance operator for all classes in the subclass hierarchy, beginning from the bottom most class in the hierarchy up to the given class. The algorithm that implements this operation is based on the partitioning of an object along class boundaries.

10. *destroy_Object (⟨oid⟩)*: Deletes all instances of a given object ⟨oid⟩. The operation proceeds by determining the root classes of the given object. The delete_Object operation is then invoked for each root class.

Category #5: Retrieve

11. *retrieve (⟨class⟩, ⟨oid-list⟩, ⟨attr-list⟩)*: Retrieves a set of specified objects ⟨oid-list⟩ from the class ⟨class⟩. If a list of attributes ⟨attr-list⟩ is specified, only these selected attributes of the objects are projected out. If the ⟨attr-list⟩ is specified as ⟨all⟩, then all attributes are projected out. Inherited attributes may be specified. If the ⟨oid-list⟩ is specified as ⟨all⟩, then oids of all instances of the given class ⟨class⟩ are used as the given oid-list. The operation returns a set of partial objects, where a partial object is a projection of the original object on the specified attributes.

12. *select (⟨class⟩, ⟨select-cond⟩)*: Selects a set of instances from the class ⟨class⟩, which satisfy the selection condition ⟨select-cond⟩. The selection condition is specified as a conjunction or disjunction of ⟨name op value⟩ triplets,

259

where op is a comparison operator. The attributes used in the selection condition must be value or descriptive attributes (inherited attributes are allowed). Returns a set of oids that satisfy the condition.

13. *star* (*(class1)*, *(oid-list)*, *(class2)*, *(assoc-name)*): Retrieves from the class ⟨class1⟩, those objects in ⟨oid-list⟩ which have object references to any objects in the class ⟨class2⟩, through the association ⟨assoc-name⟩. If the ⟨oid-list⟩ is specified as ⟨all⟩, then all objects of ⟨class1⟩ having object references to any object in the class ⟨class2⟩ are retrieved. Returns a list of *oid pairs*, each pair signifying an object of ⟨class1⟩ which is associated with a particular object of ⟨class2⟩.

14. *non_star* (*(class1)*, *(oid-list)*, *(class2)*, *(assoc-name)*): Retrieves from the class ⟨class1⟩, those objects in ⟨oid-list⟩ that have no object references to any object in the class ⟨class2⟩. The ⟨assoc-name⟩ specifies the name of the schema level association from ⟨class1⟩ to ⟨class2⟩. If the ⟨oid-list⟩ is specified as ⟨all⟩, then all objects of ⟨class1⟩ having no object references to any object in ⟨class2⟩ are retrieved. Returns a set of oids.

4 System Implementation

The system configuration of KOMS as a layer on top of a storage management layer is shown in Fig. 6, and components of KOMS are shown within this layer. Components of KOMS have been implemented in C++, and use the persistent facilities provided by ONTOS in the underlying storage layer. Details of this implementation can be found in [LAW91]. In the following section, we describe system modules and components via schema diagrams or class hierarchies.

4.1 System Extensibility

System Extensibility is the ability to modify or extend the modules that comprise the software architecture of the system. System extensibility is

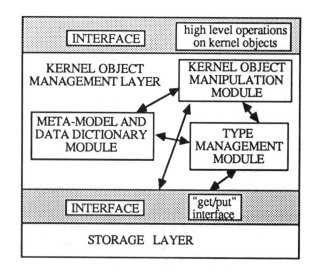

Figure 6: Configuration of KOMS

easily achieved if the software architecture of a system is developed as an *open, modular, and extensible* architecture with *well-defined interfaces*.

We develop a system architecture schema; a schema comprising system software modules and their associations (interactions) with one another. Consequently, software modules and interfaces are modeled and implemented as classes and objects for ease of extension. Thus, files, buffers, file managers, buffer managers, query processors, data dictionaries, object managers, etc., can be modeled as classes and objects. A software module is specified using several classes, and is implemented using member functions or methods in these classes. Each module has one or more interface classes.

4.1.1 System Modules and Interface Classes

An *interface class* is a special type of class that represents a particular interface to a group of other classes. For example, a module that comprises 5 classes has a *combined* interface equal to the sum of the interfaces of each class (say 30 methods). Collectively, these 5 classes represent a module which may have a much smaller interface (e.g. 6 methods). We take the *collective* (not combined) interface of these group of classes and package it into a class called an *interface class of the module*. A module thus serves as a higher level of system abstraction than a class.

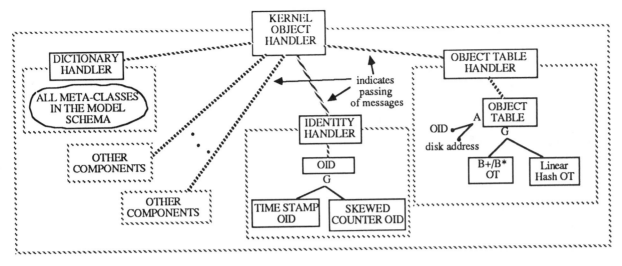

Figure 7: Several System Modules

4.1.2 Example Modules

We use some simplified examples from our system, shown in Fig. 7, to illustrate the concept of modules and interface classes.

In the first example, identity and two currently supported forms of identity, time-stamp and skewed counter, are modeled as a class and two subclasses respectively. A single interface class, ID-Handler, is used to access these different forms of identity. Thus, it it possible to easily extend the notion of identity. The second related example is that of identity-address mappings or object Tables. Two variants of object tables, a Linear Hash version and a B+/B* index version, are shown as subclasses. The class OT-Handler serves as an interface.

A more complex example is the meta-data or data-dictionary module. The classes that comprise the structure of the data dictionary are the same (meta) classes shown in Fig. 5. Interface to the data dictionary is via the DicHandler class. An external module uses the DicHandler class by first creating a DicHandler object, and then sending it a message to invoke the appropriate interface function. This is illustrated below:

```
DicHandler *aDicHandler;
aDicHandler → getAllSuperClassesOf( "TA" );
```

The action taken by the corresponding method in the DicHandler class is as follows. It examines the arguments list, and "unpacks" the argument list into various objects (belonging to classes that comprise the module). Messages are sent to these objects, and the actual method is implemented in the classes that comprise the module. The Interface class, in effect plays the role of a "message controller", and directs messages appropriately. This is illustrated (using C++ like code) below:

```
DicHandler::getAllSuperClassesOf(char* name){
    IID x;
    CLASS* y;
    KernelObjectHandler *h1;
/* unpack argument into appropriate objects */
    x = h1 → select( "CLASS", name="TA" );
        /* x is now the iid of the Class TA object */
/* get virtual pointer to TA class object */
    y = #x;
/* send message to appropriate object */
    y→ getAllSuperClassesOf();
    }
```

The actual computation of the result is done by the function *getAllSuperClassesOf()* in the meta-class CLASS. The above example also illustrates the use of the KernelObjectHandler class which represents the interface operators described in Section 3.3.

Conclusions

In this paper, we have described our experiences with designing and implementing a Kernel Object Management System (KOMS): an intermediate layer of a layered extensible object-oriented knowledge base management system called OSAM*.KBMS/X. The issues of building a generalized system have been addressed by proposing an intermediate layer with upward and downward extensibility instead of building a monolithic system. A deliberate attempt has been made to use a set of core object modeling constructs as a basis for the system. The system has been implemented with extensibility as a key goal.

By using the eXtensible Kernel Object Model (XKOM) to model itself, a well-defined model schema has been developed, which can be used by a Database Implementor (DBI) to generate customized model semantics. An initial version of this model meta-architecture has been implemented. Similarly, by modeling the system architecture using classes and objects, a well-defined schema (i.e. description and implementation) of the system architecture has been developed, which can be used by the DBI to extend the system. All current modules of KOMS have been implemented using such an extensible approach. In terms of extension, we foresee that with the standardization of classes and objects representing software components, system extension would involve *system synthesis* from pre-existing software modules. This can form the basis for rapid prototyping of software systems. Rapid prototyping is planned as one of the applications of KOMS.

We have also identified and explored several concepts that relate to the notion of core object modeling constructs. A model of storage using a partitioning of objects along class boundaries has been developed. Correspondingly, a generalized storage structure for object instances has been defined. The management of associations (or relationships) is a key issue that has been addressed by strong support for object references. A set of basic object manipulation operators have been identified and implemented.

Currently, as part of the OSAM*.KBMS/X architecture, we are extending this concept to the design and implementation of an Adjacency-Matrix-based Query Processor and an Integrated Rule Processor as upper layer clients of KOMS.

We expect to follow a similar system development approach, coupling a generalized approach with extensibility. We plan to extend the meta-architecture concept to support queries, rules, methods, etc. as first class objects. The results achieved with our current effort have been encouraging and lead us to believe that a similar approach to the development of the upper-layer software will provide us with the expected results in terms of modularity and extensibility.

Acknowledgements

This research is partially supported by the National Science Foundation (Grant# DMC-8814989), IBM (Grant# S919FM81), and the Florida High Technology and Industry Council (Grant# UPN 90090708)

Bibliography

[ALA89] A. M. Alashqur, S. Y. W. Su, and H. Lam, 'OQL: A Query Language for Manipulating Object-oriented databases,' 15th VLDB, 1989.

[AND87] T. Andrews, and C. Harris, 'Combining Language and Database Advances in an Object-oriented Development Environment,' ACM OOPSLA, 1987.

[AST76] M. Astrahan, et al. 'System R: Relational Approach to Database Management,' ACM Trans. on Database Systems, 1(2), June 1976.

[ATK89] M.P. Atkinson, et al. 'The Object-Oriented Database System Manifesto,' Altair Technical Report 30-89, Rocquencourt, France, Aug. 1989.

[BAN87] J. Banerjee, et al. 'Data Model Issues for Object- oriented Applications,' ACM Trans. on Office Information Systems, 5(1), 1987.

[BAT88] D.S.Batory, et al. 'GENESIS: An Extensible Database Management System,' IEEE Trans. on Software Engineering, 14(11), 1988.

[CAR86a] M.J. Carey, et al. 'Object and File Management in the EXODUS Extensible Database System,' 12th VLDB, August 1986.

[CAR86b] M.J. Carey, et al. 'The Architecture of the Exodus Extensible DBMS,' International

Workshop on Object-Oriented Database Systems, Sept. 1986.

[CHO85] H. T. Chou, et al. 'Design and Implementation of the Wisconsin Storage System,' Software - Practice and Experience, 15(10), Oct. 1985.

[COP84] G. Copeland, and D. Maier, 'Making Smalltalk a Database System,' ACM SIGMOD, 1984.

[DIT86] K.R. Dittrich, 'Object-Oriented Database Systems: The Notions and the Issues,' International Workshop on Object-Oriented Database Systems, 1986.

[FIS87] D. Fishman, et al. 'Iris: An Object Oriented Database Management System,' ACM Trans. on Office Information Systems, 5(1), Jan. 1986.

[HAM81] M. Hammer, and D. McLeod, 'Database Description with SDM: A Semantic Data Model,' ACM Trans. on Database Systems, 6(3), 1981.

[HULL87] R. Hull, and R. King, 'Semantic Database Modeling: Survey, Applications and Research Issues,' ACM Computing Surveys, 19(3), 1987.

[KHO86] S. Khoshfian, and G. Copeland, 'Object Identity,' ACM OOPSLA, 1987.

[KIM89] W. Kim, et al., 'Indexing techniques for object-oriented databases,' in *Object-Oriented Concepts, Databases, and Applications*, W. Kim and F. Lochovsky (Ed.), Addison Wesley, 1989.

[LAW91] S.F. Law, 'Object-oriented Design and Implementation of a Kernel Object Manager,' M.S. Thesis, University of Florida, May 1991.

[LEC88] C. Lecluse, et al., 'O_2, an object oriented data model', ACM SIGMOD, 1988.

[LOO86] M.E.S. Loomis, 'Data Modeling - The IDEF1X Technique,' IEEE Communications, March 1986.

[MAI86a] D. Maier, et al. 'Development of an Object-Oriented DBMS,' ACM OOPSLA, 1987.

[MAI86b] D. Maier, and J. Stein, 'Indexing in an Object-oriented DBMS,' International Workshop on Object-Oriented Database Systems, 1986.

[MIT89] M.J. Mitchell, et al. 'Data Model Development and Validation for Product Data Exchange,' Technical Report, National Institute of Standards and Technology, 1989.

[ONT90] Ontologic Inc., ONTOS: Object Database, System Documentation, Version 1.5, 1990.

[PAU87] H. -B. Paul, et al. 'Architecture and Implementation of the Darmstadt Database Kernel System,' ACM SIGMOD, 1987.

[SCH86] P. Schwarz, et al. 'Extensibility in the Starburst Database System,' International Workshop on Object-Oriented Database Systems, 1986.

[SHI81] D. Shipman, 'The Functional Data Model and the Data Language DAPLEX,' ACM Trans. on Database Systems, 6(1), 1981.

[SKA86] A. Skarra, S. Zdonik, and S. Reiss, 'An Object Server for an Object Oriented Database System,' International Workshop Object-Oriented Database Systems, 1986.

[SMI77] J. Smith, and C. Smith, 'Database Abstractions: Aggregation and Generalization,' ACM Trans. on Database Systems, 2(2), 1977.

[STO86] M. Stonebraker, and L.A. Rowe, 'The Design of POSTGRES,' ACM SIGMOD, 1986.

[SU89] S. Y. W. Su, V. Krishnamurthy, and H. Lam, 'An Object-oriented Semantic Association Model (OSAM*)' in AI in Industrial Engineering and Manufacturing: Theoretical Issues and Applications, Kumara, S., et al., (editors), American Institute of Industrial Engineering, 1989.

[SU91] S. Y. W. Su, and A. Alashqur, 'A Pattern-based Constraint Specification Language for Object-oriented Databases,' Proc. of Spring COMPCON, 1991.

[VEL89] F. Velez, G. Bernard, and V. Darnis, 'The O_2 Object Manager, an overview,' 15th VLDB, 1989.

[VER82] G.M.A. Verheijen, and J. Van Bekkum, 'NIAM: An Information Analysis Method,' in Information Systems Design Methodologies: A Comparative Review, T.W. Olle, H.G. Sol, Verrijn-Stuart (Ed.), North Holland, 1982.

[ZAN83] C. Zaniolo, 'The Database Language GEM,' ACM SIGMOD, 1983.

The Economics of Software Reuse
(PANEL)

Martin L. Griss, *Hewlett-Packard Laboratories,* (moderator)
Sam S. Adams, *Knowledge Systems Corporation*
Howard Baetjer, Jr., *Agorics Project, George Mason University*
Brad J. Cox, *Information Age Consulting*
Adele Goldberg, *ParcPlace Systems*

Abstract

We discuss several models of a "software components" industry and issues concerning effective reuse and object-oriented programming, and speculate on how (and whether) a vigorous components market will arise. A "software industrial revolution" requires an infrastructure, a "reuse mindset", and the treatment of software as an asset.

Background

It is widely believed that systematic application of reuse to prototyping, development, and maintenance is one of the most effective ways to significantly improve the software process, shorten time-to-market, improve software quality and application consistency, and reduce development and maintenance costs[1, 2, 3]. One of the dreams of the software engineering community is to have widely used libraries of reusable software[4, 5]. Despite the fact that many people believe that a vigorous market in software libraries would soon arise, the movement in this direction has been disappointing. The only widely used object-oriented libraries are those for data-structures and user-interface frameworks, which Smalltalk has had for over a decade.

Non-object-oriented numeric, statistical, graphics and data-structures libraries are also widely used. Many companies are developing proprietary software libraries, but a significant market in reusable software is yet to appear. This is largely because effective reuse depends on more socioeconomic than technical factors[5, 6], while most workers have concentrated on technology. Too few software developers value or appreciate the effort required to produce a quality library, and so a combination of inexperience and NIH make them unwilling to pay for good quality software. While (improved) object-oriented technology seems to be a very promising vehicle for realizing the dream, and recent work in domain analysis, object-oriented methods, library technology and architectural frameworks should lead to a consistent methodology for domain specific reuse, there remains a significant effort. People need to learn the most effective way of using[7], investing in and performing cost/benefit analysis on the technology, and in setting up processes and incentives that encourage appropriate change.

The panel will illuminate the issues, identify problems, and suggest future directions. We will address the questions:

- *Will a viable software components industry arise, and if so when and how?*

- *What impediments need to be overcome and how?*

- *Is it possible to develop a marketplace for reusable software? How do we pay for it?*

- *How do companies that develop reusable software for internal use pay for it?*
- *Are economics of reuse within a corporation different from those across corporations?*

Sam S. Adams

Providing an appropriate infrastructure for the distribution and management of reusable software is one of the most critical factors in the successful exploitation of object technology on a large scale within an organization. Since reusable software components and frameworks become more valuable as assets as they become more widely used, appropriate mechanisms must be provided to ensure and increase the quality and value of reusable software.

Reusable Software as an Asset: Economic issues have always had a strong influence on the evolution of software development practices. One historical effect of the evolution of software development in organizations is the view that the resulting software is an extremely expensive end product that constantly requires costly maintenance to retain its effectiveness - 80% of the cost of a traditional software system now comes from the maintenance and enhancement of delivered systems. The "waterfall" model of software development was meant to optimize scarce and expensive programming resources and to reduce maintenance costs by providing better initial system specifications. While reuse is sought after in the engineering community, the economic and organizational effects of reusable software as a financial asset have not been widely investigated. Most software organizations have developed management structures and engineering practices that consider the executable end-product to be a short-lived commodity that will quickly be replaced by the next revision or system. Reusable software must be treated like an asset, and managed as a value-retaining medium that can benefit from investment and provide both short term and long term financial dividends. Organizations already have elaborate and successful mechanisms and policies for the management of corporate assets such as facilities, machinery, computer systems, and personnel. Just as they spend a large percentage of their revenue on increasing the value of their other assets, investment in the quality and reusability of corporate software assets should be considered a high priority. This will be profitable, however, only if an effective mechanism exists for the collection, refinement, quality assessment and distribution of reusable software. A reuse-based infrastructure must be designed to support these activities, providing a foundation for the tracking, reporting and management of the costs and benefits of the development, testing, maintenance and reuse of an organization's software assets.

Developing a Reuse Mindset: From a software asset perspective, there is an important multiplier to consider for any given change to a software component, termed by Lynn Fogwell the "reuse factor": every change (good or bad) to a piece of reusable software must be considered as to its impact on all future users of the software, not just the current project. Even a small renaming of a method or function to be more "intention revealing" can have dramatic effects over the lifetime of the software. For example, most C programmers use very terse names for variables and functions, even though the negative effect this practice has on code readability and reuse is well documented. When something this seemingly trivial can have dramatic long term effects, how much more should the "reuse factor" be considered on major changes such as refactoring an object class hierarchy? We must continue to (incrementally) strive to increase the value of our software assets with constant consideration of both the short term and long term effects. In a large organization, there may be several libraries of reusable software, each maintained for a specific user group. Since reusable software should eventually migrate hierarchically to corporate libraries that span departments and projects, every library manager should accept only high quality software. Only the more general, broadly reusable software gets "marketed" or submitted to higher-level corporate libraries. Each "level" can incrementally assess the software quality by local standards, and provide a pathway to promote the best and most widely reusable software to the largest user base, maximizing an organization's return on its investment. It is critical that an organization explicitly recognize the point in the migration of reusable software where the greatest impact occurs. This is where a piece of software (method, class, subsystem, or design information) is exposed to a larger community. This is where costs can be estimated for the integration, education, and maintenance of the software, including any rework required to meet standards, where a financial cost/benefits analysis should take place, and where various design, coding and documentation standards should be checked and enforced, and any potential conflicts determined and analyzed.

Software Engineering in a Pervasive Reuse Environment: For the past five years, Knowledge Systems has had extensive experience in the reuse of object-oriented software across many different projects and problem domains, using Smalltalk. The Smalltalk programmer starts new projects with hundreds of reusable classes at his disposal, incorporating vendor-supplied and locally developed and acquired libraries. Unlike traditional environments, reuse is a fact of life in Smalltalk, permeating every method and class. This has provoked much research into the implications. Experienced Smalltalk programmers enjoy great productivity and freedom, but are confronted with serious new challenges in the management of reusable components and the often tangled configuration dependencies that arise in organization-wide reuse. Analysis and design activities are also markedly affected, but most methodologies for the design of object oriented systems have very little to say about the effect of reuse, and usually assume a clean slate to begin a design activity.

Software development organizations will be affected in many ways when reuse becomes a pervasive daily concern. If we are to exploit the economic advantages of object-oriented technology today, as well as in the future, we must not only consider reusable software an asset, but treat it as one.

Howard Baetjer, Jr.

A variety of active markets in software components will emerge over the next few years. Although obstacles to such markets are great, the rewards to overcoming them are greater. As our investigations of the development of other industries suggest, profit-seeking entrepreneurs will develop new kinds of markets and market institutions to answer the challenge. For instance:

How may buyers find out what is available? Electronic markets hold tremendous promise for improving communication across huge areas. Costly search of passive repositories will be replaced with active matching of buyers and sellers.

What will induce a larger supply of components for sale? Supply will increase as communication and compatibility problems ease. With lower transaction costs, developers in specialized domains who customize proprietary components will expand to new market niches. As experience increases and object-oriented technologies mature, some firms will "productize" their proprietary libraries.

How may component developers be assured of getting paid for value they provide their customers? Examinations of other industries highlight the almost infinite number of possible property right arrangements and pricing strategies. Finding those most appropriate to the special nature of software represents one of the greatest challenges facing the entrepreneur. Already, a variety of innovative pricing schemes, including bundling strategies, and charge-per-use (rather than charge-per-copy) are being developed for software. While no one innovation promises a perfect fix, various combinations of these ideas seem more than adequate to support component markets.

Brad J. Cox

The possibility of a software industrial revolution, in which programmers stop coding everything from scratch and begin assembling applications from well-stocked catalogs of reusable software compo-

266

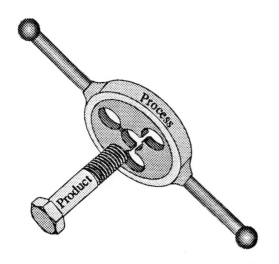

Whereas mature engineering domains define standard products and expect diverse processes to be used in making them, in software we do the reverse, defining standard languages and methodologies from which standard components are to automatically ensue.

nents, is an enduring, but elusive, dream. Although object-oriented programming systems, languages, and architectures have brought this dream closer, common-sense organizational principles like reusability and interchangeability are still the exception rather than the rule.

According to Thomas Kuhn, science does not progress continuously, by gradually extending an established paradigm. It proceeds as a series of revolutionary upheavals. The discovery of unreconcilable shortcomings in an established paradigm produces a crisis that may lead to a revolution in which the established paradigm is overthrown and replaced.

The software crisis is such a crisis, and the software industrial revolution is such a revolution. The familiar process-centric paradigm of software engineering, where progress is measured by advancement of the software development process, entered the crisis stage 23 years ago when the term, software crisis, was first coined. The paradigm that may launch the Information Age is the same one that launched the Manufacturing Age 200 years ago. It is a product-centric paradigm in which progress is measured by the accretion of standard, interchangeable, reusable components, and only secondarily by advancing the processes used

to build them.

The consumer-side benefits of reusable code are easy to demonstrate, if not to grasp in practice. But what makes reuse beneficial to those who produce it, given that reusable code costs far more to build and distribute than ordinary code? What is the economically robust basis for code reuse in particular, and for commercial interchange of intellectual properties in general?

By intellectual properties I encompass wisdom, entertainment, and information in general, along with software components of every granularity; from objects as large as entire applications to those as small as Software-IC's, string compare subroutines, and even macros.

This question has arisen repeatedly whenever technology impinges upon some established way of packaging intellectual properties. Each time it has been answered through a combination of technical, legal and economic initiatives.

Does the ease with which software can be replicated involve fundamentally different issues than those that digital music recording, or gramophones, or radio and television, posed to the entertainment industry? Or that character recognition technology, or Xerography, or photography, posed to the publishing industry? Or that numerically-controlled machine tools, or pattern lathes, or standards for interchangeable parts, posed to manufacturing? Or that the printing press posed to the knowledge workers of Guttenberg's day?

Mankind's response to technological change occurs in a stereotyped manner throughout history. The establishment usually resists strenuously, but consumer demand wins in the end. Occasionally establishments resist to the point that they are replaced by outsiders that were never successful with the old paradigm. The change never occurs overnight, but generally requires a generation or more. Ultimately, technology changes the balance of power, but a new relationship emerges in which the interests of both parties are brought into balance once again.

Change is not driven by technological push but by consumer pull. The software revolution will not be driven by the software development community, just as the industrial revolution was not driven by the cottage industry gunsmiths. It will be driven by the consumers of software products, just as the consumers of ordnance products, the U.S. Government, drove manufacturing to interchangeable parts.

Adele Goldberg

One of the powerful ideas that has attracted new attention as a result of the development of object-oriented software technology is the notion of reusable, combinable applications. Today, we see this idea being promoted at the level of operating systems, window systems, and independent software architectures (low-level, such as Microsoft's DLLs and Sun's sharable libraries, and high-level, such as Patriot Partners' Constellation project and ParcPlace's object model and frameworks approach).

Many believe that the discipline of defined, published interfaces (which the object-oriented approach naturally promotes) will create a new marketplace for reusable software components. However, from our experience with many developers and users of Smalltalk systems in many different environments, we think the key economic shift will be in a different area. A public market is a very loosely organized environment. Components placed in a market will face a very wide variety of different demands, and even well-designed components with minimally constrained interfaces will have trouble attracting a critical mass of customers. On the other hand, within a single organization, reusable components can be developed and redesigned within a context that can span a large fraction of their intended uses. In this way, the accumulation of reusable code can become an important business asset, and can be treated (as we believe is appropriate) as an investment and a capital good, rather than (as at present) simply a cost.

In an object-oriented environment where inheritance is supported, it is not only individual components that are reused. The design of interfaces between objects is often more important than the implementation of functions within objects. Frameworks can capture the structural design of software objects that address a given (partial) problem domain. As such, the frameworks developed and reused within an organization will come, over time, to capture and eventually even define the expertise of the organization, and as such can contribute to the organization's ability to meet its customers' needs. This is sometimes called competitive advantage, but it applies equally well in situations where competition is not involved. This position of advantage often means that the organization should or can not share the results publically.

Given these two beliefs, that reusable code can become an important business asset and that an important form of this asset is software frameworks, we have initiated a major data collection project. The goal of the project is to be able to propose an economic model for corporations that accounts for the costs of the introduction and management of object-oriented technology. Data is being supplied by a number of corporations with both completed and ongoing projects. The results will be reported on in the form of a recommended cost model as well as case studies. One outcome of this project will be recommendations for structuring an organization to best manage its investment in creating reusable software assets.

Martin L. Griss

Since 1984, Hewlett-Packard (HP) has had several visible software reuse projects in divisions and laboratories. Some use DBMS systems to store and distribute software components. Others use Objective-C or C++ to develop class libraries (for UI, data-structures and instrument sub-systems). Several libraries have been widely distributed within HP, and some outside. Recently, several HP entities have started multi-division domain analysis to develop common architectures, components and libraries, for instrument firmware, and for chemical and medical system software, producing frameworks and major components to be used in several products. Other divisions have set up libraries, established reuse goals, and started reuse councils and component projects. HP Laboratories has several component-based software construction research projects, exploring hypertext-based reuse library management tools, application frameworks, software-bus architectures and object-oriented analysis and design methods.

Since 1989, we have been investigating ways to make software reuse a more significant part of HP's software process for the 1990's. We now believe that a broad, well coordinated software reuse program involving a significant management, process, education, and technology infrastructure is needed to make significant progress. In October 1990, we initiated a Corporate Engineering Software Reuse program. This program consists of a core team of software reuse experts, with additional people on assignment with divisional pilot projects.

The core team will be involved in: the development and execution of a reuse assessment and metrics; the design and execution of several "pilot projects" with divisional partners to develop and test methods and tools for "design for reuse", "design with reuse", and "library management"; the collection of reuse best practices, processes and guidelines in a customizable handbook; and, consulting, training, and workshops. We have assessed several divisional reuse programs, held a Reuse Practitioner's Workshop for HP engineers and managers, and published our first reuse newsletter. We are developing a reuse curriculum. We will not build a single Corporate reuse library, nor stress a single language. Most of the processes, methods, training and tools we advocate are largely independent of particular languages, but OOA/OOD derived methods for domain analysis and design for reuse seem destined to play a significant role.

We strongly believe in the importance of providing economic incentives to divisions to "pilot", bootstrap and evaluate systematic reuse programs. It is important to develop a viable economic model, and to provide early validation of the cost/benefits

of reuse within HP. We have just started several joint pilot projects with divisions, to which we provide additional people, funding, and consulting, backed by strong management support, and Corporate Engineering's technology transfer infrastructure.

Biographies

Sam S. Adams is the Senior Technical Consultant and co-founder of Knowledge Systems Corporation. Since 1984, he has been actively developing object-oriented software systems in Smalltalk, and is widely recognized for his expertise in rapid prototyping and in the design and implementation of advanced software components and frameworks. He has also been training computer professionals in object oriented technology for over 4 years, and was instrumental in the development of KSC's Smalltalk Apprentice Program. A frequent speaker and panelist at leading industry conferences, he has recently presented tutorials on Rapid Prototyping at OOPSLA '89 and '90, and has presented several workshops on OOA and OOD.

Howard Baetjer, Jr. is Executive Director of the Agorics Project, a research project of the Center for the Study of Market Processes at George Mason University. The Agorics Project is currently engaged in a major study of the evolution of the software components industry. As part of the Agorics Project, he has co-authored articles on the evolution of programming practice, and was primary developer of the prototype of the AGORA, a framework for economic experimentation written in Smalltalk. He has a B.A. (Psychology, Princeton), an M. Litt. (English Literature, Edinburgh) and an M.A. (Political Science, Boston College). He is completing his Ph.D. (Economics, George Mason University) on "Software as Capital".

Brad J. Cox is a founder and Chief Technical Officer of The Stepstone Corporation, the author of the book, "Object-oriented Programming, An Evolutionary Approach," and the originator of Stepstone's Objective-C System-building Environment and many of its Software-IC libraries. He

269

is writing another book, "Object-oriented System-building; A Revolutionary Approach." His work is aimed at bringing about a software industrial revolution in which software is produced, not by fabricating everything from first principles, but by assembling interchangeable (reusable) software components. Previously, he worked at Schlumberger-Doll Research Laboratory (AI and OO technologies to oil field services) and in the ITT Programming Technology Center (OO for a large, highly distributed telephone exchange, System 1240). He received his Ph.D. (University of Chicago) for work now called neural networks.

Adele Goldberg is President and CEO of ParcPlace Systems. ParcPlace Systems provides a broad range of object-oriented technologies and services, including development tools for Smalltalk and for C++, that serve the applications development needs of corporate programmers. Before that, she managed a research laboratory at Xerox PARC. She wrote several books, "Smalltalk-80: The Language," with David Robson, and "Smalltalk-80: The Interactive Programming Environment", and led the effort to make Smalltalk-80 available on standard microprocessors. She is editor of the book "The History of Personal Workstations." She was President of the ACM (1984-1986), helped form ACM Press, jointly received the ACM Software System Award (1987), and PC Magazine's Lifetime Achievement Award (1990). She has a Ph.D (Information Sciences, University of Chicago, 1973).

Martin L. Griss is a senior scientist at Hewlett-Packard Laboratories, Palo Alto. He leads research on software reuse, software-bus frameworks, and hypertext-based reuse tools. He works closely with HP Corporate Engineering to systematically introduce software reuse into HP's software development processes. He was previously director of HP's Software Technology Laboratory, researching expert systems, object-oriented databases, programming technology, human-computer interaction, and distributed computing. He serves on HP software engineering councils and is a consultant to HP management on software engineering. Before that he was an associate professor of Computer Science

at the University of Utah, working on computer algebra and portable LISP systems (PSL). He has published numerous papers, and was an ACM national lecturer. He has a Ph.D. (Physics, University of Illinois, 1971).

References

[1] Ted Biggerstaff and Alan Perlis (Eds). *Software Reusability*, volume 1 & 2. ACM Press, NY, 1989.

[2] Will Tracz. *Tutorial: Software Reuse: Emerging Technology*. IEEE Computer Society Press, IEEE Catalog Number EH0278-2, 1988.

[3] Bruce Barnes and Terry B. Bollinger. Making reuse cost-effective. *IEEE Software*, 8(1):13–24, January 1991.

[4] Doug McIlroy. Mass-produced software components. In J. M. Buxton, P. Naur, and B. Randell, editors, *Software Engineering Concepts and Techniques, 1968 Nato Conference on Software Engineering*, pages 138–155 (88–98), January 1969.

[5] Brad J. Cox. Planning the software industrial revolution. *IEEE Software*, 7(6):25–33, November 1990.

[6] Gregory Aharonian. Starting a software reuse effort at your company. Distributed at NASA Workshop, *Towards a National Software Exchange*, April 1991.

[7] P. F. Smart, S. N. Woodfield, D. W. Embley, and D. T. Scott. An empirical investigation of the effect of education and tools on software reusability. In *Proceedings of the Seventh Annual International Phoenix Conference on Computers and Communications*, pages 224–228. IEEE Comput. Soc. Press, Washington, DC, USA, March 1988.

Islands: Aliasing Protection
In Object-Oriented Languages

John Hogg

Bell-Northern Research
Ottawa, Ontario

Abstract

Functions that are guaranteed not to have side effects are common in modern procedural languages, but not in object-oriented languages. Certain types of state changes are essential in object functions; the difficulty lies in permitting these while banning undesirable side effects. A simple way of doing this is presented. Using this as a base, we can introduce *islands* of objects which can statically ensure non-aliasing properties in a very non-restrictive way. Islands make construction of opaque object components more practical. They also make formal treatment of object behaviour more feasible, since the object structures they encompass can be truly opaque to their clients.

1 Introduction

Object-oriented languages have a light side and a dark side. The light side is that the programming model makes rapid prototype implementation much easier, since components can be easily reused. The dark side is that as these prototypes mature, the components can manifest strange behaviours due to unforeseen interactions and interrelationships. The big lie of object-oriented programming is that objects provide encapsulation. In order to accomplish anything, objects must interact with each other in complex ways, and understanding these interactions can be difficult.

This paper presents two ways of making object interaction more predictable. The first is well-known to the programming world, but has not yet been embraced by the object-oriented community: the division of routines into procedures, which change the system state but do not return values, and functions, which return values but are guaranteed not to change visible system state. (This distinction is made informally in some object-oriented languages. However, compliance is the responsibility of the programmer.) Since functions must be allowed to create objects, a complete ban on changing state is not acceptable, so the problem is slightly more involved than in the traditional case. Nonetheless, the solution is straightforward, and involves a new version of the traditional read-only access mode.

The second part of the paper extends access modes to present something more novel: *islands* of objects. Islands can be used to statically guarantee that an object is not aliased, while placing minimal restrictions on its use. For instance, an object can be stored in a container object, changed by being passed to an external (and possibly heavily aliased) object for use in a procedure method, and later passed on to an object totally different from the one that inserted it in the container in the first place. At the end of these operations, the new "owner" of the object can still be sure that it is unaliased. The syntactic cost of this is about three times that of providing side effect-free functions, and in addition, a fairly natural "destructive read" operation must be added.

OOPSLA'91, pp. 271–285

Islands also make proof systems that depend upon knowledge of explicit relationships between objects more feasible. Within an island, objects are treated as "friends" in the sense of C++ [Str86], and analysed together. Externally, however, the island can be dealt with as a black box. The concepts of islands are widely applicable to different languages and models, and to different theoretical and practical needs.

2 Side Effect-Free Functions

The idea that routines should be divided into those that return a result ("functions") and those that change their environment ("procedures") is now firmly established in the world of traditional procedural programming languages. To the theorist, formal analysis is greatly simplified. Boehm has presented a logic for Russell, a language with functions having side effects [Boe84], but the Russell definition of "side effect" is quite non-standard. In general, the problem is unsolved.

For the pragmatic software engineer, side effect-free functions make error detection easier, and unforeseen interactions between components are considerably decreased. It seems natural to extend this approach to the object-oriented world, and provide languages in which procedures do not return values, and functions do not have side effects.

Before this can be done, however, the term "side effect" must be defined. Intuitively, a programming construct (henceforth, an expression) has a side effect if it changes the state of the system. However, consider the simple expression $3 + 4$. Under a common model of object behaviour, this will result in the creation of a new instance of class Integer with value 7. The system state has changed, yet we do not think of addition as having side effects.

The answer, of course, is that these system changes are not *visible* to any object in the system. The newly-created instance is not accessible from any existing instance. More to the point, no instance reachable prior to the evaluation of the expression (in fact, no instance *existing* prior to the evaluation) is altered. From the theoretician's view of an expression as a mapping from states to states, no predicate on the initial state will be falsified by the mapping. A programmer will say that an assertion will always be unaffected by the evaluation of an expression. We therefore have a nice intuitive understanding of what we want to achieve, and can easily formalize it.

The tool usually used to achieve freedom from side effects in modern procedural languages is some sort of read-only access mode. An *access mode* is a statically-testable restriction on the operations that may be applied to a variable. In many languages (such as Pascal) read-only is the default mode for parameters: a parameter is read-only unless it is explicitly imported with a *var* mode. A read-only parameter may not be assigned to, and may only be exported to other routines with a read-only mode. However, this is not sufficient in an object-oriented language, in which objects are referred to using pointer semantics. It is not enough to protect the pointer; the object at the other end of it must also be guaranteed to be unaffected by an operation which purports to be free from side effects.

This requirement for protection at two levels has been recognized before, with respect to the Eiffel language [Mey88].

2.1 Eiffel

The Eiffel language has syntactic provision for value-returning functions and procedures without return values. Guaranteeing that a function will not have side effects requires recognizing the cases in which side effects may occur. Meyer presents a list of these cases. They are:

1. assignment to an attribute (instance variable) x;

2. procedure call having side effects on an attribute x;

3. local call having side effects (which in some languages could be considered a form of the previous case); and

4. using an attribute as an argument where the called routine produces a side effect on the corresponding parameter.

Meyer states that it would be simple to enforce these rules, but that side effects which only change the "concrete" state of an object and not the "abstract" state should be allowed. In other words, internal state changes that cannot be detected through any sequence of method invocations should not be considered to be side effects at all. He therefore relies on the programmmer to avoid unwanted state changes.

Unfortunately, the list given above is incomplete. Consider the following code:

```
class C export
    hiddenSideEffects
feature
    protected: MUTABLECLASS;
    hiddenSideEffects(): STRING is
        local temp: MUTABLECLASS
        do
            temp := returnParam(protected);
            temp.mutate;
            Result := "protected has just been altered"
        end;

    returnParam(arg: MUTABLECLASS):
            MUTABLECLASS is
        do
            Result := arg
        end
    end

class MUTABLECLASS export
    mutate
feature
    value: BOOLEAN;
    mutate() is
        do
            value := not value;
        end;
```

Here, all of the Eiffel side effect rules have been followed, but the attribute *protected* loses its supposed protection by being the result of a function.

When *hiddenSideEffects* returns, the object that its attribute *protected* refers to will have its value negated, even though the only call of a routine with side effects was on the local variable *temp*.

Clearly, return values are a potential source of unexpected side effects in an object-oriented language. This is especially true because we cannot just decree that all function results are *read*, for the reasons explained earlier: the function may have constructed a structure of objects which is not visible in the context (i.e., the object) from which it was called, but is to be returned for use in that context. In non-object-oriented languages, the ability to generate structures of objects in this manner is not so central to the programming paradigm. This is why the designers of the Turing language [HMRC88] could reasonably ban the creation of new collection elements in a function. When an attempt is made to simulate an object-oriented language in Turing, however, the restriction is immediately apparent. The natural way to simulate the instances of a class of objects uses a collection.

Fortunately, there is no fundamental reason why the desired behaviour of functions cannot be obtained, as we shall see.

2.2 Access Modes and Types

First, a word about typing. An interest in freedom from side effects is usually accompanied by concerns about other aspects of program predictability, and therefore side effect-free functions are found in typed languages. Furthermore, attempts to understand object behaviour are presently concentrated on types and type inheritance. To ensure that there is no misunderstanding, we will state the obvious: the access modes presented here and later on in the paper are completely orthogonal to any notion of typing, and of inheritance. Side effect-free functions (and later, islands) will be most useful in the context of a typed language, but types are not necessary. To drive the point home, the remainder of the examples in this paper will be expressed in a Smalltalk-like language [GR83]. This is not meant to suggest that Smalltalk is the most appropriate vehicle for anything presented here. The ideas are clearly translatable to other object-oriented languages. In fact, since the work presented here is orthogonal to inheritance, it applies to object-*based* languages in general and not just object-*oriented* languages, using the terminology of [Weg87].

Since parameters and results have associated access modes, each method invocation must be checked for legality. This is done by treating the set of modes associated with an invocation as an extension of the method selector. Mode conformance is therefore checked at runtime, and an implementation would supply a mechanism similar to **doesNotUnderstand** to deal with cases of mismatch between access modes of the invoking message and the methods supplied by a receiver object. In a statically-typed language, signature mode conformance would also be statically checked.

2.3   Rules for Side Effect-Free Functions

We will now provide a set of rules for ensuring freedom from side effects in functions. They are based on the traditional notion of a read-only (henceforth, *read*) access mode.[1] In an object environment, however, this mode must refer to both the variable and the object to which it refers. The restrictions on *read* are simple:

Definition 1 (Read) *A variable whose declaration has the label %read is read. If within a method the receiver (self) is read, then all instance variables are implicitly read. A read expression is a read variable or the result of a read-valued function.*

1. *A read variable may not be assigned to.*

2. *A read expression may only be exported as read. An expression is exported when it is used*

---

[1] An alternative name for this mode is *const*. However, that suggests that an object that is the value of a *const* variable cannot change. If the object or the structure of objects reachable from it is aliased, i.e., is the value of another possibly non-*const* variable, then the nomenclature is misleading, since it may change "under foot". A mode is a property of a variable and describes the way that an object and its structure may be accessed. The mode is *not* a property of the object or its structure.

as a parameter of a method invocation or the result of a function method.

3. *A read expression may not be the right side of an assignment.*

The first restriction obviously protects the *read* variable itself from being assigned to. The second restriction ensures that the object that the variable refers to is protected when it is used in other contexts. The third restriction protects the object within the current context. If a reference may be retained in an instance variable, then the protected object may be altered later in an execution by some other method. The persistent environments that are the central concept of object-oriented programming make it difficult to specify during one entry to a context (an instance) that some reference should be treated in a special way when the context is returned to later. Permitting assignment to temporary variables (which must subsequently be treated as *reads*) is somewhat simpler, but results in considerable syntactic baggage and also incompleteness, for negligible advantages.

The idea of a *read* access mode is usually expressed in a syntax that is the reverse of the one used here: no variable may be changed unless it is declared *var*. Using *var* as a default and making *read* restriction explicit is a matter of taste, and makes it easier to express what *read* entails. The difference is minor.

Definition 2 (Function) *In a function method definition, all parameters (including the receiver, self) are read.*

Within a function method, then, all instance variables (and the objects they refer to) are *read*. A function invocation will have no visible side effects.

These rules imply that there are two sorts of function: those that return *read* results, and those with "free" results. This addition to the signature of a function method is the price that must be paid for adding side effect-free functions to the pointer semantics of an object-oriented language.

2.4 A Function Example

The following example is expressed in an extended Smalltalk in which method definitions have signatures annotated by access modes. In Smalltalk, every method can have side effects, and also returns a value. Since we have divided the world into procedure and function methods, it becomes convenient to make this distinction in the language, and therefore function selectors have been distinguished from procedure selectors by an initial upper-case letter. The mode of the receiver during the execution of a method is prepended to the method name, and instance variables and parameters have their modes appended. The mode of a function result (if explicit) follows a colon appended to the signature.

The example concerns a class of complex objects having a method **MaxAbs** which returns the receiver or its parameter, depending upon which has the greater absolute value. We must ensure that regardless of the class of the components of the receiver and the parameter, this method cannot change the visible state of the system. One way of ensuring this is as follows:

class name   Complex
instance variable names   x
                             y

instance methods

...

```
%read MaxAbs: aComplex%read :%read
    ((self Abs) > (aComplex Abs))
        ifTrue: [↑self]
        ifFalse: [↑aComplex]

%read Abs :%read
    ↑((x∗x) + (y∗y)) Sqrt
```

This code does not specify the behaviour of the system by itself; that will depend upon the classes of objects used to represent the x and y values of the receiver of the method, and upon the parameter. However, the demands made by these methods are fairly severe. They return *read* results, which restricts the use to which they can be put.

An alternative to this would be the following implementation, which returns a result that can be used in further processing:

class name   Complex
instance variable names   x
                             y

instance methods

...

```
%read Max: aComplex%read
    ((self Abs) > (aComplex Abs))
        ifTrue: [↑self Copy]
        ifFalse: [↑aComplex Copy]

%read Abs :%read
    ↑((x∗x) + (y∗y)) Sqrt

%read Copy
    ↑(Complex new) x: x y: y

%read x: newX%read y: newY%read
    x ← newX Copy.
    y ← newY Copy
```

This is functionally an improvement, since the result of Max may now be assigned to a variable in the calling method since there it has no *read* mode restriction. However, it is clearly quite inefficient, since copies must be made to ensure that *read* instance variables remain protected.

The solution to this involves introducing an *immutable* mode, in the sense of [LG86]. Primitive objects are almost always defined so as to be immutable: after an immutable instance is created, it can never be changed, because there is no operation that can change it. As a result, it needs no explicit *read* protection. This mode would also be useful in the second half of this paper. An immutable object need not be protected from aliasing, because the effects of this aliasing will never be seen by any holder of an alias. Immutability can considerably simplify analysis. However, this idea will not be further described here.

3 Islands

Functions that are free from side effects are valuable in themselves to both the theoretician and the practical programmer. They also provide a good introduction to the main contribution of this paper: the notion of *islands*.

The main problem in constructing a usable formal semantics for an object-oriented language is arguably *aliasing*. An object is aliased (with respect to the context of another object and its associated state) if there are two *paths* to it. A path is a sequence of variable names with each variable name denoting a context (i.e., an object) in which the succeeding variable is evaluated. If aliasing exists, then it becomes very difficult to determine whether an operation will change the state of a seemingly-unrelated object.

The aliasing found in a "pure" object system is not the same sort of aliasing that occurs in traditional procedural languages. Every object system variable is a pointer to an object, and there is no way in which two variables can refer to the same pointer. However, the distinct pointers may refer to the same object. Readers familiar with object systems will find the following description obvious. Those new to objects (even though they may have a strong background in semantics) may find it helpful.

Figure 1 gives two examples of aliasing, one harmless and one not. In Part (a), we have a primitive object (an integer) known in the current context by two aliases, the variables x and y. If x ← x + 1 is now executed, there is no problem; x points to a new instance, and the value and behaviour of y both remain unchanged.

Now consider Part (b) of the figure. Here, x and y both refer to an instance of a user-defined class that contains a value, and methods for accessing and altering that value. A method x increment-Value (with the obvious semantics of the diagram) will now leave the *value* of y unchanged, but it will change the state of the object to which y refers, and thus its behaviour. In other words, a construct will have changed the meaning of a variable

in a way that is not syntactically detectable. Note that object-oriented aliasing problems only occur "at one level of indirection".

Aliasing can be divided into two types: *static* aliasing, and *dynamic* aliasing. An object is aliased statically if the two different access paths are both composed entirely of chains of instance variables. The aliasing is dynamic if at least one of the access paths has a prefix consisting of temporary variables or parameters. A dynamic alias will therefore disappear at the end of the execution of the method in which it appears. By contrast, a static alias may make its existence felt during some later invocation.

This persistence makes a static alias much more troublesome than a dynamic alias. A dynamic alias (i.e., the use of parameters, or most uses of temporary variables) has no effects beyond the scope in which it occurs. From an operational viewpoint, a static alias can cause unpleasant surprises at an arbitrarily distant point in an execution. By the time the bomb goes off, the chains of variables in instances by which an aliased object is known may be arbitrarily long. From a denotational perspective, a static alias causes problems because the meaning of an expression is dependent upon its context; the meaning of a function invocation may be affected by a preceding procedure invocation even though the invocations share no variables.

3.1 Previous Work

3.1.1 SPOOL

The most closely-related work in the literature to that presented here is the proof system for SPOOL [AdB90]. Some of the same ideas can be seen in the semantics constructed for the non-object-oriented language Turing [HMRC88]. The aliasing problem is that an operation involving one set of identifiers may affect the visible state of a disjoint set of identifiers. This occurs because some object is reachable from the current context through more than one chain of objects containing pointers (i.e., variables) to other objects. If these chains and their relationships can be made explicit, then the problem

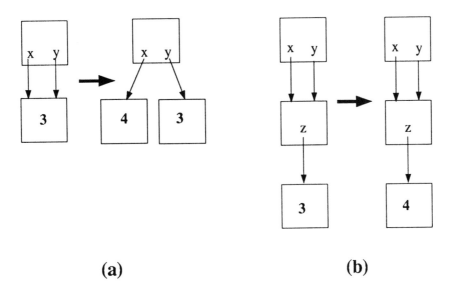

(a)

(b)

Figure 1: Aliasing problems

is solved. Changes made to an instance through one alias can be reflected in other aliases.

The SPOOL proof system is based on a Hoare logic, following the tradition of [Coo78]. Its predicate language contains not only simple variable names but also *global expressions*. A global expression g.x has the value of the variable x in the context of the global expression g. Conditionals may appear in global expressions; otherwise, they reduce to chains of variable names. The SPOOL proof system expresses predicates in terms of these chains of variables. A Hoare formula describes the body of a method as seen from within the context of its receiver. Proof rules express the same formula from the context of the caller by prepending the variable indicating the receiver to each variable chain used in the body. A formula describing an object at a high level in the system therefore has a body consisting of some set of method invocations. Its predicates, however, have no invocations, but rather variables that are long chains.

There are three obvious problems with this approach. From the description above, it is clear that the technique does not scale. It may be reasonable for small sets of classes, but is unusable in anything larger than a toy system. Long chains of variable names are not meaningful.

The use of paths also massively violates object encapsulation: to determine the behaviour of an object, not only must its implementation be examined, but also the implementation of all of its acquaintances. This bodes ill for the late binding of behaviour that is the essence of object-oriented systems.

Finally, a variable chain system is impractical because it does not provide modularity of proofs. Object-oriented libraries are supposed to provide the user with a set of components that can be used to construct larger components and entire systems. If each use of a component requires proofs about it to be reconstructed, then very little has been gained. A practical proof system must encapsulate not only code, but also specifications, so that a component can be retrieved from a library as a true black box.

3.1.2 FX

The polymorphic effect system of FX [LG88] is another attempt to solve the aliasing problem. Expressions have types, and in addition have *effects*, which describe side effects (such as reading, writing, or allocating), and *regions*, which describe where these effects may occur. Regions are explicitly specified by the programmer. One expression can be shown to have no effect on another if the effects of the first occur in a region not used by the second. Furthermore, an expression with effects can be shown to have none that are visible to the rest of the system if the region in which they occur is only visible from within the expression. An expression that only has such *masked* effects corresponds to a function as described in the first part of this paper.

Like the earlier work of Reynolds [Rey78], effects are conservative. If the programmer specifies regions with large granularity, potential interference will be indicated where none actually exists. If small regions are used, then the task of region management can overwhelm the programming underneath it. Again, calculating the *reach* (the regions accessed by an expression) can require abandonment of the simple encapsulation that we would like to see in a set of objects.

3.2 Island Strategy

In practice, programmers manage to muddle along even in the presence of aliasing without shooting themselves in the foot too often. We can speculate that this success is due to the fact that aliasing tends to be local, and between objects of closely-related classes. A programmer working within one of these classes will have a good idea of how other classes will be affected by any aliases present, and may well depend upon this knowledge. Approaches to object design such as CRC (Class, Responsibility, Collaboration) [BC89] would seem to empirically support this hypothesis.

Assuming, then, that *islands* of aliasing are used in an informal way at present, an obvious idea is to formalize the concept, and control the existence of aliases in a rigorous manner. First, we will expand upon what an island should be, and what guarantees it should provide.

An island is the transitive closure of a set of objects accessible from a *bridge* object. A bridge is thus the sole access point to a set of instances that make up an island; no object that is not a member of the island holds any reference to an object within the island apart from the bridge.

Container structures make natural examples of islands. Since it must be possible to insert other objects (and structures of objects) into a container and later remove them without destroying the alias protection of the island, several other properties are required. It must be possible to pass a structure into an island with a guarantee that no other references to it are held, and later it must be possible to retrieve the structure with the same assurance. While a structure is held within an island, it should be usable: that is, it should be possible to invoke both functions and procedures on it, and to use it as a parameter to other functions and procedures external to the island, while still maintaining the guarantees of non-aliasing.

For a more concrete view of the concept, see Figure 2. The boxes represent instances, and the ovals indicate the boundaries of islands. The arrows represent references from instance variables to objects. Here, we see a fragment of some global system state that includes a container island. An implementation of this example will be presented later.

The topmost instances are users of the container. One instance inserts items which it guarantees to be unaliased, and this allows the other to have the same guarantee when it removes the items from the container. The oval island boundary represents a wall across which no static references can exist, except through the bridge object at its top. Even dynamic references must be granted by the bridge.

Since the only access to the island is through the bridge, it follows that the state of an island remains unchanged between methods invoked on the bridge. When a bridge is itself unaliased, its sole holder is assured that any construct that does not contain a reference to the bridge cannot affect its (transitive) state. A lack of aliasing is thus a property to be jealously protected. The main bridge in the diagram here does not have that property. However, if we look inside the island, we see a set of smaller islands which are unaliased, representing the items held in the container.

These items are protected, but they are not inaccessible. Figure 3 shows the dynamic use of an item by an object outside of the island. The heavy lines

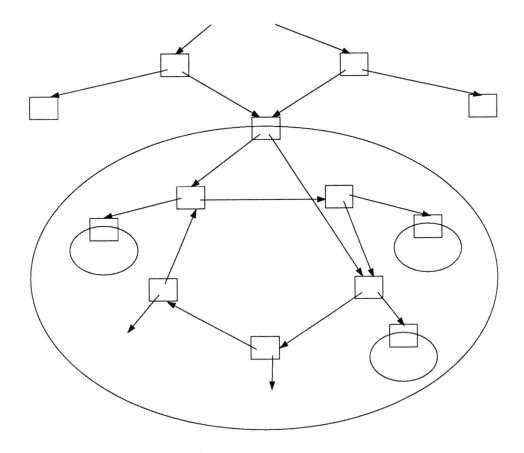

Figure 2: Static references around an island

are (temporary) references from parameters to objects. The numbers on the objects represent their order in the calling stack, and it can be seen that the external object has sent a message to the protected item, which may change its state as a result. Since this access is through the bridge, however, it is controlled: invariants on the state of the island as a whole can be proven using a proof system. Also, when the methods terminate and the calling stack has unwound, the situation of Figure 2 will return, and there will again be no references across the island boundary.

An island provides a true encapsulation of its components: all access is through a single bridge, and therefore the state of the island can never change without this change being visible to the bridge. Within the island, path variables (or other techniques) will in general be necessary to construct proofs about intra-island behaviour. However, the interface that the bridge presents to the world need not, should not, and in fact must not export references to island objects. This means that

island-based systems should scale: the complexity of a proof in terms of path lengths is limited by the size of an island, instead of the size of an entire system.

3.3 Island Implementation

We now turn to the implementation of islands. First, a "destructive read" is needed. In addition to the previously-presented *read* access mode, two more access modes are required: *unique* and *free*. They are both orthogonal to the *read* mode, but mutually exclusive, so a variable x many be unrestricted, *read*, *unique*, *free*, *read* and *unique*, or *read* and *free*. The claim that the syntactic cost of islands is about three times the cost of side effect-free functions refers to this tripling of required access modes, and to a tripling of the rules associated with them.

The destructive read is simply an atomic operation that returns the value of a variable (i.e., the identity of the object to which it points) and sets

279

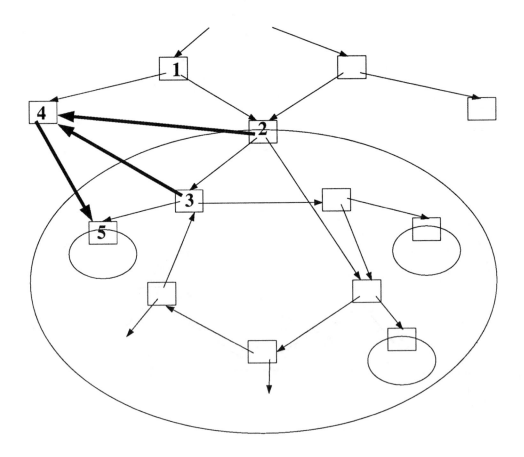

Figure 3: Dynamic references during island use

the variable to nil. It will be written as ↓ x. This can also be extended to expressions: ↓ (e) means that the value returned by the expression e is the identity of an object that is not held elsewhere—that is, the object is not the value of any instance variable.

The mode *unique* indicates that the object to which it refers has only one static reference in the entire system—i.e., its address is contained in only one instance variable. The mode *free* indicates that *no* other references to the variable exist anywhere in the system. Clearly, there can never be a *free* instance variable. A destructive read of a *unique* instance variable produces a *free* result, and a *free* value can be assigned to a *unique* instance variable.

Due to the lack of aliasing, an object held through a *unique* variable can only be affected by an expression in which the variable appears. This is extremely useful in proving properties about a system.

The rules for *read* access have already been given. The rules for *unique* are as follows:

Definition 3 (Unique) *A variable whose declaration has the label %unique is* unique. *A unique expression is a* unique *variable or the result of a* unique-*valued function.*

1. *A unique variable may only be assigned the result of a* free *expression.*

2. *A unique expression may not be assigned to anything.*

3. *A unique expression may only be exported (as receiver, parameter or result) as* unique.

4. *If a method receiver is* unique, *then every parameter and the result must be* read *or* unique *or* free.

These rules need some justification. The first says that a reference cannot be *unique* if it is held anywhere else, so an assignment to a *unique* variable can only take place if the value being assigned is released wherever else it may be held. Similarly, an expression is not *unique* if it is assigned to another variable. Access modes must be protected on export, and the third rule ensures this.

The least obvious rule is the last one. *Unique* is a transitive property. If an object's acquaintances are aliased, then the observable state of the object may be unexpectedly changed, even if there is no aliasing of the object itself. Therefore, an object being accessed as *unique* must not import or export any unprotected references. An unprotected parameter could be retained by the object, however. This is shown in Part (a) of Figure 4. The light lines indicate the original variable references, while the heavy line is a reference retained after the execution of a method. *A* has passed *B* as a parameter of a method to *C*, which has retained the reference; thereafter *B* is visible to *C*, but may be accessed without going through it. Likewise, Part (b) of Figure 4 shows how an unprotected result *B* passed from *C* to *A* may result in exactly the same situation.

Unique instance variables and *unique* parameters are somewhat different animals. Neither may be copied without respecting the *unique* status, but in addition, only an instance variable may be destructively read to generate a *free* reference. They are generally so similar, however, that the same access mode has been used to identify them to decrease keyword (and concept) proliferation.

The definition of *free* is simple:

Definition 4 (Free) *A variable whose declaration has the label* %free *is* free. *A* free *expression is the destructive read of a* unique *instance variable or a* free *variable, the result of a* **new** *method, or a the result of a* free-*valued function invocation.*

> *1. A* free *variable may only be accessed via a destructive read.*

Free variables and values are extremely transitory: as soon as they are touched, they disappear. Note that there are no restrictions on the modes of parameters methods with *free* receivers. This is because a *free* receiver has essentially already vanished over the event horizon from the original state.

The structure that it refers to may return in the result of the function, but it will not have any alias in the rest of the system.

In addition, we need to modify the meaning of *read* slightly by adding this restriction, since a destructive read has side effects:

Definition 5 (Revised Read) *4. A* read *variable may not be destructively read.*

We can now relax the definition of a function slightly:

Definition 6 (Revised Function) *In a function method definition, all parameters (including the receiver,* **self***) are* read *or* free.

Finally, we have the following definition:

Definition 7 (Bridge Classes) *If every method of a class has the property that every parameter and function result is* read, unique *or* free, *then every instance of that class is a* bridge.

A bridge class presents an external interface to a set of classes. A specification for a bridge may be given as a set of Hoare formulas, and the class may thereafter be used as a black box.[2] Classes used within the island will not be visible to the user, and will be protected by the island. Bridge class instances may then be used to construct larger islands and eventually entire systems. At each level, proofs will use path variables to refer to visible bridge instances, but not the instances within their islands.

Every structure underneath an instance of a bridge class is an island, but many islands are not headed by a bridge class instance. In particular, every structure underneath a *unique* instance (i.e., an instance referred to by a variable of *unique* mode) must be an island. However, bridge-class islands and *unique* islands are different in two major ways. A bridge-class object may be aliased, while a *unique* instance may not. Also, a *unique*

---

[2] We recognize that this is a very oversimplified and unrealistic view of the software engineering process, and that true black-box class usage will not be practical in the foreseeable future. Nevertheless, the principle still holds.

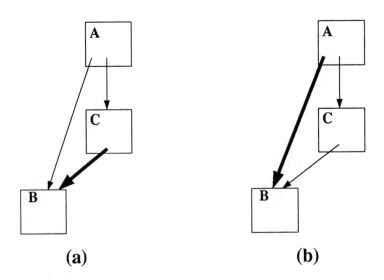

(a)   (b)

Figure 4: Alias creation through retained references

instance may later lose its uniqueness and therefore the protection of its island by being assigned to a non-*unique* variable using a destructive read. By contrast, the objects underneath an instance of a bridge class are permanently protected.

Islands have the nice property that they are not forced upon a user. A language may provide a set of access modes, but they can be ignored if the programmer so wishes, e.g. during prototyping. A set of collaborating classes can later be turned into an island by the addition of appropriate access modes. If this is not possible, it could indicate that the design provides insufficient encapsulation.

3.4　An Island Example

Figures 2 and 3 depicted an island implementation of a container class. We now present a concrete implementation of this. It is a circular queue implementation of a bounded buffer, but it also allows items in the buffer to be accessed. Items are inserted and removed in the normal way, but in addition are associated with keys. While an item is in the buffer, it may be changed by having its *intern-*

Mutate method invoked. Additionally, an object external to the island may "borrow" an item as a parameter to its *mutate* method. In other words, dynamic aliasing of an instance can be permitted, while the subsequent non-aliasing of the instance is guaranteed.

class name	DictionaryBuffer
instance variable names	head
	tail

instance methods

```
initialize: size%read
    | temp |
    head ← Slot new.
    tail ← head.
    size do: [
        temp ← Slot new.
        head next: temp.
        head ← temp ].
    head next: tail.
    tail ← head
```

insertKey: newKey%*free*
    value: newValue%*free*
  tail insertKey: ↓newKey value: ↓newValue.
  tail ← tail Next.

transfer: destination%*unique*
  head transfer: destination.
  head ← head Next

%*read* Find: searchKey%*read* :%*read*
  | temp |
  temp ← head.
  [temp Key ∼= searchKey] whileTrue:
    [temp ← temp Next].
  ↑temp

internMutate: searchKey%*read*
  (self Find: searchKey) internMutate

    externMutate: searchKey%*read*
  mutator mutate: (self Find: searchKey)

class name   Slot
instance variable names   next
                            key%*unique*
                            value%*unique*

instance methods
  next: newNext
    next ← newNext

  %*read* **Next** :%*read*
    ↑next

  %*read* **Key** :%*read*
    ↑key

  insertKey: newKey%*free*
    value: newValue%*free*
    key ← ↓newKey.
    value ← ↓newValue

transfer: destination%*unique*
  destination insertKey: ↓key value: ↓value

internMutate
  value mutate

externMutate: mutator%*unique*
  mutator mutate: value

From the class definitions given above, DictionaryBuffer is an island, but Slot is not. (The unrealistic assumption is made here that DictionaryBuffer does not inherit from classes such as Object that provide methods for downright promiscuous access to private parts. An island-based reimplementation of the Smalltalk library would look very different from the present version.) An object inserted into the DictionaryBuffer is *unique*, and therefore any objects reachable from it form an island. This *unique*ness is preserved while the object is held in the container island, but the subsequent recipient of the held island structure may remove this protection.

4   Conclusion

An object-oriented version of functions that are statically guaranteed not to have side effects has been presented. Using this, islands have been introduced. Islands are of value both to the pragmatic software engineer and to those interested in formal proofs of object behaviour.

To the software engineer, islands allow a set of objects to be nicely encapsulated. An instance of a bridge class may be used as a true black box: clients can use objects within an island, but can never do so except through a single, controllable interface. Islands are not forced upon users; the tool is an aid, not a straitjacket. However, they are one more step towards the holy grail of truly reusable, black-box components.

A component can only be a black box if it comes with some sort of behaviour specification apart from the code. The most reliable sort of specification is one that implementations can be proven to satisfy, such as a set of Hoare formulas or pre- and post-conditions on a method. Such a specification on a bridge class need not and cannot reveal the implementation of the island it protects. It is hoped that this will overcome scaling problems that make existing proof techniques for object systems inapplicable for non-trivial systems.

Only sequential languages have been treated in this paper. However, all of the ideas are directly applicable in some models of parallel object behaviour, and some of the ideas are applicable in all (reasonably mainstream) models.

Islands fit POOL [Ame89] particularly well. In that language, an object may only have one active thread of control at any point. If an object is executing one thread (either directly within its own context, or indirectly through a procedure call in the context of another object) then any messages that arrive are placed in a queue. As a result, an island will accept at most one external thread at a time. Inside an island, however, any number of threads can be active. They may be persistent, or they may be started by an external thread. In any case, the requirements and protections described in this paper all still hold.

An area for future work is the applicability of islands to models in which multiple threads can be active within an instance. The problem is that *unique* loses its meaning: the reference may be held by only one object, but two threads through that object can still clash with one another.

Bridges and islands were originally devised as a technique for making proof systems for object-oriented languages practical. However, other uses have also been suggested. Islands can greatly simplify some persistent-store and storage management problems. An island with a *unique* bridge can be moved to persistent store or freed with no possibility of dangling references.

This presentation of access modes and their applications has been informal. A formal treatment requires presenting a formal semantics of a language based on a formal model, which is beyond the scope of this forum. A complete treatment for a simplified object-oriented language is given in [Hog91].

References

[AdB90]   Pierre America and Frank de Boer. A sound and complete proof system for SPOOL. Technical Report 505, Philips Research Laboratories, May 1990.

[Ame89]   Pierre America. Issues in the design of a parallel object-oriented language. *Formal ASpects of Computing*, 1(4):366–411, 1989.

[BC89]   Kent Beck and Ward Cunningham. A laboratory for teaching object-oriented thinking. In *OOPSLA '89 Proceedings*, pages 1–6, October 1989.

[Boe84]   Hans-Juergen Boehm. A logic for the Russell programming language. Technical Report TR 84-593, Ph.D. thesis, Cornell University, February 1984.

[Coo78]   Stephen A. Cook. Soundness and completeness of an axiom system for program verification. *SIAM Journal of Computing*, 7(1):70–90, February 1978.

[GR83]   Adele Goldberg and David Robson. *Smalltalk-80: The Language and its Implementation*. Addison-Wesley, 1983.

[HMRC88]   Richard C. Holt, Philip A. Matthews, J. Alan Rosselet, and James R. Cordy. *The Turing Language: Design and Definition*. Prentice-Hall, 1988.

[Hog91]   John S. Hogg. *Formal Semantics of Opaque Objects in the Presence of Aliasing*. PhD thesis, University of Toronto, 1991. (to appear).

[LG86]   Barbara Liskov and John Guttag. *Abstraction and Specification in Program Development*. MIT Press, 1986.

[LG88]   John M. Lucassen and David K. Gif-
           ford. Polymorphic effect systems. In
           *Proceedings of the Fifteenth Annual
           ACM SIGACT-SIGPLAN Symposium
           on Principles of Programming Lan-
           guages*, pages 47–57, January 1988.

[Mey88]   Bertrand Meyer. *Object-oriented Soft-
           ware Construction.* Prentice-Hall,
           1988.

[Rey78]   John C. Reynolds. Syntactic control of
           interference. In *Conference Record of
           the Fifth Annual ACM Symposium on
           Principles of Programming Languages*,
           January 1978.

[Str86]   Bjarne Stroustrup. *The C++ Program-
           ming Language.* Addison-Wesley, 1986.

[Weg87]   Peter Wegner. Dimensions of object-
           based language design. In *OOPSLA
           '87 Proceedings*, October 1987.

Equate: An Object-Oriented Constraint Solver

Michael R. Wilk

Computer Science Department, Cornell University
Ithaca, New York 14853
wilk@cs.cornell.edu

Abstract

This paper presents a constraint-solving method that obeys the principle of object encapsulation. Under this method, constraints are translated into procedures for achieving constraint satisfaction. Neither the constraints nor their procedural translations refer directly to an object's implementation; all object references are through the interfaces provided by classes. Translation is performed using definite-clause backward chaining, a technique borrowed from logic programming. Because object classes guide the translation process, the method is applicable to objects of all data types.

1 Introduction

Although computer programs for general constraint solving have existed for thirty years, insufficient attention has been given to the problem of incorporating such programs into real-world applications. Ideally, applications should not be required to adapt to the design of the constraint solvers; instead, constraint solvers should be designed to meet the needs of the applications.

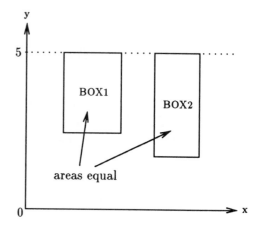

Figure 1: Two boxes with constraints.

Consider one application: a geometric figure editor. Rectangles in this editor are represented as objects called *boxes*. (Refer to Appendix A for a specification of the box class.) The editor could use a constraint solver to find arrangements of figures that meet certain conditions. Figure 1 shows a pair of boxes and two constraints: the boxes should be of equal area and their tops should coincide with the line $y = 5$.

Let us compare two approaches to solving these constraints. The first uses a constraint solver that returns a solution to a set of algebraic equations.

OOPSLA'91, pp. 286–298

Let box*n.slot* represent the state variable of box*n* with name *slot*. We could express our constraints as follows:

Areas equal: `box1.area = box2.area`
Box1 top at 5: `box1.bottom + box1.height = 5.0`
Box2 top at 5: `box2.bottom + box2.height = 5.0`
Box1 area: `box1.area = box1.width ×`
               `           box1.height`
Box2 area: `box2.area = box2.width ×`
               `           box2.height`

Here is one solution:

```
box1.bottom = 0.0      box2.bottom = 4.0
box1.width  = 1.0      box2.width  = 5.0
box1.height = 5.0      box2.height = 1.0
box1.area   = 5.0      box2.area   = 5.0
```

Although the constraint solver provided a solution to the problem it was given, we still might question whether the solver was suitable for our application. One complaint is its violation of object encapsulation. "Encapsulation is the process of hiding all of the details of an object that do not contribute to its essential characteristics. In practice, one hides the representation of an object, as well as the implementation of its methods." [Boo91]

Encapsulation was first violated by the constraint expressions. We named state variables explicitly, disclosing the representation of boxes. When referring to the tops of the boxes we disclosed the implementation of the method `top`. We also disclosed the formula used to maintain consistency between width, height, and area.

Encapsulation was also violated by the solution, which told us how to set individual state variables. These variables should not be manipulated directly: boxes should be changed using the interface provided by the box class. In circumventing this interface one might inadvertently set a state variable to an illegal value (such as giving a box negative width), or one might bypass a necessary side effect (such as triggering the redraw of an object).

The fundamental problem with this constraint solver is that it conforms more to mathematical concepts than to any principles of programming, and certainly not to principles of object-oriented programming. In contrast let us consider

the Equate constraint solver, designed with object-oriented programming in mind. This time constraints are expressed in the language of the objects:

Areas equal: `area(box1) = area(box2)`
Tops at 5:   `top(box1) = top(box2) = 5.0`

Using some guidance provided by the box class, Equate could produce the following solution:

```
move-to(box1, nil, 5.0-height(box1));
move-to(box2, nil, 5.0-height(box2));
scale(box2,
      (area(box1)/height(box2))/width(box2),
      1.0);
```

Instead of a set of variable assignments, here the solution is a program. The first instruction moves **box1** vertically so that its top is at $y = 5$; the second one does the same for **box2**; the third adjusts the width of **box2** so that its area is equal to that of **box1**. Execution of this program puts the two boxes in a state that satisfies the constraints. The solution obeys the principle of encapsulation: boxes are queried and modified using only the interface provided by the box class.

This paper explains how Equate is built. The next four sections describe the form of constraints and their solutions, the process of finding solutions, and the use of Equate within applications. An example is then presented in which Equate solves a set of overlapping constraints. The paper concludes with a review of related work, some thoughts on future directions, and a few final observations.

2   Equate Defined

The Equate constraint solver takes as input a constraint in the form of an equation:

$$exp_1 = exp_2$$

where exp_1 and exp_2 are programming language expressions[1]. Equate produces as output a set of programs called *solutions*. Any solution executing successfully will cause the constraint to be satisfied without changing the value of exp_2. Equate itself

---

[1] Examples in this paper are presented without reference to a specific programming language. A working version of Equate is implemented in the Common Lisp Object System.

does not satisfy a constraint; it translates a declarative constraint into procedural solutions. Some examples:

```
equation:  x + y = z
   solution:  x := z - y
   solution:  y := z - x

equation:  (x + y = z) = true
   solution:  x := z - y
   solution:  y := z - x
   solution:  z := x + y

equation:  left(box1) = left(box2)
   solution:  move-to(box1, left(box2), nil)
```

Because undecidable problems can easily be phrased as equations, Equate cannot always provide solutions. Indeed, Equate may return no solutions even when there exist infinitely many. Although we cannot always expect Equate to return solutions, the equational format does not limit constraint expression. For example, a request for programs that generate counterexamples to Fermat's Last Theorem can be expressed as the equation:

```
( int?(a) ∧ int?(b) ∧ int?(c) ∧ int?(n) ∧
a>0 ∧ b>0 ∧ c>0 ∧ n>2 ∧
(a^n + b^n = c^n) ) = true
```

3 The Structure of Solutions

A solution S is a program represented by a directed, acyclic graph (V, E). A vertex of S is called a *step*. Each step v_i comprises both a goal G_i and a corresponding instruction I_i for achieving that goal. A solution is executed by performing the instructions according to a topological ordering of the steps.

The solution in Figure 2 has two possible execution sequences: I_1, I_2, I_3 and I_2, I_1, I_3. Step v_2 contains a special instruction fail-unless. Some solutions, like the one in this example, work only under certain conditions; fail-unless aborts the solution when these conditions are not met. Solutions running to completion achieve the conjunction of their goals.

For simplicity of presentation, a solution is sometimes shown as a list of its instructions in an order corresponding to one topological ordering of steps.

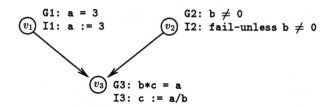

Figure 2: A solution to (a = 3 ∧ b*c = a) = true.

4 The Search for Solutions

Equate's constraint-solving method can be summarized as follows: decompose a large constraint into smaller constraints for which solutions are known, then combine those solutions into a solution that satisfies the large constraint. Constraints are recursively decomposed using definite-clause backward chaining, the search technique used in logic programming languages [Llo87] of which Prolog is the best-known example.

4.1 Rewrite Rules

The search for solutions is guided by *rewrite rules* provided by object classes. These rules are similar to the program clauses of logic programs. In Equate rewrite rules serve two purposes: to provide solutions to equations directly, and (when direct solutions cannot be given) to convert equations into equivalent sets of equations that are more easily solved. Equate's simplification strategy is to rewrite an equation until its left-hand side is simple enough that a solution can be given directly.

The form of a rewrite rule is

$$A \quad \longleftarrow \quad B_1; \ \ldots; \ B_n \quad (n \geq 1)$$

where A is called the *head* and $B_1; \ldots; B_n$ is called the *body*. To find a solution set for an equation E, Equate searches for rules whose heads match E. For each matching rule, a solution set is created by *synthesizing* the solution sets generated from each B_i in the body. The complete solution set for E is the union of the solution sets created for each of these rules. Section 4.2 explains the process of solution set synthesis.

The head of a rewrite rule is always in the form of an equation. Each B_i in the body can be in one of two forms:

- An instruction. The solution set for an instruction consists of a single solution of one step with that instruction. If the instruction is of the form **fail-unless** *predicate* then the goal of the step is *predicate*; otherwise, the goal is E.

- An equation. The solution set for an equation is found recursively.

Let us look at some rewrite rules.

```
right(box) = exp  ←
    left(box) + width(box) = exp
```

This rule says that to get the coordinate of the right edge of a box to equal some value, it is sufficient to get the sum of the coordinate of the left edge and the width to equal that value.

```
exp₁ = exp₂  ←
    fail-unless symbol?(exp₁);
    exp₁ := exp₂
```

This rule says that an assignment statement can be used to give a symbol a particular value.

```
abs(exp₁) = exp₂  ←
    fail-unless exp₂ ≥ 0;
    exp₁ = exp₂
```

This rule says that to get the absolute value of one expression to equal the value of a second, if the value of the second expression is non-negative then it is enough to make the values of the two expressions equal. Appendix B contains more examples of rewrite rules.

The search for solution sets is improved by constant folding, in which constant expressions are replaced by their values. This is particularly important when the predicate of a **fail-unless** instruction is a constant expression. If the value of the predicate is **true**, then the **fail-unless** instruction is superfluous and can be removed from any solution that contains it. If the value of the predicate is **false**, then the instruction causes any solution that contains it to abort, so that solution can be discarded.

4.2 Synthesizing Solution Sets

So far we have discussed how rewrite rules are used to break down an equation into instructions and simpler equations for which solution sets are found. Now let us discuss how to synthesize these solution sets into a single solution set for the original equation.

The process is associative, so we need describe only the synthesis of two solution sets. Let $\{S_1, S_2, \ldots, S_m\}$ be one set of solutions and let $\{T_1, T_2, \ldots, T_n\}$ be another set of solutions. A *join* of two solutions is defined to be a solution that achieves all the goals in both solutions. The synthesis of the two solution sets is the set of all joins of a solution from the first set with a solution from the second set. Using "$\bowtie$" as the join operator, we can express the synthesis of the two solution sets as $\{S_j \bowtie T_k \mid 1 \leq j \leq m,\ 1 \leq k \leq n\}$.

4.3 Computing a Join

Let $S_1 = (V_1, E_1)$ and $S_2 = (V_2, E_2)$ be two solutions. To compute $S_1 \bowtie S_2 = S_3 = (V_3, E_3)$, first let S_3 be a supergraph of S_1 and S_2 such that $V_3 = V_1 \cup V_2$ and $E_3 = E_1 \cup E_2$.

The construction is not yet complete. Whereas E_1 and E_2 guarantee that execution sequences achieve the respective goals of S_1 and S_2, execution sequences given by $E_1 \cup E_2$ may not achieve all the goals of S_3. Additional edges may need to be added to S_3 to ensure that all goals are protected during execution; that is, once achieved they stay achieved.

A step v_i with instruction I_i and goal G_i is said to *clobber* a step v_j with instruction I_j and goal G_j if G_j does not hold after the execution sequence I_j, I_i. To protect each goal in S_3, Equate inserts into S_3 an edge from v_i to v_j for all steps v_i that might clobber step v_j, forcing v_i to execute before v_j in any execution sequence. If the resulting graph is cyclic, then there is no topological ordering of steps and the solution is discarded.

289

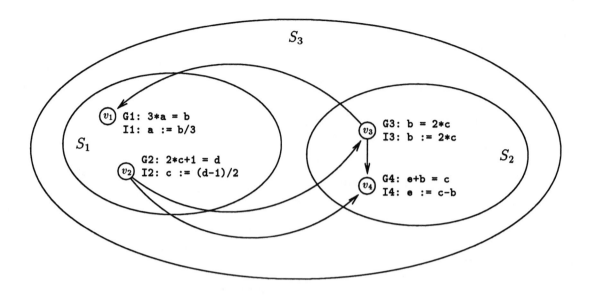

Figure 3: S_3 is the join of solutions S_1 and S_2.

Equate concludes that a step v_i might clobber a step v_j if I_i writes to any memory location that is both read by G_j and read or written by I_j. The need for the first condition is clear: G_j can be made false only if I_i writes to a location used in its evaluation. The need for the second condition is more subtle: if I_j is sure to make G_j hold, then the values in locations not read or written by I_j are of no consequence.

Figure 3 shows S_3 as the join of two solutions $S_1 = (\{v_1, v_2\}, \{\})$ and $S_2 = (\{v_3, v_4\}, \{(v_3, v_4)\})$. Because I_3 writes b and both G_1 and I_1 read b, an edge from v_3 to v_1 is included in S_3. Likewise, edges from v_2 to v_3 and from v_2 to v_4 are also included.

Equate distinguishes two types of memory location. The first is a symbol, like a or x, for which the symbol itself provides its own unique identity. The other type of location is a state variable. A unique identifier for the state variable of any object is a pair of the identity of that object with the name of the state variable. Thus the state variable of box1 that stores its width is uniquely identified by (box1,width).

4.4 Location Rules

To decide if one step might clobber another, Equate must compute the locations read and written by expressions; that is, their *read sets* and *write sets*. It does so using *location rules* provided by object classes. Location rules are similar to rewrite rules, but the information returned is not a set of programs but a set of locations. A few examples:

```
read-set(exp₁ * exp₂)  ⟵
    read-set(exp₁) ∪
    read-set(exp₂)
```

This rule says that the read set of $exp_1 * exp_2$ is the union of the read sets of exp_1 and exp_2.

```
read-set(top(box))  ⟵
    requires box?(box);
    {(box,bottom),(box,height)}
```

This rule says that to be able to compute the read set of top(*box*), *box* must be an explicit box object: the read set cannot be computed if the value of *box* is known only when the solution containing that expression is executed. Given that requirement, the locations read by top(*box*) are the bottom and height of *box*.

```
write-set(exp₁ := exp₂)    ⟵
    requires symbol?(exp₁);
    {exp₁} ∪
    write-set(exp₂)
```

This rule says that the write set of the assignment statement exp_1 := exp_2, where exp_1 is a symbol, includes exp_1 as well as any locations written by exp_2.

```
write-set(scale(box,sx,sy))    ⟵
    requires box?(box);
    if sx ≠ 1.0 then {(box,width)} ∪
    if sy ≠ 1.0 then {(box,height)} ∪
    if sx ≠ 1.0 or sy ≠ 1.0
                then {(box,area)} ∪
    write-set(sx) ∪
    write-set(sy)
```

This rule says that the execution of scale(box,sx,sy) could change the value of (box,width) unless sx is the constant 1.0; likewise for (box,height). Its execution could change the value of (box,area) unless both sx and sy are 1.0. It is unlikely that expressions sx or sy would write locations, but because they might we union in write-set(sx) and write-set(sy).

4.5   The "safe" Function

As Equate composes solutions to an equation $exp_1 = exp_2$ it sometimes generates instructions that would change the value of exp_2 while changing the value of exp_1. Consider the symbol-assignment rule from Section 4.1. Applying the rule to the equation x = 2*x-1 generates the incorrect solution x := 2*x-1. The error is avoided because Equate discards any solutions containing instructions that read and write the same location. This filtering frees the rule itself from having to prevent such instructions. (To solve equations like x = 2*x-1, rewrite rules for transforming linear equations can be written.)

Occasionally instructions that read and write the same location should be permitted. Consider this ineffective rewrite rule:

```
int?(exp) = true    ⟵
    exp = floor(exp)
```

The rule says that to get an expression exp to be an integer it is sufficient to make exp equal to the largest integer no larger than exp. Applying this rule to the equation int?(a) = true generates a := floor(a) which, although correct, would be discarded by Equate. The rule needs to tell Equate that changing exp to establish the equality will not also change floor(exp). It can do so by using the identity function safe for which there is the location rule:

```
read-set(safe(exp))    ⟵
    {}
```

The correct rewrite rule is:

```
int?(exp) = true    ⟵
    exp = safe(floor(exp))
```

With this rule the equation int?(a) = true generates a := safe(floor(a)). This looks to Equate like an instruction with an empty read set and therefore it would not be discarded. Calls to safe serve no purpose during the execution of solutions, so they vanish from instructions once read sets have been determined.

5   Using Equate

Equate only transforms an equation into a set of solutions; the application has the responsibility of managing constraints and executing solutions. This section describes how an application should accomplish these tasks.

5.1   Adding and Removing Constraints

When an application has several constraints to be solved, it should ask Equate for solutions to each, cache those results, and then call Equate's routine for synthesizing solution sets. This approach is more efficient than asking Equate to solve the conjunction of constraints directly: if an individual constraint is added or removed, only the synthesis needs to be recomputed.

291

5.2 Choosing a Solution

Once a solution set for all the constraints has been created, the application must choose a solution from that set to execute when it decides to satisfy the constraints. Although that choice may be application-specific, there are some general guidelines to follow.

First, solutions with the fewest `fail-unless` instructions are preferable as they are perhaps most likely to run to completion. Solutions with no `fail-unless` instructions will always succeed.

Second, it may be desirable to avoid changing certain locations. For example, if the user of the application has just issued a command that assigns values to some locations, solutions that do not write to those locations should be favored; otherwise, a solution might simply undo the user's operation.

Third, the execution time for each solution can be estimated by its apparent complexity. Shorter, simpler solutions should obviously be favored.

5.3 Aborted Solutions

A solution is executed by performing its instructions according to a topological ordering of its steps. If the predicate of a `fail-unless` instruction evaluates to `false` then the solution aborts: no more instructions are executed, and a failure is signaled. When a solution aborts then in all likelihood the constraints have not been satisfied. But because the solution has accessed objects using the proper interface, the objects themselves are always consistent. Depending on the application it may be possible to try another solution immediately without rolling back the effects of the failed solution.

It is sometimes desirable to restore the application to its state before a solution was attempted. Anticipating this, the application can copy out the values of all locations in the write set of a solution. If the solution aborts then these locations can be restored.

If all solutions fail, the application must somehow cope with a state where the constraints do not hold. The user of the application might attempt to change the state to one from which a solution will run to completion. Alternatively, the user might be asked to remove or change constraints.

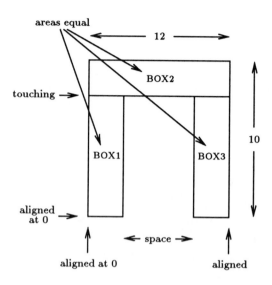

Figure 4: The constraints on the arch.

6 A Final Example

Let us examine the performance of Equate on a nontrivial example. Figure 4 shows an arch composed of three boxes; eight constraints guarantee the arch is well-formed. The following equation expresses these constraints:

```
((left(box1) = left(box2) = 0.0) ∧
 (bottom(box1) = bottom(box3) = 0.0) ∧
 (height(box1) + height(box2) = 10.0) ∧
 (width(box2) = 12.0) ∧
 (top(box1) = bottom(box2) = top(box3)) ∧
 (right(box2) = right(box3)) ∧
 (area(box1) = area(box2) = area(box3)) ∧
 (right(box1) < left(box3)))
= true
```

Using the rules in Appendix B, Equate returns four solutions. The arch is highly constrained, so in each solution only one memory location remains fixed while the others are changed to satisfy the equation. The first solution fixes the height of `box1`, the second fixes the height of box2, the third fixes the height of box3, and the fourth fixes the bottom of box2. Because of these fixed values, none of the solutions can succeed from every start state; for example, the first solution will fail if executed in a state where the height of box1 is greater than 10.

Figure 5 shows an arch that already satisfies the constraints. Let us change the arch, increasing the height of box2 from 2 to 2.5 as shown in Figure 6. (The dashed line shows the height of box2 before the change.) The arch no longer has a height of 10, so let us choose a solution to reestablish the constraints. The second solution does not write to location (box2,height), so we know that if we execute it our change to the height of box2 will remain. Here is that solution:

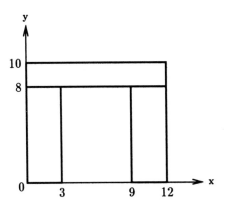

Figure 5: The arch in its original state.

```
fail-unless 10.0-height(box2) > 0.0;
move-to(box1, 0.0, nil);
move-to(box2, 0.0, nil);
move-to(box1, nil, 0.0);
move-to(box3, nil, 0.0);
scale(box1,
      1.0,
      (10.0-height(box2))/height(box1));
fail-unless top(box1)-bottom(box3) > 0.0;
scale(box2, 12.0/width(box2), 1.0);
fail-unless area(box2)/height(box1) > 0.0;
move-to(box2, nil, top(box1));
scale(box3,
      1.0,
      (top(box1)-bottom(box3))/height(box3));
fail-unless area(box2)/height(box3) > 0.0;
scale(box1,
      (area(box2)/height(box1))/width(box1),
      1.0);
scale(box3,
      (area(box2)/height(box3))/width(box3),
      1.0);
move-to(box3, right(box2)-width(box3), nil);
fail-unless (right(box1)<left(box3)) = true;
```

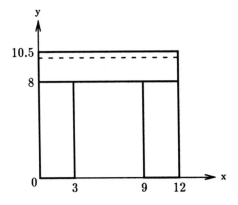

Figure 6: The arch after changing its height.

Execution of this solution gives us the arch shown in Figure 7. (The dashed lines show the arch in the state before the solution was executed.) Any of the other three solutions would have succeeded, but would have merely reduced the height of box2 back to 2, restoring the arch to its state in Figure 5.

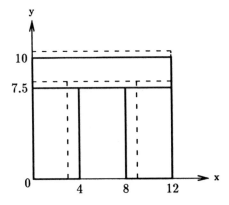

Figure 7: The arch after executing the solution.

293

7 Related Work

The constraint-solving technique most similar to Equate's is ThingLab's use of propagation of degrees of freedom [Bor79]. ThingLab also divides the constraint satisfaction process into two phases: a planning phase and a plan execution phase. (This approach had been taken in Sutherland's trailblazing Sketchpad [Sut63].) But whereas Equate composes its solutions as constraints are declared, ThingLab composes its plans when objects are asked to change. ThingLab propagates degrees of freedom within a constraint graph by finding parts that have only one constraint affecting them; Equate's better conflict detection (see Section 4.3) overcomes this limitation, yielding more solutions. Borning later enhanced ThingLab by allowing constraints of differing strengths [B+87, B+89].

ThingLab II [MBFB89, FBMB90] improved upon its predecessor by including an incremental planning algorithm so that its constraint graphs need not be recomputed from scratch with each addition or removal of a constraint. Vander Zanden [Van88] provided an incremental planner for collections of required constraints.

Concurrent to the development of ThingLab were the studies of Steele and Sussman [SS80, Ste80] on local propagation of values through hierarchical constraint networks. Their systems feature multiple views for high-level reasoning about networks, the ability to retract assumptions that led to contradictions, efficient backtracking, and the generation of explanations. Other well-known constraint solvers include IDEAL [Van82], which typesets graphics into documents by solving systems of "slightly nonlinear" equations; Magritte [Gos83], which uses algebraic techniques to eliminate cycles from constraint graphs; and TK!Solver [KJ85], a commercial product for personal computers that solves sets of equations using local propagation and relaxation. [Lel88] contains a summary of these and other systems, including Leler's own system Bertrand. Among constraint solvers, Equate is unique in its use of location rules to determine conflicts in solutions.

Some concepts in Equate (goal clobbering, backward chaining, fail conditions, solution graphs) have parallels in planning, a highly-studied subfield of artificial intelligence. Planning is the process of finding a sequence of actions that a robot (or some other agent) can take to accomplish a prespecified goal. HACKER [Sus73] introduced a subgoal protection technique to assure the satisfaction of conjunctive goals when combining plans. WARPLAN [War74] was the first Prolog planner; its successor WARPLAN-C [War76] generates plans with conditional branches. NOAH [Sac75] was the first nonlinear planner, where a plan is represented as a partial order on steps. [AHT90] is a collection of major papers on planning.

Equate's rules for transforming equations are similar to (but currently much simpler than) those found in symbolic arithmetic systems. PRESS [BW81] is an equation solver implemented in Prolog that controls its algebraic manipulations with meta-level inference rules. MACSYMA [Sym89] and Mathematica [Wol88] are well-known symbolic arithmetic packages.

Logic programming has recently been extended to include constraint satisfaction [Coh90]. A theoretical foundation for constraint logic programming has been presented by Jaffar and Lassez [JL87]. Prolog III [Col90] is an instance of the theory. Constraint logic programming allows the inclusion of constraints in program clauses. Conjunctions of constraints are simplified using domain-specific constraint solvers, such as SL resolution for boolean formulas and Gaussian elimination or the simplex method for systems of linear equations and inequations.

Although constraint satisfaction is most often the search for a direct matching of values to variables, some studies have shown particular concern for encapsulation. [Tom89] describes difficulties with placing constraints on encapsulated objects in a CAD system but offers no concrete solutions. Encapsulation comes naturally to ThingLab, primarily because its constraints come from within class definitions and are not arbitrarily imposed from outside. Apogee [HH88] is a user-interface management system that respects encapsulation, but it does not do true constraint solving because dependencies among objects are expressed procedurally (and purely functionally) rather than declaratively. [Bar86, SM88, Giu89] are other systems with procedural dependencies.

8 Future Directions

Reducing search time. A direct implementation of the search method described in Section 4 is too inefficient for solving substantial constraint problems. Currently in development are heuristics for eliminating incompatible solutions sets before those sets are computed explicitly. Also in development is a scheme for representing large solution sets economically.

Solution optimization. Before execution, solutions can be filtered so that they do not contain instructions for satisfying constraints that have not been violated. Common subexpression elimination would also improve solution efficiency.

Smarter joining. The join algorithm could detect special conditions; for example, it should know that identical steps never clobber each other.

More locations. Locations can be defined for array and list elements, for example.

Inexplicit references. Currently all constraints must refer to objects explicitly. One would like to be able to place a constraint on "the largest box," where the identity of that box is variable.

Automatic rule generation. Using modern code-analysis techniques it is sometimes possible for the computer to generate location rules.

Guarantee of termination. PRESS [BW81] guarantees termination of its search by requiring each rule to reduce some numerical property of the expression to which it is applied. Equate could support a similar requirement.

The "safe" function. The use of safe is somewhat *ad hoc*; an alternative is sought.

Polymorphism. To allow for polymorphic functions it will be necessary to consider types when matching expressions to rules.

9 Summary and Conclusions

Equate was created to provide an object-oriented paradigm for constraint programming. Equate respects the principle of object encapsulation in its constraints and solutions, easing the task of incorporating it into applications. Beyond respecting this principle, Equate has other advantages. Because each class provides the rules for decom-

posing and solving constraints placed on instances of that class, Equate is especially useful to applications with heterogenous data. Because rewrite and location rules are kept separate from the methods of an application, these methods do not need to be written in a special constraint language. Because Equate produces procedural translations of constraint equations, the application can pick the appropriate time to reestablish constraints.

The constraint-solving power of Equate depends on the rules provided by object classes. Equate uses these rules to break a large constraint into smaller, solvable constraints, then finds an ordering of solutions to these constraints that ensures that the effects of one solution are not "clobbered" by another. Any constraint for which a solution method is known can be solved using Equate, provided that the constraint is in a form that can be matched to a rule for solving it.

Finding solutions requires a considerable search. Fortunately, this is required only as constraints are declared. In most applications the constraints seldom change as the application is used. The need to reestablish constraints occurs much more frequently, and this requires only the choice and execution of a solution, not a lengthy analysis. Even when some constraints do change, the constraints that remain unchanged do not require reanalysis.

This paper has presented the basic principles of Equate. Before Equate will be ready as a fully-functioning constraint solver it will be necessary to resolve many of the issues raised in Section 8. The prototype has performed well, so the outlook is promising.

Acknowledgements

Thanks to Paul Bay, Alan Borning, Roy Hall, John Hopcroft, Kevin Novins, Rick Palmer, and Len Wanger for constructive comments on drafts of this paper. This work was supported by The Advanced Research Projects Agency of the Department of Defense under Office of Naval Research Contract N00014-88-K-0591, ONR Grant N00014-89-J-1946, and NSF Grant IRI-9006137.

Appendix A

A box is an instance of BOX-CLASS. Each box has the following state variables: LEFT, BOTTOM, WIDTH, HEIGHT, and AREA. Figure 8 shows a diagram of a box with its state variables indicated.

These methods operate on boxes:

`left(box)`
`bottom(box)`
`width(box)`
`height(box)`
`area(box)`
> returns the value of the appropriate state variable.

`right(box)`
> returns the value of LEFT + WIDTH.

`top(box)`
> returns the value of BOTTOM + HEIGHT.

`move-to(box, x, y)`
> sets LEFT to x (unless x is nil) and sets BOTTOM to y (unless y is nil).

`scale(box, sx, sy)`
> scales WIDTH by the amount sx (if $sx > 0$) and HEIGHT by the amount sy (if $sy > 0$), then assigns AREA the product of WIDTH and HEIGHT.

`box?(exp)`
> a predicate for testing if exp is a box.

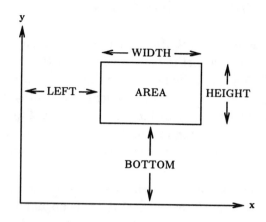

Figure 8: The state variables of a box.

$$area(box) = exp \longleftarrow$$
$$height(box) = exp/width(box)$$

$$right(box) = exp \longleftarrow$$
$$left(box) + width(box) = exp$$

$$top(box) = exp \longleftarrow$$
$$bottom(box) + height(box) = exp$$

Some rewrite rules for numbers and booleans:

$$(exp_1 + exp_2) = exp_3 \longleftarrow$$
$$exp_1 = exp_3 - exp_2$$

$$(exp_1 + exp_2) = exp_3 \longleftarrow$$
$$exp_2 = exp_3 - exp_1$$

$$(exp_1 < exp_2) = \text{true} \longleftarrow$$
$$exp_1 = exp_2 - 1.0$$

$$(exp_1 < exp_2) = \text{true} \longleftarrow$$
$$exp_2 = exp_1 + 1.0$$

$$(exp_1 < exp_2) = exp_3 \longleftarrow$$
$$\text{fail-unless } (exp_1 < exp_2) = exp_3$$

$$(exp_1 \wedge exp_2) = exp_3 \longleftarrow$$
$$exp_1 = exp_3;$$
$$exp_2 = exp_3$$

$$(exp_1 = exp_2) = \text{true} \longleftarrow$$
$$exp_1 = exp_2$$

$$(exp_1 = exp_2) = \text{true} \longleftarrow$$
$$exp_2 = exp_1$$

Appendix B

Rewrite rules from BOX-CLASS:

$$left(box) = exp \longleftarrow$$
$$move\text{-}to(box, exp, nil)$$

$$bottom(box) = exp \longleftarrow$$
$$move\text{-}to(box, nil, exp)$$

$$width(box) = exp \longleftarrow$$
$$\text{fail-unless } exp > 0.0;$$
$$scale(box, exp/safe(width(box)), 1.0)$$

$$height(box) = exp \longleftarrow$$
$$\text{fail-unless } exp > 0.0;$$
$$scale(box, 1.0, exp/safe(height(box)))$$

$$area(box) = exp \longleftarrow$$
$$width(box) = exp/height(box)$$

References

[AHT90] J. Allen, J. Hendler, and A. Tate, editors. *Readings in Planning.* Morgan Kaufmann, San Mateo, California, 1990.

[B+87] A. Borning *et al.* Constraint hierarchies. In *OOPSLA Conference Proceedings,* Orlando, Florida, pages 48–60, October 1987.

[B+89] A. Borning *et al.* Constraint hierarchies and logic programming. In *Proceedings of the Sixth International Conference on Logic Programming,* Lisbon, Portugal, pages 149–164, June 1989.

[Bar86] P. S. Barth. An object-oriented approach to graphical interfaces. *ACM Transactions on Graphics,* 5(2):142–172, April 1986.

[Boo91] G. Booch. *Object Oriented Design with Applications.* Benjamin/Cummings, Redwood City, California, 1991.

[Bor79] A. Borning. ThingLab – a constraint-oriented simulation laboratory. Technical Report SSL-79-3, Xerox PARC, Palo Alto, California, July 1979.

[BW81] A. Bundy and B. Welham. Using meta-level inference for selective application of multiple rewrite rule sets in algebraic manipulation. *Artificial Intelligence,* 16:189–212, 1981.

[Coh90] J. Cohen. Constraint logic programming languages. *Communications of the ACM,* 33(7):52–68, July 1990.

[Col90] A. Colmerauer. An introduction to Prolog III. *Communications of the ACM,* 33(7):69–90, July 1990.

[FBMB90] B. N. Freeman-Benson, J. Maloney, and A. Borning. An incremental constraint solver. *Communications of the ACM,* 33(1):54–63, January 1990.

[Giu89] D. Giuse. KR: constraint-based knowledge representation. Technical Report CMU-CS-89-142, Department of Computer Science, Carnegie-Mellon University, Pittsburgh, Pennsylvania, April 1989.

[Gos83] J. Gosling. *Algebraic Constraints.* PhD thesis, Department of Computer Science, Carnegie-Mellon University, Pittsburgh, Pennsylvania, May 1983.

[HH88] T. R. Henry and S. E. Hudson. Using active data in a UIMS. In *Proceedings of the ACM SIGGRAPH Symposium on User Interface Software,* pages 167–178, Banff, Alberta, October 1988.

[JL87] J. Jaffar and J.-L. Lassez. Constraint logic programming. In *Conference Record of the Fourteenth Annual ACM Symposium on Principles of Programming Languages,* pages 111–119, Munich, West Germany, January 1987.

[KJ85] M. Konopasek and S. Jayaraman. Constraint and declarative languages for engineering applications: the TK!Solver contribution. *Proceedings of the IEEE,* 73(12):1791–1806, December 1985.

[Lel88] W. Leler. *Constraint Programming Languages: Their Specification and Generation.* Addison-Wesley, Reading, Massachusetts, 1988.

[Llo87] J. W. Lloyd. *Foundations of Logic Programming.* Springer-Verlag, Berlin, 1987.

[MBFB89] J. H. Maloney, A. Borning, and B. N. Freeman-Benson. Constraint technology for user-interface construction in ThingLab II. In *OOPSLA Conference Proceedings,* New Orleans, Louisiana, pages 381–388, October 1989.

[Sac75] E. D. Sacerdoti. The nonlinear nature of plans. In *Advance Papers of the Fourth International Joint Conference on Artificial Intelligence,* pages 206–214, Tbilisi, USSR, September 1975.

[SM88] P. A. Szekely and B. A. Myers. A user interface toolkit based on graphical objects and constraints. In *OOPSLA Conference Proceedings,* San Diego, California, pages 36–45, September 1988.

[SS80] G. J. Sussman and G. L. Steele Jr. CONSTRAINTS – a language for expressing almost-hierarchical descriptions. *Artificial Intelligence,* 14:1–39, 1980.

[Ste80] G. L. Steele Jr. *The Definition and Implementation of a Computer Programming Language Based on Constraints.* PhD thesis, Department of Electrical Engineering and Computer Science, M.I.T., Cambridge, Massachusetts, August 1980.

[Sus73] G. J. Sussman. *A Computational Model of Skill Acquisition.* PhD thesis, Artificial Intelligence Laboratory, M.I.T., Cambridge, Massachusetts, August 1973.

[Sut63] I. E. Sutherland. Sketchpad: a man-machine graphical communication system. In *Proceedings of the AFIPS Spring Joint Computer Conference,* pages 329–346, Detroit, Michigan, May 1963.

[Sym89] Symbolics, Inc., Burlington, Massachusetts. *MACSYMA Reference Manual,* 14th edition, 1989.

[Tom89] T. Tomiyama. Object oriented programming paradigm for intelligent CAD systems. In *Intelligent CAD Systems II: Implementational Issues,* pages 3–16. Springer-Verlag, Berlin, 1989.

[Van82] C. J. Van Wyk. A high-level language for specifying pictures. *ACM Transactions on Graphics,* 1(2):163–182, April 1982.

[Van88] B. T. Vander Zanden. An incremental planning algorithm for ordering equations in a multilinear system of constraints. Technical Report 88-910, Department of Computer Science, Cornell University, Ithaca, New York, April 1988.

[War74] D. H. D. Warren. WARPLAN: a system for generating plans. Department of Computational Logic Memo 76, University of Edinburgh, Scotland, June 1974.

[War76] D. H. D. Warren. Generating conditional plans and programs. In *Proceedings of the AISB Summer Conference,* pages 344–354, University of Edinburgh, Scotland, 1976.

[Wol88] S. Wolfram. *Mathematica: A System for Doing Mathematics by Computer.* Addison-Wesley, Redwood City, California, 1988.

Object-Preserving Class Transformations

Paul L. Bergstein

Northeastern University, College of Computer Science

Cullinane Hall, 360 Huntington Ave., Boston MA 02115

pberg@corwin.CCS.northeastern.EDU

Abstract

Reorganization of classes for object-oriented programming and object-oriented database design has recently received considerable attention in the literature. In this paper a small set of primitive transformations is presented which forms an orthogonal basis for object-preserving class reorganizations. This set is proven to be correct, complete, and minimal. The primitive transformations help form a theoretical basis for class organization and are a powerful tool for reasoning about particular organizations.

Keywords: Object-oriented programming and design, object-oriented database design, class library organization.

1 Introduction

Reorganization of classes for object-oriented programming and object-oriented database design has recently received considerable attention in the literature: [BCG*87], [LBS90], [LBS91], [AH87], [BMW86], [Cas89], [Cas90], [LM91], [Pir89], [PW89]. A number of researchers have suggested algorithms and hueristics to produce "good" class organizations. A "good" class organization may be variously defined as one which promotes efficient reuse of code, one with a minimum of multiple-inheritance, a minimum of repeated-inheritance, or some other characteristics depending on the author's point of view.

In any case, it is usually desirable that reorganization of a class hierarchy should not change the set of objects which the classes define, that is the reorganization should be **object-preserving**. For object-oriented database design, this means that the database does not need to be repopulated. For object-oriented programming, this means that programs will still accept the same inputs and produce the same outputs. Furthermore, methods need not be rewritten (although they may need to be attached to different classes).

In this paper a small set of primitive transformations is presented which forms an orthogonal basis for object-preserving class organizations. This set is proven to be correct, complete, and minimal. The primitive transformations help form a theoretical basis for class organization and are useful in proving characteristics of particular organizations.

The concept of a primitive set of object-preserving class transformations was developed as part of the Demeter project to develop CASE tools for object-oriented design and programming. While the class model used in this paper is the simplified one of [LBS91], the Demeter System^{TM} actually uses an expanded model which includes optional parts, collection (repetition) classes, and the ability to specify concrete syntax used for parsing and printing objects. Each notation has the advantage of being programming language independent and is therefore useful to programmers who use object-oriented languages such as C++ [Str86], Smalltalk [GR83], CLOS [BDG*88] or Eiffel [Mey88].

The C++ Demeter System incorporates a C++

OOPSLA'91, pp. 299–313

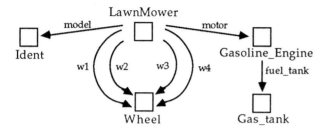

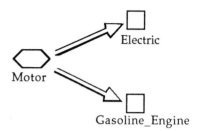

Figure 1: Construction class

Figure 2: Alternation class

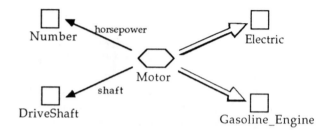

Figure 3: Common parts

code generation algorithm to translate the class definitions into C++ and generate methods for manipulating the application objects (e.g. parsing, printing, copying, comparing, traversing, etc.). The primitive transformations discussed in this paper were very helpful in developing and analyzing the latest additions to the Demeter System: tools for the abstraction of optimal class organizations from object examples, and for the optimization of existing class organizations [LBS91] [BL91].

The second section provides a brief description of the class notation. In section 3 the primitive transformations are presented along with related proofs. In section 4 some practical rules for class hierarchy optimization, which can be built from the primitive transformations, are given.

2 Class notation

The class notation of [LBS91] uses two kinds of classes: construction and alternation classes. A construction class definition is an abstraction of a class definition in a typical statically typed programming language (e.g., C++). A construction class does not reveal implementation information. Examples of construction classes are in Fig. 1 for: LawnMower, Wheel, etc.

Each construction class defines a set of objects which can be thought of as being elements of the direct product of the part classes. When modeling an application domain, it is natural to take the union of object sets defined by construction classes. For example, the motor of a lawn-mower can be either a gasoline engine or an electric motor. So the objects that can be stored in the motor part of a

lawn-mower are either gasoline_engine or electric motor objects. Alternation classes are used to define such union classes. An example of an alternation class is in Fig. 2. Gasoline_Engine and Electric are called alternatives of the alternation class. Often the alternatives have some common parts. For example, each motor has a drive shaft. The notation in Fig. 3 is used to express such common parts. Alternation classes have their origin in the variant records of Pascal. Because of the delayed binding of function calls to code in object-oriented programming, alternation classes are easier to use than variant records.

Alternation classes which have common parts are implemented by inheritance. In Fig. 3, Electric and Gasoline_Engine inherit from Motor. Class Motor has methods and/or instance variables to implement the parts horsepower and shaft.

Construction and alternation classes correspond to the two basic data type constructions in denotational semantics: cartesian products and disjoint sums. They also correspond to the two basic mechanisms used in formal languages: concatenation and alternation.

The concept of a part class which is used throughout this paper needs further explanation.

A part object does not have to be a physical part; any attribute of an object is a part of it. Object o_2 is said to be a part of object o_1 if "o_1 knows about o_2". Therefore, the part-of relation is a generalization of the aggregation relation which only describes physical containment. For example, a car is part of a wheel if the wheel knows about the car.

Definition 1 . *A* **class dictionary graph** ϕ *is a directed graph* $\phi = (V, \Lambda; EC, EA)$ *with finitely many vertices* V. Λ *is a finite set of labels. There are two defining relations* EC, EA. EC *is a ternary relation on* $V \times V \times \Lambda$, *called the (labeled) construction edges:* $(v, w, l) \in EC$ *iff there is a construction edge with label* l *from* v *to* w. EA *is a binary relation on* $V \times V$, *called the alternation edges:* $(v, w) \in EA$ *iff there is an alternation edge from* v *to* w.

Next the set of vertices is partitioned into two subclasses, called the construction and alternation vertices.

Definition 2 .

- *The* **construction vertices** *are defined by* $VC = \{v \mid v \in V, \forall w \in V : (v, w) \notin EA\}$. *In other words, the construction vertices have no outgoing alternation edges.*

- *The* **alternation vertices** *are defined by* $VA = \{v \mid v \in V, \exists w \in V : (v, w) \in EA\}$. *In other words, the alternation vertices have at least one outgoing alternation edge.*

Sometimes, it is more convenient to describe a class dictionary graph as a tuple which contains explicit references to VC and VA: $\phi = (VC, VA, \Lambda; EC, EA)$.

The definition of a class dictionary graph is motivated by the interpretation in object-oriented design given in Figure 4. During the programming process, the alternation classes serve to define interfaces (i.e., they serve the role of types) and the construction classes serve to provide implementations for the interfaces.

Graph	Object-oriented design
Vertex	Class
construction	instantiable
alternation	abstract
Edge	Class relationship
construction	part-of relationship "uses", "knows", labels are part names
alternation	inheritance relationship specialization, classification

Figure 4: Standard Interpretation

The standard interpretation implies that the labels on construction vertices are significant. Consider two class dictionary graphs each with only a single construction vertex and no edges. From a graph theoretic point of view, the graphs are equal regardless of the labels on the vertices, but if the construction vertex of one graph is labeled *Integer* and the vertex of the other graph is labeled *String*, then the two class dictionary graphs define different sets of objects in the standard interpretation.

Since the mapping from construction vertices to labels is a bijection, its explicit inclusion in the definition of class dictionary graphs would only clutter the theory. When referring to an element of the construction vertices of a class dictionary graph, the reference is sometimes to a vertex and sometimes to the label of a vertex. The meaning should be clear from the context.

The following graphical notation, based on [TYF86], is used for drawing class dictionary graphs: squares for construction vertices, hexagons for alternation vertices, thin lines for construction edges and double lines for alternation edges.

Example 1 *Fig. 5 shows a class dictionary graph for telephones. Telephones can either be standard or cordless and they also can be either rotary dial or touch-tone. Cordless phones have an antenna while standard phones have a handset cord. The dialer on a touch-tone phone is a keypad, whereas a rotary* *dial phone has a dial. For further illustration the components of the formal definition are given, i.e.:*

```
V = { Telephone, Cordless, Standard,
      Antenna, Handset_Cord,
      Dialer, Rotary, Dial,
      TouchTone, Keypad }

VC = { Cordless, Standard, Antenna,
       Handset_Cord, Rotary, Dial,
       TouchTone, Keypad }

VA = { Telephone, Dialer }

EC = { (Telephone, Dialer, dialer),
       (Rotary, Dial, dial),
       (TouchTone, Keypad, dial),
       (Cordless, Antenna, ant),
       (Standard, Handset_Cord, cord) }

EA = { (Telephone, Cordless),
       (Telephone, Standard),
       (Dialer, Rotary),
       (Dialer, TouchTone) }

Λ  = {dialer, ant, cord, dial }.
```

Definition 3 *In a class dictionary graph $\phi = (V, \Lambda;\ EC, EA)$, a vertex $w \in V$ is **alternation-reachable** from vertex $v \in V$ (we write $v \stackrel{*}{\Rightarrow} w$):*

- *via a path of length 0, if $v = w$*

- *via a path of length $n + 1$, if $\exists u \in V$ such that $(v, u) \in EA$ and $u \stackrel{*}{\Rightarrow} w$ via a path of length n.*

A legal class dictionary graph is a structure which satisfies 2 independent axioms.

Definition 4 *A class dictionary graph $\phi = (V, \Lambda;\ EC, EA)$ is **legal** if it satisfies the following two axioms:*

1. *Cycle-free alternation axiom:*

   There are no cyclic alternation paths, i.e.,
   $$\{(v, w) \mid v, w \in V, v \neq w, \text{ and } v \stackrel{*}{\Rightarrow} w \stackrel{*}{\Rightarrow} v\} = \emptyset.$$

2. *Unique labels axiom:*

   $$\forall u, v, v', w, w' \in V,\ l \in \Lambda \text{ such that}$$
   $$v \stackrel{*}{\Rightarrow} u,\ v' \stackrel{*}{\Rightarrow} u,\ \text{and } (v, w) \neq (v', w'):$$
   $$\{(v, w, l),\ (v', w', l)\} \not\subseteq EC$$

The cycle-free alternation axiom is natural and has been proposed by other researchers, e.g., [PBF*89, page 396], [Sno89, page 109: Class names may not depend on themselves in a circular fashion involving only (alternation) class productions]. The axiom says that a class may not inherit from itself.

The unique labels axiom guarantees that "inherited" construction edges are uniquely labeled. Other mechanisms for uniquely naming the construction edges could be used, e.g., the renaming mechanism of Eiffel [Mey88].

Throughout the rest of this paper, the term class dictionary graph refers to a legal class dictionary graph.

3 Primitive Object-Preserving Transformations

An informal definition of **object-preserving** has already been given in the introduction. For a formal definition we first need a definition of **object-equivalence**. [1]

Definition 5 *Given a class dictionary graph $\phi = (VC, VA, \Lambda;\ EC, EA)$, for $v \in V$ let*
$$PartClusters_\phi(v) = \{(l, \mathcal{A}(w)) \mid \exists v' :$$
$$v' \stackrel{*}{\Rightarrow} v \text{ and } (v', w, l) \in EC\}$$
where $\mathcal{A}(w) = \{w' \mid w \stackrel{*}{\Rightarrow} w' \text{ and } w' \in VC\}$.

*Then, class dictionary graphs ϕ_1 and ϕ_2 are **object-equivalent** if:*

- $VC_{\phi_1} = VC_{\phi_2}$

- $\forall v \in VC :$
  $PartClusters_{\phi_1}(v) = PartClusters_{\phi_2}(v).$

---

[1] The most straight-forward definition would be: Two class dictionary graphs, ϕ_1 and ϕ_2, are object-equivalent if $Objects(\phi_1) = Objects(\phi_2)$, where $Objects(\phi)$ is formally defined in [LBS91]. The equivalent definition of object-equivalence given here is more appropriate for this paper.

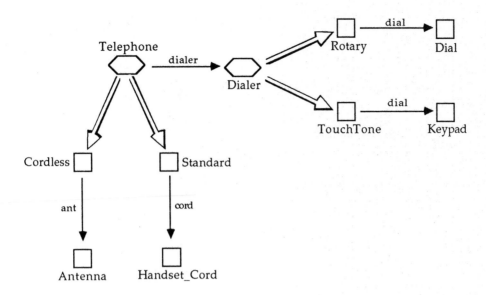

Figure 5: Telephones

Intuitively, two class dictionary graphs are object-equivalent if they define sets of corresponding construction classes with the same names, and for each construction class defined by one class dictionary graph the parts are the same as those defined for the corresponding class in the other class dictionary graph.

Example 2 *The two class dictionary graphs in Fig. 6, ϕ_1 and ϕ_2, are object-equivalent since:*

$$VC_{\phi_1} = VC_{\phi_2}$$
$$= \{\text{Undergrad, Grad, Prof, TA,}$$
$$\text{Admin\_asst, Coach, Num, Real\_Num}\}$$

$PartClusters_{\phi_1}(\text{Undergrad})$
   $= PartClusters_{\phi_2}(\text{Undergrad})$
   $= \{(\text{ssn, \{Num\}}), (\text{gpa, \{Real\_Num\}})\}$

$PartClusters_{\phi_1}(\text{Grad})$
   $= PartClusters_{\phi_2}(\text{Grad})$
   $= \{(\text{ssn, \{Num\}}), (\text{gpa, \{Real\_Num\}})\}$

$PartClusters_{\phi_1}(\text{TA})$
   $= PartClusters_{\phi_2}(\text{TA})$
   $= \{(\text{ssn, \{Num\}}), (\text{salary, \{Real\_Num\}}),$
   $(\text{assigned, \{Course, Committee\}})\}$

$PartClusters_{\phi_1}(\text{Prof})$
   $= PartClusters_{\phi_2}(\text{Prof})$
   $= \{(\text{ssn, \{Num\}}), (\text{salary, \{Real\_Num\}}),$
   $(\text{assigned, \{Course, Committee\}})\}$

$PartClusters_{\phi_1}(\text{Admin\_asst})$
   $= PartClusters_{\phi_2}(\text{Admin\_asst})$
   $= \{(\text{ssn, \{Num\}}), (\text{salary, \{Real\_Num\}})\}$

$PartClusters_{\phi_1}(\text{Coach})$
   $= PartClusters_{\phi_2}(\text{Coach})$
   $= \{(\text{ssn, \{Num\}}), (\text{salary, \{Real\_Num\}})\}$

$PartClusters_{\phi_1}(\text{Course})$
   $= PartClusters_{\phi_2}(\text{Course}) = \emptyset$

$PartClusters_{\phi_1}(\text{Committee})$
   $= PartClusters_{\phi_2}(\text{Committee}) = \emptyset$

$PartClusters_{\phi_1}(\text{Real\_Num})$
   $= PartClusters_{\phi_2}(\text{Real\_Num}) = \emptyset$

$PartClusters_{\phi_1}(\text{Num})$
   $= PartClusters_{\phi_2}(\text{Num}) = \emptyset$

Definition 6 *A class dictionary graph* **transformation**, *T, is a rule which defines an allowable modification of class dictionary graphs. Let*

$$R_T = \{(\phi_1, \phi_2) \mid \phi_2 \text{ can be obtained from}$$
$$\phi_1 \text{ by a single application of } T\}.$$

Then T is called **object-preserving** *if ϕ_1 is object-equivalent to ϕ_2 for all $(\phi_1, \phi_2) \in R_T$.*

3.1 Primitive Transformations

The following five primitive transformations form an orthogonal basis for object-preserving transformations:

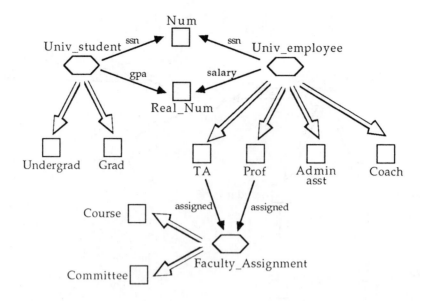

(a) Class Dictionary Graph ϕ_1

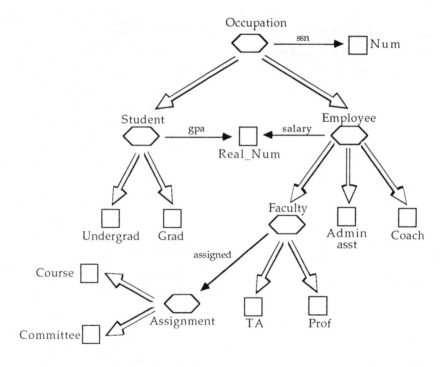

(b) Class Dictionary Graph ϕ_2

Figure 6: Object-equivalent Class Dictionary Graphs

1. **Deletion of "useless" alternation.** An alternation vertex is "useless" if it has no incoming edges and no outgoing construction edges. If an alternation vertex is useless it may be deleted along with it's outgoing alternation edges.

   Intuitively, an alternation vertex is useless if it is not a part of any construction class, and it has no parts for any construction class to inherit.

2. **Addition of "useless" alternation.** An alternation vertex, v, can be added along with outgoing alternation edges to any set of vertices already in the class dictionary graph. This is the inverse of transformation 1.

3. **Abstraction of common parts.** If $\exists v, w, l$ such that $\forall v'$, where $(v, v') \in EA : (v', w, l) \in EC$, then all of the edges, (v', w, l), can be deleted and replaced with a new construction edge, (v, w, l).

   Intuitively, if all of the immediate subclasses of class C have the same part, that part can be moved up the inheritance hierarchy so that each of the subclasses will inherit the part from C, rather than duplicating the part in each subclass.

4. **Distribution of common parts.** An outgoing construction edge, (v, w, l) can be deleted from an alternation vertex, v, if for each $(v, v') \in EA$ a new construction edge, (v', w, l) is added.

   This is the inverse of transformation 3.

5. **Part replacement.** If the set of construction vertices which are alternation-reachable from some vertex, $v \in V$, is equal to the set of construction vertices alternation-reachable from another vertex, $v' \in V$, then any construction edge $(w, v, l) \in EC$ can be deleted and replaced with a new construction edge, (w, v', l).

   Intuitively, if two class C1 and C2 have the same set of instantiable (construction) sub-

classes then the defined objects do not change when C1 is replaced by C2 in a part definition.

The set of primitive object-preserving transformation given in this section is *correct*, i.e. any sequence of primitive transformations preserves object-equivalence; *complete*, i.e. for any two object-equivalent class dictionary graphs, ϕ_1, ϕ_2, there is a sequence of primitive operations which transforms ϕ_1 to ϕ_2; and *minimal*, i.e. none of the primitive transformations can be derived from any set of the others.

3.2 Proofs

3.2.1 Correctness

Each primitive operation preserves object-equivalence.

3.2.2 Completeness

Given two object-equivalent class dictionary graphs, ϕ_1 and ϕ_2, ϕ_1 can be transformed to ϕ_2 using only primitive operations as follows:

1. Use primitive operation 2 (addition of useless alternation) to "superimpose" the alternation subgraph of ϕ_2 onto ϕ_1.

   Since there are no alternation cycles in ϕ_2, there must be some $v \in VA_{\phi_2}$ with outgoing alternation edges only to construction vertices (if there are any alternation vertices at all). For each such alternation vertex, add a new alternation vertex to ϕ_1 with alternation edges to the corresponding construction vertices.

   Now continue adding new alternation vertices corresponding to alternation vertices in ϕ_2 that have outgoing alternation edges only to construction vertices and alternation vertices which have already been added in ϕ_1 until all the alternation vertices in ϕ_2 are duplicated in ϕ_1.

2. Use primitive operation 4 (distribution of common parts) to remove the outgoing construction edges from all of the original alternation vertices in ϕ_1.

Distribution of common parts is applied repeatedly until all of the parts are attached directly to construction vertices.

3. Use primitive operation 3 (abstraction of common parts) to move construction edges up the "new" inheritance hierarchy in ϕ_1 until they are all attached to vertices corresponding to the vertices where they are attached in ϕ_2. This must be possible since ϕ_1 and ϕ_2 are object-equivalent.

   At this point ϕ_1 and ϕ_2 have the same number of construction edges and the construction edges have the same labels and the same sources, but may have different targets.

4. Use primitive number 5 (part replacement) to move any construction edge with an "old" alternation vertex or construction vertex as its target so that its target corresponds to the proper vertex in ϕ_2.

5. Use primitive transformation 1 (deletion of useless alternation) to delete the "old" alternation subgraph from ϕ_1. At this point there are no construction edges (either incoming or outgoing) attached to any of the "old" alternation vertices. Also, since there are no cycles in the old alternation subgraph, and since we have not added any edges from "new" alternation vertices to "old" alternation vertices or vice versa, at least one of the "old" alternation vertices must be "useless" (if there are any at all). After deleting that useless alternation vertex the condition still holds, so we can continue deleting the "old" alternation vertices until there are none left.

   Now $\phi_1 = \phi_2$.

3.2.3 Minimality

No primitive transformation can be derived from any set of the others since:

- No sequence of primitive operations can reduce the number of alternation vertices without deletion of useless alternations.

- No sequence of primitive operations can increase the number of alternation vertices without addition of useless alternations.

- No sequence of primitive operations can reduce the number of construction edges without abstraction of common parts.

- No sequence of primitive operations can increase the number of construction edges without distribution of common parts.

- No sequence of primitive operations can change the construction edge in-degree of a vertex from 0 to 1 or from 1 to 0 without part replacement.

Example 3 *This example illustrates the construction of the completeness proof with the class dictionary graphs of Figure 6. Note that although the labels on construction vertices are significant, the labels on the alternation vertices are only provided as a means of referring to particular vertices in the following discussion.*

Addition of Useless Alternations. In ϕ_2 there are three alternation vertices which have outgoing alternation edges only to construction vertices: Faculty, Assignment, and Student. These are added to ϕ_1 along with their outgoing alternation edges. Next, the Employee vertex is added with its outgoing alternation edges, including an edge to Faculty. Finally, the Occupation vertex is added along with its edges to Student and Employee. At this point ϕ_1 has been transformed to the class dictionary graph shown in Figure 7.

Distribution of Common Parts. The ssn and gpa parts are distributed from class Univ_student to classes Undergrad and Grad where they are inherited. Similarly, parts ssn and salary are distributed from Univ_employee to TA, Prof, Admin_asst, and Coach. The result is the class dictionary graph shown in Figure 8. In a deeper inheritance hierarchy some parts might need to be distributed repeatedly until they are attached directly to construction classes.

Abstraction of Common Parts. Parts ssn and gpa are abstracted from Undergrad and Grad to Student.

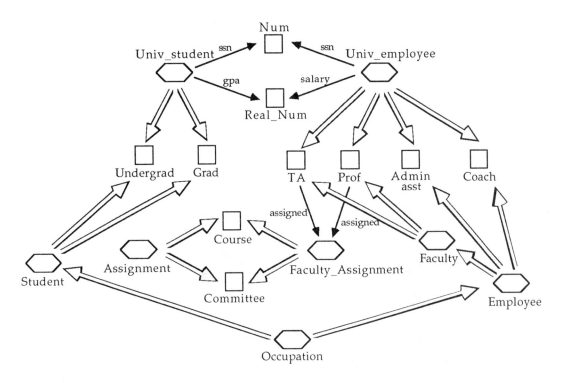

Figure 7: Addition of Useless Alternations

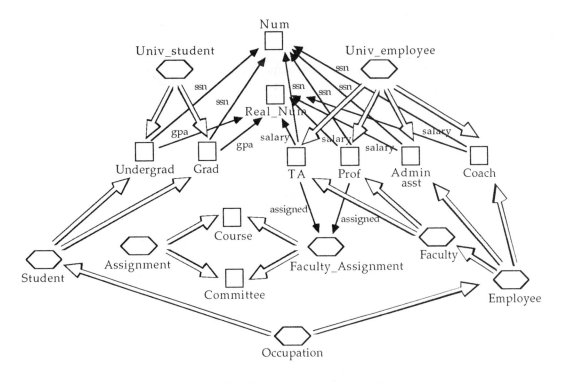

Figure 8: Distribution of Common Parts

307

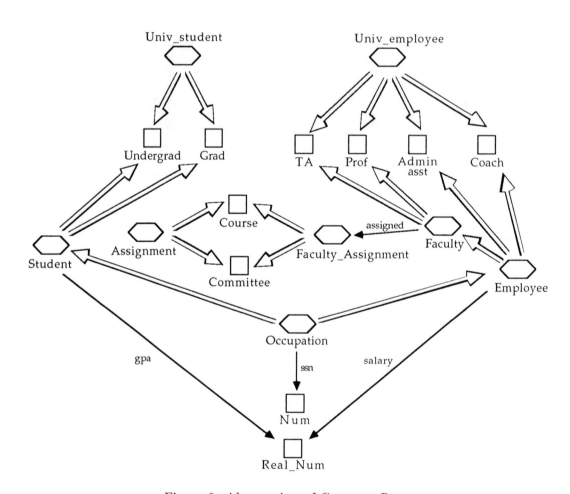

Figure 9: Abstraction of Common Parts

Next, parts ssn, salary, and assigned are abstracted from TA and Prof to Faculty. Parts ssn and salary are then abstracted from Faculty, Admin_asst, and Coach to Employee. Finally, part ssn is abstracted from Employee and Student to Occupation. The result is shown in Figure 9.

Part Replacement. The "old" alternation vertex Faculty_Assignment still has an incoming construction edge from the new vertex Faculty. In ϕ_2 the corresponding edge is to vertex Assignment, so the edge is moved accordingly in ϕ_1. This is allowed since the set of construction vertices alternation reachable from Assignment is equal to the set alternation reachable from Faculty_Assignment. Such a part replacement must always be possible since ϕ_1 is object-equivalent to ϕ_2. The result is shown in Figure 10.

Deletion of Useless Alternations. The alternation vertices Faculty_Assignment, Univ_student, and Univ_employee are now "useless" since they have no incoming edges and no outgoing construction edges. These vertices and their outgoing alternation edges are deleted, and the transformation from ϕ_1 to ϕ_2 is complete.

4 Practical Applications

There are many useful rules which can be derived from the primitive transformations and are therefore guaranteed object-preserving. The following examples show how object-preserving transformations can be used to improve class organization by reducing the number of construction edges, the number of alternation edges, or the degree of multiple inheritance in a class dictionary graph.

1. **Elimination of redundant parts.**

   If a vertex, v, has two incoming construction edges with the same label, (u, v, l) and (u', v, l), then those edges should be replaced by a single edge (w, v, l) where w is an alternation vertex with exactly u and u' as alternation successors, by *abstraction of common parts*. If necessary, w is first introduced by *addition of useless alternation*. (See Fig. 11.)

2. **Removal of singleton alternation vertices.**

   If an alternation vertex, v, has only one outgoing alternation edge, (v, w), then that vertex should be removed. Incoming construction edges (u, v, l), and alternation edges, (u, v), are replaced by edges (u, w, l) and (u, w) respectively. Outgoing construction edges, (v, x, l), are replaced by edges (w, x, l). The incoming construction edges can be moved by *part replacement* and the outgoing construction edges by *distribution of common parts*. Moving the incoming construction can be accomplished by *alternation replacement* which is analogous to *part replacement* but is not primitive. It is easy to see how *alternation replacement* can be accomplished using only primitive transformations. Finally, the vertex v is deleted by *deletion of useless alternation*. (See Fig. 12.)

3. **Complete Cover**

   If a subset, S, of the outgoing alternation edges from a vertex, u, completely cover the alternatives of another alternation vertex, v, then replace the edges in S with a single alternation edge to v. We say the alternatives of an alternation vertex, v, are completely covered by a set of edges, S, if every vertex which is the target of an outgoing alternation edge from v is also the target of an edge in S. This rule can be derived from the primitive transformations using a construction similar to that given in section 3.2.2. (See Fig. 13.)

4. **Partial Cover**

   This rule applies if two alternation vertices, u and v, cover a common set of alternatives, but neither contains a subset of outgoing alternation edges that completely covers the alternatives of the other. In this case, a new alternation vertex, w, is created with an outgoing alternation edge to each of the vertices that is a target of outgoing alternation edges from both u and v, and incoming alternation edges (u, w) and (v, w). For each edge (w, x)

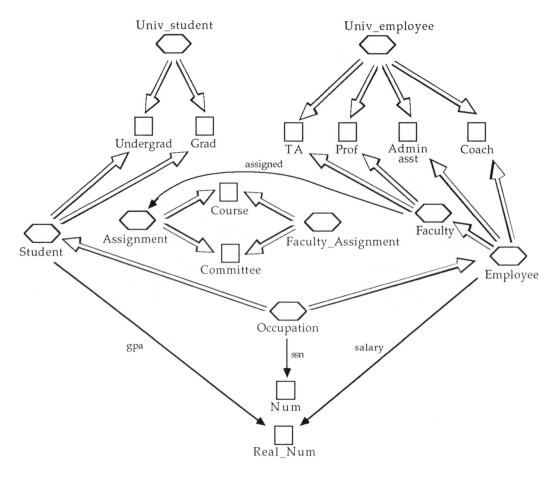

Figure 10: Part Replacement

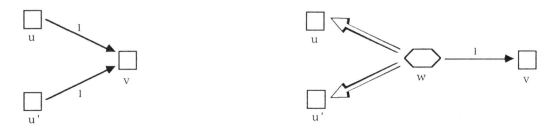

Figure 11: Elimination of redundant parts

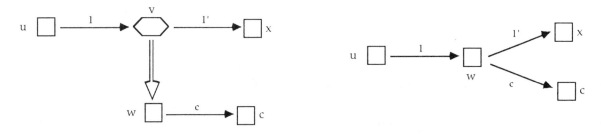

Figure 12: Removal of singleton alternation vertex

310

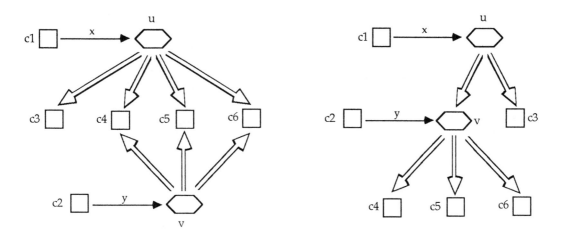

Figure 13: Complete Cover

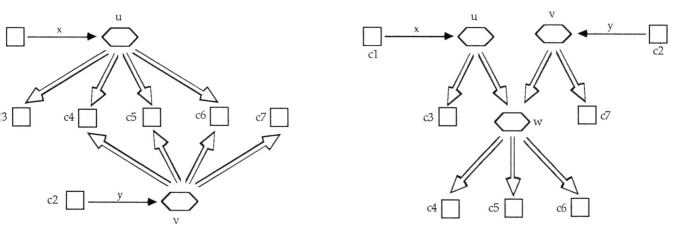

Figure 14: Partial cover

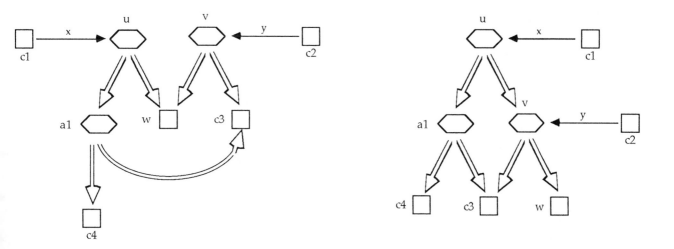

Figure 15: MI minimization

which is added, the corresponding edges (u, x) and (v, x) are deleted. (See Fig. 14.)

5. **MI Minimization**

If there are alternation edges, (u, w) and (v, w) such that for all other alternation edges from v, (v, w'), w' is alternation reachable from u, then replace the edge (u, w) with the edge (u, v). This rule reduces the amount of multiple inheritance without changing the edge size. However, it introduces repeated inheritance. (See Fig. 15.)

5 Conclusion

The primitive object-preserving class transformations presented in this paper are a powerful tool for reasoning about object-preserving transformations and optimizations. In order to determine whether a transformation is guaranteed to be object-preserving it is only necessary to show whether it can be derived from the primitive transformations.

To prove that a particular class organization is in some sense *optimal* (see, for example, [LBS91]), it is only necessary to consider improvements that might be possible through the primitive transformations.

An area for further research is the study of *object-extending* class reorganizations [LHX91]. An object-extending transformation is one which adds to the set of defined objects or adds part classes to previously defined objects. For object-oriented data base design this means that the objects can be updated automatically. For object-oriented programming it means that the programs will still accept similar inputs and produce similar outputs.

Acknowledgments: I would like to thank Karl Lieberherr for his generous support and feedback. Additional thanks go to Cun Xiao for his help in polishing some of the definitions.

References

[AH87]   S. Abiteboul and R. Hull. A formal semantic database model. *ACM Transactions on Database Systems*, 12(4):525–565, Dec. 1987.

[BCG*87] Jay Banerjee, Hong-Tai Chou, Jorge F. Garza, Won Kim, Darrell Woelk, and Nat Ballou. Data model issues for object-oriented applications. *ACM Transactions on Office Information Systems*, 5(1):3 – 26, January, 1987.

[BDG*88] D.G. Bobrow, L.G. DeMichiel, R.P. Gabriel, S.E. Keene, G. Kiczales, and D.A. Moon. Common Lisp Object System Specification. *SIGPLAN Notices*, 23, September 1988.

[BL91]   Paul Bergstein and Karl Lieberherr. Incremental class dictionary learning and optimization. In *European Conference on Object-Oriented Programming*, page ?, Springer Verlag, Geneva, Switzerland, 1991.

[BMW86]   Alexander Borgida, Tom Mitchell, and Keith Williamson. Learning improved integrity constraints and schemas from exceptions in data and knowledge bases. In Michael L. Brodie and John Mylopoulos, editors, *On Knowledge Base Management Systems*, pages 259–286, Springer Verlag, 1986.

[Cas89]   Eduardo Casais. Reorganizing an object system. In Dennis Tsichritzis, editor, *Object Oriented Development*, pages 161–189, Centre Universitaire D'Informatique, Genève, 1989.

[Cas90]   Eduardo Casais. Managing class evolution in object-oriented systems. In Dennis Tsichritzis, editor, *Object Management*, pages 133–195, Centre Universitaire D'Informatique, Genève, 1990.

[GR83]   A. Goldberg and D. Robson. *Smalltalk-80: The Language and its Implementation*. Addison Wesley, 1983.

[LBS90]   Karl J. Lieberherr, Paul Bergstein, and Ignacio Silva-Lepe. Abstraction of object-oriented data models. In Hannu Kangassalo, editor, *Proceedings of International Conference on Entity-Relationship*, pages 81–94, Elsevier, Lausanne, Switzerland, 1990.

[LBS91] Karl J. Lieberherr, Paul Bergstein, and Ignacio Silva-Lepe. From objects to classes: algorithms for optimal object-oriented design. *Software Engineering Journal*, 1991. Accepted for publication.

[LHX91] Karl J. Lieberherr, Walter L. Hürsch, and Cun Xiao. *Object-Extending Class Transformations*. Technical Report NU-CCS-91-8, Northeastern University, July 1991.

[LM91] Qing Li and Dennis McLeod. Conceptual database evolution through learning. In Rajiv Gupta and Ellis Horowitz, editors, *Object-oriented Databases with applications to CASE, networks and VLSI CAD*, pages 62–74, Prentice Hall Series in Data and Knowledge Base Systems, 1991.

[Mey88] Bertrand Meyer. *Object-Oriented Software Construction*. *Series in Computer Science*, Prentice Hall International, 1988.

[PBF*89] B. Pernici, F. Barbic, M.G. Fugini, R. Maiocchi, J.R. Rames, and C. Rolland. C-TODOS: an automatic tool for office system conceptual design. *ACM Transactions on Office Information Systems*, 7(4):378–419, October 1989.

[Pir89] Fiora Pirri. Modelling a multiple inheritance lattice with exceptions. In *Proceedings of the Workshop on Inheritance and Hierarchies in Knowledge Representation and Programming Languages*, pages 91–104, Viareggio, February 1989.

[PW89] Winnie W. Y. Pun and Russel L. Winder. *Automating Class Hierarchy Graph Construction*. Technical Report, University College London, 1989.

[Sno89] Richard Snodgrass. *The interface description language*. Computer Science Press, 1989.

[Str86] B. Stroustrup. *The C++ Programming Language*. Addison Wesley, 1986.

[TYF86] T.J. Teorey, D. Yang, and J.P. Fry. A logical design methodology for relational data bases. *ACM Computing Surveys*, 18(2):197–222, June 1986.

Experiences in DBMS Implementation Using an Object-oriented Persistent Programming Language and a Database Toolkit

Eric N. Hanson[†]   Tina M. Harvey[‡]   Mark A. Roth[§]

Abstract

The EXODUS database toolkit, and in particular the E persistent programming language, have been used in two substantial database system implementation efforts by the authors (the Ariel database rule system and the Triton nested relation DBMS). Observed advantages of using a persistent programming language for database system implementation include ease of implementation of special-purpose persistent objects used by the DBMS such as catalogs, data indexes, rule indexes, and nested relational structures. Other advantages of using E (a persistent version of C++) that are independent of the persistence issue are the usefulness of object-oriented programming in developing large software systems, and the utility of the *Collection* abstraction in E. Observed disadvantages include (1) the inability to map the type system of the DBMS to the type system of the underlying programming language while still retaining good performance for

ad-hoc queries, and (2) software engineering difficulties due to the distinction in E between database types and main-memory types.

1   Introduction

It is well-known in the database community that implementing DBMS code is difficult and time-consuming. Recent research on persistent programming languages and other tools to support database implementation has given hope that the burden of implementing DBMS code could be substantially reduced. In an attempt to simplify the implementation of two different prototype database systems (the Ariel database rule system [13, 14] and the Triton nested relational database system [15, 27]) we have used the EXODUS database toolkit extensively [7]. In particular, we have made significant use of the E programming language of EXODUS [24], a version of C++ [32] extended with persistent objects. This paper reviews the advantages and disadvantages of using a database toolkit and a persistent programming language (E) that we observed while implementing non-trivial DBMS software.

The next section describes the EXODUS toolkit. Section 3 discusses the impact of persistence on our implementations, as well as issues related to the type systems of the DBMS and the underlying programming language. Section 4 discusses the impact of features of the language and toolkit unrelated to persistence, including the impact of object-oriented programming, collections, and the EXODUS optimizer generator [12]. Section 5 covers issues related to performance, Section 6 briefly reviews related research, and Section 7 summarizes and presents

---

[†]Eric Hanson is with the Artificial Intelligence Technology Office (WL/AAA-1), Air Force Wright Laboratory, Wright-Patterson AFB, OH 45433, and with Wright State University. His work was supported in part by the Air Force Office of Scientific Research under grant number AFOSR-89-0286.

[‡]Tina Harvey's work was done while with the Department of Electrical and Computer Engineering Air Force Institute of Technology. She is currently with the 7th Communications Group/DOWI, The Pentagon, Washington DC 20330.

[§]Mark Roth is with the Department of Electrical and Computer Engineering (AFIT/ENG), Air Force Institute of Technology, Wright-Patterson AFB, OH 45433.

conclusions. We now turn to the discussion of EX-ODUS.

2 Overview of EXODUS

EXODUS provides some powerful tools to help automate the generation of application-specific database systems, including a storage manager, the persistent programming language E, a rule-based query optimizer generator and a B+tree class generator. One possible architectural framework for using EXODUS to build a database system is shown in Figure 1.

The EXODUS storage manager is accessed via procedural calls which allow creation and destruction of database files containing sets of objects, and iteration through the contents of files. Objects can be inserted in and deleted from a file at any offset in the file, and explicit clustering of objects on disk can be specified. The storage manager provides procedures for transaction and version management.

The E programming language provided by the EXODUS toolkit is an extension of C++ with persistent objects. Persistence in E is implemented on top of the EXODUS storage manager. E extends C++ types and defines a corresponding **db** type (database type) for each C++ and user defined type. These db types are used to define objects in the database. There are four kinds of db types in E:

- fundamental db types – dbshort, dbint, dblong, dbfloat, dbdouble, dbchar, and dbvoid

- dbclass, dbstruct and dbunion (every sub component of a dbclass must be of a db type)

- pointer to a db type object

- arrays of db type objects

If the **persistent** keyword is used before the declaration of a db type, EXODUS will map the persistent db variables to a permanent storage location.

In E, a *collection* is an unordered set of objects. E also has a feature called *generator classes* which allows defining a generic template for a C++-style class. Customized classes can then be declared using the generator class name plus additional parameters for customization. Collections are supported in E using a built-in generator class called collection, which is invoked by *collection [T]* where T is any db type. A collection must be instantiated for a specific type before it can be used to declare collection objects. EXODUS provides a generator class for B+trees to allow straightforward creation of indexes for different data types. A typical way to create an indexed data set is to create a collection, and then create a B+tree as an index on the objects in that collection.

In E, *iterators* are controlled looping functions that are used to step through a sequence of values such as collections. An iterator is made up of an iterator function and an interate loop. The iterate loop consumes values that the iterator function produces. The iterator function yields values to the iterate loop.

The EXODUS optimizer generator takes as input (1) a set of operators, (2) a set of methods that implement the operators, (3) transformation rules that describe equivalence-preserving transformations of query trees, and (4) implementation rules that describe how to replace an operator with a specific method. Using these rules, a specific optimizer is generated for the particular application. Neither the Ariel nor Triton developers made use of the optimizer generator, so we are not able to comment extensively on it. The developers of Ariel made the decision to implement a custom optimizer rather than use the optimizer generator. One reason for this is that the original optimizer generator required use of C functions and structures, and we were committed to using object-oriented programming in C++. The latest version of the optimizer generator now also handles C++ and E objects, so we would no longer object to using the optimizer generator on these grounds. Another reason we decided against using the optimizer generator was the need to be able to optimize a set of commands in the action of an Ariel rule. We felt it might be difficult to implement special-purpose optimization

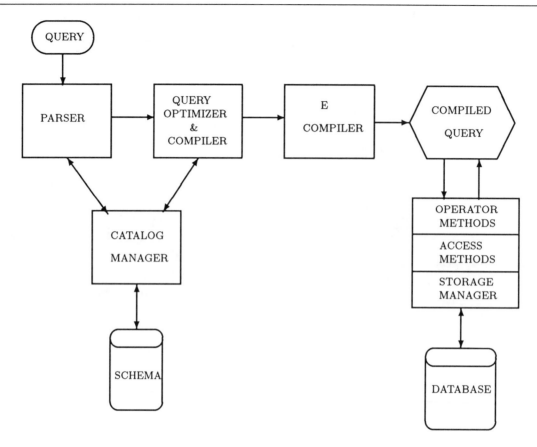

Figure 1: An architecture for a DBMS based on EXODUS

3 The Impact of Persistence

routines for rule actions using the optimizer generator. The Triton optimizer has not been developed, but the intent is to use the optimizer generator. A more thorough discussion of the merits of the optimizer generator awaits more experience using it.

In the next section we comment on the impact of persistence in the programming language based on our experiences with E.

The availability of persistent objects and collections in E has definitely proved worthwhile to use, significantly simplifying implementation of system catalogs, data indexes, rule indexes, and data storage structures. Having persistent objects in the programming language is a convenient interface to

the storage manager that frees the programmer from most of the details of mapping data between disk and main-memory data structures. The primary disappointment with persistence in E is related to issues of interaction between the database type system and E language type system, which will be discussed later in Section 4. Also, our experiences reinforce the belief that persistence should be a property of data independent of type. This property was defined as *persistence data type orthogonality*, in the design of PS-algol [4], and is also sometimes called simply *persistence orthogonality*.

3.1 Catalogs

The catalogs in Ariel have been implemented using persistent E objects. The *Relation* catalog consists of a collection of objects of type Relation. The

Relation object has methods on it to set and get information about attributes, presence of indexes, statistics about relation size, number of unique values per attribute and so on. Instance variables of the Relation object include a list of *Attribute* objects to describe the attribute names, data types, and other information about each attribute. Using E provided high-performance access to the catalog data without the need to implement any code for mapping the catalog information into special internal data structures. Typically, relational database systems store catalog information in relations, and map data about a recently-accessed set of relations into a main-memory *catalog cache* (this is the approach used in POSTGRES [31]). Using persistent objects for the catalogs freed us from having to implement a catalog cache.

The only drawback to our approach was that it is not possible to use the query language to query our catalogs. Special-purpose commands have been provided to get information from the catalogs to make up for this, but these commands do not give access in as flexible a manner as a general-purpose query language. Similar advantages to using persistent data for the catalogs have been realized in the Triton project.

3.2 Indexes

Using persistent objects definitely simplifies the implementation of complex permanent storage structures such as data indexes and other special purpose indexes such as rule indexes. As with the catalogs, the primary simplification is that the programmer does not need to be concerned with mapping data between the disk and main-memory data structures. Hence, it becomes essentially no more difficult to implement a persistent index structure such as a B+-tree than it would be to implement a main-memory index structure, except that performance artifacts such as node size and clustering must be addressed more carefully in the persistent implementation.

The amount of code saved by using a persistent language to implement indexes depends on a number of factors including the complexity of the index being implemented, the programming language features available independent of persistence, etc. Research prototypes using PS-algol have shown that code size can be reduced by a factor of 3 in some cases [18]. The Ariel implementors are using persistent objects to implement a fairly complex rule index [14]. We believe that this rule index would have been infeasible to implement without the aid of a persistent programming language.

3.3 Data Storage Structures and Language and Database Type System Issues

Implementation of data storage structures for relations and nested relations was made simpler than it would have been otherwise by the availability of persistent collections provided in E. There are two main approaches to building database storage structures using E, and using them to process database queries (these approaches also apply for other persistent programming languages that do all type checking at compile time and use conventional compiler and linker technology). The first approach, which we call the *compiled approach*, is to compile database type definitions and object (e.g., relation) creation commands into E code, and compile this code into object files using the E compiler. To compile a query, the system generates another file of E code, which is compiled and linked with the object files containing the compiled type definitions. The resulting executable is then run to process the query. This approach has the appealing property that database types are mapped directly into types in the underlying programming language. It can also provide fast query execution since queries are compiled directly into machine code. Unfortunately, it results in a severe performance problem for query compilation if a conventional compiler and linker are used by the persistent programming language, as they are in E (we will discuss performance figures later).

The second approach, which we call the *interpreted* approach, does not use the persistent programming language at all for compiling types and queries. Instead, type definitions and queries are interpreted directly by the DBMS. Data is stored in persistent collections of generic storage objects (e.g., byte strings) for which one type (e.g., TupleCollection in Ariel) is defined when the database system itself is compiled. Implementing code to interpret the format of these generic objects stored in the persistent collections of data is left to the DBMS implementor. Execution of queries is done by compiling a query into an execution plan, which is then interpreted. A drawback of this approach is that interpreted queries will run slower than the compiled queries in the first approach, given that the same query plan is used in both approaches. However, response time for any query generated in text form and sent to the DBMS for execution is dramatically better in the second approach (a fraction of a second vs. many seconds). Such long response time for ad-hoc queries is not tolerable.

We chose to implement the interpreted approach in Ariel since we felt the response time of the compiled approach was unacceptable. Relations in Ariel are persistent collections of byte strings. Tuples are mapped onto these byte strings explicitly. A **TupleDescriptor** object describes how tuple fields are arranged in the byte strings in a collection representing a relation. An alternative to this approach would have been to map a relation definition directly into E language constructs, and then compile the resulting E code with the E compiler.

The Ariel type system allows separate commands for defining relation types and constructing instances of relations with those types, similar to the mechanism provided in the EXCESS query language [8]. The following is an example definition of a relation type and a relation in Ariel:

```
define relation type
    emp_type(name=c20, age=int,
              salary=float, dept_no= int)
create relation emp : emp_type
```

The E code that would be generated to represent the same information is:

```
dbclass emp_type
{
    dbchar name[20];
    dbint age;
    dbfloat salary;
    dbint dept_no;
};
```

```
dbclass emp_Collection :
  collection[emp_type];
persistent emp_Collection emp;
```

Compiling a source file containing the E code above into an object file takes 3 seconds on a Sun SPARCstation 1 computer. Compiling an E source file containing a trivial one-relation selection query and linking that file with the appropriate object file for the relation and the E library to create an executable file takes more than 15 seconds.

An alternative approach to implementing a persistent language to support DBMS development would be to start with a language supporting incremental compilation of both types and program code, such as Smalltalk [11] or Lisp and CLOS [17]. This would allow direct mapping of database types into language types, and fast compilation of both types and queries, making the "compiled" approach discussed earlier practical. However, this approach would bring with it the larger run-time overhead associated with Smalltalk or Lisp.

3.4 Type System Mapping Example

As another more sophisticated example of a translation from a database type to underlying E types, in Triton, a nested relation definition is mapped directly into a persistent collection of E objects, which in turn have fields which contain collections of objects. Figure 2 shows a nested relation that holds information on VHSIC Hardware Description Language (VHDL) systems[3]. Figure 3 gives the E code representation of the *Systems* relation.

This implementation illustrates the ease with which nested relation types can be mapped into E and also allows compilation of Triton queries

number	name	comps comp#	ports name	mode	type	start_bit	stop_bit
43191	COUNTER	15899	STRT	in	BIT	0	0
			STROBE	in	BIT	0	0
			CON	in	BIT_V	0	1
		30018	DATA_BUS	in	BIT_V	0	3
			CNT	out	BIT_V	0	3
14701	FULL_ADDER	41572	X	in	BIT	0	0
			Y	in	BIT	0	0
			CIN	in	BIT	0	0
		81909	Z	out	BIT	0	0
			COUT	out	BIT	0	0

Figure 2: The *Systems* Relation

into machine code. However, it suffers from the performance problem mentioned above for ad hoc queries and thus an interpreted implementation of the Triton type system and query processor is being considered for use by Triton application developers. On the other hand, Since the Triton system is targeted for use by embedded database applications (such as CAD or CASE tools), extended SQL commands [25] will be embedded in a host programming language and compiled as part of the application. Thus, ad hoc queries will not normally be performed.

It is unfortunate that the difficulty in making use of the E compiler to compile database types and queries negates some of the advantages of using a persistent programming language. Essentially the only language feature necessary to support stored data using the "interpreted" approach to DBMS implementation is the persistent collection of byte strings. It would thus be about the same amount of work to implement stored relations using a direct interface to the storage manager (e.g., a C++ class called PersistentCollection with the same methods provided by E collections, including get_first, get_next, get_last and get_prev). This would not require extensions to the C++ compiler on the part of the EXODUS implementors. Moreover, it would have allowed use of a standard C++ programming environment including code inspectors, debuggers,

etc., without modification. It would also be possible to build on the PersistentCollection class by creating subclasses. The E language does not allow subclasses to be derived from the built-in collection classes of E, although there appears to be nothing preventing this. Although object persistence in E was not especially useful for storing relations in Ariel, we still believe persistence is worthwhile in a database implementation language because of its usefulness for implementing indexes, catalogs, and any other data structures with object types that cannot change at run time.

Another difficulty we have faced implementing Ariel is a distinction in E between database classes defined using the **dbclass** notation, and normal classes. There is a slight overhead to accessing a **dbclass** object compared to a normal object since **dbclass** objects reside in the storage manager, and a pointer to a dbclass object is a 16-byte record, compared to a 4-byte word for a main-memory pointer. The designers of E wanted to give the implementor a choice whether or not to use classes or dbclasses to have more control over performance. Objects that needed to be persistent would be defined using dbclasses, and the rest of the objects would be defined using classes.

This design choice in E violates the principle of persistence orthogonality, which states that all data objects should be allowed the full range of

```
dbstruct port {
  dbchar name[12];
  dbchar mode[4];
  dbchar type[6];
  dbint  start_bit;
  dbint  stop_bit;
public:
  port (char *, char *, char *, int, int);
  char * get_name();
  void change_name (char *);
  char * get_mode();
  void change_mode (char *);
  char * get_type();
  void change_type (char *);
  int get_start_bit();
  void change_start_bit (int);
  int get_stop_bit();
  void change_stop_bit (int);
  void print (port *);
};
dbstruct comp {
  dbint  comp_num;
public:
  comp (int);
  int get_comp_num();
  void change_comp_num (int);
  void print (comp *);
};

dbstruct system {
  dbchar name[12];
  dbint  number;
  dbclass compRVA:collection[comp];
  compRVA comps;
  dbclass portRVA:collection[port];
  portRVA ports;
public:
  system (char *, int);
  char * get_name();
  void change_name (char *);
  int get_number();
  void change_number (int);
  void print (system *);
};

dbclass systemRVA:collection[system];
persistent systemRVA systems;
```

Figure 3: The E Code Representation of the *Systems* Relation

persistence. Our experience in implementing Ariel reveals that the lack of persistence orthogonality causes software engineering difficulties since a DBMS implementor does *not* know in advance all the types for which he or she would like to create persistent instances. For example, at first we did not intend to store query plan operator objects in the Ariel database, but now we have decided that it would be natural to store compiled queries as persistent plan objects. Accomplishing this will involve a significant modification to our code. In E it is not trivial to simply change all classes to db-classes since all subobjects of a db-object must also be db-objects, which can cause a single change to propagate through many objects. Also, some basic library routines such as string manipulation functions are not the same for db-objects as they are for main-memory objects. This mismatch can result in the need to extensively modify a class definition in order to make it into a dbclass, creating an inordinate workload on the programmer. This extra work inhibits the process of prototyping a complex software system.

In the design of persistent programming languages, we thus feel that it is very important to make no distinction between database types and main-memory types, even if it involves a small sacrifice in performance. It will be a challenge to the language implementors to make access to both kinds of objects as efficient as possible. Investigation of efficient ways to implement a persistent language in this manner is worthy of continued research. We are encouraged by recent developments in the area of transaction-based virtual memory storage systems, including work on Cricket [29], ObjectStore [21] and Bubba [6, 10], which potentially can provide access to persistent objects with no overhead beyond that needed for concurrency control and recovery. In these systems, once a persistent object is in memory, it can be accessed at the speed of a main-memory object.

In summary, the main area where we felt that the persistent programming language features of E were the most useful was in creating special-purpose persistent data structures, such as catalogs, data indexes, and rule indexes. If good ad-hoc query response time is required, the persistent features of the language have approximately the same utility for actually storing database data as a direct interface to a storage manager providing transaction support would have. Finally, it is best to make no distinction between database and main-memory types.

4 The Impact of Object-Oriented Programming

In this section we discuss the impact of the C++-derived features of E that support object-oriented programming, as well as E's extensions to C++ including generator classes and collections. The implementations of Ariel and Triton have derived substantial benefits from using the C++ object-oriented programming features of E. In Ariel, we have implemented a terminal monitor, lexer, parser, semantic analyzer, system catalogs, query optimizer and query executor, and system utilities in about 16000 lines of code written using E and the Unix compiler generation tools LEX and YACC [20, 16]. A system of similar, or slightly greater complexity is the terminal monitor, front-end, query executor, and utilities of the university INGRES system [30], which contain approximately 32000 lines of C code. It is hard to make a precise comparison, but it appears that a savings of somewhere between 25 to 50% in the amount of code written can be achieved using object-oriented programming in E (or C++) relative to using C to implement a DBMS. Moreover, object-oriented implementation has provided us with some reusable code which will facilitate extensions as Ariel grows.

Object-oriented programming features including classes, polymorphism, and inheritance are used throughout Ariel. Use of inheritance and polymorphism has been particularly beneficial in the design of the Ariel syntax tree structure generated by the parser, the internal representation of built-in data types, and the query plan operator tree representation. As an example, the class hierarchy for the

```
QueryPlanOp
    Scan
        RelationScan
        SequentialScan
        IndexScan
        StoreTemporary
    Join
        NestedLoopJoin
            NestedLoopJoinIndexInner
        SortMergeJoin
    Project
```

Figure 4: Class hierarchy for query plan operators in Ariel.

query plan operators in Ariel is shown in Figure 4.

Methods on these object types include those for accessing result tuples, getting statistics on the expected cost of execution, and constructors and destructors. C++ *virtual* functions are used so that methods are inherited from above unless they are reimplemented in a subclass. Polymorphism proved useful – for example, every object in the class hierarchy shown responds to the *get_next* method. It is not necessary to know the type of the node to get the next tuple from it. A substantial number of instance variables and some methods are inherited by the subclasses of Scan and Join.

There is an inherent benefit from the organization enforced on the code by designing the code using C++ classes. Subjectively, the code seems easier to understand and modify than a C program accomplishing a similar task with which the authors are familiar (e.g., the front-end of university INGRES).

Another object-oriented feature of E is generator classes, a mechanism for creating parameterized types. For example, EXODUS provides a generator class for building B+-trees for different data types [35]. A simplified and shortened version of

```
dbclass BplusTree [
  // keys for entities stored in the tree
  dbstruct key_type {
    void print();   },

  // key comparison function
  int compare(const key_type &,
    const key_type &),
  // entities to be stored in the tree
  dbstruct entity_type {},
]{

  // Definitions of instance variables for
  // BplusTree
  ...

public:
  // Constructors, destructors, functions for
  // building an index, inserting and deleting
  // records etc.
  ...
};
```

Figure 5: Sketch of B+-tree class generator in E.

the definition of this generator class is shown in Figure 5.

Users of this class generator create a new class by specifying parameters for the items in the square brackets (key_type, compare, and entity_type). For example, this piece of code defines an instance of BplusTree for keys of type integer and entities of type Tuple (IntKey is a structure type containing an integer, and IntKeyCompare is a function that takes two IntKeys and compares them):

```
dbclass IntBtreeIndex :
  BplusTree[IntKey, IntKeyCompare, Tuple];
```

The ability to derive classes using a generator can be useful, significantly reducing the amount of code that needs to be written to implement closely related types. However, one difficulty with the E implementation of generator classes is that classes created with a generator class cannot be made sub-

types of another type. In Ariel, this made implementing the IndexScan query plan operator more complex than necessary by not allowing use of polymorphism with types derived from BplusTree.

In object-oriented programming, a commonly used, powerful technique is to define a base class B and subclasses of B, say $b_1, b_2, \ldots, b_k$. Each of the subclasses responds to the same set of messages. Then, another class C can be implemented generically, storing one of B's subtypes in a variable of type B. Messages can be sent to the object contained in that variable, and the object will respond correctly, regardless of its type. This generic implementation, which makes use of polymorphism, can save a substantial amount of code in the implementation of C, by letting a single line of the form

```
object->message(parameters...)
```

replace a multi-line SWITCH statement with one CASE for each of B's subclasses b_1–b_k. We believe that an implementation of generator classes should provide a way to create a hierarchy of types, with virtual (inheritable, polymorphic) methods, so that the object-oriented programming technique described above can be used when working with classes derived from a generator class. The experimental parameterized class facility for C++ described in [33] appears to support the desired features, although it is not yet part of the C++ standard.

An alternative to using generator classes that allows object-oriented implementation style is to provide *base classes* from which sub-classes can be derived. This sub-classing approach to genericity does not require any extensions to an object-oriented programming language (no generator class facility is needed). For example, the BplusTree class in EXODUS could have been implemented as a standard E class with virtual functions. A guideline could have been written for deriving subclasses from BplusTree by re-implementing a very small amount of code in each subclass (e.g., the key-comparison function). The vast majority of the complex code for implementing BplusTree would be inherited by the subclasses. This approach does not completely eliminate the need for a generator class facility (e.g., the key-comparison function would have to be re-implemented for each type), but it provides a workable alternative in many cases, and it does not interfere with object-oriented programming style.

The *collection* generator class available in E proved very useful in implementing data storage structures. The Triton system is built on the nested relational data model, which allows relation-valued attributes in relations. The nested relational data model is mapped very nicely using E collections. Nested relational attributes are represented by using collections of collections. The EXODUS storage manager automatically uses *near* hints to group collections and sub-collections together on disk to increase efficiency. Unfortunately, EXODUS only provides the capability for sequential scanning of collections, making access via a search key slow for large relations. The only way around this shortcoming is to build indexes on every frequently accessed or sufficiently large relation. One way we feel EXODUS could be improved to simplify the programmer's task would be to provide a library of additional types of collections including ordered and hashed collections. This would be somewhat simpler to use than a separate index mechanism.

5 Performance Issues

Obtaining good performance from a DBMS implemented with a persistent programming language is crucial, as it is in any DBMS implementation. We currently do not have a great deal of information on performance of our database implementations based on E – no extensive application benchmarks have been done. However, subjectively we feel that the speed at which individual persistent objects can be accessed using the E language, which has a built-in interface to the EXODUS storage system, is excellent. For example, access to Ariel catalog information stored in a persistent data structure made up of a hash table and linked lists is extremely fast.

A performance study done on the EXODUS storage system shows that the overhead for accessing an E persistent object that is already in the buffer pool is about 47 MIPS RISC architecture machine cycles greater than the overhead to access a C++ main-memory object [28]. Our experience suggests that this level of performance is adequate for implementing system catalogs without the need for a special cache. Performance is also good for scanning persistent collections of objects or collections of collections as in the Triton system. The ability to map nested relations directly to nested collections of tuples in the EXODUS storage system allows us to directly benefit from the "nearness" of nested tuples to decrease object access time. A comparison of a relational and nested relation database design for a software engineering CASE tool, using the Triton system on a Sun 3 computer, showed code generation and compilation times in the range of 2 to 3 seconds for relational queries and 3 to 7 seconds for more complex nested relational queries. Query execution times were about 0.1 seconds for the relational queries and about 0.5 seconds for more complex nested relational queries. Given an equivalent *set* of relational queries and a single nested relational query, code generation and compilation times were 70 to 80% faster and query execution times were 10 to 75% faster for the nested relational query [15]. In summary, the speed of object access in E, or any similarly implemented persistent language, does not seem to be an impediment to implementing a DBMS using the language.

Transaction throughput is another performance issue. An important question is whether a DBMS implemented with a persistent language can achieve high transaction rates (e.g., greater than 100 transactions per second). Currently, we have no data on transaction rates using E since a multi-user version of EXODUS is not yet available. However, a DBMS implemented using a persistent programming language will clearly be limited to a transaction rate no greater than that which can be supported by the storage system underlying the language. We see no fundamental reason why such a storage system cannot be performance-tuned to provide high transaction throughput, using techniques similar to those used in other DBMS implementations such as splitting the log tail, group commit, etc. [22]. Thus, in the long run, the native transaction rate of the persistent language's storage system should not hinder DBMS implementors using the language.

Variables related to throughput which the DBMS implementor can control include the CPU utilization per transaction, and contention for system-wide shared resources such as catalogs and indexes. The majority of CPU cycles utilized by the DBMS will probably be outside the storage system of the persistent language, and it is the DBMS implementor's responsibility to keep it to a minimum to achieve high transaction rates. As in any DBMS implementation, when using a persistent programming language, care must be taken to avoid creating concurrency control bottlenecks around *hot-spots* such as a tuple-count field in the system catalogs and other meta-data. If handled improperly, hot spot bottlenecks can drastically reduce concurrency and hence transaction throughput. For example, having each transaction set a write-lock on tuple count and hold it until the end of the transaction will severely limit throughput. This is exactly what will happen if the tuple count is treated as ordinary data by a concurrency control system based on two-phase locking.

In most DBMS implementations, hot-spots such as tuple-count are handled as special cases. In the case of tuple-count, updates to it are normally not logged, and write locks are held only while physically updating the tuple count, not until the end of the transaction. Given a persistent programming language such as E, it would be difficult or impossible to implement special-case treatment of hot-spots in a DBMS based on the language if the hot-spot data was implemented using persistent language objects. We feel that persistent programming language implementors should give more attention to this issue, perhaps providing an interface to their storage systems designed to handle hot-spots in a way which will allow high transac-

tion rates to be achieved.¶ If they don't, then DBMS implementors using the persistent language who want to achieve high transaction throughput will have to resort to ad-hoc approaches to storing hot-spot data such as using data files directly to by-pass the persistent programming language.

6   Review of Related Research

In this section we compare and contrast EXODUS to three other extensible systems, GENESIS, DAS-DBS, and POSTGRES, and discuss the relationship of E with four other persistent programming languages, O++, Vbase, O_2, and Object Design's ObjectStore that are all based on C or C++. Then we discuss other efforts to implement database systems using database toolkits or persistent programming languages.

6.1   Database Toolkits and Extensible Databases

GENESIS [5], like EXODUS, provides a modular approach to extensibility. This approach is supported by providing a library of modules with completely compatible interfaces. GENESIS provides a data definition language to define the schema of relations, as well as a data manipulation language that provides access to the basic objects in the database (which are records, files, and links).

The lowest layer of GENESIS is the file management system, JUPITER. Like the EXODUS storage manager, JUPITER provides buffer and recovery management; unlike EXODUS, JUPITER is extensible in that different buffer and recovery management schemes can be supported by replacing the appropriate module in JUPITER with a new one. JUPITER supports both single-keyed and multi-keyed file structures, such as indexing, B^+-trees, heap structures, and multi-key hash structures.

The Darmstadt Database System (DAS-DBS) [26] supports extensibility through the use

---

¶The need to support special protocols for handling meta-data was briefly mentioned in [23].

of a kernel storage component that allows flexible, application-specific front ends. The DASDBS kernel provides access (such as reading, insertion, and deletion) to sets of complex objects as opposed to a one-record-at-a-time interface by fetching or storing lists of pages via a variable size buffer. Thus, a single scan of a complex object retrieves all of the values of its sub-objects, which limits the number of disk accesses. This is very similar to the way the EXODUS storage manager works. The kernel provides operations to read, insert, and delete an object. Like the EXODUS storage manager, the DASDBS kernel provides concurrency control capabilities. Instead of using tuple indices, the kernel appends a virtual address attribute to each tuple which can be used in the application layers to build access paths (e.g., B^+-index trees) and provides direct access to the tuple. To enhance performance, the DASDBS kernel attempts to group pages representing a complex object together on disk.

POSTGRES [31] supports extensibility by allowing users to define new data types, operators, built-in functions, and access methods. Like EXODUS, built-in types support both scalar type fields and variable length records. However, unlike EXODUS, POSTGRES supports two interesting built-in types, which are POSTQUEL and procedure types. POSTQUEL types are data manipulation commands, while procedure types are programming language procedures with embedded data manipulation commands. POSTGRES provides these two types to allow users to represent and manipulate complex objects.

6.2 Persistent Programming Languages

Database programming languages are unique in that they should not only support strong typing of objects, but must allow the specification of persistent objects that can last beyond the programs that created them. These two objectives can either be met by providing a single language that does both (as does the E programming language of EXODUS), or providing a separate data definition language and data manipulation language.

O++ [1] is implemented as an extension of C++ with persistent objects, and is thus closely related to E. In addition, O++ also provides additional language statements for defining queries. The main difference between O++ and E is that in O++ there is no distinction between database classes and in-memory classes, but there is a distinction between database pointers and in-memory pointers (there is also a third pointer type called a *dual* pointer that can point to a persistent of volatile object). The O++ approach to persistence is essentially the dual of the E approach. Neither O++ nor E completely separates the issue of persistence from the definition of types.

Vbase [2] and O_2 [19] are database systems that support a separate data definition language and data manipulation language. In both systems, the data manipulation language is based on an extension of C. In Vbase, the data definition language, called TDL, allows strong typing and inheritance. All objects are persistent until they are explicitly deleted, which is good in that persistent and volatile object interaction is not an issue. However, explicit deletion of objects can be tedious.

The Data Definition Language of O_2 is also strongly typed and supports inheritance. Persistent objects are declared from a persistent super object called *tuple*. All objects of type tuple or declared from a subtype of tuple are persistent, and sets of tuple objects can be identified. Methods for types are specified when the type is declared, and types are inherited down the type hierarchy unless they are redefined for a specific subtype. Methods are first order functions and are implemented in C.

The ObjectStore system [21] treats persistent data and persistent data access the same way as conventional virtual memory access. "During ObjectStore application sessions, referenced persistent data is dynamically mapped into the workstation's virtual address space." If persistent data is called for and it not in memory, a "memory fault" occurs and the missing data is retrieved from the database. ObjectStore also supports data caching, concurrency control and restart/recovery. The programmer can create persistent data via several methods:

a variant of the C++ **new** operator which also allows clustering hints, use of a **persistent** keyword, or use of a library call. Any C or C++ type can be made persistent; in addition, ObjectStore includes a collection class, and the Set, Bag, and List subclass of collection, and iterator functions over these classes.

6.3 Use of Database Toolkits and Persistent Languages

Relatively little has been published on experiences using database toolkits to implement a DBMS. Cooper *et al.* [9] discuss three systems implemented using PS-algol [4], a persistent version of Algol with the property of persistence orthogonality. One of the systems covered used PS-algol to implement a DBMS based on an extended functional data model (EFDM) [18]. The benefits of using PS-algol cited in the EFDM implementation were (1) automatic movement of persistent data to/from memory, (2) reduction in misuse of data due to strong typing, (3) usefulness of a universal pointer type, (4) fast access to persistent language objects. Our findings corroborate theirs, particularly (1) and (4) above.

7 Conclusions

The EXODUS system has proven to be a powerful tool for implementing a database system, although it is by no means an antidote for the all the complexities of DBMS implementation. At a minimum, DBMS designers still have to specify a data model, query language parser, catalogs, index and data storage structures, a query optimization strategy (with or without using the optimizer generator), and a query execution strategy.

Using a persistent programming language to implement a DBMS has proven very useful for implementing special-purpose persistent structures such as catalogs, data indexes, and rule indexes, and somewhat less useful for storing the data itself. The problem with using persistent collections in E to store data is due to the fact that one must resort to using persistent collections of generic objects (byte strings) to hold data in order to get adequate response time for ad hoc queries. In systems where ad hoc query capability is not necessary (as in Triton), or where all persistent types can be specified at compile time (e.g., in a computer-aided design database) this is not a major problem. A difficulty we experienced with the E implementation of persistence is the lack of persistence orthogonality in E, which led to software engineering problems in the implementation of Ariel. We assert that it is impossible for the designer of complex software system to know at the outset what data types will need to be persistent. Research on virtual-memory based storage systems (e.g., Cricket) may eliminate the incentive to distinguish between database and main-memory types. We highly encourage this and other research on ways to improve the speed of storage systems for persistent languages.

Language features of E independent of persistence, especially object-oriented programming capability, clearly helped simplify our systems. Ariel shows a significant reduction in code size relative to parts of university INGRES with comparable complexity. E generator classes were useful, but the inability to use polymorphism and inheritance with generated classes is a problem. Generator class facilities in an object-oriented language need to allow use of object-oriented style with generated classes. We were not able to adequately evaluate the usefulness of the optimizer generator. A useful evaluation of the optimizer generator would be to implement an optimizer with the generator and also code the optimizer by hand, and compare the resulting optimizers.

In terms of performance, we are pleased with the speed of access to persistent objects in E. Performance seems adequate for catalogs, indexes, and data storage structures. Any improvements in speed of persistent object access would, however, be welcome. The speed of the underlying storage system does not appear to stand in the way of achieving high transaction throughput. However, we are concerned about having the persistent language storage system handle meta-data such as catalogs and indexes. Since the storage system will use a standard two-phase locking, write-ahead log strategy for all data, it almost certainly will cause a transaction throughput bottleneck around the system catalogs. Database toolkit designers need to provide some sort of support for meta-data to avoid the creation of a transaction bottleneck.

Using EXODUS has been a worthwhile experience for us. We encourage continued research on ways to improve database toolkits and persistent programming languages so that the job of DBMS implementors who follow in our footsteps might be simpler.

References

[1] R. Agrawal and N. H. Gehani. Rationale for the design of persistence and query processing facilities in the database programming language, O++. In Richard Hull, Ron Morrison, and David Stemple, editors, *Proceedings of the Second International Workshop on Database Programming Languages*, pages 25–40, Gleneden Beach, Oregon, June 1989.

[2] Timothy Andrews. The Vbase object database environment. In Alfonso F. Cardenas and Dennis McLeod, editors, *Research Foundations in Object-Oriented and Semantic Database Systems*, pages 221–240. Prentice-Hall, Englewood Cliffs, NJ, 1990.

[3] James R. Armstrong. *Chip-Level Modeling with VHDL*. Prentice-Hall, Englewood Cliffs, NJ, 1989.

[4] M. P. Atkinson, P. J. Bailey, K. J. Chisholm, P. W. Cockshott, and R. Morrison. An approach to persistent programming. *The Computer Journal*, 26(4), 1983. (reprinted in [34]).

[5] D. S. Batory, J. R. Barnett, J. F. Garza, K.P. Smith, K. Tsukuda, B. C. Twichell, and T. E. Wise. GENESIS: An extensible database management system. In Stanley B. Zdonik and David Maier, editors, *Readings in Object-Oriented Database Systems*, pages 500–518. Morgan Kaufmann, San Mateo, CA, 1990.

[6] H. Boral. Prototyping Bubba, a higly parrallel database system. *IEEE Transactions on Data and Knowledge Engineering*, 2(1), May 1990.

[7] M. Carey, D. DeWitt, D. Frank, G. Graefe, J. Richardson, E. Shekita, and M. Muralikrishna. The architecture of the EXODUS extensible DBMS. In *Procedings of the International Workshop on Object-Oriented Database Systems*, September 1986.

[8] M. J. Carey, D. J. DeWitt, and Scott L. Vandenberg. A data model and query language for EXODUS. In *Proceedings of the 1988 ACM SIGMOD International Conference on Management of Data*, June 1988.

[9] R. L. Cooper, M. P. Atkinson, A. Dearle, and D. Abderrahmane. Constructing database systems in a persistent environment. In *Proceedings of the 13th VLDB Conference*, 1987.

[10] G. Copeland. Uniform object management. In *Proceedings of the Intl. Conf. on Extending Database Technology*, March 1990.

[11] Adele Goldberg and David Robson. *Smalltalk-80: The Language*. Addison Wesley, 1989.

[12] G. Graefe and D. J. DeWitt. The EXODUS optimizer generator. In *Proceedings of the 1987 ACM SIGMOD International Conference on Management of Data*, May 1987.

[13] Eric N. Hanson. An initial report on the design of Ariel: a DBMS with an integrated production rule system. *SIGMOD Record*, 18(3), September 1989.

[14] Eric N. Hanson, Moez Chaabouni, Chang-ho Kim, and Yu-wang Wang. A predicate matching algorithm for database rule systems. In *Proceedings of the 1990 ACM SIGMOD International Conference on Management of Data*, May 1990.

[15] Capt Tina M. Harvey. Access and operator methods for the Triton nested relational database system. Master's thesis, School of Engineering, Air Force Institute of Technology (AU), Wright-Patterson AFB, OH, December 1990.

[16] S. C. Johnson. YACC – yet another compiler compiler. Technical Report CSTR-32, Bell Laboratories, Murray Hill, NJ, 1975.

[17] Sonya E. Keene. *Object-Oriented Programming in Common Lisp.* Addision-Wesley, 1989.

[18] K. G. Kulkarni and M. P. Atkinson. Implementing an extended functional data model using PS-algol. *Software Practice and Experience*, 17(3):171–185, Marche 1987.

[19] Christophe Lécluse, Philippe Richard, and Fernando Velez. O_2, an object-oriented data model. In Stanley B. Zdonik and David Maier, editors, *Readings in Object-Oriented Database Systems*, pages 227–241. Morgan Kaufmann, San Mateo, CA, 1990.

[20] M. E. Lesk. LEX – a lexical analyzer generator. Technical Report CSTR-39, Bell Laboratories, Murray Hill, NJ, 1975.

[21] Object Design, Inc. ObjectStore technical overview, release 1.0, August 1990.

[22] Andreas Reuters, editor. *Proceedings of the 2nd International Workshop on High Performance Transaction Systems.* Springer Verlag, 1987.

[23] Joel E. Richardson and Michael J. Carey. Programming constructs for database system implementation in EXODUS. In *Proceedings of the 1987 ACM SIGMOD International Conference on Management of Data*, May 1987.

[24] Joel E. Richardson, Michael J. Carey, and Daniel T. Schuh. The design of the E programming language. Technical report, University of Wisconsin, 1989.

[25] Mark A. Roth, Henry F. Korth, and Don S. Batory. SQL/NF: A query language for ¬1NF relational databases. *Information Systems*, 12(1):99–114, 1987.

[26] Hans-Jeorg Schek et al. The DASDBS project: Objectives, experiences, and future prospects. *IEEE Transactions on Knowledge and Data Engineering*, 2(7):25–43, March 1990.

[27] Capt Craig W. Schnepf. SQL/NF translator for the Triton nested relational database system. Master's thesis, School of Engineering, Air Force Institute of Technology (AU), Wright-Patterson AFB, OH, December 1990.

[28] Dan Schuh, Michael Carey, and David Dewitt. Persistence in E revisited – implementation experiences. In *Proceedings of the 1990 Persistent Object Systems Workshop*, Fall 1990.

[29] Eugene Shekita and Michael Zwilling. Cricket: A mapped, persistent object store. Technical report, University of Wisconsin, Fall 1990.

[30] M. Stonebraker, E. Wong, P. Kreps, and G. Held. The design and implementation of INGRES. *ACM Transactions on Database Systems*, 1976.

[31] Michael Stonebraker, Lawrence Rowe, and Michael Hirohama. The implementation of POSTGRES. *IEEE Transactions on Knowledge and Data Engineering*, 2(7):125–142, March 1990.

[32] Bjarne Stroustrup. *The C++ Programming Language.* Addision Wesley, 1986.

[33] Bjarne Stroustrup. Parameterized types for C++. In *Proceedings of the Usenix C++ Conference*, 1988.

[34] Stanley B. Zdonik and David Maier, editors. *Readings in Object-Oriented Databases.* Morgan Kaufmann, 1990.

[35] Michael Zwilling. B+-tree external documentation, 1989. EXODUS Project Documentation.

Symbolic and Spatial Database for Structural Biology

Dan Benson, Greg Zick
Department of Electrical Engineering, FT-10
University of Washington / Seattle, WA 98195
benson@ee.washington.edu
zick@ee.washington.edu

ABSTRACT

This paper describes the development of a database to support three-dimensional image reconstruction of structural biology using object-oriented technology. The requirements of this system encompass many of the popular justifications for the application of object-oriented technology, such as non-standard data types and complex composite data, but we also find advantage in the increased functionality obtained for spatial relationship operations and access methods. We focus attention on the implementation of the spatial data, its representation, operations, indexing, and queries.

1 INTRODUCTION

Biomedical imaging is making a tremendous impact on medical knowledge, teaching, and practice due to the fact that images provide a great deal of information that is otherwise unobtainable. Improvements on the acquisition, dissemination, understanding, and use of this information comprise the bulk of imaging research activities. A brief summary of them includes the development of new image modalities, image acquisition techniques, image processing, feature extraction, object recognition, and applications which make use of the extracted information. As these technologies advance, and even become automated, the crucial missing component is the organization and management of the underlying data that is generated [DUER83]. Shown graphically in Figure 1, data generated by these biomedical imaging activities can be organized in a database that supports multiple data types and multi-level models.

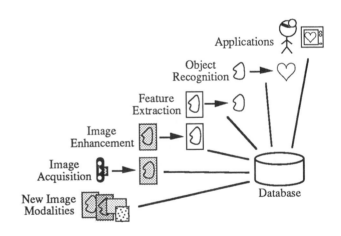

Figure 1. The role of a Biomedical Imaging Database

Images contain information about real world objects. Once acquired, each stage in the process carries this information along while "squeezing out" certain elements of the image contents forming an internal model or representation that can be used by applications. These stages are all related, in fact, they build off of each other.

OOPSLA'91, pp. 329–339

Likewise, there exists relationships among the data each stage generates.

There are two basic categories of data a biomedical imaging database must support, symbolic and spatial. Symbolic data is the sort of alphanumeric data commonly found in traditional databases, such as patient accounting information, or employee records. Spatial data, on the other hand, consists of geometric information, such as maps, images and their contents, or three-dimensional anatomical objects.

A traditional relational database stores information describing real world entities but is limited in the ways these entities can be represented and accessed. There exists a semantic gap between the user's representation of the world and the representation in the database. This gap is substantially narrowed through an object-oriented implementation that provides multiple layers of abstractions closely modeling the user's world view.

In this paper, we describe the development of a database to support three-dimensional image reconstruction of structural biology using object-oriented technology. This application involves all of the stages of biomedical imaging mentioned above. The requirements of this system encompass many of the popular justifications for the application of object-oriented technology, such as non-standard data types and complex composite data, but we also find advantage in the increased functionality obtained for spatial relationship operations and access methods. We place particular attention to the implementation of the spatial data, its representation, operations, indexing, and queries.

The current prototype consists of the GemStone [GEMS90] object-oriented database running as a server on an IBM RS/6000 and Objectworks for Smalltalk-80 v. 2.5 [PARC90] running on a Macintosh IIfx as the application interface. We based our selection of these tools on their prototyping capabilities, data impedance matching, and availability at the time the project was initiated.

The organization of this paper is as follows: Section 2 provides the background and context of the application domain. Section 3 describes the spatial data representation and operations of spatial relationship. Section 4 presents an object-oriented spatial index that augments the vendor-supplied access to object sets. Section 5 describes spatial queries and how the application of object-oriented technology improves accuracy and precision in spatial search. Section 6 concludes with a summary and discussion of future work.

2 BACKGROUND

For a number of years, researchers in the department of Biological Structures at the University of Washington have been developing and refining methods for 3-D image reconstruction [STIM88, PROT89, MCLE91] in which three-dimensional images of anatomical objects are reconstructed from sets of ordered 2-D cross-sectional slices, somewhat like a loaf of sliced bread. The images and animations produced by these techniques reveal anatomical structures in ways never seen before and allow interactive manipulation of accurate quantified data in anatomy.

The data acquisition process leading up to the 3-D reconstruction begins with various specimens prepared in ways that allow millimeter-thin slices to be removed as images are acquired of each new surface. The objects of interest are then traced manually by professional anatomists for each image taken, similar to contour lines on a map. These surface boundaries are labeled and digitized into computer-readable form for input to a 3-D graphics editor where the data is edited and displayed as three-dimensional surface reconstructions.

Currently underway is a project to acquire data encompassing the entire human body, providing the foundation for a distributed knowledge base of structural biology that will be used to solve problems in basic science, teaching, and clinical medicine [BRIN89]. Because anatomy is a fundamental framework upon which most of the basic medical sciences rest, a knowledge base of biological structure would have profound implications in many areas of medicine. A key aspect to the success of this system is the underlying management of the exceptionally large amount of data, the complexity and structure of the data, and its relationships. The organization of this data must also provide efficient symbolic as well as spatial access to the anatomical objects. Symbolic access is retrieval based on attribute values such as, "*Select all images of the liver taken after October 6, 1991,*" whereas spatial access is based on spatial properties such as, "*Select all objects within 10 mm of the heart.*"

Up to now, this data has been stored in flat files and organized in a file directory hierarchy. While this has been adequate for relatively small sets of data, knowledge of the relevancy and structure of objects, as well as relationships among various objects, exists in the minds and memories of the biologists rather than as an integrated part of the data itself and information retrieval does not go beyond simple filename lookup. This method of organization fails as the amount of data increases, the relationships become more complex, and access to the data more sophisticated.

Conventional relational database technology does not meet the needs of modern imaging applications, characterized by highly complex and structured data, multiple data types and relationships, and non-traditional database processing. It lacks adequate data models and poses a rigid table structure for the definition of the relationships between data records, thus preventing efficient representation and access of spatial or complex data structures.

We believe that an object-oriented database approach offers many advantages in supporting biomedical applications having spatial data. It shortens the semantic gap between real-world objects and their corresponding abstractions and thus offers a more flexible model for dealing with complex data. The data modeling capabilities provided by the object-oriented model make it possible to support not only multiple types of images but also highly structured data such as graphics. Furthermore, the extensibility of an object-oriented database allows us to implement user-defined index structures which are essential in achieving adequate performance in spatial data access.

3 SPATIAL DATA

Spatial data can be defined as anything having a location in a given global space with zero size (point) or non-zero size (occupies space). A spatial database, then, supports data structures for the representation of spatial data, efficient spatial access capabilities, and may also support a subset of geometric operators on the data [GÜNT88]. Spatial data is found in many application areas including anatomy, solid modeling, geography, computer aided design (CAD), robotics, and others.

Anatomical objects make up the primary data set for the structural biology database. Each three-dimensional object is described spatially in terms of its boundary. This information is obtained from a series of images taken of 2-D cross-sectional slices in which objects of interest are identified explicitly as ordered sets of points that trace their contours. Each set of ordered 2-D contours describe an object in three dimensions. The relationship between the original images, the 2-D contours, and the 3-D surface reconstruction is depicted in Figure 2.

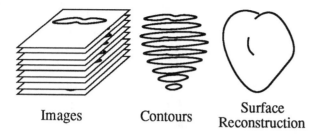

Images   Contours   Surface
                      Reconstruction

Figure 2. Spatial data abstractions

In an object-oriented implementation, the internal representation is hidden and can be modified with minimal effect on the overall system. No matter which representation is used internally, the object interface reflects generalizations about all spatial objects. For instance, each object is located at a point in space. All spatial objects, therefore, respond to the message requesting their location. Another generalization is that all spatial objects occupy a portion of space (a point having zero size). Because the description of the regions occupied by objects can be arbitrarily complex, a common approximation of an object's extent is a bounding box, defined by an n-dimensional rectangle describing intervals in n dimensions that completely enclose the bounds of the object.

We represent spatial data types through a class hierarchy defining 3-D objects, shown in Figure 3.

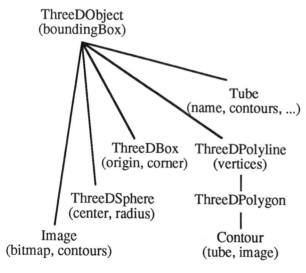

Figure 3. ThreeD class hierarchy.

The generalizations of all 3-D objects are captured in the common superclass called ThreeDObject. Some of the basic attributes ThreeDObjects can be asked for include:

boundary	returned in various forms such as points, lines, contours, etc.
bounding box	defined as the minimum ThreeDBox containing all of the object's extent
center	defined as the center point of the object's bounding box
location	defined as the closest point of the object's bounding box to the origin
surface area	area of object's surface
volume	volume of object's bounds

Each subclass of ThreeDObject may override these basic methods and may have additional specialized attributes. ThreeDPolygons, for instance, are confined to a plane and can therefore be asked for their area and perimeter; a ThreeDPolyline can answer its length and a ThreeDSphere can provide its radius.

The basic 3-D anatomical object is called a Tube. A Tube has instance variables describing symbolic information and one instance variable describing spatial data called *contours* that is an ordered collection of instances of the class Contour. As a subclass of ThreeDPolygon, each Contour is defined by an ordered collection of ThreeDPoints and is associated with its Tube and Image that contains the original bitmap data. Besides the general-purpose polyhedra objects, other specialized 3-D object classes are defined that are useful for spatial queries: ThreeDBox, ThreeDPolyline, and ThreeDSphere.

The various attributes that can be obtained from 3-D objects are used in determining spatial relationships between objects. The two basic spatial relationships are intersection and containment between two objects. For example, an object can determine whether it intersects or contains another object through the messages, *intersects: aSpatialObject* and *contains: aSpatialObject,* respectively. The argument to these messages, *aSpatialObject*, can be any spatial object.

Each class of spatial object may rely on a specific set of tests when determining its relationship with other spatial objects. A brute-force implementation of the *intersects:* method would be to first determine the type of object passed and then invoke the appropriate algorithm for intersection test based on the argument type. For example, the *intersects:* method for the Tube class would look like:

```
intersects: aSpatialObject
    (aSpatialObject isKindOf: Tube)
      ifTrue: [ … code to test for intersection
                  with another Tube …].
    (aSpatialObject isKindOf: ThreeDPolygon)
      ifTrue: [ … code to test for intersection
                  with a ThreeDPolygon …].
    (aSpatialObject isKindOf: ThreeDSphere)
      ifTrue: [ … code to test for intersection
                  with a ThreeDSphere …].
    …
```

This, however, results in a lengthy case-like statement that is both inefficient and difficult to maintain for each type of spatial object in the system.

For spatial relationship operations, we prefer to implement a double-dispatching technique, similar to that used in the Smalltalk-80 kernel classes for handling arithmetic operations among Number subclasses [GOLD83]. In double-dispatching, the receiver object returns the result of sending the argument object a more specific message with itself as the argument. It is a useful technique for efficiently choosing an algorithm based on the class of the argument of a message and the class of the receiver. Using the previous example, the Tube *intersects:* method becomes:

```
intersects: aSpatialObject
    ^aSpatialObject intersectsTube: self
```

A complete implementation requires that all spatial object classes implement an *intersectsTube:* method containing the appropriate code to test specifically for intersection with a Tube object. The same would apply for other types of spatial objects. Double-dispatching provides significant speed at the expense of a large number of typed methods and makes it possible to send the generic *intersects:* message to all types of spatial objects. If the number of classes participating in double-dispatching becomes too large, other techniques can be incorporated, such as coercion [PARC90].

The intersection relationship is commutative so double-dispatching simply reverses the arguments. However, the containment relationship must be rephrased to an equivalent relationship when double-dispatching. For instance, the *contains:* method would return the result of sending *containedIn[selfClassName]: self* to the argument object.

4 SPATIAL ACCESS

An important aspect of a database containing spatial information is providing efficient spatial access to objects. For large data sets, indices can aid the search process in order to obtain adequate performance. Retrieval of spatial objects in the database is based on symbolic and/or spatial properties. Current database systems support conventional indices, such as B-tree, ISAM, and hashing on simple data types, but do not provide spatial data indexing [ULLM88]. Spatial access, then, is limited to linear iterative search across the entire collection of objects.

An object-oriented database, being extensible, allows us to construct a user-defined indexing structure using high-level objects. An ideal solution would implement the index at a low level inside the database kernel as close to the disk activity as possible. Although implemented at a higher level than conventional indices, an object-level index does offer several advantages. The database administrator has direct control and design of the index and it can be tuned for specific applications. If desired, the index can be easily replaced if an improved index is found. Care must be taken, however, to see that the index maintains consistency and operates as a built-in index would.

A number of index structures for organizing spatial data have been proposed. The most common consist of variations of hierarchical and bucket methods such as quad-trees, oct-trees, k-d trees, k-d-B trees, grid files, RTrees, and cell trees [GÜNT88]. Most methods are designed primarily for point data. Of those that support objects of non-zero size, we chose the RTree as the most suitable structure for the anatomical data because it readily supports extended objects, such as lines, regions, and volumes, it does not sub-divide objects, and does not restrict occupancy to fixed-grid cells.

We have designed and implemented an object-oriented R*Tree [BECK90] spatial index. The R*Tree, an enhanced variant of the original RTree [GUTT84], is in the family of spatial access methods that are based on the approximation of complex spatial objects by their bounding boxes. This approximation makes the R*Tree efficient in terms of both space and time because the information stored at each node in the tree consumes a limited number of bytes and simple rectangular regions can be compared quickly.

The R*Tree organizes spatial objects in a height-balanced tree structure by essentially grouping objects into neighborhoods. Each tree has one root node; each node can have a maximum of M children. Leaf nodes contain references to the actual spatial objects and intermediate nodes contain references to children nodes and a parent node. Each node also stores its own bounding box representing the total region covered by its children.

Based on a high-level tree-structure, the R*Tree is inherently object-oriented. It lends itself well to data and behavior encapsulation and is designed to intermix spatial objects of multiple dimensions. The basic behavior of an R*Tree object is specified through the actions of insertion, deletion, and searching.

Database objects are stored in the database in container objects, such as Sets or Bags, similar to the function of a relation storing records in a relational database. For spatial objects the container class, IndexedSpatialSet, is defined that has two instance variables, *objectSet*, an instance of Set that acts as the holder for all spatial objects inserted into the container, and *spatialIndex*, an instance of R*Tree that provides spatial access to the set of objects.

When an object is inserted into an IndexedSpatialSet it is inserted into the *objectSet* and the *spatialIndex*, where the *objectSet* organizes objects based on a hashing method and the *spatialIndex* organizes them based on their spatial properties. Deletion of objects occurs in a similar fashion. An IndexedSpatialSet, with its instance variables, is depicted graphically in Figure 4.

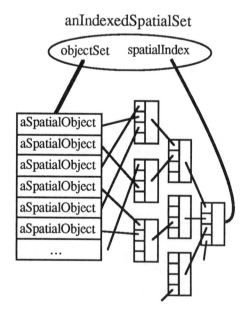

Figure 4. An IndexedSpatialSet

During insertion, the R*Tree object needs to know the bounding box of the object to be inserted, obtained through the *boundingBox* message. The R*Tree object need not be concerned with the type of spatial object it is inserting as long as the object responds appropriately to the *boundingBox* message. In fact, an *n*-dimensional R*Tree is able to accept a spatial object of *n* dimensions or lower since all comparisons between bounding boxes are done by the bounding box objects themselves which can handle differences in dimensionality.

5 SPATIAL QUERIES

Spatial queries on objects are formulated in terms of spatial properties such as location and regions of occupancy. The two most common queries are:

- *Object intersection query*: Given a spatial object S, find all objects, O, where $O \cap S \neq \emptyset$
- *Object containment query*: Two variations: Given a spatial object S, find all objects, O, where (1) $S \supseteq O$, and (2) $O \supseteq S$

Two problems encountered with spatial search, accuracy of results and precision of query region, are related to the index structure. Conventional implementations of non-point spatial indices cannot provide completely correct answers to spatial queries [OREN90]. Furthermore, each index structure imposes a restriction on the type of query region that can be specified. Most methods, for example, allow for only a rectangular region parallel to the global object space coordinate axes. While this may be adequate for some applications, there is often a need to specify other types and more precise search regions. For instance, given a set of three-dimensional anatomical objects, a possible query might be, "*Find all objects inside the skull.*" Restricting the search region to a rectangular cube makes it impossible to describe precisely the volume inside the skull.

We have shown that an object-oriented spatial index overcomes the problems of inaccuracy and precision of query region [BENS91]. Spatial index search operations are inaccurate because they are each based on an approximation of the data objects (e.g., bounding box) so the accuracy of the search is only as good as the approximation. The object-oriented R*Tree returns completely accurate answers because each candidate object, identified at the leaf node level, is interrogated as to whether or not it actually does fulfill the search criteria rather than only its approximation. Secondly, through polymorphism and late binding, any arbitrary spatial object may be specified as the search region so that the precision of the query depends only on the precision of the query object. The object-oriented R*Tree uses the query object's bounding box during the tree traversal but the final intersect or contain operation is performed with the actual query object, thereby guaranteeing accurate results.

The flexibility of the IndexedSpatialSet class is seen in its ability to perform symbolic queries, spatial queries, or combined symbolic and spatial queries. For purely symbolic queries, such as "*Find all objects with names between 'K' and 'M',*" the query request is redirected to the *objectSet* where the built-in accessing methods are utilized. For purely spatial queries, such as "*Find all objects intersecting object O,*" the query request is redirected to the *spatialIndex* which is more efficient in finding objects spatially.

Queries that combine symbolic and spatial predicates are more complicated. The current system relies on the spatial access for any queries containing spatial predicates. However, at the leaf nodes, when the actual objects are interrogated, the symbolic predicates are checked before the final spatial requirements. This heuristic is based on experience gained from testing various combinations of queries and appears to provide the best performance so far. Additional investigation is needed in query optimization for a more thorough solution to this problem.

We have constructed a very simple interface to experiment with spatial query concepts on a data set of randomly generated two-dimensional objects. Figure 5 shows the layout of the query interface with a set of 1000 spatial objects from classes we've named City, Crop, Lake, River, and Road.

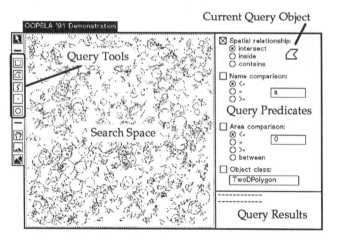

Figure 5. A simple spatial query interface

The set of possible spatial query objects are displayed as drawing tool icons on the left-hand side as: rectangle, polygon, polyline, point, and circle. The two-dimensional search space is shown as a bitmap image (Smalltalk Form) containing all the objects in the data set. This image can be scaled and scrolled in all directions within its window.

Spatial and symbolic query predicates are specified on the right-hand side of the interface. Check boxes indicate inclusion/exclusion of the predicate in the query, currently combined only by the AND operator. Specific operations for each type of predicate are selected through radio buttons. The set of objects returned by the query appear as a scrolling list in the lower right-hand corner of the interface.

Spatial queries are formulated graphically. The spatial query object is specified by selection of an appropriate drawing tool and is drawn directly in the search space, denoting its location and boundary. Figure 6 shows the result of executing a spatial intersect query with a polygon object. For purely spatial queries such as this example, the R*Tree index uses the bounding box of the polygon object during tree traversal but relies on the polygon query object itself to check the final spatial predicate. The objects returned are listed by name and are drawn in the search space.

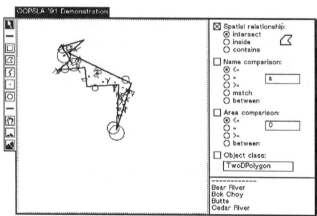

Figure 6. All objects intersecting a polygon

Combinations of spatial and symbolic queries are formulated by checking multiple check boxes in the query predicate area. Figure 7 shows the result of a query involving all four possible predicates. The query asks for instances of the class Lake that are inside the circle object having names <= 'West' and areas between 400 and 600. In this case, the R*Tree index uses the bounding box of the circle object during tree traversal. As each candidate object is found, the symbolic predicates are checked before the final spatial predicate using the circle query object.

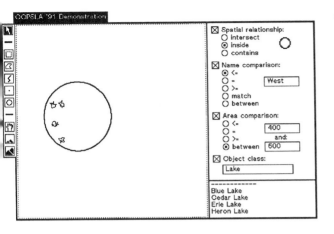

Figure 7. Combination spatial and symbolic query

Queries in an object-oriented database can be done in many ways. As yet there does not exist an equivalent SQL-like declarative language for specifying arbitrary queries. The GemStone database includes the OPAL language, which closely resembles Smalltalk, for data definition and data manipulation. In the current prototype we generate a GemStone Block object for symbolic predicates. This block is passed to the IndexedSpatialSet object in the database for evaluation. For queries involving spatial and symbolic predicates, the block object is passed to the R*Tree where it is evaluated at the leaf node level.

6 SUMMARY & FUTURE WORK

In this paper, we have described the development of a database to support three-dimensional image reconstruction of structural biology using object-oriented technology. The application domain is characterized by multiple data types and multi-levels of abstraction of data obtained from images. Much of this information is spatial data, so particular attention was placed on the implementation of the spatial data, its representation, operations, indexing, and queries.

We represent spatial data through the class hierarchy of three-dimensional objects. The ThreeDObject class contains generalizations of all 3-D objects and serves as the superclass for current and future specializations. We implement spatial relationship operations through double-dispatching techniques that provide an efficient method of choosing appropriate algorithms based on the class of the argument of a message and the class of the receiver.

A container class for spatial objects was defined that has two instance variables, a Set object that holds the spatial objects and provides access based on symbolic attributes, and an R*Tree index object that provides efficient spatial access to the object set. We have shown how the object-oriented R*Tree extends the functionality of spatial indices through accuracy of query results and precision of query region. This was possible because of the object-oriented features of polymorphism and late binding.

Our work presented here accomplishes the framework for a database schema that outlines the representation, operations, and access methods for spatial objects and a spatial/symbolic query interface. As a prototype, the current system is in its development stage and requires further refinement before it can be integrated with the data acquisition and production system in Biological Structures. Once completed, it will have an impact on and improve the 3-D reconstruction efforts in Biological Structures by providing advanced data management capabilities with increased functionality and support for spatial data.

The spatial query examples shown in this paper were done with a set of two-dimensional objects. Formulation of 3-D query objects will be accomplished through an enhancement to the 3-D editor application currently in use [PROT89] to include support for arbitrary 3-D query object construction and connection to the database. The R*Tree spatial index is designed to support objects of any dimension so it requires no modifications.

One path of research currently underway is the presentation of symbolic queries in a more generalized fashion. The interface should be dynamic such that the choices presented reflect the set of instance variables in the scope of target objects. For instance, queries over all ThreeDObjects can be formulated according to those instance variables common to all ThreeDObjects. However, if the query is narrowed to only Contour objects, then the predicate choices should include those variables common to all Contours. In this way, the presentation of query predicates can be generated as the query is formulated interactively.

One observation we have regarding spatial queries is the proportion of time spent on computation of spatial relationships done by the objects compared to the time spent in traversal of the index. Intersection seems to be the most computationally intensive operation and appears to be the bottleneck that overshadows the index search. As some spatial operations are hindered by the data representation, we are looking at alternative representations, the roles they play in aiding spatial operations, and the feasibility of object conversions in the database.

ACKNOWLEDGEMENTS

We wish to thank the 3D Reconstruction researchers in the Department of Biological Structures for their assistance on the work presented here. We also wish to thank IBM for support provided through a Graduate Student Fellowship awarded to the first author, and the W. M. Keck Foundation for initial support of this research.

REFERENCES

BECK90   N. Beckmann, H-P Kriegel, R. Schneider, B. Seeger. The R*Tree: An Efficient and Robust Access Method for Points and Rectangles. *Proceedings ACM-SIGMOD International Conference on the Management of Data*, 322-331, 1990.

BENS91   D. Benson, G. Zick. Obtaining Accuracy and Precision in Spatial Search. *Technical Report DEL-91-01*, Department of Electrical Engineering, University of Washington, 1991.

BRIN89   J. F. Brinkley, J. S. Prothero, J. W. Prothero, C. Rosse. A Framework for the Design of Knowledge-Based Systems in Structural Biology. *Proceedings Thirteenth Annual Symposium on Computer Applications in Medical Care*, IEEE Computer Society Press, 61-65, 1989.

DUER83   A. J. Duerinckx, S. J. Dwyer. Guest Editors' Introduction: Digital Picture Archiving and Communication Systems in Medicine. *Computer, Vol. 16, No. 8, Special Issue on Digital Image Archiving in Medicine*, 14-16, August 1983.

GEMS90   Gemstone Object-Oriented Database Management System, Version 2.0, Servio Corporation, 1990.

GOLD83   A. Goldberg, D. Robson. *Smalltalk-80 The Language and its Implementation.* Addison-Wesley, 714 pgs., 1983.

GUTT84   A. Guttman. R-Trees: A Dynamic Index Structure for Spatial Searching. *Proceedings ACM-SIGMOD International Conference on the Management of Data*, 47-57, 1984.

GÜNT88   O. Günther. *Efficient Structures for Geometric Data Management*, Lecture Notes in Computer Science 337, edited by G. Goos and J. Hartmanis, Springer Verlag, 1988.

MCLE91 M. McLean, J. Prothero. Three-dimensional reconstruction from serials sections. V. Calibration of dimensional changes incurred during tissue preparation and data processing. Analytical & Quantitative Cytology and Histology (in press), 1991.

OREN90 J. Orenstein. A Comparison of Spatial Query Processing Techniques for Native and Parameter Spaces. *Proceedings ACM-SIGMOD International Conference on the Management of Data*, 343-352, 1990.

PARC90 Objectworks for Smalltalk-80, Version 2.5, ParcPlace Systems, Inc. 1990.

PROT89 J. S. Prothero, J. W. Prothero. A software package in C for interactive 3-D reconstruction and display of anatomical objects from serial section data. *NCGA Conference Proceedings*. I:187-192, 1989.

STIM88 G. K. Stimac, J. W. Sundsten, J. S. Prothero, J. W. Prothero, R. Gerlach, R. Sorbonne. Three-dimensional Contour Surfacing of the Skull, Face, and Brain from CT and MR Images and from Anatomic Sections. *AJR* 151:807-810, 1988.

ULLM88 J. Ullman. *Principles of Database and Knowledge-Base Systems, Vol. 1.* Computer Science Press, 1988.

Re-engineering of old systems to an object-oriented architecture.

Ivar Jacobson

Fredrik Lindström

Objective Systems SF AB
Torshamnsgatan 39
BOX 1128
S-164 22 Kista, Sweden
Phone: +46 8 703 45 41
Fax: +46 8 751 30 96

Abstract

Most of our present-day information systems have been in use for a long time. They have been developed using the system development methods, programming tools, data base handlers, etc. that were available when the development work started. Even if the systems are adapted to changed requirements from the surrounding world, the basic structure and the original technical and methodological ties have been retained. Our goal is to show how an object-oriented development method can be used to gradually modernize an old system, i.e re-engineer the system. We do this by showing how three typical cases of re-engineering are related to object-oriented development. The technique is based on experiences from real projects.

1.   Introduction

More and more system owners face the following questions: How do you build a model of your system that enables you to reason about modifications? How do you gradually replace parts of the system? How can you integrate a modern programming technique such as object-oriented programming into an existing system? This paper will summarize a technology that will answer these questions.

The basis of our technology is system development using object-oriented technique. The technology implies that occurrences from the application domain are modelled as objects and associations between objects. The resulting system model will be used as a mapping between the occurrences of the application domain and programming elements in the existing system.

Changes in the objects of the application domain can be traced directly to the same objects in the model. Different discussions about changes in the system will therefore be more precise. For example, if a new type of communication protocol shall be used, you can easily identify which program elements in the existing system are candidates for a change.

The technique is founded on two assertions:

1.   A change in the application domain is frequently local in the sense that it concerns a behaviour or an occurrence with a clear delimitation.

2.   An object-oriented system model can be used to describe a system designed in a non object-oriented manner.

OOPSLA'91, pp. 340–350

t is generally unrealistic to replace an old system by a completely new system; such a change requires too much resources. You must find ways of gradually replacing older system parts without completely losing the investments made so far. Our basic principle is that an old system must be modernized gradually. Figure [1] shows how changes successively can carve out the original system. Eventually, the entire system will be replaced.

The rest of this paper is organized in the following way. First, a presentation of re-engineering, its goals and definitions. Next, we introduce a combination of object-oriented system development and re-engineering. Third, experiences from three projects are presented. Last, a conclusion. Throughout this paper we assume a familiarity of concepts like object, inheritance, encapsulation, analysis, and design.

2. Re-engineering.

All systems have a limited lifetime. Each implemented change erodes the structure which makes the following change more expensive. As time goes on, the cost to implement a change will be too high, and the system will then be unable to support its intended task. This is

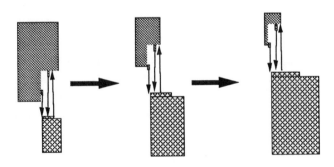

Figure [1]. We gradually want to replace an existing implementation with an object-oriented.

true of all systems, independent of their application domain or technological base.

Before the system reaches this state something must be done. Depending on its position in a "changeability - business value" matrix one of four actions is possible, see figure [2].

We will assume that the old system is difficult to change but has a high business value, in this case we choose to re-engineer the system. A system with a satisfactory degree of changeability or a low business value either does not need the re-engineering investment or is not worth it. What then is "re-engineering"? *Re-engineering is the process of creating an abstract description of a system, reason about a change at the higher abstraction level, and then re-implement the system.* Re-engineering is subsequently defined in terms

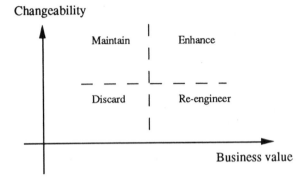

Figure [2]. Decision matrix, what to do with an old system

of relations between different levels of abstraction. Intuitively and similar to (1), this can be expressed with the following formula:

> Re-engineering =
> Reverse engineering+ Δ + Forward
> engineering.

The first element of re-engineering, "Reverse engineering", is the activity of defining a more abstract, and easier to understand, representation of the system.

The second, "Δ" represents change of the system. Changes have two major dimensions, change of functionality and change of implementation technique. The third, "Forward engineering" (i.e normal system development) is the activity of creating a representation that is executeable, e.g. finally a program written in Smalltalk or C. Since the concept of forward engineering is familiar to most readers we will not discuss it further in this section.

2.1. Reverse engineering

The goal of reverse engineering is to capture an understanding of the behavior and the structure of the system and be able to communicate this to others. To do this we need at least the three following things:

a)   A concrete graph that describes the components of the system and their interrelationship.

b)   An abstract graph showing the behavior and the structure of the system.

c)   A mapping between the two, i.e how something in the abstract graph relates to the concrete graph and vice versa.

The abstract graph should be free of implementation details. For example, mechanisms for persistent storage or partitioning into processes should not appear on this graph . The concrete graph must, on the other hand, show these details. The mapping between the two should tell us how the ideal world of analysis is implemented the way the concrete graph describes.

2.2. Change

From the perspective of re-engineering we classify changes into two orthogonal dimensions, change of functionality and change of implementation technique. The first is the most common of the two but a change of implementation technique seems to be in increasing demand, see (2) and (3).

A change of functionality comes from a change of the business rules. Thus, modifications of the busines rules results in modifications of the system. Change of functionality doesn't affect how the system is implemented, i.e how the forward engineering is carried out: an end user of a system need never know if the system is implemented with Smalltalk or C.

A new implementation technique of an information management system could mean that the organization will use C++ instead of C, or use an object-oriented database management system instead of a relational one. Needless to say, a change of implementation technique is not an easy process, even if there are tools that can do part of the job automatically.

The dimensions are orthogonal in the sense that it is meaningful to talk about changes in one without changes in the second. We can change the functionality without changing the implementation technique and vice versa. When only part of the system changes its implementation technique it is necessary to enable communication between the two parts. Different languages and operating systems are more or less supportive in this task, a basic functionality that must be supported is that an application can be called on request from another application. (General reasoning about this is found in (4)).

2.3. A small example

Let us consider an invoice system as a small and trivial example to illustrate the process of re-engineering. We assume that the only available description of the system is a number of files of C-code and a database description in SQL. The changes involve both functionality and implementation technique. The change in functionality is that two limitations of the current system have to be removed. It only allows one address per customer and a user can only work with one invoice at the time. The change of implementation technique will be to rewrite part of the system in C++.

The first step, reverse engineering, means that we identify how the components of the system relate to each other and then create a more abstract description of the system. The relationships between components are identified, e.g. the dependencies between the files and the C-functions, the C-functions and the database descriptions, etc. After that, an abstract description (in the sense that we deliberately leave out implementation relevant information) of the system is created, e.g. a dataflow diagram for the C-functions and an entity relationship model of the database description. The process of creating a more abstract description can in theory be repeated as many times as necessary. Practically, it is enough with two levels (design and analysis).

After the first step, we will have an abstract model that shows the business rules of the invoice system and a number of mappings between the different levels of abstraction. Part of the abstract model represents how invoices are regulated by the legal system, other parts represent how the organization that once ordered the system wanted the invoice system to work. The mappings comprise the design decisions that occur when transforming an abstract representation to a concrete one.

The second step, reasoning about the changes in functionality, is done at a more abstract level. Without the abstract model we would have to reason with low-level non-problem domain concepts and make statements like "add one more table that contains the references between customers and addresses". Instead, at the higher level of abstraction, we can say "change the association between the entities Customer and Address".

Next, we redesign the system from the abstract representation to the more concrete representation, i.e forward engineering. In this process we must take the changes of implementation technique into consideration. Since we only change the technique for part of the system we have to answer the question "Where should the border between the old and the new system be"? When we formulate the answer we have to consider what mechanisms there are available that make the communication possible. When implementing the system we also must take all recaptured design decisions into consideration.

To summarize, when we re-engineer a system we need:

a) A representation of the system "as it is", at some level of abstraction.

b) A logical representation of the system, at a level that makes it possible to reason about changes in functionality.

c) A way to capture design decisions, or knowing why the system is implemented the way it is.

d) A technique that enables two different implementations to communicate.

e) A technique to delimit the part of the system that we want to explore (without this it is impossible to re-engineer a large sytem)

3. Different scenarios for re-engineering .

This chapter outlines a combination of object-oriented system development and re-engineering. Since there are many issues involved in the process we introduce the necessary concepts one at the time using three different scenarios. Scenarios that can be combined in a straightforward manner. We will describe re-engineering with:

1. A complete change of implementation technique and no change in the functionality.

2. A partial change in implementation technique and no change in functionality.

3. A change in functionality.

3.1. Complete re-engineering with no change in functionality.

A complete change of implementation technique will seldom occur for a large system. Nevertheless, we will use the scenario to illustrate part of the re-engineering process, namely reverse engineering and introduce some concepts. Figure [3] shows an overview of the transformation process. In the figure, the rectangles describe different representations of the system. The dark grey represents the existing system, the light grey

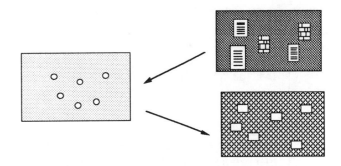

Figure [3]. The figure describes how all of the old system is transformed into an object-oriented implementation.

represents the analysis model, and the middle grey represents the object-oriented implementation, i.e the lighter a rectangle is, the more abstract it is. Rectangles inside the existing system represent the primitive description elements(defined in 3.1.1). Circles inside the analysis model represent analysis objects. Rectangles inside the object-oriented implementation represent design objects.

343

The main steps of the re-engineering process are:

1. Prepare an analysis model. Described in 3.1.1.
2. Map each analysis object to the implementation of the old system. Described in 3.1.2
3. Redesign the system using a forward engineering technique for object-oriented system development. The last step of this re-engineering scenario is to implement the analysis model. This is achieved through a forward engineering process as described in (5).

3.1.1. Prepare an analysis model

The first step, prepare an analysis model, requires that we assimilate the existing information about the system. The existing information has many different forms, e.g. requirements specifications, user operating instructions, maintenance manuals, training manuals, design documentation, source code files, and database schema descriptions. We call them here description elements. An important subset of the description elements is the set of description elements that represent the true system, e.g. source code or documentation that is consistent with the source code, these are called "primitive" description elements.

What is then a primitive description element? Naturally, their nature depends on the quality of the documentation. In the worst case, e.g. when we only trust the source code, their granularity is on the level of methods of a class.

> D is the set of all description elements.
>
> $D_{Primitive}$ is a subset of D, where $D_{Primitive}$ represents a description of the system that is consistent with the source code.

From the set of description elements we prepare an analysis model, see figure [4]. This is done by using the criterias for finding objects that are described in the object-oriented method we use, e.g. see (5), (6), (7), (8). The resulting analysis model can be regarded as a graph, we have a number of analysis objects A_i that are connected to one another with a set of directed edges, E. The edges have different semantics in the

analysis model, but these are ignored at this stage (they all imply some kind of dependency of the terminal object).

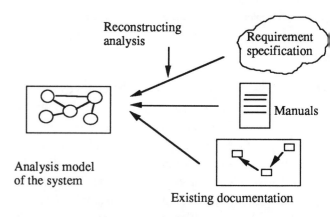

Figure [4]. Preparation of the analysis model.

> The analysis model is represented by a directed graph (A, E, $f(a_i, a_j)$).
>
> A, the nodes, is the set of all analysis objects identified from the description elements, E is the set of all arcs between the nodes, and f is a function that associates an arc with an ordered pair of nodes. The function represents a dependency between the analysis object.

3.1.2. Map each analysis object to the implementation of the old system.

Part of the reverse engineering process is to have a mapping between the analysis model and the system.

We have two constraints on the analysis model:

a) All analysis objects must be motivated by at least one primitive description element. We can express that with is_motivated_by, a mapping from the analysis model to the set of primitive description elements.

> For each analysis object A_i, there must exist at least one element $D_{Prim\,j}$ such that is_motivated_by(A_i, $D_{Prim\,j}$) exists.

) All edges in the analysis model must be motivated by at least one primitive description element. This is also expressed with is_motivated_by.

> For each edge E_i of the analysis model, there must exist at least one element $D_{Prim\,j}$ such that is_motivated_by($E_{i,}\ D_{Prim\,j}$) exists.

Also abstract analysis objects and inheritance associations can be motivated by description elements.

We use the analysis objects, the description elements (both primitive and non-primitive), and the guidance from the experts of the system to map the analysis objects to the implementation of the old system. This is comparable with the normal process of analyzing a system, except for the vast amount of information.

After this step we have a situation as described in figure [5].

3.2. Partial re-engineering with no change in functionality.

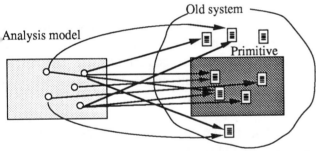

Figure [5] All analysis objects and edges must be motivated by at least one primitive description element. Note that they also can be motivated by non-primitive description elements.

The goal is to make the object-oriented application believe that the whole system consists of objects, the process is visualized in figure [6]. The thick arrows symbolizes the transformations between different levels of abstraction. The thin lines shows the communication between the object-oriented system and the remaining part of the old system.

The main steps of this process are:

1. Identify the part of the system that will be reimplemented using object-oriented technique.
2. Prepare an analysis model of the part to be exchanged and its environment.
3. Map each object to the old implementation of the system .
4. Iterate the previous steps until the interface between the part to be exchanged and the rest of the existing system is acceptable.
5. In parallel:
5.1 Design the new subsystem and its interface to the rest of the old system.
5.2 Modify the old system and add an interface to the new subsystem.
6. Integrate and test the new subsystem and the modified old system.

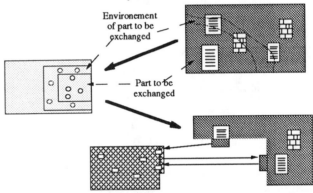

Figure [6]. Part of the system is implemented with an object-oriented technique. The thick arrows symbolizes the transformations between different levels of abstraction. The thin lines shows the communication between the object-oriented system and the remaining part of the old system.

3.2.1. Identify the part of the old system that will be reimplemented using object-oriented technique.

Two subsets of $D_{Primitive}$ are created. The first is D_x, which contains the elements that the new subssystem exchange. The second subset is D_{Env}, which contains the neighbours of D_x. A neighbour is an element that:

a) isn't already included in D_x.
b) is adjacent to elements in D_x in a dependency graph, i.e either a terminal or a initial node.

Thus, there must be a graph that shows the dependencies between the primitive description elements. The graph is either implicit, i.e exists in the minds of the technical experts, or explicit, i.e exists in a readable form. In an ideal situation, we would like to have the complete graph. However, due to the size of such a graph we only make it explicit for the part we need to study.

A readable form is always preferable. Although advanced tools and techniques exist, technical experts will always make the task substantially easier.

> A directed graph $(D_{Primitive}, E_D, g(D_{Pi}, D_{Pj}))$ is created.
>
> $D_{Primitive}$, the nodes, is the set of all primitive description elements, E_D is the set of arcs between the nodes, and g is a function that associates an arc with an ordered pair of nodes. The function represents a dependency between the primitive description elements.

3.2.2. Prepare an analysis model of the part to be exchanged and its environment.

This step is similar to the corresponding step in the previous scenario. The difference is that we only have to concentrate our efforts of understanding the system to a limited part of D. Thus, prepare an analysis model representing the union of D_x and D_{Env}.

3.2.3. Map each analysis object to the implementation of the old system.

We use the function is_motivated_By(x, D_{Pj}) to map the objects and edges of the analysis model to the elements in $D_{Primitive}$. We can then divide the analysis model into two subsets:

a) A_x, which represents the part of the model that definitely will be implemented with the new technique.

b) A_{Env}, analysis objects will serve as wrappers of the old system. They represent objects that A_x is related to.

3.2.4. Evaluate the interface between the part to be exchanged and the remaining part of the old system.

When we have decided what part of the old system that we want to change, we can create an interface between the new and the old system. At this stage, when a better understanding of the old system is reached, it is time to evaluate the interface, i.e we have to examine the partition of $D_{Primitive}$. Through changing the set D_x it is possible to get a set D'_x that, through D'_{Env}, gives a better interface between the old and new subsystems. When we do this we have to repeat the previous steps until we have an interface that is acceptable in terms of implementation cost.

During the evaluation of the interface we must take technical aspects in consideration, e.g. see (9) who describes the technical problems that occurred when an object-oriented language was built on top of an existing system. In general, most of these aspects arises from the problem of communicating the state of one instance between the new and the old subsystem. The basic problem is atomicity of transactions, i.e no intermediate states of the instance should be visible for its clients. As a goal, the cut between the subsystems should be made so that only one of them manages the state of an object and works as a server to the other subsystems. Despite this goal, implementation restrictions may make it unattainable. In that case, we must allow multiple copies of the instance.

3.2.5. Design the new subsystem and its interface to the old system.

The new system is implemented as the object-oriented method prescribes. Objects in A_{Env} are implemented with a set of classes that let the object communicate with the old system, see figure [7].

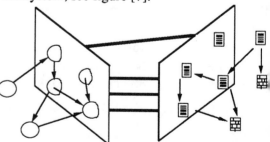

Figure [7]. The objects half-buried in the interface encapsulate the old system.

This way, the other objects of the application only sees objects. The objects of A_{Env} behave like objects from the new subsystem and like old software from the old subsystem

Thus, the encapsulation property of objects makes it possible to successively move the plane further and further into the old system. This way it is possible to gradually replace the old system with an object-oriented system.

3.2.6. Modify the old system and add an interface to the new system.

In parallel, we have to modify the old system. All parts that communicate with D_x, i.e. calls procedures or uses data in D_x, are replaced. Instead of their original code, they have to use the interface to the new system. The set D_{Env} contains these parts. Also, we must modify the parts in D_x so that a call or an access to them results in an error. An activation of them means that we have missed redirecting communication meant for the new subsystem.

3.3. Re-engineering with change of functionality.

This scenario is a normal forward engineering process. We add changes in functionality in the analysis model and implement them using the object-oriented technique. The result of this process is described in figure [8].

The main steps of the process are:
1. Change the analysis model according to requirements.
2. Design the system.

Only the first step is described, for a description of the second see (5).

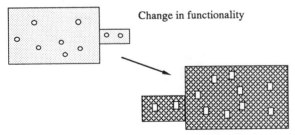

Change in functionality

Figure [8] A change of functionality. In this case an addition is depicted.

3.3.1. Change analysis model according to requirements

We change the analysis model in accordance with the requirements on changes in functionality. New objects and edges are added as described in the normal forward engineering process. Objects identified from the old system either are deleted or receive new attributes and edges. Thus, the resulting analysis model can be partitioned into three subgraphs, one that contains all the new objects, one that contains the changed ones, and one that contains the unchanged. We then have three different subsets of the analysis model:

a) A_{New}, which represents the new objects.
b) $A_{\Delta func}$, which represents the elements with a new functionality.
c) $A_{No\Delta func}$, which represents the elements not affected by the change in functionality.

4. Case studies

We have used ObjectOry to re-engineer a number of systems, including two major systems. The first system was a military system for handling spare parts, and the second system was a telecommunication system. One of the others, a traffic control system is also presented.

Our experiences with re-engineering come from using ObjectOry™ (see (5)), an industrial software development process. ObjectOry is a mature object-oriented technique with many important features for supporting the reverse engineering process. Particulary, one unique concept of ObjectOry, use cases, have been an excellent tool for reverse engineering. Briefly, a use case is a sequence of user interactions with the system. Its purpose is to define a typical way of using the system. In the context of reverse engineering, we explore an old system with use cases. That is, together with an expert of the old system, the system analyzer identify a use case. Then, they follow the use case through the existing documentation of the system.

Another important aspect of ObjectOry is the separation of analysis and design. As a result of the projects with re-engineering, our belief in this has been enforced. With an analysis model that clearly, without implementation details, captures the business rules of an organization, it is much easier to understand and change a system. The role of the design model is to capture all the necessary modifications dependent on the implementation environment. Today, all the systems we have reversed or re-engineered have only been documented with at most a design model. They have completely lacked an analysis model.

4.1. Spare part system

The goal of the first project was to demonstrate practically how an object-oriented system development method can be used when designing distributed information systems. The example used for the work was DELTA, a system for redistribution of stock. The system is used by all defence branches in the Swedish Armed Forces. The project was executed on assignment from the Defence Materiel Administration FMV, and our work amounted to about 4 to 5 manyears.

The re-engineering has been done down to class level on a smaller part of the system that concerns spare parts, for example customer orders and redistribution of material between storage places. These functions have been implemented in an object-oriented environment including an object-oriented data base.

We have also specified and implemented the changes required to make the system a geographically distributed system.

The same DELTA system has been used in a parallel study to demonstrate how a conventional, form-based user interface in a terminal environment can be extended with window handling, graphics, and direct manipulation in a personal computer environment.

The main categories of the description elements of the project were:
a)   database schemas
b)   Cobol code
c)   user manuals
d)   interviews with users and technical experts

Before the project had started, the organisation responsible for the system had planned to replace the whole system at once. However, after evaluating the initial results of the project they changed their minds. The effort to replace the whole system was found too large. Instead it was decided that a way of gradual replacement must be found.

4.2. Telecommunication system

The communication system was reverse engineered in a small project of about 1 manyear. The original work of the system was about 120 manyears and it was developed with an object-based technology. The purpose of the project was to make an analysis model that will be used to restructure the system. After the project, the organisation responsible for the system estimated that a complete reverse engineering process would take about 10 manyears. Due to the understandibility of the analysis model, they also concluded that the model should make it possible to reduce the time to get experienced system engineers from 5 to 2 years.

4.3. Traffic control system

Basically, the traffic contol system involves three different systems. A resource allocation system, a traffic control system, and a communication system. Historically, the traffic control system was developed first, then the resource allocation system, and last the communication system.

Related to figure [2], the traffic control system is the most difficult to change, closely followed by the resource allocation system. But, the resource allocation system has a high business value and it depends on the traffic control system. Therefore, the company has choosen to re-implement part of the traffic control system and part of the resource allocation system. The communication system is left untouched since its degree of changeability is considered sufficiently high.

The project has both a partial change of implementation technique and a change in functionality. To get a complete understanding of the three systems we studied functions that spanned over all of the systems . After that, we created an analysis model and its motivations, see figure [9].

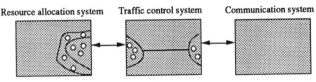

Figure [9]. The delimitations and the objects of the trafic control system.

The desired result is found in figure [10]. Part of the resource allocation system and part of the traffic control system will be implemented with object-oriented technology. The change is that the new technology will only be used for a part of the traffic control system, the other part will be left out. Thus, we have to create an interface between the different subsystems and modify them accordingly. On the other hand, the communication system will not be effected by any changes and can be left as it is.

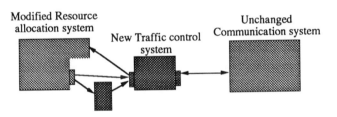

Figure [10]. The desired result of the re-engineering of the resource allocation system.

Based on these projects, we estimate that it requires 1/10 - 1/20 of the total development time of the old system to create an analysis model. That is, if the total development time of a system is 10 manyears, the analysis model takes about 0.5 - 1 manyear to reverse engineer. Of course this figure is uncertain, but we believe that the magnitude is correct.

5. Conclusions

The life span of an information system comprises specification, design and maintenance. The maintenance phase dominates in time and often also with respect to resources. During this phase the system is subjected to a number of changes and additions. The gap between the older technology in the system and the new technology that becomes available increases successively. Changes in the activities of an organization also mean that systems grow old.

Gradually the system approaches a limit where it no longer is cost-efficient or even technically motivated to continue the maintenance. But the cost of enforcing the required changes is usually very high. This poses a serious dilemma for system managers and similar personnel. A possible way out of this dilemma is to define well delimited system parts that are candidates for modernization. Provided this delimitation is made in an efficient manner, replacement can be made with moderate changes in the existing system. This is where re-engineering can help.

We have described a practical method for re-engineering. The method is based on an object-oriented modelling. We have described how the work can be divided into a number of steps from analysis to design and finally design and testing, i.e. the method can be performed in a systematic manner.

We have achieved the following: In a simple manner and with limited efforts you can make a model of an existing system. By means of the model you can reason about where a change can be made, its extent and how it shall be mapped on the existing system. The new model is object-oriented and can serve as a basis for a future development plan. The extensions can be designed as additions outside the existing systems with a minimum of adaptations in the form of interfaces.

Today, we think that the subject of re-engineering is too focused on tools. Despite their importance they are not sufficient. We think it is necessary to change the focus of re-engineering to the complete life-cycle of the system, i.e. try to incorporate re-engineering as a part of a development process, and not as a substitute for it.

In the long run, we want to industrilize reenginering techniques so that they will be incorporated as a part of ObjectOry. We belive that Objectory has a good foundation for this. Besides beeing object-oriented, it is based on a mature forward enginering process (see 5). This means that a new system will keep a high degree of changeability.

6.   References

(1) J. Chikovsky and J. H. Cross. "Reverse enginee-ring and Design Recovery: A Taxonomy.". IEEE Software 1990;(January):13-17.

(2) Economist. "How computers can choke companies". 1990 June 9:71-72.

(3) J. Duntemann and C. Marinacci. "New objects for old structures". Byte 1990 April:261-266.

(4) P. Zave. "A Compositional Approach to Multiparadigm Programming". IEEE Software 1989;(September):15-25.

(5) I. Jacobson. "Object Oriented Development in an Industrial Environment.". In: Proc. OOPSLA. Orlando, Florida.: ACM Press, 1987: 183-191.

(6) P. Coad. *Object-Oriented Analysis*.Englewood Cliffs, New Jersey: Prentice-Hall, 1990:232. (E. Yourdon, ed.) Yourdon Press Computing Series

(7) G. Booch. *Object Oriented Design*.Redwood City, California: The Benjamin/Cummings Publishing Company, Inc., 1990:580. (G. Booch, ed.) The Benjamin/ Cummings Series in Ada and Software Engineering

(8) R. Wirfs-Brock, B. Wilkerson and L. Wiener. *Designing Objec-Oriented Software*.Englewood Cliffs, New Jersey: Prentice-Hall, 1990:341.

(9) C. Dietrich, L. R. Nackman and F. Gracer. "Saving a Legacy with objects". In: Proc. OOPSLA. New Orleans: ACM Press, 1989: 77-83.

350

OOP and AI
(PANEL)

Mamdouh Ibrahim, *EDS/Artificial Intelligence Services*, (moderator)
Daniel Bobrow, *Xerox PARC*
Carl Hewitt, *MIT*
Jean-Francois Perror, *LAFORIA*
Reid Smith, *Schlumberger Research Laboratories*
Howard Shrobe, *Symbolics/MIT*

Background

Recently, object-oriented programming has gained recognition as a powerful paradigm for structuring and programming complex systems. At the same time, the AI community is still in pursueit of new representational and software engineering techniques for developing complex applications.

Given the similarities (at least from the surface) between constructs such as objects and frames, and notions such as classification hierarchies and class inheritance, it is natural to ask questions such as:

1. what can object-oriented programming and AI offer each other?

2. how do the two areas differ from each other?

3. where are they heading? and can each shape the future of the other?

4. what should the OOPSLA community do to further contribute to the integration of OOP and AI?

As part of their positions, the panelists are asked to address specific questions related to OOP and AI. Examples of such questions are:

- are objects suitable for some but not all of AI tasks?

- is the class/instance mechanism flexible enough to represent natural operations on concepts such as partial specializations?

- what is missing from existing OOP class hierarchies that prevents them from being used in AI applications?

- What would object-oriented languages (specifically CLOS) contribute to the AI community that LISP would not provide?

- given the OOP lack of formalisms and semantics, can we expect object- oriented knowledge representation to achieve real advances in AI?

- how can concurrent object-oriented programming benefit AI systems?

- how can OOP support tools be of advantage in designing knowledge-based systems and second generation expert systems?

Daniel Bobrow

OOP is really AI. Much AI will really be done under the guise of developing appropriate class hierarchies for different applications. What will be missing is the declarative descriptions of specifications for the hierarchies. We must learn to work with real (commercial) OOP systems, and add declarative knowledge rather than just inventing our own OOP systems.

Carl Hewitt

Scientific communities are large scale, ongoing concerns, which investigate a multitude of phenomena. They are inherently concurrent systems with no known bounds to the amount of concurrency that is possible. I am concerned with addressing issues of how such methods can be abstracted and incorporated in programming systems.

Mamdouh Ibrahim

The benefits of OOP for both knowledge representation and as software engineering tools have already been recognized and proven in many domains. AI is no exception. In fact, there is no doubt in my mind that further advances in AI will not be possible without OOP.

However, we must recognize that there are AI tasks for which existing OOP languages, techniques and methodologies might be inappropriate. For example, AI classification problems are difficult to implement with the current class-based languages. The problem is that in OOP we must create the classes before we create their instances. In classification problems, we actually start with the instances and try to find their classes. This involves tasks such as inexact pattern matching and discovery and learning, which are also difficult to implement with the current state of the art in OOP.

Delegation-based systems may address some of the classification problems; and the advantages of using mature reflective languages will be impossible to ignore when developing real learning systems. Further research in these and other related areas should broaden the AI application base for which OOP can be of great advantage.

J-F Perrot

The role of Objects in AI is twofold : as a first-rate programming tool (see also their importance in Software Engineering), and as a basis for Knowledge Representation. Both of these aspects rely ultimately on the fundamental fact that the Class/Instance mechanism provides a crude but highly efficient computer implementation of the Concept/Instance distinction that we use in our normal way of thinking. On the other hand, the inheritance mechanism, which is supposed to be of such paramount importance for defining OOP, has a much more dubious status as a cognitive tool (see the running battle about Multiple vs. Single Inheritance).

It is essential to get a clear picture of how and why OOP works so well, in order to use it better (see the universal need of methodologies) and to avoid asking from it what it cannot provide. For example, to take a point made by Terry Winograd in his invited talk at OOPSLA '90, not all "real-world objects" are readily modelized with OOP techniques. Also, what one has to say about a perfectly solid object may involve unexpected aspects of it.

¿From the use of (Smalltalk) objects as a firm basis for knowledge representation a number of interesting ideas have already emerged:

- the need to provide a more flexible mechanism than Class/Instance to represent such natural operations on concepts as partial specialization (e.g. from class Wheel deduce "Wheels of diameter X") in a disciplined way (as opposed to ad hoc solutions as with frames) see Wolinski/Perrot, ECOOP '91

- the possibility to endow classes with a few additional properties which make them amenable to a form of "conceptual computation" (doctoral thesis of R.Bourgeois, 1990)

- subjecting ordinary objects to first-order production rules in the OPUS fashion (Laursen & Atkinson, OOPSLA '87) reveals the need to introduce 'aspectual' properties of objects in order to obtain the full power of rule-based deduction that one normally expects to-day (metarules, truth maintenance etc.) - work in progress by F. Pachet.

It is expected that this work will shed some light not only on the way Knowledge should be represented in AI programs, but also on the way industrial programmers, designers and analysts could use their present- day OO tools more effectively.

Howard E. Shrobe

Object oriented programming is valuable advanced programming technique useful in the construction of a variety of AI systems. Having been using OOP techniques since the late 1970's in the Lisp Machine environment, I can attest to its power in the construction of integrated systems in CAD and AI.

However, it would be a mistake to identify the concerns of OOP and AI or to overlook other advanced programming techniques which are of equal importance to AI people as well as other developers of complex software systems. I would rank amongst these other techniques, the package of Symbolic Computing techniques (list processing, garbage collection, associative retrieval, condition management) that are commonly available in Lisp (even without its OOP extension CLOS). I would also include the elegant pattern matching capabilities made available through unification in Prolog and its related languages. Finally, I would emphasize that powerful, integrated programming environments such as those developed originally in InterLisp and to an even greater extent in the Lisp Machine environment provide indispensable leverage. Advanced programmers need all of these and more.

The concerns of AI and those of OOP are not the same.

AI is concerned with modelling people's understanding of the world; in the particular part of AI with which I am personally involved the main concern is modelling the problem solving behavior of experts. The key intellectual elements of this exploit are the study of problem solving paradigms, knowledge representations and programming languages which faithfully embody such services.

OOP on the other hand is concerned with providing a powerful and extensible programming medium. Its key intellectual elements are the nature of classes and inheritance, method combination, dispatching techniques, type inference etc.

Much confusion has arisen from the fact that many ontologies of the world are object centered. This has led the AI community to pioneer in the development of OOP. In many cases, however, the AI community has lost site of the original AI insights that had motivated the exploration. Minsky's original paper on Frames eventually led to a number of "Frame-like" languages (KEE, HyperClass, Loops) these in turn have influenced the design of CLOS, the object-oriented extension of Common Lisp. However, Minsky's original paper was primarily about the observation that human problem solving is anticipatory, centers around prototypical representations, and involves approximate matching of a variety of types. Notice that none of these are concepts relevant to OOP per se and that they have been lost in the course of OOP developments in the AI community.

In my view the exploit of building a knowledge based system consists of studying the ways experts in a domain conceive of the world, how they organize their problem solving efforts, what abstractions they employ, etc. These are then given life in the form of problem solving paradigms and knowledge representations. Finally one looks for programming vehicles that faithfully give life to these constructs. When these are indeed object-oriented, OOP techniques seem particularly relevant; but one should not assume that everything in AI takes this form. Often it doesn't.

Even when OOP doesn't provide a direct representation for an AI construct it may play a role in building the appropriate mechanism. For example, the Joshua system which my colleagues at Symbolics and I developed, is an assertionally oriented system which uses the polymorphism of OOP (in particular Flavors or CLOS). In Joshua there is a Protocol of Inference which is an abstract description of the inferential process. Different types of statements handle elements of this protocol in different ways to exploit specific constraint within their domain. This also allows us to embed a variety of problem solving paradigms, knowledge representations and reasoning techniques within a system which is nevertheless homogeneous at its highest level.

Managing the Transition to Object-Oriented Technology
(PANEL)

Tim Korson, *Clemson University*, (moderator)
Nelson Hazeltine, *NCR*
Tim Hilgenberg, *Hewitt Associates*
Reed Philip, *Knowledge Systems*
David Taylor, *Taylor Consulting*

Overview

This panel will examine the issues an organization faces when moving to object-oriented technology (OOT).

Some of the obvious issues include the choice of languages, databases, environments, CASE tools, and analysis and design methodologies.

However, once these choices are made, an organization is still faced with the task of successfully introducing the new software technology. The panel will discuss the impact of OOT at all levels:

- activities, productivity, and assessment of each person on the technical staff

- project organization

- project and corporate management

- the structure of the organization itself

Some specific questions to be addressed in this area are:

- How should corporate reuse be managed?

- What changes in project management, metrics, and deliverables are necessary?

- How are accounting procedures and project funding affected?

- How is corporate strategy and policy affected?

- What corporate and project positions are affected, and how does that affect individual career paths?

Nelson Hazeltine

It is probably still too early for most corporations to decide to implement object technologies at the exclusion of procedural technologies. What is recommended for most corporations is a corporate staff function that acts as the corporate-wide champion and at least one serious line project that is dedicated to developing systems that utilize object technologies. The purpose of the project is for the corporation to gain confidence with the technologies and understand the benefits and barriers to success. Once the corporation is comfortable with the technologies, then guidelines can be established at the Corporate level to better assure success with other object-oriented projects.

Factors, within the experience of the author and at this point in time, that are thought to lead to project developement success follow:

1. A strong process of development

2. A strong methodology or mentoring program

3. Ample architecture support for the development team

4. A relatively flat development organization

5. Rewards for developers summiting reusable classes to the library

6. Rewards for developers using classes

7. Good source control

8. Training of management as well as developers

Tim Hilgenberg

When Hewitt Associates decided to redevelop its mission critical software, we were looking for an approach that would provide us with the flexibility we needed to develop and deliver software to to a client population that has a diverse range of requirements in an ever changing regulatory environment. We felt that Object-Oriented Technology would provide us the techniques we needed to develop software that would be flexible, adaptable and easily changeable into the future.

This panel is discussing the issues an organization faces when deploying object-oriented technology. Briefly, we have encountered the following issues:

- Education of the Project Team

  Our experience has shown that the training of object-oriented concepts and the experience gained in prototyping small applications of these concepts is instrumental to the successful introduction of O-O technology. We trained the entire team; managers, analysts, programmers, testers and users in object-oriented techniques. Even with this training, we found that it still took some time for the team to make the paradigm shift from a process orientation to an object orientation. Once O-O techniques have been learned, they should also be re-enforced through small prototyping projects. These projects should be done in

a true object-oriented environment, not a hybrid environment. This forces the individual to think only in terms of objects and their behaviors and gives them no opportunity to solve their problems in a procedural manner.

- Development of a Technical Platform

  A critical decision in our project was the selection of development tools and the integration of these tools into a technical platform. The business application logic would then be built on this platform. This process included the selection of a language, a data base, communication software, a transaction processor and a Graphical User Interface (GUI) development tool. Being a vendor of human resources software, our client base has mainly large IBM mainframe equipment. In order to be "socially acceptable" in this environment, we felt we had to integrate object-oriented technology within the IBM System Application Architecture (SAA) environment. Our objective was to build an O-O environment within a cooperative processing architecture. This architecture would use a PC with a GUI front-end, CICS as our back-end communication server and transaction processor, and DB2 as our data base. Another critical decision was selecting the language we would use to write our mainline business logic. Since our clients are primarily mainframe, we felt they would only accept a system that was primarily built in COBOL. Since there is no standard object-oriented COBOL language, we developed internally a COBOL pre-processor that would translate our object-oriented source syntax into ANSI COBOL source code.

- Organizing the Development Project Organization

  We felt that in order to meet our flexibility requirements, we had to effectively manage the design of our base application classes and ensure that we were properly reusing the system classes and methods. We also have a large analysis staff and we need to provide a level of conceptual integrity across this team. To satisfy these needs, we established a new functional entity in the project team called the "Repository". The charter of the repository is to maintain and register the critical information related to the application. This includes class and method definition and logic specifications, class hierarchies and data base table and attribute definitions. The Repository is staffed with application content experts trained in object-oriented techniques. They review and register all specifications developed by the analysis team before they are sent to the development team for construction. The Repository is a quality assurance checkpoint insuring that the specifications satisfy the stated requirements and that the base application class are being reused.

- Development of an Object-Oriented Methodology

In order to utilize object-oriented technologies on a large scale project, an organization needs to have a comprehensive O-O development methodology in place to support this type of development project. Tested analysis, design and construction techniques, along with a complete definition of project deliverables are critical to delivering the product in a timely manner. The best approach to developing a methodology is to design the process and then test it on a small prototype application. A new methodology and selection of a CASE tool particularly in an object-oriented development environment should not be used on a large mission critical application. Currently, a lack of established methodologies and CASE tools for object-oriented development will inhibit some organization from developing large scale projects using object-oriented technology.

Reed Philip

There are many characteristics about managing the transition to object technologies (OT) that are well understood and documented from previous experience applying strategic technologies. These include:

- the need for extensive education

- access to experts that can provide early guidance

- support from senior management

- applications that carry an appropriate level of risk reward

As a result, I will focus on issues that make the move to objects unique. But first I would like to place the whole issue of transitioning to OT in perspective.

Within the last five years organizations have been promised incredible improvements in application quality and productivity if they would only adopt relational databases, 4GL's, CASE, distributed processing, artificial intelligence, cooperative processing, etc. It's no wonder senior management is skeptical when another "silver bullet" called OT appears on the scene. It takes at least five years for any new technology to demonstrate a significant positive impact on the corporate bottom line. Since most corporations are measured by the quarterly earnings report, decisions whether or not to adopt a new technology is measured the same way. As a result management is constantly seeking the irrefutable evidence of the elusive 10:1 productivity increase and we as technologists are eager to provide it. While significant productivity improvements have been measured within certain organizations it would be unwise to extrapolate this success or failure to all organizations.

Our experience tells us that success or failure is determined before the first line of code is written. It is critical that expectations are properly set, proper training is in place, and good project management skills employed.

The promise of reusable code and designs, is one of the topics that gets considerable play during the selling phase. While corporate management of reuse is the key to the OT promise, there is currently little or no infrastructure to support it. KSC and its clients have benefited greatly from the availability of a large body of internally produced reusable components and frameworks. In several cases application to application reuse exceeded 85%. We have shown that significant code reuse for small to medium teams is possible, but the business systems required to enable reuse pervasively throughout an organization do not yet exist. The whole issue of design reuse, specially on the enterprise level, is still evolving. (Much of the ongoing enterprise repository and information modeling standards activities should produce a context for management of design reuse).

(Note: In the absence of tools there is a geographical relationship between code creators and code reusers. The amount of reuse (R) is inversely proportional to the distance (D) from the creator, $R=L*1/D$. The other factor is the readability (L) of the code. Highly readable code tends to get reused).

Even with excellent management and an emphasis on quality designs it is foolish for an organization to expect significant reuse from the first two or three projects. Time is required for a body of reusable design and code to accumulate, and skill is required to build designs and implementations to be reused. A focus on reuse must be pervasive from design to implementation, even before there is much to reuse! The effectiveness of reuse at all levels and, therefore, its impact on organizational productivity is a management issue!. Technology is certainly needed to support the management directions and practices. More complete tools and processes will need to be in place to effectively manage corporate wide reuse of designs and code. And until that time effective reuse will be, at best, hard to achieve and harder to replicate throughout the organization.

All is not lost. Until better tools are available:

- focus on quality design
- develop coding standards that enhance readability
- use tools like Envy to manage the process
- create a work environment that encourages reuse
- create a sense of ownership

David Taylor

The more broadly a company adopts object-oriented technology, the more it must transform itself to get the maximum benefit from this technology. Just as American manufacturers learned that adopting just-in-time (JIT) manufacturing required far more than a change in technology, conversion to object-oriented information systems will require changes on many levels. And, as with JIT, the return is proportional to the investment. The companies that are willing to invest in change will reap the greatest competitive benefits.

Like JIT, object technology affects an organization on four major levels: old technologies must give way to new ones; managers and staff must be educated to a new way of thinking about software and trained in new techniques; the corporate organization must change in order to accommodate a new approach to software; and the corporate culture must change to reward a new way of developing systems. Adopting object technology without investing in education, reorganization and cultural changes will modest benefits at best.

For example, if a company cuts corners on education, continues to build monolithic applications and parsists in rewarding programmers based on the amount of new code they create, converting to C++ or Smalltalk may actually do more harm than good. By contrast, the surest way to succeed with this technology is to throughly educate all parties in the advantages of building software by assembly, realign job descriptions according to a layered approach to software construction, and reward programmers for producing the most functionality with the fewest additional lines of code.

Appendix

How to Get Your Paper Accepted at OOPSLA

Alan Snyder
Hewlett-Packard Laboratories
P.O. Box 10490
Palo Alto CA 94303-0969

Introduction

The primary goal of the program committee of a major conference like OOPSLA is to put together a high quality program of technical papers. The program is created by soliciting contributed papers from authors and then selecting the best papers according to some criteria. The process is reactive: the authors submit, the committee selects from those submissions. Because of time constraints, it is generally not possible for the committee to interact with an author to improve the quality of a paper that fails to meet the acceptance criteria in its submitted form. Although the reviewers may offer helpful comments to the author of a rejected paper, the author must find some other forum for the paper (hopefully in an improved form).

As program chair for the 1991 OOPSLA conference, I decided to address this situation proactively by writing this article. The purpose of this article is to provide advice to prospective OOPSLA paper authors, based on my past experience. If you are a prospective author of an OOPSLA paper, I hope you will be able to use this advice to make improvements to your paper *before* submitting it to the program committee, thus improving its chances for acceptance.

This article will also offer some suggestions to help you decide whether to submit a paper to OOPSLA at all. Members of the program committee spend a considerable amount of time reviewing a large number of papers. You should avoid unnecessarily adding to this workload, by not submitting a paper that is clearly inappropriate.

Criteria

The 1991 OOPSLA conference is looking for papers in two basic categories. **Research papers** are papers that describe work whose purpose is to advance the state of the art of object technology. **Experience papers** are papers that describe work in which object technology has been applied for some purpose. The evaluation criteria for these papers are somewhat different; these differences are noted in the remaining discussion. Tutorial papers and surveys are not solicited for the 1991 conference; they should not be submitted. (This policy could change for future conferences; check the call for papers.)

The primary requirement is that your paper must contribute to our understanding of object technology. It must have something new to say, and its message must be of sufficient importance and interest to warrant the attention of the OOPSLA community.

If your paper is a research paper, it should describe a new idea or a new technique. It must

OOPSLA'91, pp. 359–363

describe original work. Your paper should present supporting evidence, not just conjecture. Idea papers should be backed up by a convincing analysis.

If your paper is an experience paper, it should present new data based on actual experience that demonstrates the effectiveness (or ineffectiveness) of object technology, describes problems encountered, and makes suggestions for improvements. It should provide new evidence, either positive or negative, to evaluate existing ideas or techniques. It should help provide direction for future research, as well as provide new insights of value to other practitioners using object technology.

The distinction between research and experience papers is not absolute. It is possible to gain experience in a research setting, and it is possible to develop new ideas or techniques while applying a technology. However, if you focus on one of these two aspects, you will write a better paper.

Your paper should make its contribution abundantly clear. It is not the job of the program committee to ferret out this information. One aspect of identifying the contribution is to cite and make appropriate comparisons with previous work. A research paper should compare and contrast the work with prior work, demonstrating novelty. An experience paper should compare its results with other papers that present similar or opposing data. An experience paper that merely confirms that which is well known (as opposed to that which is widely believed) is of little value.

Obviously, your paper must not have been published elsewhere in the same or similar form. Less obviously, your paper must not be under consideration elsewhere in the same or similar form. While the desire for authors to "hedge their bets" by submitting the same or similar paper to multiple conferences and/or journals is understandable, this practice plac-

es an unnecessary burden on the peer review process. It can also cause embarrassment or confusion if the same paper is accepted at more than one conference. If you believe that unusual circumstances warrant simultaneous submission to more than one forum, you *must* notify *all* the program chairs and editors involved; simultaneous submission without notice is considered highly unethical. (Note that archival journals frequently accept versions of papers that have already appeared in conferences, but usually it is in your best interest to get feedback from the conference presentation *before* submitting a polished and revised version to a journal.) It is also considered inappropriate to submit multiple papers to the same conference that cover substantially similar or overlapping material. (It may be appropriate, however, for multiple papers to be submitted concerning distinct aspects of a single project, particularly if the various papers have different authors.)

If you have published previous papers on the same subject, your paper should clearly indicate the relationship between your new paper and the previous papers.

Finally, your paper must be well written. It must clearly communicate its message to the intended audience.

Purpose

You should answer some key questions before submitting a paper:

The first question you should answer is "**Why am I writing this paper?**" If the answer is of the form "to document what I have been doing for the past two years", then you are in danger of writing a bad paper. It may be a shock to your pride, but most people are not interested in what you have done for the past two years. If you need to document your efforts, write a memo or a tech report. Another poor answer is "to help build my case for tenure". Tenure may be your initial motivation for writing a paper, but it should not be the only motivation.

The purpose of your paper should be to communicate *something* to *someone*. So, the next questions are "**What is my paper trying to say?**" and "**Who is the audience for my paper?**" If you cannot clearly answer these questions, then the paper is likely to be poor.

A focused paper is better than a scattered paper. Resist the temptation to describe every great idea you had while working on your project. Pick a primary message and communicate it well.

After deciding what the paper is trying to say, the next question to answer is "**Is it worth saying?**" Is it a new message, or just a rehash of an old message? Is the message of value, or potential value, or is it trivial? Is it conjecture, or have you demonstrated the soundness of your conclusions?

After deciding who the audience is, the next question to answer is "**Is OOPSLA a good way to reach my audience?**" Does my message have value to researchers and developers of object technology? Does my message have value to practitioners using object technology?

Is it Premature?

Many papers are rejected because they are "premature". This characterization means that the work appears to be interesting, but it has not progressed far enough to be worth reporting in a conference paper. The paper may have more conjectures or opinions than results. Perhaps there are ideas that look promising, but they have not been worked out in enough detail. Perhaps more analysis of the issues is needed. Perhaps the proposed technique sounds interesting, but its value cannot be determined until it has been implemented.

An experience paper may be called premature if it offers conjectures about expected results rather than reporting observed results. For example, if you are just about to release a product, it is premature to claim improvements in software maintenance until the product undergoes a maintenance cycle. If you have just created a "reusable" library, it is premature to declare it reusable until actual reuse occurs.

One area of difficulty is portability. Experience has shown that designing a portable system of any kind can be surprisingly difficult. One cannot convincingly claim to have designed a portable system unless the portability of that system has been tested in least two environments.

The decision to accept or reject a paper that is premature is a judgement call by the program committee. A committee may choose in some cases to accept a paper that presents early work of a profound or provocative nature. However, you should honestly evaluate the maturity of your work before deciding to submit a paper on it. You may be able to write a much stronger paper for next year's conference!

Is it Sound?

Your paper should convince the program committee that your work is technically correct. The burden of proof is on you, the author. It is not the job of the program committee to prove your paper incorrect. If the correctness of your work is in doubt, your paper will probably be rejected. Soundness of ideas or techniques can often be demonstrated by the depth and clarity of the analysis, or by reference to a working implementation. Questions of soundness often arise for papers that present algorithms or proofs (see the next two sections).

Algorithms

It is self-evident that complex algorithms are difficult to get right. Garbage collection algorithms in particular have gained a degree of notoriety amongst members of previous OOPSLA program committees. In general, a description of a complex algorithm will not by itself be sufficient to convince the program committee that your algorithm is correct. The committee will be much more likely to accept your algorithm paper if it contains at least one of the following elements: a formal proof of correctness (but see the next section), reference to a working implementation, or (marginally) a formal analysis of its complexity.

Proofs

A formal proof is of value only if it is convincing. While a reviewer may be able to spot an error in a faulty proof, one cannot expect a reviewer to validate a proof. Therefore, any sloppiness in the formalism is grounds for suspicion (and likely rejection of the paper). It is better to avoid formality than to misuse it.

In addition to being convincing, a proof must prove something worth proving. It is not worth anyone's time to read a paper that proves an irrelevant result. Be careful about including a proof in an effort to make your paper more "prestigious". This approach may backfire, as a sloppy or unmotivated proof can easily cause a paper to be rejected that otherwise might have been accepted.

Generality

The audience at OOPSLA includes people from many communities. You will improve your paper if you can address a broad audience, wherever possible. While specific examples can be given, the problem and solution should be presented in general terms.

I will explore this question in the context of object-oriented programming languages, although it applies to other areas as well. Many papers submitted to OOPSLA are written in the context of a specific object-oriented programming language. In many cases, the papers are actually addressing more general issues.

As a hypothetical example, suppose you want to write a paper on "extending the *Foo* programming language to support distributed computing". A paper on this subject could easily address many issues that are not specific to the *Foo* programming language, although some might be. Such general issues might include naming, storage management, concurrency, and distributed schema (type) management. Your paper would be much stronger, and much more likely to be accepted, if it addresses these issues in general terms wherever possible, using the *Foo*-specific work as examples. If your paper is inherently *Foo*-specific, then you should consider submitting it to a more appropriate forum, such as the *Foo* Conference, the *Foo* Journal, or a meeting of the *Foo* Users Group.

A gray area arises if your paper deals with a distinctive aspect of the *Foo* language. A paper that can demonstrate the value (or disadvantage) of a language-specific feature could be of great interest to all language researchers.

What about Applications?

Suppose you've written an application using object technology. Should you submit a paper to OOPSLA about it? That depends. What is interesting about it? Is it the novelty of the application? That might not be sufficient. For example, a novel application for allowing users to find library books might better be reported at a conference on library technology. Is the novelty of the application directly enabled by using object technology? That could be a good OOPSLA paper! Is the interesting aspect your experience in using object technology? Then concentrate on reporting your experience;

don't devote an undue amount of verbiage to describing the application itself.

Don't be Isolated

Object technology overlaps many established areas of computer science, such as programming languages, databases, and distributed computing. If you are writing a research paper, it is important that you be familiar with the larger area, and not isolate yourself to the narrower domain of object technology. For example, if you are writing a paper on object-oriented distributed computing, you should think of yourself as writing a paper on distributed computing (that happens to involve an "objects" approach). The fact that your approach is object-oriented does not excuse you from relating the work to the existing distributed computing literature. Similar comments could be made about many different areas.

Writing

Effective communication is important for a successful paper. A paper has little value if its intended audience cannot understand it. An incomprehensible paper cannot even be reviewed.

Most authors will benefit from having their paper reviewed by a skilled writer. If your native language is not English, you have an extra burden. If at all possible, try to have your paper reviewed by a native or fluent speaker of English.

Final Advice

In my experience, most papers are substantially improved by getting feedback from other people. Giving a talk to a small group is an excellent way to get feedback and to force yourself to organize your thoughts. Also, have your paper reviewed by your colleagues *before* submitting it to OOPSLA. After all, you can change your paper based on their feedback; if the program committee rejects it, there is no second chance (for that conference).

Do not hesitate to attach a cover letter to your paper if there is additional information that would be useful to the program committee. For example, if you have published previous papers on the same subject, you might attach a cover letter to explain in more detail the novel contributions of the paper you are submitting.

Finally, as has been noted elsewhere [Wegman], the conference review process is necessarily imperfect. The reviewers operate under strict time constraints, and the committee must make quick decisions. A paper will not receive the careful attention that it would from a journal. Furthermore, the committee may need to satisfy other constraints in putting together a successful program. As a result, some good papers will be rejected. Authors should carefully consider any reviewer comments and get opinions from experienced colleagues before deciding whether to abandon the effort or to revise the paper and submit it elsewhere.

Additional insight can be obtained from the excellent paper by Smith [Smith] that describes the review process from the point of view of the referee.

Acknowledgments

This article has benefited from the collective experience of the current and five previous OOPSLA program committees.

References

[Smith] Alan Jay Smith. The Task of the Referee. *Computer* (April 1990), 65-71.

[Wegman] Mark N. Wegman. What it's like to be a POPL Referee, or How to write an extended abstract so that it is more likely to be accepted. *Sigplan Notices 21:5* (May 1986), 91-95.

Title Index

Author Index

--NOTES--

--NOTES--

--NOTES--

--NOTES--

--NOTES--

--NOTES--